2000 Qu

Prove ufficiali commentate e **simulazioni d'esame**
per la preparazione ai **test di ammissione**

MEDICINA IN LINGUA INGLESE

Accedi ai servizi riservati

Il codice personale contenuto nel riquadro dà diritto a servizi esclusivi riservati ai nostri clienti. Registrandoti al sito **edises.it**, dalla tua area riservata potrai accedere a:

- **Infinite esercitazioni**
  Scegli se esercitarti su singole materie, sulle prove ufficiali o se simulare una prova d'esame con le stesse modalità della prova reale
- **Ulteriori materiali di interesse**
  Contenuti extra, test attitudinali, prospettive e sbocchi occupazionali ed altro ancora su **www.ammissione.it**

CODICE PERSONALE

Grattare delicatamente la superficie per visualizzare il codice personale.
Le **istruzioni per la registrazione** sono riportate nella Prefazione
Il volume NON può essere venduto né restituito se il codice personale risulta visibile
L'accesso ai servizi riservati ha la **durata di 18 mesi** dall'attivazione del codice
e viene garantito esclusivamente sulle edizioni in corso.

2000 Quiz

Prove ufficiali commentate e **simulazioni d'esame**
per la preparazione ai **test di ammissione**

MEDICINA IN LINGUA INGLESE

editest

EdiTest – 2000 Quiz per Medicina in lingua inglese – VII edizione

9 8 7 6 5 4 3 2 1 0
2026 2025 2024 2023 2022

Le cifre sulla destra indicano il numero e l'anno dell'ultima ristampa effettuata

Cover Design and Front Cover Illustration: Digital Followers S.r.l.

Progetto grafico: curvilinee

Fotocomposizione: doma book di Massimo Di Grazia

Stampato presso: PrintSprint S.r.l. – Napoli

per conto della EdiSES edizioni S.r.l. – Piazza Dante, 89 – Napoli

ISBN 978 88 9362 559 3

www.edises.it
assistenza.edises.it

I curatori, l'editore e tutti coloro in qualche modo coinvolti nella preparazione o pubblicazione di quest'opera hanno posto il massimo impegno per garantire che le informazioni ivi contenute siano corrette, compatibilmente con le conoscenze disponibili al momento della stampa; essi, tuttavia, non possono essere ritenuti responsabili dei risultati dell'utilizzo di tali informazioni e restano a disposizione per integrare la citazione delle fonti, qualora incompleta o imprecisa.

Realizzare un libro è un'operazione complessa e, nonostante la cura e l'attenzione poste dagli autori e da tutti gli addetti coinvolti nella lavorazione dei testi, l'esperienza ci insegna che è praticamente impossibile pubblicare un volume privo di imprecisioni. Saremo grati ai lettori che vorranno inviarci le loro segnalazioni e/o suggerimenti migliorativi sulla piattaforma *assistenza.edises.it*

PREFAZIONE

Rivolto a tutti i candidati agli esami di ammissione in **Medicina e Chirurgia in lingua inglese**, questo volume costituisce un utile strumento di preparazione.

Una prima parte è dedicata alle **simulazioni d'esame**, simili per struttura e composizione al test reale e utili per esercitarsi nella soluzione di quiz analoghi a quelli ufficiali e per una **verifica trasversale delle conoscenze**.

Una seconda parte comprende tutte le **prove assegnate dal 2012 a oggi risolte e commentate** consentendo di familiarizzare con le tipologie di quiz generalmente somministrate e al contempo di favorire il ripasso delle nozioni teoriche previste dal programma d'esame, così da individuare gli argomenti in cui si è più deboli e procedere a uno studio mirato della teoria.

Il **codice personale**, contenuto nella prima pagina del volume, consente di accedere a una serie di servizi riservati ai clienti tra cui:

- il **software di simulazione online** (infinite esercitazioni per materia, sulle prove ufficiali degli anni passati e simulazioni d'esame gratuite);
- materiali di approfondimento e **contenuti extra**.

Tutti i materiali e i servizi associati al volume sono accessibili dall'**area riservata** che si attiva mediante registrazione al sito **edises.it**. Per accedere alla tua area riservata segui le istruzioni riportate nella pagina seguente.

ISTRUZIONI PER ACCEDERE AI CONTENUTI E AI SERVIZI RISERVATI

Collegati al sito edises.it

• Se sei registrato al sito

- clicca su **Accedi al materiale didattico**
- inserisci email e password
- inserisci le ultime 4 cifre del codice ISBN, riportato in basso a destra sul retro di copertina
- inserisci il tuo **codice personale** per essere reindirizzato automaticamente all'area riservata

• Se non sei già registrato al sito

- clicca su **Accedi al materiale didattico**
- registrati al sito **edises.it**
- attendi l'email di conferma per perfezionare la registrazione
- torna sul sito **edises.it** e segui la procedura già descritta per utenti registrati

Per problemi tecnici connessi all'utilizzo dei supporti multimediali e per informazioni sui nostri servizi puoi contattarci sulla piattaforma **assistenza.edises.it**.

INDICE

SIMULAZIONI D'ESAME

PROVE UFFICIALI

IMAT a.a. 2014/2015

IMAT a.a. 2015/2016

IMAT a.a. 2016/2017

IMAT a.a. 2017/2018

IMAT a.a. 2018/2019

IMAT a.a. 2019/2020

IMAT a.a. 2020/2021

IMAT a.a. 2021/2022

SIMULAZIONI D'ESAME

Test 1

Read the following passage and answer the questions nr. 1-3.

"But I did not want to shoot the elephant. I watched him beating his bunch of grass against his knees, with the *preoccupied grandmotherly* air that elephants have. It seemed to me that it would be murder to shoot him. I had never shot an elephant and never wanted to. (Somehow it always seems worse to kill large animal). Besides, there was the beast's owner to be considered. But I had got to act quickly. I turned to some experienced-looking Burmans who had been there when we arrived, and asked them how the elephants had been behaving. They all said the same thing; he took no notice of you if you left him alone, but he might charge if you went too close to him".

1) The phrase "*preoccupied grandmotherly air*" signifies:

A. being totally unconcerned
B. pretending to be very busy
C. a very superior attitude
D. calm, dignified and affectionate disposition
E. being happy for grandmother

2) From the passage it appears that the author was:

A. an inexperienced hunter
B. kind and considerate
C. possessed with fear
D. a worried man
E. carefree and light-hearted

3) The author did not want to shoot the elephant because he:

A. was afraid of it
B. did not have the experience of shooting big animals
C. did not wish to kill animal which was not doing anybody any harm
D. did not find the elephant to be ferocious
E. was attached to the elephant

4) *A* can do a work in 15 days and *B* in 20 days. If they work on it together for 4 days, then the fraction of the work that is left is:

A. 1/4
B. 1/10
C. 7/15
D. 8/15
E. 3/5

5) *A*, *B* and *C* can do a piece of work in 20, 30 and 60 days respectively. In how many days can *A* do the work if he is assisted by *B* and *C* on every third day?

A. 12 days
B. 15 days
C. 16 days
D. 18 days
E. 20 days

6) The sum of ages of 5 children born at the intervals of 3 years each is 50 years. What is the age of the youngest child?

A. 4 years
B. 8 years
C. 10 years
D. 5 years
E. 7 years

7) *A* is two years older than *B* who is twice as old as *C*. If the total of the ages of *A*, *B* and *C* be 27, the how old is *B*?

A. 10
B. 12
C. 20
D. 5
E. Cannot be determined

8) In the table below are shown some of the broad classifications used by a town bookshop in cataloguing books and the number of books in stock per classification.

Book classifications	Current stock level
Paperback Fiction	12,750
Biography	3,800
History	5,700
Science	3,450
Geography	2,275
Medical	3,500
Nature	4,125
Education	7,600
Reference	10,300
Ancient World	1,900

To the nearest whole number, what percentage of stock in the bookshop is classified as "history"?

A. 3%
B. 5%
C. 7%
D. 10%
E. 12%

9) Below is a line drawing of a church made by a surveyor as seen from directly above in an aeroplane. When the surveyor returns to the ground she wants to identify which particular church it was she drew.

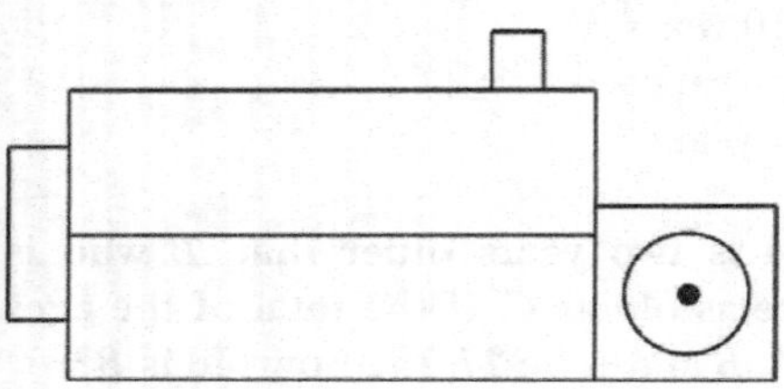

Which one of the churches drawn below, as seen from ground level, could NOT be the one drawn above?

A.

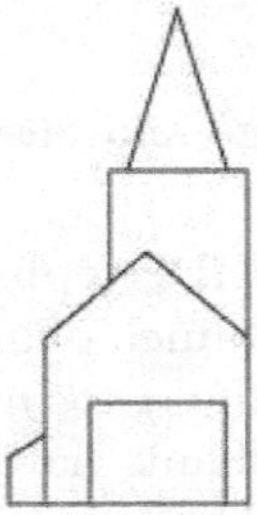

B.

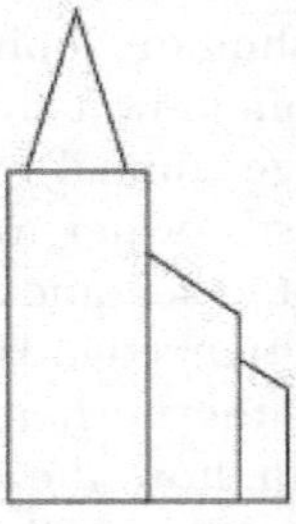

C.

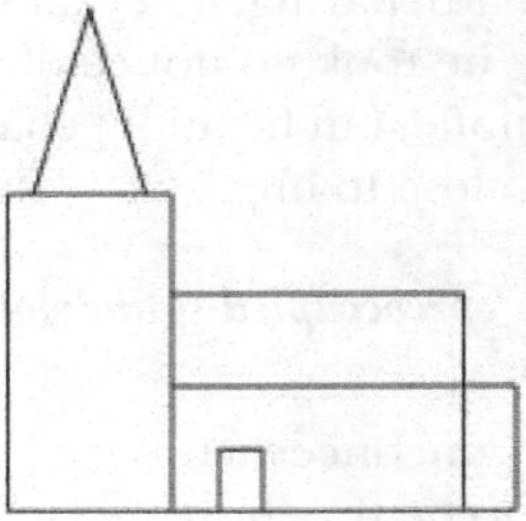

D.

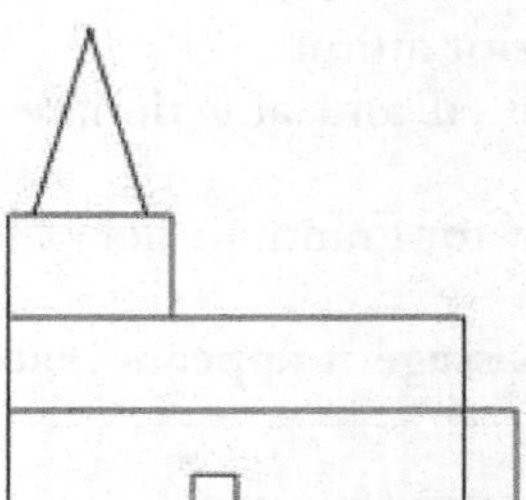

E.

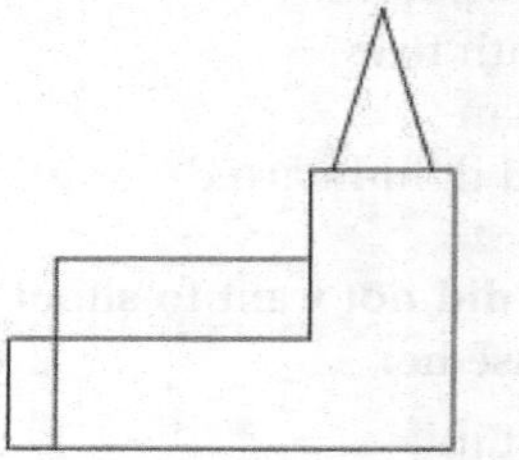

10) A student multiplied a number by 3/5 instead of 5/3. What is the percentage error in the calculation?

A. 34%
B. 44%
C. 64%
D. 54%
E. 24%

11) Clouds are caused by what?

A. Evaporation
B. Humidity
C. Water vapour condensing
D. Melting ice crystals
E. Transpiration

12) Where is the tropic of Capricorn?

A. North of the Equator
B. On the Equator
C. South of the Equator
D. Both sides of the Equator
E. On the Greenwich Meridian

13) In which of the following Shakespearean plays can we find the character of *Titania*?

A. Romeo and Juliet
B. Othello
C. King Lear
D. The Tempest
E. A Midsummer Night's Dream

14) The Commonwealth of Nations was created as:

A. a statement of British colonialism
B. an association of states politically and economically subject to Britain
C. a free association of independent states with strong economic and cultural links with Great Britain
D. the first step towards a European Community
E. the first step towards the birth of the United Nations

15) The two major British parties are:

A. Democratic and Republican
B. Conservative and Liberal
C. Conservative and Democratic
D. Labour and Conservative
E. Republican and Conservative

16) The steam engine was invented by:

A. Stevenson
B. Meucci
C. Newton
D. Edison
E. Watt

17) The term survival of the fittest was originally associated with:

A. sport
B. war games
C. darwinism
D. politics
E. economics

18) Which river flows through Paris?

A. Tiber
B. Rhine
C. Danube
D. Loire
E. Seine

19) What was Stanley Kubrick's nationality, the director of the famous movie *Shining* (1980)?

A. German
B. English
C. Hungarian
D. American
E. Czech

20) *1984* by George Orwell was written in:

A. 1935
B. 1954
C. 1948
D. 1939
E. 1944

21) Which of the following countries is NOT a founding member of the European Union?

A. Sweden
B. Belgium
C. France
D. Germany
E. Italy

22) Which of the following personalities was NOT awarded the Nobel Medicine Prize?

A. Renato Dulbecco
B. Konrad Lorenz
C. Harold Pinter
D. Rita Levi Montalcini
E. Ivan Petrovič Pavlov

23) A common functional group found in glucose and fructose is a(n):

A. amine
B. glycerol
C. hydroxyl
D. sulfhydryl
E. carbonyl

24) Which of the following is not found in the urine of a normal healthy adult?

A. Uric acid
B. Ammonia
C. Glucose
D. Urea
E. Sodium chloride

25) Which one of the following is NOT found in naturally occurring eukaryotic DNA?

A. Genes
B. Alleles
C. Carbohydrate
D. Phosphodiester bonds
E. Lipid

26) What is the name of the jelly-like substance that is inside the cell?

A. Ectoplasm
B. Cytokinesis
C. Cytoplasm
D. Endoplasmic reticulum
E. Golgi apparatus

27) What cell feature is responsible for storing water?

A. Mitochondria
B. Vacuole
C. Lysosome
D. Cell membrane
E. Nucleus

28) A monomer is:

A. a type of covalent bond in organic molecules
B. a building block of an organic molecule
C. a neurotransmitter in the brain
D. a type of amino acid
E. a membrane-bound organelle found in nearly all animal cells

29) Saturated fats are:

A. derived from animals
B. derived from plants
C. most closely related to protein structure
D. very closely related to nucleic acid structure
E. fatty acids in which there is one or more double bond in the fatty acid

30) The functional group NH_2 can be found in:

A. carbohydrates
B. nucleic acids
C. lipids
D. proteins
E. vitamins

31) Movement of cell against concentration gradient is called:

A. osmosis
B. active transport
C. diffusion
D. passive transport
E. meiosis

32) Photosynthesis generally takes place in which parts of the plant?

A. Leaf and other chloroplast bearing plants
B. Steam and leaf
C. Roots and chloroplast bearing plants
D. Bark and leaf
E. Steam only

33) Most fish do not sink in water because of the presence of:
I: swim bladder;
II: air bladder;
III: air sacs;
IV: air in spongy bones

A. I and II are correct
B. II and III are correct
C. III and IV are correct
D. I, II, III and IV are correct
E. III and I are correct

34) Plants synthesize proteins from:

A. starch
B. sugar
C. amino acids
D. fatty acids
E. calcium

35) One of the following is not a function of bones.

A. Place for muscle attachment
B. Protection of vital organs
C. Secretion of hormones for calcium regulation in blood and bones
D. Production of blood corpuscles
E. All of the listed are functions of bones

36) Plants absorb most part of water needed by them through their:

A. embryonic zone
B. growing point
C. zone of elongation
D. root hairs
E. leaves

37) Proces of cell division can take place by:

A. heterosis
B. fusion
C. mitosis
D. meiosis
E. none of the listed

38) Most highly intelligent mammals are:

A. whales
B. dolphins
C. elephants
D. kangaroos
E. foxes

39) Photosynthesis takes place faster in:

A. yellow light
B. white light
C. red light
D. darkness
E. green light

40) Nucleus, the genetic material containing rounded body in each cell, was first discovered in 1831 by:

A. Robert Hooke
B. Robert Brown
C. Rudolf Virchow
D. Theodore Schwann
E. Terry H. Brown

41) When atoms of different elements are joined together into groups, they create ___________.

A. compounds
B. molecules

C. mixtures
D. isomers
E. none of the others

42) The temperature at which a substance changes from a liquid to a gas is called:

A. boiling point
B. freezing point
C. melting point
D. condensation point
E. fusion point

43) When HCl(aq) is exactly neutralized by NaOH(aq), the hydrogen ion concentration in the resulting mixture is:

A. always less than the concentration of the hydroxide ions
B. always greater than the concentration of the hydroxide ions
C. always equal to the concentration of the hydroxide ions
D. sometimes greater and sometimes less than the concentration of the hydroxide ions
E. none of the listed

44) Which compounds are isomers?

A. 1-propanol and 2-propanol
B. Methanoic acid and ethanoic acid
C. Methanol and methanal
D. Ethane and ethanol
E. Methanoic acid and ethanol

45) Which statement explains why the element carbon forms so many compounds?

A. Carbon atoms combine readily with oxygen
B. Carbon atoms have very high electronegativity
C. Carbon atoms active oxygen process
D. Carbon readily forms ionic bonds with other carbon atoms
E. Carbon readily forms covalent bonds with other carbon atoms

46) In a molecule of CH_4, the hydrogen atoms are spatially oriented toward the centers of a regular:

A. pyramid
B. tetrahedron
C. square
D. circle
E. rectangle

47) The reaction $CH_2CH_2 + H_2 \rightarrow CH_3CH_3$ is an example of:

A. substitution
B. addition
C. esterification
D. melting
E. fermentation

48) Which molecule contains a total of three carbon atoms?

A. 2-methylpropane
B. 2-methylbutane
C. Propane
D. Butane
E. Ethanol

49) What substance is made up of monomers joined together in long chains?

A. Ketone
B. Protein
C. Ester
D. Acid
E. Gas

50) Which type of reaction is occurring when a metal undergoes corrosion?

A. Oxidation-reduction
B. Neutralization
C. Naturalisation
D. Polymerization
E. Saponification

51) Which substance functions as the electrolyte in an automobile battery?

A. PbO_2

B. $PbSO_4$
C. H_2SO_4
D. H_2O
E. HSO

52) Arrange the following in ascending order of the number of molecules present.
1 5.00 g Br_2
2 2.00 g CH_4
3 1.12 dm^3 So_3 (g)
Use relative atomic mass: H = 1; C = 12; O = 16; S = 32; Br = 80.
Take the volume of 1 mole of gas to be 22.4 dm^3.

A. 1, 2, 3
B. 1, 3, 2
C. 2, 1, 3
D. 3, 1, 2
E. 2, 3, 1

53) The value of the expression $(x - 5)^{-2}$ depends on *x*. Which are the possible values for *x* that make this expression negative?

A. $x < -5$
B. $-5 < x < 5$
C. $x > 5$
D. No value for *x* makes the expression negative
E. $x < 0$

54) The cube of the binomial $(a + b)^3$ is equal to:

A. $a^3 + 3a^2b + 3ab^2 + b^3$
B. $a^3 - 3a^2b + 3ab^2 - b^3$
C. $a^3 + b^3 + 3ab$
D. $a + b + 3a + 3b$
E. $a^3 - b^3 - 3$

55) If the sum of all the forces acting on a moving object is zero, the object will:

A. slow down and stop
B. change the direction of its motion
C. accelerate uniformly
D. continue moving with constant velocity
E. none of the listed

56) Which of the following values is the most accurate approximation for the square root of 814.420?

A. 90
B. 900
C. 9000
D. 81442
E. 407270

57) An aeroplane is flying horizontally with a velocity of 600 km/h and at a height of 1960 m. When it is vertically at a point *A* on the ground a bomb is released from it. The bomb strikes the ground at point *B*. The distance *AB* is:

A. 1200 m
B. 0.33 km
C. 3.33 km
D. 33 km
E. 15 km

58) A 1200-kilogram car traveling at 10 meters per second hits a tree and is brought to rest in 0.10 second. What is the magnitude of the average force acting on the car to bring it to rest?

A. 1.2×10^2 N
B. 1.2×10^3 N
C. 1.2×10^4 N
D. 1.2×10^5 N
E. 1.4×10^3 N

59) A 3.0-kilogram block is initially at rest on a frictionless, horizontal surface. The block is moved 8.0 meters in 2.0 seconds by the application of a 12-newton horizontal force, as shown in the diagram below. What is the average power developed while moving the block?

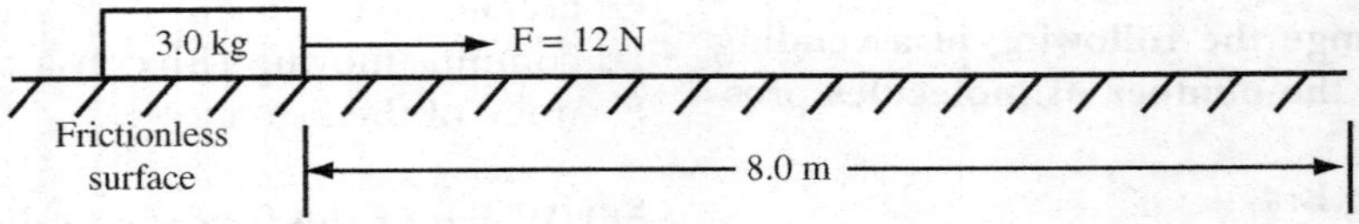

A. 24 W
B. 32 W
C. 48 W
D. 96 W
E. 85 W

60) One nanometer is equal to:

A. 10^{-6} m
B. 10^{-8} m
C. 10^{-9} m
D. 10^{-5} m
E. 10^{-3} m

RISPOSTE CORRETTE

1) D	11) A	21) A	31) B	41) B	51) C
2) B	12) C	22) C	32) A	42) A	52) B
3) B	13) E	23) C	33) A	43) C	53) D
4) D	14) C	24) C	34) C	44) A	54) A
5) B	15) D	25) E	35) C	45) E	55) D
6) A	16) E	26) C	36) D	46) B	56) B
7) A	17) C	27) B	37) C	47) B	57) C
8) D	18) E	28) B	38) B	48) C	58) D
9) D	19) D	29) A	39) B	49) B	59) C
10) C	20) C	30) D	40) B	50) A	60) C

Test 2

1) Read the following passage and answer the question.

Homo erectus appeared 1.9 million years ago. It was 60% larger than its *Australopithecine* predecessor and had a significantly increased brain size, as well as a smaller, flatter gut, differently angled ribs and smaller teeth and mouth. The trigger for this huge evolutionary change has to be the advent of cooking, despite the scant evidence for human control of fire earlier than 400,000 years ago. Heating breaks down indigestible molecules and makes them digestible. Starch in uncooked roots, for example, is often in crystalline form. Until it's heated, our digestive systems can't use it. That means our ancestors could obtain as much nutrition from one roasted tuber as they could from several raw ones, and therefore needed to eat less. Cooking also softens food, diminishing the need for big teeth that can shear and pulverise.

Smaller teeth also mean smaller faces, as well as much smaller mouths.

Which one of the following best expresses the main conclusion of the above argument?

A. The appearance of *Homo erectus* brought about huge evolutionary changes in the species
B. By diminishing the need for big powerful teeth, cooking gave our ancestors smaller faces and smaller mouths
C. *Homo erectus* needed to eat less than its predecessor, *Australopithecus*, to obtain the same amount of nutrition
D. There is little evidence for human use of fire for cooking until long after the appearance of *Homo erectus*
E. Cooking must be the explanation for the evolutionary changes that came with the appearance of *Homo erectus*

2) Read the following passage and answer the question.

The worst of what ensued when the Exxon Valdez spilled 40,000 tons of crude oil into Alaska's coastal waters in 1989 is not that it was the most damaging oil spill in history but that it isn't yet history. Despite the intense research on the ecosystem, this 10,000-squaremile tapestry of ice fields, mountains, forests and sea is far from recovered. Lingering and unanticipated injuries abound. A 2001 study found more than 100 tons of toxic oil remaining on dozens of the beaches, oil that seeps out with every tide, and that - because incomplete weathering left behind higher concentrations of toxins - is even more poisonous now than when it gushed from the ripped tanker. This oil will remain on these beaches for decades to come.

(Adapted from *The Lingering Lessons of the EV* by Marybeth Holleman, *Ecologist*. May 2004, p 12)

Which of the following best summarises the main conclusion of the argument?

A. Despite the research on the coastal ecosystem, the affected environment has not returned to normal
B. The worst aspect of the Exxon Valdez oil spill is that its consequences are not yet played out
C. Much of the damage caused by the Exxon Valdez oil spill was due to the oarticular nature of the coastal line

D. The harmful effects of the oil are greater now than they were when the Exxon Valdez spilled its cargo
E. There will be oil on Alaska's beaches decades from now

3) The length of the bridge, which a train 130 metres long and travelling at 45 km/hr can cross in 30 seconds, is:

A. 250 m
B. 225 m
C. 245 m
D. 200 m
E. 215 m

4) In a group of 6 boys and 4 girls, four children are to be selected. In how many different ways can they be selected such that at least one boy should be there?

A. 220
B. 205
C. 154
D. 209
E. 159

5) How many 3-digit numbers can be formed from the digits 2, 3, 5, 6, 7 and 9, which are divisible by 5 and none of the digits is repeated?

A. 20
B. 18
C. 15
D. 5
E. 10

6) The table below details the deals available from broadband providers.

Provider	Speed	Downloads	Contract	Cost (monthly)
Chat-Chat	20 MB	20 GB	12 months	£ 12.00
Yellow	24 MB	unlimited	12 months	£ 12.50
E20	24 MB	40 GB	18 months	£ 7.50
Pure Media	24 MB	unlimited	12 months	£ 12.00
DTT	20 MB	40 GB	18 months	£ 15.00

All the providers except E20 have "special" offers for new customers: Chat-Chat – 40% reduction for 6 months; Yellow – first 3 months free; Pure Media - £ 40.00 off; DTT - £ 1.00 a month for the first 3 months.
Irrespective of the speed, downloads and contract period, which one of the providers would be the cheapest over the first 6 months?

A. Chat-Chat
B. Pure Media
C. Yellow
D. E20
E. DTT

7) Look at this series: 53, 53, 40, 40, 27, 27, ... What number should come next?

A. 53
B. 12
C. 34
D. 14
E. 27

8) Elated is to despondent as enlightened is to:

A. poor
B. miserable
C. tolerant
D. aware
E. ignorant

9) Arrange the words given below in a meaningful sequence.
1. Family; 2. Community;
3. Member; 4. Locality; 5. Country

A. 3, 1, 2, 4, 5
B. 3, 1, 2, 5, 4
C. 3, 1, 4, 2, 5
D. 3, 1, 4, 5, 2
E. 1, 3, 4, 2, 5

10) Choose the word which is different from the rest.

A. Yoghurt
B. Butter
C. Oil
D. Cheese
E. Cream

11) What is the former name of the Indian city of Mumbai?

A. Balhi
B. Bombay
C. Calcutta
D. Madras
E. Poona

12) Which mountain range extends from the Czech Republic to Romania?

A. Carpathians
B. Urals
C. Alps
D. Apennines
E. Pyrenees

13) Which royal dynasty was born at the end of the War of the Roses?

A. Windsor
B. Hannover
C. Stuart
D. Tudor
E. Lancaster

14) What is meant by the term «Chartism»?

A. A document advocating women's rights
B. The environmental movement of the 1970's
C. An exchange of letters and documents
D. A document in favour of universal suffrage
E. An English movement in defense of social rights

15) In which country were the Boer Wars fought (1880-81 and 1899-1902)?

A. South Africa
B. Congo
C. Bangladesh
D. Birmania
E. India

16) *Apocalypse Now*, the film on Vietnam, directed by Francis Ford Coppola, draws its inspiration from:

A. G. Orwell's apocalyptic novel 1984
B. A. Huxley's *Brave New World*
C. J. Conrad's apocalyptic vision of colonialism in *Heart of Darkness*
D. S. Beckett's apocalyptic view of the post war world
E. P.K. Dick's *Clans of the Alphane Moon*

17) The American Declaration of Independence dates back to:

A. 1789
B. 1777
C. 1861
D. 1776
E. 1799

18) James Joyce is noted for:

A. the simplicity of his plots
B. his lyrical poetry which celebrates the natural beauty and cultural heritage of his native Ireland
C. his ability to reproduce the speech patterns of the common man
D. his highly symbolic description of the characters

E. his groundbreaking experimentation in the structure, language and themes of his novels

19) The Nobel Laureate Derek Walcott for Literature is from:

A. British West Indies
B. New Zealand
C. Australia
D. South Africa
E. Ireland

20) In which country would you find the Taj Mahal?

A. Thailand
B. Uraguay
C. India
D. Pakistan
E. North Korea

21) A *Pun* is:

A. the same as a proverb
B. a humorous ambiguous expression
C. a very short poem
D. a type of rock music
E. a bitter satire

22) The *Magna Charta* was sealed by:

A. King John (1215)
B. Oliver Cromwell (1654)
C. King Richard I (1190)
D. King James I (1608)
E. King Henry VIII (1510)

23) How is energy transformed in an ecosystem?

A. Energy is brought in from oxygen, transformed during photosynthesis, converted into Adenosine Diphosphate and then stored as carbohydrates
B. Energy is brought in from the sun, transformed during photosynthesis, converted into Adenosine Triphosphate (ATP) and then stored as carbohydrates
C. Energy is brought in from the sun, converted into Adenosine Triphosphate (ATP) and then scored as lipids
D. Energy is brought in from the sun, transformed during photosynthesis, converted into carbohydrates and then stored as Adenosine Triphosphate (ATP)
E. Energy is brought in from oxygen, converted into Adenosine Diphosphate and then stored as lipids

24) The monomer of a carbohydrate is:

A. a nucleotide
B. an amino acid
C. monosaccharide
D. fatty acid and glycerol
E. disaccharide

25) A functional group found in lipids is:

A. a carbonyl
B. a hydroxyl
C. a carboxyl
D. an amine
E. none of the others

26) Look at the table of hormones involved in glucose homeostasis. Which combinations of hormones would be seen in a healthy individual?

	Blood sugar	Insulin	Glucagon
A.	↓	↑	↑
B.	↑	↓	↑
C.	↓	↓	↑
D.	↑	↑	↓
E.	↓	↓	↓

Which of the following formulae for ethanol is correct?

A. C_2H_6
B. C_2H_5OH
C. CH_2OH
D. $C_2H_5OH_2$
E. C_2H_6OH

27) Which labelled component on the diagram of a cell produces pyruvate (pyruvic acid) during respiration?

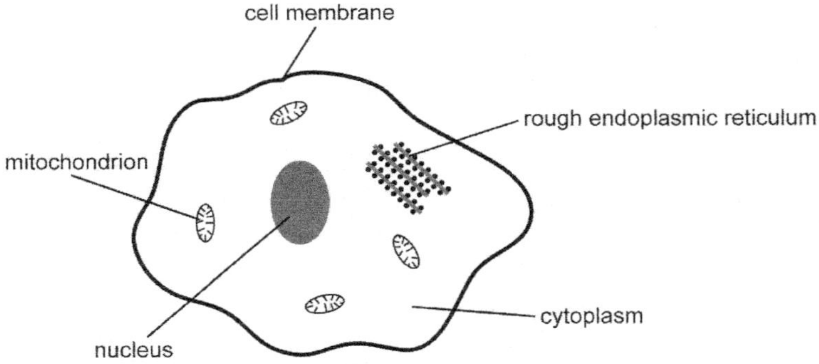

A. Cell membrane
B. Nucleus
C. Mitochondrion
D. Cytoplasm
E. Rough endoplasmic reticulum

28) A sample of mitochondria was isolated from an animal cell and provided with the substrates its enzymes can act on. Which one of the following reactions would NOT be able to take place?
[Assume the sample is not contaminated]

A. Decarboxylation reactions that produce carbon dioxide
B. The oxidation of reduced NAD
C. The phosphorylation of glucose
D. The formation of acetyl coenzyme A
E. The synthesis of ATP from ADP and inorganic phosphate

29) The graph shows the energy levels of a reaction as it progresses, without an enzyme.

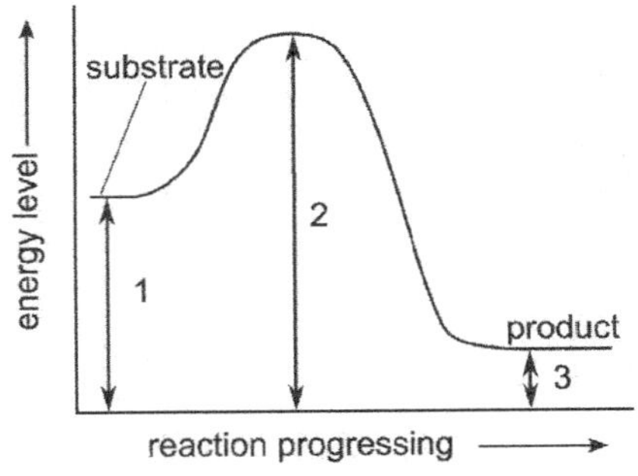

Which of the energy levels, represented by the arrows above, would change if an enzyme that catalysed the reaction was present?

A. 1 and 3 only
B. 2 only
C. 1 only
D. 3 only
E. 1 and 2 only

30) In a mature mRNA molecule, which of the following binds to the phosphate?
1. ribose sugar
2. uracil
3. thymine

A. 2 only
B. 3 only
C. 2 and 3 only
D. 1 only
E. 1 and 2 only

31) Primary phloem develops from:

A. lateral meristem
B. protoderm
C. extrastelar cambium
D. provascular tissue
E. embryonic zone

32) Other than spreading malaria, anopheles mosquitoes are also vectors of:

A. dengue fever
B. filariasis
C. encephalitis
D. yellow fever
E. cholera

33) Pyorrhoea is a disease of the:

A. nose
B. heart
C. gums
D. lungs
E. fingers

34) O_2 released in the process of photosynthesis comes from:

A. CO_2
B. water
C. sugar
D. pyruvic acid
E. calcium

35) Placenta is the structure formed:

A. by the union of foetal and uterine tissue
B. by foetus only
C. by fusion of germ layers
D. by uterine tissue only
E. none of the listed

36) Neurospora is used as genetic material because:

A. it has short life cycle of 10 days
B. the product of single meiosis can be easily analysed
C. meiotic products are linearly arranged in the form of ordered tetrads
D. is a diploid fungus
E. none of the listed

37) Phloem is a tissue found in:

A. reproductive organs of animals
B. plants
C. insects
D. mammals
E. animal tissues

38) N_2 content is kept constant in the biosphere due to:

A. N_2 fixation
B. industrial pollution
C. nitrogen cycle
D. absorption of N_2
E. absorption of O_2

39) Prothrombin which helps in clotting of blood is released by:

A. lymphocytes
B. erythrocytes
C. monocytes
D. blood platelets
E. diploid cells

40) Myopia is connected with:

A. ears
B. eyes
C. lungs
D. breast
E. heart

41) There are alternate acid base theories that define an acid as any species that can:

A. donate a proton
B. donate an electron
C. accept a proton
D. accept an electron
E. decrease an electron

42) Which 0.1 M solution will turn phenolphthalein pink?

A. HBr(aq)
B. CO_2(aq)
C. OH(aq)
D. CH_3OH(aq)
E. Cl(aq)

43) Given the equation: $H^+ + OH^- \leftrightarrow H_2O$, which type of reaction does the equation represent?

A. Esterification
B. Gasification
C. Decomposition
D. Hydrolysis
E. Neutralization

44) Given the following data: volume of acid (HCl) used = 14.4 mL; volume of base (NaOH) used = 22.4 mL; molarity of standard base (NaOH) = 0.20 M; what is the molarity of the acid solution?

A. 1.6 M
B. 12 M
C. 0.64 M
D. 0.31 M
E. 0.13 M

45) The temperature levels in a nuclear reactor are maintained primarily by the use of:

A. shielding
B. coolants
C. moderators
D. electrons
E. control rods

46) Which radioactive emanations have a charge of –1?

A. Neutrons
B. Protons
C. Gamma rays
D. Alpha particles
E. Beta particles

47) What kind of radiation will travel through an electric field on a pathway that remains unaffected by the field?

A. A proton
B. A gamma ray
C. An electron
D. An alpha particle
E. A beta ray

48) Which radioactive isotope is used in geological dating?

A. Uranium-238
B. Iodine-131
C. Cobalt-60
D. Technetium-99
E. Cobalt-90

49) Minimum number of unequal vectors which can give zero resultant is:

A. two
B. three
C. four
D. more than four
E. five

50) What is the popular name for deuterium oxide?

A. Acid rain
B. Dry ice
C. Heavy water
D. Laughing gas
E. Ice

51) As Group 17 (VII) of the Periodic Table is descended (F → At), which of the following properties decrease?

A. Number of electrons in the outer orbital
B. Number of occupied orbitals
C. Both electronegativity and number of electrons in the outer orbital
D. Both electronegativity and number of occupied orbitals
E. Electronegativity (Pauling scale)

52) The position of the first 20 elements in the Periodic Table are shown below.

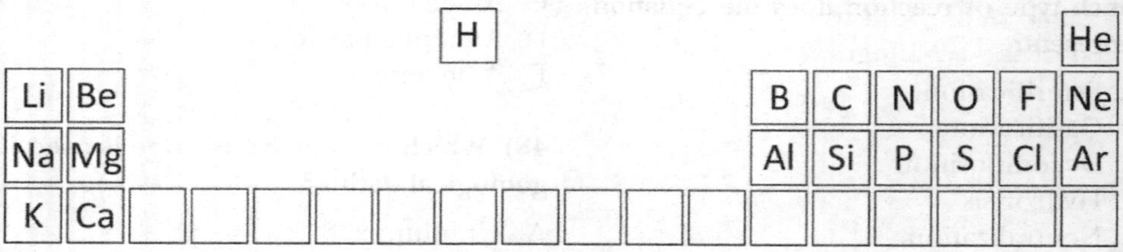

Which one of the following pairs have the same electronic structure?

A. KF and two atoms of Ar
B. $CaCl_2$ and three atoms of Ar
C. BH_3 and NH_3
D. MgF_2 and K_2O
E. PO_3^- and SO_3^{2-}

53) The expression $k = y^2 + z^2 - 1 - 2\,yz$ can be written as:

A. $k = (y + z)(y - z) - 1$
B. $k = (y - z + 1)(y - z - 1)$
C. $k = (y + z + 1)(y - z - 1)$
D. $k = (yz + 1)(yz - 1)$
E. $k = (yz)(y + 1)(y - 1)$

54) Which of the following numbers is a root of the equation $2^{x+2} \cdot 3^x = \frac{1}{9}$?

A. 2
B. 0
C. –2
D. $\frac{1}{2}$
E. $\frac{2}{3}$

55) $Log_3 81 = \ldots$

A. 27
B. 4
C. 8
D. 9
E. 18

56) Consider the expression $y = A/x$. Keeping the value of *A* constant, if *x* halves:

A. then *y* halves
B. then *y* doubles
C. then *y* is multiplied by 5
D. then *y* does not vary
E. then *y* is undetermined

57) A net force of 10 newtons accelerates an object at 5.0 meters per second^2. What net force would be required to accelerate the same object at 1.0 meter per second^2?

A. 1.0 N
B. 2.0 N
C. 5.0 N
D. 50 N
E. 20.2 N

58) A 2.0×10^3-kilogram car travels at a constant speed of 12 meters per second around a circular curve of radius 30 meters. As the car goes around the curve, the centripetal force is directed:

A. toward the center of the circular curve
B. away from the center of the circular curve
C. tangent to the curve in the direction of motion
D. tangent to the curve opposite the direction of motion
E. tangent to the center in direction of motion

59) A 1.2-kilogram block and a 1.8-kilogram block are initially at rest on a frictionless, horizontal surface. When a compressed spring between the blocks is released, the 1.8-kilogram block moves to the right at 2.0 meters per second, as shown. What is the speed of the 1.2-kilogram block after the spring is released?

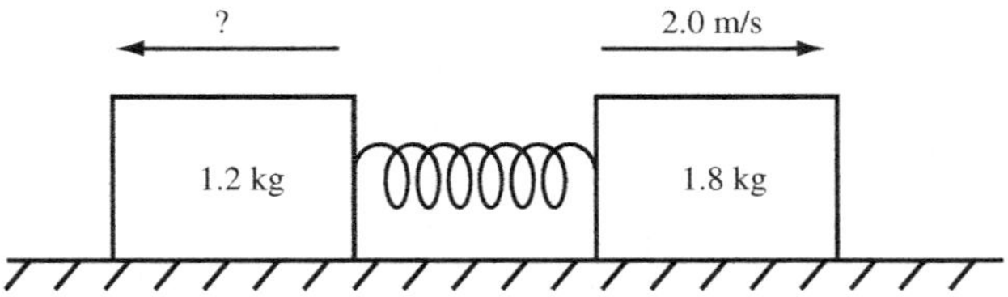

A. 1.4 m/s
B. 2.0 m/s
C. 3.0 m/s
D. 3.6 m/s
E. 2.8 m/s

60) An object weighing 15 newtons is lifted from the ground to a height of 0.22 meter. The increase in the object's gravitational potential energy is approximately:

A. 310 J
B. 32 J
C. 3.3 J
D. 0.34 J
E. 0.009 J

RISPOSTE CORRETTE

1) E	11) B	21) B	31) D	41) A	51) E
2) B	12) A	22) A	32) B	42) C	52) B
3) C	13) D	23) D	33) C	43) E	53) B
4) D	14) E	24) C	34) B	44) D	54) C
5) A	15) A	25) C	35) A	45) B	55) B
6) B	16) C	26) B	36) A	46) E	56) B
7) D	17) D	27) D	37) B	47) B	57) B
8) E	18) E	28) C	38) C	48) A	58) A
9) A	19) A	29) B	39) D	49) B	59) C
10) C	20) C	30) D	40) B	50) C	60) C

Test 3

Read the following passage and answer the questions nr. 1-4.

"At this stage of civilisation, when many nations are brought in to close and vital contact for good and evil, it is essential, as never before, that their gross ignorance of one another should be diminished, that they should begin to understand a little of one another's historical experience and resulting mentality. It is the fault of the English to expect the people of other countries to react as they do, to political and international situations. Our genuine goodwill and good intentions are often brought to nothing, because we expect other people to be like us. This would be corrected if we knew the history, not necessarily in detail but in broad outlines, of the social and political conditions which have given to each nation its present character".

1) According to the author, "mentality" of a nation is mainly product of its:

A. history
B. international position
C. politics
D. present character
E. social status

2) The need for a greater understanding among nations:

A. was always there
B. is no longer there
C. is more today than ever before
D. will always be there
E. will show itself in the future

3) The character of a nation is the result of its:

A. mentality
B. cultural heritage
C. gross ignorance
D. socio-political conditions
E. wealth

4) According to the author, his countrymen should:

A. read the story of other nations
B. have a better understanding of other nations
C. not react to other actions
D. have vital contacts with other nations
E. know the past of their nation

5) A person crosses a 600 m long street in 5 minutes. What is his speed in km per hour?

A. 5
B. 7.2
C. 3.6
D. 8.4
E. 10

6) If a person walks at 14 km/hr instead of 10 km/hr, he would have walked 20 km more. The actual distance travelled by him is:

A. 36 km
B. 80 km
C. 56 km
D. 70 km
E. 50 km

7) A train can travel 50% faster than a car. Both start from point *A* at the same time and reach point *B* 75 kms away from *A* at the same time. On the way, however, the train lost about 12.5 minutes while

stopping at the stations. The speed of the car is:

A. 140 kmph
B. 120 kmph
C. 100 kmph
D. 110 kmph
E. 130 kmph

8) A picture of a boat with 8 rowers is shown below. The distance between the entry and exit point of each oar is 6 m (relative to the boat) and the oars are in the water for 50% of the time. The rowers are 1.5 m apart in a boat 17 m long. When the stroke rate is 30 per minute, the boat is moving forward at 5 m/s.

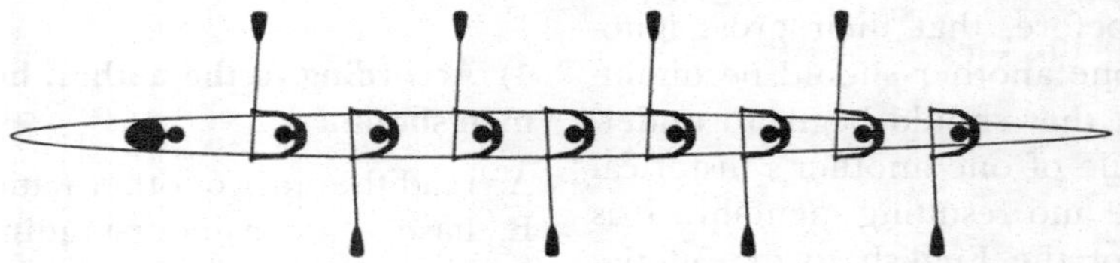

Relative to the water, what is the relationship between the oar entry and exit points?

A. The oar exits 1 m ahead of where it enters the water
B. The oar exits 5 m ahead of where it enters the water
C. The oar exits 6 m behind where it enters the water
D. The oar exits 1 m behind where it enters the water
E. The oar exits 6 m ahead of where it enters the water

9) Look at this series: 4, 5, 8, 9, 12, 13, 16, ... What number should come next?

A. 19
B. 16
C. 14
D. 17
E. 15

10) Play is to actor as concert is to:

A. orchestra
B. piano
C. symphony
D. percussion
E. musician

11) Romanticism was:

A. a short-lived literary movement that evolved from Classicism
B. a poetic style that rejected the spontaneity of eighteenth-century poetry
C. a European movement that involved all forms of art
D. a philosophical school of thought XIX century
E. an artistic movement of the XVII century

12) Which of the following writers dealt with the problems caused by the Industrial Revolution?

A. P.B. Shelley
B. C. Dickens
C. J. Joyce
D. L. Carroll
E. O. Wilde

13) The War of the Roses was fought between:

A. House of Lancaster and House of York
B. House of Tudor and House of York

C. House of Spencer and House of York
D. House of Tudor and House of Lancaster
E. House of Spencer and House of Tudor

14) Who won the Nobel Prize for peace in 2019?

A. Carola Rackete
B. Abiy Ahmed Ali
C. Greta Thunberg
D. Amnesty International
E. Reporter Without Borders

15) The study of the origins and history of the form and meaning of words is known as:

A. entomology
B. lexicography
C. lexicology
D. etymology
E. philology

16) Of which country is Vaduz the capital?

A. Montenegro
B. Estonia
C. Liechtenstein
D. Iceland
E. Belarus

17) Which of the following did not occur in the 1960's?

A. Signing of the Treaty of Rome
B. First man on the moon
C. Kennedy's assassination
D. Che Guevara's death
E. Prague Spring

18) Which of the following words is not related to *computer language*?

A. Infopoverty
B. Trapdoor
C. Malware
D. Hacker
E. Laymen

19) Which sentence is correct?

A. Badminton is played by women only
B. Badminton is played by a team of five players
C. Badminton is played by a team of four players
D. Badminton is played by two or four people
E. Badminton is played by men only

20) Who wrote *Heart of Darkness*?

A. Edgar Allan Poe
B. Franz Kafka
C. Vladimir Nabokov
D. Emily Bronte
E. Joseph Conrad

21) Where was the International Red Cross founded in 1864?

A. Geneva
B. Paris
C. Basel
D. Bern
E. Zurich

22) In which year did Hitler's Germany annexe Austria?

A. 1937
B. 1930
C. 1938
D. 1933
E. 1936

23) All endocrine glands can secrete:

A. antibodies
B. enzymes
C. hormones
D. antibodies and enzymes
E. antibodies and hormones

24) When resting, the inside of a nerve cell contains more chloride ions than sodium ions and so is negatively charged. When the cell fires, sodium ions, but not

potassium ions, enter the cell through a channel and the voltage becomes positive.
What feature of the chemistry of sodium and potassium could explain why sodium ions and not potassium ions enter the cell during firing?

A. The ions have different sizes
B. The chlorides have different solubilities
C. The ions have different colours
D. The metals have different reactivity
E. The ions have different masses

25) The four statements below are about evolution. Which of the statements are correct?

1 All variation is inherited.
2 Better adapted individuals tend to survive and reproduce.
3 Individuals of a species have variation caused by their alleles.
4 New species develop from variants that are better adapted to the environment.

A. 2, 3
B. 3, 4
C. 2, 3, 4
D. 1, 2, 4
E. 1, 2, 3, 4

26) The short-term removal of the nucleus from an Amoeba would alter which one of the following?

A. Osmosis (the movement of water across a membrane)
B. Metabolic processes
C. Diffusion (the movement of particles)
D. Volume of cytoplasm
E. Nutrition

27) Which one of the following describes the function of ligase in the production of recombinant DNA by scientists?

A. Break bonds in DNA
B. Break bonds in tRNA
C. Form bonds in DNA
D. Form bonds in mRNA
E. Break bonds in mRNA

28) Red blood cells live for about:

A. 120 days
B. 250 days
C. 80 days
D. 30 days
E. 180 days

29) Cells that help human body form clots to stop bleeding are called:

A. erythrocytes
B. leukocytes
C. blastomeres
D. hormones
E. platelets

30) The Hardy-Weinberg Law predicts that the genetics of a population will remain in equilibrium as long as there is no ……………..

A. vegetative propagation
B. asexual reproduction
C. sporulation
D. genetic drift
E. mutation

31) Plants absorb dissolved nitrates from soil and convert them into:

A. free nitrogen
B. urea
C. ammonia
D. proteins
E. vitamins

32) Our skin, when exposed to excess sunlight, becomes dark. This is because of our skin pigment called:

A. flavoxanthin
B. melanin
C. carotene
D. xanthophyll
E. none of the listed

33) Ramapithecus and Cro-Magnon man are considered:

A. ancestors of modern man
B. ancestors of monkey
C. ancestors of lion
D. ancestor of dinosaurs
E. none of the listed

34) Outer covering of virus made up of protein is:

A. coat
B. virion
C. viriod
D. enzymes
E. capsid

35) Normal adult human male has:

A. 10 gram of haemoglobin/100 gram of blood
B. 14 gram of haemoglobin/100 gram of blood
C. 18 gram of haemoglobin/100 gram of blood
D. 24 gram of haemoglobin/100 gram of blood
E. 34 gram of haemoglobin/100 gram of blood

36) Most abundant tissues of our body are:

A. muscular
B. connective
C. epithelial
D. nervous
E. epidermis

37) Osmosis is the flow of solution from higher concentration to a solution of lower concentration through a semi permeable membrane. What is incorrect in this statement?

A. Exact concentration of solution is not given
B. Character of semi permeable membrane is not given
C. The flow of solution is not possible through semi permeable membrane
D. All are incorrect
E. Nothing is incorrect

38) Norepinephrine increases:

A. respiration
B. urine production
C. saliva production
D. blood pressure
E. concentration

39) Night blindness is cause by lack of which vitamin?

A. Vitamin A
B. Vitamin B
C. Vitamin C
D. Vitamin D
E. Vitamin E

40) Organic substances which, in very small amounts, control growth and development are called:

A. vitamins
B. cells
C. enzymes
D. protein
E. hormones

41) One molecule of ozone contains how many oxygen atoms?

A. 1
B. 2
C. 3
D. 4
E. 8

42) Compared to the rate of inorganic reactions, the rate of organic reactions generally is:

A. slower because organic particles are ions
B. slower because organic particles contain covalent bonds

C. slower because organic particles contain ions
D. faster because organic particles are ions
E. faster because organic particles contain covalent bonds

43) Which solution will change red litmus to blue?

A. HCl(aq)
B. NaCl(aq)
C. CH_3OH(aq)
D. NaOH(aq)
E. $NaHCl_3$(aq)

44) What is the name of the compound that has the molecular formula C_6H_6?

A. Butane
B. Butene
C. Benzene
D. Butyne
E. Benzolene

45) Which compound is a saturated hydrocarbon?

A. Ethane
B. Ethene
C. Butane
D. Ethyne
E. Ethanol

46) Given the reaction: ZnO + X + heat → Zn + XO, which element, represented by X, is used industrially to reduce the ZnO to Zn?

A. Cu
B. C
C. SN
D. Pb
E. Xe

47) Which quantities are conserved in all oxidation-reduction reactions?

A. Charge only
B. Mass only
C. Temperature only
D. Both charge and mass
E. Neither charge and mass

48) Which formula represents a salt?

A. KOH
B. KCl
C. CH_3OH
D. CH_3COOH
E. CH_2COH

49) What is the pH of a 0.00001 molar HCl solution?

A. 1
B. 9
C. 5
D. 4
E. 6

50) What is the pH of a solution with a hydronium ion concentration of 0.01 mole per liter?

A. 1
B. 2
C. 10
D. 14
E. 16

51) The electrostatic force that holds oppositely charged particles together is called:

A. chemical bond
B. covalent bond
C. metallic bond
D. none of the others
E. ionic bond

52) What is the family name of the group 1A elements?

A. Alkali metals
B. Alkaline Earth metals
C. Halogens
D. Noble Gases
E. Metalloids

53) What is the smallest prime factor of 1001?

A. 3
B. 5
C. 11
D. 7
E. 13

54) For which values of $a \neq 0$ are the two lines $x - ay + 3 = 0$ and $(a + 1)x + ay - 3 = 0$ not parallel?

A. $a \neq -1$
B. $a \neq 3$
C. $a \neq \frac{1}{2}$
D. $a \neq -2$
E. $a \neq +2$

55) The domain of the function $f(x) = \sqrt{\lg_{1/2} x}$ is:

A. $x > 0$
B. $0 < x < 1$
C. $0 < x \leq 1$
D. $x > 1/2$
E. none of the listed

56) The cosine of an angle measuring 110° is:

A. negative
B. greater than ½
C. greater than the sine of the same angle
D. equal to the cosine of an angle measuring 290°
E. none of the listed

57) One should not connect a number of electrical appliances to the same power socket because:

A. this can damage the appliances due to overloading
B. this can damage the domestic wiring due to overloading
C. this can damage the electrical meter
D. the appliance will not get full voltage
E. this can damage the power socket

58) Rainbow is produced when sunlight fall on drops of rain. Which of the following physical phenomena are responsible for this?
I. Diffusion; II. Refraction;
III. Internal reflection

A. I, II and III
B. I and II
C. II and III
D. I and III
E. Only I

59) Natural radioactivity was discovered by:

A. Marie Curie
B. Ernest Rutherford
C. Henri Becquerel
D. Enrico Fermi
E. Albert Einstein

60) Planets are:

A. luminous heavenly bodies revolving around a star
B. non-luminous heavenly bodies
C. luminous heavenly bodies that twinkle
D. luminous heavenly bodies that do not twinkle
E. luminous stars

RISPOSTE CORRETTE

1) A	11) C	21) A	31) A	41) C	51) E
2) C	12) B	22) C	32) B	42) B	52) A
3) D	13) A	23) C	33) A	43) D	53) D
4) B	14) B	24) A	34) E	44) C	54) D
5) B	15) D	25) C	35) B	45) A	55) C
6) E	16) C	26) B	36) A	46) B	56) A
7) C	17) A	27) C	37) C	47) D	57) B
8) D	18) E	28) A	38) D	48) B	58) C
9) D	19) D	29) E	39) A	49) C	59) C
10) E	20) E	30) D	40) E	50) B	60) B

Test 4

1) Motorway speed limits should no longer be restricted to 70 mph. More than half of all motorists admit to driving at 80 mph or above so it may as well be made legal. Driving at 10 mph above the current limit is not frowned upon and few drivers believe that they will be prosecuted for doing so.

Which of the following best expresses the main point of the passage?

A. It is as safe to drive at 80 mph as it is at 70 mph
B. Most drivers are quite happy to disobey speed limits
C. Drivers frequently exceed 80 mph on motorways
D. Driving at 80 mph on motorways is accepted behaviour
E. Cars can be driven at 80 mph without fear of prosecution

2) Non-smokers should take priority over smokers where NHS treatment is concerned. People who engage in smoking are responsible for their own health problems. Those people who have made efforts to maintain their health should not have to wait for treatment behind smokers who have ignored it.

Statement: If all the non-smokers who failed to exercise, watch their weight or avoid excessive alcohol consumption went to the back of the queue there would be few people left at the front.

Which of the following best describes how the short statement relates to the argument?

A. It lends significant support to the argument
B. It presents a significant challenge to the argument
C. It restates the conclusion of the argument
D. It restates one of the premises of the argument
E. It neither supports nor challenges the argument

3) Nuclear power provides cheap and clean electricity. Almost 80 per cent of the electricity needs of France are met by nuclear power plants compared to a paltry 20 per cent in the UK. Coal-fired power stations produce 50 times more carbon dioxide per kilowatt-hour than do nuclear power plants, and fossil fuels will eventually run out. The government should support a new generation of nuclear power stations to tackle climate change and ensure sustainable energy supplies in the future. The UK lags behind France in nuclear technology so the power stations will have to be built and run by French companies.

Which one of the following, if true, would most seriously weaken the above argument?

A. The UK has a better spread of energy sources than France and can look towards 'renewables' for additional power
B. The UK will lose its independence in power generation if nuclear power stations dominate energy sources
C. The construction and decommissioning of nuclear reactors are expensive, and have a large carbon footprint
D. Cutting back on energy consumption would reduce carbon dioxide emissions without the risks from nuclear power

E. France's lack of natural resources meant that it had to embrace nuclear power

4) Wind farms are a poor source of power. When the wind stops blowing, not a single watt of power is produced. Which of the following is an implicit assumption of the above argument?

A. The wind must blow continuously for power to be produced
B. Lack of wind makes wind farms an unreliable power source
C. Wind farms can only produce power intermittently
D. Wind farms are an expensive means of producing power
E. Failure to produce power makes wind farms a poor power source

5) Cellulitis is a bacterial skin infection that mainly affects the extremities. It can be treated with anti-microbial therapy directed by blood culture and antibiotic sensitivity results. However, contamination by other bacteria on the skin usually leads to a high proportion of false positives.
Which of the following can safely be inferred from the above paragraph?

A. It is best to wait for the results of a blood culture and sensitivity test before initiating anti-microbial therapy
B. Cellulitis will only respond to one antibiotic
C. Bacterial contamination leads to a low proportion of false negatives
D. The taking of blood cultures is often of no help in directing the treatment of cellulitis
E. Cases of cellulitis are restricted to the arms and legs

6) What fraction of the square is shaded if A and C are the mid-points of the two sides?

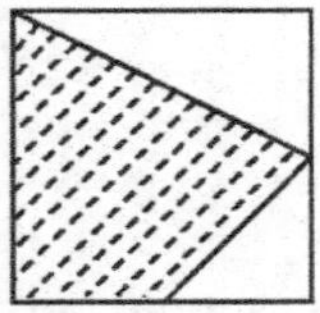

A. 5/8
B. 6/8
C. 5/10
D. 7/8
E. 3/8

7) The bar chart compares the hospital admissions for asthma per 100 000 population, for children in selected European countries. There are 12 million children in the UK and 10 million in Spain. **How many children in the UK have been admitted to hospital with asthma?**

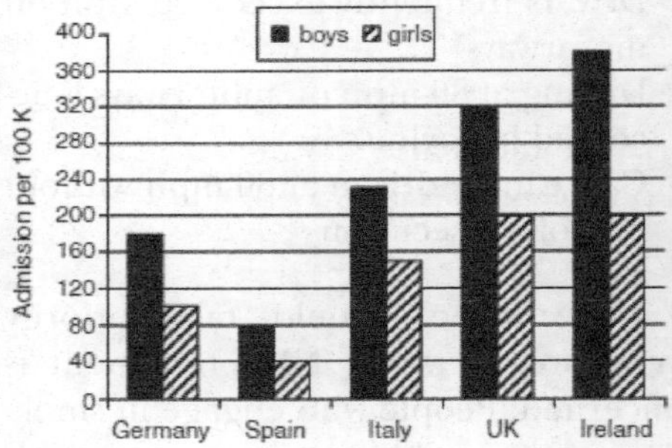

A. 24000
B. 32000
C. 52000
D. 62400
E. 84000

8) Which shape comes next in the following sequence of shapes?

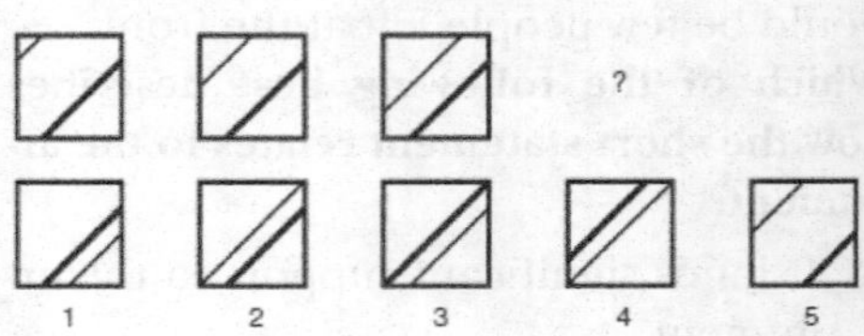

A. 1
B. 2

C. 3
D. 4
E. 5

9) The diagram shows a square wedding cake iced on all sides excluding the base. It measures 30 cm × 30 cm × 15 cm deep. It is to be cut into identical portions measuring 5 cm × 5 cm × 5 cm. How many portions will have icing on them?

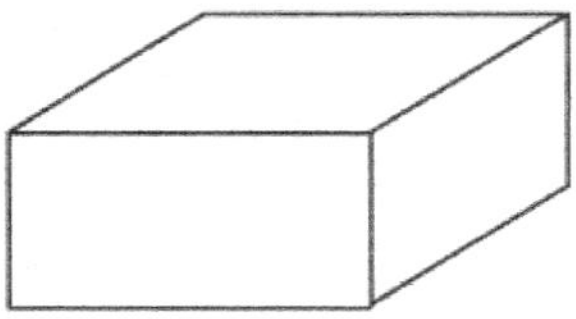

A. 90
B. 76
C. 60
D. 48
E. 40

10) The pie charts show the distribution of A-level grades in two different schools, X and Y.

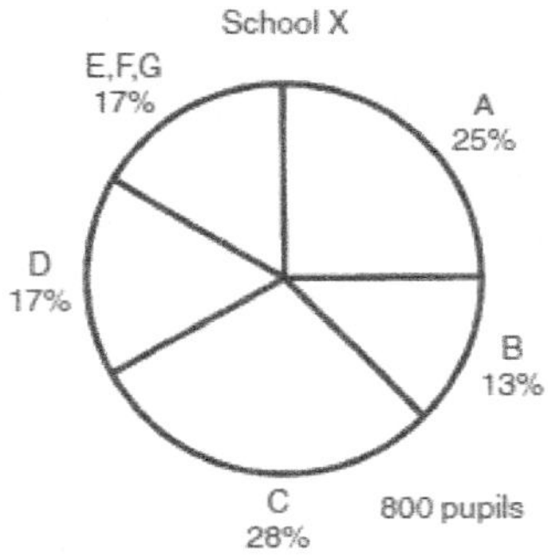

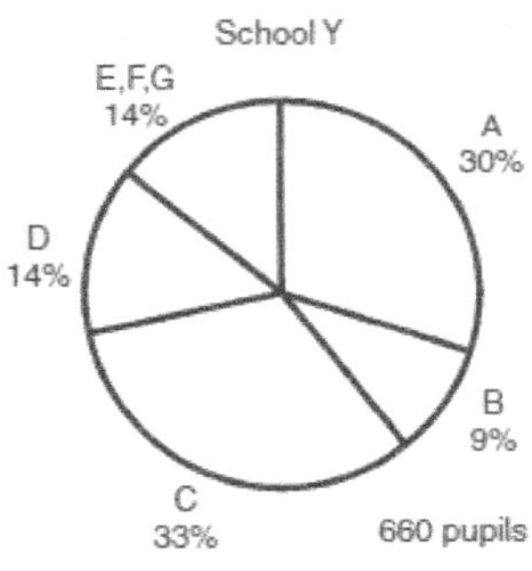

Which of the following can be deduced from the pie charts?
1. School X achieved more A-grades at A level than School Y.
2. The number of pupils achieving grade C or above in School X is 528.
3. The A–C pass rate in School Y was 5 per cent above that in School X.

A. 1 and 2
B. 2 and 3
C. 1 and 3
D. All
E. None

11) What is the name of the movement of the second half of the 19th century which claimed that art was independent of any moral implication?

A. Modernism
B. Aestheticism
C. Classicism
D. Romanticism
E. Renaissance

12) Which American president signed the agreement reached at the Yalta Conference?

A. Thomas Jefferson
B. Franklin D. Roosevelt
C. Harry S. Truman
D. Theodore Roosevelt
E. Herbert Hoover

13) Napoleon was defeated at Waterloo by:

A. Bismark
B. Wellington
C. Nelson
D. Metternich
E. Churchill

14) Which of the following is an American cult movie about the hippie generation?

A. Blade Runner

B. Pulp Fiction
C. Easy Rider
D. Apocalypse Now
E. The Graduate

15) What is the Marshall Plan?

A. An aid programme sponsored by the Soviet Union to help East and West Germany to build up the Berlin Wall
B. A political programme sponsored by the Soviet Union to dismantle the UNO
C. An aid programme sponsored by the USA to support the economies of Western European countries
D. A political programme sponsored by the USA to help European poorest countries
E. An aid programme sponsored by the USA to support the economies of East European countries

16) With which of the following would you NOT associate the Russian scientist Pavlov?

A. Reflex actions
B. Genetics
C. Dogs
D. Bells
E. Salivation

17) With which country would you associate the name Salvador Allende?

A. Chile
B. Brazil
C. Mexico
D. Guatemala
E. Honduras

18) Which of the following would normally be associated with *perestroika*?

A. Breshnev
B. Stalin
C. Chomsky
D. Engels
E. Gorbachev

19) The Domino theory refers to:

A. a board game
B. an artistic movement
C. a political concept
D. a geological theory
E. a philosophical concept

20) The Kyoto Protocol sets out a series of desirable actions in the field of:

A. Japanese culture
B. Chinese culture
C. intercultural relations
D. ecology
E. human rights

21) What was the name of Instanbul until 1930?

A. Constantinople
B. Byzantium
C. Ankara
D. Adrianopolis
E. Izmir

22) Which ancient kingdom had Prague as its capital?

A. Transylvania
B. Bohemia
C. Carpathia
D. Moravia
E. Silesia

23) Which of the following sequences described one half of a complete cycle of breathing?

A. Chest muscles contract, chest expands, chest pressure rises, air is expired
B. Chest muscles contract, chest contracts, chest pressure rises, air is expired
C. Chest muscles contract, chest expands, chest pressure falls, air is inspired
D. Chest muscles relax, chest contracts, chest pressure falls, air is expired

E. Chest muscles relax, chest expands, chest pressure falls, air is inspired

24) A schematic diagram of a nephron is shown below. Where is the concentration of salt the highest?

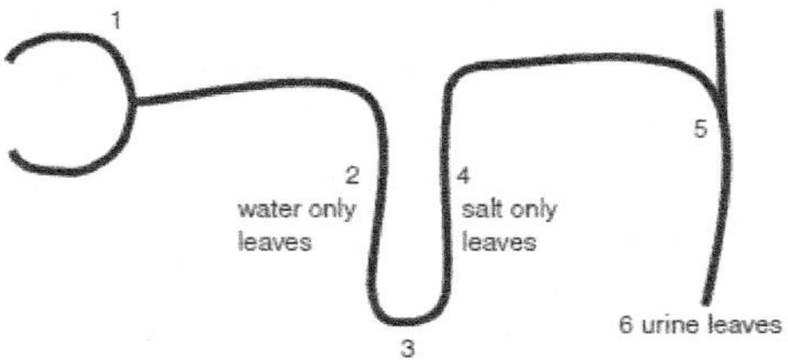

A. 1
B. 2
C. 3
D. 4
E. 5

25) According to the pedigree chart shown below, what is the probability of male M passing on an affected gene if he marries and has children, assuming that his wife is neither affected nor a carrier?

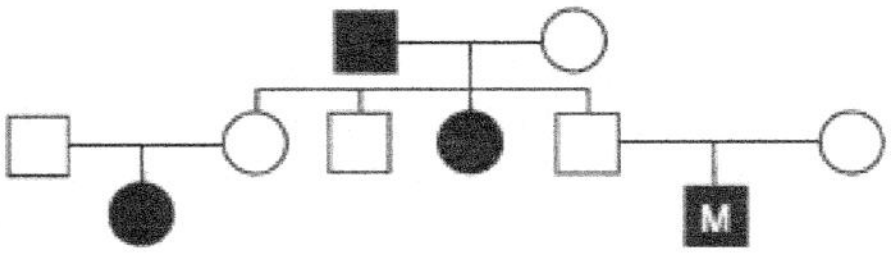

A. 100%
B. 50%
C. 33.3%
D. 25%
E. 0%

26) How many strands of DNA are there in the chromosome shown below?

A. 0
B. 1
C. 2
D. 4
E. 8

27) Which vessel has the highest pressure during systole of the heart?

A. Pulmonary artery
B. Superior vena cava
C. Inferior vena cava
D. Aorta
E. Pulmonary veins

28) Progesterone is secreted by:

A. the implanted blastocyst
B. the ovary
C. amnion
D. placenta
E. uterus

29) Hormones involved in glucose homeostasis are:

A. insulin and glucagon
B. adrenaline and oestrogen
C. FSH and progesterone
D. HCG and oestradiol
E. LH and adrenaline

30) Vitamin B12 is present:

A. in vegetables
B. in all the foods
C. in cereals
D. exclusively in foods of animal origin
E. in fruit

31) Fibres create short-chain fatty acids which:

A. accelerate cholesterol synthesis
B. accelerate carbohydrate synthesis
C. slow down carbohydrate synthesis
D. accelerate protein synthesis
E. slow down cholesterol synthesis

32) HIV virus was first identified in:

A. 1988

B. 1995
C. 1983
D. 2000
E. 1975

33) The genetic condition in which a person cannot metabolise the amino acid phenylalanine in the liver is called:

A. phenylketonuria
B. DNA syndrome
C. phosphorylation
D. glycolysis inhibition
E. pyruvate inhibition

34) Which of the following statements is FALSE?

A. Glycolysis can occur with or without oxygen
B. Glycolysis occurs in the mitochondria
C. Glycolysis is the first step in both aerobic and anaerobic respiration
D. Glycolysis produces 2 ATP, 2 NADH, and 2 pyruvate
E. Glycolysis is a series of enzymatic processes

35) The process that begins with the production of Acetyl-CoA is:

A. chemiosmosis
B. fermentation
C. oxidative phosphorylation
D. Calvin cycle
E. Krebs cycle

36) Cramps during exercise are caused by:

A. alcohol fermentation
B. glycolysis inhibition
C. lactic acid fermentation
D. hydrolysis
E. oxidation

37) Enzymes are composed of what organic molecule?

A. Sugars
B. DNA
C. Fatty acids
D. Proteins
E. Nucleic acids

38) Which of the following sentences about fungi is FALSE?

A. The cells of fungi contain nuclei with chromosomes
B. They usually reproduce by means of spores
C. Fungi absorb their food
D. They mostly develop very diffuse bodies made up of a spreading network of very narrow, tubular, branching filaments called hyphae
E. Fungi can photosynthesize like plants

39) The test used to identify bacteria by the composition of their cell walls is called:

A. Gram stain
B. Shape stain
C. Metabolic model
D. Pathogenic model
E. Movement pattern

40) Tuberculosis is due to:

A. Staphilococcus aureus
B. Koch bacillus
C. Streptococcus pneumoniae
D. Streptococcus pyogenes
E. Lactobacillus acidophilus

41) What is the combined total of protons, neutrons and electrons in Cu^{2+} cations?

$$^{64}_{29}CU$$

A. 91
B. 93
C. 95
D. 97
E. 100

42) 95 RON unleaded petrol contains 95 per cent octane, which combusts to produce carbon dioxide and water according to the following equation: $2C_8H_{18}$ + $aO_2 = bCO_2 + cH_2O$.
How many moles of water are produced from one mole of octane?

A. 10
B. 11
C. 12
D. 9
E. 13

43) Which one of the following elements will not form an ionic compound with fluorine?

A. Potassium
B. Aluminium
C. Carbon
D. Caesium
E. None of them

44) Which two of the following gases dissolve in water and turn litmus paper red?

A. O_2 and CO
B. NH_3 and CH_4
C. CO_2 and HF
D. NH_3 and CO
E. CH_4 and O_2

45) In a vehicle catalytic exhaust system the following pollutants are converted to less harmful emissions as follows:
i) Carbon monoxide to carbon dioxide.
ii) Hydrocarbons to carbon dioxide and water.
iii) Nitrogen oxides to nitrogen and oxygen.
Select the correct option (A to E) from the table below to describe the chemical reactions taking place in i), ii) and iii).

A. i) oxidation; ii) reduction; iii) reduction
B. i) oxidation; ii) de-hydration; iii) reduction
C. i) reduction; ii) oxidation; iii) reduction
D. i) oxidation; ii) oxidation; iii) reduction
E. i) oxidation; ii) reduction; iii) oxidation

46) Elements within the same group of the periodic table have the same number of:

A. protons
B. neutrons
C. protons and neutrons
D. electrons in their inner electron shells
E. electrons in their outer electron shells

47) Which of the following is classified as a metal?

A. Ge
B. As
C. F
D. V
E. Ar

48) Which of the following is a weak acid?

A. H_2SO_4
B. $HClO_3$
C. HF
D. HCl
E. HNO_3

49) What alkaline earth metal is located in period 3?

A. Li
B. Na
C. Ca
D. Mg
E. Sr

50) Which one of the following is likely to be the most soluble base?

A. $Ca(OH)_2$
B. $Cu(OH)_2$
C. $Ga(OH)_3$

D. $Zn(OH)_2$
E. $Zr(OH)_3$

51) Which one of the following statements is true?

A. One mole of any acid will ionize completely in aqueous solution to produce one mole of H^+ ions
B. Solutions of weak acids always have lower concentrations of H^+ than solutions of strong acids
C. There are several common acids that are insoluble
D. All of the IA and IIA metal hydroxides are soluble
E. All weak acids are insoluble

52) Which one of the following salts is insoluble?

A. NH_4Cl
B. $Ca(NO_3)_2$
C. $BaCO_3$
D. Na_2S
E. $Zn(CH_3CO)_2$

53) A wallet contains £400 in £5, £10 and £20 notes. The number of £10 notes is twice the number of £5 notes and there are six fewer £20 notes than £10 notes. How many £5 notes are there?

A. 8
B. 10
C. 12
D. 13
E. 15

54) Which of the following values of x satisfy the inequality $x(x - 3) \leq 10$?

A. –3, –2, –1, 1, 0, 1, 2
B. 1, 2, 3, 4, 5, 6, 7
C. –4, –3, –2, –1, 0, 1
D. –1, 0, 1, 2, 3, 4, 5
E. 5, 6, 7, 8, 9, 10

55) Which of the following is equivalent to 114/2000?

A. 5/10 + 7/10
B. 5/10 +7/100
C. 5/100 +7/1000
D. 5/100 +7/100
E. 5/1000 +7/1000

56) Let $X = 12{,}75 \times 0{,}0143$. Which of the following values is the correct result for X?

A. $X = 0{,}182321$
B. $X = 0{,}182323$
C. $X = 0{,}182322$
D. $X = 0{,}182324$
E. $X = 0{,}182325$

57) Mica is used in electrical appliances such as electric iron because mica is:

A. a good conductor of heat but a bad conductor of electricity
B. a bad conductor of heat but a good conductor of electricity
C. a good conductor of heat as well as electricity
D. a bad conductor of heat as well as electricity
E. a good conductor of light as well as electricity

58) A 2.0×10^3-kilogram car travels at a constant speed of 12 metres per second around a circular curve of radius 30 metres. What is the magnitude of the centripetal acceleration of the car as it goes around the curve?

A. $0.40\ m/s^2$
B. $4.8\ m/s^2$
C. $800\ m/s^2$
D. $9600\ m/s^2$
E. $99.7\ m/s^2$

59) A golf ball is hit from a tee. The vertical component of its velocity is 30 me-

tres per second (m × s^{-1}). Calculate the maximum height that it will reach, ignoring the influence of spin and air resistance. (1 kg = 10 N).

A. 25 m
B. 24 m
C. 45 m
D. 71 m
E. 65 m

60) The head pivots on the atlas vertebra ('C1') at the top of the spine. The weight of the head acts 4 cm in front of the pivot and the neck muscles act 6 cm behind the pivot to support the weight. What is the force in newtons, to the nearest newton, exerted by the neck muscles to support a head weighing 4 kg? (Take g = 10 m s^{-2}).

A. 6 N
B. 36 N
C. 60 N
D. 40 N
E. 27 N

RISPOSTE CORRETTE

1) D	11) B	21) A	31) E	41) A	51) B
2) E	12) B	22) B	32) C	42) D	52) C
3) C	13) B	23) C	33) A	43) C	53) A
4) E	14) C	24) C	34) B	44) C	54) D
5) D	15) C	25) E	35) E	45) D	55) C
6) A	16) B	26) D	36) C	46) E	56) E
7) D	17) A	27) D	37) D	47) D	57) A
8) B	18) E	28) B	38) E	48) C	58) B
9) B	19) C	29) A	39) A	49) D	59) C
10) A	20) D	30) D	40) B	50) A	60) E

Test 5

1) Place the following four sentences in the order in which they form the most coherent passage.

A. Deep sea organisms do not replenish their carbon from the air so they contain a higher proportion of inactive carbon.

B. Carbon-14 dating is not an infallible method of determining the age of ancient artefacts and organic matter.

C. Consequently they can have an anomalous carbon-dating age that appears much older than the true age.

D. It works best on once-living remains that consumed carbon from the air where the carbon-14 to carbon-12 ratio is fixed.

A. B, D, A, C
B. A, D, B, C
C. B, A, C, D
D. C, D, A, B
E. A, B, C, D

2) Today, medical paternalism has given way to patient autonomy. This means that each individual has the right to accept, choose or refuse a treatment based on what each believes to be in his or her own best interests. Failure to consent to a life-saving treatment no longer implies that the patient is incapable of making the 'right decision'. Doctors have a duty to ensure that patients are able to make an informed choice, including why one course of treatment might be the preferred option, but they cannot exert any pressure beyond that of 'gentle persuasion'.

Which of the following best summarizes the passage?

A. The patient's viewpoint is the only one that is important when deciding upon a medical treatment
B. The doctor should assist a patient in making decisions that are consistent with the patient's own beliefs and values
C. The doctor must respect the patient's wishes at all times even when the patient's life is at risk
D. The doctor must act in the patient's best interests by identifying the preferred treatment option
E. None of the listed

3) Pensioners account for one-fifth of the population and will need 75 per cent of their former earnings, amounting to 15 per cent of gross domestic product (GDP), if they are to avoid a sharp decline in living standards. The state pension amounts to a paltry 4 per cent of GDP and private pensions can barely match this meagre amount, leaving a large gap. Clearly many people of retirement age are going to find it hard to make ends meet in the future.

Which two of the following show that the conclusion is unsafe even if the evidence is correct?

1. It might be the case that many people of retirement age will choose to carry on working to make up the gap.
2. It might be that in the future GDP will increase, which means that pensions will also rise.
3. It might be the case that the stock market will improve and income from private pensions will increase twofold.
4. It might be the case that many pensioners will make ends meet on less than three-quarters of their former earnings.

A. 1 and 2
B. 1 and 4

C. 3 and 1
D. 4 and 2
E. 2 and 3

4) If most members of a ramblers' group are members of a hikers' group and a few of the hikers are members of a climbers' group, then which of the following statements must be true?
1. Most members of the climbers' group are not ramblers.
2. Most members of the hikers' group are ramblers.
3. No members belong to all three groups.

A. 1 only
B. 2 only
C. 3 only
D. 1 and 2 only
E. None

5) Consider the following two statements and the conclusion that follows:
i) Aptitude tests are a reliable predictor of degree performance (*major premise*).
ii) The IMAT is an aptitude test (*minor premise*).
iii) The IMAT is a reliable predictor of degree performance (*conclusion*).
Which one of the following is invalid?

A. If i) is false then iii) is unsafe
B. If ii) is false then iii) is unsafe
C. If iii) is true then i) and ii) are true
D. If iii) is unsafe then i) and/or ii) are false
E. If i) and ii) are true then iii) is safe

6) The bar chart compares the hospital admissions for asthma per 100 000 population, for children in selected European countries. There are 12 million children in the UK and 10 million in Spain.

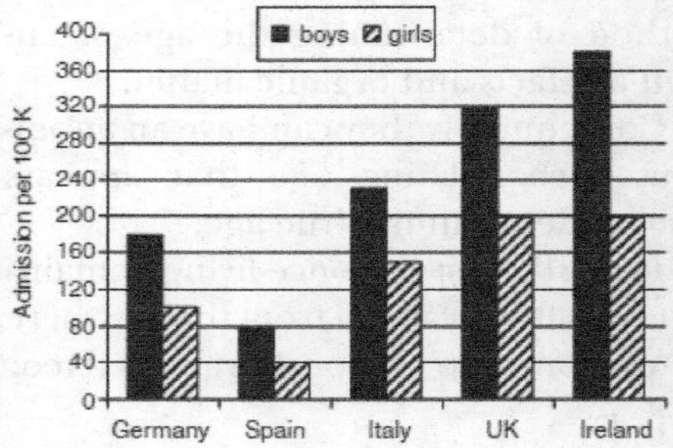

What is the difference between the UK and Spain in the number of hospital admissions for boys?

A. 24 000
B. 22 400
C. 30 400
D. 20 000
E. 32 000

7) The table shows the percentage of females with a cardiovascular-related condition, by age and diagnosis.

Diagnosis/Age	25-34	35-44	45-54	55-64	65-74	75+
Angina	0.0	0.2	1.3	3.1	6.3	9.1
Heart murmur	1.0	0.9	1.2	1.4	1.8	2.2
Arrhythmia	1.0	1.5	2.2	2.5	3.3	4.2
Myocardial infarction	0.0	0.2	0.3	0.6	0.7	1.7
Stroke	0.1	0.1	0.1	0.3	0.4	1.8
Diabetes	0.3	0.9	1.5	2.5	4.8	5.3
Hypertension	1.5	3.7	7.8	20.5	27.9	26.8

The incidence of which conditions varies the least with age?

A. Heart murmur
B. Stroke
C. Angina
D. Hypertension
E. Arrhythmia

8) Which one of the following letters will not look correct if it is turned upside down and reflected in a mirror?

B C I E X S

A. B
B. I
C. X
D. S
E. F

9) The line graph shows the trend in the number of households with regular use of a car from 1960 to 2000. The graph shows that the number of one-car-only households has been stable at 45 per cent from about 1970.

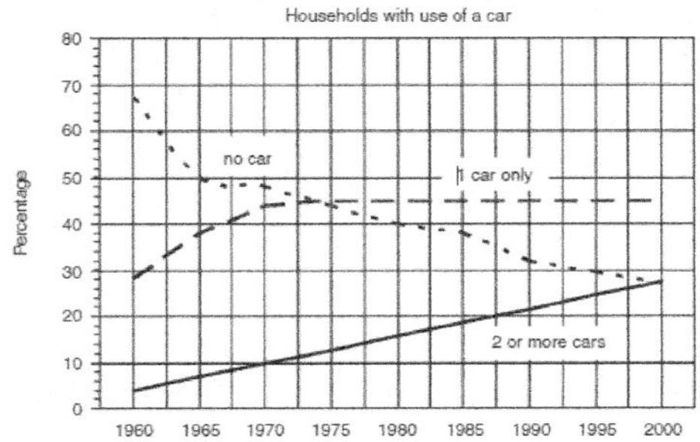

If trends continue, approximately when will the number of two or more car households equal the number of one-car households?

A. 2010
B. 2012
C. 2015
D. 2020
E. 2030

10) Considering the graph of the question n. 14, if in the future, half of all households have the use of two or more cars, what percentage increase will this be compared with the 1970 figure?

A. 40%
B. 400%
C. 450%
D. 500%
E. 550%

11) Modernism was:

A. an artistic revolution that produced masterpieces in both the literary and visual arts worlds
B. a cultural movement that had a great impact on drama in the first half of the 20th century but produced no great writers of fiction or poetry
C. an early 20th-century movement in poetry that was characterized by a nostalgic looking back to the pre-industrial age
D. a philosophical school of thought of the XIX century
E. a poetic style that evolved from Romanticism

12) In World War I England was allied with:

A. France, Bulgaria and the United States
B. France, Italy, Spain and the United States
C. France, Spain and the United States
D. Italy, United States, Austria
E. Italy, France and the United States

13) Ferdinand de Saussure is best associated with:

A. anthropology
B. physics
C. political theory
D. linguistics
E. economics

14) What does the CIA stand for?

A. Covert International Assassins

B. Crime In Action
C. Criminal Investigation Association
D. Central Investigation Agency
E. Central Intelligence Agency

15) Which of these descriptions best fits Fellini's *La Dolce Vita*?

A. A love story
B. An exposure of fashionable decadence
C. A study of controlled violence
D. A tribute to the fashion world
E. A tribute to the world of television

16) In Greek mythology, a multi-headed hound which guards the gates of Hades is called what?

A. Polypheme
B. Cerberus
C. Barabas
D. Gnasher
E. Minotaur

17) What is the earliest known writing system in the world?

A. Arabic script
B. Sanskrit
C. Mishnaic Hebrew
D. Prakrit
E. Cuneiform script

18) In which country will you find Machu Picchu?

A. Peru
B. Chile
C. Brazil
D. Uraguay
E. Mexico

19) What does NASA stand for?

A. National Astronauts and Space Adventures
B. National Aeronautics and Space Administration
C. Nebulous Air and Starry Atmosphere
D. New Airways and Spatial Asteroids
E. National Aeronautic and Space Air

20) The two American Houses of Congress comprise the Senate and which other?

A. The House of Commons
B. The House of Deputies
C. The House of Representatives
D. The House of Parliament
E. The House of Lords

21) What territory did Britain gain at the Treaty of Berlin in 1878?

A. Corsica
B. Ascension Island
C. Cyprus
D. Falkland Islands
E. Malta

22) In which decade did Swedish physicist Alfred Nobel patent dynamite?

A. 1850s
B. 1860s
C. 1840s
D. 1880s
E. 1900s

23) Look at the list (1 to 7) below and then choose the correct path for blood flowing through the heart to the lungs.
1. right ventricle; 2. bicuspid valve (mitral); 3. right atrium; 4. pulmonary artery; 5. pulmonary vein; 6. left atrium; 7. tricuspid valve.

A. 1, 2, 3, 4
B. 6, 2, 1, 5
C. 3, 2, 1, 5
D. 3, 7, 1, 4
E. 3, 2, 1, 4

24) The oxygen dissociation curve shows the percent saturation of haemoglobin versus the oxygen partial pressure. Which of the following statements is true if the curve shifts to the right (dotted line) when a person begins to exercise?

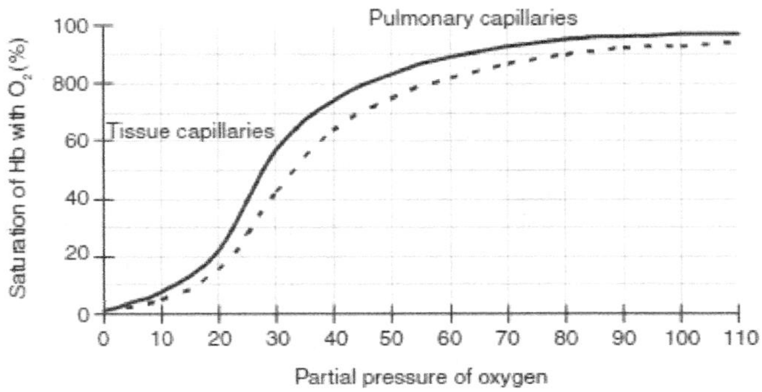

A. There is an increase in the oxygen saturation of haemovglobin at the lungs
B. There is a decrease in the oxygen saturation of haemoglobin at the tissues
C. There is an increase in the partial pressure of oxygen at the tissues
D. There is a decrease in the partial pressure of oxygen at the tissues
E. None of the sentences is correct

25) Identify the correct path for blood flowing through the heart to the body.

A. Left atrium, tricuspid valve, left ventricle, aorta
B. Left atrium, bicuspid (mitral) valve, left ventricle, pulmonary artery
C. Left atrium, bicuspid (mitral) valve, left ventricle, aorta
D. Right atrium, pulmonary valve, right ventricle, pulmonary artery
E. Right atrium, tricuspid valve, right ventricle, pulmonary artery

26) A schematic diagram of a nephron is shown below. Identify the correct transport processes from 1 through to 5.

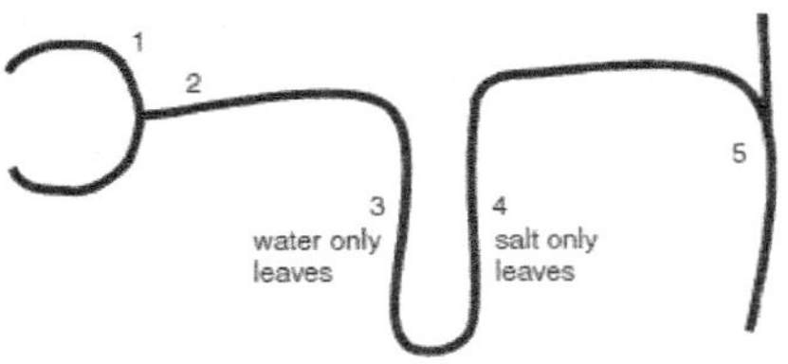

A. Diffusion, active transport, osmosis, active transport, osmosis
B. Ultrafiltration, re-absorption, countercurrent, active transport, excretion
C. Ultrafiltration, osmosis, active transport, osmosis, diffusion
D. Ultrafiltration, active transport, osmosis, active transport, osmosis
E. Ultrafiltration, re-absorption, diffusion, active transport, active transport

27) The pH of blood is maintained at 7.4 by the carbonic acid hydrogen carbonate ion buffer as follows: $CO_2 + H_2O = H^+ + HCO_3^-$. Which of the following statements is consistent with respiratory acidosis of the blood?

A. CO_2 levels rise and the pH falls
B. CO_2 levels rise and the pH remains unchanged
C. CO_2 levels rise and the pH rises
D. CO_2 levels fall and the pH rises
E. None of the listed

28) What type of inheritance is shown in the diagram below if F is not a carrier for the disease?

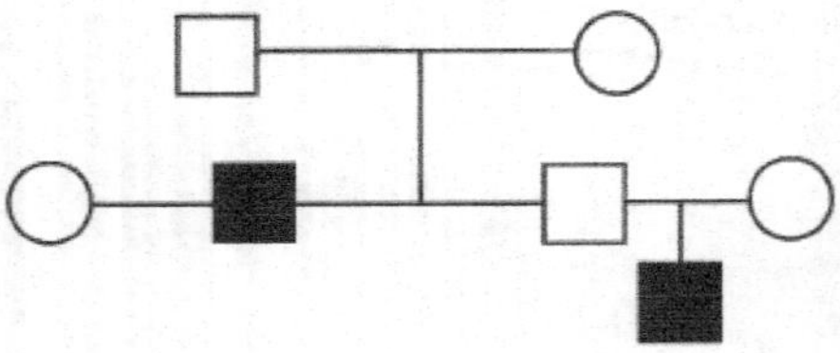

A. Autosomal dominant
B. Autosomal recessive
C. X-linked dominant
D. X-linked recessive
E. Autosomal recessive or X-linked recessive

29) Which of the following sequences describes the path of a nerve impulse in a reflex arc?

A. Receptor, efferent neurone, PNS, motor neurone, effector
B. Receptor, afferent neurone, PNS, motor neurone, effector
C. Receptor, effector, CNS, afferent neurone, efferent neurone
D. Receptor, efferent neurone, CNS, afferent neurone, effector
E. Receptor, afferent neurone, CNS, efferent neurone, effector

30) The capillary network comprises the greatest cross sectional area of blood vessels in the body with the highest resistance to blood flow. In a healty individual the highest blood pressure would most likely be found in:

A. the aorta
B. the vena cava
C. the systemic capillaries
D. the pulmonary arthery
E. the pulmonary vein

31) Which of the following does not belong to the class of anti-hypertensive drugs?

A. ACE inhibitors
B. Beta-blockers
C. Calcium channel blockers
D. Diuretics
E. Catecholamines

32) The human brain contains a ______ gland which is considered the master gland of the body.

A. pineal
B. pituitary
C. medulla
D. cerebra
E. thyroid

33) In the human stomach, ________ are digested by the enzyme, pepsin, and most ________ are killed by the low pH from HCl.

A. starch, amoebas
B. starch, fungi
C. proteins, bacteria
D. proteins, fungi
E. proteins, amoebas

34) In the alveolus of humans, ________ enters the blood and ________ exits the blood.

A. oxygen, carbon dioxide
B. carbon dioxide, oxygen
C. nitrogen, oxygen
D. oxygen, water
E. water, carbon dioxide

35) The excretory system of humans includes the ________ where nitrogenous wastes are removed from the blood, and essential water and salts are resorbed.

A. stomach
B. kidney
C. heart

D. lungs
E. liver

36) A common neurotransmitter is:

A. glucose
B. TSH
C. oxygen
D. acetyl choline
E. FT3

37) Viruses are considered non-living because:

A. they don't reproduce but can grow
B. they don't have nucleic acids
C. they don't metabolize
D. they don't contain cytoplasm
E. they don't have mitochondria

38) Diseases that are passed from person to person are said to be:

A. contagious
B. air-borne
C. non-fectious
D. pathogens
E. pathologic

39) Bacteria play a very important role in Earth's ecosystems because they:

A. use oxygen
B. produce carbon dioxide
C. deposit valuable minerals
D. decompose dead organisms
E. use nitrose

40) If bacteria have a round shape, they are said to be:

A. spirillum
B. bacillus
C. coccus
D. oval
E. round

41) Which of the following statements is true about propene?

A. It is an alkane
B. It burns in air to produce carbon monoxide and hydrogen
C. It is an unsaturated hydrocarbon
D. It has carbon–carbon triple bonds
E. All the statements are true

42) Which of the following atoms is most often found acting as hydrogen bond acceptor?

A. Hydrogen
B. Carbon
C. Calcium
D. Oxygen
E. All of them

43) How many bigger is the volume of 2 moles of oxygen (O_2) compared to the volume of 1 mole of Argon gas (Ar)? Assume that the temperature and pressure are equal.

A. 4
B. 2
C. 0,25
D. 0,5
E. 1

44) What salt is formed in the following acid/base reaction?

$$HClO_3 + Ba(OH)_2 \rightarrow \dots\dots\dots\dots$$

A. $BaCl_2$
B. ClOBa
C. H_2O
D. $BaClO_3$
E. $Ba(ClO_3)_2$

45) The precipitate formed when barium chloride is treated with sulfuric acid is:

A. BaS_2O_4
B. $BaSO_3$
C. $BaSO_2$
D. $BaSO_4$
E. BaS

46) Which element has the highest first ionization energy?

A. B
B. Be
C. N
D. C
E. O

47) Which of the following elements has the greatest attraction for electrons in a covalent bond?

A. Ge
B. As
C. Se
D. Br
E. Bi

48) All of the following properties of the alkaline earth metals increase going down the group, except:

A. atomic radius
B. first ionization energy
C. ionic radius
D. atomic mass
E. atomic volume

49) Which of the following is an ionic hydride?

A. PH_3
B. H_2S
C. HI
D. KH
E. CH_4

50) Which of the following is the most basic oxide?

A. N_2O_3
B. N_2O_5
C. P_4O_6
D. P_4O_{10}
E. Bi_2O_5

51) Which of the following pairs of elements and valence electrons is incorrect?

A. Al; 3
B. Br; 7
C. S; 4
D. Sr; 2
E. Tl; 3

52) Which one of the formulas for ionic compounds below is INCORRECT?

A. $SrCl_2$
B. Cs_2S
C. $AlCl_3$
D. Al_3P_2
E. CaSe

53) A microwave oven is on sale with a 20 per cent discount. The following month the price is reduced by a further 10 per cent. What is the overall price reduction in percentage terms?

A. 25%
B. 30%
C. 37%
D. 40%
E. 28%

54) A round of toast and a portion of margarine cost £ 1.10. The toast costs £ 1 more than the margarine. How much does the round of toast cost?

A. £ 0.90
B. £ 0.95
C. £ 1.00
D. £ 1.05
E. £ 1.15

55) Calculate $\dfrac{25+\dfrac{1}{8}}{7-\dfrac{3}{10}}$.

A. 2/5
B. $3^{3/4}$
C. 1/6
D. $2^{1/5}$
E. 1/9

56) If $x = (y + 1)^{0.25} + 0.5$, calculate the value of y when $x = 2.5$.

A. 12
B. 14
C. 16
D. 15
E. 18

57) A motorist travels from Birmingham to Blackpool, a distance of 120 miles, at an average speed of 60 miles per hour and then leaves Blackpool and returns to Birmingham at an average speed of 40 miles per hour. What was the average speed for the round trip?

A. 45 mph
B. 48 mph
C. 50 mph
D. 54 mph
E. 58 mph

58) What is the approximate cost of boiling 1.75 litres of water in a kettle that draws 13 amps at 230 volts for four minutes, if electricity costs 15 pence per kilowatt-hour?

A. 1 p
B. 0.5 p
C. 2 p
D. 3 p
E. 4 p

59) Mains water flows through a series of pipes and taps as shown below:

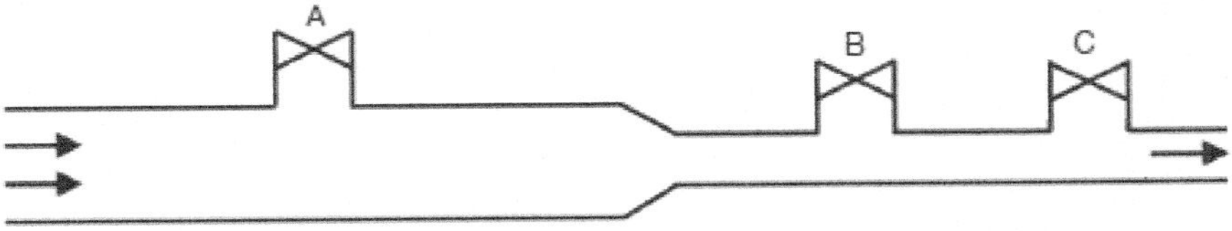

Choose the correct answer from the choices given.

A. The water pressures at taps A, B and C are all equal
B. The water pressure at tap A is greater than at tap B
C. The water pressures at taps A and B are equal
D. The water pressure at tap A is less than at tap C
E. None of the answers is correct

60) What is the total equivalent resistance for the resistors arranged below?

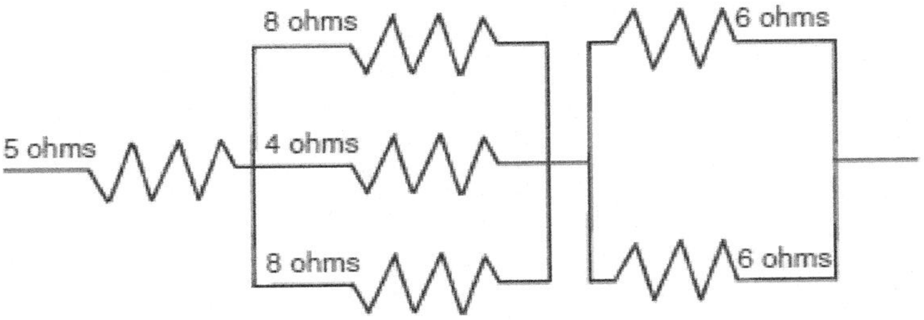

A. 10 ohms
B. 13 ohms
C. 15 ohms
D. 20 ohms
E. 22 ohms

RISPOSTE CORRETTE

1) A	11) A	21) C	31) E	41) C	51) C
2) B	12) E	22) B	32) B	42) D	52) D
3) B	13) D	23) D	33) C	43) B	53) E
4) E	14) E	24) C	34) A	44) E	54) D
5) C	15) B	25) C	35) B	45) D	55) B
6) C	16) B	26) D	36) D	46) C	56) D
7) A	17) E	27) A	37) C	47) D	57) B
8) D	18) A	28) B	38) A	48) B	58) D
9) E	19) B	29) E	39) D	49) D	59) B
10) B	20) C	30) A	40) C	50) E	60) A

Test 6

1) Fruit juice has often been marketed as a health product, and it is easy to understand why. Fruit, from which juice is derived, is a relatively healthy balance of fibre, vitamins, minerals and sugars. In particular, the presence of fibre adds bulk, and slows the progression of digestion. This means that the sugars are absorbed over a prolonged period. Juice, on the other hand, misses out this key ingredient, but still contains the high sugar load. The issue here arises from the way our body reacts to sugar: if it detects too much, too fast, it releases a burst of insulin, a hormone which drives the sugar into muscles and converts them to stored energy. As you can imagine, juice is digested quickly, and the sugar stored as a result of the insulin. The result? Rapid weight gain and all of its consequences, from diabetes to cardiovascular risk. Fruit juice is not a health product, and should be avoided by most of the population.

Which of the following statements can be correctly deduced from the above passage?

A. Fruit juice is harmful to health
B. Fruit juice is a healthy product
C. Fruit juice prevents diabetes and cardiovascular diseases
D. Fruit juice contains little sugar
E. Drinking fruite juices helps to lose weight

2) Referring to the passage of question n. 1, only one of the following statements is true. Which?

A. Digestion of juice is slow
B. Fruit contains a high quantity of sugar
C. Fruit juice should be avoided by most of the population
D. If our body detects too much sugar, it reduces the production of insulin
E. The presence of fibre in fruit accelerates the progression of digestion

3) Referring to the passage of question n. 1, which of the following sentences is FALSE?

A. Juice is digested quickly and the sugar is stored as a result of insulin
B. Fruit juice has never been marketed as a health product
C. The presence of fibre adds bulk during digestion
D. The fact that fruit juice derives from fruit does not mean it is a healthy product
E. Juice contains a high sugar load

4) The misuse of antibiotics has led to the spread of superbugs like MRSA. Doctors should know that most ear, nose and throat infections are self-limiting, which means that 90 per cent of prescriptions are unnecessary. The rise of superbugs is due to the over-eagerness of doctors to prescribe antibiotics.

Which one of the following shows that the conclusion is unsafe even if the evidence is correct?

A. Patients with an infection expect their doctor to prescribe them antibiotics
B. In healthy people most MRSA infections are self-limiting
C. Doctors are only happy about writing prescriptions for the 10 per cent of patients who really need them

D. Superbugs would not have proliferated if antibiotics had not been over-prescribed
E. 90 per cent of infections would have cleared up without the use of antibiotics

5) Common sense dictates that in the event of an accident, the driver of a smaller car is more likely to be injured than the driver of a large car. Therefore, it is preferable to drive a big, polluting car and ignore the damage to the environment than to drive a small, environmentally friendly car and put your own safety at risk.
Which of the following is an unwarranted assumption of the above argument?

A. Car safety in an accident is a matter of common sense
B. Bigger cars usually burn more fuel than smaller cars
C. Personal safety is more important than damaging the environment
D. You should never put your own safety at risk
E. Occupants of smaller cars are more likely to be injured in an accident than occupants of larger cars

6) The graph shows the motion of a car over seven time intervals H, I, J, K, L and M.

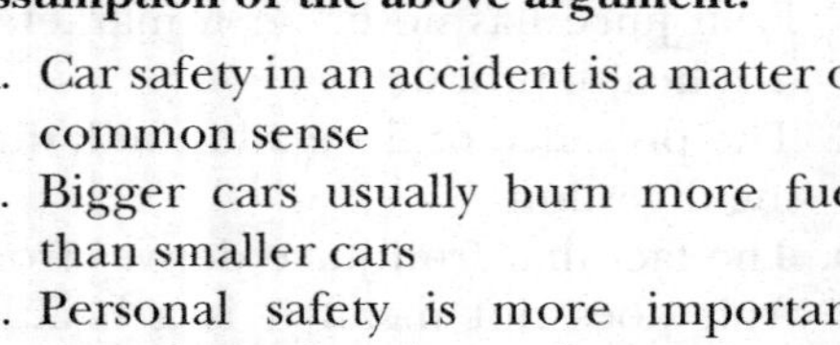

Which two intervals correspond with the greatest acceleration and the least displacement (distance)?

A. H and I
B. H and K
C. J and I
D. J and M
E. H and M

7) A radioisotope is being used for a medical procedure. The table shows how the sample decays with time. What was the activity of the sample when it was prepared?

Time: days	Activity: counts per minute
0	
1	3.2×10^5
2	8×10^4
3	2×10^4
4	5000

A. 6.4×10^4
B. 1.28×10^6
C. 2.56×10^6
D. 5.12×10^5
E. 3.4×10^8

8) If the shapes drawn below are placed inside the square frame, what fraction of the frame will be empty?

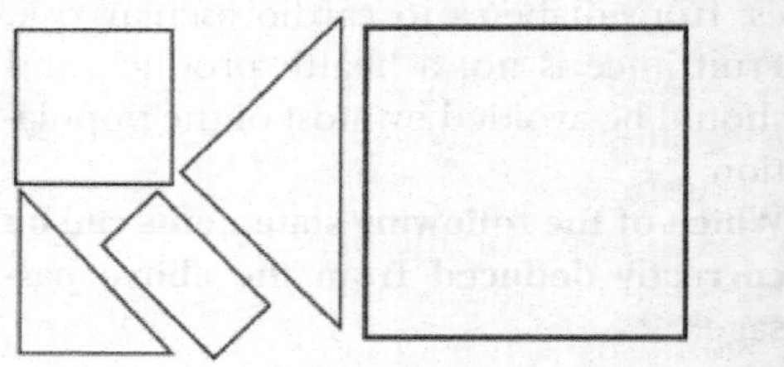

A. 1/16
B. 1/10
C. 1/8
D. 1/6
E. 1/4

9) John has 36 books that are either paperbacks or hardbacks. One-quarter are fiction books and 24 are paperbacks. There are six times as many paperback non-fiction books as hardback fiction books. How many books does he have that are both hardback and non-fiction?

A. 2
B. 4
C. 6
D. 9
E. 8

10) Water drips from a tap at a rate of one drop every three seconds. The volume of water in each drop is 0.1 ml. If the tap is left to drip for 25 hours, how many litres of water will be wasted?

A. 2 1
B. 3 1
C. 4 1
D. 7 1
E. 1 1

11) In which country will you find Machu Picchu?

A. Brazil
B. Chile
C. Uraguay
D. Peru
E. Mexico

12) What does NASA stand for?

A. New Airways and Spatial Asteroids
B. National Astronauts and Space Adventures
C. Nebulous Air and Starry Atmosphere
D. National Aeronautics and Space Administration
E. National Aeronautic and Space Air

13) The first Academy Awards ceremony took place in:

A. 1915
B. 1940
C. 1929
D. 1935
E. 1980

14) Who pronounced the famous sentence *Homo homini lupus*?

A. Karl Marx
B. Thomas Hobbes
C. Francis Bacon
D. Thomas More
D. Friedrich Nietzsche

15) Who was Aristotle a student of?

A. Parmenides
B. Plato
C. Democritus
D. Alexander the Great
E. Socrates

16) Between 1887 and 1888 Vincent van Gogh produced a series of still life paintings depicting which flowers?

A. Roses
B. Daffodils
C. Sunflowers
D. Geraniums
E. Poppies

17) Which body of water separates England from Ireland?

A. The Channel Tunnel
B. The Atlantic Ocean
C. The Celtic Sea
D. North Sea
E. The Irish Sea

18) For which of the following disciplines is Nobel Prize awarded?

A. Physics, Chemistry, Peace
B. Physiology or Medicine
C. Literature, Peace and Economics
D. Peace, Literature, Economics and Chemistry
E. Peace, Literature, Medicine, Physics, Chemistry and Economics

19) What is the official title of *The Maastricht Treaty*?

A. Treaty on European Economy
B. Treaty on European Citizenship
C. Treaty on European Consolidation

D. Treaty on European Union
E. Treaty establishing the European Economic Community

20) Which religious leader was assassinated on 4th April 1968?

A. Mahatma Gandhi
B. Martin Luther King
C. Mother Theresa
D. Jesse Jackson
E. Malcom X

21) The death of which philosopher in 1804 marked the end of the Enlightenment?

A. Hegel
B. Wolff
C. Hume
D. Kant
E. Descartes

22) Who was the first Roman emperor to convert to Christianity?

A. Diocletian
B. Constantine
C. Nerva
D. Aurelian
E. Hadrian

23) Identify the correct path for food passing through the digestive system.

A. Pharynx, oesophagus, stomach, small intestine, large intestine
B. Larynx, pharynx, oesophagus, stomach, duodenum, colon
C. Pharynx, oesophagus, stomach, large intestine, small intestine
D. Larynx, oesophagus, stomach, small intestine, large intestine
E. Pharynx, oesophagus, stomach, ileum, duodenum, colon

24) If brown eyes (B) are dominant and blue eyes (b) are recessive, what is the probability that a child will inherit blue eyes if it has a heterozygous mother and a father who has homozygous brown- and blue-eyed parents?

A. 33.3 per cent
B. 50 per cent
C. 25 per cent
D. 75 per cent
E. 100 per cent

25) A mother expressing an X-linked dominant disease (A) and a father not expressing the disease have one affected son, one unaffected son and one unaffected daughter. Which of the following statements is true?

A. The father is X^AY
B. The mother is X^aX^a
C. The father is X^aY
D. The father is X^aY^A
E. No child is homozygous

26) Identify the substances i, ii and iii corresponding with the dominant transport processes for molecules passing through the nephron of a normal kidney.

	Transport process		
	Filtration	**Re-absorption**	**Secretion**
i	YES	NO	YES
ii	NO	NO	NO
iii	YES	YES	NO

A. i = glucose; ii = creatinine; iii = protein
B. i = creatinine; ii = protein; iii = urea
C. i = protein; ii = salt; iii = glucose
D. i = creatinine; ii = protein; iii = glucose
E. i = urea; ii = protein; iii = creatinine

27) Two haploid gametes fertilize to give a diploid zygote that replicates by mitosis to give two identical daughter cells. How many copies of each chromosome are present in a daughter cell when the cells separate at the end of mitosis?

A. 0
B. 1
C. 2
D. 4
E. 8

28) The classification level in which classes with similar characteristics are grouped are called a (n):

A. class
B. order
C. phylum
D. taxonomy
E. domain

29) Bacteria ore prokaryotic organisms made of cells that have strong exterior

____

A. cell membranes
B. domain
C. cell walls
D. taxonomy
E. reticulum

30) How many kingdoms of classification are there for organisms?

A. 4
B. 6
C. 5
D. 7
E. 8

31) The control group in any experiment is that group which:

A. is tested only once
B. is exposed only to the experimental condition
C. is exposed to all conditions in the experiment
D. is exposed to all conditions except the experimental condition
E. should be a relatively small group to achieve viable results

32) Metabolic processes are:

A. those which alter homeostasis in an organism
B. only carried out at the "organ" level of an organism
C. only anabolic and at the "cellular" level
D. those which produce energy in an organism
E. the sum total of all anabolic and catabolic activities in an organism

33) The organization of life is arranged according to a hierarchy of complexity. Which of the following outlines the correct hierarchy?

A. molecule, organ system, population, community, ecosystem
B. molecule, cell, tissue, organ system, organ
C. cell, molecule, tissue, organ, organ system
D. organ, organ system, ecosystem, population, community
E. molecule, tissue, organ, population

34) During his studies on the genetics of peas, Mendel discovered three laws of inheritance:

A. dominance, recombination, recessiveness
B. dominance, independent assortment, segregation
C. hybridation, heterozygosis, recombination
D. segregation, replication, recessiveness
E. none of the listed

35) In a monohybrid cross between a homozygous dominant parent and a homozygous recessive parent, the F1 offspring will all have ________ genotypes, and the F1 phenotypes will resemble the ________ parent.

A. heterozygous, recessive
B. homozygous, dominant
C. heterozygous, dominant

D. heterozygous, recessive
E. recessive, homozygous

36) If a monohybrid, heterozygous F1 generation is crossed with itself (selfed), the phenotypic ratio of the F2 generation will be:

A. 2:2
B. 4:0
C. 1:1
D. 2:1
E. 3:1

37) In a cross using dihybrid plants, the probability of the offspring being tall is 3/4 and the probability of being yellow is 1/4. The probability that the offspring will be both tall and yellow is ______.

A. 1/6
B. 13/16
C. 1/8
D. 3/16
E. 1/4

38) In humans, some traits such as color-blindness and hemophilia are carried only on the X chromosomes. These are known as __________ traits.

A. sex-linked
B. autosomal
C. chromosomal
D. homozygous
E. heterozygous

39) The molecular structure of DNA is a:

A. hairpin loop
B. double helix
C. single strand
D. tetramer
E. triple helix

40) After replication, one strand of the new DNA is from the old DNA, and one strand has been newly synthesized. This is known as __________.

A. conservative replication
B. transcription
C. translation
D. traduction
E. semi-conservative replication

41) The species ^{72}N, ^{75}As and ^{74}Ge have the same:

A. number of electrons
B. number of protons
C. number of neutrons
D. number of protons and neutrons
E. mass number

42) The neutral atoms of all the isotopes of the same element have:

A. different number of protons
B. equal number of neutrons
C. the same number of electrons
D. the same mass number
E. the same masses

43) The maximum number of electrons that can be accommodated in a sublevel for which $l = 3$ is:

A. 2
B. 10
C. 6
D. 14
E. 8

44) The outer electronic configuration ns^2np^4 corresponds to which one of the following elements in its ground state?

A. As
B. Ca
C. Cr
D. Br
E. S

45) How many p electrons are there in an atom of rubidium?

A. 12
B. 18

C. 24
D. 9
E. 6

46) Select the term that best describes the series of elements: Mn, Fe, Co, Ni, Cu.

A. D-transition metals
B. Representative elements
C. Metalloids
D. Alkaline earth metals
E. Halogens

47) Which element has the largest atomic radius?

A. Li
B. Na
C. Rb
D. F
E. I

48) Which element has the lowest first ionization energy?

A. He
B. Ne
C. Ar
D. Kr
E. Xe

49) Which of the compounds below is most likely to be ionic?

A. GaAs
B. $ScCl_3$
C. NO_2
D. CCl_4
E. ClO_2

50) What is the total number of electrons in the correct Lewis dot formula of the sulphite ion?

A. 8
B. 24
C. 26
D. 30
E. 32

51) In the Lewis structure for the OF_2 molecule, the number of lone pairs of electrons around the central oxygen atom is:

A. 0
B. 1
C. 2
D. 3
E. 4

52) Which one of the following violates the octet rule?

A. PCl_3
B. CBr_4
C. NF_3
D. OF_2
E. AsF_5

53) A solid sphere fits neatly inside a hollow cube. The volume of the sphere is given by its radius cubed multiplied by four-thirds pi (π). What is the ratio of the volume of the sphere to the volume of the cube?

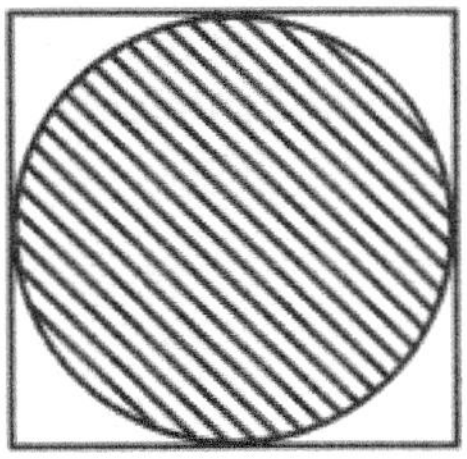

A. 6π
B. $32/3\pi$
C. $2/3\pi$
D. $6/\pi$
E. $\pi/6$

54) What is $5.2 \times 10^{12} + 4.8 \times 10^{11} - 1.0 \times 10^{10}$ in scientific notation?

A. 5.68×10^{12}
B. 5.67×10^{12}
C. 5.67×10^{11}
D. 56.7×10^{10}
E. 5.60×10^{12}

55) The three-car train shown below accelerates at 0.4 m s^{-2}. What is the tension in each of the three couplings?

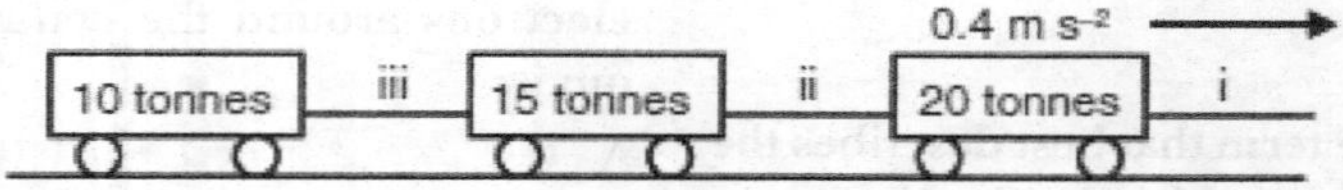

A. i) 8 kN; ii) 6 kN; iii) 4 kN
B. i) 18 kN; ii) 18 kN; iii) 18 kN
C. i) 18 kN; ii) 12 kN; iii) 8 kN
D. i) 18 kN; ii) 10 kN; iii) 4 kN
E. i) 15 kN; ii) 3 kN; iii) 8 kN

56) If the area of the square is 9 cm^2, what is the area of the circle?

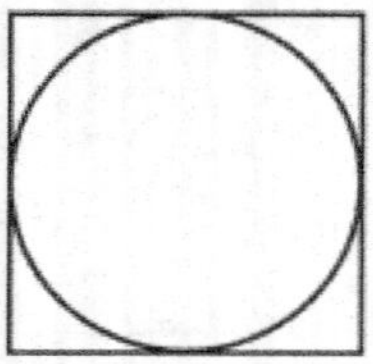

A. 2π
B. 2.25π
C. 2.5π
D. 3π
E. 3.25π

57) What is the length of the diagonal line drawn inside the cube of side *x*?

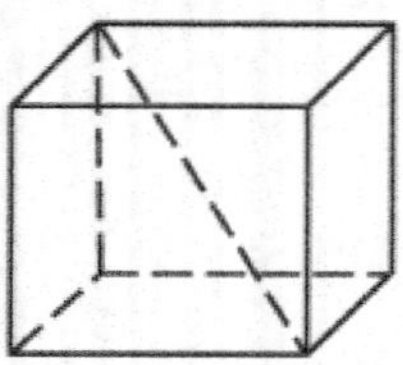

A. $2x$
B. $x\sqrt{2}$
C. $x\sqrt{3}$
D. $3\sqrt{2}\,x$
E. $(x/2)\sqrt{3}$

58) The energy of x-ray photons is given by *E* = *Fh* where *f* is the frequency of the photons in hertz (Hz), *h* is Planck's constant (6.63×10^{-34}). If an x-ray photon has 1.2×10^{-15} joules of energy, how many photons are produced every second?

A. 1.8×10^{18}
B. 5.5×10^{48}
C. 4.0×10^{34}
D. $8.3 \times 10^{2}0$
E. 2.5×10^{18}

59) The specific heat capacity of a substance is the energy required to raise 1 g by 1 °C; for water it is 4.2 J g^{-1} °C^{-1}. The heat of vaporization of a substance is the energy required to convert 1 g of liquid at its boiling point to gas at the same temperature; for water it is 2.3 kJ g^{-1}. **Calculate the amount of energy required to raise 1 kg of water at 0 °C to boiling point and convert 200 g of it to steam. Give your answer in kilojoules.**

A. 820 kJ
B. 900 kJ
C. 880 kJ
D. 750 kJ
E. 800 kJ

60) A train running at the speed of 60 km/hr crosses a pole in 9 seconds. What is the length of the train?

A. 200 metres
B. 324 metres
C. 120 metres
D. 180 metres
E. 150 metres

RISPOSTE CORRETTE

1) A	11) D	21) D	31) D	41) C	51) C
2) C	12) D	22) B	32) E	42) C	52) E
3) B	13) C	23) A	33) A	43) D	53) E
4) C	14) B	24) C	34) B	44) E	54) B
5) A	15) B	25) C	35) C	45) B	55) D
6) D	16) C	26) D	36) E	46) A	56) B
7) B	17) E	27) A	37) D	47) C	57) C
8) E	18) E	28) C	38) A	48) E	58) A
9) D	19) D	29) C	39) B	49) B	59) C
10) B	20) B	30) B	40) E	50) C	60) E

Test 7

1) Fractures of the hip are a leading cause of disability and mortality in elderly people. A high proportion of these patients have osteoporosis, which leads to fragile bones. All elderly people should take calcium and vitamin D supplements to help to prevent osteoporosis. This inexpensive treatment will reduce the risk of a hip fracture after a fall.
Which one of the following, if true, would seriously weaken the above argument?

A. Most falls in the elderly do not lead to bone fractures
B. Preventive treatments are not cost-effective
C. Most fractures involve vertebrae and not the hip
D. Most elderly people do not have falls
E. Regular exercise is the best way to strengthen bones

2) Placebo-controlled drug trials are unethical if participants are denied new therapeutic treatments that might prove effective. Any new treatment should be tested alongside the existing standard therapies to offer candidates the possibility of a better outcome and not just a 'nothing' treatment.
Which of the following, if true, would most seriously weaken the above argument?

A. There is no guarantee that any new treatment will be any more effective than a placebo
B. It is unethical to employ treatments that have not been proven safe or effective in a placebo-controlled drug trial
C. In a placebo-based drug trial the participant loses the benefit of the standard treatment
D. Placebo treatments are never effective and are justly describe as 'nothing' treatments
E. None of the listed

3) A five-year study has shown that obesity is caused by a sedentary lifestyle and not by over-eating. Participants with sedentary lifestyles put on more weight than participants who ate more.
Which of the following statements, if true, would make the findings of the study unsafe?

A. Participants who put on more weight also dieted more
B. Participants who over-ate preferred fast food
C. Not all of the participants with a sedentary lifestyle put on weight
D. A sedentary lifestyle led to an increased food intake
E. A few participants lost weight during the five-year study

4) The box and whisker plot summarizes the performance of 200 students in the first two sections of the IMAT.

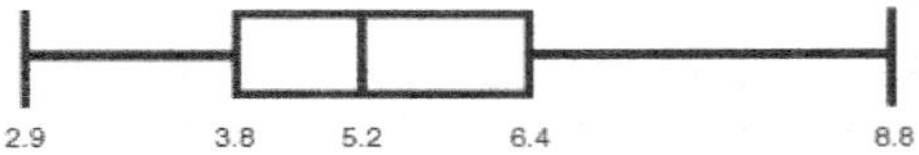

Indicate the true statement.

A. Only one student achieved 8 marks on the IMAT scale
B. Half the students scored between 3.8 and 6.4 marks
C. One-quarter of the pupils scored more than 3.8 marks

D. The mean mark was 5.2
E. The probability that two students chosen at random achieved more than 6.4 marks is 8 per cent

5) Which of the columns in the table shows the correct number of excess winter deaths per 1000 of population consistent with the bar chart?

Age range	A	B	C	D	E
under 65	2	1	3	3	3
65-74	1.9	1.2	2.9	2.9	2.9
75-84	2.2	3.9	6.1	6.1	6.9
over 85	4.1	7.9	12	7.9	14

A. A
B. B
C. C
D. D
E. E

6) A high-calorie drink is available to patients in neutral, vanilla and chocolate flavours.
The pie chart shows the popularity of the three flavours amongst patients.

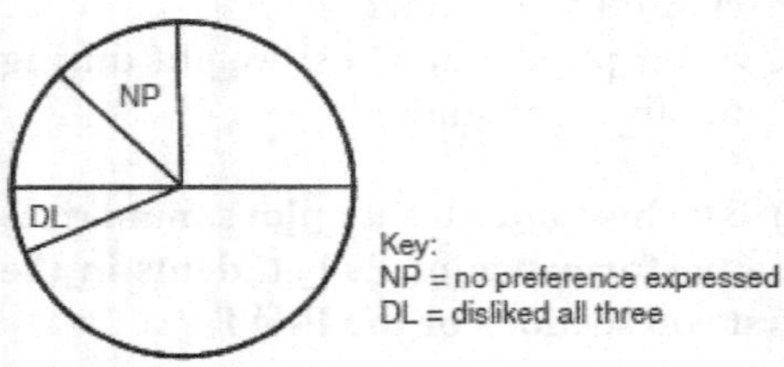

Which one of the following columns might represent preferences expressed?

Flavour	A	B	C	D	E
neutral	30	90	160	500	160
vanilla	60	120	320	300	80
chocolate	120	400	320	200	280

A. A
B. B
C. C
D. D
E. E

7) The stacked bar chart shows retailers' annual book sales in four categories: children's (CH), adult non-fiction (AN), adult special (AS) and adult fiction (AF).

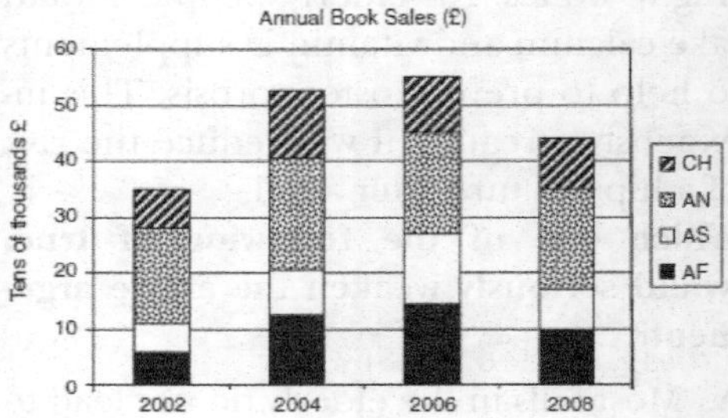

In which year did the smallest proportion of sales come from children's books?

A. 2002
B. 2004
C. 2008
D. 2006
E. None of them

8) Considering the stacked bar chart of the question n. 7, approximately what is the increase in per cent in annual sales between the years with the greatest difference?

A. 20 per cent
B. 40 per cent
C. 49 per cent
D. 57 per cent
E. 66 per cent

9) According to the stacked bar chart of the question n. 7, approximately what was the greatest increase in adult fiction sales over any two-year span?

A. £ 10 000
B. £ 60 000
C. £ 120 000

D. £ 150 000
E. £ 175 000

10) Which shape does not belong with the other four?

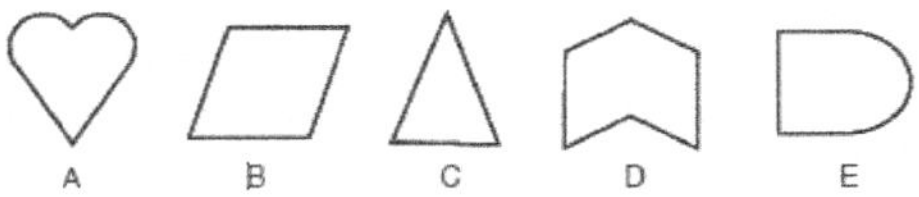

A. A
B. B
C. C
D. D
E. E

11) Where was the International Red Cross founded in 1863?

A. Basel
B. Paris
C. Geneva
D. Bern
E. Berlin

12) Who was called the Iron Lady?

A. Hillary Clinton
B. Margaret Thatcher
C. Queen Elizabeth II
D. Condoleezza Rice
E. Indira Gandhi

13) The mission of OPEC is the one:

A. to maintain international peace and security
B. to coordinate and unify the petroleum policies of its Member Countries and ensure the stabilization of oil markets
C. to promote collaboration and dialogue among civilizations, cultures and peoples
D. to contribute to the growth of the world economy
E. to promote the health and well-being of children in the world

14) Galileo was an Italian astronomer who:

A. developed the telescope
B. discovered four satellites of Jupiter
C. discovered that the movement of pendulum produces a regular time Measurement
D. wrote a book called Dialogue Concerning the Two Chief World Systems
E. all of the above

15) Who discovered the Land of Fire?

A. Vasco da Gama
B. Ernest Henry Shackleton
C. Ferdinand Magellan
D. James Clark Ross
E. James Cook

16) Who is considered to be the father of Gothic Novel in England?

A. H. Fielding
B. G. Chaucer
C. A. Radcliffe
D. W. Scott
E. H. Walpole

17) Hermeneutics is:

A. the study of the method for comparing different versions of a text
B. the study of the esoteric level of meaning of literary texts
C. the study of the arrangement of words in a sentence and of sentences in a paragraph
D. the science concerning the principles and methods of the interpretation of literary texts
E. a literary movement

18) Which of the following cities is the capital of Australia?

A. Sidney
B. Melbourne
C. Adelaide
D. Canberra
E. Wellington

19) *The Brothers Karamazov* was written by:

A. Aleksandr Puškin
B. Fëdor Dostoevskij
C. Boris Pasternak
D. Anton Čechov
E. Valdimir Majakovskij

20) Which English king had six wives?

A. Henry VI
B. Henry VIII
C. James IV
D. Richard II
E. Richard III

21) The Munich Agreement (1938) was a settlement permitting Nazi Germany's annexation of portions of:

A. Czechoslovakia
B. Poland
C. Hungary
D. France
E. Belgium

22) The worst world financial crisis after 1929 started in:

A. 2005
B. 2001
C. 1990
D. 2010
E. 2008

23) The 3-nucleotide sequence on DNA which specifies a particular amino acid is known as a __________.

A. codon
B. anti-codon
C. triplet
D. transcription factor
E. gene

24) A _________ is a change in the order of nucleotides on DNA which cause an alteration in proteins being synthesized.

A. transcription
B. replication
C. mutation
D. translation
E. traduction

25) Just because a gene or allele exists, it is not always expressed. The control of expression (for example by operons in bacteria) is known as ________.

A. dominance
B. recessiveness
C. heterozygosity
D. gene regulation
E. recombination

26) ______ DNA is hybrid DNA from two or more sources.

A. Redundant
B. Recombinant
C. Plasmid
D. Single-stranded
E. Autosomal

27) What is the name of the phase represented by the letter X? This is the first stage where the chromosomes become visible and the nuclear envelope disappears.

A. Metaphase
B. Telophase
C. Prophase
D. Anaphase
E. Meiosis

28) Centrioles, the little cylindrical objects within a cell, are represented by which number?

A. Three
B. Four
C. Five
D. Six
E. Seven

29) Compounds are considered organic if they contain:

A. phosphorus and water
B. carbon and hydrogen
C. nucleotides and silicon
D. water and oxygen
E. nitrogen and carbon

30) Carbon is the element that is the foundation of organic compounds. Which of the following characteristic of carbon makes this element so diverse?

A. It has four valence electrons
B. It can form large macromolecules
C. It can form up to four covalent bonds
D. All of the above
E. None of the above

31) What is the chemical formula for a ketone/aldehyde?

A. $—NH_2$
B. —COOH
C. C=O
D. —SH
E. —CO

32) A disaccharide such as sucrose can be broken down into its monomers by:

A. hydrolysis
B. a condensation reaction
C. the breaking of ionic bonds
D. the formation of covalent bonds
E. a fusion reaction

33) In which of the following compounds does oxygen have the highest oxidation number?

A. H_2O
B. O_2
C. H_2O_2
D. CO_2
E. OF_2

34) Where in the soil are the greatest number of plant roots?

A. Top 3 inches of soil
B. Top 12 inches of soil
C. Top 3 feet of soil
D. Below 5 feet of soil
E. Top 4 inches of soil

35) Lipids are:

A. hydrophilic
B. inorganic
C. hydrophobic
D. macromolecules which have carbonyls as a sole functional group
E. organic

36) Two examples of energy storage polysaccharides are:

A. glucose and sucrose
B. glucose and fructose
C. chitin and glycogen
D. starch and glycogen
E. fructose and chitin

37) Glycogen can be found primarily in what types of cells?

A. Those that make up the cell membrane of fungi
B. Vertebrate lung and kidney cells
C. Vertebrate liver and muscle cells
D. Cells that make up vascular and cardiac tissue
E. Epithelial tissue

38) A hydrophilic compound is one which:

A. is water-soluble
B. has at least two isomers
C. is always inorganic
D. has at least four isomers
E. is not water-soluble

39) Monosaccharides:

A. are considered polymers
B. have a 3:1 ratio of carbon : hydrogen
C. have a 1:2:2 ratio of carbon : hydrogen : nitrogen
D. have a 1:2:1 ratio of carbon : hydrogen : oxygen
E. have a 2:1 ration of nitrogen : oxygen

40) Chitin can be found in:

A. glandular tissue
B. the muscle tissue of vertebrates
C. epithelial tissue of humans
D. liver cells
E. exoskeleton of animals such as cockroaches and crabs

41) What volume of 1.0 molar saline solution must be added to 500 ml of 6.0 molar saline solution to dilute it to a 2.0 molar solution? (1 molar = 1 mol/L)

A. 750 ml
B. 1.0 L
C. 1.5 L
D. 1.75 L
E. 2.0 L

42) Calcium hydrogen carbonate $Ca(HCO_3)_2$ is a buffer in the body. How many moles of oxygen are present in 0.5 mole of $Ca(HCO_3)_2$?

A. 0.5
B. 2.0
C. 1.5
D. 6.0
E. 3.0

43) Which of the following statements could be true for the element krypton? $^{83.8}_{36}Kr$

A. 36 protons, 36 neutrons, 36 electrons, 6 isotopes
B. 83 protons and neutrons and 36 electrons
C. 36 protons and 36 electrons, 6 isotopes
D. 6 isotopes, 36 protons, 36 electrons, 84 neutrons
E. 40 protons, 24 neutrons, 16 isotopes

44) Bromine water can be used to distinguish between alkanes and alkenes because bromine reacts with alkenes by adding to both sides of the double bond. Which two of the following hydrocarbons will turn bromine water colourless?

A. C_2H_6
B. C_3H_6
C. $C_{12}H_{26}$
D. $C_{20}H_{42}$
E. $C_{60}H_{100}$

45) Determine the oxidation number of carbon in K_2CO_3.

A. 0
B. +2
C. +4
D. -2
E. +1

**46) Consider the following reaction: $4NH_3 + 5O_2 \rightarrow 4NO + 6H_2O$.
The element being oxidized and the oxidizing agent are:**

A. N and NH_3
B. N and O_2
C. O and NH_3
D. O and O_2
E. H and NH_3

47) Which name/formula combination is wrong?

A. Phosphorous acid/H_3PO_4
B. Nitrogen oxide/NO
C. Acetate ion/CH_3COO^-
D. Sodium chromate/Na_2CrO_4
E. Calcium hypobromite/$Ca(BrO)_2$

48) Which assignment of oxidation number is INCORRECT for the blinking element?

A. $K_2Cr_2O_7$; +6
B. NH_3; +3
C. $H_2PO_2^-$; +1
D. SeO_3^{2-}; +4
E. $Cu(NO_3)_2$; +2

49) Of the following symbol/name combinations of elements, which one is wrong?

A. C/carbon
B. F/fluorine
C. B/barium
D. N/nitrogen
E. U/uranium

50) The weight of a millimole of $(NH_4)HPO_4$ is:

A. 132 g
B. 114 g
C. 1.14×10^{-3} g
D. 0.132 g
E. 6.02×10^{20} g

51) How many atoms are in one mole of CH_3OH?

A. 6
B. 6.0×10^{23}
C. 12.0×10^{23}
D. 3.6×10^{24}
E. 3

52) Which one of the samples has the largest mass?

A. 1 mol of $CO_2(g)$
B. 1 mol of $UF_6(g)$
C. 1 mol of $CH_3COCH_3(l)$
D. 1 mol of He(g)
E. All the listed have the same mass

53) What is the area of the shaded region if the diameter of the circle is x?

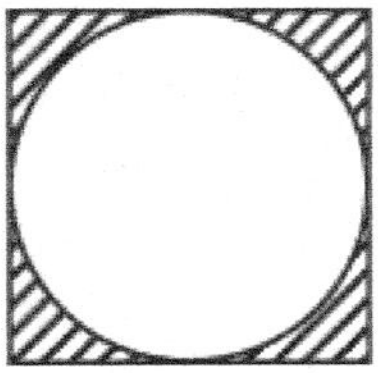

A. $x^2 - \pi x^2$
B. $x^2(1 - 4\pi)$
C. $x^2(1 - \pi)/4$
D. $x^2(4 - \pi)/4$
E. $x^2\ \pi/4 - \pi$

54) Calculate $\dfrac{5+\frac{3}{8}}{2-\frac{3}{4}}$.

A. 3.6
B. 4.0
C. 4.3
D. 4.4
E. 4.8

55) Calculate the following, giving your answer in scientific notation.

$$\frac{32+\log_{10}(10^8)}{8\times10^{-7}\times(10^3)^4}$$

A. 5.0×10^{-5}
B. 7.0×10^{-5}
C. 5.0×10^{5}
D. 7.0×10^{3}
E. 5.0×10

56) If $y = 0$ when $x = 2$ or -2, what is the value of y when $x = 0$?

A. +4
B. −4
C. +2
D. −2
E. 0

57) A golf ball of mass 46 g is hit from a tee peg at a speed of 50 m s^{-1}. If the ball is in contact with the golf club for 10 milliseconds, what force is exerted on the club face?

A. 200 N
B. 230 N
C. 250 N
D. 330 N
E. 180 N

58) In the diagram, what current flows through the bulb?

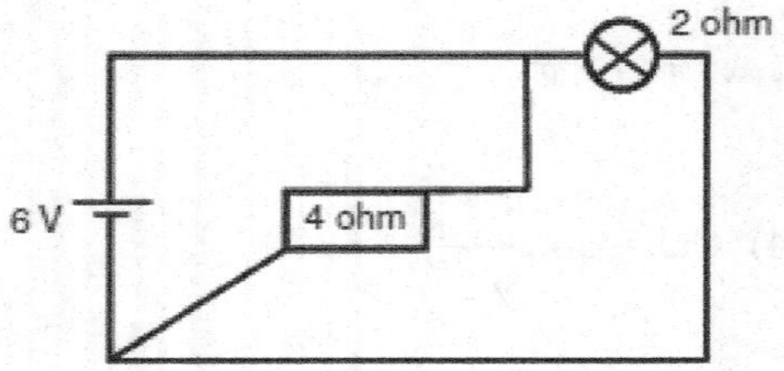

A. 1 A
B. 4 A
C. 3 A
D. 8 A
E. 6 A

59) Lead ingots measuring 200 mm × 100 mm × 50 mm are stacked with their largest face on the ground. (1 kg = 10 N).

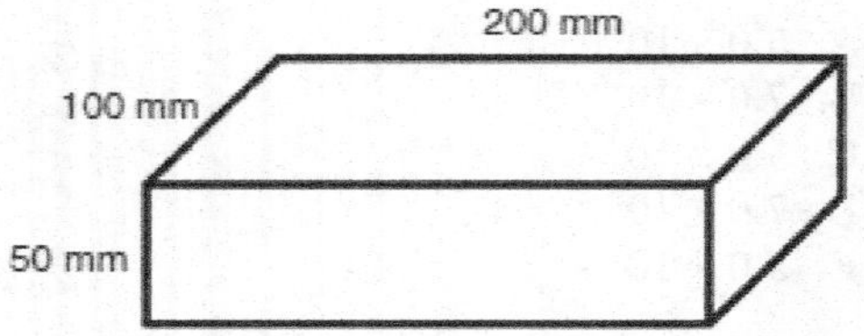

If the density of lead is approximately 11 gram per cm^3, what pressure in pascals (Pa) will an ingot exert on the ground?

A. 5500 Pa
B. 3100 Pa
C. 5700 Pa
D. 2700 Pa
E. 6000 Pa

60) A rightward force is applied to a 12-kg object to move it across a rough surface at constant velocity. The object encounters 30 N of frictional force.

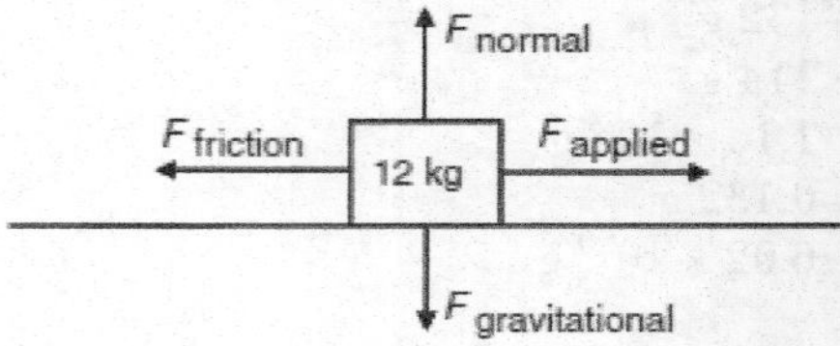

($g = 10\ ms^{-2}$)
Use the diagram to determine to the gravitational force.

A. 30 N
B. 60 N
C. 100 N
D. 120 N
E. 180 N

RISPOSTE CORRETTE

1) E	11) C	21) A	31) C	41) E	51) D
2) B	12) B	22) E	32) A	42) E	52) B
3) D	13) B	23) A	33) E	43) C	53) D
4) B	14) E	24) C	34) B	44) B	54) C
5) C	15) C	25) D	35) C	45) C	55) A
6) E	16) E	26) B	36) D	46) B	56) B
7) D	17) D	27) C	37) C	47) A	57) B
8) D	18) D	28) C	38) A	48) B	58) C
9) B	19) B	29) B	39) D	49) C	59) A
10) B	20) B	30) D	40) E	50) D	60) D

Test 8

1) The hypothesis that the earth's atmosphere is warming because of anthropogenic greenhouse gases is clearly true. Carbon dioxide emitted from power stations and car e hausts is the principal culprit. Methane, the second most important greenhouse gas, arises from the decomposition of organic matter on agricultural farms.

Which one of the following, if true, would seriously weaken the above argument?

A. Climate change is a complex process and predicting it with any certainty is impossible in the short term
B. Carbon dioxide makes up less than 0.05 per cent of the earth's atmosphere so it cannot be responsible for global warming
C. Greenhouse gases released by human activities are not the primary source of greenhouse gases in the atmosphere
D. A thousand years ago atmospheric temperatures were higher than today and anthropogenic greenhouse gases were lower
E. Global warming did not begin until after the industrial devolution

2) A survey of managers aged 35 and under found that 2/3 of employers monitor staff use of the Internet during working hours and block access to sites deemed irrelevant to the job.

This has been branded as "old fashioned", with senior executives not encouraging the benefits of exploiting new technology. 16% of managers described their senior executives as dinosaurs. Senior executives were pessimistic that staff wanted access to the Internet for research, professional development and other aspects of getting the job done. 65% of organisations monitored Internet usage, and this rose to 88% in the police. Also, 65% blocked acess to "inappropriate" sites, with this rising to 89% in local government and 90% in the utilities.

Which of the following statements is true?

A. 2/3 of employers use Internet during working hours
B. Senior executives who encourage the benefits of exploiting new technology are called "old fashioned"
C. Managers aged 35 and under block access to sites considered relevant to the job
D. 16% of senior executives describe managers under 35 as dinosaurs
E. The percentage of employers who block access to "inappropriate" sites rises to 90% in the utilities

3) Access to education for people with disabilities and learning difficulties is now being helped by new technology. Sophisticated software now turns speech into written form for the hearing impaired, while printed words are transformed into sounds at the click of a button for the blind. Those suffering from dyslexia can alter the size or colour on a printed document to make it easier to read. The ability to make effective use of this new technology can depend on a student's age an IT literacy. This is particularly true of mature disabled in accessing learning tend to lie not in the student's disability or learning problem, but in the task they are expected to perform where time may be a crucial factor. What can take an able-bodied person a few minutes can mean hours of work for someone with a disability. Overall disabled students have generally become agile users of new technologies, developing personal strategies depending on their needs and making full use of whatever technical support is on offer.

Which of the following statements is absolutely FALSE?

A. New technology helps disabled people
B. Disabled students are generally agile users of new technologies
C. Sophisticated software transforms speech into written form and printed words into sounds
D. Every disabled person can use new technology independently on his age and IT literacy
E. Disabled people who are advantaged by new technologies are above all the hearing impaired, the blind and dyslexic

4) Johnson has entered her "firebrand" dinghy in a race being held in her twin town of La Rochelle in France organised by the local yacht club. The race consists of completing a course measuring 3 kilometres marked out by a series of orange buoys. She decides to practise the course the day before the race. The wind is difficult with gusts and calms in almost equal measures. In sailing the course John manages an average speed of 3 knots for 10 minutes, 10 knots for 20 minutes and 7 knots for 30 minutes.

How many laps of the marked course did Johnson complete, to one decimal place?
(1 knot = 1.852 km/h)

A. 3.5 laps
B. 4.5 laps
C. 6.0 laps
D. 6.7 laps
E. 12.3 laps

5) What is the missing number in the following series of numbers?
1, 2, 9, 64, 625, ?, 117 649.

A. 1110
B. 2048
C. 6072
D. 7776
E. 8824

6) The scatter graph compares the IMAT test results of 25 candidates in Tests 1 and 2.

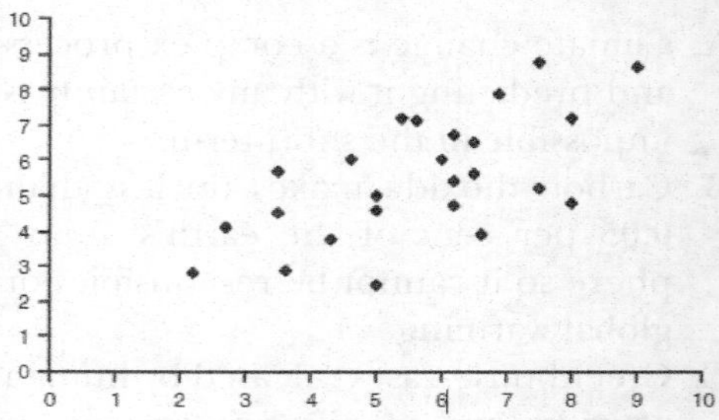

Which one of the following statements is true when comparing the test results in the two tests?

A. There is a strong positive correlation
B. There is a weak negative correlation
C. There is a weak positive correlation
D. There is a strong negative correlation
E. There is no correlation negative or positive

7) If Paul can paint a house in six hours and Julie can paint a house in nine hours, how long will it take them to paint a house if they both work together?

A. 7 hours 30 minutes
B. 4 hours 32 minutes
C. 4 hours 24 minutes
D. 3 hours 45 minutes
E. 3 hours 36 minutes

8) The group categories the items of food into low to high calorie content and produces the following table.

Calorie count per serving	Number of items
<80	7
>80 but <109	3
>109 but <149	3
>149 but <189	2
189 and over	6

The group then checks its table.
Is there anything wrong with the total number of items in the table?

A. One too few of calorie count >149 but <189
B. Two too many of calorie count <80
C. One too many of calorie count 189 and over
D. Total number of calorie count correct
E. One too few of calorie count >109 but <149

9) Referring to the table of question n. 8, a group member wants to ascertain the median calorie count for all the items in the table.
Which one of the following should he do?

A. Re-arrange the numbers into numerical order, find the tenth number and divide by 2
B. Add all the numbers together and divide by 20
C. Find the average of all the numbers and divide by 2
D. Find the calorie count number that occurs most frequently
E. Re-arrange the numbers into numerical order, add the tenth and eleventh numbers and divide by 2

10) Referring to the table of question n. 8, it is the birthday of one of the group and another member wants to buy a chocolate cake, large enough for each member to have one serving size. However, before going shopping she wants to know what weight of cake she will need for the group, measured in ounces. Grams are converted to ounces by dividing grams by 28.3.
If *X* is the weight of the required cake in ounces, and *G* is the weight of one serving size in grams, which one of the following options is the correct formula?

A. $X = 12\left(\frac{G}{28.3}\right)$

B. $G = \frac{12X}{28.3}$

C. $G = \frac{12}{28.3X}$

D. $X = 28.3\left(\frac{G}{12}\right)$

E. $X = \frac{28.3}{12G}$

11) The European Economic Community was set up in:

A. 1950
B. 1960
C. 1973
D. 1957
E. 1949

12) Who wrote *Doctor Zhivago*?

A. Fyodor Dostoyevsky
B. Anton Chekhov
C. Boris Pasternak
D. Lev Tolstoy
E. Mikhail Bulgakov

13) Who was King of the United Kingdom during the Second World War?

A. Richard I
B. George III
C. George IV
D. George V
E. George VI

14) Which 51-mile waterway opened to traffic in August 1914?

A. Manchester Ship Canal
B. Panama Canal
C. St Lawrence Seaway
D. Suez Canal
E. Corinth Canal

15) The Spanish flag consists of which two colours?

A. Black and red
B. Red and yellow
C. Blue and yellow
D. Green and blue
E. Red and blue

16) What does the Greek word for "diamond" mean?

A. Brilliance
B. Precious
C. Unbreakable
D. Priceless
E. Transparent

17) What is the biggest planet in the Solar System?

A. Mercury
B. Mars
C. Saturn
D. Earth
E. Jupiter

18) Scurvy is a disease resulting from a deficiency of what?

A. Vitamin A
B. Vitamin B
C. Vitamin C
D. Vitamin E
E. Vitamin D

19) In which year was the Cannes Film Festival founded?

A. 1952
B. 1949
C. 1948
D. 1950
E. 1946

20) Which ancient Greek is referred to as the father of Western medicine?

A. Hippocrates
B. Aristotle
C. Aristophanes
D. Plato
E. Socrates

21) The great Victoria Desert is located in:

A. Canada
B. West Africa
C. Australia
D. North America
E. New Zealand

22) Who is the author of the book *Nineteen Eighty Four*?

A. Thomas Hardy
B. George Orwell
C. Emile Zola
D. Walter Scott
E. Thomas Beckett

23) The gland responsible for metabolism is:

A. pineal gland
B. pituitary gland
C. thyroid
D. liver
E. parathyroid

24) Look at the list (1 to 6) below and then choose the correct path for carbon dioxide leaving the body during exhalation.

1 trachea; 2 bronchioles; 3 bronchi; 4 larynx; 5 pharynx; 6 alveoli.

A. 5, 4, 1, 3, 2, 6
B. 6, 2, 3, 1, 5, 4
C. 6, 2, 3, 1, 4, 5

D. 6, 2, 3, 4, 1, 5
E. 6, 3, 2, 1, 4, 5

25) Type 2 diabetes is often associated with:

A. blindness
B. obesity
C. infections
D. diuretic problems
E. sleeping disorders

26) Melatonin is:

A. a vitamin
B. a carbohydrate
C. a hormone
D. a fatty acid
E. a pyrimidine base

27) Which of the following effects are not produced by caffeine?

A. Increases emotional stress
B. Stimulates the respiratory system
C. Increases alertness
D. Reduces cholesterol
E. Provokes tachycardia

28) Most abundant tissues of our body are:

A. muscular
B. connective
C. epithelial
D. nervous
E. cartilaginous

29) Mumps is a disease caused by:

A. fungus
B. bacterium
C. virus
D. mosquito
E. fly

30) In cold weather the brain signals the ________ gland to release more ______.

A. pineal; T3
B. pituitary; TSH
C. medulla; T4
D. pineal; insulin
E. medulla; glucagon

31) Which of the following is most suitable for study of mutations?

A. Haploid
B. Diploid
C. Tetraploid
D. Polyploid
E. Both diploid and tetraploid

32) Pulses are a good source of:

A. carbohydrates
B. fats
C. proteins
D. vitamins
E. minerals

33) Nymph is the name of young one of:

A. butterfly
B. beetle
C. housefly
D. cockroach
E. frog

34) Oxyreductases, transferases, hydrolases, lyases, isomerases and ligases are all classes of:

A. hormones
B. enzymes
C. proteins
D. vitamins
E. fatty acids

35) Nitrogen is fixed in ecosystems in ways stated below. Which one of the statements below is false?

A. By cyanobacteria
B. By electrical discharges in the atmosphere
C. By industrially synthesised fertilizer
D. By denitrification

E. By cyanobacteria and by electrical discharges in the atmosphere

36) Ptyalin is an enzyme produced in the:

A. salivary glands
B. pituitary gland
C. thyroid glands
D. pancreas
E. liver

37) *Mycobacterium leprae* causes leprosy, *Corynebacterium diphtheria* causes diphtheria and *Vibrio comma* causes:

A. tetanus
B. yellow fever
C. cholera
D. influenza
E. typhoid

38) Greater levels of terrestrial biodiversity are found in the:

A. Antarctic
B. temperate grasslands
C. deserts
D. Arctic
E. tropics

39) The removal of electrons from a molecule is called ______, and is an ______ reaction.

A. oxidation, exergonic
B. oxidation, endergonic
C. reduction, exergonic
D. reduction, endergonic
E. hydrolysis, endergonic

40) What is the purpose of a lysosome?

A. Produces energy
B. Stores proteins
C. Contains cell's genetic material
D. Transports proteins
E. Breaks down large molecules

41) Nitric oxide reacts with oxygen to produce nitrogen dioxide according to the following equation:

$$2NO_{(g)} + O_{2(g)} = 2NO_{2(g)}$$

Which one of the following statements is FALSE?

A. Nitric oxide is a mixture of nitrogen and oxygen
B. Oxygen is an element and a diatomic molecule
C. Nitrogen dioxide is a compound and a molecule
D. The mass of reactants equals the mass of products
E. Three moles of reactants produce two moles of products

42) Calcium is in the second group in the forth row of the periodic table. To which family of elements does it belong?

A. Alkali metals
B. Noble gases
C. Alkaline earth metals
D. Halogens
E. None of them

43) What is the percentage of hydrogen in water, atomic mass 18? Give your answer to one decimal place.

A. 7,8%
B. 9,8%
C. 12,3%
D. 11,1%
E. 10%

44) Which one of the following describes correctly the chemical behaviour of fluorine?

A. High electron affinity and a strong reducing agent
B. Most electronegative element and readily oxidized
C. Most electropositive element and readily reduced

D. Most non-metallic element and readily oxidized
E. High electron affinity and a strong oxidizing agent

45) Quantitative analysis of a 5 g sample of an unknown compound showed that it contained 2 g of copper. Which of the following could be its chimica formula? (Atomic mass: Cu = 64, C = 12, O = 16, S = 32)

A. CuO
B. Cu_2O
C. $CuCO_3$
D. $CuSO_4$
E. Cu_2SO_4

46) A mouthwash contains 0.2% w/w sodium fluoride. What is the concentration of the fluoride ion in parts per million (ppm) if sodium fluorid is 45% fluoride ion by weight? (Per cent w/w = g/100 g water; ppm = g/million g water).

A. 45 ppm
B. 450 ppm
C. 90 ppm
D. 900 ppm
E. 650 ppm

47) Sodium hydroxide is a strong base. A 0.01 molar solution has a pH of 12 and turns litmus blue. If 100 ml of the solution is titrated against 25 ml of 0.02 molar sulphuric acid the products are a salt and water; the final pH is:

A. 5
B. 6
C. 4
D. 3
E. 7

48) The pH of blood is maintained at 7.4 by the carbonic acid hydrogen carbonate ion buffer as follows: $CO_2 + H_2O = H^+ + HCO_3^-$.

What is the normal response to an increase in carbon dioxide levels in the blood?

A. The equilibrium shifts to the right and the pH rises
B. The equilibrium shifts to the right and the pH falls
C. The equilibrium shifts to the right and the pH is unchanged
D. The equilibrium shifts to the left and the pH rises
E. The equilibrium shifts to the left and the pH falls

49) In its normal state arsenic is:

A. coloured and odorous
B. coloured but odourless
C. colourless but odorous
D. colourless and odourless
E. totally insoluble

50) What are the main factors that affect solubility?

A. Temperature
B. Pressure
C. Nature of the solute
D. Nature of the solvent
E. All the listed

51) The rate of solution is a measure of how fast a substance dissolves. Which of the following factors does not determine the rate of solution?

A. Stirring
B. Temperature
C. Amount solute already dissolved
D. Time
E. All the listed factors determine the rate of solution

52) The compound deriving from carboxylic acids for elimination of a water molecule between two carboxyl is:

A. anhydride
B. weak acid
C. strong acid

D. weak base
E. strong base

53) The area of circle A is 16 times that of circle B, which is nine times that of circle C. If the diameter of circle A is 6 cm, what is the diameter of circle C?

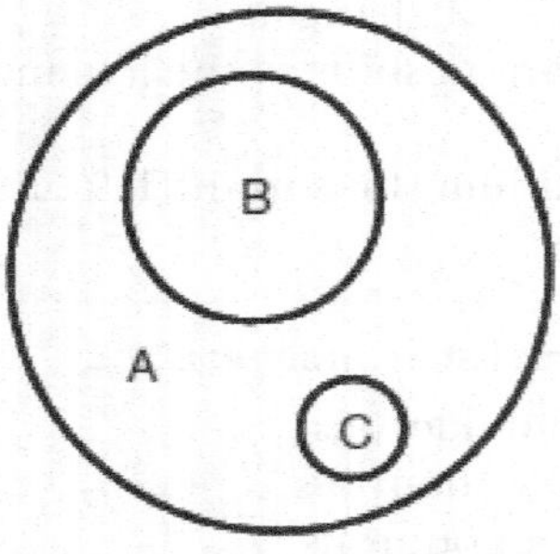

A. 0.25 cm
B. 0.5 cm
C. 0.75 cm
D. 1.0 cm
E. 1.2 cm

54) If $y^2(x^2 - 2x + 1) = 9x^2 + 6x + 1$, what is y in terms of x?

A. $y = 9x^2 + 6x + 1$
B. $y = x^2 + 3x + 1$
C. $y = (3x + 1)(3x - 1)$
D. $y = (3x + 1)/(x - 1)$
E. $y = (3x + 1)/x$

55) If $x > 5000$ then what is the closest value of $x/(2x + 1)$?

A. 1/6
B. 1/3
C. 10/21
D. 3/2
E. 1/2

56) By how much does 0.756 exceed 3/4?

A. 6/25
B. 3/125
C. 1/250
D. 3/250
E. 3/500

57) In a hammer-throwing contest a competitor whirls a mass of 4 kg around her body in a circle. If the speed of rotation of the hammer is one revolution per second before letting go, what is the size of the force acting on the competitor's arms?
The acceleration (a) of a rotating mass (m) towards the centre of rotation is given by $a = v^2/r$ where r is the radius of the circle and v the tangential velocity.

A. $16\pi^2 r$ N
B. $8\pi^2 r$ N
C. $4\pi r$ N
D. πr N
E. $8\pi^2 r^2$ N

58) A car can drive one perimeter of a circular track of radius 1,000m in 6 minutes. What is his average velocity?

A. 2,8 m/s
B. 7 m/s
C. 7.5 m/s
D. 17,5 m/s
E. 20,5 m/s

59) From a standing start, a Boeing 747 takes off in 40 seconds. If the speed at the point of lift-off is 80 m s^{-1}, what is the average acceleration?

A. 2 m s^{-1}
B. 80 m s^{-2}
C. 20 m s^{-2}
D. 2 m s^{-2}
E. 40 m s^{-1}

60) In the circuit shown below, what is the value of the current *I*?

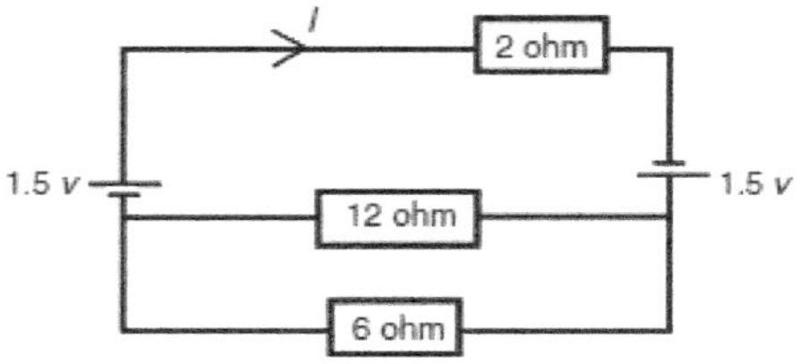

A. 2 A
B. 0.5 A
C. 1 A
D. 0.4 A
E. 3 A

RISPOSTE CORRETTE

1) D	11) D	21) C	31) A	41) A	51) D
2) E	12) C	22) B	32) C	42) C	52) A
3) D	13) E	23) C	33) D	43) D	53) B
4) B	14) B	24) C	34) B	44) E	54) D
5) D	15) B	25) B	35) D	45) D	55) E
6) C	16) C	26) C	36) A	46) D	56) E
7) E	17) E	27) D	37) C	47) E	57) A
8) C	18) C	28) B	38) E	48) C	58) D
9) E	19) E	29) C	39) A	49) D	59) D
10) A	20) A	30) B	40) E	50) E	60) B

Test 9

1) Different people use the word "normal" in different ways. A philosopher views the normal as the most usual. Psychologists and statisticians refer to normal as the middle range of a distribution of values (i.e. statistically normal). A sociologist defines "normal" as that which is in line with a rule for a particular social or cultural group in society. The Oxford English Dictionary defines "normal" as "conforming to a standard". In medicine "normal" is often used to mean an absence of physiological pathology. In common speech, "normal" may simply mean "not abnormal, not strange".

Which of the following statements is completely FALSE?

A. In medicine "normal" indicates an absence of pathology
B. In common speech "normal" means "not strange"
C. Statisticians refer to normal as "conforming to a standard"
D. Sociologists define "normal" all what is in line with a rule for a social or cultural group in society
E. The word "normal" is used with different meanings by the different categories of people

2) The patterns of communicable disease are the result of the interactions between the infectious agent, the host and the environment. The source of infection may be human, there may be animal reservoirs such as brucellosis in cattle or leptospirosis rats, or reservoirs may exist in the environment in the water or soil. There are a number of modes of transmission between the source and the host through direct or indirect transmission (by vectors or vehicles).
Vehicles such as water or food carry the infective agent while vectors such as mosquitoes for malaria are part of the circle cycle. The transmission of infection may be by inhalation, ingestion, direct skin or mucosal contact, sexual contact, injection, or cross-placental routes. The susceptibility of the host is influenced by age, natural immunity, artificial immunity (active or passive), nutritional status and immune suppression.

Which of the following statements is TRUE?

A. The atmosphere is a vehicle that can carry an infective agent
B. Immunisation cannot protect people from contacting certain communicable diseases
C. Communicable diseases are continually changing and new communicable diseases emerging
D. A person's age, diet and lifestyle choices have little impact on their susceptibility to disease
E. The transmission of infection never takes place by inhalation

3) Social stigma and prejudice are examples of discrimination, and mental health service users can often find that society and the community are unwilling to engage with them. This can be expressed directly in the form of explicit rejection, ridicule or aggression, or indirectly in the form of dismissal or avoidance. This is largely based on fear and misunderstanding of what mental health means, and it is not uncommon for questions of

capability and risk to be presented as reasons for exclusions. Indirect discrimination is often more complex to identify, as it results from a misunderstanding and adaptation rather than a direct and explicit rejection pr exclusion. For those with mental health issues it is based more on attitudes and social norms. Some types of stigma and stereotyping can be defined as indirect discrimination, for example presuming that an individual is unable to make decisions or unable to take part in a cognitive activity.

Which of the following statements can be correctly deduced?

A. Discrimination affects the recipient's sense of self-worth and overall self-image
B. A lack of awareness can lead to people with mental health issues being excluded from society
C. Rarely questions of capability and risk are presented as reasons for excluding those with mental health problems
D. Mental health creates a barrier to social interaction, services, employment and training
E. None of the sentences can be deduced

4) If your GP refers you to a specialist you can choose the hospital you want to be treated at.

You can choose any hospital in England that meets the NHS standards and this could include independent or private hospitals which are free as part of the Choice agenda. To support Choice, most GP practices use a national IT system called Choose and Book. You can choose the hospital with the best reputation, shortest waiting times, or simply the one that is most convenient. Choice of hospitals may not be appropriate for all services. Services where speedy access to diagnosis and treatment are particularly important are not required to offer a choice of hospitals. This includes: emergency attendances or admissions, patients attending a Rapid Access Chest Pain Clinic under the two-week maximum waiting time, and patients attending cancer services under the two-week maximum waiting time. Mental health and maternity services are also not included, although your GP may offer you a choice of providers if you are referred for these services.

Only one of the following statements is true. Which?

A. Because of the Choice agenda you will always be able to choose the hospital which you want to be treated at except for mental health and maternity services
B. GPs in Wales and Scotland do not have access to the Choose and Book IT system
C. Rapid Access Chest Pain Clinics and cancer services are not provided by independent and private hospitals
D. Patients suffering from cancer and chest pains do not have to be offered a choice of which hospital they can attend
E. It is not possible to choose any hospital in England that meets the NHS standards

5) Statement: Money is the root cause of all the problems in a family.

Assumptions:

1. Every problem is caused by something.
2. There are always some problems in a family.

A. Only assumption I is implicit
B. Only assumption II is implicit
C. Either I or II is implicit
D. Neither I nor II is implicit
E. Both I and II are implicit

6) Statement: "Two months ago, it was announced that Central Government pensioners would get dearness relief with immediate effect but till date, banks have not credited the arrears." – A statement from a Pensioners' Forum.

Assumptions:

1. Most of the banks normally take care of the pensioners.
2. Two months time is sufficient for the government machinery to move and give effect to pensioners.

A. Only assumption I is implicit
B. Only assumption II is implicit
C. Either I or II is implicit
D. Neither I nor II is implicit
E. Both I and II are implicit

7) Look at this series: 2, 1, (1/2), (1/4), ... What number should come next?

A. 1/3
B. 1/8
C. 2/8
D. 1/16
E. 1/6

8) The following table contains examples of the tallest skyscrapers across the USA with the height in metres shown in parenthesis:

Trump International Chicago (423)
Bank of America Atlanta (312)
Devon Energy Oklahoma City (258)
Detroit Marriott Detroit (222)
Key Tower Cleveland (289)
IDS Tower Minneapolis (241)
RSA Battle House Mobile (227)
Aon Centre Chicago (346)
30 Hudson Street Jersey City (238)
Southeast Financial Centre Miami (233)
Comcast Centre Philadelphia (297)
Bank of America Charlotte (265)
Transamerica San Francisco (258)
Hancock Place Boston (241)
Republic Plaza Denver (218)
JP Morgan Chase Houston (305)
Empire State Building New York (381)
Bank of America Houston (238)
Columbia Centre Seattle (284)
John Hancock Centre Chicago (344)
U.S. Steel Tower Pittsburgh (256)
U.S. Bank Los Angeles (310)
Chase Tower Indianapolis (253)
Bank of America Dallas (281)

What fraction of the skyscrapers are over 300 metres but less than 400 metres in height?

A. 1/2
B. 1/3
C. 1/4
D. 1/5
E. 1/6

9) A college has 19,876 students registered and 8,241 of these are studying a science subject. Also 6,037 of the students are part-time. It is not possible to study a science subject part-time.
Approximately, what is the percentage of students who are part-time?

A. 7%
B. 15%
C. 20%
D. 25%
E. 30%

10) Considering the college of the question n. 16, what is the approximate ratio of students studying science compared to the rest of students at the college?

A. 2:5
B. 3:2
C. 2:3

D. 3:4
E. 3:5

11) Who is the director of *Gangs of New York*?

A. Leonardo Di Caprio
B. Steven Spielberg
C. Martin Scorsese
D. David Lynch
E. Francis Ford Coppola

12) In which century did Michelango paint the ceiling of the Sistine Chapel?

A. 15th
B. 16th
C. 14th
D. 17th
E. 18th

13) Which founding father of communism was a German philosopher?

A. Keir Hardy
B. Che Guevara
C. Michail Bakunin
D. Karl Marx
E. Leon Trotsky

14) A polyglot is able to do what?

A. Write equally well with both hands
B. Breathe in and out at the same time
C. See in the dark
D. Speak several languages
E. Select and employ individual elements from a variety of sources

15) Which is the highest mountain in Europe?

A. Rysy Peak
B. Mount Elbrus
C. Eiger
D. Finsteraarhorn
E. Matterhorn

16) The Austrian geneticist Gregor Mendel based his theories of heredity on his studies of which plants?

A. Green beans
B. Grasses
C. Ferns
D. Orchids
E. Peas

17) Which American President resigned from office in 1974?

A. Bill Clinton
B. John Kennedy
C. Richard Nixon
D. Jimmy Carter
E. George Bush

18) The Head of Church in England is:

A. the King (Queen)
B. the Archbishop of Canterbury
C. the Prince of Wales
D. the Prime Minister
E. the chancellor of the exchequer

19) One of the best known writers of "The Lost Generation" is:

A. Mark Twain
B. John Steinbeck
C. Allan Poe
D. Scott Fitzgerald
E. Charles Bukowski

20) Which 1957 Treaty created the European Economic Community?

A. Rome
B. Madrid
C. Paris
D. Brussels
E. London

21) The latitudinal differences in pressure delineate a number of major pressure zones, which correspond with zones of:

A. oceans
B. land
C. cyclonic depressions
D. climate
E. rivers

22) Which country was once ruled by warlords called shoguns?

A. China
B. Australia
C. France
D. Japan
E. Russia

23) Pine, fir, spruce, cedar, larch and cypress are the famous timber-yielding plants of which several also occur widely in the hilly regions of India. All these belong to:

A. angiosperms
B. gymnosperms
C. monocotyledons
D. dicotyledons
E. thallophytes

24) Pollination is best defined as:

A. transfer of pollen from anther to stigma
B. germination of pollen grains
C. growth of pollen tube in ovule
D. visiting flowers by insects
E. growth of pollen grains tank to the insects

25) Plants receive their nutrients mainly from:

A. chlorophyll
B. atmosphere
C. light
D. soil
E. oxygen

26) Movement of cell against concentration gradient is called:

A. osmosis
B. active tran sport
C. diffusion
D. passive tran sport
E. homeostasis

27) Most fish do not sink in water because of the presence of:

I. swim bladder
II. air bladder
III. air sacs
IV. air in spongy bones

A. I and II are correct
B. II and III are correct
C. III and IV are correct
D. I, II, III and IV are correct
E. I and III are correct

28) Plants absorb dissolved nitrates from soil and convert them into:

A. urea
B. ammonia
C. free nitrogen
D. proteins
E. chlorophyll

29) Nucleus, the genetic material containing rounded body in each cell, was first discovered in 1831 by:

A. Robert Hooke
B. Robert Brown
C. Rudolf Virchow
D. Theodore Schwann
E. None of the others

30) Other than spreading malaria, anopheles mosquitoes are also vectors of:

A. dengue fever
B. encephalitis
C. yellow fever
D. toxoplasmosis
E. filariasis

31) Plants that grow in saline water are called:

A. hydrophytes
B. mesophytes
C. thallophytes
D. halophytes
E. angiosperms

32) Neurospora is used as genetic material because:

A. it has short life cycle of 10 days
B. the product of single meiosis can be easily analysed
C. meiotic products are linearly arranged in the form of ordered tetrads
D. is a diploid fungus
E. all the answers are correct

33) N_2 content is kept constant in the biosphere due to:

A. N_2 fixation
B. nitrogen cycle
C. industrial pollution
D. absorption of N_2
E. absorption of O_2

34) Most of the red, blue and purple colours of plants are due to a pigment called:

A. anthocyanin
B. carotene
C. chlorophyll
D. xanthophylls
E. eumelanin

35) Plants growing on sand are called as:

A. chasmophytes
B. oxylophytes
C. lithophytes
D. psammophytes
E. none of the listed

36) Normal adult human has:

A. 10 gram of haemoglobin/100 gram of blood
B. 14 gram of haemoglobin/100 gram of blood
C. 20 gram of haemoglobin/100 gram of blood
D. 24 gram of haemoglobin/100 gram of blood
E. 6 gram of haemoglobin/100 gram of blood

37) Monotremes are unique mammals because they:

A. posses hair
B. secret milk in a pouch
C. lay eggs
D. give birth to live young
E. all of the listed

38) Poison glands of snakes are homologous to:

A. electric organs of fishes
B. sting of rays
C. sebaceous glands of mammals
D. salivary glands of vertebrates
E. human tonsils

39) Plants have __________ While animals lack it.

A. starch
B. fat
C. protein
D. carbohydrates
E. cellulose

40) Night blindness is caused by lack of which vitamin?

A. Vitamin A
B. Vitamin B
C. Vitamin C
D. Vitamin D
E. Vitamin E

41) There are approximately ______ elements.

A. 90
B. 100
C. 115
D. 130
E. 145

42) An important characteristic of compounds is that their composite elements combine in definite proportions by mass. This law is called:

A. law of multiple proportions
B. law of conservation mass

C. law of definite proportions
D. law of conservation of matter
E. law of ideal compounds

43) A process that does not require energy is called:

A. easy
B. spontaneous
C. gravity
D. emission
E. fluoridation

44) The process by which unstable atoms lose energy in a spontaneous way is called:

A. radiation
B. nuclear emission
C. instability
D. decay
E. gravity

45) How many types of radiation are emitted when a nucleus undergoes radioactive decay?

A. 3
B. 4
C. 2
D. 5
E. 6

46) Alpha radiation contains two protons and two neutrons. It is sometimes called a helium-4 nucleus. When an unstable element, such as radium-226 decays, an alpha particle is produced. Using Diagram 1, select the best answer that results from the alpha decay of Ra-226.

A. C-14
B. Rn-86
C. N-14
D. Th-234
E. C-10

47) Monatomic ions simply use the ____ of the element.

A. oxidation state
B. charge
C. name
D. number
E. atomic mass

48) Gasoline and diesel generate:

A. nitrogen
B. ethanol
C. octane
D. propane
E. carbon dioxide

49) The number of moles of solute present in 1 kg of a solvent is called its:

A. molality
B. molarity
C. normality
D. formality
E. proportionality

50) The metal used to recover copper from a solution of copper sulphate is:

A. Na
B. Ag
C. Hg
D. Fe
E. Li

51) The metallurgical process in which a metal is obtained in a fused state is called:

A. smelting
B. roasting
C. calcinations
D. froth floatation
E. fluoridation

52) The oldest rocks in the earth's crust were once molten, and came from deep inside the earth. The molten rock, called magma, spewed out in volcanic eruptions during the earth's early life and solidified into hard rock's called:

A. granite

B. basalt
C. sedimentary rocks
D. igneous rocks
E. none of the listed

53) One marble jar has several different coloured marbles inside of it. It has 1 red, 2 green, 4 blue, and 8 yellow marbles. All the marbles are the same size and shape. If Peter takes out a marble from the jar without looking, what is the probability that he will NOT choose a yellow marble.

A. 8/15
B. 7/15
C. 7/8
D. 8/7
E. 3/7

54) What is the median of the following set of numbers? {12, 8, 13, 4, 7, 6, 3, 3, 15}

A. 12
B. 8
C. 7
D. 7.5
E. 3

55) The PE room at school has a variety of colored balls that can be used to play in the school yard. There are 16 red balls, 12, blue balls, 8 yellow balls, and 11 pink balls. What is the probability that you are going to get a pink ball?

A. 11/36
B. 11/47
C. 36/47
D. 12/25
E. 18/37

56) What is the range of the following set of data? {2, 5, 2, 8, 45, 8, 17, 9, 16}

A. 43
B. 45
C. 40
D. 15
E. 20

57) Three resistors are connected to a power supply.

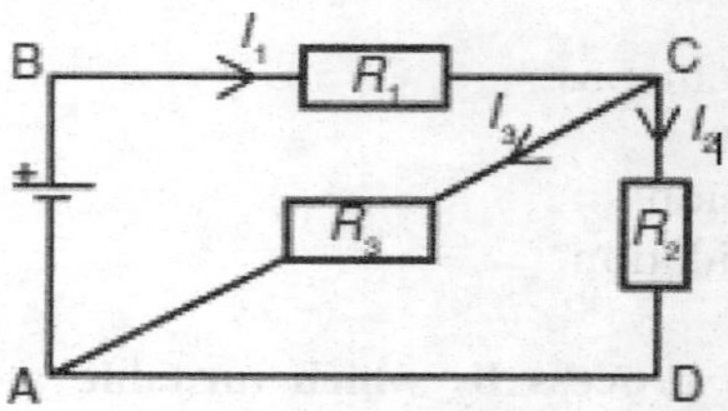

Which of the following statements are true and which are false, according to Kirchhoff's laws?

A. $I_1 = I_2 + I_3$
B. $V - I_1R_1 - I_3R_3 = 0$
C. $V - I_1R_1 + I_2R_2 = 0$
D. $V - I_1R_1 - I_2R_2 - I_3R_3 = 0$

A. A true; B true; C true; D false
B. A true; B true; C false; D false
C. A false; B false; C true; D true
D. A false; B true; C true; D true
E. A true; B false; C true; D false

58) The diagram shows the position of two positively charged points, 1C and 2C in a grid. In which square does the electric field have the greatest magnitude?

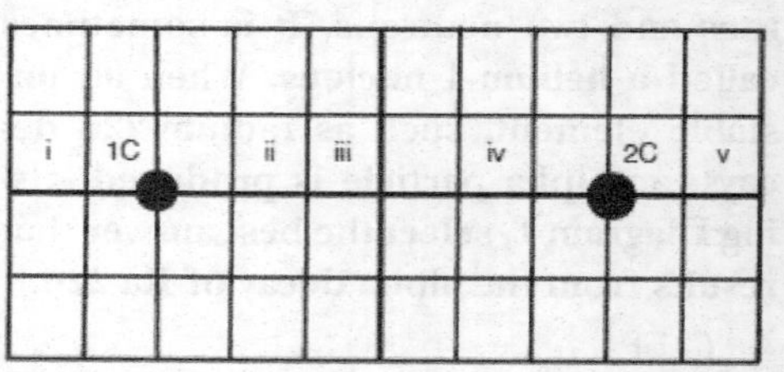

A. i
B. ii
C. iii
D. iv
E. v

59) In a crown green bowling match, a bowl of mass $3M$ strikes a jack of mass M head on.

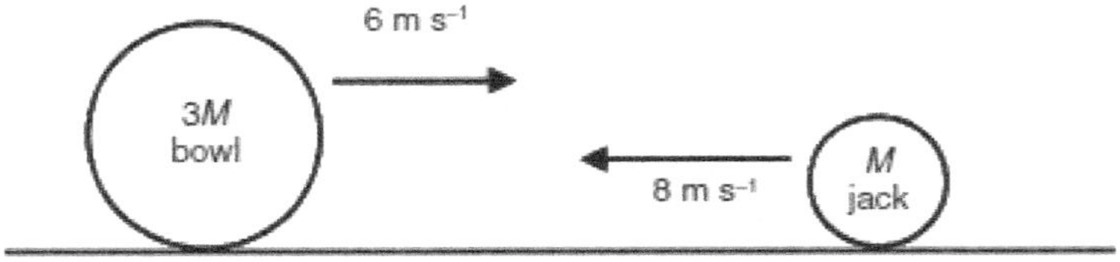

Before the collision the bowl has a velocity of 6 m s^{-1} to the east and the jack has a velocity of 8 m s^{-1} to the west.
If the velocity of the bowl after the collision is 1 m s^{-1} west, what is the velocity of the jack? Assume that the collision is perfectly elastic.

A. 13 m s^{-1} east
B. 13 m s^{-1} west
C. 14 m s^{-1} east
D. 14 m s^{-1} west
E. 12 ms^{-1} east

60) The transformer shown below has an output rated at 240 volts and 7.5 amperes. What voltage and current are required at the primary coil?

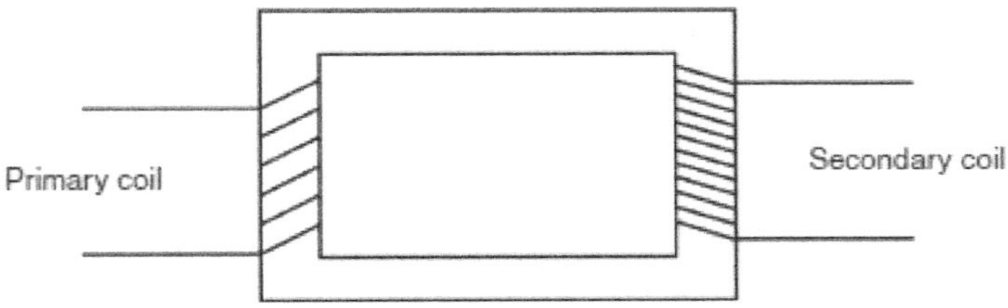

A. 60 V, 15 A
B. 120 V, 30 A
C. 240 V, 15 A
D. 120 V, 15 A
E. 360 V, 50 A

RISPOSTE CORRETTE

1) C	11) C	21) D	31) D	41) C	51) A
2) A	12) B	22) D	32) A	42) C	52) D
3) B	13) D	23) B	33) B	43) B	53) B
4) D	14) D	24) A	34) A	44) D	54) C
5) D	15) B	25) D	35) D	45) A	55) B
6) B	16) E	26) B	36) B	46) B	56) A
7) B	17) C	27) A	37) C	47) C	57) B
8) C	18) A	28) C	38) D	48) E	58) E
9) E	19) D	29) B	39) E	49) A	59) A
10) C	20) A	30) E	40) A	50) D	60) D

Test 10

1) The railroad was not the first institution to impose regularity on society, or to draw attention to the importance of precise timekeeping. For as long as merchants have set out their wares at daybreak and communal festivities have been celebrated, people have been in rough agreement with their neighbours as to the time of day. The value of this tradition is today more apparent than ever. Were it not for public acceptance of a single yardstick of time, social life would be unbearably chaotic: the massive daily transfers of goods, services, and information would proceed in fits and starts; the very fabric of modern society would begin to unravel.
What is the main idea of the passage?

A. In modern society we must make more time for our neighbours
B. The traditions of society are timeless
C. An accepted way of measuring time is essential for the smooth functioning of society
D. Society judges people by the times at which they conduct certain activities
E. Regularity of society depends on the attention given to the value of relationship with neighbours

2) Referring to the passage of question n. 1, in the second paragraph the phrase "this tradition" refers to:

A. the practice of starting the business day at dawn
B. friendly relations between neighbours
C. the railroad's reliance on time schedules
D. people's agreement on the measurement of time
E. celebration of communal festivities

3) The Alaska pipeline starts at the frozen edge of the Arctic Ocean. It stretches southward across the largest and northernmost state in the United States, ending at a remote ice-free seaport village nearly 800 miles from where it begins. It is massive in size and extremely complicated to operate. The steel pipe crosses windswept plains and endless miles of delicate tundra that tops the frozen ground. It weaves through crooked canyons, climbs sheer mountains, plunges over rocky crags, makes its way through thick forests, and passes over or under hundreds of rivers and streams. The pipe is 4 feet in diameter, and up to 2 million barrels (or 84 million gallons) of crude oil can be pumped through it daily. Resting on H-shaped steel racks called "bents," long sections of the pipeline follow a zigzag course high above the frozen earth. Other long sections drop out of sight beneath spongy or rocky ground and return to the surface later on. The pattern of the pipeline's up-and-down route is determined by the often harsh demands of the arctic and subarctic climate, the tortuous lay of the land, and the varied compositions of soil, rock, or permafrost (permanently frozen ground). A little more than half of the pipeline is elevated above the ground. The remainder is buried anywhere from 3 to 12 feet, depending largely upon the type of terrain and the properties of the soil. One of the largest in the world, the pipeline cost approximately $8 billion and is by far the biggest and most expensive construction project ever undertaken by private industry. In fact, no single business could raise that much money, so 8 major oil companies formed a consortium in order to share the costs. Each company controlled oil rights to particular shares of land in the oil fields and paid into the pipeline-construction fund according to the size of its holdings. Today, despite enormous problems of climate, supply shortages, equipment breakdowns, labor disagreements, treacherous terrain, a certain amount of mismanagement, and even theft, the Alaska pipeline has been completed and is operating.

The passage primarily discusses the pipeline's:

A. operating costs
B. employees
C. consumers
D. construction
E. companies

4) According to the passage of question n. 3, 84 million gallons of oil can travel through the pipeline each:

A. day
B. week
C. month
D. year
E. semester

5) Referring to the passage of question n. 3, the author mentions all of the following as important in determining the pipeline's route EXCEPT the:

A. climate
B. lay of the land itself
C. kind of soil
D. kind of rock
E. local vegetation

6) The figure given on the left hand side in each of the following questions is folded to form a box. Choose from the alternatives (1), (2), (3) and (4) the boxes that is similar to the box formed.

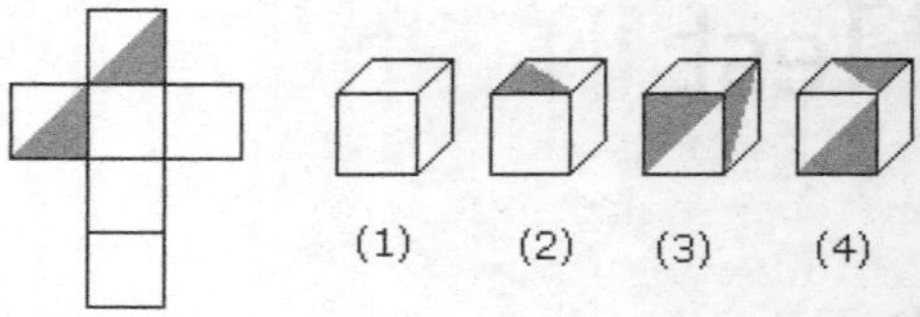

A. 3 and 4 only
B. 1 and 2 only
C. 1, 2 and 4 only
D. 1 and 3 only
E. 1, 2 and 3 only

7) Dan is Joshua's son and Guy's brother. Margaret is Guy's mother and Judy's daughter. Which of the statements below is true?

A. Judy is Dan's mother-in-law
B. Margaret is Dan's mother
C. Judy is Joshua's grandmother
D. Judy is Dan's sister
E. None of the above

8) All Germans speak Italian. All Italian speakers ride bicycles. Which of the following statements must be true?

A. All Italians speak German
B. All bicycle riders are German
C. All Germans ride bicycles
D. Some of the Italians riding bicycles are Germans
E. Some Germans who speak Italian ride bicycles

9) All owls have night vision, and birds that have night vision aren't black. Which of the following statements must be true?

A. Black ravens don't have night vision
B. All owls are not black
C. Birds that are black lack night vision
D. All of the above
E. None of the above

10) Six girls are sitting in a circle facing to the centre of the circle. They are P, Q,

R, S, T and V. T is not between Q and S but some other one. P is next to the left of V. R is 4th to the right of P. If P and R interchange their positions then which of the following pair will sit together?

A. RT
B. PV
C. VT
D. QV
E. QR

11) Which of the following mathematicians cracked Nazi Code in World War II?

A. Gustave Solomon
B. John Nash
C. Ettore Majorana
D. Bertrand Russell
E. Alan Turing

12) The ulna is a long bone in which part of the body?

A. Pelvis
B. Arm
C. Ear
D. Leg
E. Neck

13) *The Great Gasby* was written by:

A. Oscar Wilde
B. John Fante
C. Francis Scott Fitzgerald
D. Jack Kerouac
E. Thomas Stearns Eliot

14) Which of the following states is NOT a permanent member of the UN Security Council?

A. France
B. Japan
C. China
D. United Kingdom
E. USA

15) In which century did Leonardo paint the Mona Lisa?

A. 17th
B. 15th
C. 13th
D. 18th
E. 16th

16) Which of the following events took place during Caravaggio's life?

A. Birth of the United States of America
B. French Revolution
C. Adoption of the Gregorian calendar
D. Discovery of pennicillin
E. Death of Francesco Petrarca

17) A syllogism consists of:

A. three premises and one conclusion
B. one premise and one conclusion
C. two premises and two conclusions
D. two premises
E. three parts: a major premise, a minor premise and a conclusion

18) Who painted "Breakfast on the Grass"?

A. Vincent van Gogh
B. Claude Monet
C. Pablo Picasso
D. Pierre-Auguste Renoir
E. Édouard Manet

19) How many member countries of the European Union in 2019 adopt the euro as a single currency?

A. 20
B. 27
C. 21
D. 19
E. 22

20) When did the Pilgrim Fathers sail from Plymouth, England, in the Mayflower?

A. In 1621
B. In 1521
C. In 1620

D. In 1622
E. In 1776

21) What name was given to people who believed that James II and his descendants were the rightful rulers of Britain?

A. Scots on the rocks
B. Charlietans
C. Bonny Lads
D. Jacobites
E. Round heads

22) Seas and oceans make up roughly what proportion of the earth's surface?

A. 70%
B. 85%
C. 40%
D. 60%
E. 50%

23) Monocot root differs from dicot root in having:

A. open vascular bundles
B. scattered vascular bundles
C. well developed pith
D. radially arranged vascular bundles
E. only one vascular bunder

24) Outer covering of virus made up of protein is:

A. coat
B. virion
C. viriod
D. capsid
E. RNA

25) The common cold is cause by:

A. a virus
B. a bacterium
C. a fungus
D. an insect
E. a plant

26) Bacterial infections in humans can be treated with:

A. antiviral
B. antimycotic
C. antibiotic
D. no drug
E. both antiviral and antimycotic

27) A single piece of coiled DNA is called:

A. gene
B. allele
C. chromosome
D. helix
E. code

28) A group of dog offspring is known as:

A. progeny
B. litter
C. descendants
D. lineage
E. generation

29) The area of biology devoted to the study of fungi is known as:

A. genetics
B. bacteriology
C. virology
D. mycology
E. physiology

30) The death of every member of a particular species is known as:

A. disappearance
B. evolution
C. cognition
D. species death
E. extinction

31) The process of programmed cell death is called:

A. apoptosis
B. fragmentation
C. blebbing
D. cell shrinkage
E. phagocytosis

32) The name of the process used by plants to convert sunlight into food is:

A. light reaction
B. cellular respiration
C. photolysis
D. photosynthesis
E. transpiration

33) A salamander is:

A. a cold blooded animal
B. a warm blooded animal
C. an insect
D. a mosquito
E. a mammal

34) Adenine always pairs with:

A. cytosine
B. thymine
C. guanine
D. ribose
E. glucose

35) The "rungs" of the DNA ladder are made of:

A. phosphates and hydrogen
B. glucose and sugars
C. sugars and phosphates
D. base pairs
E. ribose

36) The DNA molecule is held together by:

A. magnetism
B. glucose
C. glue
D. deoxyribose
E. hydrogen bonds

37) The sugar found in DNA is:

A. equal
B. deoxyribose
C. ribose
D. fructose
E. glucose

38) The first organisms to develop a hardened endoskeleton were the:

A. echinoderms
B. annelids
C. arthropods
D. chordates
E. troglodytes

39) The symmetry exhibited by echinoderms is:

A. bilateral
B. spherical
C. radial
D. mirror image
E. trilateral

40) Pheromones are used by ants to:

A. guide members of a colony back to their own nest
B. determine which ants will become queens of future colonies
C. ensure that females mate with only one male
D. warn members of a colony of adverse environmental conditions
E. produce eggs and collect food for other bees

41) The law which states that the amount of gas dissolved in a liquid is proportional to its partial pressure is:

A. Dalton's law
B. Gay Lussac's law
C. Henry's law
D. Raoult's law
E. Newton's law

42) The main buffer system of the human blood is:

A. $H_2CO_3 - CO_3^{2-}$
B. $CH_3COOH - CH_3COO^-$
C. $H_2CO_3 - HCO_3$
D. $NH_2CONH_2 - NH_2CONH^+$
E. $NH_3CO_2 - COO^-$

43) The gas present in the stratosphere which filters out some of the sun's ultraviolet light and provides an effective shield against radiation damage to living things is:

A. helium
B. ozone
C. oxygen
D. methane
E. sodium

44) The most commonly used bleaching agent is:

A. alcohol
B. carbon dioxide
C. chlorine
D. sodium chlorine
E. glycerine

45) The nucleus of a hydrogen atom consists of:

A. 1 proton only
B. 1 proton + 2 neutrons
C. 1 neutron only
D. 1 electron only
E. 1 proton + 1 neutron

46) The metal that is used as a catalyst in the hydrogenation of oils is:

A. Pb
B. Ni
C. Cu
D. Pt
E. Fe

47) The most abundant rare gas in the atmosphere is:

A. He
B. Ne
C. Ar
D. Xe
E. Na

48) The heat energy produced when the human body metabolises 1 gram of fat is:

A. 30 KJ
B. 1 KJ
C. 39 KJ
D. 29 KJ
E. 16 KJ

49) What are the number of moles of CO_2 which contains 16 g of oxygen?

A. 0.2 mole
B. 0.3 mole
C. 0.4 mole
D. 0.5 mole
E. 0.25 mole

50) The luster of a metal is due to:

A. its high density
B. its high polishing
C. its chemical inertness
D. its mass
E. presence of free electrons

51) The number of water molecules present in a drop of water (volume 0.0018 ml) at room temperature is:

A. 1.568×10^3
B. 6.023×10^{19}
C. 4.84×10^{17}
D. 6.023×10^{23}
E. 4.54×10^4

52) The most malleable metal is:

A. platinum
B. silver
C. iron
D. gold
E. cupper

53) An industrial colour printer can print 4 pages per second. How many minutes will it take to print 6,000 pages?

A. 20
B. 25
C. 38
D. 40
E. 44

54) Skippy and his mother are both jumping clockwise along the perimeter of the field (33 m long). In one second, Skippy jumps a ground distance of 20 cm whilst his mother jumps a ground distance of 50 cm. After 25 seconds, Skippy gets tired and stops. He remains still, waiting for his mother to catch up with him.
From that moment on, how many seconds will it take his mother to reach him, assuming she carries on jumping on his clockwise circuit along the field perimeter at the same speed?

A. 24 s
B. 38 s
C. 41 s
D. 51 s
E. 76 s

55) Reginald Smythe has entered the biannual Laconda Touring Rally driving his vintage Laconda motor vehicle from London to Le Mans in France.
The first stage of the rally is from London to Dover, a distance of 70 miles. Smythe drives the first 20 miles at an average speed of 30 mph, the next 40 miles at an average of 60 mph and the last 10 miles at an average of 30 mph.
How long did it take Smythe to drive from London to Dover?

A. 1 hour 35 minutes
B. 1 hour 40 minutes
C. 1 hour 45 minutes
D. 1 hour 50 minutes
E. 1 hour 55 minutes

56) Referring to the Laconda Touring Rally of the question n. 55, shortly after leaving the ferry in Calais, Smythe joins the E1 motorway in the direction of Paris. After three hours he pulls into a service area. For the first ¼ of this journey he travels at a steady 90 kilometres per hour (kph) and for the remainder of the journey travels at 120 kph.
How far has Smythe travelled in miles (to 2 decimal places) between Calais and the service area? (1 mile = 1.6 kilometres).

A. 170.67 miles
B. 192.35 miles
C. 210.94 miles
D. 277.27 miles
E. 337.50 miles

57) The graph shows the time–temperature curve of a liquid when cooled at atmospheric pressure.

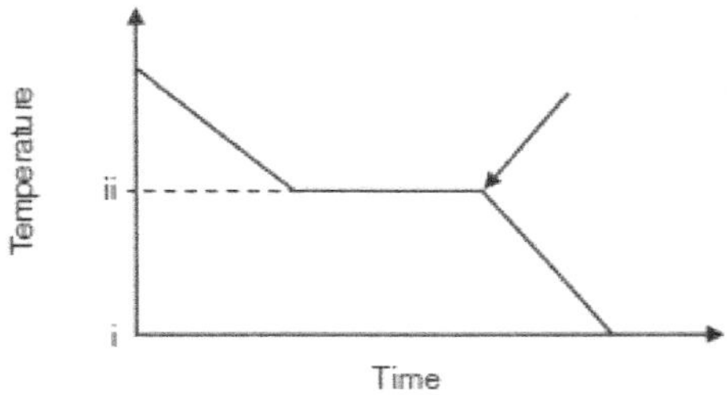

Which of the following statements are true and which are false?

A. The temperature remains constant during solidification
B. Two phase changes take place
C. All the liquid has solidified at the point shown by the arrow
D. Impurities depress the freezing point
E. The melting and freezing points are the same

58) The charge (Q) in coulombs stored by a capacitor C is given by the formula $Q = CV$ where C is in farads and V in volts. How long will it take to charge a 0.1 F capacitor with a 12 V power supply and a 100 mA charging current?

A. 0.12 s
B. 1.2 s
C. 12 s
D. 120 s
E. 1200 s

59) Two international explorers look at their own thermometers. One is graduated in Fahrenheit, the other in Celsius but they both show the same number. What is this number?

A. –50
B. –48
C. –40
D. –36
E. –32

60) Currently, the average temperature of the Earth's surface is 15 °C. With warming, scientists expect a rise of the average Celsius temperature by 16% over the next century. What will be the average Earth surface temperature in the next century, expressed in Fahrenheit?

A. 63.21
B. 63.32
C. 65.36
D. 66.58
E. 68.44

RISPOSTE CORRETTE

1) C	11) E	21) D	31) A	41) C	51) B
2) D	12) B	22) A	32) D	42) C	52) D
3) D	13) C	23) C	33) A	43) B	53) B
4) A	14) B	24) D	34) B	44) C	54) D
5) E	15) E	25) A	35) D	45) A	55) B
6) C	16) C	26) C	36) E	46) B	56) C
7) B	17) E	27) C	37) B	47) C	57) B
8) C	18) E	28) B	38) A	48) C	58) C
9) D	19) D	29) D	39) C	49) D	59) C
10) C	20) C	30) E	40) A	50) E	60) B

PROVE UFFICIALI

IMAT
a.a. 2012/2013

General knowledge and logical reasoning

1) Approximately 1 in 14 men over the age of 50 has prostate cancer. The level of 'prostate specific antigen' (PSA) is used as a preliminary screening test for prostate cancer. 7% of men with prostate cancer do not have a high level of PSA. These results are known as 'false negatives'. 75% of those men with a high level of PSA do not have cancer. These results are known as 'false positives'.

If a man over 50 has a normal level of PSA, what are the chances that he has prostate cancer?

A 0.5%
B. 0.7%
C. 5%
D. 7%
E. 25%

2) Three friends, Adam, David and Sue are sharing out a bag of marbles. To do this more quickly, they take 10 marbles each time and repeat until the bag is empty. There are not enough marbles for Sue to take 10 on the last turn. Adam and David then give her two marbles each and they all have the same.

How many marbles did Sue take on the last turn?

A. 4
B. 2
C. 3
D. 6
E. 8

3) I wish to repaint the walls of my garage. It is 3 metres high, 4 metres wide and 9 metres deep. I shall not need to paint the electronic door which covers one 3 × 4 metre end, nor the window, which is 2 metres wide and 1 metre high, nor the rear door which is 1 metre wide and 2 metres high. 1 litre of paint covers 3 square metres.

How many 1 litre tins will be needed to complete the painting?

A. 25
B. 18
C. 22
D. 21
E. 26

4) Tom shared out some money between his three children in the ratio 5:3:2. He later had an extra €6 which he gave to the child who received the least originally. This meant that the money had been shared into one large and two equal smaller shares.

How much money in total did Tom give to the three children?

A. € 20
B. € 66
C. € 26
D. € 36
E. € 60

5) Three months ago, Jane had 5 times as many DVDs as Duncan. Since then they have both bought 12 more DVDs. Jane now has twice as many as Duncan.

How many DVDs does Jane have now?

A. 72
B. 42
C. 52
D. 62
E. 32

6) There are four rivers in Bolandia, each claiming to be the longest. Tourist board brochures in the regions containing the rivers, make the following statements:
1 The Dile is shorter than the Cubba.
2 The Bongo is shorter than the Esun.
3 The Esun is longer than the Cubba.
If all of the above are correct, which one of the following statements is definitely true?

A. The Bongo is longer than the Cubba
B. The Dile is shorter than the Bongo
C. The Cubba is longer than the Bongo
D. The Dile is longer than the Esun
E. The Esun is longer than the Dile

7) The table below shows the number of people who voted for each candidate in the recent school election:

Name	Alison	Harold	Kevin	Peter	Rachel
Votes	84	100	72	126	63

When drawing a pie chart of the results one of the numbers above was not read correctly (the other four were correct). The angles were calculated as 113.4 degrees, 90 degrees, 75.6 degrees, 56.7 degrees, and 24.3 degrees.
Whose score was copied incorrectly when the pie chart was constructed?

A. Kevin
B. Alison
C. Harold
D. Peter
E. Rachel

8) **In a children's story there are three types of monster, Bongles, Crannies and Dervies. Some, but not all, Bongles are Crannies and all Crannies are Dervies. Which one of the following is definitely NOT true?**

A. Some Dervies are both Bongles and Crannies
B. No Dervies are Bongles
C. Some Dervies are neither Bongles nor Crannies
D. Some Bongles are Dervies
E. All Crannies are either Bongles or Dervies or both

9) The ingredients list on a tin of baked beans reads as follows (in order of descending weight):
- Navy beans (51%)
- Water
- Sugar
- Tomato puree (4.5%)
- Modified maize starch
- Salt
- Natural flavourings
- Onion powder
- Paprika

What is the maximum percentage of water the tin could contain?

A. 44.5%
B. 17.5%
C. 22.2%
D. 40.0%
E. 49.0%

10) A regular train service operates between Jayford and Kayton, a 16 km journey which takes 19 minutes. The trains travel at a constant speed of 60 km per hour in both directions except through a tunnel, where they are limited to 20 km per hour. Trains travelling towards Kayton enter the tunnel 4 km after setting off from Jayford.

How long is the tunnel?

A. 3.5 km
B. 0.5 km
C. 2.5 km
D. 1.5 km
E. 4.5 km

11) In preparation for my holiday in Bolandia last June, I changed € 300 into Bolandian dollars every pay day from January to May (I am paid monthly).
The exchange rates were as follows:

	January	February	March	April	May
€ 1	$ 2.74	$ 2.79	$ 2.76	$ 2.83	$ 2.81

How many more Bolandian dollars would I have received altogether if, instead, I had changed the whole € 1500 in May?

A. 180
B. 48
C. 66
D. 105
E. 36

12) After a long period of dry weather, the water container in my garden contained only 28% of its capacity of water. Last week's rain, however, increased the amount of water in the container by 25%, and according to the weather forecast, a similar amount of rain is expected to fall this coming week.
If, as expected, the container gets the same amount of rainwater this coming week as it did last week, what percentage of its capacity will it then contain?

A. 42.00%
B. 43.75%
C. 60.00%
D. 66.25%
E. 78.00%

13) A student gives his friends small, short-term loans for periods of 1, 2 or 3 weeks after which time they must be repaid in full. He always lends on a Friday afternoon. He starts with € 120 and loans out the following amounts each week:

Week	1	2	3	4
Amount	€ 45	€ 25	€ 18	€ 20

What is the smallest amount of money he has by the end of the 4th Friday?

A. € 100
B. € 12
C. € 77
D. € 82
E. € 57

14) The following information appears on a 200g packet of biscuits:

Typical values per 100 g		
Energy	Kj	2137
	Kcal	510
Protein		5 g
Carbohydrate		65.7 g
of wich sugars		38.5 g
Fat		25.3 g
of which saturates		14.6 g
Fibre		1.7 g
Sodium		0,21 g
Equivalent as salt		0.52 g

Each biscuit contains:

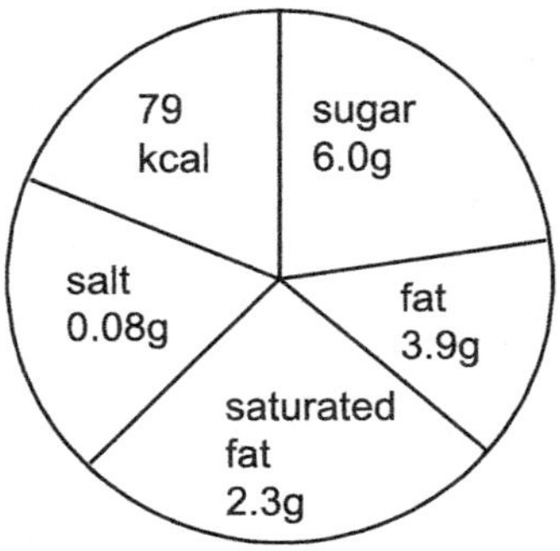

How many biscuits are there in a full packet?

A. 7
B. 6
C. 13
D. 11
E. 22

15) The 100W light bulb (cost € 0.60) is not going to be used anymore and is being replaced with the 20W (cost € 3) low energy light bulb.
If electricity is charged at € 0.15 per kWh, for how many hours must the low energy bulb be used in order for the lower cost of running it to exactly compensate for its higher initial cost?

A. 720.00
B. 0.25
C. 200.00
D. 250.00
E. 160.00

16) Alice works until 5pm each day from Monday to Friday. On Friday she is planning to go to the cinema with friends. There is a local bus service which passes her workplace, home and cinema. Part of the bus timetable is shown in the table below. Alice plans to take the bus home, where she will get ready to go to the cinema and then she will catch the bus to get to the cinema. It will take Alice 45 minutes to get ready and she will also need 10 minutes when she reaches the cinema to buy her ticket before a film starts. Films start every 15 minutes starting from 6pm.

Work	16:39	17:04	17:39	18:04
	18:39	19:04	19:39	
Home	17:08	17:33	17:58	18:33
	18:58	19:33	19:58	
Cinema	17:33	17:58	18:33	18:58
	19:33	19:58	20:33	

What is the earliest time that she can watch a film?

A. 19:00
B. 18:15
C. 18:30
D. 18:45
E. 19.15

17) In a street, a survey showed that out of a hundred households 60 had a cat, 40 had a dog, and 20 had neither a cat nor a dog.
How many households had a cat but no dog?

A. 20
B. 10
C. 40
D. 30
E. 50

18) As John walks along the High Street, the numbers to his left increase while the numbers to his right decrease, as in the diagram below.

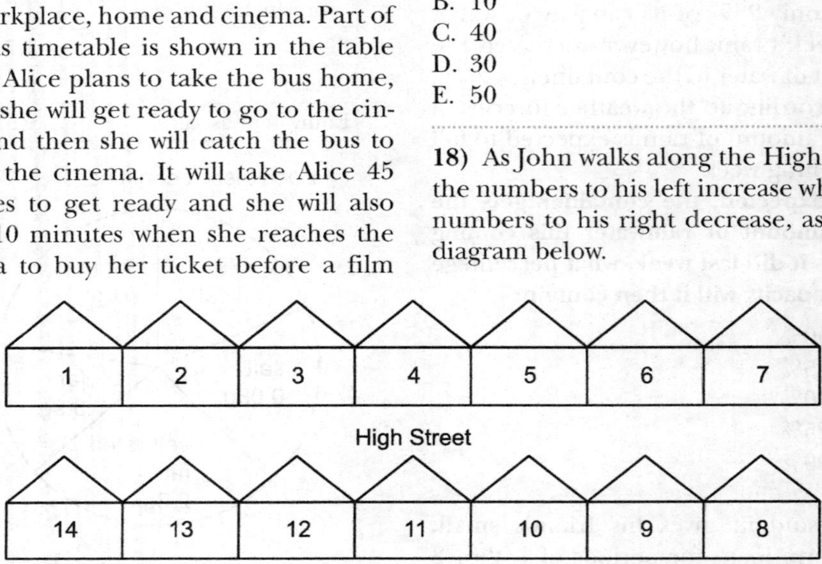

The street where he lives is numbered in the same way. He lives at number 8 Princess Road and the house directly opposite his house is number 11.
How many houses are there on Princess Road?

A. 18
B. 14
C. 16
D. 19
E. 20

19) The volume of water expands by 9% when it freezes.
If you want a block of ice 40 cm^3, how much water would you need to put into a freezer?

A. 36.7 cm^3
B. 40.0 cm^3
C. 38.2 cm^3
D. 38.0 cm^3
E. 37.0 cm^3

20) One radioactive substance, P, is gradually changed by radioactive decay into another, Q. Q itself decays into a third substance, R, which does not decay. The graphs below show how the quantities of P, Q and R varied with time during an experiment.

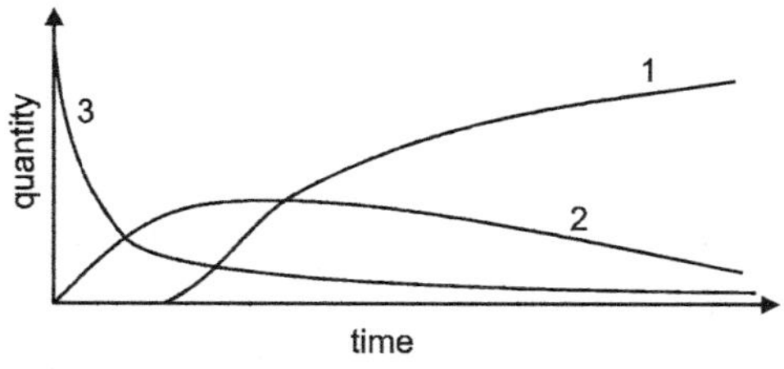

What do the graphs 1, 2 and 3 represent?

A. 1:P 2:Q 3:R
B. 1:R 2:Q 3:P
C. 1:Q 2:P 3:R
D. 1:Q 2:R 3:P
E. 1:R 2:P 3:Q

21) Modern technology has given us the power to use renewable natural resources faster than they can be replaced. The decline of fish numbers provides one example of the way in which modern technology can rapidly use up a natural resource. Modern fishing ships equipped with fish detecting systems and huge nets can gather up vast quantities of fish quicker than the sea can renew them. Because high technology gives us such harmful powers, we must learn to use the renewable resources of the earth carefully, rather than waste them.
Which one of the following best expresses the main conclusion of the above passage?

A. Most people are unaware of the damaging effects of modern technology
B. Fish need to be carefully protected to prevent them from being destroyed
C. Modern technology simply takes from the environment and destroys its resources
D. Humans must preserve renewable resources by learning how to use them carefully
E. Fishing is now a serious threat to the world's environment and should cease

22) Shower gel is now used much more than soap when people take a shower. This is unfortunate. Shower gel requires much more packaging which means more rubbish. There is also a tendency for people to use more of it when washing in comparison with soap. Therefore more natural resources are consumed in the manufacturing process than would be if people used only soap. So, the trend towards shower gel is bad for the environment. This is because it creates more problems of waste disposal and uses up more resources than soap. We should

make people more aware of the environmental impact of such simple decisions.
Which one of the following is an expression of the main conclusion of the above argument?

A. The use of shower gel increases the problems of waste disposal
B. It is unfortunate that shower gel has become more popular than soap
C. The manufacture of shower gel is more wasteful of natural resources
D. The increased popularity of shower gel is bad for the environment
E. People should be made more aware of the environmental consequences of choosing shower gel

---

23) The Chief Executive of the Royal Opera House has recently offered 100 seats on any Monday night for £10. Normally these seats can cost up to £175 therefore it represents a considerable saving. However the hopes of the Chief Executive that this will attract a broader audience are likely to be disappointed. It is not the financial costs that put people off opera – it is simply that they do not like it. Many young people spend considerable sums of money going to premier football matches or 'clubbing'. This suggests, therefore, that the problem of attracting a more diverse audience to opera is more a question of culture than economics.
Which one of the following is an expression of the main conclusion of the above argument?

A. A considerable amount of money can be saved as a result of this offer
B. The intention of the 'cheap seats' policy is that it will attract a broader audience
C. Attracting a broader audience for opera is a problem of taste rather than expense
D. Many young people do not like the idea of going to the opera
E. The 'cheap seats' policy is unlikely to attract a more diverse audience

---

24) Health services should find better ways to take blood pressure readings for patients thought to be suffering from high blood pressure (hypertension). One third of patients thought to have high blood pressure may actually have 'white coat' hypertension, according to a new study. 'White coat' hypertension means that a patient's blood pressure is high at the doctor's surgery, probably due to anxiety, but normal in everyday life. In the study, patients said to have hypertension had their blood pressure measured in a normal environment; more than one third of these patients' blood pressures were in the normal range when they were at home or participating in their usual activities. It is worrying that patients are being treated with drugs with some negative side effects to reduce high blood pressure which they do not actually have.
Which one of the following best expresses the conclusion of the argument above?

A. More effective ways of measuring blood pressure are needed
B. 'White coat' hypertension has no medical significance
C. Anxiety is the most common cause of high blood pressure
D. Two thirds of patients said to have hypertension are being wrongly treated
E. Health services could save money currently spent on unnecessarily prescribed drugs

---

25) Ten years ago in many European cities, offices typically had spaces for six bicycles, half of which were never used and spaces for 50 cars which were always full.

Today, there are fewer car spaces and many more spaces for bicycles which are always full. This change to cycling may seem strange to some as cycling is more effort. Possible causes are rising fuel prices, the introduction of higher parking charges for drivers in major cities, increasing awareness of environmental issues, expensive public transport and traffic jams.

Which one of the following can be drawn as a conclusion from the above passage?

A. Using a bicycle is now the most popular way of travelling to work
B. More people cycle to work now than 10 years ago
C. Travellers are now much more environmentally aware than they were 10 years ago
D. People will not cycle to work unless employers provide more cycle spaces on site
E. Travellers are now less happy to pay the costs of car use than they were ten years ago

26) Child actors tend to become addicted to drink and drugs in later life, usually when they become adults but are not as successful as they were previously. The actors frequently blame their parents, who often manage their children's career and so have a reason to work them hard when they are young and enjoy the wealth their children generate for them. The child actors who avoid this are often the ones who were encouraged to keep up their schooling and explore other career options.

Which one of the following can be drawn as a conclusion from the above passage?

A. Young actors who continue to work live happy, healthy lives
B. Parents should not be allowed to manage the careers of their children
C. Child actors should have other interests that allow for other career opportunities
D. Drug abuse is common in the entertainment industry
E. There are fewer jobs available for adult actors

27) Nicotine chewing gum is already available in chemists. Nicotine is an addictive drug, but by itself it causes little, if any, harm. Unlike other addictive substances it does not reduce the brain's performance, make people lazy, anti-social, or have more accidents. But until recently nicotine has been taken only in the form of tobacco, which also contains cancer-causing chemicals and deadly gases that kill one third of the people who smoke it. The chewing gum does not contain these chemicals, and is not dangerous in any other way.

Which one of the following is a conclusion which can be drawn from the above passage?

A. Nicotine chewing gum is a relatively safe alternative to tobacco for those addicted to nicotine
B. Nicotine chewing gum should be banned as it is addictive
C. Tobacco companies should put money into the manufacture and marketing of nicotine chewing gum
D. Tobacco smokers can get rid of their addiction by chewing nicotine gum
E. Nicotine chewing gum will make nicotine addiction more common by removing some of its risks

28) Roughly 60 percent of today's world population is bilingual or multilingual and it is argued that this is a new phenomenon. Today Spanish and Arabic are widely spoken whilst English is the world's most commonly spoken and written language. However, 500 years ago it was Latin which was the main language of education, religion, commerce and government in the Western World despite this not being most people's first language. In the 17th century, French and Italian gained in importance as languages of international trade.

Which one of the following can be drawn as a conclusion of the above passage?

A. English will one day be replaced as the main language of communication
B. English is the most common world language today because of the spread of the internet
C. The number of bilingual or multilingual people in the world will continue to grow
D. Speaking another language has always been an important practical consideration
E. The majority of bilingual or multilingual people speak English

29) In 2010 there were over 110,000 incidents of arson (deliberately setting fire to buildings) in the UK in which over 100 people were killed, usually in attacks on people's homes. Only a small percentage of homes have smoke alarms. If more homes had smoke alarms, the number of domestic fires would be significantly reduced. There should be a campaign to persuade people to install smoke alarms in their home as this would reduce the number of deaths.

Which one of the following identifies the flaw in the above argument?

A. It assumes that people will be willing to install smoke alarms
B. It overlooks the fact that smoke alarms may not work
C. It assumes that having smoke alarms will prevent fires
D. It assumes that all arson attacks are on people's homes
E. It assumes that all deaths in fires are from arson attacks

30) Television programmes that show young people in a school environment continue to feature highly in viewing schedules. Few of the programmes, however, give any emphasis on the time spent studying and the work required for academic success. Many of the actors used are far older than the characters they portray, suggesting attitudes, behaviour and appearances that are inaccurate and sometimes inappropriate. Broadcasters and producers should try to correct this.

Which one of the following must be assumed in the above argument?

A. Young people may feel that their social life is dull compared with that shown in television programmes
B. Television programmes about other areas such as the police are not accurate
C. School work and academic success are important to all students
D. It is often impractical to use young people in television programmes given the restrictions on how many hours they can work
E. It is important to represent school life accurately

31) It has been argued that since there has to be some limit on the funding of university education by governments, it would be best to target such funding, giving a lower priority to subjects which provide little benefit to society. Some subjects, such as Medicine, Engineering and Computing should be well funded, because they are clearly of great worth to the community. Subjects such as Classics, Literature and Art should be funded at a much lower level. These subjects are primarily of interest to the individual, and a wealthy society should give some subsidy to hobby subjects. However, it must be recognised that the future of society lies in the training and development of those people who will contribute the most.

Which one of the following must be assumed in the above argument?

A. Medicine, Engineering and Computing are not very interesting subjects to study
B. The study at universities of Classics, Literature and Art provides little benefit to society
C. Subjects which are of interest to individuals can also provide benefit to society
D. A wealthy society should not subsidise subjects which are of interest only to individuals
E. The training of those people who will contribute most to society requires an increase in government funding in university education

32) Global warming is threatening the survival of California's redwoods. These trees benefit from coastal fog which is captured by the trees, causing water to drip onto the soil and therefore watering them. Since fog is now 30 percent less frequent than it was 50 years ago the trees will not have this source of water and are therefore likely to begin to die out.

Which one of the following must be assumed in the above argument?

A. The levels of fog will continue to decline
B. Rainfall has also reduced over the past 50 years
C. Redwoods in other areas of the world are being similarly affected
D. Global warming is to blame for the reduction in coastal fog
E. Other trees will not be able to thrive in these conditions

33) After Northern Europe experienced the coldest weather for several years last winter, people are claiming that the theories of global warming are incorrect. This is not a conclusion that can be drawn from the information as it is only based on a single year's data. Global warming is based on long term changes in average temperature. It therefore does not mean that the temperature will increase every year. The extreme weather last winter was caused by cold air from the Arctic which is normally kept there by strong winds around the pole. Last winter those winds were not as strong.

Which one of the following, if true, would most strengthen the above argument?

A. Some of the people claiming that the theories of global warming are incorrect do not come from areas that had very cold weather last winter
B. Although the weather was very cold last winter, the winter before was of average temperature
C. The claims that theories of global warming are incorrect are supported by further evidence
D. All the people claiming that theories of global warming are incorrect come from areas that had very cold weather last winter
E. Other regions of the Northern Hemisphere were hotter last winter than in previous years

34) According to the Food Standards Agency, film goers should be told how many calories there are in the popcorn, ice cream and fizzy drinks that they buy in cinemas and smaller portions of popcorn and drinks should also be available. As two thirds of adults and a third of children are already obese or overweight, with serious risk of heart disease, diabetes and cancer, the need for proper labelling to warn people about the calorie content of these items is urgent.

Which one of the following, if true, most strengthens the argument in the passage above?

A. Many people think that the food and drink consumed at the cinema is as important to the visit as the film
B. Cinemas rely on sales of food and drink to boost their profits
C. A large box of salted popcorn contains as many calories as a three course meal
D. Trials show that consumers alter their eating habits when food is calorie-labelled
E. People who are overweight are sometimes more concerned with their looks than the long term health risks

35) Rating figures for music are now much more difficult to calculate compared to a decade ago. The introduction of new formats for selling music means that figures have to be calculated based on more methods such as downloads, in addition to the sales of CDs in shops. Additionally, the availability of more formats means that there is more potential for copies of works to be shared with other fans, who do not pay for them. These fans do not show up in the ratings, so the official ratings do not reflect the relative popularity of a work.

Which one of the following, if true, would most strengthen the above argument?

A. The calculation of ratings based on downloads and sales together is not difficult
B. Sharing copies of purchased works with others is against the law
C. The sharing of works with other fans is more widespread for certain types of music
D. Artists are not interested in the popularity of their work, just the sales figures
E. Official ratings have never reflected popularity very well

36) Hundreds of miles of motorways are lit by unnecessary street lights. There is a need to save energy usage in all public services and it is time that the government considered turning off street lighting. Modern cars have powerful headlights which provide a clear view of the road ahead even without overhead lighting. There is also evidence to suggest that when drivers move from an area with lighting to an area without they are more likely to have an accident than those drivers who have driven exclusively on roads without lighting.

Which one of the following, if true, would most strengthen the above argument?

A. There is evidence that there are fewer daytime accidents on those motorways without lighting
B. Street lighting costs less than other types of road maintenance
C. Many drivers find driving on unlit roads difficult
D. Research suggests that older drivers find driving without lighting more difficult
E. Driving in well-lit areas at night can lead to a lack of concentration

37) A restaurant owner who has put grey squirrel on the menu has called it the 'ultimate ethical food'. The grey squirrel, a small, tree-dwelling rodent introduced to Britain over a century ago, is breeding so rapidly that the native red squirrel is disappearing. Encouraging the consumption of the grey species as food may help protect the red one, in her view. The owner added that squirrel meat was free range, low fat and low on air miles. However, we can challenge this, as it is all just a cheap publicity stunt to increase business in the restaurant. Squirrels should not be on the menu!

Which one of the following is the best statement of the flaw in the above argument?

A. It attacks the owner's motive rather than her reasons
B. It assumes that red squirrels don't need protecting
C. It assumes that eating grey squirrels will protect the red squirrel
D. It assumes the disappearance of the red squirrel justifies eating the grey squirrel
E. It attacks the whole notion of an ethical food

38) One of the fastest-growing beauty treatments in Britain, fish pedicures – where tiny toothless fish called garra rufa smooth feet by eating dead skin – has come under scrutiny from animal rights campaigners. One campaigner said, 'Fish are covered by the Animal Welfare Act. They need a stable environment and clean water, uncontaminated by perfume or lotions.' A spa in London's West End was closed recently by the local council when many of the fish in its pedicure pool died. There should be a complete ban on this type of pedicure, or else there will soon be no garra rufa.

Which one of the following is the best statement of the flaw in the above argument?

A. Fish in the wild are likely to die if their environment changes
B. It would be less harmful if people washed their feet before using the spa
C. The death of the fish in the London spa may not be a typical occurrence
D. The public does not immediately associate fish with the Animal Welfare Act
E. Beauty spas which offer fish pedicures are not especially numerous at present

39) The National Farmer's Union (NFU) approves of controlled killing of badgers to reduce their numbers, saying that it is needed to help farming. Badgers are animals believed to be responsible for the spread of bovine tuberculosis which results in large numbers of cows having to be destroyed every year. Animal rights supporters have criticised the proposal, but it is clear that the lives of more cattle can be saved by destroying a smaller number of badgers. This controlled killing should be allowed to go ahead.

Which one of the following is the best statement of the flaw in the above argument?

A. It assumes that the animal rights supporters believe that badgers have a greater right to life than cows
B. It assumes that the arguments from the animal rights supporters are about the number of deaths
C. It assumes that the animal rights supporters believe that animals that are living freely have a greater right to life than those that are being bred on farms
D. It attacks the animal rights supporters rather than their argument
E. It assumes that animal rights supporters always disagree with the NFU

40) Many people argue that the many government programmes intended to increase road safety have caused a steady decline in the number of accidents on our roads. However, some observers report that the real number of accidents may be much higher than is shown in the official records as many accidents are not reported by drivers. They also say that during the time when accident figures have decreased, the number of people going to hospitals because of road accidents has stayed constant.

Which one of the following can be drawn as a conclusion from the above passage?

A. Positive views about continually improving road safety may not be supported by what actually happens
B. Government programmes have been unsuccessful in reducing the number of accidents
C. Hospital admissions are a good way of measuring changes in the number of accidents on our roads
D. Road safety has improved greatly in recent years
E. Drivers should be required to report all accidents that occur on the road

Biology

41) The following organelles are involved in processing amino acids into glycoprotein:
1 Golgi apparatus
2 Ribsomes
3 RER
Which sequence is correct for this process?

A. 3 → 1 → 2
B. 1 → 3 → 2
C. 2 → 1 → 3
D. 2 → 3 → 1
E. 1 → 2 → 3

42) Which of the following is/are true about hydrogen bonds between water molecules?
1 They are weak bonds.
2 They are strong bonds.
3 They are temporary bonds.
4 They require hydrolysis to break.

A. 2 and 3 only
B. 1 only
C. 1 and 3 only
D. 1 and 4 only
E. 2 and 4 only

43) Which of the following transport mechanisms require the use of protein molecules found in membranes and ATP?
1 Active transport
2 Diffusion
3 Facilitated diffusion

A. 1 only
B. 2 and 3 only
C. 3 only
D. 1 and 2 only
E. 1 and 3 only

44) The diagram below represents the fluid mosaic model of the cell (surface) membrane.

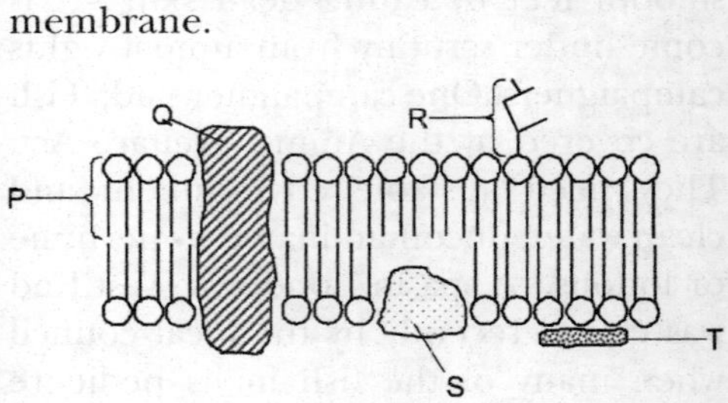

Only two of the labelled molecules have both hydrophobic and hydrophilic areas. Which two molecules are they?

A. P and T
B. P and Q
C. R and S

D. S and T
E. Q and R

45) If a glucose molecule became incorporated as a non-terminal component of starch, which two regions, labelled i to v, would be involved in forming glycosidic bonds?

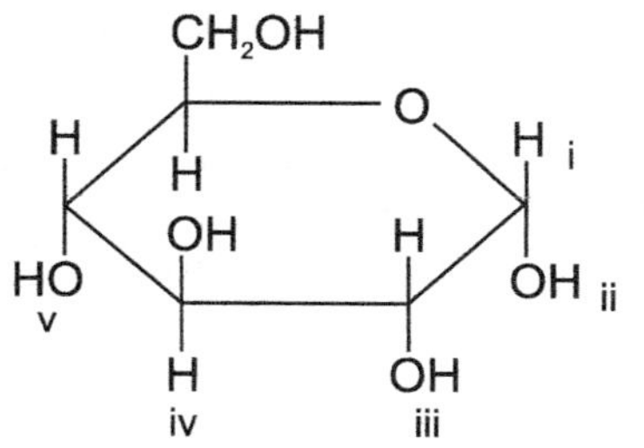

A. i and iv
B. ii and iv
C. i and iii
D. iii and v
E. ii and v

46) Which one of the following molecules will contain the greatest number of different elements?

A. Lipids
B. Water
C. Amino acids
D. Polysaccharide carbohydrates
E. Monosaccharide carbohydrates

47) Which one of the following is NOT correct about human chromosomes?

A. They are sometimes not found in pairs
B. They are made of DNA and protein
C. They are sometimes found in pairs
D. They contain regions called genes
E. They can attach to the spindle at the centriole

48) Which one of the following labels, i to v, represents a nucleotide?

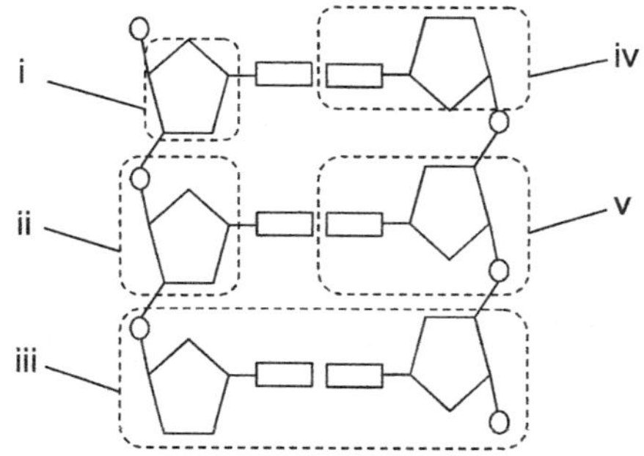

A. v
B. ii
C. iii
D. i
E. iv

49) Which one of the following would be different in a pair of non-identical twins?

A. Alleles
B. The total of adenine plus guanine
C. Amount of nuclear DNA
D. Genes
E. Chromosome number

50) In a set of genetic crosses the offspring produced showed the same phenotype ratio of 9:3:3:1.
Which of the following statements could be true?

1 Two genes each with two alleles were studied
2 All parents were heterozygous
3 Some offspring had a phenotype different to the parents
4 Some offspring had a phenotype the same as the parents

A. 3 and 4 only
B. 1, 2, 3 and 4
C. 1 and 2 only
D. 1 only
E. 2 and 3 only

51) Which of the following crosses is most likely to produce offspring of genotype GgNn?

A. ggNn × GGNN
B. GGNn × GgNn
C. GgNn × GgNn
D. ggNN × GGNn
E. GGNN × ggnn

52) Gene expression can be regulated by:

A. rough endoplasmic reticulum
B. RNA polymerase
C. transcription factors
D. the position of the genes on the alleles
E. DNA replication factors

53) Which row of the table correctly identifies a blood vessel that has a low concentration of carbon dioxide and a vessel that has a low concentration of urea?

	Low carbon dioxide	Low urea
Row 1	renal vein	Pulmonary artery
Row 2	Pulmonary vein	Renal vein
Row 3	Renal artery	Pulmonary vein
Row 4	Pulmonary vein	Renal artery
Row 5	Pulmonary artery	Renal vein

A. Row 1
B. Row 2
C. Row 3
D. Row 4
E. Row 5

54) Which of the examples of homeostasis do NOT require the brain to be involved in the control process?

1 Temperature regulation
2 Osmoregulation (regulation of the water content of blood)
3 Blood glucose concentration regulation

A. 1 only
B. 3 only
C. 2 only
D. 1 and 2 only
E. 2 and 3 only

55) Which one of the following is NOT true of human hormones?

A. They travel at the speed of blood flow
B. They are all chemicals
C. Some, such as testosterone and oestrogen, can be steroids
D. They are all released from glands and flow down ducts into the bloodstream
E. A hormone may affect one or more structures in the body

56) In a reflex arc that comprises a pain receptor cell in the skin, three neurones and a muscle (effector), the number of synapses found in the central nervous system (CNS) is:

A. 3
B. 1
C. 2
D. 4
E. 5

57) Antibiotics are becoming less effective due to:

A. people not finishing the full course
B. people becoming immune to them
C. people becoming resistant to them
D. artificial selection
E. new antibiotics being available

58) Which of the following are increased when the level of adrenaline rises in a human?

1 Heart rate
2 Breathing rate
3 Impulse rate in a sensory neurone

A. 1 and 3 only
B. 1 only
C. 2 and 3 only
D. 1 and 2 only
E. 1, 2 and 3

Chemistry

59) Which one of the following could NOT be the formula of an aldehyde?

A. $C_5H_{12}O$
B. $C_6H_{12}O$
C. $C_6H_{12}O_2$
D. $C_5H_{10}O$
E. $C_5H_{10}O_2$

60) The positions of some elements in the Periodic Table are shown below.

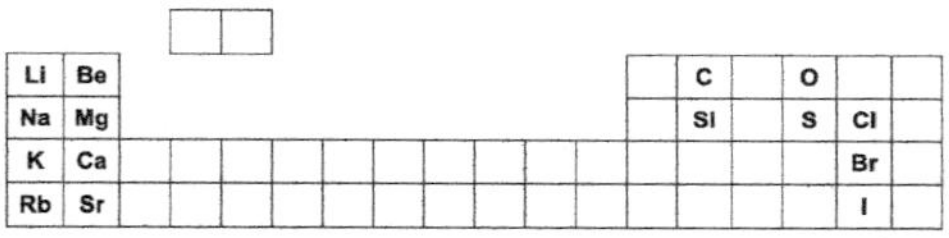

Which one of the following pairs of elements is most likely to form a covalent bond?

A. Beryllium and iodine
B. Potassium and chlorine
C. Magnesium and bromine
D. Strontium and oxygen
E. Calcium and chlorine

61) Which one of the following is NOT the correct formula for a lithium compound?

A. Li_2S
B. $LiHSO_4$
C. CH_3CO_2Li
D. Li_3N
E. $LiCO_3$

62) The Avogadro constant is 6.0×10^{23} mol^{-1}. How many hydrogen atoms are there in 0.420 g of cyclohexane? [Ar: H = 1; C = 12]

A. 1.8×10^{22}
B. 3.0×10^{21}
C. 1.8×10^{23}
D. 3.0×10^{22}
E. 3.6×10^{22}

63) Which one of the following is correct about the first and second electron affinities of oxygen?

A. first = slightly endothermic; second = very exothermic
B. first = slightly exothermic; second = very exothermic
C. first = slightly exothermic; second = very endothermic
D. first = slightly endothermic; second = very endothermic
E. first = very exothermic; second = very exothermic

64) In the following reactions, which substances are acting as oxidising agents?
$C(s) + O_2(g) \rightarrow CO_2(g)$
$2Fe^{3+}(aq) + 2I^-(aq) \rightarrow Fe^{2+}(aq) + I_2(aq)$
$Mg(s) + 2H^+(aq) \rightarrow Mg^{2+}(aq) + H_2(g)$

A. $O_2(g)$, $I^-(aq)$, $H^+(aq)$
B. $C(s)$, $Fe^{3+}(aq)$, $H^+(aq)$
C. $O_2(g)$, $I^-(aq)$, $Mg(s)$
D. $O_2(g)$, $Fe^{3+}(aq)$, $H^+(aq)$
E. $C(s)$, $Fe^{3+}(aq)$, $Mg(s)$

65) Which of the following statements are correct about the solvent properties of water?
1 All ionic substances dissolve in water.
2 All covalent substances are insoluble in water.
3 The solubility of solids usually increases with a rise in temperature.

A. 2 and 3 only
B. 1 only
C. 2 only
D. 3 only
E. none

66) What is the total number of electrons in the ions of sodium chloride?

A. sodium ion = 10; chloride ion = 17
B. sodium ion = 8; chloride ion = 8
C. sodium ion = 10; chloride ion = 18
D. sodium ion = 11; chloride ion = 17
E. sodium ion = 11; chloride ion = 18

67) Which rows of the table correctly describe the reactions of the aqueous acids with amines and amides?

	Amines	Amides
Row 1 **Ethanoic acid**	reacts	does not reacts
Row 2 **Nitrous acid**	reacts	reacts
Row 3 **Sulphuric acid**	does not reacts	Hydrolyses

A. Rows 1 and 2
B. None of the rows
C. Rows 1 and 3
D. Rows 2 and 3
E. All of the rows

68) Consider the following reactions.
$C_2H_5Br + OH^- \rightarrow C_2H_5OH + Br^-$
$Ba^{2+}(aq) + SO_4^{2-}(aq) \rightarrow BaSO_4(s)$
$Mg(s) + Cu^{2+}(aq) \rightarrow Mg^{2+}(aq) + Cu(s)$
Which one of the following types of reaction is NOT included in this list?

A. Oxidation/reduction
B. Substitution
C. Displacement
D. Precipitation
E. Elimination

69) Which one of the following is NOT correct about Fe, Cu and Zn, which are in the first row of the transition metals?

A. They all have densities greater than those of Group 1 metals
B. Only two of them form coloured ions
C. They all form basic oxides
D. They are all reactive metals
E . All of them form M^{2+} ions

Physics and Mathematics

70) In a group of students, exactly 2/5 are male and exactly 1/3 study mathematics. The probability that a male student chosen at random from the group studies mathematics is *p*.
Which of the following is the range of possible values of *p*?

A. $\frac{1}{3} \leq p \leq 1$

B. $0 \leq p \leq \frac{1}{3}$

C. $\frac{1}{3} \leq p \leq \frac{2}{5}$

D. $0 \leq p \leq \frac{5}{6}$

E. $\frac{2}{5} \leq p \leq \frac{5}{6}$

71) ABCDE is a regular pentagon. The transformation R is a rotation about the origin and maps A to B, B to C, C to D, etc. The transformation S is a reflection in the *y*-axis.

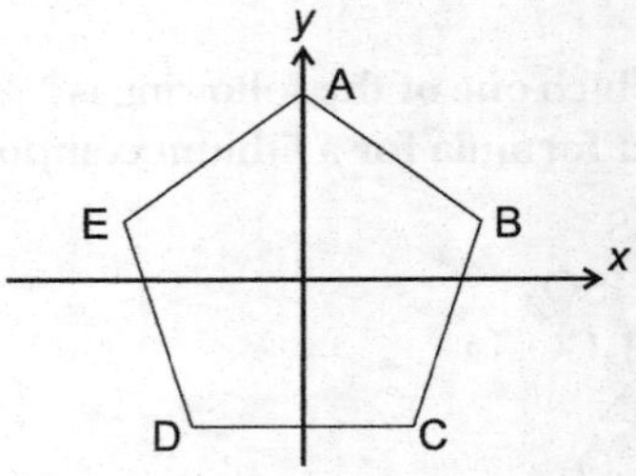

Which of the following sequences of transformations (performed in the order that they are listed) would NOT leave vertex D in the same position?

A. S R R S R S

B. R S R S
C. S R
D. R S R R
E. R R S R S R

72) The line L has equation $y = 2x - 1$. Four of the following five points are the same distance from the line L. Which one is at a different distance?

A. (1, 3)
B. (1, –1)
C. (5, 13)
D. (4, 9)
E. (6, 9)

73) Which of the following is equivalent to $\ln(x^2y) - 2\ln(xy) + 3\ln y$?

A. $2 \ln y$
B. $\ln x + 2 \ln y$
C. 0
D. $\ln x + \ln y$
E. $2 \ln x + 2 \ln y$

74) What is the set of values of x for which $x^2 < 9$ and $2x + 3 \geq 5$?

A. $x \geq -1$
B. $x > 3$
C. $x > -3$
D. $x < -3$ or $x \geq 1$
E. $1 \leq x < 3$

75) A block of iron at 100°C is transferred to a plastic cup containing water at 20°C. Which one of the following is NOT necessary in order to find the specific heat capacity of iron?

A. The final temperature
B. The mass of water
C. The thermal conductivity of the iron
D. The mass of the block of iron
E. The specific heat capacity of water

76) Three identical capacitors are connected as follows:

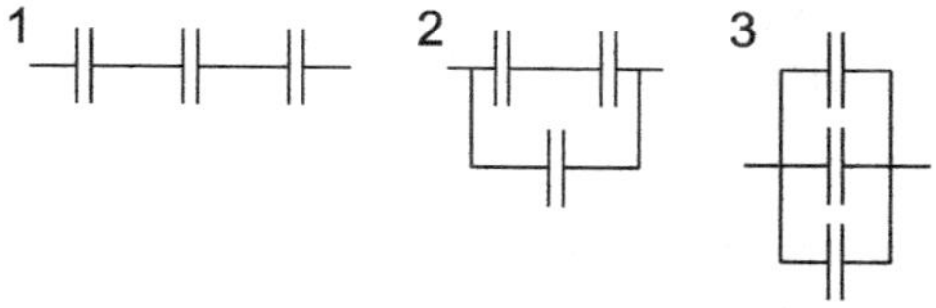

Which of the following shows the order of increasing capacitance (smallest first)?

A. 1, 3, 2
B. 1, 2, 3
C. 2, 1, 3
D. 2, 3, 1
E. 3, 2, 1

77) Which one of the following is NOT a vector?

A. Weight
B. Velocity
C. Electric charge
D. Acceleration
E. Electric field

78) A man of mass 75 kg lies on a bed of 10 000 nails. The tip of each nail has an area of 1.0 square millimetre. What pressure does the man experience? [g = 10 N/kg]

A. 7.5×10^4 Pa
B. 7.5×10^3 Pa
C. 7.5×10^7 Pa
D. 7.5×10^6 Pa
E. 7.5×10^5 Pa

79) When cooled below 4.2 K, mercury becomes a superconductor, which means it has no electrical resistance. When a current is passed through mercury under these conditions, which of the following effects will be present?

1 Thermal
2 Chemical
3 Magnetic

A. 2 only
B. 1 only
C. 3 only
D. 1 and 3 only
E. 1, 2 and 3

80) At the melting point, which of the following are correct about paraffin wax?
1 The substance becomes more disordered
2 The wax takes in heat but its temperature stays the same
3 Bonds between the carbon and hydrogen atoms are broken

A. 2 and 3 only
B. 2 only
C. 1 and 3 only
D. 1 and 2 only
E. 1, 2 and 3

RISPOSTE COMMENTATE • IMAT a.a. 2012/2013

Cultura generale e ragionamento logico

1) B. Sia C l'evento "l'uomo ha il cancro" e $\bar{C}$ l'evento contrario, cioè "l'uomo è sano". Dalla definizione classica di probabilità:

$$P = \frac{n \text{ casi favorevoli}}{n \text{ casi possibili}},$$

la probabilità $P(C)$ che un uomo sopra i 50 anni abbia il cancro alla prostata è 1/14.
Siano, inoltre, H l'evento "alti livelli di PSA" e $\bar{H}$ l'evento contrario, ossia "i livelli di PSA non sono alti".
La probabilità che un uomo non abbia alti livelli di PSA condizionata al fatto che l'uomo abbia il cancro è, dal testo:

$$P(\bar{H} / C) = 7\% = 0.07 = \frac{7}{100}.$$

Sempre dal testo, la probabilità che un uomo non abbia il cancro condizionata al fatto che i livelli di PSA siano alti è:

$$P(\bar{C} / H) = 75\% = 0.75,$$

cosicché l'evento contrario ha probabilità:

$$P(C / H) = 1 - 0.75 = 0.25 = \frac{1}{4}.$$

La probabilità $P(H/C)$ che un uomo abbia alti livelli di PSA condizionata al fatto che abbia il cancro è data dalla formula della probabilità contraria:

$$P(H / C) = 1 - P(\bar{H} / C) = 1 - \frac{7}{100} = \frac{93}{100}.$$

Dalla formula di Bayes:

$$P(C / H) = \frac{P(C) \cdot P(H / C)}{P(H)}$$

si ottiene la probabilità $P(H)$ che un uomo abbia alti livelli di PSA:

$$P(H) = \frac{P(C) \cdot P(H / C)}{P(C / H)} = \frac{\frac{1}{14} \cdot \frac{93}{100}}{\frac{1}{4}} = \frac{93}{350}.$$

La probabilità dell'evento contrario che un uomo non abbia alti livelli di PSA è:

$$P(\bar{H}) = 1 - P(H) = 1 - \frac{93}{350} = \frac{257}{350}.$$

Infine, riapplicando la formula di Bayes, otteniamo la probabilità che un uomo con livelli normali di PSA abbia il cancro:

$$P(C/\bar{H}) = \frac{P(C)\cdot P(\bar{H}/C)}{P(\bar{H})} = \frac{\frac{1}{14}\cdot\frac{7}{100}}{\frac{257}{350}} = \frac{1}{200}\cdot\frac{350}{257} = \frac{7}{1028} \approx 0.007 = 0.7\%$$

---

2) A. Indichiamo con x il numero di biglie rimaste alla fine nel sacchetto e prese da Sue. Nell'ultimo turno i tre amici si trovano col seguente numero di biglie:

Adam: 10
David: 10
Sue: x

Se Adam e David danno a Sue due biglie ciascuno, i tre amici avranno il seguente numero di biglie:

Adam: $10 - 2 = 8$
David: $10 - 2 = 8$
Sue: $x + 2 + 2 = x + 4$

Imponendo che ognuno abbia lo stesso numero di biglie, otteniamo infine:

$$8 = x + 4$$
$$x = 8 - 4 = 4.$$

---

3) D. La superficie laterale di un parallelepipedo di dimensioni $4 \cdot 9 \cdot 3$ è:

$$S_l = 2(4 + 9) \cdot 3 = 78 \text{ m}^2.$$

La superficie totale da dipingere si ottiene sottraendo dalla superficie laterale totale le superfici da non dipingere:

$$S = S_l - S_{porta,\ elettronica} - S_{finestra} - S_{porta,\ posteriore} =$$
$$= 78 - 3 \cdot 4 - 2 \cdot 1 - 1 \cdot 2 = 78 - 16 = 62 \text{ m}^2.$$

Con ogni latta di vernice si possono dipingere 3 metri quadrati. Poiché:

$$\frac{S}{3} = \frac{62}{3} \approx 20{,}7,$$

allora serviranno 21 latte di vernice per dipingere tutti i muri.

---

4) B. Indicando con S la somma di denaro iniziale, i tre bambini ricevono le seguenti quantità:

bambino 1: $\frac{5}{10}S = \frac{1}{2}S$

bambino 2: $\frac{3}{10}S$

bambino 3: $\frac{2}{10}S = \frac{1}{5}S$

Il bambino 3 riceve altri 6 euro, cosicché alla fine possiede:

$$\frac{1}{5}S+6.$$

Se i bambini 2 e 3 hanno alla fine la stessa quantità di denaro, allora:

$$\frac{3}{10}S=\frac{1}{5}S+6$$
$$\frac{3}{10}S-\frac{1}{5}S=6$$
$$\frac{1}{10}S=6,$$

da cui la somma iniziale di denaro risulta: S = 60
e, di conseguenza, considerando anche i 6 euro aggiuntivi, la somma totale di denaro ricevuta dai tre bambini è:

$$S_{tot} = S + 6 = 60 + 6 = 66 \text{ euro.}$$

---

5) E. Siano J e D il numero di CD posseduti tre mesi fa, rispettivamente, da Jane e Duncan. Si ha $J = 5D$.
Se ogni ragazzo compra altri 12 DVD e alla fine Jane ha il doppio dei DVD di Duncan, allora:

$$J + 12 = 2\ (D + 12)$$
$$J + 12 = 2\ D + 24.$$

Risolvendo il sistema:

$$\begin{cases} J=5D \\ J+12=2D+24 \end{cases}$$

otteniamo:

$$J+12=2\frac{J}{5}+24$$
$$5J+60=2J+120$$
$$3J=60$$
$$J=\frac{60}{3}=20.$$

Quindi, adesso il numero di DVD posseduti da Jane è:

$$J + 12 = 20 + 12 = 32.$$

---

6) E. Le tre affermazioni possono essere riscritte come:

1) Dile < Cubba
2) Bongo < Esun
3) Esun > Cubba

Per la proprietà transitiva della relazione d'ordine stretto:

$$\text{Dile} < \text{Cubba} < \text{Esun}$$
$$\text{Dile} < \text{Esun}$$

Poiché è anche Bongo < Esun, allora Esun è il fiume più lungo.

7) A. Poiché ad un numero alto di voti corrisponde un valore alto in termini di gradi, allora dovrebbe essere:

- Peter: 126 voti – 113.4 gradi → 113.4/126 = 0.9
- Harold: 100 voti – 90 gradi → 90/100 = 0.9
- Alison: 84 voti – 75.6 gradi → 75.6/84 = 0.9
- Kevin: 72 voti – 56.7 gradi → 56.7/72 = 0.7875
- Rachel: 63 voti – 24.3 gradi → 24.3/63 ≈ 0.381

Quindi la lettura sbagliata è o quella di Kevin o di Rachel.
Poiché $63 \cdot 0.9 = 56.7$ gradi, che è proprio uno degli angoli calcolati, mentre $72 \cdot 0.9 = 64.8$, che non è tra gli angoli calcolati, allora la lettura errata è quella relativa a Kevin.

8) B. È falso affermare che nessuno dei Dervies è anche Bongles, dal momento che esistono Crannies che sono anche Bongles e tutti i Crannies sono Darvies. Il seguente diagramma di Eulero-Venn può aiutare a visualizzare il ragionamento appena fatto:

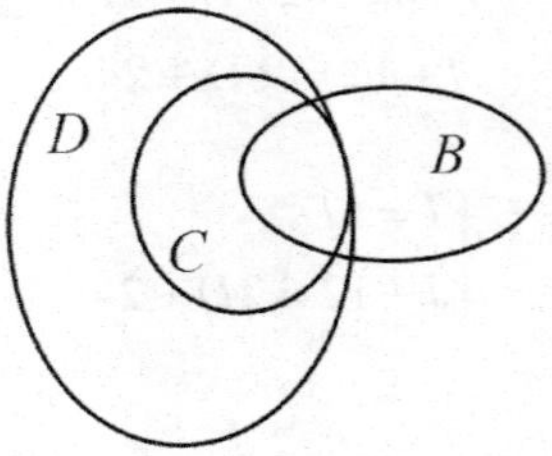

9) D. Lo zucchero si trova nella lista sopra il purè di patate, per cui la sua percentuale è almeno del 4.5%. Poiché la percentuale totale di tutti gli ingredienti è del 100%, la percentuale W dell'acqua non può superare il valore dato da:

$$W_{max} = 100\% - 51\% - 4.5\% - 4.5\% = 40\%.$$

10) D. Il dato della posizione del tunnel è superfluo. Indicando con x la lunghezza del tunnel che il treno percorre a 20 km/h, il tratto rimanente che viene percorso a 60 km/h è lungo $16 - x$. Il tempo totale impiegato è di 19 minuti, pari in ore a $\frac{19}{60}h$.

Inoltre, il tempo impiegato su ogni singola tratta è dato dal rapporto tra la distanza percorsa e la velocità del treno.
Infine, il tempo del tragitto è dato dalla somma del tempo impiegato per percorrere il tunnel e del tempo impiegato per la rimanente tratta.

Si può scrivere quindi:

$$t_{tot} = t_{tunnel} + t_{16-x}$$

$$\frac{19}{60} = \frac{x}{20} + \frac{16-x}{60}$$

$$19 = 3x + 16 - x$$

$$2x = 3$$

$$x = \frac{3}{2} = 1.5 \text{ km.}$$

11) E. La conversione mese per mese porta alla somma:

$$300\ (2.74 + 2.79 + 2.76 + 2.83 + 2.81) = 300 \cdot 13.93 = \$\ 4179.$$

Effettuando il cambio interamente a maggio, invece, si ha:

$$1500 \cdot 2.81 = \$\ 4215,$$

per cui la differenza risulta:

$$\$\ 4215 - \$\ 4179 = \$\ 36.$$

12) A. Per semplicità supponiamo che la capacità del contenitore sia di 100 l. Questo significa che inizialmente contiene 28 ml di acqua. Dopo la prima pioggia la quantità di acqua aumenta del 25% di 28 ml, ossia di $0.25 \cdot 28 = 7$ ml. Se anche a seguito della seconda pioggia l'acqua aumenta di 7 ml, allora la quantità di acqua totale alla fine sarà 28 + 7 + 7 = 42 ml, che rappresenta il 42% della capacità totale.

13) E. Alla fine del 4° venerdì, dei 120 euro iniziali ne sono stati prestati 45 + 25 + 18 + 20 = 108 euro, ma i primi 45 euro sono stati restituiti perché sono già passate 3 settimane dal primo prestito, per cui il denaro totale è: 120 – 108 + 45 = 57 euro.

14) C. Se in 100 g ci sono 510 kcal, allora in 200 g ci sono $2 \cdot 510 = 1020$ kcal. Poiché ogni biscotto contiene 79 kcal, allora il numero totale di biscotti è:

$$\frac{1020}{79} \approx 13.$$

15) E. Il costo totale per ciascuna lampada è dato dalla somma del costo della lampada e del costo dell'energia. Quest'ultima si calcola moltiplicando il costo dell'energia per la potenza e per il tempo, con un fattore 1/1000 che tiene conto del fatto che il costo è espresso in euro per kW.
Dopo un tempo t il costo totale, nel caso della lampada a basso consumo, uguaglia il costo totale relativo all'utilizzo dell'altra lampada, per cui:

$$0.6 + (0.15/1000) \cdot 100t = 3 + (0.15/1000) \cdot 20t$$

$$0.012t = 2.4$$

$$t = 200 \text{ h}$$

16) E. Uscendo dal lavoro alle 17:00, Alice può prendere il bus alle 17:04, arrivando a casa alle 17:33. Ha bisogno di 45 minuti per prepararsi, quindi non può uscire prima delle 18:18. Il primo bus utile passa da casa sua alle 18:33 ed arriva al cinema alle 18:58. Dopo 10 minuti, necessari per acquistare il biglietto, saranno le 19:08, per cui Alice potrà vedere il film delle 19:15.

17) C. Su 100 intervistati, 20 non hanno né un cane né un gatto, per cui 80 hanno almeno uno tra il cane e il gatto.
Aiutiamoci adesso con un diagramma di Eulero-Venn:

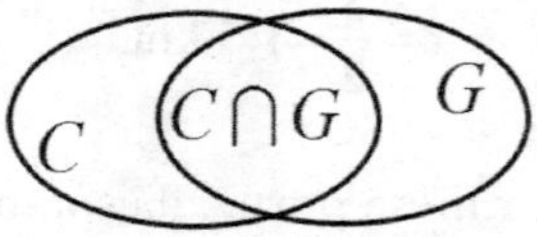

Il numero di persone che hanno sia il cane sia il gatto (intersezione tra *C* e *G*) è dato dal numero di persone che hanno il cane (insieme *C*) più il numero di persone che hanno il gatto (insieme *G*) meno il numero di persone che hanno almeno uno dei due (unione tra *C* e *G*):

$$N_{C \cap G} = N_C + N_G - N_{C \cup G} = 40 + 60 - 80 = 20.$$

Infine, il numero di persone che hanno il gatto ma non il cane è dato dalla differenza tra il numero di persone che hanno il gatto e il numero di persone che hanno entrambi gli animali:

$$N_G - N_{C \cap G} = 60 - 20 = 40.$$

18) A. Poiché andando in una qualunque direzione i numeri su un lato aumentano di un'unità e i numeri sul lato opposto diminuiscono di un'unità, allora la somma dei numeri di due case di fronte è costante. Ad esempio, se n è il numero di case, il numero della prima casa da un lato è 1 mentre sul lato opposto è n, per cui la somma è $n + 1$. Il numero di case si ottiene quindi sommando i numeri di due case di fronte e togliendo un'unità. Nel nostro caso, $n = 8 + 11 - 1 = 18$.

19) A. Se indichiamo con x il volume iniziale, dopo l'aumento del 9%, il volume sarà $1.09x$. Quindi: $1.9x = 40$, da cui: $x = 40/1.9 \approx 36.7$ cm^3.

20) B. La sostanza P, decadendo, diminuisce, per cui l'unico grafico che rappresenta una curva decrescente è il n. 3. La sostanza R viene creata dal decadimento di Q e non decade, per cui va rappresentata con il grafico 1, che è l'unica curva crescente. Il grafico 2 rappresenta, infine, la sostanza Q, che da un lato viene creata dal decadimento della sostanza P, dall'altro lato decade essa stessa in R; per tempi molto grandi il contributo negativo del decadimento supera quello positivo della creazione e, quindi, la curva inizia a decrescere.

21) D. L'elevata velocità con cui la tecnologia moderna ci consente di usufruire delle risorse naturali rinnovabili fa sì che spesso si corra il rischio di consumarle più velocemente rispetto al *rate* di produzione della natura. Per questo, le risorse rinnovabili dovrebbero essere utilizzate con cautela.

22) E. Usare il sapone gel invece del sapone tradizionale comporta un maggiore consumo di risorse e crea più problemi in termini di smaltimento dei rifiuti. Quindi, la gente dovrebbe essere resa consapevole delle conseguenze di tale scelta.

23) E. Il motivo per cui la gente non ama andare all'Opera non è di carattere economico, ma di carattere culturale. Infatti, la gente spende cifre considerevoli per andare a vedere le partite di calcio o per andare in giro nei locali. Quindi, la proposta di creare "posti economici" non risolverebbe la questione dell'aumento del pubblico.

24) A. Spesso, ad alcuni pazienti viene rilevata una pressione più alta di quella che hanno nella vita quotidiana, probabilmente a causa dell'ansia che essi provano quando si trovano in uno studio medico. Si rende necessario, quindi, un metodo più efficace per misurare la pressione, così da avere delle misurazioni più oggettive.

25) B. Dieci anni fa i posti per le biciclette erano occupati per metà, mentre quelli per le macchine erano sempre impegnati. Oggi, invece, ci sono meno posti per le macchine e un maggior numero di posti per le biciclette, che tra l'altro sono sempre occupati. Si può concludere, quindi, che le persone che oggi vanno al lavoro con la bicicletta sono molte di più di dieci anni fa.

26) C. Gli attori bambini che, crescendo non hanno più successo, incolpano di ciò i propri genitori e diventano dipendenti da alcool e droga. Questo succede più raramente agli attori bambini che vanno a scuola e che contemplano sin da piccoli altre opportunità lavorative. Si può quindi concludere che i bambini che recitano dovrebbero coltivare altri interessi per avere maggiori possibilità lavorative.

27) A. La nicotina di per sé non causa dei danni apprezzabili. Tuttavia, quando viene assunta insieme al tabacco, le altre sostanze presenti sono cancerogene. Si può concludere che le *chewing gum* alla nicotina sono un'alternativa relativamente sicura per i fumatori di tabacco.

28) D. Parlare almeno due lingue ha sempre avuto una grande valenza pratica. Come oggi l'inglese, lo spagnolo e l'arabo sono ai primi posti (con l'inglese in testa), così già 500 anni fa il latino, pur non essendo parlato dal popolo, era la lingua più usata in ambito commerciale, religioso, politico e scolastico. Allo stesso modo, nel XVII secolo si rivelarono di grande utilità pratica l'italiano e il francese.

29) C. Se i rilevatori di fumo, di cui molte case sono sprovviste, prevenissero gli incendi, allora la loro installazione ridurrebbe le morti causate dagli incidenti dolosi che avvengono nelle abitazioni.

30) E. A causa delle scelte di produzione, i programmi televisivi rappresentano la scuola in modo diverso da com'è nella realtà, non evidenziando abbastanza il tempo speso nello studio e l'impegno necessario per raggiungere determinati risultati. Spesso, anche i personaggi, gli atteggiamenti e i comportamenti rappresentati risultano inappropriati. Pertanto, a fronte dell'esigenza di rappresentare la vita scolastica in modo più aderente alla realtà, i produttori dovrebbero correggere le loro scelte.

31) B. Lo studio delle materie classiche ed artistiche fornisce alla società un contributo minore rispetto alla scienza e alla tecnologia, per cui in un'ottica di risparmio queste ultime andrebbero salvaguardate maggiormente.

32) D. La riduzione della nebbia del 30% rispetto a 50 anni fa sta provocando la morte di molti alberi; se il riscaldamento globale è responsabile della riduzione della nebbia, allora lo è anche per la conseguente morte degli alberi.

33) E. Se effettivamente l'inverno più gelido del solito in Nord Europa è stato causato da uno spostamento imprevisto di aria fredda, allora nelle regioni da cui proveniva quell'aria si deve essere registrata contestualmente una temperatura più alta di quella media per quel periodo dell'anno.

34) D. Se la presenza sui cibi di etichette con i valori nutrizionali modifica le abitudini alimentari della gente, allora etichettare opportunamente il cibo venduto nei cinema renderebbe le persone consapevoli di ciò che mangiano, dando così una mano al problema dell'obesità.

35) C. Se per certi tipi di musica sono più diffuse le copie delle canzoni – che i fan condividono tra loro scaricandole gratuitamente – rispetto ai CD regolarmente venduti, allora le classifiche ufficiali che si basano solo su queste canzoni non ne rappresentano la reale popolarità.

36) E. Quando i guidatori transitano da un'area ben illuminata ad una buia hanno maggiori probabilità di avere un incidente rispetto ai guidatori in strade totalmente buie. Se la presenza di illuminazione stradale può disturbare la concentrazione, allora togliere l'illuminazione da alcuni tratti stradali, oltre ad essere una misura di salvaguardia dell'ambiente, ridurrebbe anche il numero di incidenti stradali.

37) A. Nell'articolo la proprietaria del ristorante viene accusata di aver scelto quel menu per ragioni di natura commerciale e non, come da lei sostenuto, per motivi legati alla salvaguardia dell'ambiente. Tuttavia, la scelta da lei effettuata comporta davvero dei benefici per la fauna del luogo, per cui la motivazione utilizzata come pretesto per attaccarla non è sufficiente per dissuadere la proprietaria dal proporre quel menu.

38) C. Non è detto che la morte dei pesci nel centro benessere di Londra sia un evento tipico, per cui non è detto che la pratica in questione possa portare all'estinzione della specie.

39) B. Uccidere i tassi per salvare una maggiore quantità di bestiame non sembra essere un'argomentazione abbastanza valida, dato che si basa solamente sul numero di animali e non tiene conto di altri fattori, quali ad esempio l'impatto ambientale o le conseguenze per l'uomo.

40) A. Poiché molte persone oggi non denunciano gli incidenti stradali e, considerato che il numero di pazienti che hanno avuto un incidente e che vengono ricoverati negli ospedali è rimasto costante nel tempo, allora non si può affermare con certezza che il numero di incidenti sia effettivamente diminuito come riportato nel report ufficiale.

Biologia

41) D. La sintesi delle proteine avviene nel citoplasma. A livello dei ribosomi gli amminoacidi, ciascuno legato al proprio tRNA (RNA di trasferimento), vengono legati l'uno all'altro attraverso i legami peptidici, secondo la successione dei codoni (triplette di basi azotate) del mRNA (RNA messaggero). Le proteine elaborate vengono riversate nei canali del reticolo endoplasmatico rugoso (RER) dal quale successivamente gemmano delle vescicole che si fondono con le membrane dell'apparato di Golgi. All'interno delle cisterne di questa struttura le proteine vengono assemblate con molecole di carboidrati formando le glicoproteine. Queste vengono così stoccate e poi trasferite ad un sito cellulare specifico della cellula (della membrana plasmatica o di un particolare organulo). Pertanto la sequenza corretta è 2 → 3 → 1.

42) C. I legami idrogeno si formano quando l'atomo di idrogeno è legato ad un atomo molto elettronegativo (ossigeno, azoto). Si tratta di legami di tipo elettrostatico, presenti tra le molecole dell'acqua e in molte molecole, come le proteine e gli acidi nucleici, dove contribuiscono a mantenere la stabilità strutturale. Essi si formano tra le parziali cariche positive degli atomi di idrogeno e le parziali cariche negative degli atomi di ossigeno o azoto. Si tratta di legami deboli che si rompono facilmente e che sono temporanei poiché tendono a riformarsi a seconda delle condizioni ambientali e funzionali.

43) A. Il trasporto di sostanze attraverso le membrane cellulari avviene attraverso meccanismi di trasporto passivo e attivo. Il trasporto passivo non richiede energia sottoforma di ATP e comprende: la diffusione semplice, dovuta al gradiente di concentrazione della sostanza considerata; e la diffusione facilitata attraverso proteine di membrana che lasciano passare le sostanze secondo il gradiente di concentrazione. Altre proteine di membrana lasciano passare le molecole contro un gradiente di concentrazione, cioè da una zona a minore concentrazione ad una a maggiore concentrazione delle molecole in esame. Questo tipo di trasporto è attivo poiché, oltre a specifiche proteine di membrana, richiede ATP.

44) B. La membrana cellulare è costituita da un doppio strato di fosfolipidi (P), da proteine che attraversano lo spessore della membrana (Q, proteine integrali), da colesterolo (S). Sul lato citoplasmatico si trovano altre proteine (T, proteine periferiche). Sul versante esterno sono presenti anche molecole glucidiche ramificate (R). Le molecole lipidiche e le proteine si muovono lateralmente all'interno del doppio strato dando origine a configurazioni diverse (mosaico fluido). I fosfolipidi presentano una estremità polare (gruppo fosfato) che forma legami di tipo idrofilico con l'ambiente acquoso e due catene laterali idrofobiche o apolari. Anche le proteine integrali presentano gruppi apolari, sulla superficie a contatto con la componente idrofobica del doppio strato fosfolipidico, e gruppi polari rivolti verso l'ambiente acquoso interno ed esterno rispetto alla membrana. Pertanto solo i fosfolipidi (P) e le proteine integrali (Q) presentano estremità sia di tipo idrofilico che idrofobico.

45) E. Il glucosio è il monosaccaride più diffuso in natura sia come zucchero semplice che sotto forma di polimeri (amido, glicogeno, cellulosa). È un aldoesoso poiché presenta una funzione aldeidica –CHO e una catena di sei atomi di carbonio ($C_6H_{12}O_6$). Nella sua forma ciclica, per condensazione ed eliminazione di una molecola di acqua, dà origine ai suoi polimeri, come l'amido. Il legame tra una molecola di glucosio e la successiva (legame glicosidico) si forma grazie alla reazione tra un gruppo –OH, legato al carbonio C1 (nel grafico posizione ii) di una molecola di glucosio, con il gruppo –OH legato al C4 (posizione v). Nell'amido così le molecole di glucosio sono legate fra loro da ponti di ossigeno C_1-O-C_4 (legame glicosidico di tipo etereo) che coinvolgono le regioni contrassegnate con ii e v.

46) C. Gli amminoacidi sono i monomeri delle proteine (polipeptidi). Sono composti quaternari poiché contengono carbonio, idrogeno, ossigeno e azoto. Gli organismi viventi utilizzano 20 amminoacidi diversi che hanno in comune un gruppo carbossilico (–COOH) e un gruppo amminico (–NH_2) legati allo stesso atomo di carbonio (carbonio α). Differiscono l'uno dall'altro nei gruppi laterali che possono essere lineari o ciclici, costituiti da un numero variabile di atomi di carbonio. Negli amminoacidi cisteina e metionina è presente zolfo (amminoacidi solforati). Gli amminoacidi pertanto sono le molecole che contengono il più elevato numero di elementi diversi.

47) E. I cromosomi umani sono le unità strutturali in cui il DNA è associato con proteine specifiche (istoni). Essi sono localizzati nel nucleo e costituiscono la sede dell'informazione genetica. Sono corpi che si colorano intensamente (*chroma* "colore", *soma* "corpo"), di forma bastoncellare, visibili nel nucleo della cellula durante la mitosi. L'informazione ereditaria è localizzata a livello di regioni specifiche (sequenze di DNA) dei cromosomi stessi chiamate geni. Nella mitosi ogni cromosoma è presente in due copie (coppia di cromosomi omologhi), uno di origine paterna e uno di origine materna. Il numero dei cromosomi può essere alterato. In alcune anomalie cromosomiche il cromosoma 21 è rappresentato da tre cromosomi X (XXX, trisomia 21) o dalla assenza di un cromosoma in una coppia di omologhi (monosomia). Essi sono legati alle fibre del fuso mitotico tramite il centromero (regione costituita da proteine e DNA che appare come una costrizione del cromosoma) ma non direttamente ai centrioli (come invece si evince dalla risposta esatta – secondo cui essi possono legarsi attraverso i fusi ai centrioli – che è pertanto l'unica non corretta).

48) A. Un nucleotide è l'unità strutturale degli acidi nucleici (DNA e RNA). Ogni nucleotide è costituito da una base azotata, da uno zucchero a 5 atomi di carbonio e da un gruppo fosforico. Nella doppia catena polinucleotidica del DNA le basi azotate sono la timina, la citosina, l'adenina e la guanina mentre lo zucchero è il desossiribosio. Nell'RNA, al posto della timina, si trova l'uracile e lo zucchero ribosio. Nel DNA le basi azotate sono rivolte verso l'interno della sua struttura mentre il gruppo fosforico è rivolto verso l'esterno e lega i nucleotidi l'uno all'altro. In ogni nucleotide sia la base azotata che il gruppo fosforico sono legate allo zucchero. Nello schema riportato pertanto un nucleotide completo è indicato da v.

49) A. Una coppia di gemelli non identici (eterozigoti o dicoriali) deriva da due cellule uovo fecondate da due gameti maschili diversi. Sia le cellule uovo (gameti femminili) che i gameti maschili hanno una diversa informazione genetica dovuta alla diversa ricombinazione del materiale genetico (*crossing over*) durante il processo di divisone cellulare da cui derivano (meiosi). Il numero dei cromosomi, il numero e il tipo di geni, la quantità e la qualità di DNA nucleare (genoma) e quindi di basi azotate è identico mentre diversi sono gli alleli cioè le varianti di uno stesso gene. Si tratta di fratelli, che possono essere anche di sesso diverso, che derivano da una stessa gravidanza.

50) B. Il rapporto 9:3:3:1 è giustificato dalla legge dell'assortimento indipendente (2^a legge di Mendel). Quando vengono incrociati due individui che differiscono per due caratteri fenotipici, controllati ciascuno da due alleli dominanti (AABB) in un individuo e da due alleli recessivi (aabb) nell'altro, nella prima generazione (F1) il genotipo di tutti gli individui risulta eterozigote o diibrido (AaBb) . Essi presentano il fenotipo controllato dagli alleli dominanti. Se gli individui della prima generazione F1 vengono incrociati fra loro (AaBb × AaBb) nella seconda generazione F2 la maggior parte dei discendenti (9:16) presenta il fenotipo dominante dei genitori, alcuni, a causa delle nuove combinazioni degli alleli, presentano un fenotipo diverso (3:16; 3:16), mentre pochi esprimono il fenotipo controllato dagli alleli recessivi (1:16) della generazione parentale (aabb). Tutte le opzioni 1, 2, 3, 4 pertanto sono vere.

51) E. Quando si incrociano individui che presentano il genotipo dominante GGNN con individui che presentano il genotipo recessivo ggnn (GGNN × ggnn), i discendenti sono caratterizzati dal genotipo GgNn (eterozigote o diibrido). Il risultato è coerente con la seconda legge di Mendel (assortimento indipendente) secondo la quale quando si formano i gameti gli alleli di un gene "segregano" in modo indipendente dagli alleli dell'altro gene.

52) C. L'espressione genica è il processo attraverso il quale l'informazione contenuta in un gene, costituito da DNA, viene convertita in una proteina. Nelle cellule degli eucarioti viene regolata dai fattori di trascrizione cioè da proteine che si legano direttamente al DNA in una regione specifica detta promotore. Il promotore è il sito di legame per l'RNA polimerasi, il luogo in cui inizia la trascrizione di un gene che sarà poi tradotto in una specifica proteina. I fattori di trascrizione possono essere attivati o disattivati selettivamente da altre proteine.

53) B. I vasi sanguigni caratterizzati da una bassa concentrazione di diossido di carbonio, CO_2, e di urea, $CO(NH_2)_2$, sono rispettivamente la vena polmonare e la vena renale. Infatti quando il sangue ricco di anidride carbonica, proveniente dalla periferia, raggiunge la parte destra del cuore passa nei polmoni dove viene ossigenato. Il sangue ricco di ossigeno ritorna all'atrio sinistro del cuore attraverso le vene polmonari e ritorna in circolo attraverso l'aorta. L'urea, prodotta dal metabolismo delle sostanze azotate, come gli amminoacidi, viene eliminata attraverso il processo di filtrazione renale che porta alla formazione dell'urina. Il sangue filtrato ritorna in circolo attraverso la vena renale, è ricco di diossido di carbonio, prodotto dalle cellule del rene, ma privo di urea.

54) B. Il controllo omeostatico della concentrazione del glucosio nel sangue non dipende dal cervello ma da due ormoni, prodotti dal pancreas, che hanno un'azione antagonista: l'insulina e il glucagone. L'insulina promuove il deposito del glucosio alimentare nel fegato e nei muscoli sotto forma di glicogeno mentre il glucagone promuove la liberazione di glucosio (idrolisi del glicogeno) durante il digiuno, quando la concentrazione di glucosio nel sangue diminuisce. La regolazione della temperatura corporea e l'osmoregolazione (regolazione del contenuto acquoso del sangue), sono invece sotto il controllo dei centri nervosi ipotalamici.

55) D. Gli ormoni sono molecole organiche, secrete generalmente in quantità minime, dalle ghiandole endocrine (pancreas endocrino, tiroide, gonadi, ipofisi). Vengono riversati direttamente nel sangue, non attraverso dotti (da cui si deduce la risposta esatta), e con la corrente sanguigna raggiungono le cellule bersaglio di tutti gli organi e tessuti localizzati anche lontano dalla regione in cui vengono prodotti. Possono essere di natura proteica (insulina pancreatica) o di natura steroidea (estrogeni e progesterone). Le ghiandole ad attività esocrina, invece, secernono i loro prodotti direttamente nelle cavità che comunicano con l'esterno attraverso dotti escretori (ghiandole salivari → saliva → dotti salivari → cavità boccale).

56) C. L'arco riflesso è la risposta del SNC ad uno stimolo esterno e coinvolge tre tipi di neuroni: sensitivi, di correlazione o interneuroni, motori. Il riflesso nocicettivo (o flessorio) è una risposta motoria riflessa a stimoli dolorosi (nocicettivi) applicati alla cute, ad esempio degli arti, e consiste nel brusco allontanamento dell'arto. È un riflesso polisinaptico. In questo caso le sinapsi coinvolte sono due. Il recettore della cute, attraverso il neurone sensitivo (afferente), trasferisce lo stimolo al SNC (midollo spinale) dove contrae una sinapsi con un interneurone. Questo, con una seconda sinapsi, trasferisce la risposta alla periferia, attraverso un motoneurone (efferente), all'effettore cioè al muscolo che si flette come risposta allo stimolo doloroso.

57) A. Gli antibiotici sono medicinali che combattono le infezioni batteriche che colpiscono l'uomo e gli animali. Questi farmaci uccidono o impediscono la proliferazione dei batteri in modo da curare le infezioni ma stanno diventando meno efficaci poiché spesso vengono usati in modo non corretto. Non completando il periodo di trattamento, cioè riducendo la dose, la quantità di farmaco presente nell'organismo sarà insufficiente per combattere efficacemente i batteri che sopravvivono e possono così sviluppare resistenza. Gli antibiotici vanno sempre usati secondo le modalità e i tempi indicati dal medico.

58) D. L'adrenalina è un ormone prodotto dalle ghiandole surrenali e un neurotrasmettitore liberato a livello delle terminazioni nervose del sistema neurovegetativo che controlla i visceri. La sua concentrazione nel sangue aumenta in condizioni particolari di emergenza, stress o paura. Legandosi a recettori specifici delle cellule mette l'organismo nelle condizioni fisiologiche per sfruttare le sue risorse in modo ottimale (reazione "combatti o fuggi"). La frequenza cardiaca e la frequenza degli atti respiratori aumentano poiché aumenta il consumo di molecole ricche di energia come il glucosio.

Chimica

59) A. Un'aldeide possiede il gruppo funzionale

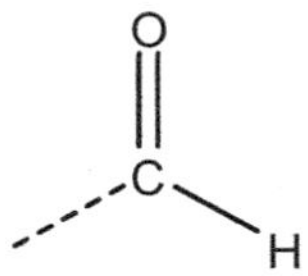

Pertanto, in un'aldeide generica è presente almeno un doppio legame, ovvero un'insaturazione. Ricordiamo che un'insaturazione rappresenta il numero delle coppie di protoni che devono essere rimosse dalla formula di un alcano per ottenere la formula corrispondente; il numero di insaturazioni (n.i.) rappresenta il numero di cicli e/o doppi legami eventualmente presenti nella molecola. Per un generico composto $C_CH_HN_NO_OX_X$ (dove X è un alogeno), il numero di insaturazioni si può calcolare secondo la formula:

$$n.\ i. = \frac{2C + 2 - (H - N + X)}{2}$$

Per un'aldeide il numero di insaturazioni deve essere almeno pari a 1 perché è presente un doppio legame. Calcoliamo il n.i. per le molecole in esame:

Formula bruta	Numero di insaturazioni
$C_5H_{12}O$	0
$C_6H_{12}O$	1
$C_6H_{12}O_2$	1
$C_5H_{10}O$	1
$C_5H_{10}O_2$	1

Tutte, tranne $C_5H_{12}O$, potrebbero rappresentare un'aldeide.

60) A. In genere tra elementi che hanno una differenza di elettronegatività elevata (> 1,9) si formano legami ionici (come nel cloruro di sodio NaCl), mentre se la differenza di elettronegatività è bassa si formano legami covalenti. In particolare, se la differenza di elettronegatività è nulla, si hanno legami covalenti puri o omopolari, come accade nell'idrogeno e nell'ossigeno gassosi (H_2 e O_2), che si ritrovano normalmente sotto forma di molecole biatomiche. Il metodo non è rigoroso, ma dà un'idea del tipo di legame. Calcoliamo quindi la differenza di elettronegatività (ΔEn) per tutte le combinazioni in questione:

Elementi	ΔEn
Be/I	1.0
K/Cl	2.2
Mg/Br	1.6
Sr/O	2.5
Ca/Cl	2.0

La minore differenza di elettronegatività si riscontra tra Be (berillio) e I (iodio). Tra questi la formazione di un legame di tipo covalente è più probabile.

61) E. Mentre nelle formule $LiHSO_4$, CH_3CO_2Li, Li_3N, Li_2S il litio assume numero di ossidazione +1, nella formula $LiCO_3$ esso dovrebbe avere numero di ossidazione +2. Dato che il litio appartiene al primo gruppo della tavola periodica, può assumere solo n.o. +1. Pertanto, la formula corretta del carbonato di litio è Li_2CO_3.

62) E. Una mole di qualsiasi elemento o composto contiene rispettivamente un numero di Avogadro ($N_A = 6{,}02 \cdot 10^{23}$) di atomi o di molecole. Per risolvere l'esercizio bisogna conoscere innanzitutto le moli di idrogeno, H. Queste possono essere ricavate dalle moli di cicloesano (C_6H_{12}) che a loro volta si possono calcolare conoscendo i grammi di C_6H_{12} forniti dal problema e la sua massa molecolare (data dalla somma delle masse atomiche di 6 atomi di C e 12 atomi di H: 84 g/mol). Quindi, le moli di C_6H_{12} sono date da:

$$n(C_6H_{12}) = \frac{0{,}420\,g}{84\,\frac{g}{mol}} = 0{,}005\ mol$$

In ogni mole di cicloesano sono presenti 12 moli di H, quindi: n(H) = 12 · 0,005 mol = 0,06 mol. Il numero di atomi di H si ricavano risolvendo la proporzione:

$$1 \text{ mole H}: 6{,}02 \cdot 10^{23} \text{ atomi} = 0{,}06 \text{ moli H} : x$$

da cui:

$$x = 3{,}6 \cdot 10^{22} \text{ atomi}$$

63) C. L'affinità elettronica è l'energia liberata da un atomo A quando addiziona un elettrone secondo il processo:

$$A + e^- \rightarrow A^-$$

Se l'anione che si forma è più stabile dell'atomo neutro, allora il processo avviene liberando una certa quantità di energia, viceversa se è meno stabile. In generale, i valori di affinità elettronica dei metalli sono molto minori rispetto a quelli dei non metalli. Essa aumenta da sinistra verso destra in un periodo e dal basso verso l'alto in un gruppo. Nel caso dell'ossigeno, infatti, l'affinità elettronica relativa al processo:

$$O + e^- \rightarrow O^-$$

è abbastanza elevata (141 kJ/mol) e il processo è esotermico. Lo ione O^- che si forma è più stabile dell'atomo neutro perché l'ultimo livello energetico è quasi pieno.

La seconda affinità elettronica dell'ossigeno invece riguarda il processo:

$$O^- + e^- \rightarrow O^{2-}$$

Questo processo non è favorito (per avvenire ha bisogno di molta energia ed è quindi endotermico) perché porta alla formazione di uno ione in cui due cariche negative sono concentrate su un atomo di piccole dimensioni, che quindi è molto instabile.

64) D. In una reazione redox, la specie ossidante è quella che si riduce, ossia acquista elettroni dalla specie che si ossida (che quindi cede elettroni). Nella prima reazione il carbonio si ossida (passa dallo stato di ossidazione 0 a +4), quindi la specie ossidante è l'ossigeno che passa da 0 a −2 (si riduce). Nella seconda reazione la specie ossidante è il ferro che riduce il suo stato di ossidazione da +3 a +2. Nell'ultima reazione, invece, a fungere da ossidante è H^+ che si riduce allo stato di ossidazione zero in H_2.

65) D. I processi di dissoluzione sono spesso endotermici e quindi favoriti da un aumento della temperatura. Non è corretto invece affermare che tutte le sostanze covalenti sono insolubili in acqua, perché dipende dalla loro polarità. Ad esempio, gli zuccheri sono sostanze organiche covalenti molto polari e generalmente solubili in acqua. Allo stesso modo non è corretto dire che i composti ionici sono tutti solubili in acqua, perché ne esistono alcuni, quali quelli contenenti lo ione Ag^+, che mostrano scarsa solubilità in acqua.

66) C. Il cloruro di sodio è costituito da ioni Na^+ e Cl^- uniti insieme attraverso un legame ionico. Lo ione Na^+ contiene un elettrone in meno rispetto all'atomo neutro, quindi 10 elettroni. Lo ione cloruro invece contiene un elettrone in più rispetto all'atomo neutro e quindi 18 elettroni.

67) A. La prima riga è corretta, infatti mentre le ammidi non reagiscono con gli acidi carbossilici, le ammine reagiscono con questi, portando alla formazione di ammidi:

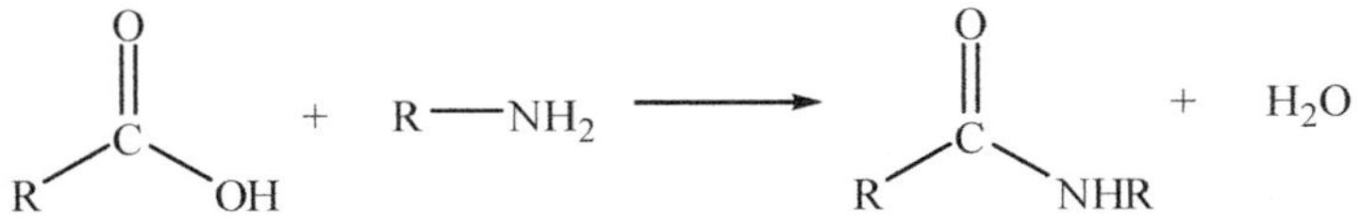

Anche la seconda riga è corretta, infatti sia le ammine che le ammidi reagiscono con acido nitroso. In particolare la reazione con le ammidi e le ammine primarie comporta lo sviluppo di azoto. Le ammidi reagiscono con acido nitroso, portando alla formazione dell'acido carbossilico azoto e acqua.

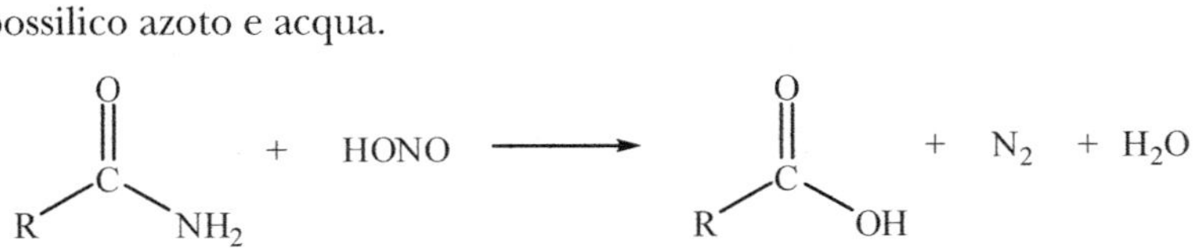

Le ammine primarie invece portano alla formazione di una miscela di alcheni e alcoli.

$$R{-}NH_2 + HONO \longrightarrow \text{miscela di alcoli e alcheni} + H_2O + N_2$$

68) E. La prima è una reazione di scambio semplice in cui OH va a sostituire Br. In particolare, si tratta di una delle reazioni più comuni che avvengono a carico degli alogenuri alchilici, ovvero una sostituzione nucleofila. Nella seconda reazione, a partire da ioni solvatati, si ha la formazione del sale $BaSO_4$ solido, quindi si tratta di una precipitazione. L'ultima è una reazione di ossidoriduzione in cui Mg si ossida e Cu si riduce. Manca quindi una reazione di eliminazione.

69) D. L'affermazione "sono tutti metalli molto reattivi" è falsa perché il rame appartiene al gruppo 11 della tavola periodica, che è quello dei metalli nobili, di cui fanno parte anche l'oro e l'argento. Questi sono metalli poco reattivi, infatti è possibile ritrovarli in natura allo stato puro.

Fisica e matematica

70) D. Sia n il numero di studenti del gruppo.
Sia E_1 = Evento studente del gruppo è maschio
Sia E_2 = Evento studente del gruppo studia matematica
Sia $P(E_1)$ la probabilità che estraendo a caso uno studente dal gruppo, sia maschio. Si avrà:

$$P(E_1) = \frac{\frac{2}{5}n}{n} = \frac{2}{5}$$

Sia $P(E_2)$ la probabilità che estraendo a caso uno studente dal gruppo, esso studi matematica. Sarà:

$$P(E_2) = \frac{\frac{1}{3}n}{n} = \frac{1}{3}$$

Gli eventi E_1, E_2 sono compatibili nel senso che ci può essere una parte degli studenti maschi che studiano matematica. Quindi in generale:

$$E_1 \cap E_2 \neq \varnothing$$

Poiché risulta in generale che:

$$P(E_1 \cup E_2) = P(E_1) + P(E_2) - P(E_1 \cap E_2)$$

Nel nostro caso ponendo per semplicità:

$$p = P(E_1 \cup E_2)$$

Sarà:

$$P(E_1) + P(E_2) - \max(P(E_1 \cap E_2)) \leq p \leq P(E_1) + P(E_2) - \min(P(E_1 \cap E_2))$$

Poiché:

$$\min(P(E_1 \cap E_2)) = 0$$

E questo si ha quando nessuno degli studenti maschi studia matematica. Mentre:

$$\max(P(E_1 \cap E_2)) = \frac{1}{3}$$

Questo si ha quando tutti gli studenti che studiano matematica sono maschi. Quindi:

$$\frac{2}{5}+\frac{1}{3}-\frac{1}{3}\leq p\leq\frac{2}{5}+\frac{1}{3}-0$$

$$\frac{2}{5}\leq p\leq\frac{11}{15}$$

La risposta corretta è che:

$$0<\frac{2}{5}\leq p\leq\frac{11}{15}<\frac{5}{6}$$

71) E. Si cerca la composizione di trasformazioni che non lascia D nella stessa posizione. Tutte le composizioni di trasformazioni portano D nella stessa posizione eccetto la sequenza RRSRSR, infatti: R (rotazione di $\frac{2\pi}{5}$ in senso orario) porta D in E e quindi $D \equiv E$; successivamente R con una successiva rotazione porta D in A e quindi $D \equiv A$; a questo punto una riflessione S rispetto all'asse y, porta D in D perché D si trova sull'asse y; successivamente con una ulteriore rotazione R si porta D in B per cui $D \equiv B$; in seguito S porta D in E, quindi $D \equiv E$; un'ulteriore rotazione porta D in A, e quindi $D \equiv A$.
Si può verificare facilmente, con lo stesso criterio, che tutte le altre sequenze di trasformazioni riportano D esattamente ella stessa posizione di partenza.
Quindi l'unica sequenza di trasformazioni che non porta D nella stessa posizione è la RRSRSR.

72) C. La distanza punto retta è per una retta con equazione in forma esplicita $y = mx + q$:

$$d_{(x_0,y_0)}=\frac{|y_0-mx_0-q|}{\sqrt{m^2+1}}$$

$$d_{(5,13)}=\frac{|13-10+1|}{\sqrt{4+1}}=\frac{4}{\sqrt{5}}$$

$$d_{(1,-1)}=\frac{|-1+2+1|}{\sqrt{4+1}}=\frac{2}{\sqrt{5}}$$

$$d_{(1,3)}=\frac{|3-2+1|}{\sqrt{4+1}}=\frac{2}{\sqrt{5}}$$

$$d_{(4,9)}=\frac{|9-8+1|}{\sqrt{4+1}}=\frac{2}{\sqrt{5}}$$

$$d_{(6,9)}=\frac{|9-12+1|}{\sqrt{4+1}}=\frac{2}{\sqrt{5}}$$

73) A. Si ha:

$$\ln(x^2y)-2\ln xy+3\ln y=\ln x^2+\ln y-2\ln x-2\ln y+3\ln y=$$
$$2\ln x+\ln y-2\ln x-2\ln y+3\ln y=2\ln y$$

74) E. Quanto chiesto equivale a risolvere il sistema:

$$\begin{cases} x^2 < 9 \\ 2x + 3 \geq 5 \end{cases}$$

La prima disequazione del sistema ha per soluzioni $-3 < x < 3$. La seconda disequazione ha soluzioni le $x \geq \frac{5-3}{2} = 1$. Le soluzioni del sistema sono date quindi nell'intervallo in cui entrambe le disequazioni sono contemporaneamente verificate, ovvero nell'intervallo $1 \leq x < 3$.

75) C. Indicando con T_f la temperatura finale di equilibrio e trascurando la capacità termica della tazza di plastica, si ha:

$$Q_{tot} = Q_{ass} + Q_{ced} = 0$$

$$m_{water}c_{water}(T_f - 20) + m_{iron}c_{iron}(T_f - 100) = 0$$

$$c_{iron} = \frac{m_{water}c_{water}(T_f - 20)}{m_{iron}(100 - T_f)},$$

da cui si evince che l'unica grandezza, tra quelle proposte, che non è necessaria per trovare il calore specifico del ferro, è la sua conduttività termica.

76) B. Nel primo caso la capacità totale della serie di condensatori è:

$$C_1 = \left(\frac{1}{C} + \frac{1}{C} + \frac{1}{C}\right)^{-1} = \left(\frac{3}{C}\right)^{-1} = \frac{C}{3},$$

che risulta la più piccola possibile della combinazione dei tre elementi condensatori. Nel secondo caso, invece, si deve considerare che la serie di due condensatori è in parallelo con il terzo condensatore:

$$C_2 = \left(\frac{1}{C} + \frac{1}{C}\right)^{-1} + C = \left(\frac{2}{C}\right)^{-1} + C = \frac{C}{2} + C = \frac{3}{2}C.$$

Infine, nel terzo caso i condensatori sono in parallelo, per cui:

$$C_3 = C + C + C = 3C.$$

77) C. La carica elettrica non è un vettore, bensì uno scalare. Invece la velocità, la forza peso, l'accelerazione ed il campo elettrico sono dei vettori, in quanto sono identificati da un'intensità e da una direzione orientata.

78) A. La superficie totale è $A = 10000 \cdot (1\ mm^2) = 10^4 \cdot (10^{-6}\ m^2) = 10^{-2}\ m^2$, per cui la pressione risulta:

$$p = \frac{F}{A} = \frac{mg}{A} = \frac{75 \cdot 10}{10^{-2}} = 7.5 \cdot 10^4\ Pa.$$

79) C. Non presentando alcuna resistenza elettrica, la corrente non produce alcun effetto Joule, per cui il mercurio non si riscalda. Inoltre, non possono avvenire reazioni chimiche. Quello che invece succede è che il mercurio espelle il campo magnetico presente al suo interno.

80) D. Al punto di fusione, la sostanza diventa più disordinata, aumentando i gradi di libertà delle molecole, e la temperatura della cera non varia con l'assorbimento di calore, perché quest'ultimo serve inizialmente per la transizione di fase solido-liquido. Invece, i legami tra gli atomi non possono venire distrutti, altrimenti la cera subirebbe una reazione chimica, mentre il processo di fusione è un processo fisico che lascia inalterata la natura della sostanza.

IMAT
a.a. 2013/2014

Thinking skills

1) Ever since Uranus was discovered, astronomers have thought there might be more planets in the Solar System. Because of small deviations in the orbits of Uranus and Neptune – deviations which would occur if another planet existed – some astronomers think there must be an undiscovered planet – Planet X. But these deviations cannot tell us whether Planet X exists, because they would occur if the orbits had been wrongly predicted. Since Uranus and Neptune take many decades to circle the sun, astronomers rely on old data to calculate their orbits. As this is likely to be inaccurate, the calculated orbits are probably wrong, and so Uranus and Neptune will deviate from them even if there is no Planet X.
Which one of the following best expresses the main conclusion of the above argument?

A. Astronomers are right to think that there must be an undiscovered planet
B. The deviations in the orbits of Uranus and Neptune cannot tell us whether Planet X exists
C. The calculations of the orbits of Uranus and Neptune are probably wrong
D. Uranus and Neptune will deviate from the predicted orbits whether or not Planet X exists
E. The use of old and inaccurate data indicates that Planet X cannot exist

2) Coffee granules are available in two jar sizes, regular and large. The regular jar contains 250 grams and costs € 4.50. The large jar is 60% bigger, containing 400 grams, but at € 6.30 costs only 40% more than the regular jar.
By how much per kilogram is the large jar of coffee better value for money than the regular jar?

A. € 3.60
B. € 0.90
C. € 2.25
D. € 3.15
E. € 6.00

3) According to a recent analysis of university entrance records, you are more likely to go to university if your name is John than if it is Wayne. Therefore, if you want your child to go to university, you are better off calling him John than Wayne.
Which one of the following is the best statement of the flaw in the argument above?

A. It confuses a correlation with a cause
B. It jumps to a conclusion without any evidence
C. It fails to consider other names than Wayne or John
D. It draws a general conclusion from specific evidence
E. It confuses a necessary condition with a sufficient one

4) Horrific images of the earthquake in Haiti were seen immediately all over the world, and by the next day the full extent of the damage was seen by the entire world. Clearly, the main problem was moving aid from the airport to distant areas, and with the roads largely blocked the only practical method was to use helicopters. The great nations of the world should be ashamed that food was not getting to the people who needed it, and that even a week later their relief still depended on the ability of courageous and skillful drivers to reach them in trucks.

Which one of the following is an underlying assumption of the argument above?

A. There was enough food in Haiti to supply all the people in the weeks after the earthquake
B. The images failed to prompt the great nations of the world into relief operations after the earthquake
C. The great nations of the world had helicopters at their disposal which could reach Haiti within a week
D. The relief agencies were able to import trucks to Haiti but not helicopters
E. The people of Haiti were able to clear their roads within a week of the earthquake

5) The pasta that I buy in the local supermarket usually costs € 1.60 per packet. This week the packet is marked '€ 0.20 off normal price'. In addition the following sign is on display '10% off all bills when you spend € 10 or more'.

Assuming that I spend over €10 altogether, how much will the packet of cereal cost?

A. € 1.18
B. € 1.12
C. € 1.24
D. € 1.30
E. € 1.26

6) There is an increasing number of historical or significant buildings in the UK which are said to be 'At Risk'. Without a change in the law most of these buildings are doomed to crumble into the ground. This is because these buildings are no longer structurally sound. The exisiting strict renovation laws mean that they are too expensive or impractical for private individuals or developers to renovate or repair. There are certainly people out there who would be willing to maintain these buildings if they could use more modern and less expensive techniques and materials. Surely it is better to sacrifice some of the original building's character rather than lose the entire structure.

Which one of the following best expresses the main conclusion of the above argument?

A. Historians can learn more from buildings which have not been modernised by modern developers
B. Existing laws make 'At Risk' buildings too expensive for most developers
C. 'At Risk' buildings need to be renovated according to strict rules
D. A change in the law is needed if we hope to preserve more 'At Risk' buildings
E. There is nothing wrong with changing the character of historic buildings

7) A nationwide survey showed that the majority of people would not be willing to give up their car in favour of public transport. However, in a recent survey of people living in an area with heavy traffic problems, 76% stated that they would prefer to travel to work by public transport if the system was made more reliable. This shows that the previous findings were wrong. We should, therefore, restrict car use and start a programme of improving the nation's public transport network as soon as possible.

Which one of the following is the best statement of the flaw in the argument above?

A. It does not consider the 24% who would not prefer to use public transport
B. It fails to specify which types of public transport are to be improved
C. The statistic presented may not be representative of the whole population
D. The counter arguments are not explained in detail
E. It fails to explain how the public transport system can be improved

8) The low level of literacy among science undergraduates is an issue across all universities. One of the biggest problems is that pupils in school spend more time perfecting their SMS text messaging and emailing skills than they do writing grammatically correct pieces of literature. It is important to get across to undergraduates that good writing matters. Employers take on scientists believing they can communicate their findings fluently and accurately. We need to deliver science graduates with these skills.

Which one of the following best expresses the main conclusion of the above argument?

A. Employment often depends on good ability in literacy
B. Students do not concentrate properly in lessons in school
C. Education is failing those who leave with poor writing skills
D. Many science graduates are unable to write in a grammatically correct way
E. Students must be helped to recognise the importance of good literacy skills

9) Stephen is currently involved in a long distance charity walk from Alphcaster to Omegham. He left Alphcaster 9 days ago and has just completed 60% of his journey.
He hopes to complete 60% of the rest of the walk during the next 4 days. This will leave him just 60 miles from Omegham, which he aims to complete in a further 2 days.

How far is it from Alphcaster to Omegham?

A. 250 miles
B. 225 miles
C. 375 miles
D. 300 miles
E. 450 miles

10) A significant social trend in the 20th century was for people to move away from their place of birth in order to access education and work. This gave individuals more opportunities and helped the economy by producing mobility within the workforce. The negative side of this is now being felt as more and more elderly people face the problems of old age without family members nearby to care for them. This has negative effects on the economy as well as on the individual, as more and more state funding for care is needed.

Which one of the following could be drawn as a conclusion of the above passage?

A. Elderly people are expecting the state to provide care for them rather than relying on their children
B. People should make caring for their elderly parents a priority over choice of work opportunities
C. People should try to find education and work close to their place of birth
D. The benefits of a mobile workforce have to be compared with the costs to elderly people and the economy

E. The state should provide care for elderly people to make mobility of the workforce possible

11) It has recently been suggested that some degrees can be completed in two years instead of the traditional three years. But staff teaching engineering and medicine at degree level say that the current first year mostly involves getting students up to a common level of maths and physics, which in the past was achieved by high school teaching. By the end of the second year few students have reached the level of attainment that students did 40 years ago. Two year degrees are not realistic – certainly not for engineering.
Which one of the following is an assumption of the argument in the passage above?

A. School examinations are easier now than they were 40 years ago
B. Engineering students are less motivated than they were 40 years ago
C. Maths and physics are more important elements of engineering than they were 40 years ago
D. Two year degree courses will have the same amount of teaching per year as three year courses
E. Two year degree courses will be more popular with students than three year courses

12) A multi-storey car park has eight levels. On the top seven levels there are eight rows of parking. Two of these rows hold 15 cars each whilst the others hold 10 cars each. On the road level there are two rows holding 15 cars but only four rows holding 10 cars each. The entry control system counts cars in and out. The system stops admitting cars once 90% of the total capacity is in use. Four spaces on the road level are reserved for staff parking and these are not available to the public.
What is the maximum number of public cars which can be admitted?

A. 644
B. 500
C. 630
D. 626
E. 696

13) The table below shows the consumer price inflation and unemployment rate for 5 countries:

Consumer price inflation % rate	March	February
United States	+0.4	+0.3
Japan	+0.2	+0.5
Germany	+0.1	+0.1
France	+0.3	0.0
UK	+0.2	+0.5

Unemployed % rate	March	February
United States	5.9	6.1
Japan	3.0	3.0
Germany	9.2	9.3
France	12.6	12.6
UK	9.1	9.2

A newspaper comparing March to February reported that: 'Unemployment has fallen but there has been a rise in the inflation rate'.
Which country is the statement referring to?

A. Japan
B. United States
C. Germany
D. France
E. UK

14) One in four deaths caused by road accidents involving commercial vehicles is caused by the driver falling asleep at the wheel. The problem even affects police men and women, who are now more likely to die due to driving when tired than by physical attacks. Evidence at the scene (such as tyre marks) can tell investigators how quickly the car driver braked: late breaking would indicate lack of concentration which might be caused by tiredness. The problem with this evidence is that it is not conclusive, whereas conclusive evidence can be offered for other offences such as drink driving.

Which one of the following can be drawn as a conclusion of the passage above?

A. It would be unfair to prosecute people for falling asleep at the wheel
B. The number of hours per day that commercial drivers should be allowed to drive should be reduced
C. It will not be as easy to prosecute drivers for falling asleep at the wheel as it is for drink driving
D. Accidents caused by drivers falling asleep at the wheel are a greater problem than drink driving
E. Commercial vehicle drivers and the police are more prone to falling asleep at the wheel because of the long hours they work

15) At a society meeting, 1000 people are entitled to vote in the elections for Chair-person with a oneperson-one-vote system. The election rules state if no candidate obtains more than 50% of the votes cast in the first ballot, a second ballot must be held between the top two candidates. 350 votes were cast for a particular candidate in the first ballot. Then a second ballot took place.

Under these circumstances which one of the following is possible?

A. The candidate came third
B. The candidate won the election, came second, or came third
C. The candidate definitely won the election
D. The candidate came second or third, but did not win
E. The candidate either won the election or came second

16) A safe has external dimensions as follows:
Width 48cm
Depth 44cm
Height 52cm
The entire safe is made of steel 4cm thick except the base which is 8cm thick.

What are the internal dimensions of the base of the safe?

A. 40cm × 40cm
B. 36cm × 36cm
C. 40cm × 36cm
D. 40cm × 32cm
E. 44cm × 40cm

17) My watch is a twenty four hour digital watch, so that, for instance 4.17am appears as:

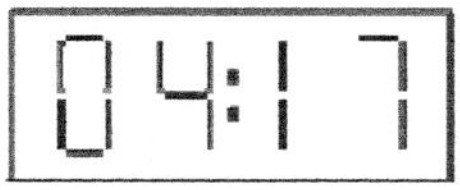

and 4.17pm appears as:

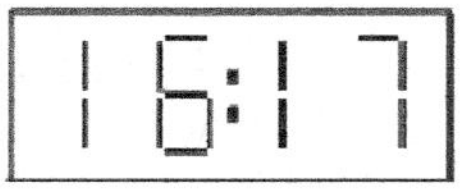

One morning recently I woke up, picked up my watch and saw:

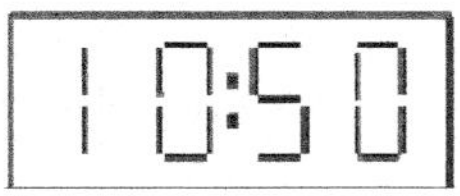

I panicked, thinking that I had overslept, until I realised I had picked up the watch upside down and it was only one minute past five.

At which one of the following times would the display appear the same whichever way I picked it up?

A. 5.51 pm
B. 1.01 am
C. 5.51 am
D. 3.51 pm
E. 3.21 pm

18) A study on identical twins concluded that genes contribute roughly half of the attributes we need to be happy. People often find such studies scary, seeing something sinister about us being mere puppets of our biology. However, put in non-scientific terms, it sounds like common sense. Parents talk about how their children had different personality traits from a very young age. Perhaps it's nicer to think this is caused by something 'fluffy' like a soul – but even if that were true, why is that more reassuring than the thought that genes are responsible? Either way, you're born as you are.

Which one of the following statements is best supported as the conclusion of the passage above?

A. Whether or not you are happy in life is either determined by your soul or your genes
B. We may as well accept the idea that our potential for happiness in life is to some extent decided at birth
C. Whether or not you are happy in life is not something over which you yourself have any control
D. Roughly half of what we need to be happy is decided by our genetic make up
E. The person you are at birth is the person you will be throughout your life

19) The table below shows the winning time for the men's 200m run in the Olympic Games since 1900, when the event was first held, until 1988.

year	seconds	year	seconds
1900	22.2	1924	21.6
1904	21.6	1928	21.8
1908	22.6	1932	21.2
1912	27.1	1936	20.7
1916	*	1940	*
1920	22.0	1944	*

year	seconds	year	seconds
1948	21.1	1972	20.00
1952	20.81	1976	20.23
1956	20.75	1980	20.19
1960	20.62	1984	19.80
1964	20.36	1988	19.75
1968	19.83	–	–

* Olympics not held in these years.

What is the longest number of years for which the Olympic record stood unbroken?

A. 24
B. 28
C. 20
D. 16
E. 6

20) Any company that wishes to sell a new drug must provide the government with details of research about its safety and possible side effects. At present, this information is confidential, but there are plans to make it available to the public. While patients are surely entitled to more information about the drugs they are prescribed, this will also inevitably make public vital details about the ingredients of certain drugs and how they are manufactured. Drug companies are naturally reluctant to release this information to their competitors. Therefore, through fear of imitators, drug companies will no longer introduce new and important drugs into the country.

Which one of the following, if true, would most weaken the above argument?

A. People may be reluctant to use certain drugs when they have fuller information about them
B. The drug industry is a very competitive business and secrecy is vital if companies are to survive
C. People are better informed about the side effects of drugs abroad than they are in this country
D. There are sufficient drugs already on the market and so there is no necessity to introduce new ones
E. Strong patent laws prevent companies from using the information to create rival drugs

21) After looking at interviews conducted with a number of adult learners, our research suggested that the learners who felt they were most successful were all highly motivated. We noticed that early success had heightened motivation in some cases and saw that both success and motivation may be due to a special aptitude for learning. We also noticed that many of those who felt they were most motivated were also learning in favourable conditions or for fun, which meant they may have become motivated since starting their classes. Though these conditions seemed persuasive, the results led us to the same conclusion. It's impossible to learn anything without motivation.
Which one of the following is NOT a flaw in the above argument?

A. It assumes that in order to be motivated you have to have a special aptitude for learning
B. The research is only concerned with adult learners
C. It assumes that those who felt they were successful actually were
D. The research does not establish that there are no successful learners who lacked motivation
E. It assumes that those who felt they were motivated actually were

22) Many people believe that foreign travel broadens the mind and that there is some inherent benefit in spending some time in a culture different from your own. Many students are taking 'gap' years where they spend time in another country. Whilst this may offer some benefits in terms of confidence and independence, it is wrong to assume that foreign travel alone can provide this. Global travel can have negative impacts on local cultures and the environment. Home country based 'gap' projects are often seen as unglamourous but the benefit of working with different groups and cultures within our own society can be equally rewarding.
Which one of the following is the main conclusion of the above passage?

A. Foreign travel is not the only way to gain confidence and independence
B. There is inherent benefit in spending some time abroad
C. It is important that gap year students consider the impact of their travel on the communities they work in
D. Projects within our own society can be as rewarding as foreign travel
E. Foreign gap year projects must have an element of community work for them to be worthwhile

23) My packet of washing powder claims to contain enough powder for 24 washes. This claim is based on using the plastic scoop supplied with the packet and filling it once for each wash. Living in a soft water area I find I only need to fill the scoop three-quarters full.

How many washes can I get from this packet?

A. 32
B. 30
C. 42
D. 18
E. 26

24) Two companies have just started a round-the-clock air taxi service between Rome and Milan. They use the same flight path and fly at constant speeds at different altitudes. Planes owned by the company Alpha-Air take off from Rome every 10 minutes and take 90 minutes to reach Milan.
Planes owned by the company Beta-Air take off every 5 minutes and take 60 minutes to reach Milan. Captain Johnston, who flies for Beta-Air, takes off from Rome 5 minutes after the previous Alpha-Air flight has departed.
How many Alpha-Air planes (flying from Rome to Milan) will Captain Johnston have passed as he lands in Milan?

A. 0
B. 3
C. 1
D. 2
E. 4

25) A novelty shop sells a rather unusual clock designed to puzzle users. There is only one hand, which points upwards. It has two faces.
The larger hour face rotates clockwise and the smaller minute face rotates anti-clockwise. Each face has one big dot, representing 12 o' clock or 0/60 minutes and 11 smaller marks counting one hour or five minute divisions. There are no numbers.

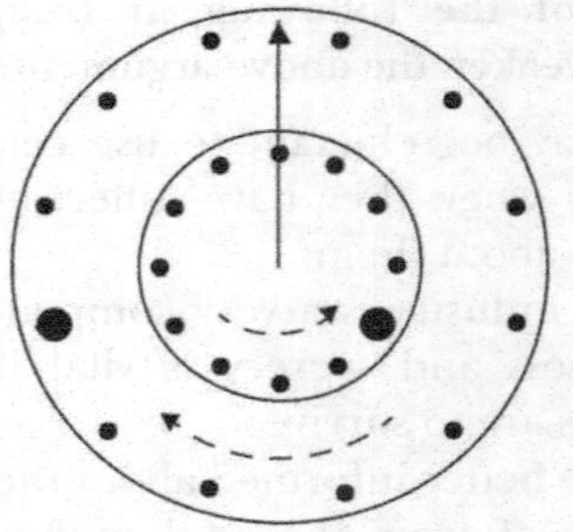

What time is it when the clock looks as shown in the diagram?

A. 3:20
B. 3:40
C. 8:20
D. 8:40
E. 9:20

26) The headquarters of the World Health Organisation (WHO) is found in which of these cities?

A. Nairobi
B. Washington DC
C. London
D. Rome
E. Geneva

27) A placebo is:

A. an inactive drug or treatment
B. a form of mild stimulant
C. a type of pain killer
D. a form of local anaesthetic
E. a sedative

28) Which general famously crossed the Alps with his army?

A. Augustus
B. Hamilcar
C. Antony
D. Octavius
E. Hannibal

29) In which modern day country was the Inca civilization centred?

A. Bolivia

B. Brazil
C. Chile
D. Ecuador
E. Peru

30) Which one of these did Galileo NOT do?

A. Design a thermometer
B. Design an electric battery
C. Discover the movement of a pendulum produces a regular time measurement
D. Develop the microscope
E. Develop the telescope

Biology

31) A sample of DNA contains 32% guanine. Which answer shows the percentage of thymine in the same sample?

A. 18
B. 23
C. 24
D. 32
E. 34

32) Which one of the following does not contain amino acids?

A. Cell membranes
B. Enzymes
C. Viruses
D. Antibodies
E. Amylose

33) The diagram below shows a phospholipid.

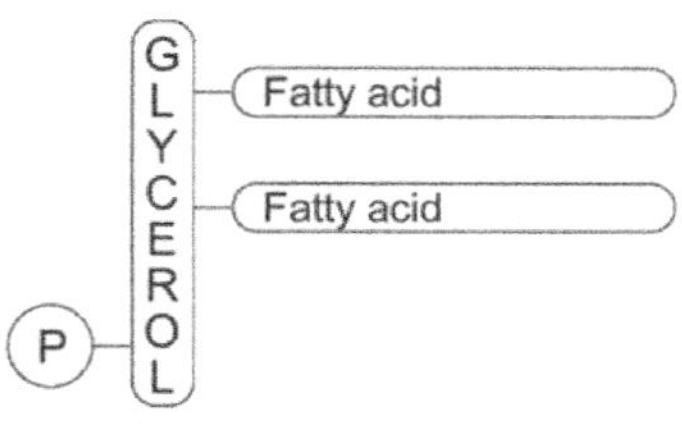

P = phosphate

When this molecule is broken into a phosphate, glycerol and two fatty acids, the number of water molecules released is:

A. 2
B. 1
C. 0
D. 3
E. more than 3

34) A liver cell in the metaphase of mitosis can be identified as being eukaryotic because it has:
1. mitochondria
2. ribosomes
3. a nucleus

A. 1 and 3 only
B. 1 and 2 only
C. 1 only
D. 2 and 3 only
E. 1, 2 and 3

35) In which of the following stages of mammalian respiration is CO_2 released?
1. Glycolysis
2. Anaerobic respiration
3. Krebs cycle

A. 2 and 3 only
B. 1 only
C. 1 and 2 only
D. 2 only
E. 3 only

36) Which one of the following molecules is made in both photosynthesis and respiration?

A. Oxygen
B. Glucose
C. ATP
D. Carbon dioxide
E. Reduced NADP

37) Which of the following comes immediately after anaphase in mitosis?

A. Prophase

B. Interphase
C. Cytokinesis
D. Metaphase
E. Telophase

38) Which statement about ribosomes is NOT correct?

A. Ribosomes can be found in the cytoplasm
B. Ribosomes are involved in protein synthesis
C. Ribosomes can be found on rough endoplasmic reticulum (RER)
D. Ribosomes can have RNA associated with them
E. Ribsosomes can carry out transcription

39) A section of one strand of DNA has a base sequence of: ACG-GCT-GGT-TCC. Which of the following are correct?
1. The other DNA strand would include a CGA triplet
2. If adenine always binds with 2 H bonds to its complementary base and guanine with H bonds, then each of these triplets will have a total of 8 H bonds
3. The mRNA sequence transcribed from this DNA sequence would contain 3 uracil bases

A. 3 only
B. 1 only
C. 2 only
D. 1 and 2 only
E. 2 and 3 only

40) The direct product of transcription of recombinant DNA can be:

A. monoclonal antibodies
B. insulin
C. mRNA
D. the primary structure of a protein
E. a replicate DNA molecule

41) The family pedigree shows that boy C has a genetic condition. No other member of the family shows the same genetic condition.

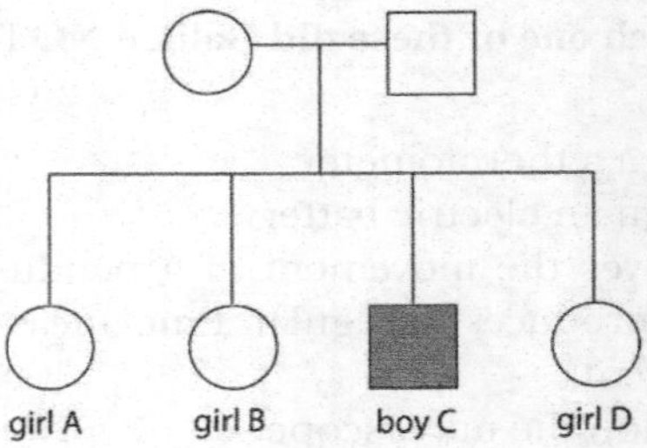

Which one of the following could NOT explain why boy C has the condition?

A. Autosomal recesive condition
B. Sex-linked recessive condition
C. Mutation
D. Both arents are carriers
E. Sex-linked dominant condition

42) The increase in the frequency of one phenotype in a wild population of fish could be due to:
1. an advantageous mutation
2. increased reproductive success of individuals with that phenotype
3. a change in the environment

A. 3 only
B. 1 only
C. 1, 2 and 3
D. 2 and 3 only
E. 1 and 2 only

43) Which one of the following is found below the diaphragm in a human?

A. Pulmonary vein
B. Pulmonary artery
C. Liver
D. Alveoli
E. Heart

44) Which one of the following is not involved in defending the body against infection?

A. Phagocyte
B. B cell
C. Antibodies
D. T cell
E. Beta cell

Chemistry

45) Which name of the following phase changes is NOT correct?

A. Liquid to gas = Evaporation
B. Solid to liquid = Melting
C. Solid to gas = Sublimation
D. Gas to liquid = Condensation
E. Gas to solid = Freezing

46) The positions of the main group elements in the Periodic Table are shown below:

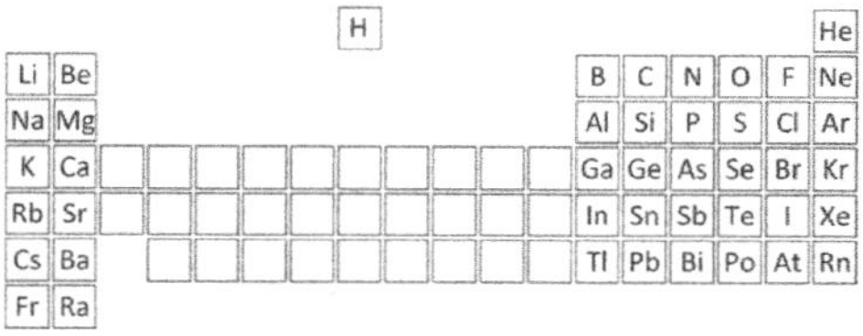

Which one of the following formulae is NOT correct?

A. $Ba(HCO_3)_2$
B. $CsNO_3$
C. $GaCO_3$
D. $BeSO_4$
E. SnS_2

47) What value does c need to be so that the following equation can be balanced?
$4KMnO_4 + aH_2SO_4 + 5C_2H_5OH \rightarrow$
$4MnSO_4 + bK_2SO_4 + 5CH_3CO_2H + cH_2O$

A. 17
B. 16
C. 11
D. 26
E. 21

48) The following are some compounds of nitrogen:
$NOCl$, KNO_2, NO_2, NO_2Cl, $Ca(NO_3)_2$
What oxidation numbers are shown by nitrogen in these compounds?

A. 4, 5, 6
B. 2, 3, 4, 5
C. 3, 4, 5, 6
D. 3, 4, 5
E. 2, 3, 4, 5, 6

49) Which of the following are correct about carbon to carbon bonds?
1. The length of carbon to carbon bonds increases in the order C≡C, C=C, C-C
2. The strength of the C=C bond is less than twice the strength of the C-C bond
3. The carbon atoms are joined by six electrons in the C≡C bond

A. 1, 2 and 3
B. 1 and 2 only
C. 1 and 3 only
D. 2 and 3 only
E. 3 only

50) The compound $(CH_3)_2CHCH_2NH_2$ can be synthesised by the following route.

$$CH_3CH{=}CH_2 \xrightarrow{1} CH_3CHBrCH_3 \xrightarrow{2} (CH_3)_2CHCN \xrightarrow{3} (CH_3)_2CHCH_2NH_2$$

What types of reaction are used in stages 1, 2 and 3?

A. 1 = substitution; 2 = addition; 3 = hydrolysis
B. 1 = addition; 2 = substitution; 3 = hydrolysis
C. 1 = addition; 2 = addition; 3 = reduction
D. 1 = addition; 2 = substitution; 3 = reduction

E. 1= substitution; 2 = addition; 3 = reduction

51) **How many atoms of hydrogen are there in 3.0kg of ethane?**
[relative atomic mass: H = 1, C = 12; Avogadro constant = 6.0×10^{23} per mol]
A. 3.6×10^{26}
B. 3.6×10^{23}
C. 3.9×10^{26}
D. 6.0×10^{22}
E. 6.0×10^{25}

52) **Which of the following must be correct about organic isomers?**
1. They have the same molecular formulae
2. Their physical properties are very similar
3. They have different structural formulae
A. 1, 2 and 3
B. 1 only
C. 1 and 2 only
D. 2 and 3 only
E. 1 and 3 only

Physics and Mathematics

53) In the expressions below: g = gravitational acceleration; h = height; m = mass; R = electrical resistance; t = time; v = velocity; V = voltage.
Which of the following expressions have units of power?

1. $\frac{mv^2}{2t}$

2. $\frac{V^2}{R}$

3. $\frac{mgh}{t}$

A. 1 and 3 only
B. 1 only
C. 1 and 2 only
D. 1, 2, and 3
E. 2 and 3 only

54) A uniform beam, 3.0m long, of weight 100N has a 300N weight placed 0.50m from one end. The beam is suspended by a string 1.0m from the same end.
A diagram of the weights placed on the beam is given below:

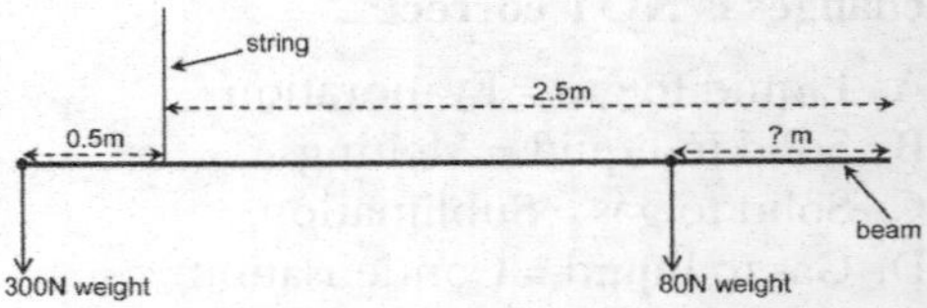

How far from the other end must a weight of 80N be placed for the beam to be balanced?
A. 2.25 m
B. 1.25 m
C. 0.75 m
D. 1.875 m
E. 0.125 m

55) **In an AC (alternating current) generator, a coil of wire rotates in a magnetic field.**

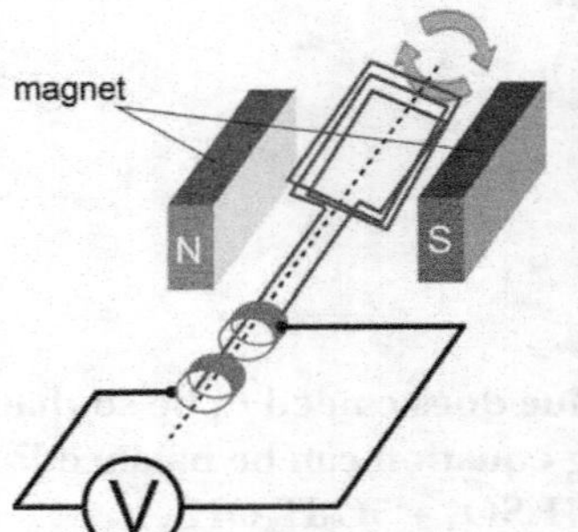

Which of the following would change the potential difference measured by the voltmeter in the system above?

1. Use more turns of wire in the coil
2. User thicker wire
3. Change the speed of rotation

A. 1 and 2 only
B. 2 only
C. 3 only
D. 1 and 3 only
E. 1, 2 and 3

56) A mass is connected to a spring and it vibrates up and down, forming a simple harmonic system. Which of the following are correct?
1. The kinetic energy of the mass is at a maximum half way up
2. The potential energy of the system is at a maximum at the top of the mass's motion
3. The potential energy of the system is at a maximum at the bottom of the mass's motion

A. 1 and 2 only
B. 1, 2 and 3
C. 1 only
D. 2 only
E. 3 only

57) Simplify $\ln\frac{x^2}{4y} + \ln xy + \ln 8$.

A. $3\ln x + 2\ln y + \ln 32$
B. $3\ln x + \ln 2$
C. $4\ln x + \ln 2$
D. $3\ln x + 2\ln 2$
E. $\ln\frac{x^2 + 4xy^2 + 32y}{4y}$

58) Which of the following is the equation of the circle with centre (–1.5, 0.5) and radius 3?

A. $2x^2 - 6x + 2y^2 + 2y - 13 = 0$
B. $2x^2 + 6x + 2y^2 - 2y - 13 = 0$
C. $2x^2 - 6x + 2y^2 - 2y - 13 = 0$
D. $2x^2 + 6x + 2y^2 - 2y - 23 = 0$
E. $2x^2 + 6x + 2y^2 - 2y - 14 = 0$

59) What is the set of values for which $12 - x^2 > 8$ and $2x + 3 \geq 5$?

A. $1 \leq x$
B. $-1 \leq x < 2$
C. $2 < x$
D. $1 < x \leq 2$
E. $1 \leq x < 2$

60) The diagram shows a quarter of a circle surrounded by an isosceles triangle. The radius of the circle is r.

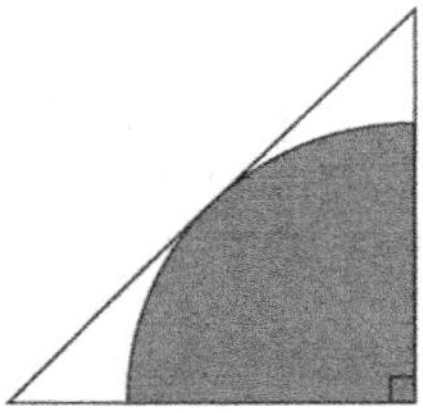

Which one of the following expressions represents the unshaded area?

A. $r^2 - \frac{\pi r}{2}$
B. $(4 - \pi)r^2$
$r^2 - \frac{\pi r}{2}$
C. $r^2 - \frac{\pi r^2}{2}$
D. $\left(2 - \frac{\pi}{4}\right)r^2$
E. $\left(1 - \frac{\pi}{4}\right)r^2$

RISPOSTE COMMENTATE • IMAT a.a. 2013/2014

Abilità logiche

1) B. Le deviazioni nelle orbite di Urano e Nettuno non possono dirci se il Pianeta X esiste, poiché gli scienziati fanno riferimento a misurazioni datate che potrebbero essere imprecise.

2) C. Calcoliamo per ciascuna confezione quanto costa 1 kg di caffè:
– confezione da 250 g: 4.50 euro / 0.25 kg = 18 euro
– confezione da 400 g: 6.30 euro / 0.4 kg = 15.75 euro
Quindi la differenza di prezzo per kg di caffè è 15.75 – 18 = 2.25 euro.

3) A. Si osserva una correlazione tra il nome e la probabilità di frequentare l'Università; tuttavia, una correlazione non implica necessariamente un rapporto causa-effetto.

4) C. Nell'articolo si criticano i grandi Stati per non aver portato provviste per oltre una settimana. È implicita l'assunzione che fossero a disposizione da parte delle nazioni elicotteri in grado di giungere ad Haiti in meno di una settimana.

5) E. (*Quesito segnalato come errato: nel calcolo del punteggio ciascuna delle alternative risulta corretta*). Dopo il primo sconto, ogni pacchetto costa 1.6 – 0.2 = 1.4 euro. Se si spendono in totale più di 10 euro, viene applicato un secondo sconto del 10% sulla spesa totale, che equivale ad applicare il 10% di sconto su ogni singolo prodotto, per cui il costo di ogni singolo pacchetto diventa $0.9 \cdot 1.4 = 1.26$ euro.

6) D. Solo apportando una modifica alla legge attualmente in vigore la gente sarebbe disposta a rinnovare gli edifici storici "a rischio" con tecniche e materiali più moderni e meno costosi, sacrificando tuttavia alcune caratteristiche originali di questi edifici. Allo stato attuale le restrizioni imposte per legge rendono troppo costose o impraticabili le opere di ristrutturazione, senza le quali gli edifici non rimarranno in piedi ancora per molto tempo.

7) C. La statistica si limita ad analizzare un'area campione con un traffico molto intenso, per cui non è rappresentativa dell'intera popolazione. I risultati del rilevamento non sono quindi estendibili al resto del paese, senza avere prima campionato altri tipi di zone.

8) E. Gli studenti devono essere aiutati a riconoscere l'importanza del saper leggere e scrivere correttamente, in quanto rappresenta un'abilità comunicativa fondamentale. Allo stato attuale, passano più tempo a scrivere sms ed e-mail piuttosto che brani grammaticalmente corretti.

9) C. Indichiamo con x la distanza totale tra *Alphcaster* e *Omegham*. Dopo aver camminato per 9 giorni, a Stephen rimane da percorrere il 40% di x. Negli ultimi 2 giorni Stephen cammina per 60 miglia, che rappresentano il 40% dell'ultimo tratto, ossia il 40% del 40% di x. Quindi:

$$40\%(40\%x) = 60$$
$$0.4(0.4x) = 60$$
$$0.16x = 60$$
$$x = \frac{60}{0.16} = 375\, miles.$$

10) D. La mobilità produce, per chi si sposta, benefici sia in termini di istruzione sia in termini di lavoro. Tuttavia, la società paga un costo non indifferente: ci sono sempre più anziani che rimangono soli e che necessitano di cure, con un impatto negativo anche sull'economia del paese.

11) D. Dei tre anni necessari per la laurea, il primo è dedicato sostanzialmente alle conoscenze di base di matematica e fisica. Se i corsi biennali di laurea avessero lo stesso numero di materie di quelli triennali, sarebbero improponibili e non realistici.

12) D. Sui primi 7 piani ci sono 8 file, 2 con 15 posti e 6 con 10 posti. In ogni fila vi sono, quindi, $2 \cdot 15 + 6 \cdot 10 = 90$ posti per piano, per un totale di $7 \cdot 90 = 630$ posti nei primi 7 piani. Nell'ultimo piano vi sono 2 file con 15 posti l'una e 4 file con 10 posti, per un totale di $2 \cdot 15 + 4 \cdot 10 = 70$ posti.
In tutto l'edificio vi sono, quindi, $630 + 70 = 700$ posti. Tuttavia, 4 posti sono riservati, per cui i posti effettivamente liberi sono $700 - 4 = 696$.
Poiché il sistema di controllo ammette le macchine fino al riempimento del 90% dei posti liberi, allora il massimo numero di macchine pubbliche ammesse è:

$$0.9 \cdot 696 = 626.4 \approx 626.$$

13) B. L'unico paese in cui il tasso di inflazione del prezzo per i consumatori diminuisce mentre il tasso di disoccupazione aumenta sono gli Stati Uniti. Infatti, il primo scende da 0.4 a 0.3, mentre il secondo sale da 5.9 a 6.1.

14) C. (*La risposta esatta è stata così corretta*). È più facile perseguire un guidatore per stato di ebbrezza piuttosto che per un colpo di sonno. Infatti, non vi sono metodi che permettano di stabilire con precisione se un incidente è stato causato da un colpo di sonno del guidatore, mentre è invece possibile stabilire in modo affidabile se il guidatore si trovava in stato di ebbrezza.

15) E. Poiché il secondo ballottaggio coinvolge solo i due candidati più votati, allora il candidato che vi è pervenuto o vincerà le elezioni oppure arriverà secondo.

16) C. Le dimensioni esterne della base sono 48 cm · 44 cm. Il rivestimento interno di acciaio è spesso 4 cm, per cui vi è una riduzione delle dimensioni interne di 4 cm per lato, ossia 8 cm per dimensione. Quindi le dimensioni interne della base sono (48 – 8) cm · (44 – 8) cm = 40 cm · 36 cm.

17) D. L'orario 3.51 p.m. corrisponde a 15:51 nel formato a 24 ore, che è un numero palindromo, cioè che letto in un verso o nell'altro non cambia, ed in più è costituito da cifre che capovolte rimangono uguali.

18) B. La possibilità di un'anima indipendente dai geni, anche se priva di fondamenti scientifici, rassicura maggiormente rispetto all'ipotesi per cui la nostra felicità è decisa alla nascita dai nostri geni. Tuttavia, nonostante più rassicurante, la prima possibilità è tanto ammissibile quanto la seconda, come si evince peraltro dalla domanda retorica conclusiva.

19) B. Il record col periodo più lungo è quello di 21.6 secondi stabilito nel 1904. Infatti, tale record rimase imbattuto fino al 1932, quando fu stabilito il nuovo record di 20.7 secondi. Tra il 1932 ed il 1904 intercorrono 28 anni.

20) E. Le compagnie farmaceutiche potrebbero immettere sul mercato nuovi farmaci anche se fossero costrette a rivelare i dettagli di produzione al pubblico e, di conseguenza, alla concorrenza, nel caso in cui fossero tutelate da forti leggi sui brevetti.

21) A. La ricerca afferma che sia il successo sia la motivazione possono essere dovuti ad una speciale attitudine per l'apprendimento.

22) D. I progetti realizzati nella nostra società possono essere tanto gratificanti quanto i viaggi all'estero. Infatti, tanto i primi quanto i secondi possono trarre beneficio dal lavoro con differenti gruppi e culture.

23) A. Se invece di usare un intero misurino se ne utilizzano 3/4, allora si incrementa di 4/3 il numero totale dei lavaggi, che sarà quindi:

$$24 \cdot \frac{4}{3} = 32.$$

24) B. Il Capitano Johnston supererà 3 aerei della compagnia Alpha-Air, in particolare quelli partiti 5, 15 e 25 minuti prima. Non riuscirà a superare l'aereo partito 35 minuti prima, dato che gli mancherà un tempo di (90 – 35) = 55 minuti, inferiore ai 60 minuti impiegati complessivamente dall'aereo del Capitano Johnston.

25) D. La ruota dei minuti gira in senso antiorario, per cui ruotando mentalmente in senso orario fino al cerchio grande, osserviamo che i minuti già trascorsi sono 40. La ruota delle ore, invece, gira in senso orario. Aggiungendo i 40 minuti precedentemente determinati, scopriamo che mancano altre 3 h alle 12, per cui sono le 8:40.

26) E. L'Organizzazione Mondiale della Sanità (OMS), in inglese *World Health Organization* (WHO), ha sede in Svizzera, a Ginevra. Dal 1948 è uno degli istituti specializzati delle Nazioni Unite ed ha lo scopo di promuovere la cooperazione internazionale nel settore della sanità, in particolare nella lotta contro le malattie infettive e nella gestione delle emergenze sanitarie globali. Tra le sue funzioni ricordiamo: indirizzare la ricerca sanitaria, stabilire norme e standard e formulare scelte di politica sanitaria basate sull'evidenza scientifica, garantire assistenza tecnica agli Stati membri, monitorare e valutare le tendenze in ambito sanitario, finanziare la ricerca medica e fornire aiuti di emergenza in caso di calamità. Elabora, inoltre, raccomandazioni, convenzioni e altri atti internazionali nei settori di sua competenza. Lavora anche per risolvere in tutto il mondo problemi legati alla nutrizione, all'igiene e alle condizioni abitative e lavorative. Vi aderiscono 194 Stati membri e i suoi organi di governo sono il Segretariato, l'Assemblea Mondiale e il Consiglio Esecutivo. L'OMS è divisa in sei regioni – regione Europea, Africana, del Mediterraneo Orientale, del Sud-Est Asiatico, delle Americhe e del Pacifico Occidentale – proprio per poter far fronte alle diverse realtà dei suoi Stati membri.

27) A. Il placebo è una forma farmaceutica che, pur non contenendo sostanze biologicamente attive, viene presentata al paziente come rimedio efficace e somministrata così da indurre suggestione psicoterapeutica, oppure per effettuare confronti con farmaci tradizionali nelle sperimentazioni cliniche. La somministrazione di queste sostanze di per sé inerti a pazienti persuasi della loro efficacia spesso produce risultati sorprendenti. Si parla di "effetto placebo" quando il paziente sente di star guarendo o di essere guarito pur senza essere ricorso alla medicina tradizionale. È molto evidente nelle terapie del dolore, dell'ansia, della depressione ed è condizionato dal contesto in cui viene effettuata la somministrazione. Essendo fortemente influenzato da una serie di variabili soggettive, quali la personalità e l'atteggiamento del medico nonché le aspettative del paziente, se l'ambiente di somministrazione non è adeguato, può provocare un effetto opposto, denominato effetto "nocebo", in cui il paziente sperimenta uno stato di malessere simile agli effetti indesiderati di un farmaco. In ogni caso, i vantaggi che il paziente trae dall'effetto placebo non sono soltanto psicologici, ma anche obiettivamente quantificabili: favorevoli modificazioni della frequenza cardiaca, della pressione arteriosa, del ritmo respiratorio, della durata del sonno, dell'appetito, ecc.

28) E. Il più grande capitano cartaginese e più tenace nemico di Roma (il padre gli fece giurare da piccolo odio eterno verso quella città), Annibale (249-183 a.C.) occupò Sagunto, alleata di Roma, provocando la Seconda Guerra Punica. Il suo scopo non era tanto annientare la città, quanto indebolirla e distruggere la federazione italica. Così, nel 218, partito con un esercito di sessantamila uomini e un certo numero di elefanti, attraversò le Alpi, superando enormi difficoltà. Sottovalutato dai Romani, Annibale conseguì in successione una serie di vittorie contro quelli presso il Ticino, il Trebbia, il lago Trasimeno e Canne. Quest'ultima straordinaria vittoria permise ai Cartaginesi di indebolire fortemente il dominio di Roma nell'Italia meridionale. Gli eserciti romano e cartaginese si affrontarono nella battaglia decisiva a Zama nel 202, dove però Annibale subì una devastante sconfitta ad opera di Publio Cornelio Scipione, grazie alla sostanziale saldezza degli alleati italici e la strategia di logoramento insegnata dal dittatore Quinto Fabio Massimo. Isolato e osteggiato, il condottiero cercò rifugio presso il re di Bitinia, Prusia, e quando i Romani imposero al re di consegnare

Annibale, questi, per sottrarsi all'umiliazione di essere portato prigioniero a Roma, nel 183 si avvelenò.

29) E. Il vastissimo impero fondato dagli Inca nell'America meridionale aveva come capitale la città di Cuzco, nell'odierno Perù. Quando giunse nell'area, nel XIII secolo, questo popolo controllava un territorio che si estendeva lungo la Cordigliera delle Ande dall'Ecuador all'Argentina. La durata dell'impero inca si protrasse per circa cinquecento anni; il suo declino cominciò dopo la morte del re, a causa della durissima lotta per la successione al trono tra i suoi figli, che indebolì fortemente l'impero facendolo diventare facile preda dei *conquistadores* spagnoli giunti nel 1532, comandati da Francisco Pizarro. La civiltà inca è tra le più importanti dell'età precolombiana. Lo Stato, fortemente centralizzato, costituiva un esempio di straordinaria organizzazione politica e amministrativa, con al vertice un sovrano investito di somma autorità politica, militare e religiosa, in quanto considerato direttamente discendente del Sole, divinità suprema di quel popolo. Dell'architettura inca resta una grande quantità di costruzioni monumentali in pietra. Famosissimi, in tutto il mondo, il sito di Machu Picchu, nel Perù centro-meridionale, e il Tempio del Sole a Cuzco.

30) B. Tra le tante invenzioni di Galileo Galilei non compare la pila elettrica, progettata da Alessandro Volta nell'Ottocento. Galileo (1564-1642) è, però, il fondatore della scienza moderna, con il suo metodo scientifico sperimentale: sua la scoperta della legge dell'isocronismo del pendolo, della bilancia idrostatica, il termoscopio, il compasso di proporzione e il telescopio con cui scoprì i cosiddetti "pianeti medicei", cioè i quattro satelliti di Giove. Secondo la nuova concezione di scienza sperimentale, Galileo rese note le sue scoperte astronomiche nel *Sidereus nuncius* ("Messaggero stellare"). Ormai giunto alla certezza che la teoria formulata da Copernico nel 1543, secondo la quale la Terra si muove intorno al Sole, fosse essenzialmente esatta, nel 1632 pubblicò la sua opera principale, *Dialogo sopra i massimi sistemi del mondo*, che gli procurò un processo per eresia culminante con un'abiura solenne da parte dello scienziato e con la sua condanna alla prigionia a vita commutata in confino. Quest'opera fondamentale, scritta sotto forma di dialogo, rappresenta una profonda critica da parte della scienza nuova alla concezione aristotelica che manteneva ancora, nella cultura ufficiale del tempo, gli atteggiamenti superati della Scolastica medievale. Il senso della realtà, la rigida argomentazione di una ragione che penetra lucidamente nel mondo fisico, si oppongono alla cultura dogmatica degli aristotelici. Sostenuta la necessità dell'esperienza, Galileo seppe formulare un sistema per valorizzarla scientificamente, secondo l'assunto che la scienza non può conoscere l'essenza del fenomeno, ma solo i rapporti fra i suoi vari elementi.

Biologia

31) A. La molecola del DNA è costituta da due catene complementari nelle quali una base purinica (adenina, guanina) di una catena è sempre legata ad una base pirimidinica (timina, citosina). L'adenina è sempre legata alla timina (A-T; T-A), la citosina è sempre legata alla guanina (C-G; G-C). Pertanto il numero di residui di A è uguale al numero di residui di T e il numero di residui di G è uguale al numero di residui di C. Se un campione di DNA contiene il 32% di guanina il contenuto di citosina sarà lo stesso. Il contenuto dei residui di G-C è il 64%, il 36% rappresenta il contenuto dei residui di T-A. Pertanto il contenuto di timina, come quello di adenina, è pari al 18%.

32) E. Gli amminoacidi sono le molecole organiche che costituiscono le unità ripetitive delle proteine, legati fra loro attraverso il legame peptidico. Gli enzimi e gli anticorpi sono esempi di proteine funzionali poiché i primi aumentano la velocità di una trasformazione chimica (catalizzatori), i secondi intervengono nella difesa immunitaria. Alcune proteine svolgono una funzione strutturale come le proteine del capside virale o le proteine della membrana cellulare. L'amilosio è invece un polisaccaride costituito da unità di glucosio.

33) C. I fosfolipidi costituiscono la membrana cellulare nella quale si dispongono in modo da formare un doppio strato. I fosfolipidi sono costituiti da una componente polare idrosolubile e una componente apolare idrofobica. La prima contiene un gruppo fosfato mentre la seconda è costituita da glicerolo legato, attraverso due legami esterei, a due acidi grassi. Quando viene sintetizzato un fosfolipide si liberano due molecole di acqua (condensazione). Nella trasformazione inversa la molecola di un fosfolipide viene decomposto in fosfato, glicerolo e due acidi grassi in presenza di due molecole di acqua. Pertanto non viene liberata nessuna molecola di acqua.

34) C. Una cellula epatica, durante la metafase della mitosi, presenta tutti gli organuli citoplasmatici che sono stati duplicati durante l'interfase. La membrana nucleare, durante la profase, si è dissolta e i cromosomi sono localizzati a livello del piano centrale della cellula. La cellula epatica pertanto, può essere identificata come eucariotica grazie alla presenza dei mitocondri (risposta corretta), gli organuli citoplasmatici coinvolti nella decomposizione degli zuccheri e nella produzione di ATP. I ribosomi invece si osservano anche in una cellula procariotica in divisione.

35) E. Dalla decomposizione ossidativa del glucosio ($C_6H_{12}O_6$), si liberano anidride carbonica, acqua ed energia sotto forma di ATP. Questa trasformazione avviene attraverso la glicolisi, nel citoplasma, il ciclo di Krebs e la catena respiratoria, nei mitocondri. L'anidride carbonica (CO_2), nei mammiferi, è rilasciata durante il ciclo di Krebs (risposta esatta) dalla ossidazione degli zuccheri. Nello stesso processo CO_2 si libera anche dalla ossidazione dei lipidi.

36) C. La fotosintesi clorofilliana e la respirazione cellulare avvengono rispettivamente nei cloroplasti, nella cellula vegetale, e nei mitocondri sia nella cellula vegetale che animale. La fotosintesi trasforma l'energia luminosa in energia chimica che viene accumulata nel glucosio e nelle molecole da esso derivate, come l'amido, mentre la respirazione cellulare demolisce gli zuccheri e gli acidi grassi allo scopo di liberare l'energia di legame per compiere lavoro. Sia nella fotosintesi che nella respirazione cellulare viene prodotto ATP (risposta corretta). L'ATP prodotto nella fase luminosa della fotosintesi attiva la fissazione di CO_2 in uno zucchero a cinque atomi di carbonio (ribulosio); nella respirazione l'ATP rappresenta il prodotto principale (38 molecole) in cui viene accumulata energia.

37) E. Nella mitosi si distinguono cinque fasi, che si susseguono, in cui l'aspetto e la struttura del nucleo cambiano: interfase, profase, metafase, anafase, telofase. Dopo l'interfase, in cui i cromosomi si sono duplicati, segue la profase durante la quale i cromosomi si ispessiscono e sono visibili. Nella metafase essi raggiungono il piano equatoriale della cellula legati, tramite il centromero, alle fibre del fuso mitotico. In anafase si verifica la migrazione delle unità che costituiscono ogni cromosoma (cromatidi) verso i poli opposti della cellula. Dopo l'anafase, nella telofase, i due nuovi nuclei si separano e il citoplasma si divide in parti uguali (citochinesi). Si formano così due cellule identiche fra loro e rispetto alla cellula madre (divisione equazionale).

38) E. La sintesi delle proteine è un processo attraverso il quale il codice genetico, contenuto nel DNA nucleare è costituito dalla sequenza di nucleotidi, viene trascritto nel mRNA e poi tradotto nelle sequenza di amminoacidi delle proteine. I ribosomi, costituiti da RNA ribosomico (rRNA) non intervengono nella fase di trascrizione (DNA $\rightarrow$ mRNA) ma di traduzione (mRNA $\rightarrow$ proteine).

39) D. Poiché le due catene polinucleotidiche del DNA sono fra loro complementari, se in una delle due è presente la sequenza GCT, a questa corrisponderà la sequenza CGA nella catena complementare. Inoltre poiché l'adenina è sempre legata con due legami H alla sua base complementare, la timina, e poiché la guanina è legata alla citosina con tre legami H, in ognuna delle 4 triplette di basi si avranno 8 legami H.

40) C. Il termine DNA ricombinante indica una sequenza di DNA ottenuta con le tecniche e gli strumenti della ingegneria genetica. Il materiale genetico di un plasmide, contenente il gene di interesse, può essere integrato nel DNA ospite ed essere replicato. Dal DNA ricombinante viene direttamente trascritto mRNA (prodotto di trascrizione) che darà origine, nella successiva fase di traduzione, alla proteina ricombinante.

41) E. Se una determinata condizione genetica, come una sindrome o una malattia, fosse legata ai cromosomi sessuali (XX e XY) e fosse dominante (risposta esatta in quanto non corretta), anche la discendenza femminile ne sarebbe affetta, non solo il figlio maschio. Tutti gli altri casi invece sono possibili: se è presente un allele recessivo legato al sesso, se si verifica una mutazione, se l'allele è presente negli autosomi (cromosomi non sessuali) e perciò nel caso che entrambi i genitori siano portatori.

42) C. Le cause che possono determinare un aumento della frequenza di un particolare fenotipo, in una popolazione selvatica di una determinata specie animale, possono essere sia la comparsa di una mutazione vantaggiosa, sia l'aumentato successo riproduttivo di individui con quel particolare fenotipo, sia un cambiamento ambientale che lo abbia favorito. Tutte e tre le possibilità (la 1, la 2 e la 3) sono coerenti con la teoria dell'evoluzione in cui la selezione naturale è il fattore stesso della evoluzione. La legge di Hardy-Weinberg ($p^2 + 2pq + q^2 = 1$) descrive una situazione modello in cui le frequenze degli alleli, e perciò dei genotipi e dei fenotipi degli individui di una popolazione, rimangono costanti. L'analisi della variazione delle frequenze geniche permette di studiare i cambiamenti in atto nella popolazione considerata.

43) C. Il diaframma è una struttura muscolare che, nei mammiferi, separa la cavità toracica da quella addominale. Nell'uomo, ha forma di cupola a convessità superiore; con la contrazione si appiattisce, favorendo l'espansione inspiratoria della cavità toracica e l'ingresso di aria atmosferica ricca di ossigeno. Il fegato (risposta esatta), come gli altri organi della cavità addominale si trova pertanto al di sotto del diaframma.

44) E. Sia le cellule B (linfociti B), gli anticorpi, le cellule T (linfociti T) e i fagociti sono coinvolti nella difesa immunitaria dell'organismo da batteri, virus o altri organismi estranei che possono provocare malattie infettive. Sono invece estranee a questa funzione le cellule beta (risposta esatta) delle isole di Langherans del pancreas. Queste secernono insulina, un ormone che interviene nel controllo omeostatico del livello di glucosio nel sangue.

Chimica

45) E. Generalmente, il passaggio dallo stato gassoso allo stato solido avviene in due step: un primo passaggio dallo stato gassoso allo stato liquido (condensazione) e un secondo passaggio dallo stato liquido allo stato solido (solidificazione). Quando la sostanza si trova al di sotto del suo punto triplo (condizioni di T e P alle quali le tre fasi sono in equilibrio) il passaggio dallo stato gassoso allo stato solido può avvenire in modo diretto. Tale processo è detto *brinamento*. Il passaggio di stato inverso (da solido a gas) è detto invece sublimazione.

46) C. Tutti gli elementi del gruppo 13 possono assumere n.o. +3 (gallio e tallio assumono anche n.o. +1). Nel composto $GaCO_3$ invece il Ga dovrebbe avere numero di ossidazione +2, pertanto tale composto non esiste.

47) C. Data la reazione:

$$4KMnO_4 + \mathbf{a}H_2SO_4 + 5C_2H_5OH \rightarrow 4MnSO_4 + \mathbf{b}K_2SO_4 + 5CH_3CO_2H + \mathbf{c}H_2O$$

possiamo determinare **b** bilanciando gli atomi di potassio: a sinistra sono 4, pertanto b = 2.

$$4KMnO_4 + \mathbf{a}H_2SO_4 + 5C_2H_5OH \rightarrow 4MnSO_4 + \mathbf{2}K_2SO_4 + 5CH_3CO_2H + \mathbf{c}H_2O$$

Di conseguenza, possiamo determinare **a** bilanciando gli atomi di zolfo: a destra sono 6, pertanto a = 6.

$$4KMnO_4 + \mathbf{6}H_2SO_4 + 5C_2H_5OH \rightarrow 4MnSO_4 + \mathbf{2}K_2SO_4 + 5CH_3CO_2H + \mathbf{c}H_2O$$

Infine, ricaviamo **c** bilanciando gli atomi di ossigeno: a sinistra abbiamo 45 atomi di ossigeno e per bilanciare quest'ultimo, poniamo c = 11.

48) D. Quando un atomo entra a far parte di una molecola mette in compartecipazione, cede o acquista elettroni. La distribuzione della nuvola elettronica varia a seconda dei valori di elettronegatività posseduti da ciascun atomo. A ogni atomo che entra a far parte di una molecola o ione poliatomico può essere assegnato un numero di ossidazione. Esso rappresenta la carica elettrica che ogni atomo assumerebbe se si rompessero tutti i legami della molecola e si assegnassero gli elettroni all'atomo più elettronegativo. Nei suoi composti l'azoto può assumere diversi numeri di ossidazione. Il più alto è +5 (pari al numero del gruppo a cui appartiene, ossia al numero di elettroni di valenza). Ricordando che la somma dei numeri di ossidazione di tutti gli atomi all'interno di una molecola neutra deve essere zero, possiamo calcolare il numero di ossidazione dell'azoto in tutti questi composti: NOCl, KNO_2, NO_2, NO_2Cl, $Ca(NO_3)_2$. Consideriamo NOCl. Bisogna tener presente che l'ossigeno assume quasi sempre numero di ossidazione –2 (tranne nei perossidi, dove è –1 e nel suo composto col fluoro dove è +2). Per quanto riguarda il Cl, in questo composto esso è l'elemento più elettronegativo, quindi il suo n.o. sarà negativo (–1). Per differenza possiamo ricavare il n.o. di N.
Sappiamo infatti che:

$$n.o._N + n.o._{Cl} + n.o._O = 0$$

e quindi:

$$n.o._N = -n.o._{Cl} - n.o._O = +1 +2 = +3$$

In modo analogo si ricavano i n.o. anche per gli altri composti:

$$\overset{+1}{K}\overset{+3}{N}\overset{-2}{O}_2 \quad \overset{+4}{N}\overset{-2}{O}_2 \quad \overset{+5}{N}\overset{-2}{O}_2\overset{-1}{Cl} \quad \overset{+2}{Ca}\left(\overset{+5}{N}\overset{-2}{O}_3\right)_2$$

Pertanto i n.o. assunti dall'azoto in questi composti sono +3, +4 e +5.

49) A. Tra due atomi di carbonio si può avere la formazione di legami singoli, doppi e tripli, mettendo in compartecipazione rispettivamente una, due o tre coppie di elettroni. Il legame doppio è costituito da un legame di tipo symb e uno di tipo π, quello triplo da un legame σ e due legami π. I due atomi di carbonio dell'etano, ad esempio, danno luogo alla formazione di quattro legami semplici (σ), utilizzando 4 orbitali ibridi uguali di tipo sp^3. Tali orbitali si formano dal "mescolamento" di un orbitale s e 3 orbitali p (ibridazione). Invece, i due atomi di carbonio dell'etilene sono uniti attraverso un legame doppio e formano legami semplici con gli atomi di H (come mostrato in figura). In tali atomi di C si ha la formazione di tre orbitali ibridi sp^2 (costituiti da un orbitale s e due orbitali p), mentre un orbitale p resta non ibridato. La sovrapposizione di due orbitali sp^2 porta alla formazione del legame σ, mentre la sovrapposizione laterale dei due orbitali p porta alla formazione del legame π.

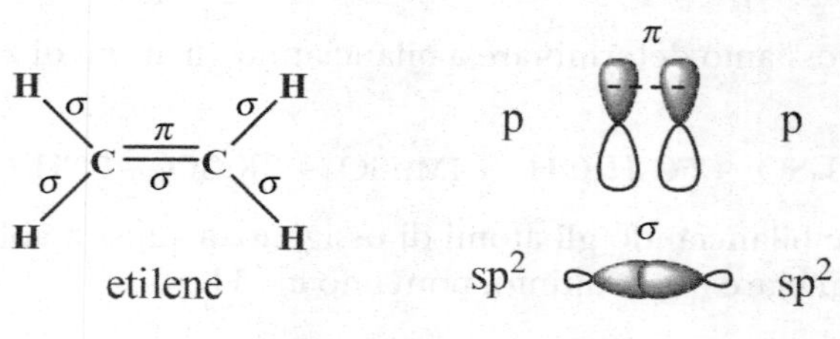

La sovrapposizione degli orbitali sp^2 è completa, mentre tra gli orbitali p è parziale. Per questo motivo il legame σ è più forte di quello π, da cui segue che la forza di un legame doppio (σ + π) è inferiore a quella di due legami σ. Ad ogni modo, un legame triplo è più forte di un legame doppio che a sua volta lo è più di un legame semplice, vale a dire che la distanza di legame è minore per il legame triplo.

50) D. Gli alcheni subiscono essenzialmente reazioni di addizione al doppio legame. Lo step 1 infatti è una reazione di addizione di HBr. Il bromoalcano che si forma invece è suscettibile di sostituzione nucleofila, infatti $(CH_3)_2CHCN$ si ottiene per reazione di sostituzione nucleofila da parte dello ione cianuro (–CN) al bromoalcano. Infine, il nitrile può essere trasformato in un'ammina attraverso una riduzione con idruro di litio e alluminio ($LiAlH_4$) o idrogenazione catalitica. L'inserimento di un gruppo CN in una molecola organica è spesso sfruttato per allungare la catena alchilica: si noti infatti che da un alchene con 3 atomi di carbonio è stata ottenuta un'ammina con 4 atomi di carbonio.

51) A. Una mole di qualsiasi elemento o composto contiene rispettivamente un numero di Avogadro ($N_A = 6{,}02 \cdot 10^{23}$) di atomi o molecole. Per risolvere l'esercizio bisogna conoscere innanzitutto le moli di idrogeno, H. Queste possono essere ricavate dalle moli di etano (C_2H_6) che a loro volta si possono calcolare conoscendo i grammi di C_2H_6 forniti dal problema e la sua massa molecolare (data dalla somma delle masse atomiche di 2 atomi di C e 6 atomi di H: 30 g/mol). Quindi, le moli di etano sono date da:

$$n(C_2H_6) = \frac{3000g}{30\frac{g}{mol}} = 100\,mol$$

In ogni mole di etano sono presenti 6 moli di H, quindi: n(H) = 6 · 100 mol = 600 mol. Il numero di atomi di H si ricava risolvendo la seguente proporzione:

$$1 \text{ mole H}: 6{,}02 \cdot 10^{23} \text{ atomi} = 600 \text{ moli H} : x$$

da cui:

$$x = 3{,}6 \cdot 10^{26} \text{ atomi}$$

52) E. In chimica organica esistono diversi tipi di isomeri: quelli costituzionali hanno la stessa formula molecolare e si differenziano per il modo in cui gli atomi sono legati tra loro. Si tratta, quindi, di composti anche molto diversi tra loro per quanto riguarda le proprietà chimico-fisiche. Ad esempio, etanolo e dimetil etere hanno la stessa formula molecolare (C_2H_6O), ma formula di struttura diversa:

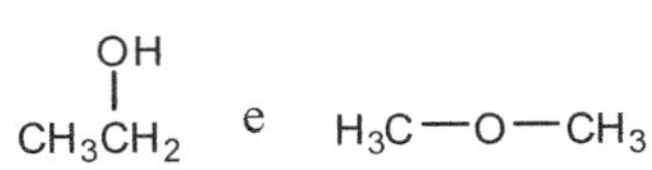

etanolo   dimetil etere

Appartengono, infatti, a due distinte classi di composti: uno è un alcool, l'altro è un etere. Di conseguenza, hanno proprietà chimico-fisiche molto diverse. Tuttavia, altri tipi di isomeri, pur avendo diversa struttura, hanno proprietà simili. Ad esempio, il

2-esanolo e il 3-esanolo sono alcoli secondari, isomeri con proprietà chimico-fisiche simili.

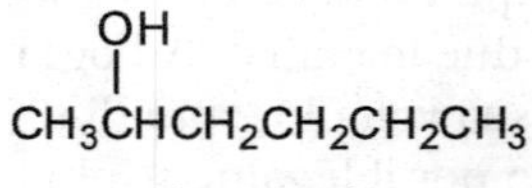

2-esanolo

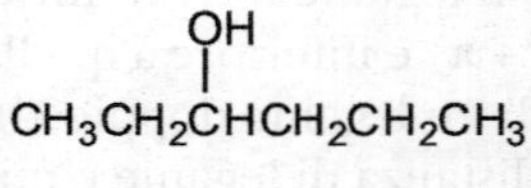

3-esanolo

Fisica e Matematica

53) D. La potenza ha le dimensioni di un'energia su un tempo.

L'espressione $\frac{mv^2}{2t}$ può essere riscritta come $\frac{\frac{1}{2}mv^2}{t}$, dove notiamo che al numeratore compare l'energia cinetica, mentre al denominatore vi è un tempo. Quindi, essa rappresenta una potenza.

L'espressione $\frac{V^2}{R}$, invece, è la potenza dissipata da una resistenza per effetto Joule.

Infine, anche $\frac{mgh}{t}$ rappresenta una potenza, in quanto al numeratore vi è l'energia potenziale gravitazionale ed al denominatore vi è un tempo. Pertanto tutte le 3 espressioni rappresentano la potenza.

54) C. (*Quesito segnalato come errato: nel calcolo del punteggio ciascuna delle alternative risulta corretta*). Affinché il sistema sia in equilibrio, la somma dei momenti torcenti deve essere nulla:

$$\sum \vec{\tau} = 0$$

$$\sum \tau_z = 0.$$

Ricordando che il momento torcente di una forza è dato dal prodotto vettoriale tra il vettore forza ed il vettore distanza rispetto ad un polo arbitrario e scegliendo come polo il punto in cui la corda sostiene la trave, così da annullare il momento torcente della tensione della corda e non doverla quindi calcolare, otteniamo:

$$\sum \tau_z = 300 \cdot 0.5 - 100 \cdot 0.5 - 80 \cdot (2 - x) = 0$$

$$80x = 60$$

$$x = \frac{60}{80} = 0.75m.$$

Riproduciamo nuovamente l'immagine proposta dal quesito riportando in scala le giuste proporzioni.

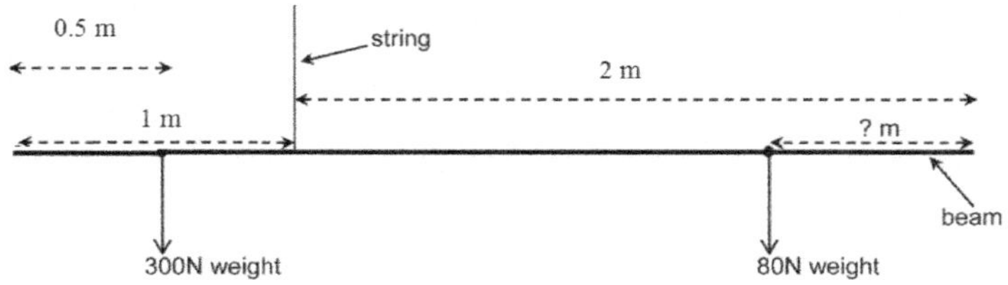

55) D. La forza elettromotrice indotta è direttamente proporzionale al numero di avvolgimenti del filo ed alla rapidità con cui il flusso del campo magnetico varia. Quindi aumentare il numero di avvolgimento comporterebbe un cambiamento della differenza di potenziale misurata, così come cambiare la velocità di rotazione. Invece, usare un filo più spesso non produrrebbe nessun effetto in termini di tensione misurata.

56) B. A metà altezza l'allungamento della molla è nullo e la velocità è massima, per cui anche l'energia cinetica è massima.
L'energia potenziale elastica e l'energia potenziale gravitazionale possono essere ridotte ad un'unica energia potenziale di tipo elastico se si sostituisce alla posizione a riposo della molla la posizione di equilibrio. In questo caso l'oscillatore armonico "verticale" diventa del tutto equivalente ad un oscillatore armonico "orizzontale", per cui l'energia potenziale è massima quando l'allungamento x della molla è massimo, essendo dato da: $U_{el} = \frac{1}{2}kx^2$, cosa che avviene nel punto più alto e nel punto più basso di oscillazione.

57) B. Si ha applicando le proprietà dei logaritmi:

$$\ln\frac{x^2}{4y} + \ln xy + \ln 8 = \ln\frac{x^2xy^8}{4y} = \ln 2x^3 = 3\ln x + \ln 2$$

58) B. Data una circonferenza di equazione:

$$x^2 + y^2 + ax + by + c = 0$$

Le coordinate del centro sono date da: $C = \left(-\frac{a}{2}, -\frac{b}{2}\right)$; il raggio è dato da:

$$r = \sqrt{\left(\frac{a}{2}\right)^2 + \left(\frac{b}{2}\right)^2 - c}$$

Quindi per comodità algebrica conviene dividere tutte le equazioni per 2 perché hanno tutte i termini quadratici moltiplicati per 2. In tal caso si osserva che l'equazione

$$2x^2 + 2y^2 + 6x - 2y - 13 = 0$$

si può riscrivere come:

$$x^2+y^2+3x-y-\frac{13}{2}=0$$

da cui si ottiene:

$$C=\left(-\frac{3}{2},\frac{1}{2}\right)$$

e il raggio è:

$$r=\sqrt{\left(-\frac{3}{2}\right)^2+\frac{1}{4}+\frac{13}{2}}=3$$

che è ciò che è richiesto dal testo.

59) E. Basta risolvere il sistema di disequazioni:

$$\begin{cases}12-x^2>8\\2x+3\geq 5\end{cases}$$

$$\begin{cases}x^2<4\\x\geq 1\end{cases}$$

$$\begin{cases}-2<x<2\\x\geq 1\end{cases}$$

Quindi l'intervallo soluzione è $1\leq x<2$.

60) E. La parte non scura della figura è data dall'area del semiquadrato meno l'area del quarto di circonferenza grigia. Dalla figura si evince che il lato del quadrato è $r\sqrt{2}$, dove r è il raggio del quarto di circonferenza. Quindi l'area cercata sarà:

$$\frac{\left(r\sqrt{2}\right)^2}{2}-\frac{\pi r^2}{4}=r^2-\frac{\pi r^2}{4}=r^2\left(1-\frac{\pi}{4}\right)$$

IMAT
a.a. 2014/2015

General knowledge and logical reasoning

1) Research reveals that, in a given period of the 20th century, top footballers (defined as those who had played for their country's team) lived, on average, almost 5 years longer than middle ranking footballers. We can conclude therefore that for the top footballers, success had a beneficial effect on their lifespan.
Which one of the following is the best statement of the flaw in the argument above?

A. The study was limited to footballers in a given period of time
B. It assumes that the longer lifespan could not be explained by other factors
C. Playing football regularly may have health benefits which contribute to longer lifespan
D. Living longer is not necessarily a good thing
E. Life expectancy increased generally in the 20th century

2) One of the foolish but persisting fantasies of the Olympic movement is that the Games are, or were, or will be, or even ought to be, completely free of politics. It is difficult to understand how this foolish belief continues, but the facts are these: the nations lining up to host the games are motivated not by unattainable ideals but by a legitimate desire to promote the excellence of their citizens; and the nations who have boycotted the games in the past have done so to make genuine political points.
Which one of the following is a conclusion which can be drawn from the above passage?

A. If some countries use the Olympic movement to further their own ends, they are guilty only of exposing a myth
B. Although everyone knows the Olympics are caught up in politics, no one is brave enough to admit it
C. National interests are ruining the Olympics
D. We should do everything possible to ensure that the Olympics do not become further politicised
E. Just because the Olympic games have been politicised, it doesn't mean that they should be

3) There is concern at the moment about the way in which football referees are treated by players during games. The Football Association and the Referees' Association feel that there is too much verbal (and physical) abuse directed at referees. Various solutions have been suggested such as only allowing the captain of each team to approach and talk to the referee. The major difficulty is how such new rules should be introduced. The preferred suggestion seems to be that the rules should be changed first in the amateur game, the aim being to improve discipline in the game from the bottom upwards, until the whole game is improved.

Which one of the following, if true, would most weaken the argument above?

A. Referees should use their existing powers to control abusive players
B. Amateur players are more likely to abuse referees than are professionals
C. By introducing it first to amateur players, it reaches those who spend the least time playing football
D. Referees in the amateur game are less proficient than those in the professional games
E. Not many professional players start out in the amateur leagues

4) The purpose of an election is to decide what policies are supported by the people. However, in elections the concept of 'tactical voting' is becoming increasingly common. The argument is a simple one:
Party X will never be beaten by party Y but party Z could win with a few extra votes. Therefore, you should transfer your vote from party Y to party Z to make sure that party X is beaten.
This reasoning is perfectly sound if your main objective is to vote a party out. Unfortunately, if you support party Y then there is no guarantee that party Z will support the same principles.
Which one of the following is the conclusion that could best be drawn from the above passage?

A. Tactical voting is an important part of the electoral process
B. Elections are often thought of in terms of voting for or against the party in office, rather than as voting for your preferred party
C. Tactical voting will not achieve the purpose of an election
D. Party X policies are not popular
E. It is important that party X does not win the election

5) Despite much opposition to the idea, modern musical trends such as hip-hop have a place in the world of opera. Traditional opera is a powerful musical experience. However, modern musicians should not necessarily stick with the traditional form. Modern musical forms which fuse staged drama, singing and contemporary or ethnic trends in music are also powerful musical experiences. Glydebourne's youth operas "Misper" and "Zoe", and its Mozart hiphopera, "School 4 Lovers', enjoyed critical and box office success and attracted hip-hop audiences. Moving away from the snobbery of tradition gives a much wider audience access to transformative musical experience.
Which one of the following best expresses the main conclusion of the passage?

A. Musicians are entitled to fuse new forms and old to create exciting musical experiences
B. Hip-hop is as powerful and dramatic as opera
C. Contemporary music has a place in the musical world in addition to traditional operatic performances
D. Contemporary music forms have a place in performances of opera
E. Creating new operatic performances allows more people to access this exciting art form

6) Over 30 years ago, the smallpox virus was eradicated (removed) from the natural environment, but examples of it are still preserved in two laboratories. It is planned, however, to destroy these remaining viruses. Given that this will be the first example of a deliberate destruction of an entire species, we should think again before destroying these viruses. Years ago we thought we had the right to kill as many creatures as we liked, but now we realise we have no such right.

Furthermore, we cannot know the future; we cannot justify destroying something that could be of enormous value to us one day, valuable in ways we cannot even think of now. And anyway, what possible harm can captive viruses do to us?

Which one of the following best expresses the main conclusion of the above argument?

A. Captive smallpox viruses are not going to harm us
B. We do not have the right to destroy the smallpox virus
C. We cannot justify destroying something which may one day be valuable to us
D. The planned destruction of the smallpox virus should be given more thought
E. The deliberate destruction of an entire species should never be allowed

7) When driving, if the car in front of you brakes suddenly, you need to be able to stop without crashing into it. The easiest rule-of-thumb is the two second rule. You choose a reference point that the vehicle in front of you is passing then say aloud: 'Only a fool breaks the two second rule'. If you reach the reference point before you have finished the saying you need to pull back. This works at all speeds. However, when there are adverse road conditions or the road is narrow you need to double your braking distance. These practices will enable you to avoid such crashes.

Which one of the following is an underlying assumption of the argument above?

A. It will not take less than two seconds to repeat the saying.
B. Some drivers brake more suddenly than others
C. Those who do not use the rule do not value road safety
D. Adopting the "two second rule" will avoid all accidents
E. Most crashes are caused by cars running into the car in front

8) If for a number of hours each day you're having experiences on the computer where there are no consequences, that may have an implication for antisocial behaviour. In real life you can't undo something; you can't bring someone back to life once you've stabbed them. On a computer you can play the game again. It may be that for people who spend most of their time playing computer games involving killing others, real bleeding to death has no meaning. Studies of brain activity show that there is less pre-frontal cortex activity in the brains of screenobsessed teenagers than in the brains of those who spend little time on computer games. The pre-frontal cortex area of the brain is where we process ideas of sequence, consequences and empathy.

Which one of the following can be drawn as a conclusion of the passage above?

A. Brain structure is altered by environmental factors
B. There may be a link between use of computer games and violence
C. People who spend a lot of time playing computer games are the main culprits in knife crime
D. Young people cannot distinguish the difference between fantasy and reality
E. Computer games should not be available for children under 18 years of age

9) We constantly split our attention between the people we are with and what's happening on our mobile phone screens. On-screen multi-tasking makes us less efficient as well as less emotionally engaged with others. It takes 64 seconds to recover our train of thought after interruption by a message (that's 8.5 hours a week wasted if we check our screens every five minutes) and when we've sent an email or SMS text message, the brain goes through a series of semi-conscious calculations as we wonder when and how the recipient will reply. The result is that we're not "present" for several minutes afterwards. In order to function effectively in the workplace, we need to switch off our communication hardware.

Which one of the following is the best statement of the flaw in the above argument?

A. It may only be the younger workers who use mobile phone technology to excess
B. In many work environments you may not be allowed to use personal mobile phones
C. People may be unwilling to make less use of their mobile phones
D. We may need to have some 'down time' in order to recharge our mental batteries
E. Without the means to send and receive information instantly, our effectiveness may be compromised

10) If the media give publicity to certain types of crime, it may encourage criminals to carry out "copy cat" offences. If, however, they were forbidden to divulge details of crimes, this would amount to censorship. The freedom of speech of the media is too important to sacrifice, so the media should be free to report crime even if this means some crimes are committed which would not otherwise be committed.

Which one of the following expresses the main conclusion of the above argument?

A. Censorship of the media would reduce the crime rate
B. Freedom of speech is a right that is too important to give up
C. The media should be permitted to report crimes even if other crimes sometimes result from this reporting
D. Publicity about crimes can encourage others to commit similar offences
E. The media should not report all the details of a crime

11) Smoking cigarettes causes a speeding up in the rate of blood flow, which in turn increases the risk of heart disease. It was thought that this speeding up of blood flow was caused solely by the gas carbon monoxide, which is absorbed during smoking, and not by nicotine, which is also absorbed from the smoke in the lungs. However, tests have shown that using nicotine patches (from which nicotine is absorbed through the skin) or chewing nicotine gum also causes the rate of blood flow to increase. This shows that the nicotine in cigarettes is also responsible for the increased risk of heart disease among smokers.

Which one of the following is not an assumption of the argument in the passage above?

A. There is nothing else in nicotine patches and chewing gum which might cause an increase in the rate of blood flow
B. The effect of nicotine on the body does not depend on the way in which it was absorbed
C. Any differences between the amount of nicotine absorbed from smoking and the amount absorbed from nicotine patches and chewing gum can be disregarded
D. Carbon monoxide is not absorbed from nicotine patches and nicotine chewing gum

E. Carbon monoxide would not produce a rise in the rate of blood flow in the absence of nicotine

12) In many countries shocking images of the damage smoking can do to the body are displayed on cigarette packets. Images of rotting teeth, mouth tumours and cancerous lungs are among the grim pictures. A review concluded that shocking pictures of the damage smoking can do are a cost effective way to help smokers to quit and discourage others from starting. All countries should introduce these kinds of images to discourage smoking.

Which one of the following, if true, most weakens the above argument?

A. In countries using the images there are high taxes on tobacco and a ban on advertising
B. Smokers are likely to die younger than nonsmokers
C. The USA is planning to display shocking images on cigarette packets
D. Pictures that arouse emotions are especially effective
E. Governments receive a significant amount of revenue from taxes on tobacco products

13) There is a special offer on jars of coffee this week. Customers who buy two jars at the normal price have the option to buy up to four more jars at one quarter of the normal price.

For customers buying coffee this week, which of these bar graphs shows how the average cost per jar (as a percentage of the normal cost) varies with the number of jars bought?

A.
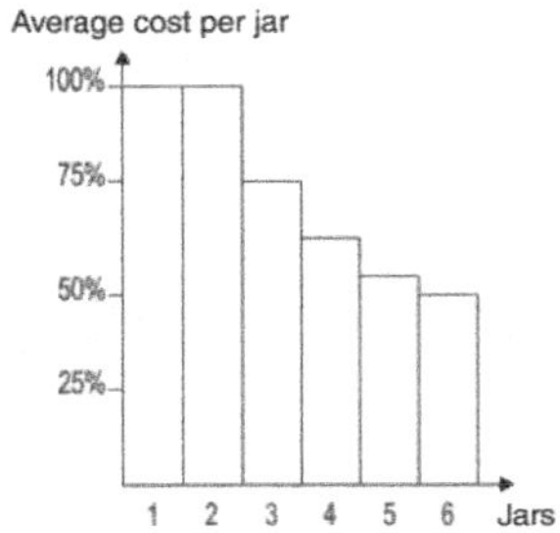

B.
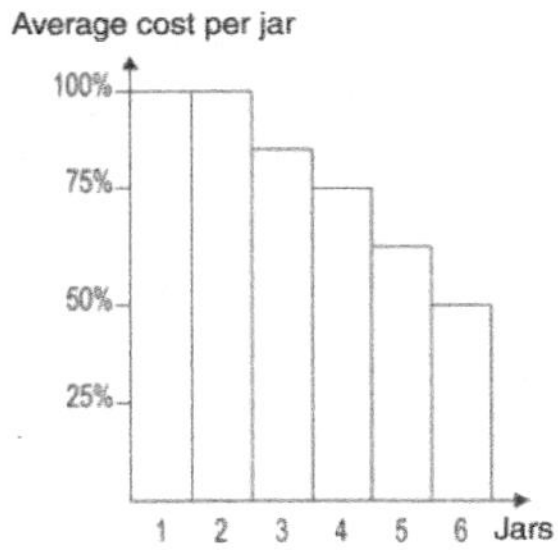

C.
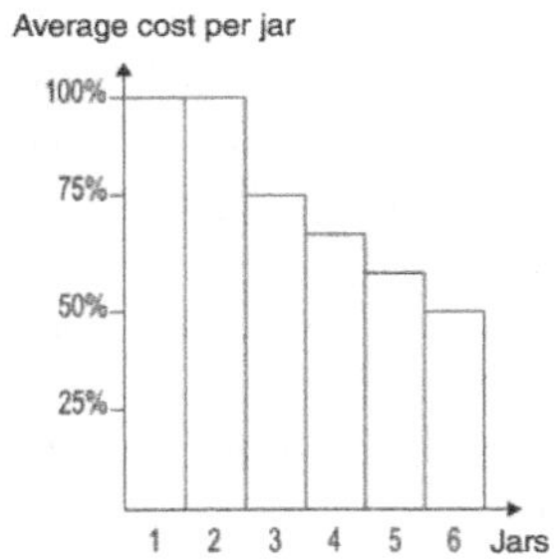

D.
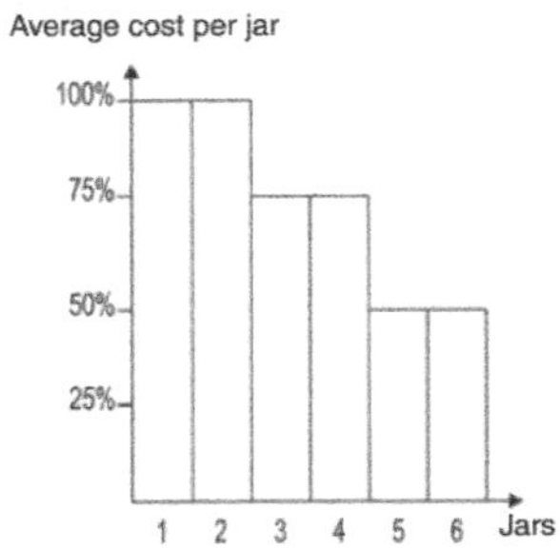

E.

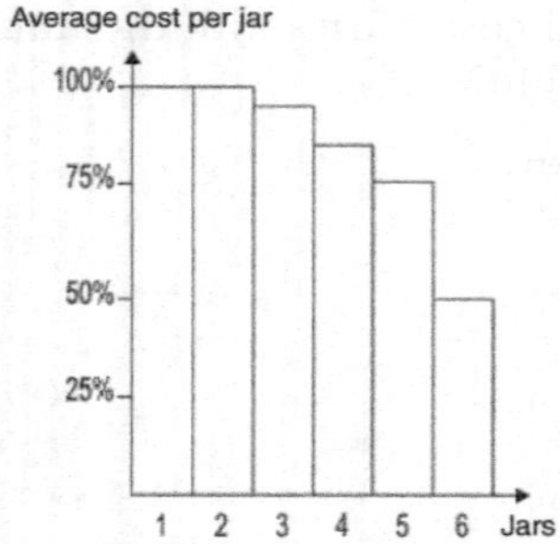

14) During a recent storm the plastic company logo fell off the outside of the office building of Fleesam Ltd. and broke cleanly into the two pieces shown below:

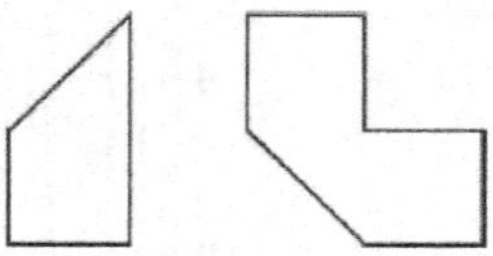

A junior clerk took the two pieces to a signmaker to show what had happened, and asked him to make a new logo. Unfortunately after the clerk had left, the signmaker realised that he didn't know how the two pieces had fitted together originally.

Which one of the following could not be Fleesam's logo?

A. 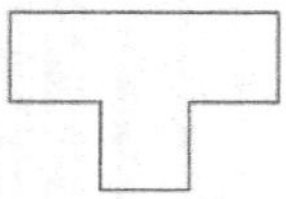

B. 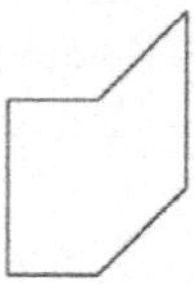

C. 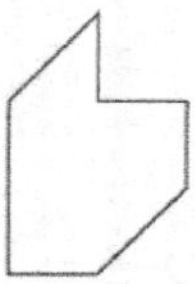

D. 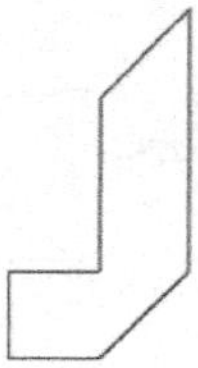

E. 

15) A golf tournament is played over 10 rounds, on successive Saturdays. The winner of each round scores 3 points and the player finishing second scores 1 point. The tournament is won by the competitor with the most points over the 10 rounds.

Alan Vinci, Barry Durand, Carl Johansson and Daniel and Eric Lim were the participants in this year's tournament. All five won at least one round, but either Barry, Daniel or Eric finished second on each occasion. The 12 finishing order was different every round, and the Lim brothers didn't both score points in the same round at any time.

Who won this year's tournament?

A. Alan Vinci
B. Eric Lim
C. Barry Durand
D. Carl Johansson
E. Daniel Lim

16) The owner of a hotel needs to decorate 20 rooms. He has found prices for four different types of interior wood paint and calculated the volume of paint he needs for each room. He will use the same type of paint for all the rooms.

Type of paint	375 ml	750 ml	1.25 l	2.5 l	Volume needed per room
Non Drip Gloss	€ 4.50	€ 8.00	€ 10.00	€ 16.00	1.4 litres
Satinwood	€ 5.00	€ 8.00	€ 11.00	€ 20.00	1.1 litres
Quick Dry Gloss	N/A	€ 10.00	N/A	€ 20.00	1.0 litres
Once Gloss	€ 4.50	€ 8.00	€ 12.00	€ 18.00	0.8 litres

What is the least amount he needs to spend on paint?

A. € 108
B. € 116
C. € 120
D. € 112
E. € 126

17) The diagram below shows the layout of a game playing board with the square board numbered as indicated. The numbers on the board start with 1 on the bottom left and finish with 25 at the top right.

21	22	23	24	25
20	19	18	17	16
11	12	13	14	15
10	9	8	4	6
1	2	3	4	5

A larger, square playing board is numbered in a similar way and divided into pieces which fit together to make the whole board. One piece of this larger board is shown below:

27	26	
16	17	18
	12	

How many squares are there on this larger board?

A. 49
B. 25
C. 64
D. 121
E. 81

18) Sally owns a small business which produces handcrafted jewellery. The materials used to create a necklace cost € 1.50 on average. She pays her staff € 5.40 an hour. For a standard piece of jewellery she charges 70% more than it costs to produce.
To make a particular Italian-style glass necklace it takes 30 minutes. How much does she sell this single necklace for?

A. € 5.40
B. € 11.34
C. € 11.73
D. € 2.94
E. € 7.14

19) The diagram below is a plan of the raised flower beds and a chair in my garden.

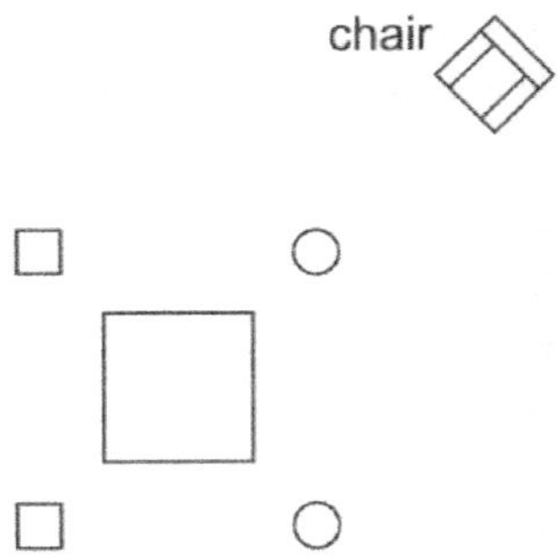

Which one of the following can not be a view of the raised beds from my chair?

A.
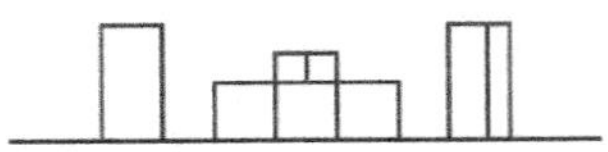

B.
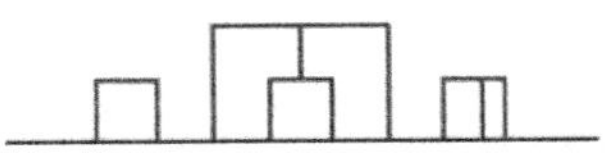

C.

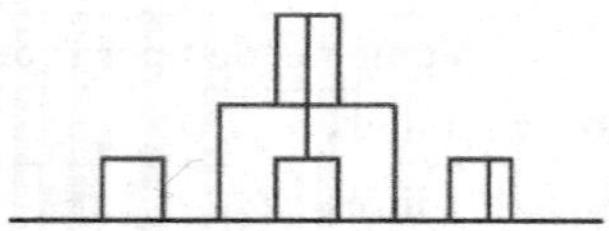

D.

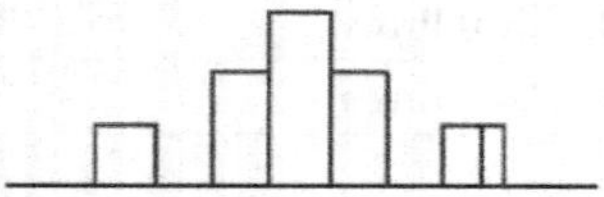

E.

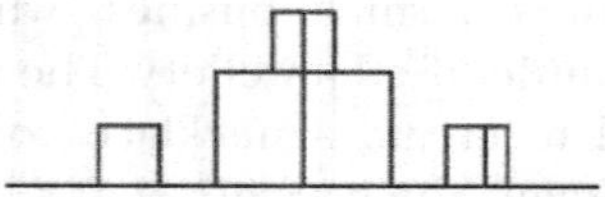

20) Last month Karl walked from Starton to Endham, raising money for charity. His target, successfully achieved, was to complete the walk in ten days. He started later than intended and had only completed 12 km by the end of the first day. However, he walked 45 km on each of the second, third and fourth days, and after the fifth day he was exactly half way. Poor weather on the sixth day restricted his progress, but 41 km on both the seventh and eighth days meant that he had completed exactly three-quarters of the walk with two days left. On the ninth day he covered three-fifths of the remaining distance, completing the last 36 km on the tenth day.
How far did Karl walk from Starton to Endham?

A. 240 km
B. 360 km
C. 294 km
D. 384 km
E. 328 km

21) The net shown can be folded to make a tetrahedron with each of the shapes showing on the outside.

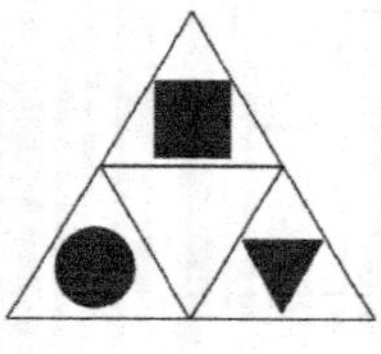

Which one of the following nets can be folded to make a tetrahedron identical to the one shown above?

A.

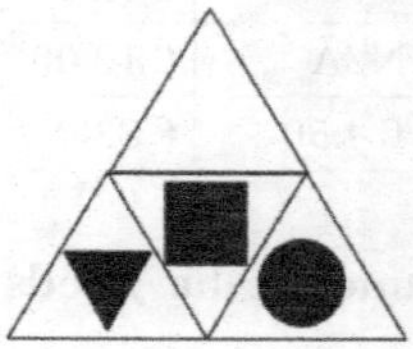

B.

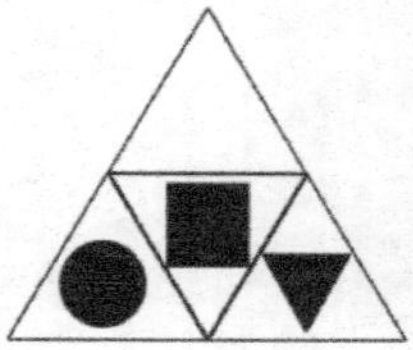

C.

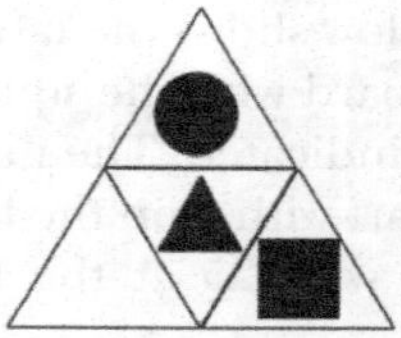

D.

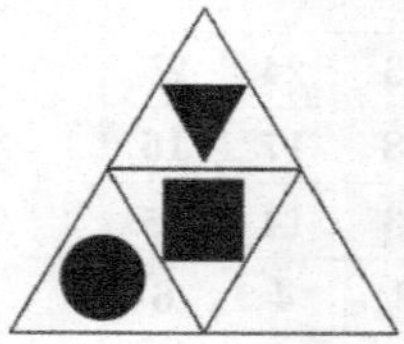

E.

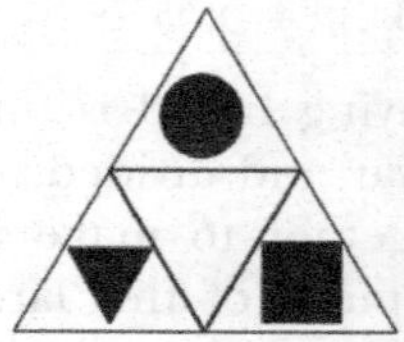

22) Tessa makes bracelets. She works five days each week, from Monday to Friday. Her contract requires her to make a minimum of 150 bracelets every working day, for which she is paid a basic wage of $ 320 per week. She can also earn a bonus of $ 3 per bracelet for every one above 175 that she makes on any particular day.
Last week, Tessa earned $ 515 in total. On Friday she made 205 bracelets, the most she has ever made in one day.

What is the minimum number of bracelets that Tessa made last week?

A. 805
B. 815
C. 890
D. 865
E. 940

23) 15 runners took part in this year's Marathon of Marathons (eight marathon races on consecutive days). Points were awarded to the first seven to finish in each race, as follows:

Winner	11 points
Second	8 points
Third	6 points
Fourth	4 points
Fifth	3 points
Sixth	2 points
Seventh	1 point

All 15 runners finished in the first three at least once, but only Philip, who was the overall winner with a total of 61 points, finished in the first three every time.

How many of the eight races did Philip win?

A. 3
B. 2
C. 1
D. 4
E. 5

24) William Harvey, who wrote the book commonly referred to as 'De Motu Cordis' is famous for his description:

A. of the circulation of the blood
B. of how anaemia can be caused by a lack of iron
C. of how blood plasma carries heat and urea as well as carbon dioxide
D. of the different forms of blood cells and platelets
E. of the interaction between antigens and antibodies

25) Which popular website was founded in 2004 by Mark Zuckerberg?

A. Wikipedia
B. eBay
C. YouTube
D. Twitter
E. Facebook

26) The artists Claude Monet and Pierre Auguste Renoir were associated with which art movement?

A. Fauvism
B. Pointillism
C. Abstract expressionism
D. Impressionism
E. Cubism

27) What does the letter P stand for in the international organisation OPEC?

A. Piracy
B. Plastics
C. Petroleum
D. Philosophy
E. Physics

Biology

28) The diagram shows a section of rough endoplasmic reticulum (RER).

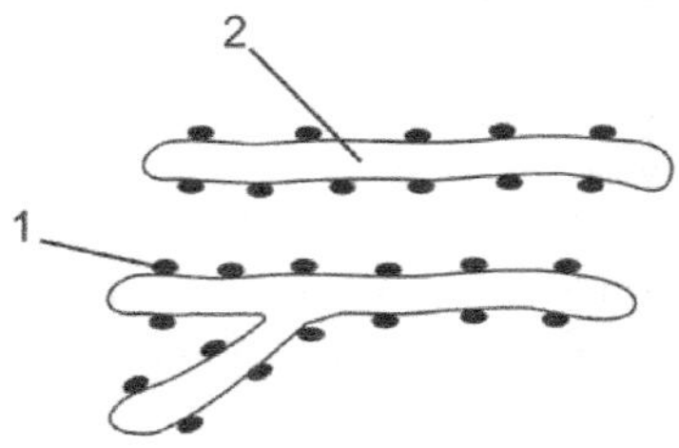

Which answer correctly identifies the substances associated with structures 1 and 2?

A. 1: tRNA; 2: polypeptide
B. 1: DNA; 2: carbohydrate
C. 1: phospholipids; 2: mRNA

D. 1: amino acids; 2: tRNA
E. 1: proteins; 2: DNA

29) The diagram below shows a pair of homologous chromosomes and the site of crossing over.

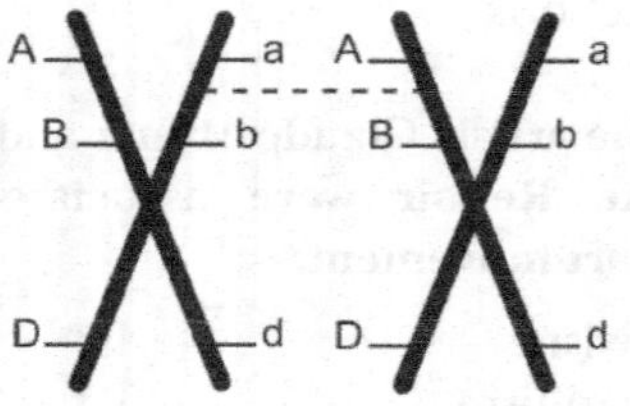

- - - - = site of crossing over

Which answer in the table is correct when meiosis is complete?

	Number of recombinant daughter chromosomes produced	Number of daughter chromosomes that are genetically distinct form each other
Row 1	1	2
Row 2	2	1
Row 3	4	2
Row 4	2	4
Row 5	4	4

A. Row 5
B. Row 1
C. Row 2
D. Row 3
E. Row 4

30) Which curves show the results of calculating the initial rate of reaction of an enzyme:
1. when the substrate concentration is varied, under optimal conditions and without an inhibitor;
2. when the substrate concentration is varied, under optimal conditions and fixed, low concentration of a competitive inhibitor?

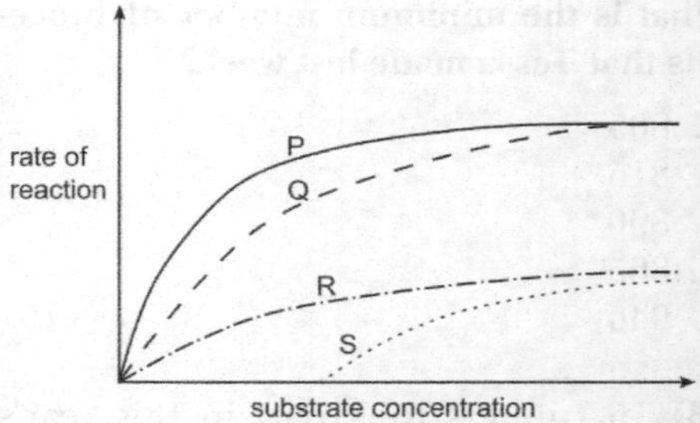

A. (1) curve R; (2) curve P
B. (1) curve R; (2) curve S
C. (1) curve Q; (2) curve R
D. (1) curve P; (2) curve Q
E. (1) curve P; (2) curve S

31) In cells of winter wheat (*Triticum aestivum*), the fluidity of the cell membrane can be varied by the plant, depending upon the environmental temperature. As the weather becomes colder, the cell membrane changes to maintain its fluidity. **Which type of bond would be more common in cell membranes of winter wheat plant cells as their growing conditions become colder?**

A. C–N
B. C–C
C. C–H
D. C=C
E. C–O

32) The transmission of nerve impulses at a synapse is unidirectional. Which of the features of the transmission of nerve impulses given below have a role in maintaining the unidirectional transmission?
1. Exocytosis of neurotransmitter at the presynaptic membrane
2. Neurotransmitter hydrolysing enzyme found on the postsynaptic membrane
3. Neurotransmitter receptors found on the postsynaptic membrane
4. Sodium gated channels on the postsynaptic membrane

A. 1, 3 and 4 only
B. 1, 2 and 3 only
C. 1, 2 and 4 only
D. 2 and 4 only
E. 1 and 4 only

33) Which one of the following names the structure, in humans, that directly detects a change in blood glucose level and then the structure that responds to the change?

A. Liver and adrenal gland
B. Adrenal gland and pancreas
C. Hypothalamus and pituitary gland
D. Pituitary gland and liver
E. Pancreas and pancreas

34) One set of semilunar valves in the human heart closes when:

A. the oxygen level in blood decreases at the respiring tissues
B. the blood pressure in the right ventricle is less than in the pulmonary artery
C. the blood pressure is greater in the left ventricle than in the aorta
D. another set of semilunar valves opens
E. the blood pressure in the aorta is greater than in the vena cava

35) The diagram shows the respiration process in the cytoplasm of a yeast cell or an animal cell when O_2 is limiting:

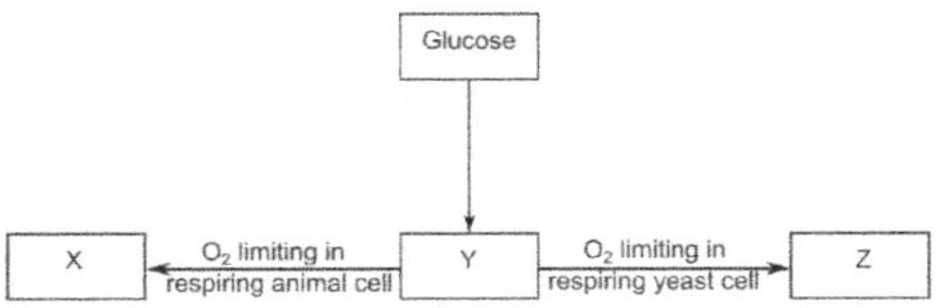

Which option correctly identifies substances X, Y and Z?

A. X = pyruvate; Y = lactate; Z = ethanol
B. X = ethanol; Y = pyruvate; Z = lactate
C. X = lactate; Y = pyruvate; Z = ethanol
D. X = lactate; Y = ethanol; Z = pyruvate
E. X = pyruvate; Y = ethanol; Z = lactate

36) The diagram below shows the inheritance of a nonlethal recessive sexlinked condition.

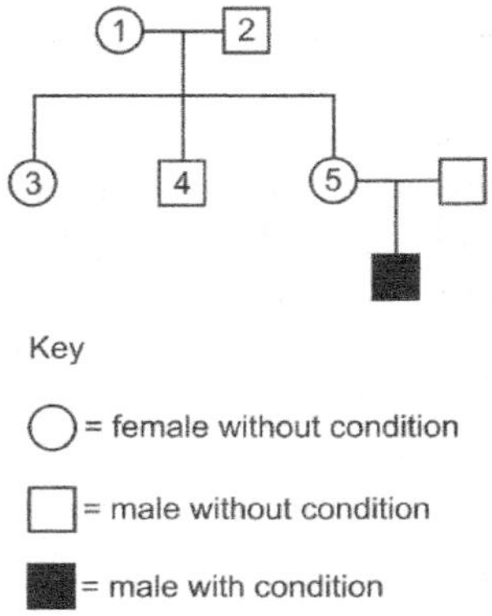

Which row in the table below does not correctly state the probability for each person possessing one copy of the allele for the condition?

Person	Maximum probability (%)
1	50
2	0
3	50
4	0
5	100

A. Person 2
B. Person 1
C. Person 3
D. Person 4
E. Person 5

37) Which of the following molecules are associated with the Human Immunodeficiency Virus (HIV)?
1. DNA
2. RNA
3. Phospholipids
4. Reverse transcriptase

A. 1, 2, 3 and 4
B. 1 and 2 only

C. 2 and 3 only
D. 1, 2 and 4 only
E. 2, 3 and 4 only

38) A circular bacterial plasmid consists of 1000 base pairs (bp). A specific restriction enzyme has three recognition sites within this plasmid. The sites are at 150 bp, 250 bp and 950 bp. After complete restriction, what size are the fragments?

A. 50 bp, 100 bp, 150 bp and 700 bp only
B. 100 bp, 150 bp, 200 bp only
C. 50 bp, 100 bp and 700 bp only
D. 100 bp, 200 bp and 700 bp only
E. 50 bp, 100 bp, 150 bp, 200 bp and 700 bp

39) Which of the following can produce vesicles?
1. RER
2. Golgi
3. Cell surface membrane

A. 1, 2 and 3
B. 1 and 2 only
C. 2 and 3 only
D. 1 and 3 only
E. 2 only

40) Two disease-free cells, P and Q, were studied. Which option correctly identifies cell P as a typical plant cell and cell Q as a typical prokaryote?

	Cell P	Cell Q
Row 1	Gene for RuBisCo is present	Susceptible to penicillin
Row 2	Plasmids present	Centrioles found as a pair
Row 3	Outermost layer is selecriely permeable	SERpresent
Row 4	Glycogen can be present	Cell wall is present
Row 5	Organelle with grana present	Nucleolus may be present

A. Row 3
B. Row 2
C. Row 1
D. Row 4
E. Row 5

41) The diagram shows a sequence of bases on a DNA template:

CAC GTT CGC ATA GAC

Which one of the following shows the sequence of bases on the complementary mRNA strand with one substitution mutation?

A. GTG CAA GGG TAT CTG
B. CUC GTT CGC UTT GUC
C. GUG CAA GCG UAU GUC
D. GUG CAA CCG UAU CUG
E. GTG CAA GCG TAT CTG

42) Which one of the following statements about both asexual and sexual reproduction is correct?

A. Mutations only occur in sexual reproduction and not in asexual reproduction
B. Only the gametes (and not body cells) undergo meiosis in sexual reproduction compared with both cell types in sexual reproduction
C. Mitosis leads to sperm formation in asexual reproduction and sexual reproduction
D. Variation is only required for sexual reproduction and not for asexual reproduction
E. Some organisms can carry out both asexual and sexual reproduction

Chemistry

43) A battery has lead plates dipped in sulfuric acid. When charged, the positive plate is covered with PbO_2. After discharge both plates are covered with $PbSO_4$.

Which option below correctly describes the overall change in the oxidation number of the lead involved in the chemical reaction during discharge?

A. Positive plate: 4 → 2; Negative plate: 2 → 0
B. Positive plate: 4 → 2; Negative plate: 0 → 2
C. Positive plate: 4 → 0; Negative plate: 0 → 2
D. Positive plate: 4 → 1; Negative plate: 0 → 1
E. Positive plate: 4 → 1; Negative plate: 1 → 0

44) Excess lead (II) nitrate solution is added to 1.30 g of zinc powder and the mixture is stirred. When the reaction is finished the lead formed is filtered, dried and weighed. It has a mass of 3.31 g.
What is the percentage yield of the lead?

A. 100%
B. 90%
C. 80%
D. 70%
E. 60%

45) How many of the following compounds are acidic, alkaline or amphoteric (react with both acids and alkalis)?

Al_2O_3	Cl_2O_7	CO_2	HCl	H_3PO_4
K_2O	KOH	MgO	Na_2O	NO_2
P_4O_{10}	SiO_2	SO_2		

A. Acidic = 8; Amphoteric = 1; Alkaline = 4
B. Acidic = 7; Amphoteric = 1; Alkaline = 5
C. Acidic = 6; Amphoteric = 1; Alkaline = 6
D. Acidic = 9; Amphoteric = 2; Alkaline = 2
E. Acidic = 10; Amphoteric = 2; Alkaline = 4

46) The following are some compounds that can be made from ethene, C_2H_4:

$$C_2H_6,\ C_2H_5Br,\ C_2H_5OH,\ CH_2BrCH_2Br,\ -(CH_2CH_2)_{n}-$$

Which one of the compounds is made by oxidising ethene?

A. $-(CH_2CH_2)_{n}-$
B. C_2H_6
C. C_2H_5Br
D. C_2H_5OH
E. CH_2BrCH_2Br

47) The reaction scheme below shows some reaction conversions of organic molecules.

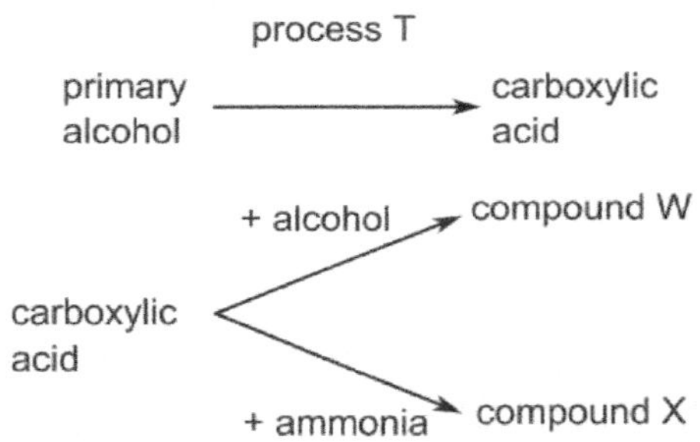

Which is the correct combination of process and compounds for this scheme?

A. process T: reduction; compound W: ketone; compound X: nitrile
B. process T: reduction; compound W: ketone; compound X: amide
C. process T: oxidation; compound W: ester; compound X: nitrile
D. process T: oxidation; compound W: ester; compound X: amide
E. process T: reduction; compound W: ester; compound X: amide

48) The atomic numbers of five atoms are given below. Which atom would have an electronic configuration ending in a p^5?

A. 8
B. 9

C. 7
D. 6
E. 5

49) The relative molecular mass of calcium carbonate is 100. What is the minimum volume of 2.0 M hydrochloric acid that would be needed to completely react with 2.0 g of calcium carbonate?

A. 20 cm^3
B. 10 cm^3
C. 5 cm^3
D. 30 cm^3
E. 40 cm^3

50) What is the pH of 0.1 M HCl?

$$pH = -\log_{10}[H^+]$$

A. 0
B. 0.1
C. −1
D. −0.1
E. 1

51) A student carried out an experiment to find the rate of decomposition of hydrogen peroxide into water and oxygen gas. The student used 100 cm^3 of a 1M solution of hydrogen peroxide at 25°C and 1 atm pressure.
1 g of powdered MnO_2 as a catalyst was added and the solution was constantly stirred. The student measured the total volume of oxygen produced.
The procedure was repeated, but this time using 100 cm^3 of 2M hydrogen peroxide, under identical conditions.
Which option below shows the effect on (R) the rate of reaction, (V) the total volume of oxygen collected, by using the 2M solution compared to the 1M solution?

A. R: Doubled; V: No effect
B. R: No effect; V: Doubled
C. R: Doubled; V: Doubled
D. R: No effect; V: No effect
E. R: Doubled; V: Halved

52) Which two of the following molecular substances in the gaseous state have the strongest permanent molecular dipole?

GeH_4 ICl SiF_4 CH_2Cl_2 Co_2

A. ICl and CH_2Cl_2
B. GeH_4 and SiF_4
C. CO_2 and SiF_4
D. ICl and CO_2
E. CH_2Cl_2 and CO_2

Physics and Mathematics

53) Evaluate:

$$\frac{8\times10^{-5}}{\sqrt{1.6\times10^{7}}}\times(1.2\times10^{3})^{2}$$

A. 2.88×10^4
B. 2.88×10^{-1}
C. 2.88×10^{-3}
D. 2.88×10^{-2}
E. 2.88×10^{-5}

54) Four individual spheres have radii:

$\frac{r}{2}$, r, $2r$ **and** $3r$

What is the sum of their surface areas?

A. 57 πr^2
B. 58 πr^2
C. 26 πr^2
D. 25 πr^2
E. 169 πr^2

55) What is the equation of the straight line which passes through (−6, 2) and is perpendicular to $4y + 3x = 8$?

A. $3y + 4x = 30$
B. $3y - 4x = 18$
C. $4y - 3x = 26$
D. $3y + 4x = -18$
E. $3y - 4x = 30$

56) A computer game is on sale for € 32.00. The price ticket shows that this cost is a reduction of 20% of the original price. What was the original price?

A. € 52.00
B. € 40.00
C. € 33.60
D. € 38.40
E. € 25.60

57) An ornamental thermometer, commonly known as a Galileo thermometer, contains a number of spheres of hollow coloured glass, representing different temperatures, immersed in a column of ethanol. A particular sphere (X) rises from the bottom to the top of the column of liquid when the temperature falls below the value it represents.

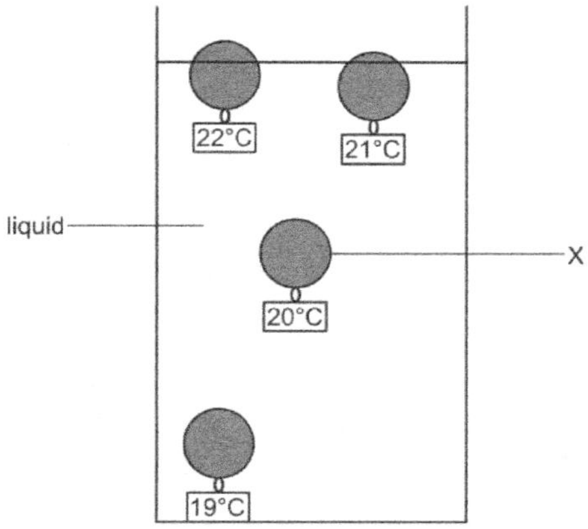

Which statement best explains why the sphere rises when the temperature falls?

A. The pressure exerted by the liquid has decreased
B. The mass of the sphere has decreased
C. The density of the liquid has increased
D. The temperature of the sphere is different from that of the liquid
E. The volume of gas inside the sphere has increased

58) The circuit shown contains three identical resistors, two ammeters X and Y, and a voltmeter Z. The internal resistance of the battery is negligible.

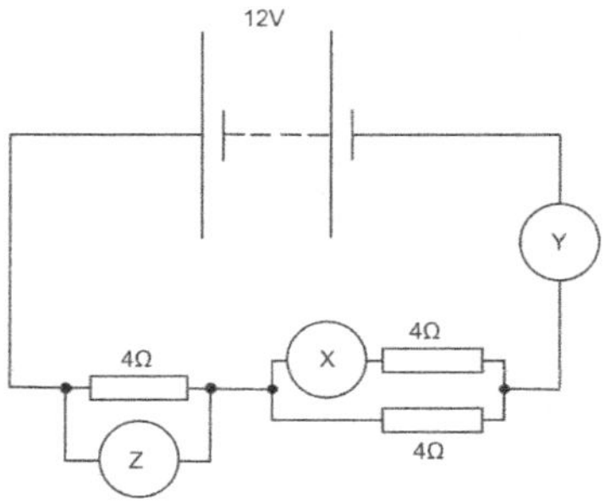

Which option shows the readings on the three meters?
[Assume the ammeters have negligible resistance, and negligible current flows through the voltmeter.]

A. X = 1.0 A; Y = 0.0 A; Z = 12 V
B. X = 1.0 A; Y = 2.0 A; Z = 8.0 V
C. X = 1.0 A; Y = 2.0 A; Z = 6.0 V
D. X = 3.0 A; Y = 6.0 A; Z = 12 V
E. X = 2.0 A; Y = 0.0 A; Z = 4.0 V

59) A book of mass 0.40 kg rests on a horizontal surface with which it has a coefficient of dynamic friction of 0.50. **If this book is now pushed by an external horizontal force of 10 N, what will be its acceleration immediately after it has started to move?**
[Assume the gravitational field strength is 10 Nkg^{-1}, that air resistance is negligible and that the orientation of the book does not change.]

A. 20.0 ms^{-2}
B. 15.0 ms^{-2}
C. 12.5 ms^{-2}
D. 25.0 ms^{-2}
E. 50.0 ms^{-2}

60) An earthed magnet is near a bar of material which is seen to be repelled by the magnet.
What could the bar of material be?
[The system is isolated and no currents are induced.]

A. A bar of unmagnetised cobalt
B. A bar of electrostatically charged aluminium
C. A bar of electrostatically charged copper
D. A bar of unmagnetised soft iron
E. A bar of magnetised steel

RISPOSTE COMMENTATE • IMAT a.a. 2014/2015

Cultura generale e ragionamento logico

1) B. Il ragionamento esposto nella traccia ha un difetto che fa sì che il passaggio logico dalle premesse alla conclusione non sia accettabile. È dunque indispensabile individuare innanzitutto le premesse e la conclusione dell'argomentazione. Nel brano si afferma che in base ai risultati di una ricerca secondo la quale in un determinato periodo del Ventesimo secolo giocatori di football di livello elevato sono vissuti in media almeno 5 anni in più rispetto ai giocatori di livello medio, si può concludere che per i giocatori di football di livello alto il successo ha avuto effetti benefici sulla durata della loro vita. Una tesi del genere può essere sostenuta solo presupponendo che non possano esservi, oltre al successo, altri fattoti in grado di determinare una durata maggiore della vita come sostenuto dall'alternativa corretta "*It assumes that the longer lifespan could not be explained by other factors*".

2) A. Questo tipo di quesito richiede di stabilire quale, fra le cinque alternative, riporti l'affermazione che, pur non essendo effettivamente asserita nel brano può essere supportata da esso in quanto sua conclusione. Nel testo si legge che il movimento olimpico nutre l'insensata fantasia della estraneità dei Giochi olimpici alla politica. Tuttavia, i fatti testimoniano l'ingerenza degli interessi politici degli Stati nei Giochi. Analizziamo le cinque alternative per individuare la conclusione del brano:
– "*Although everyone knows the Olympics are caught up in politics, no one is brave enough to admit it*". L'alternativa non può essere presa in considerazione in quanto nel brano si parla solo del movimento olimpico e della sua erronea convinzione che non vi sia l'ingerenza della politica nei giochi;
– "*National interests are ruining the Olympics*". L'autore descrive una situazione e nulla nel brano ci autorizza a concludere che secondo lui gli interessi nazionali – tra l'altro da sempre presenti come specificato – stiano rovinando i Giochi olimpici;
– "*We should do everything possible to ensure that the Olympics do not become further politicized*". Come la risposta precedente, sulla base delle notizie fornite dal testo, non è possibile concludere che secondo l'autore bisogna impedire un'ulteriore politicizzazione dei Giochi;
– "*Just because the Olympic games have been politicized, it doesn't mean that they should be*". Anche in questo caso l'affermazione riportata costituisce una deduzione non autorizzata da quanto espresso nel testo, pertanto deve essere scartata.
Tra le cinque alternative la sola a costituire la conclusione del ragionamento è la seguente: "*If some countries use the Olympic movement to further their own ends, they are guilty only of exposing a myth*", secondo cui se gli Stati si servono del movimento olimpico per perseguire i propri scopi non fanno nient'altro che sfatare un mito.

3) E. La domanda chiede di identificare quale delle cinque alternative di risposta riporti l'affermazione che, se fosse aggiunta alle premesse dell'argomentazione, ne in-

debolirebbe la conclusione. Secondo quest'ultima bisognerebbe cominciare a cambiare le regole partendo dal basso nei campionati amatoriali di football per migliorare la disciplina durante le partite con giocatori professionisti. Analizziamo dunque le cinque alternative per individuare l'affermazione che toglierebbe forza alla conclusione:
– "*Amateur players are more likely to abuse referees than are professionals*". Se ciò fosse vero, avremmo un altro motivo per accogliere il suggerimento di introdurre le nuove regole prima nel campionato dilettanti, pertanto tale alternativa rafforzerebbe il ragionamento anziché indebolirlo;
– "*Referees should use their existing powers to control abusive players*", "*By introducing it first to amateur players, it reaches those who spend the least time playing football*", "*Referees in the amateur game are less proficient than those in the professional games*".
Tali alternative non inciderebbero sul passaggio dalle premesse alla conclusione, passaggio che riguarda specificamente l'introduzione di nuove regole e, soprattutto, la questione di come introdurle, pertanto vanno scartate.
L'unica risposta corretta è la seguente: "*Not many professional players start out in the amateur leagues*". Infatti, se ciò fosse vero, sarebbe indebolito il concetto esposto dalla conclusione come l'obiettivo dell'introduzione delle nuove regole prima nel campionato dilettanti, ossia «*to improve discipline in the game from the bottom upwards, until the whole game is improved*».

---

4) C. Questo tipo di quesito richiede di stabilire quale, fra le cinque alternative di risposta, riporti l'affermazione che, pur non essendo effettivamente asserita nel brano, costituisce la sua conclusione. Dunque, per risolvere il quesito è necessario ricavare la conclusione del testo in questione partendo dalle premesse. Nel brano si afferma che lo scopo principale di una elezione è stabilire quali politiche siano sostenute dalle persone, sebbene il concetto di voto tattico, usato per impedire che un determinato partito vinca le elezioni e attui le sue politiche, stia diventando sempre più comune. Analizzando le risposte se ne ricava che due, "*Tactical voting is an important part of the electoral process*" e "*Elections are often thought of in terms of voting for or against the party in office, rather than as voting for your preferred party*", vanno scartate perché introducono informazioni e concetti che non si evincono dal ragionamento; se, infatti, come si afferma nel brano, «*the concept of 'tactical voting' is becoming increasingly common*», la conclusione del ragionamento non potrà essere che il voto tattico è già una parte importante del processo elettorale così come nel testo non si fa mai riferimento alla distinzione tra partiti in carica e partiti preferiti. Anche le alternative "*Party X policies are not popular*" e "*It is important that party X does not win the election*" non possono essere prese in considerazione in quanto sono entrambe possibili presupposti della scelta del "voto tattico" ma non costituiscono la conclusione del brano. L'unica affermazione che meglio potrebbe essere tratta come conclusione dal testo è "*Tactical voting will not achieve the purpose of an election*". Infatti, come già detto, si afferma che lo scopo di un'elezione è decidere quali politiche sono sostenute dalle persone, ma il "voto tattico" impedisce che un partito X, benché supportato dalla gente, vinca le elezioni e attui le sue politiche. Dunque, la conclusione non può che essere che il voto tattico non realizza l'intento di un'elezione.

5) D. Il quesito richiede di individuare fra le cinque alternative di risposta quella che esprime al meglio la conclusione del ragionamento. Dunque bisogna individuare in primo luogo la conclusione e le premesse espresse nel brano.
Conclusione: "*Despite much opposition to the idea, modern musical trends such as hip-hop have a place in the world of opera. Traditional opera is a powerful musical experience. However, modern musicians should not necessarily stick with the traditional form*".
Prima premessa: "*Modern musical forms which fuse staged drama, singing and contemporary or ethnic trends in music are also powerful musical experiences*".
Seconda premessa: "*Glydebourne's youth operas "Misper" and "Zoe", and its Mozart hiphopera, "School 4 Lovers', enjoyed critical and box office success and attracted hip-hop audiences. Moving away from the snobbery of tradition gives a much wider audience access to transformative musical experience*".
Analizzando le alternative si ricava che le seguenti tre "*Musicians are entitled to fuse new forms and old to create exciting musical experiences*", "*Hip-hop is as powerful and dramatic as opera*", "*Creating new operatic performances allows more people to access this exciting art form*", rimandano in vario modo alle premesse e, poiché noi cerchiamo la conclusione, vanno scartate.
L'alternativa "*Contemporary music has a place in the musical world in addition to traditional operatic performances*", invece, presenta un'affermazione che non è espressa nel brano; dal momento che noi cerchiamo la conclusione effettivamente asserita nel ragionamento, anch'essa non è valida. Se si legge con attenzione il testo, osserviamo che secondo l'autore "*modern musical trends ... have a place in the world of opera*», non «*in the musical world in addition to traditional operatic performances*". La risposta corretta è dunque "*Contemporary music forms have a place in performances of opera*".

6) D. Per trovare la risposta al quesito è necessario in primo luogo identificare la conclusione del ragionamento e, poi, individuare fra le cinque alternative quella che la esprime al meglio. Nel brano si afferma che ancora oggi sono conservati in due laboratori alcuni campioni del virus del vaiolo, malattia eradicata oltre 30 anni fa, e che è in programma la distruzione definitiva di questo virus. L'autore giunge alla conclusione che però sarebbe meglio pensarci ancora su riguardo alla distruzione di un virus che in futuro potrebbe esserci utile. Analizzando le alternative, la seguente, "*The planned destruction of the smallpox virus should be given more thought*" corrisponde alla conclusione dell'argomentazione in esame: "*we should think again before destroying these viruses*".

7) A. Questa tipologia di quesito richiede di determinare quale, fra le cinque alternative di risposta, contiene la supposizione implicita del ragionamento, ossia il presupposto che non è affermato nel brano ma sul quale poggia la conclusione. Nel testo si parla della "regola dei due secondi", che se rispettata consente di evitare incidenti stradali, in particolare tamponamenti, mantenendo la giusta distanza di sicurezza. La regola consiste nel mantenere una distanza tale che prima di passare per lo stesso punto dove è passata l'auto che è davanti, bisogna avere il tempo di pronunciare ad alta voce la frase "Solo uno sciocco infrange la regola dei due secondi". È evidente che per affermare ciò l'autore deve quindi assumere implicitamente che non ci vogliono meno di due secondi per ripetere la frase e valutare così la distanza dall'auto davanti. Pertanto la risposta corretta è: "*It will not take less than two seconds to repeat the saying*".

8) B. In questo quesito si chiede di trovare, fra le cinque alternative, l'affermazione che, pur non essendo effettivamente asserita nel passo, ne costituisce la sua conclusione. Questo genere di domanda, quindi, comporta di dover trarre la conclusione del ragionamento in questione esclusivamente sulla base delle idee che l'autore asserisce nel brano e che si possono considerare come le premesse del suo ragionamento. Nel brano si afferma che un comportamento antisociale potrebbe essere sviluppato da persone che trascorrono molto tempo a giocare al computer. Da studi su adolescenti di questo tipo emerge, infatti, una minore attività dell'area del cervello che elabora le idee di sequenzialità, consequenzialità ed empatia. Le alternative "*Brain structure is altered by environmental factors*", "*Young people cannot distinguish the difference between fantasy and reality*" e "*Computer games should not be available for children under 18 years of age*" vanno scartate poiché presentano informazioni e concetti non coerenti con quanto espresso nel brano. Anche l'alternativa "*People who spend a lot of time playing computer games are the main culprits in knife crime*" non è valida, in quanto presenta come una certezza che le persone che trascorrono molto tempo giocando con videogiochi siano i principali colpevoli di crimini con arma bianca, mentre l'autore si esprime in termini di possibilità quando parla di comportamento antisociale ("*may have an implication for antisocial behavior*"). L'alternativa corretta è dunque "*There may be a link between use of computer games and violence*". Tale affermazione è sostenuta dal brano come sua conclusione; in esso infatti vengono citati studi che potrebbero attestare un'implicazione del genere. La conclusione coerente è la possibilità, espressa appunto dall'alternativa in questione, di un legame tra videogiochi e violenza.

9) E. La richiesta del quesito è di individuare quale delle cinque alternative contenga l'affermazione che meglio mostra il difetto nell'argomentazione. Nel brano si parla delle difficoltà di attenzione che derivano dall'uso costante del cellulare. La conclusione cui giunge il testo è che per essere efficienti sul posto di lavoro bisogna spegnere i dispositivi di comunicazione. Analizziamo di seguito le cinque alternative per identificare quella che esprime l'errore su cui poggia il ragionamento.
Le tre alternative seguenti esprimono concetti non collegati o direttamente collegabili a quelli dai quali dipende il passaggio dalle premesse alla conclusione, pertanto vanno scartate:
– "*It may only be the younger workers who use mobile phone technology to excess*". In nessun punto del brano si parla di lavoratori più giovani;
– "*In many work environments you may not be allowed to use personal mobile phones*". Dato un fatto del genere, il ragionamento resta comunque valido rispetto a quei luoghi di lavoro in cui l'uso del cellulare personale è permesso;
– "*People may be unwilling to make less use of their mobile phones*". Nel testo non è in questione la volontà delle persone, ma solo l'opportunità di ridurre l'uso del cellulare.
Considerando ora la risposta "*We may need to have some 'down time' in order to recharge our mental batteries*". Dati i problemi di relazione con gli altri derivanti dall'uso del cellulare, la conclusione afferma che bisogna spegnere i dispositivi di comunicazione per lavorare efficacemente sul luogo di lavoro. Tuttavia, l'eventualità che l'uso del cellulare

sia un modo per rilassare la mente e, implicitamente, per essere più efficaci sul lavoro, renderebbe meno corretta la conclusione. Dunque questa alternativa potrebbe indicare un difetto del ragionamento. Tuttavia, il quesito chiede di individuare l'affermazione che lo esprime meglio e ciò avviene nel caso della restante opzione di risposta. Infine, analizziamo l'alternativa "*Without the means to send and receive information instantly, our effectiveness may be compromised*". Il brano giunge alla conclusione che nei luoghi di lavoro bisogna spegnere i dispositivi di comunicazione perché il loro uso pregiudica l'attenzione e quindi l'efficienza. L'alternativa presa in considerazione, però, mette in evidenza una carenza in questo ragionamento: essa sottintende l'utilità a lavoro dell'uso di dispositivi per inviare e ricevere informazioni in tempo reale. Spegnendo i dispositivi di comunicazione, infatti, la disattenzione potrebbe essere ridotta, ma non si avrebbero più i mezzi per comunicare in tempo reale, per cui l'efficacia lavorativa potrebbe essere compromessa piuttosto che garantita. È chiaro che, collegandosi esplicitamente alle idee di comunicazione e di efficacia presenti nelle premesse e nella conclusione del brano, l'alternativa in questione è quella che coglie meglio il difetto del ragionamento.

10) C. Per identificare quale delle cinque alternative esprime meglio la conclusione, bisogna innanzitutto individuare quest'ultima. La ricerca è agevolata dal fatto che la conclusione appare dopo le due premesse da cui deriva, come mostrato di seguito:
Prima premessa: "*If the media give publicity to certain types of crime, it may encourage criminals to carry out "copy cat" offences*".
Seconda premessa: "*If, however, they were forbidden to divulge details of crimes, this would amount to censorship. The freedom of speech of the media is too important to sacrifice*".
Conclusione: "*so the media should be free to report crime even if this means some crimes are committed which would not otherwise be committed*".
Passando in rassegna le cinque alternative è evidente che l'unica a riportare la conclusione principale del ragionamento è la seguente: "*The media should be permitted to report crimes even if other crimes sometimes result from this reporting*".
Le altre alternative esprimono concetti contenuti nelle premesse ("*Freedom of speech is a right that is too important to give up*"; "*Publicity about crimes can encourage others to commit similar offences*") o che non sono coerenti con quanto asserito nel testo ("*Censorship of the media would reduce the crime rate*"; "*The media should not report all the details of a crime*").

11) E. Quattro delle cinque alternative di risposta presentano affermazioni che non sono asserite esplicitamente nel ragionamento della traccia, ma che sono assunte come supposizioni implicite di tale ragionamento. Per individuare l'unica a non essere una di esse, come richiede il quesito, si procede con l'analisi delle singole risposte:
– "*There is nothing else in nicotine patches and chewing gum which might cause an increase in the rate of blood flow*"; "*Carbon monoxide is not absorbed from nicotine patches and nicotine chewing gum*". Entrambe queste alternative rappresentano delle assunzioni implicite del ragionamento. Infatti, se esse non fossero vere, i test di cui si parla nel brano non potrebbero costituire una base significativa per concludere che la nicotina, come il monossido di carbonio, è anch'essa responsabile di un aumento del flusso sanguigno e dei connessi rischi cardiaci tra i fumatori;

– "*The effect of nicotine on the body does not depend on the way in which it was absorbed*". Questo è un chiaro presupposto del ragionamento che giunge alla conclusione sugli effetti della nicotina in cui si considerano due forme di assorbimento di tale sostanza: "*in the lungs*" e "*through the skin*";
– "*Any differences between the amount of nicotine absorbed from smoking and the amount absorbed from nicotine patches and chewing gum can be disregarded*". Se ciò non fosse vero, gli effetti della nicotina contenuta nei cerotti e nelle gomme da masticare, evidenziati dai test, non sarebbero un termine di confronto sufficiente per trarre la conclusione sugli effetti della stessa sostanza presente nelle sigarette.
L'unica alternativa che non costituisce una supposizione del ragionamento è la seguente "*Carbon monoxide would not produce a rise in the rate of blood flow in the absence of nicotine*". Infatti, essa è in contrasto con quanto asserito nel brano stesso, ossia "*It was thought that this speeding up of blood flow was caused solely by the gas carbon monoxide*".

12) A. La domanda chiede di identificare quale delle cinque alternative di risposta riporti l'affermazione che, se fosse aggiunta alle premesse dell'argomentazione, ne indebolirebbe la conclusione. Il tema di tutto il ragionamento è la dissuasione dal fumo e l'utilizzo, a tale scopo, in molti paesi di immagini scioccanti degli effetti del fumo sui pacchetti delle sigarette. Posto che tali immagini possono avere un effetto dissuasivo, è tratta la conclusione circa l'opportunità che tutti i paesi dovrebbero adottare lo stesso metodo per scoraggiare le persone dal fumo. Analizzando le alternative, l'unica corretta è la seguente: "*In countries using the images there are high taxes on tobacco and a ban on advertising*". Infatti, se fosse vero che nei paesi in cui si usano le immagini scioccanti sui pacchetti di sigarette vi sono tasse alte sul tabacco e il divieto di pubblicità, ne deriverebbe che il metodo delle immagini non sarebbe l'unica forma di dissuasione e di conseguenza ciò andrebbe a indebolire la conclusione per la quale invece tale metodo dovrebbe essere adottato da tutti i paesi.

13) A. Per giungere alla soluzione del quesito, bisogna innanzitutto calcolare come il costo medio per barattolo vari in base al numero dei barattoli comprati. Per fare ciò dobbiamo calcolare la media ponderata in funzione del numero dei barattoli. La formula della media ponderata è la seguente:

$$CM = \frac{2 \times 100\% + n \times 25\%}{2 + n}$$

dove *CM* è il costo medio per barattolo, 2 è il numero dei barattoli fissi e *n* è il numero dei barattoli aggiuntivi dell'offerta.
Calcoliamo *CM* in funzione di *n* nella seguente tabella:

$$n = 1 \quad \Rightarrow \quad CM = \frac{200\% + 25\%}{3} = 75\%$$

$$n = 2 \quad \Rightarrow \quad CM = \frac{200\% + 50\%}{4} = 62,5\%$$

$$n = 3 \quad \Rightarrow \quad CM = \frac{200\% + 75\%}{5} = 55\%$$

$$n = 4 \qquad \Rightarrow \qquad CM = \frac{200\% + 100\%}{6} = 50\%$$

Nei diagrammi delle cinque alternative di risposta n è rappresentato sull'asse delle ascisse e CM su quello delle ordinate. Se ora consideriamo i valori di CM ottenuti in funzione di n, possiamo osservare che il diagramma A rappresenta tali valori.

14) B. Per risolvere più facilmente il quesito, coloriamo in grigio uno dei due pezzi in cui si è rotto il logo di plastica della compagnia:

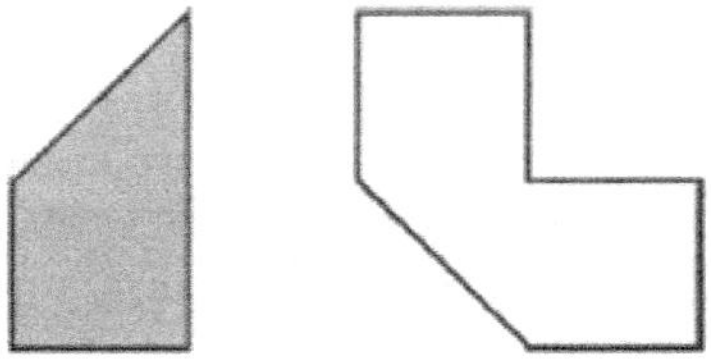

Adesso associamo i due pezzi in modo da riprodurre le figure rappresentate nelle cinque alternative di risposta. Così facendo, possiamo ottenere le quattro figure seguenti:

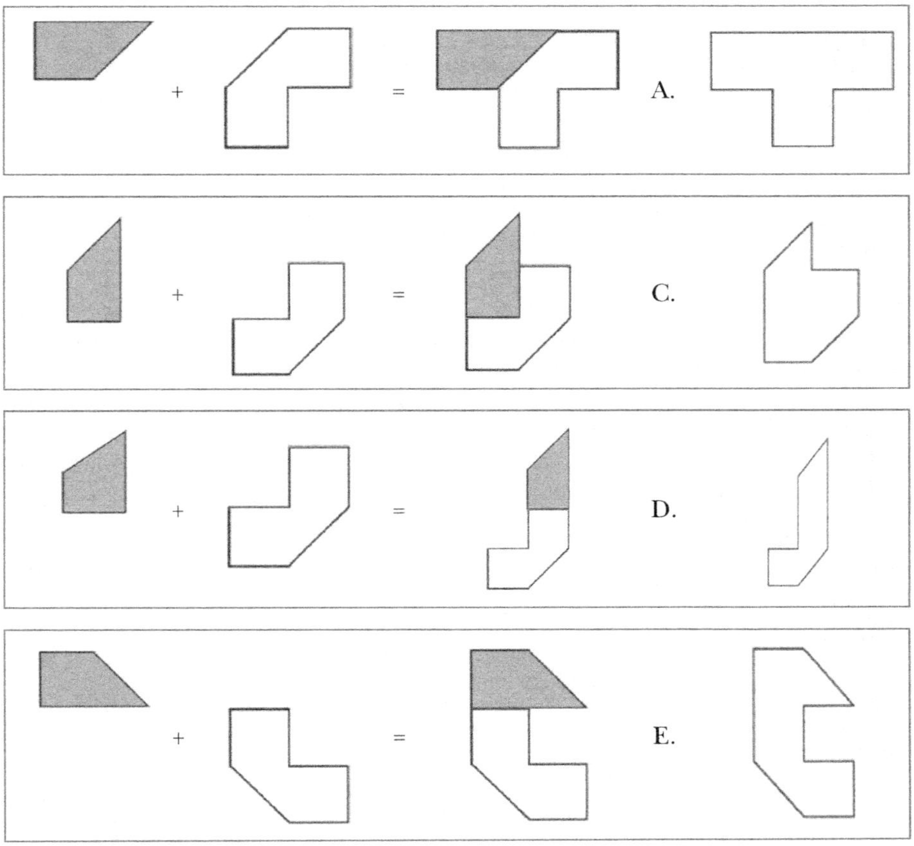

È chiaro che la figura B non corrisponde a nessuna delle possibili associazioni dei due pezzi. Ciò significa che essa non può essere il logo della compagnia.

15) C. Per risolvere il quesito, riportiamo tutti i dati forniti dalla traccia in una tabella. Per facilitare l'analisi, indichiamo i cinque giocatori con le iniziali del loro nome: Alan Vinci = A; Barry Durand = B; Carl Johansson = C; Daniel Lim = D; Eric Lim = E.
Sappiamo che ciascuno dei cinque giocatori vince almeno un round, cioè arriva al primo posto almeno una volta. Scriviamo al primo posto in ciascuno dei primi 5 round un nome diverso. Nel caso dei restanti 5 round, invece, non conosciamo il nome di chi sia arrivato primo.
Nella traccia si dice che al secondo posto in tutti i round arrivano sempre B o D o E. Scriviamo "B o D o E" in tutti i casi. Tuttavia, è chiaro che quando B arriva primo (nella nostra tabella nel round 2), egli non può essere arrivato anche secondo. Perciò, cancelliamo B nel secondo posto del round 2. Ragioniamo analogamente per D ed E rispettivamente nei round 4 e 5.
Sappiamo ancora che i due fratelli, cioè D ed E, non ottengono mai punti nello stesso round. Questo vuol dire che nel round 4 dovremo cancellare anche E, poiché D è arrivato primo, e nel round 5 dovremo cancellare anche D, poiché E è arrivato primo.

ROUND / POSTI PUNTI	1	2	3	4	5	6	7	8	9	10
I posto 3 punti	A	B	C	D	E	?	?	?	?	?
II posto 1 punto	B o D o E	B o D o E	B o D o E	B o D o E	B o D o E	B o D o E	B o D o E	B o D o E	B o D o E	B o D o E

Infine, sappiamo che l'ordine dei giocatori che arrivano al primo e al secondo posto è sempre diverso in ogni round. Considerando questa informazione, possiamo concludere che, ad esempio, se nel round 1 A arriva primo e B secondo, tale combinazione non si presenterà più negli altri round. Se ora calcoliamo in questo modo tutte le possibili combinazioni diverse di giocatori al I e II posto, otteniamo il quadro dei risultati di ogni round:

ROUND / POSTI PUNTI	1	2	3	4	5	6	7	8	9	10
I posto 3 punti	A	B	C	D	E	A	A	B	C	C
II posto 1 punto	B o D o E	B o D o E	B o D o E	B o D o E	B o D o E	B o D o E	B o D o E	B o D o E	B o D o E	B o D o E

Calcoliamo il punteggio ottenuto da ogni giocatore:
A = 9; B = 10; C = 9; D = 6; E = 6.
Pertanto il giocatore che ottiene il punteggio più alto nei dieci round è Barry Durand.

16) C. I volumi indicati devono essere intesi come barattoli interi, cioè abbiamo barattoli da 375 ml, da 750 ml, ecc. Per questo motivo dobbiamo ragionare in numero di barattoli e determinare il numero necessario per dipingere le 20 stanze e il cui costo totale è minimo. Escludiamo subito il terzo tipo di pittura, Quick Dry Gloss, di cui non conosciamo tutti i dati ('N/A' significa «non disponibile»). Analizziamo quindi i restanti tre tipi di pittura:

Non Drip Gloss
– Volume necessario per le 20 stanze = 1,4 *l* × 20 stanze = 28 *l* – Numero e tipo dei barattoli dal costo totale minimo: 11 barattoli da 2,5 *l* + 1 barattolo da 750 *ml* – Costo totale per dipingere le 20 stanze: 11 barattoli × 16 € + 1 barattolo × 8 € = 184 €
Satinwood
– Volume necessario per le 20 stanze = 1,1 *l* × 20 stanze = 22 *l* – Numero e tipo dei barattoli dal costo totale minimo: 9 barattoli da 2,5 *l* – Costo totale per dipingere le 20 stanze: 9 barattoli × 20 € = 180 €
Once Gloss
– Volume necessario per le 20 stanze = 0,8 *l* × 20 stanze = 16 *l* – Numero e tipo dei barattoli dal costo totale minimo: 6 barattoli da 2,5 *l* + 1 barattolo da 1,25 *l* – Costo totale per dipingere le 20 stanze: 6 barattoli × 18 € + 1 barattolo × 12 € = 120 €

Il prezzo più basso, dunque, si ha con l'ultimo tipo di pittura, Once Gloss.

17) A. Per risolvere il quesito prendiamo innanzitutto il

pezzo in questione.

27	**26**	
16	**17**	**18**
	12	

Poiché l'ordine dei numeri nella riga centrale è crescente da sinistra verso destra (16 → 17 → 18) e poiché sappiamo che l'ordine si inverte ad ogni riga, l'ordine dei numeri nella riga con il 12 e quello nella riga con il 26 e il 27 deve essere crescente da destra verso sinistra. Su tale base inseriamo i numeri mancanti immediatamente a sinistra e a destra del riquadro con il 12 e a destra del riquadro con il 26.

← **27**	**26**	**25**
16	**17**	**18** →
← **13**	**12**	**11**

Poiché solo i numeri 14 e 15 separano il 13 e il 16, ciò significa che a sinistra del 13 vi sarà solo un riquadro con il 14, mentre a sinistra del 16 vi sarà solo un riquadro con il 15. Poiché il 18 e il 25 sono separati dai numeri 19, 20, 21, 22, 23 e 24, ciò significa che a destra del 18 vi saranno tre riquadri, rispettivamente con il 19, il 20 e il 21, mentre a destra del 25 vi saranno altri tre riquadri, rispettivamente con il 22, il 23 e il 24.

	27	26	25	24	23	22
15	16	17	18	19	20	21
14	13	12	11			

Guardando la figura ottenuta al punto 3 e contando i riquadri della riga centrale (15 → 16 → 17 → 18 → 19 → 20 → 21), capiamo che la larghezza del tabellone di gioco è costituita da 7 riquadri. Poiché il tabellone è un quadrato, ciò significa che anche la sua altezza sarà composta da 7 riquadri.
Pertanto, in base all'esame appena compiuto è possibile concludere che il tabellone di gioco è composto da 7 × 7 = 49 riquadri.

43	44	45	46	47	48	49
42	41	40	39	38	37	36
29	30	31	32	33	34	35
28	27	26	25	24	23	22
15	16	17	18	19	20	21
14	13	12	11	10	9	8
1	2	3	4	5	6	7

18) E. Per produrre una sola collana di vetro in stile italiano, Sally deve spendere:
- 1,50 € in materiali;
- 2,7 € per il suo staff, poiché quest'ultimo riceve 5,4 € per un'ora di lavoro e per produrre la collana ci vogliono 30 minuti.

In totale la produzione della collana costa 1,50 € + 2,7 € = 4,2 €.
Poiché Sally fa pagare la collana il 70 % in più di quanto è costato produrla, il prezzo di una singola collana sarà pari alla somma di quanto è costata la produzione di un singolo pezzo, cioè 4,2 €, e del 70 % di 4,2 €, cioè 2,94 €. Dunque, il prezzo di una singola collana sarà: 4,2 € + 2,94 € = 7,14 €.

19) E. Per rendere più facile la risoluzione del problema, coloriamo le due aiuole rotonde in questo modo:

Dalla mappa appena colorata non possiamo sapere quali siano le rispettive altezze di tutte le aiuole. Tuttavia, è chiaro che, quali che siano le altezze relative, guardando dalla sedia dovremo sempre vedere le due aiuole colorate.

Ora passiamo al vaglio le figure riportate nelle cinque alternative di risposta e vediamo se le due aiuole colorate appaiono sempre.

Nella figura A vediamo le due aiuole:

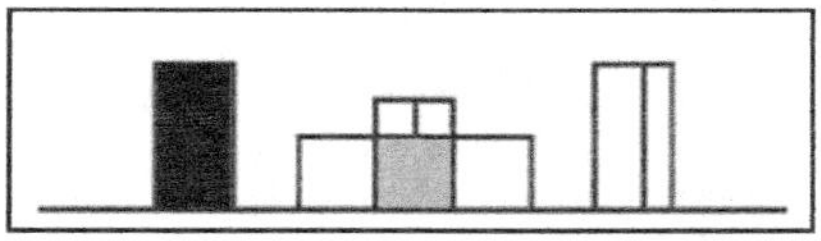

Nella figura B vediamo le due aiuole:

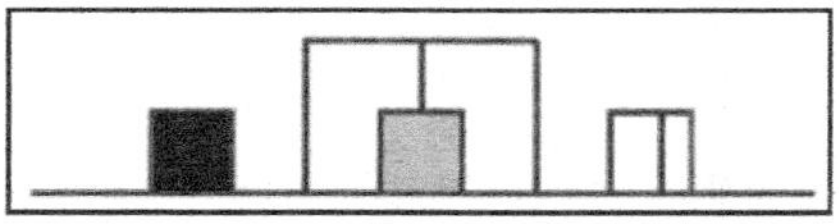

Nella figura C vediamo le due aiuole:

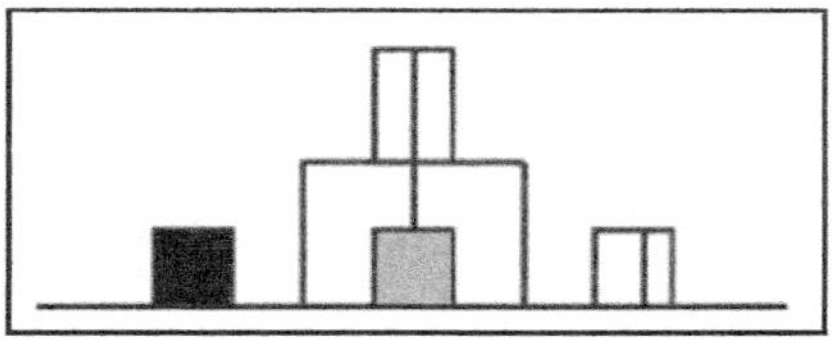

Nella figura D vediamo le due aiuole:

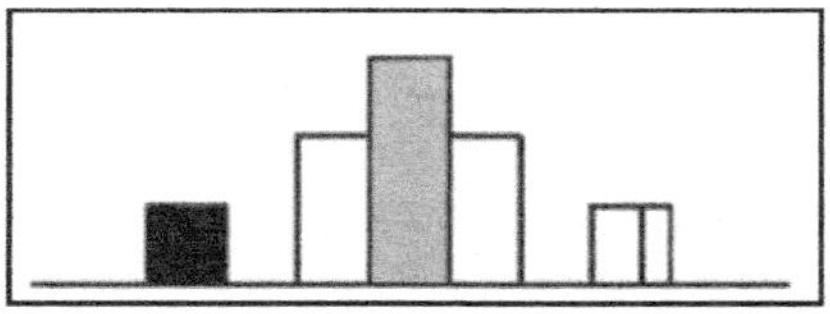

Nella figura E non vediamo l'aiuola grigia:

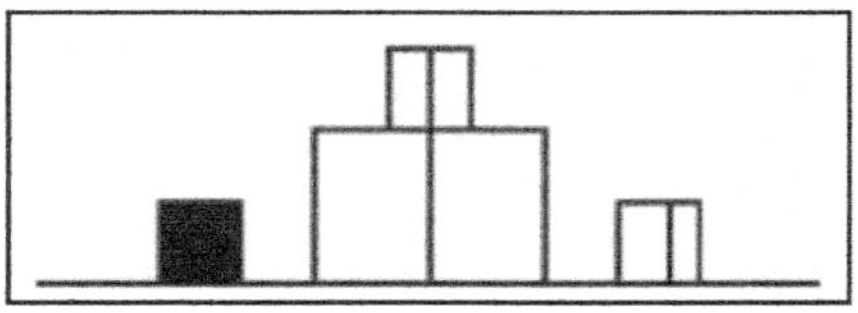

Basandoci sull'analisi appena realizzata, concludiamo che la figura E non può essere una delle possibili visuali delle aiuole guardando dalla sedia.

20) B. Indichiamo con 'D' la distanza tra Starton e Endham che Karl percorre in 10 giorni. Riportiamo i dati forniti dalla traccia nella seguente tabella.

Giorni	Strada percorsa		
1	12 km	$^{1}/_{2}$ D	$^{3}/_{4}$ D — Poiché nei primi 8 giorni Karl percorre i tre quarti di D, chiaramente nei due giorni rimanenti egli deve percorrere ancora un quarto di D
2	45 km		
3	45 km		
4	45 km		
5	?		
6	?		
7	41 km		
8	411 km		
9	$^{3}/_{20}$ D	Poiché il nono giorno Karl percorre i tre quinti della DISTANZA CHE ANCORA GLI RESTA DA PERCORRERE, cioè un quarto di D, in questo giorno egli percorre: $^{3}/_{5}D \cdot {}^{1}/_{4}D = {}^{3}/_{20}D$	
10	$36\,Km = D - {}^{3}/_{4}\,D - {}^{3}/_{20}D$	Sappiamo che il decimo giorno Karl percorre 36 km e che questi corrispondono esattamente alla distanza che ancora gli resta da percorrere, cioè la distanza totale D meno la distanza percorsa nei primi 8 giorni $({}^{3}/_{4}D)$ e meno la distanza percorsa il nono giorno $({}^{3}/_{20}D)$	

Ora svolgiamo l'equazione: $D - {}^{3}/_{4}\,D - {}^{3}/_{20}D = 36\,Km$. Dal calcolo, dunque, risulta che la distanza è di 360 Km.

21) A. Innanzitutto per risolvere il quesito bisogna immaginare di ripiegare la figura della traccia in modo da formare un tetraedro con le immagini nere del cerchio, del quadrato e del triangolo visibili all'esterno. A tale scopo immaginiamo di lasciare il triangolo bianco fermo in alto e di muovere verso il basso gli altri tre triangoli, quelli con le immagini nere.

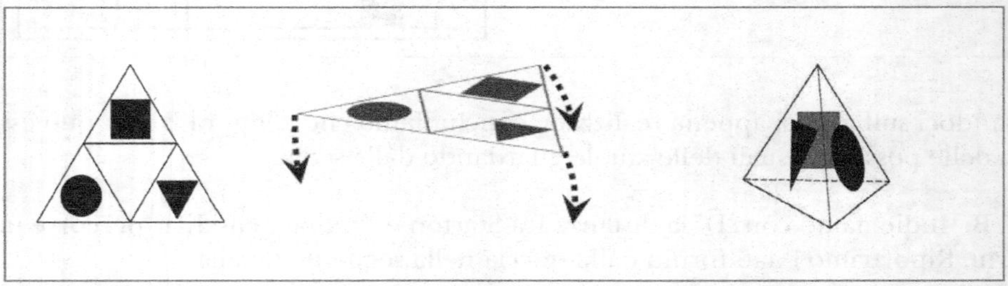

Ora immaginiamo di ripiegare ciascuna delle figure riportate nelle cinque alternative in modo da formare un tetraedro secondo gli stessi criteri della traccia. Così facendo, osserviamo che solo la figura della seguente alternativa dà un tetraedro identico a quello della traccia.

A. 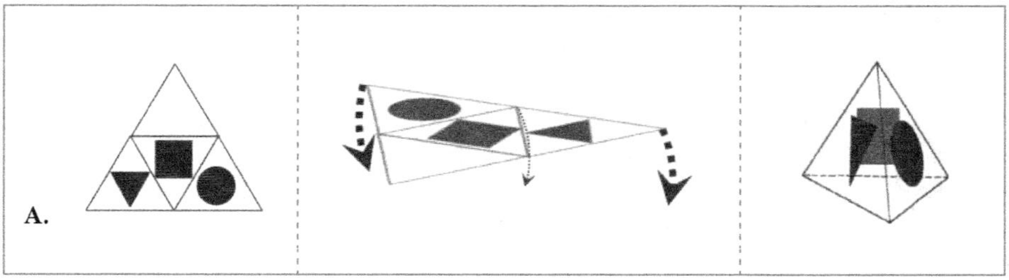

22) C. Se la scorsa settimana Tessa ha guadagnato 515 $ in totale, ciò significa che ha guadagnato un bonus pari a: 515 $ - 320 $ = 195 $. Poiché il bonus è di 3 $ a braccialetto (simbolo 'B') per ogni braccialetto extra – cioè per ogni braccialetto che in una data giornata sia fabbricato dopo averne già realizzati 175 –, il bonus dipende dalla produzione di 195 $: 3 $ = 65B extra.
Se venerdì Tessa ha fabbricato 205B, ciò significa che in quella giornata ha prodotto 205B – 175B = 30B extra. Perciò, nelle altre giornate lavorative della scorsa settimana Tessa deve aver prodotto 65B extra – 30B extra = 35B extra.
Tuttavia, sappiamo anche che 205 è il numero massimo di braccialetti prodotti da Tessa in una giornata lavorativa della scorsa settimana. Ciò significa che in nessuna delle altre giornate di quella settimana (lunedì, martedì, mercoledì e giovedì) Tessa può avere prodotto più di 205B. A sua volta questo significa che i restanti 35B extra non possono essere stati tutti prodotti in una sola delle altre quattro giornate, perché altrimenti in quest'unica giornata Tessa avrebbe prodotto 175B + 35B extra = 210B, numero superiore al livello massimo di 205B giornalieri. Dobbiamo quindi concludere che i 35B extra devono essere stati fabbricati in almeno altre due giornate lavorative X e Y, chiaramente dopo che in ciascuna delle due è stato superato il numero di 175B.
Alla luce di quest'analisi possiamo dire che il numero minimo di braccialetti prodotti da Tessa la scorsa settimana è dato sommando i seguenti dati:

Braccialetti fabbricati venerdì	175B + 30B extra =	205B
Braccialetti fabbricati nelle due giornate lavorative X e Y	175B + 175B + 35B extra =	385B
Braccialetti fabbricati nelle restanti due giornate lavorative	150B + 150B =	300B
	TOTALE:	890B

23) C. Ricordando che in totale le corse della maratona della traccia sono 8, esaminiamo le cinque alternative di risposta:
– **5 CORSE VINTE**. Se avesse vinto 5 corse, Philip avrebbe ottenuto 5 × 11 = 55 punti. A questi bisogna aggiungere i punti ottenuti nelle restanti 3 corse, poiché sappiamo che in ogni corsa Philip si è classificato tra i primi 3. A questo proposito basta considerare l'ipotesi peggiore, cioè che Philip sia arrivato terzo in ciascuna delle restanti 3 corse, per un totale di 3 × 6 = 18 punti. Infatti, già ammettendo l'ipotesi peggiore di 3 terzi posti, nel complesso delle 8 gare Philip avrebbe ottenuto 55 + 18 = 73 punti, cioè un punteggio superiore ai 61 punti da lui effettivamente ottenuti. Questo caso è da scartare;

– **4 CORSE VINTE**. Ragioniamo in modo analogo al caso precedente. Se avesse vinto 4 corse, Philip avrebbe ottenuto $4 \times 11 = 44$ punti. Considerando di nuovo l'ipotesi peggiore di 4 terzi posti nelle restanti 4 corse – per un totale di $4 \times 6 = 24$ punti – nell'insieme delle 8 gare Philip avrebbe ottenuto $44 + 24 = 68$ punti, cioè un punteggio superiore a 61 punti. Anche questo caso è da scartare;
– **3 CORSE VINTE**. Ragioniamo ancora in modo analogo ai due casi precedenti. Se avesse vinto 3 corse, Philip avrebbe ottenuto $3 \times 11 = 33$ punti. Considerando ancora l'ipotesi peggiore di 5 terzi posti nelle restanti 5 corse – per un totale di $5 \times 6 = 30$ punti –, nell'insieme delle 8 gare Philip avrebbe ottenuto $33 + 30 = 63$ punti, cioè un punteggio superiore a 61 punti. Dobbiamo scartare pure questo caso;
– **2 CORSE VINTE**. In questo caso dobbiamo seguire un ragionamento un po' diverso da quello fatto nei tre casi precedenti. Se avesse vinto 2 corse, Philip avrebbe ottenuto $2 \times 11 = 22$ punti. Indipendentemente da quante volte fosse arrivato secondo e quante terzo nelle restanti 6 gare, comunque in queste 6 corse Philip avrebbe ottenuto un numero pari di punti. Infatti, 8 punti per il secondo posto in x gare e 6 punti per il terzo posto in y gare danno insieme un punteggio pari. Sommando questo punteggio ai 22 punti delle 2 gare vinte, avremmo ancora un punteggio pari, che non corrisponde al punteggio dispari di 61 punti di Philip. Si tratta di un altro caso da scartare;
– **1 CORSA VINTA**. Se Philip avesse vinto 1 corsa, avrebbe ottenuto 11 punti. Arrivando secondo in altre 4 corse e terzo nelle restanti 3, avrebbe ricevuto $(4 \times 8) + (3 \times 6) = 50$ punti. Sommando questi 50 punti con gli 11 della sua unica vittoria, Philip avrebbe conquistato 61 punti, cifra corrispondente al punteggio da lui realmente ottenuto.

24) A. Il medico inglese William Harvey, vissuto tra il XVI e il XVII secolo, è stato il primo scienziato a descrivere in maniera accurata il sistema circolatorio umano. Nel suo trattato *Exercitatio anatomica de motu cordis et sanguinis in animalibus* (1628), infatti, Harvey descrisse il cuore come un muscolo che funziona come una pompa, emettendo sangue quando si contrae.

25) E. Nel febbraio del 2004 il diciannovenne Mark Zuckerberg, studente di Harvard, diede vita a Facebook, social network ad accesso gratuito, il cui nome rimanda agli annuari con le foto di ogni singolo soggetto (*facebook* in inglese) che alcuni college americani mettono a disposizione dei nuovi studenti e del personale, come mezzo per conoscere le persone del campus. Il sito di *e-commerce* eBay è stato fondato nel 1995 da Pierre Omidyar mentre l'enciclopedia online Wikipedia nel 2001 da Jimmy Wales e Larry Sanger. Infine, YouTube, piattaforma web che consente la condivisione e visualizzazione in rete di video, è stata fondata nel 2005 da Chad Hurley, Steve Chen e Jawed Karim, mentre il sito di microblogging, Twitter, è stato creato da Jack Dorsey nel 2006.

26) D. L'Impressionismo prende il nome da un quadro di Claude Monet dal titolo *Impression: soleil lèvant* (*Impressione al sorgere del Sole*). Questa definizione, accolta dagli stessi impressionisti, descrive pienamente il modo di dipingere di questo gruppo di artisti che operò in Francia dal 1860 fino agli inizi del 1900. Il loro intento era di riportare sulla tela, con maggiore fedeltà possibile, la realtà così come si presentava ai loro occhi (paesaggi naturali, paesaggi urbani, ritratti), per macchie di colore, con le ombre colorate e senza linee di contorno. Abbandonando la tradizionale pratica dell'atelier, che prevedeva che il pittore rielaborasse in studio gli schizzi presi dal vero, gli impressionisti cominciarono a dipingere il paesaggio *en plein air*. Tra i massimi esponenti del movimento insieme a Monet, è Pierre-Auguste Renoir le cui opere ritraggono frammenti di vita colti nell'atto di svolgersi.

27) C. L'Organizzazione dei Paesi produttori di petrolio (OPEC) è stata fondata nel 1960 e raggruppa i maggiori paesi che producono petrolio e che hanno nella sua esportazione la loro maggiore fonte di entrate economiche. Il fine dell'OPEC è di coordinare e limitare la produzione di petrolio da parte dei paesi membri controllando così l'offerta e dunque il prezzo del greggio sui mercati internazionali.

Biologia

28) A. Il reticolo endoplasmatico (RE) è un organello delle cellule eucariotiche costituito da un reticolo di sacculi delimitati da membrane. Il reticolo endoplasmatico ruvido (RER) è così denominato per la presenza di ribosomi adesi alla sua superficie esterna, caratteristica che lo differenzia dal reticolo endoplasmatico liscio (REL), che invece non presenta ribosomi. La presenza dei ribosomi sul RER è dovuta al fatto che questo organello è deputato alla sintesi delle proteine destinate alla secrezione, alla membrana plasmatica o ad altri organelli. Pertanto, la struttura 1 in questa sezione rappresenta un ribosoma, a livello del quale avviene la sintesi proteica con l'intervento dei tRNA, mentre la struttura 2 è il lume del reticolo, che contiene i polipeptidi sintetizzati a livello dei ribosomi e penetrati nel lume del RER.

29) E. Durante la profase della prima divisione meiotica, i due cromosomi omologhi di ogni coppia, ciascuno duplicato e perciò costituito da due cromatidi fratelli, si appaiano, formando le cosiddette tetradi. A seguito dell'appaiamento, due cromatidi non fratelli possono scambiarsi materiale genetico attraverso il processo di crossing over, producendo cromatidi ricombinanti. Nel caso illustrato, solo due dei quattro cromatidi sono interessati dal crossing over, che comporta lo scambio degli alleli *a* e *A*, pertanto i cromosomi figli ricombinanti saranno due. Poiché questi avranno una combinazione di alleli differente da quella dei cromatidi che non hanno subito crossing over, i quattro cromosomi figli saranno tutti diversi nella loro costituzione genetica.

30) D. Il grafico della velocità iniziale di una reazione catalizzata da un enzima in funzione della concentrazione del substrato è un'iperbole rettangolare che si avvicina asintoticamente alla velocità massima per una determinata concentrazione di enzima. La velocità iniziale della reazione aumenta all'aumentare della concentrazione di substrato, ma a concentrazioni elevate di substrato la velocità non aumenta ulteriormente, in quanto le molecole di enzima sono saturate dal substrato. In presenza di un inibitore competitivo, che compete con il substrato per il legame con l'enzima, la velocità iniziale della reazione risulta diminuita per basse concentrazioni di substrato, mentre arriva ad eguagliare quella della reazione in assenza di inibitore per concentrazioni elevate di substrato.

31) D. La membrana cellulare è costituita da un doppio strato fosfolipidico in cui sono immerse le proteine. Il doppio strato fosfolipidico si comporta come un cristallo liquido, un fluido bidimensionale in cui le molecole possono muoversi lateralmente all'interno di uno strato. I fosfolipidi sono formati da una testa polare rivolta verso l'esterno del doppio strato e da code apolari di acidi grassi rivolte verso l'interno del doppio strato. Gli acidi grassi insaturi (contenenti doppi legami C=C) solidificano a temperature più basse rispetto a quelli saturi (contenenti solo legami semplici C–C), in quanto i doppi legami C=C determinano la formazione di ripiegamenti nelle molecole lipidiche che impediscono alle catene idrocarburiche di avvicinarsi e interagire mediante le forze di van der Waals. Pertanto, alle basse temperature, la fluidità delle membrane può essere preservata attraverso l'aumento dei doppi legami C=C nelle catene degli acidi grassi, ovvero attraverso l'aumento del loro grado di insaturazione.

32) A. La trasmissione dell'impulso nervoso a livello sinaptico è un processo unidirezionale diretto da un neurone presinaptico a una cellula postsinaptica. All'arrivo di un potenziale d'azione, la membrana presinaptica si depolarizza; ciò determina l'esocitosi del neurotrasmettitore dal neurone presinaptico nella fessura sinaptica. Il neurotrasmettitore rilasciato attraversa la fessura sinaptica e si lega a recettori presenti sulla membrana postsinaptica, determinando una risposta nella cellula postsinaptica. Se tali recettori sono canali del sodio ligando-dipendenti, il loro legame con il neurotrasmettitore ne causa l'apertura, aumentando la permeabilità agli ioni Na^+, con conseguente depolarizzazione della membrana postsinaptica e genesi di un potenziale postsinaptico. Il neurotrasmettitore presente nella fessura sinaptica viene poi idrolizzato ad opera di enzimi idrolitici, ma questo processo non ha alcuna correlazione con la unidirezionalità della trasmissione dell'impulso nervoso.

33) E. Il pancreas è una ghiandola che ha funzioni sia esocrine che endocrine. Il pancreas endocrino è formato da gruppi di cellule chiamati isolotti di Langerhans, responsabili della produzione dei due ormoni principalmente coinvolti nella regolazione della concentrazione plasmatica di glucosio (glicemia): l'insulina, prodotta dalle cellule beta, e il glucagone, prodotto dalle cellule alfa. Il glucosio ha un effetto diretto sulle cellule beta del pancreas, per cui un aumento della glicemia determina un incremento della produzione di insulina, mentre una sua diminuzione determina un decremento della produzione di insulina. La produzione di glucagone subisce una regolazione opposta a quella della produzione di insulina, per cui aumenta all'abbassarsi della glicemia e diminuisce all'innalzarsi della glicemia.

34) B. Le valvole semilunari sono valvole cardiache poste tra i ventricoli e le arterie: la valvola aortica è collocata tra il ventricolo sinistro e l'aorta, la valvola polmonare tra il ventricolo destro e l'arteria polmonare. La presenza di tali valvole serve a garantire l'unidirezionalità del flusso sanguigno dai ventricoli alle arterie, impedendo il reflusso di sangue in senso inverso. Le valvole semilunari si aprono quando la pressione ventricolare supera quella arteriosa a valle. Pertanto, la valvola polmonare si apre quando la pressione ematica nel ventricolo destro supera la pressione ematica nell'arteria polmonare.

35) C. Il metabolismo del glucosio (zucchero a sei atomi di carbonio) per la produzione di energia chimica in forma di ATP inizia con la sua scissione in due molecole di piruvato (a tre atomi di carbonio) attraverso una via metabolica chiamata glicolisi, costituita da dieci reazioni catalizzate da enzimi che si svolgono nel citosol. In presenza di ossigeno, il piruvato viene ossidato completamente ad anidride carbonica e acqua attraverso il ciclo di Krebs e la fosforilazione ossidativa all'interno dei mitocondri. In condizioni di scarsa disponibilità di ossigeno, nelle cellule animali il piruvato funge da substrato nel processo di fermentazione lattica, con produzione di lattato, mentre nelle cellule di lievito va incontro al processo di fermentazione alcolica, con produzione di etanolo.

36) B. L'allele che determina la condizione in esame è associato al cromosoma X. Infatti, essendo recessivo, se fosse associato al cromosoma Y, la condizione dovrebbe manifestarsi anche nel marito della donna 5. Quest'ultima, avendo trasmesso al figlio l'allele in esame, deve essere una portatrice eterozigote, per cui possiede certamente l'allele (probabilità del 100%). L'allele è stato trasmesso alla donna 5 dalla madre (individuo 1), che pertanto è certamente una portatrice eterozigote (probabilità del 100%). Gli individui 2 e 4 non posseggono l'allele (0%), in quanto non manifestano il carattere. L'individuo 3 ha il 50% di probabilità di aver ereditato l'allele in questione dalla madre.

37) E. Il virus dell'immunodeficienza umana (HIV), agente eziologico della sindrome dell'immunodeficienza acquisita (AIDS), è un retrovirus. Esso penetra nei linfociti T CD4+ a seguito della fusione tra il proprio involucro fosfolipidico e la membrana plasmatica del linfocita. All'interno della cellula umana, il genoma del virus, costituito da due copie di RNA a singolo filamento, viene retrotrascritto in cDNA a doppio filamento dall'enzima virale trascrittasi inversa, una DNA polimerasi RNA-dipendente. Il cDNA si integra nel genoma della cellula ospite e viene trascritto insieme ad esso, con produzione dell'RNA virale, il quale dirige la sintesi delle proteine virali e fornisce anche l'RNA genomico per l'assemblaggio delle nuove particelle virali, che fuoriescono dalla cellula per gemmazione attraverso la membrana plasmatica del linfocita.

38) D. Gli enzimi di restrizione sono enzimi batterici che tagliano il DNA a doppio filamento in siti di riconoscimento con sequenze specifiche. Partendo da un'ipotetica posizione 0, l'enzima di restrizione taglia il DNA plasmidico a livello di siti che distano 150 bp (sito 1), 250 bp (sito 2) e 950 bp (sito 3) dalla posizione 0. Pertanto, i tagli in 1 e in 2 rilasciano un frammento di 100 bp (250 – 150), i tagli in 2 e in 3 rilasciano un frammento di 700 bp (950 – 250) e i tagli in 3 e in 1 rilasciano un frammento di 200 bp (1000 – 950 + 150).

39) A. Le proteine sintetizzate nel reticolo endoplasmatico ruvido (RER), ossia quelle destinate alla secrezione, alla membrana plasmatica o ad altri organelli, vengono trasferite ai compartimenti di destinazione da vescicole di trasporto che gemmano dalla membrana del RER. Le proteine sintetizzate nel RER che devono subire modificazioni nel complesso del Golgi vengono trasportate alla superficie *cis* di quest'ultimo da vescicole di trasporto; il trasferimento tra le varie cisterne del Golgi avviene sempre all'interno di vescicole; infine, le proteine modificate nel Golgi vengono inserite in vescicole che gemmano dalla sua superficie *trans* per essere trasportate nei compartimenti di destinazione. La membrana cellulare produce vescicole che si liberano all'interno della cellula nel processo di endocitosi e all'esterno della cellula nel processo di gemmazione.

40) C. La RuBisCo (ribulosio bisfosfato carbossilasi/ossigenasi) è un enzima tipico delle cellule vegetali che catalizza la prima reazione del ciclo di Calvin, ossia la reazione tra anidride carbonica e ribulosio bisfosfato con produzione di fosfoglicerato (fissazione del carbonio). La penicillina è un antibiotico che interferisce con la sintesi del peptidoglicano, un polimero complesso che costituisce la parete cellulare dei batteri. I plasmidi sono tipici dei procarioti, i quali non contengono alcun organello cellulare (centrioli, SER, nucleolo). Il glicogeno è il polisaccaride di riserva tipico degli animali, mentre nelle piante si ritrova la cellulosa.

41) D. L'mRNA trascritto da un filamento stampo di DNA presenta una sequenza di basi complementare a quella dello stampo. Le coppie di basi complementari nel DNA sono CG (citosina e guanina) e AT (adenina e timina); nell'RNA la timina (T) è sostituita dall'uracile (U). La sequenza di basi dell'mRNA complementare alla sequenza di DNA stampo indicata è GUG CAA GCG UAU CUG. Tale sequenza è riportata nella risposta GUG CAA CCG UAU CUG con una mutazione in posizione 7, dove la G è sostituita da una C.

42) E. Esistono organismi che possono mostrare sia riproduzione sessuata che asessuata. Ad esempio, nelle angiosperme la riproduzione sessuata avviene attraverso la meiosi con produzione dei gameti e la fusione tra il gamete femminile (cellula ovulo) e il gamete maschile (cellula spermatica) nel processo di fecondazione, che avviene all'interno dell'ovario del fiore. Molte angiosperme, però, mostrano anche riproduzione asessuata, un processo che non richiede la formazione di semi, fiori e frutti. La progenie ha origine da un organo vegetativo (come un fusto, una radice o una foglia) che si accresce e si separa dal resto della pianta.

Chimica

43) B. Durante la fase di scarica della pila, il PbO_2 che ricopre l'elettrodo positivo si trasforma in $PbSO_4$. Ricordiamo che la somma dei numeri di ossidazione degli atomi che costituiscono una molecola neutra deve essere uguale a zero. Il numero di ossidazione dell'ossigeno è -2, per cui in PbO_2 il numero di ossidazione del piombo è $+4$ $[+4 + (-2 \cdot 2) = 0]$; il numero di ossidazione dello zolfo è $+6$, per cui in $PbSO_4$ il numero di ossidazione del piombo è $+2$ $[+2 +6 + (-2 \cdot 4) = 0]$. Pertanto, il piombo sull'elettrodo positivo si riduce. All'elettrodo negativo, il Pb si trasforma in $PbSO_4$. Il numero di ossidazione del piombo allo stato elementare è 0, mentre in $PbSO_4$ è $+2$. Pertanto, all'elettrodo negativo il piombo si ossida.

44) C. La reazione è la seguente: $Pb(NO_3)_2 + Zn \rightarrow Pb + Zn(NO_3)_2$. Il rapporto stechiometrico tra il piombo e lo zinco che reagiscono è di 1:1, per cui il numero di moli di Pb che reagiscono è uguale al numero di moli di Zn consumate. Il numero di moli di Zn che reagiscono si ricava dal rapporto tra la massa di Zn consumata e la massa molare di Zn: mol(Zn) = 1.30 g/65.4 g mol^{-1} = 0.02 mol. Il numero di moli di Pb che reagiscono è quindi 0.02. La massa di Pb che si otterrebbe con una resa del 100% è data dal prodotto tra il numero di moli di Pb consumate e la massa molare di Pb: g(Pb) = 0.02 mol · 207.2 g mol^{-1} = 4.14 g. La resa del piombo è ricavabile dal rapporto percentuale tra la massa di Pb ottenuta e quella ottenibile con una resa del 100%: resa(Pb) = 3.31 g/4.14 g · 100% = 80%.

45) A. Secondo la teoria acido-base di Lewis, una base è una qualunque specie che può donare coppie elettroniche solitarie, mentre un acido è una qualunque specie che può accettare coppie elettroniche solitarie. In base a tale definizione, le specie acide nella tabella in esame sono le seguenti: Cl_2O_7, CO_2, HCl, H_3PO_4, NO_2, P_4O_{10}, SiO_2, SO_2; mentre quelle basiche sono: K_2O, KOH, MgO, Na_2O. La specie anfotera è Al_2O_3, che può reagire sia con gli acidi (comportandosi da base) che con le basi (comportandosi da acido).

46) E. Lo stato di ossidazione dell'etene fa riferimento allo stato di ossidazione degli atomi di carbonio che lo compongono. Poiché la somma dei numeri di ossidazione degli atomi che compongono una molecola neutra deve essere uguale a zero e poiché il numero di ossidazione dell'idrogeno è +1, i due atomi di carbonio nell'etene hanno numero di ossidazione pari a −2; infatti, $2 \cdot [-2 + (+1 \cdot 2)] = 0$. L'unico dei composti riportati in cui si riscontra una variazione del numero di ossidazione del carbonio è CH_2BrCH_2Br; infatti, essendo il numero di ossidazione di H pari a +1 e quello di Br pari a −1, il numero di ossidazione del carbonio in questo composto è uguale a −1: $2 \cdot [-1 + (+1 \cdot 2) + (-1)] = 0$. Pertanto, essendo aumentato il numero di ossidazione del carbonio, il composto risulta ossidato rispetto all'etene.

47) D. La conversione di un alcool primario in un acido carbossilico è una reazione di ossidazione, in quanto implica l'aumento del numero di atomi di ossigeno e la diminuzione del numero di atomi di idrogeno (es. $CH_3CH_2OH + O_2 \rightarrow CH_3COOH + H_2O$). La reazione tra un acido carbossilico e un alcool produce un estere (es. $CH_3COOH + CH_3OH \rightarrow CH_3COOCH_3 + H_2O$), mentre la reazione tra un acido carbossilico e l'ammoniaca produce un'ammide (es. $CH_3COOH + NH_3 \rightarrow CH_3CONH_2 + H_2O$).

48) B. La configurazione elettronica di un atomo rappresenta il riempimento degli orbitali atomici da parte degli elettroni. Il primo livello energetico (a energia più bassa) comprende un solo orbitale (1*s*), che può ospitare due elettroni. Il secondo livello energetico (a energia superiore al primo) comprende un orbitale 2*s* e tre orbitali 2*p* ($2p_x$, $2p_y$, $2p_z$) a maggiore energia, ciascuno dei quali può ospitare due elettroni. Poiché gli elettroni occupano gli orbitali secondo un ordine di energia crescente, una configurazione elettronica che termina con p^5 indica che sono stati collocati due elettroni nell'orbitale 1*s*, 2 elettroni nell'orbitale 2*s* e 5 elettroni negli orbitali 2*p*

($1s^2 2s^2 2p^5$). Pertanto, tale configurazione elettronica corrisponde a un atomo che possiede 9 elettroni.

49) A. La reazione bilanciata è la seguente: $CaCO_3 + 2\ HCl \rightarrow CaCl_2 + H_2CO_3$. Il numero di moli di carbonato di calcio che reagiscono è dato dal rapporto tra la massa e la massa molecolare relativa: $mol(CaCO_3) = 2.0\ g/100\ g\ mol^{-1} = 0.02\ mol$. Il numero di moli di HCl necessarie è: $mol(HCl) = 2 \cdot mol(CaCO_3) = 2 \cdot 0.02\ mol = 0.04\ mol$. Il volume di HCl richiesto è dato dal rapporto tra il numero di moli e la concentrazione molare: $V(HCl) = mol(HCl)/M(HCl) = 0.04\ mol/2.0\ mol \cdot L^{-1} = 0.02\ L = 20\ mL = 20\ cm^3$.

50) E. In soluzione, l'acido cloridrico si dissocia completamente (acido forte) secondo la seguente reazione: $HCl \rightarrow H^+ + Cl^-$. Poiché ciascuna molecola di HCl libera un solo protone, ovvero si tratta di un acido monoprotico, la concentrazione molare di H^+ in una soluzione di HCl è uguale alla concentrazione molare dell'acido. Pertanto, $[H^+] = 0.1\ M$ e $pH = -\log[H^+] = -\log(0.1) = -(-1) = 1$.

51) C. La reazione bilanciata di decomposizione del perossido di idrogeno è la seguente: $2\ H_2O_2 \rightarrow 2\ H_2O + O_2$. Tale reazione ha una cinetica del primo ordine, il che significa che la velocità di reazione è direttamente proporzionale alla concentrazione del reagente. La legge cinetica della reazione è la seguente: velocità = $k\ [H_2O_2]$. Pertanto, raddoppiando la concentrazione molare del perossido di idrogeno (da 1 M a 2 M), la velocità della reazione raddoppia. Poiché nel secondo esperimento viene raddoppiata la concentrazione molare della soluzione di H_2O_2, ma se ne utilizza lo stesso volume, il numero di moli di H_2O_2 che si decompongono risulta raddoppiato; poiché per ogni mole di H_2O_2 che si decompone si producono 0.5 mol di O_2, raddoppia anche il numero di moli di ossigeno prodotte e quindi raddoppia il volume di O_2 raccolto.

52) A. La forza del dipolo molecolare permanente di una molecola dipende dalla polarità dei legami covalenti tra gli atomi e dalla loro distribuzione nello spazio. Un legame chimico è tanto più polare quanto maggiore è la differenza di elettronegatività tra gli atomi coinvolti. Se la differenza di elettronegatività è inferiore a 0.4 il legame è covalente non polare, se è superiore a 2.0 il legame è ionico, se è compresa tra 0.4 e 2.0 il legame è covalente polare. I legami Ge–H non sono polari; il legame I–Cl è covalente polare e la molecola ha geometria lineare, perciò presenta un momento dipolare; i legami S–F sono molto polari, ma la molecola di SiF_4 ha geometria tetraedrica, per cui la simmetria dei quattro legami uguali porta all'annullamento reciproco dei dipoli di legame e la molecola nel complesso non presenta momento dipolare; i legami C–Cl sono polari e i legami C–H non sono polari e, poiché la molecola di CH_2Cl_2 presenta due legami C–H e due legami C–Cl, la geometria tetraedrica non determina l'annullamento del momento dipolare molecolare; i legami C–O sono polari, ma la molecola di CO_2 ha geometria lineare, per cui i due dipoli di legame si annullano per simmetria e la molecola non presenta momento dipolare.

Fisica e Matematica

53) D. Il quesito deve essere risolto senza l'uso della calcolatrice, pertanto, è importante utilizzare le giuste strategie per rendere il calcolo accessibile e rapido, anche se svolto con le sole regole algebriche.
Per i numeri scritti in notazione esponenziale, rammentiamo che:

– per ogni spostamento di una posizione della virgola verso sinistra, l'esponente va aumentato di una unità;

– per ogni spostamento di una posizione della virgola verso destra, l'esponente va diminuito di una unità.

Mediante questa regola, è utile modificare la scrittura del numero sotto radice, per due motivi:

– rendere il coefficiente del numero uguale ad un quadrato perfetto;

– scrivere la potenza di 10 con un esponente pari, per semplificarla con la radice.

Allo stesso modo si può modificare il numero in parentesi, per eliminare la virgola, avendo cura di variare la rispettiva potenza di 10 all'interno della parentesi.
Alla luce di quanto detto, si può scrivere:

$$\frac{8\times10^{-5}}{\sqrt{1,6\times10^{7}}}\times\left(1,2\times10^{3}\right)^{2}=\frac{8\times10^{-5}}{\sqrt{16\times10^{6}}}\times\left(12\times10^{2}\right)^{2}=$$

$$=\frac{8\times10^{-5}}{\sqrt{16}\sqrt{10^{6}}}\times(12)^{2}\left(10^{2}\right)^{2}=\frac{8\times10^{-5}}{4\times10^{3}}\times\left(144\times10^{4}\right)$$

Si raccolgono separatamente i coefficienti e le potenze di dieci:

$$\frac{8\times144}{4}\times\frac{10^{-5}\times10^{4}}{10^{3}}=(2\times144)\times10^{-5+4-3}=288\times10^{-4}=2,88\times10^{-2}$$

54) A. La superficie S di una sfera di raggio r è data da $S = 4\pi r^2$. Pertanto, le superfici delle quattro sfere sono rispettivamente pari a:

$$S_1=4\pi\left(\frac{r}{2}\right)^{2}=4\pi\frac{r^{2}}{4}=\pi r^{2}$$

$S_2 = 4\pi r^2$

$S_3 = 4\pi(2r)^2 = 4\pi \cdot 4r^2 = 16\pi r^2$

$S_4 = 4\pi(3r)^2 = 4\pi \cdot 9r^2 = 36\pi r^2$

Pertanto, la somma delle quattro superfici è pari a:

$S_{tot} = S_1 + S_2 + S_3 + S_4 = \pi r^2 + 4\pi r^2 + 16\pi r^2 + 36\pi r^2 = 57\pi r^2$

55) E. Dapprima scriviamo il fascio di rette passante per il punto di coordinate

$P = (x_p; y_p) = (-6; 2)$.

$(y - y_p) = m(x - x_p)$

Sostituendo le coordinate del punto otteniamo:

$(y-2) = m(x+6)$

Di questo fascio dobbiamo considerare la retta perpendicolare alla retta $4y + 3x = 8$, i cui coefficienti sono $a = 3$, $b = 4$, $c = -8$.

Il coefficiente angolare di questa retta è pari a:

$$-\frac{a}{b} = -\frac{3}{4}$$

Per ottenere il coefficiente angolare m da inserire nel fascio di rette, dobbiamo calcolare l'antireciproco di questo numero. In altre parole, occorre considerare il reciproco (con numeratore e denominatore invertiti) a cui dobbiamo cambiare segno. Pertanto si ha:

$$m = \frac{4}{3}$$

Quindi possiamo scrivere:

$$(y-2) = \frac{4}{3}(x+6)$$

$3(y-2) = 4(x+6)$

$3y - 6 = 4x + 24$

$3y - 4x = 6 + 24$

$3y - 4x = 30$

---

56) B. Se p è il prezzo originale del gioco, sappiamo che tale prezzo, scontato del 20%, diventa pari a € 32. Pertanto si può scrivere che il prezzo p, a cui sottraiamo il 20% di p, è pari a € 32:

$p - 20\% \cdot p = € 32$

Sapendo che $20\% = \frac{20}{100} = 0{,}20$, scriviamo:

$p - 0{,}20 \cdot p = € 32$

$(1 - 0{,}20) \cdot p = € 32$

$0{,}80 \cdot p = € 32$

Da cui:

$$p = \frac{€ 32}{0{,}80} = \frac{€ 32}{\frac{80}{100}} = \frac{€ 32}{\frac{8}{10}} = \frac{€ 32}{\frac{4}{5}} = € 32 \cdot \frac{5}{4} = € 8 \cdot 5 = € 40$$

---

57) C. Applichiamo il secondo principio della dinamica a una delle sfere del termometro, immerse nell'etanolo. Su tale sfera agiscono:

– la forza peso $P = mg$, dove m è la massa della sfera e $g = 9{,}8\ m/s^2$ è l'accelerazione gravitazionale terrestre.

– La spinta di Archimede $A = m_e g$, dove m_e è la massa dell'etanolo spostata dalla sfera.

Le due forze sono rappresentate in figura.

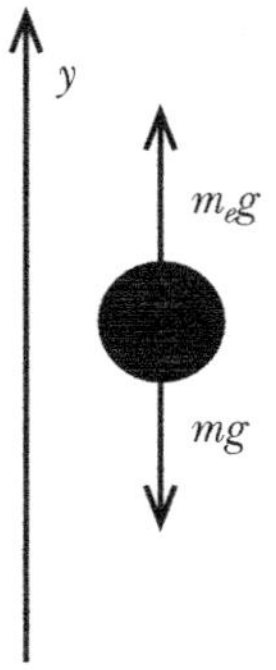

Applicando il secondo principio della dinamica lungo l'asse mostrato in figura, possiamo scrivere:

$$-mg + m_e g = ma$$

Dove a è l'accelerazione della sfera.
Dai segni attribuiti alle forze, si nota che se è maggiore la forza peso, allora la sfera scende verso il fondo (l'accelerazione è negativa e diretta verso il basso), mentre se è maggiore la spinta di Archimede, la sfera sale a galla (l'accelerazione è positiva e diretta verso l'alto).
Esprimendo le masse (m, m_e) come prodotto delle densità (δ, δ_e) per i volumi V e considerando la sfera totalmente immersa nell'etanolo, possiamo scrivere:

$$-\delta Vg + \delta_e Vg = \delta Va$$

$$-\delta g + \delta_e g = \delta a$$

$$(\delta_e - \delta)g = \delta a$$

$$a = (\delta_e - \delta)\frac{g}{\delta}$$

Considerando che g, $\delta > 0$, si nota che il segno dell'accelerazione a è dato dalla differenza $\delta_e - \delta$.
In particolare:

– se la densità dell'etanolo è maggiore di quella della sfera, ossia $\delta_e > \delta$, allora $\delta_e - \delta > 0$ e quindi $a > 0$. Pertanto, l'accelerazione ha verso concorde con l'asse y e la sfera si dirige verso l'alto e sale in superficie;

– se la densità dell'etanolo è minore di quella della sfera, ossia $\delta_e < \delta$, allora $\delta_e - \delta < 0$ e quindi $a < 0$. Pertanto, l'accelerazione ha verso discorde con l'asse y e la sfera si dirige verso il basso e scende sul fondo.

La temperatura incide sulla densità dei corpi. In particolare, per escursioni termiche caratteristiche delle temperature dell'ambiente, è possibile sostenere che la densità dei solidi sia poco variabile. Pertanto, nella formula dell'accelerazione, al variare della temperatura ambientale, la densità δ del solido, con una certa approssimazione, può essere considerata costante. Tuttavia, per escursioni termiche caratteristiche delle temperature dell'ambiente, la densità dei liquidi può variare sensibilmente. Questo

avviene anche per l'etanolo. Dunque, è necessario assumere che δ_e sia funzione della temperatura T, ossia $\delta_e(T)$.
In generale, sappiamo che i liquidi si dilatano all'aumentare della temperatura e, pertanto, la loro densità tende a diminuire. Viceversa, al diminuire della temperatura, la densità del liquido aumenta. Questa regola vale per l'etanolo (mentre l'acqua è un liquido che fa parzialmente eccezione). Quindi, vi può essere un valore specifico della temperatura T per il quale $\delta_e(T) > \delta$, da cui si ha che $a > 0$ e quindi la sfera sale verso la superficie.
Ne consegue che il funzionamento del termometro di Galileo si spiega mediante il principio appena esposto. Ciascuna delle sfere ha una densità differente, che corrisponde alla densità dell'etanolo a una certa temperatura. Ad esempio, la sfera con etichetta 20°C ha una densità pari a quella che assume l'etanolo a 20°C. Quando la temperatura dell'ambiente si abbassa sotto i 20°C, anche l'etanolo e la sfera, che sono in equilibrio termico tra loro e con l'ambiente, hanno una temperatura sotto i 20°C. Pertanto, la densità dell'etanolo diventa superiore a quella della sfera con etichetta 20°C e tale sfera tenderà a salire verso la superficie. Quando la temperatura raggiunge i 19°C, accade la stessa cosa alla sfera con l'etichetta di 19°C e così via.
Pertanto, la risposta corretta è che la sfera sale a galla perché la densità del liquido è aumentata.
La risposta "*The pressure exerted by the liquid has decreased*" non è corretta, in quanto la pressione esercitata dal liquido non è diminuita. La pressione è direttamente proporzionale alla densità del liquido, in base alla legge di Stevino. Dunque, se la densità del liquido aumenta, allora aumenta anche la pressione.
L'alternativa "*The mass of the sphere has decreased*" non è corretta, in quanto la massa della sfera è costante.
La risposta "*The temperature of the sphere is different from that of the liquid*" deve essere scartata, poiché, come specificato in precedenza, la massa è in equilibrio termico con il liquido; anche su questo aspetto si basa il funzionamento del termometro.
Infine, l'opzione "*The volume of gas inside the sphere has increased*" non è corretta, poiché la sfera è rigida e il suo volume non ha variazioni apprezzabili, perciò il volume del gas al suo interno è costante.

58) B. Considerando che la resistenza degli elementi X e Y della batteria è trascurabile, e che la corrente che attraversa l'elemento Z è trascurabile possiamo calcolare la resistenza equivalente data dalle tre resistenze (A, B e C) del circuito, tutte con valore pari a 4Ω (vedi figura).

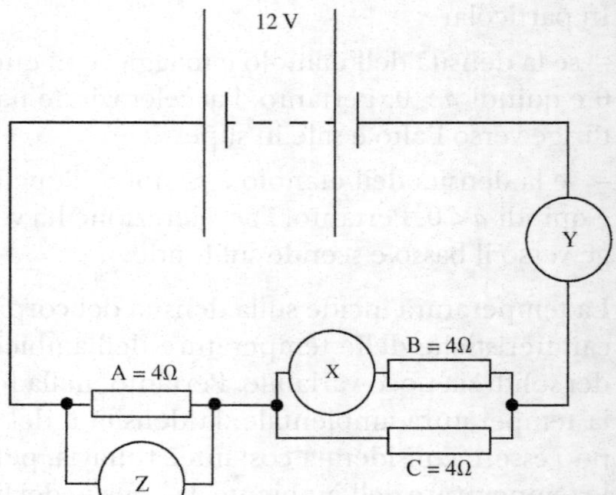

Innanzitutto, vi sono le due resistenze B e C in parallelo che equivalgono ad una resistenza pari a:

$$\frac{4\Omega \cdot 4\Omega}{4\Omega + 4\Omega} = \frac{16}{8}\Omega = 2\Omega$$

Questa resistenza va considerata in serie con l'altra resistenza A di 4Ω. Pertanto, la resistenza equivalente di A, B e C è pari a:

$R_{eq} = 2\Omega + 4\Omega = 6\Omega$

Dalla prima legge di Ohm, ricaviamo la corrente che attraversa il circuito, sapendo che la batteria genera ai suoi capi una differenza di potenziale di 12*V*. Quindi si ha:

$$I = \frac{\Delta V}{R_{eq}} = \frac{12V}{6\Omega} = 2A$$

Pertanto l'amperometro *Y* misura 2*A*.
Questa corrente è la stessa che attraversa la resistenza A. Pertanto, ai capi della resistenza A, è applicata la seguente differenza di potenziale:

$\Delta V = 2A \cdot 4\Omega = 8V$

Quindi il voltmetro *Z* misura 8*V*.
Calcoliamo anche la corrente che passa attraverso la resistenza B. Se la batteria applica ai capi del circuito una differenza di potenziale di 12*V* e ai capi della resistenza A vi è una caduta pari a 8*V*, vuol dire che ai capi delle due resistenze in parallelo B e C vi sarà una differenza di potenziale pari a $12V - 8V = 4V$. Di conseguenza la corrente che attraversa la resistenza B vale:

$$I = \frac{4V}{4\Omega} = 1A$$

Pertanto, l'amperometro *X* misura 1*A*.

59) A. In figura è mostrato il libro poggiato sul tavolo. Su tale libro sono applicate le seguenti forze:
- la forza esterna orizzontale $F = 10N$;
- la forza peso $P = m \cdot g = 0{,}40Kg \cdot 10NKg^{-1} = 4N$;
- la reazione vincolare R;
- la forza d'attrito $f_a = \mu \cdot R$.

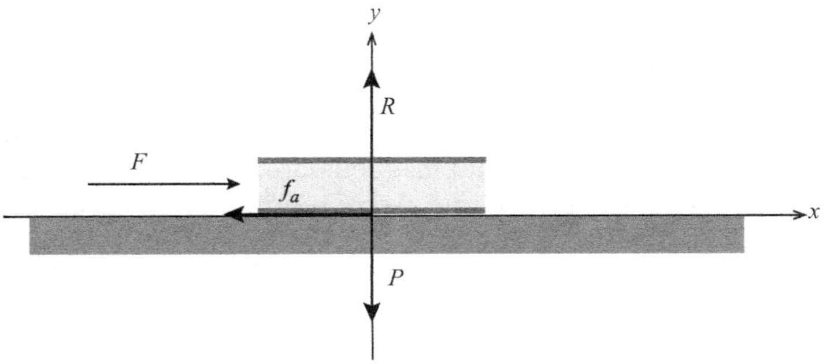

Applicando il secondo principio della dinamica lungo l'asse *y* in figura, ricaviamo la reazione vincolare *R*

$R - mg = 0$

$R = mg = 4N$

Applicando il secondo principio della dinamica lungo l'asse x in figura, ricaviamo l'accelerazione a.

$F - f_a = ma$

$F - \mu \cdot R = ma$

$$a = \frac{F - \mu \cdot R}{m}$$

Sostituendo i valori si ottiene:

$$a = \frac{F - \mu \cdot R}{m} = \frac{10N - 0,50 \cdot 4N}{0,4kg} = \frac{10N - 2N}{0,4kg} = \frac{8N}{0,4kg} = \frac{8N}{\frac{4}{10}kg} =$$

$$= \frac{8 \cdot 10m}{4s^2} = 2 \cdot 10\frac{m}{s^2} = 20\frac{m}{s^2}$$

60) E. La risposta "*A bar of unmagnetised cobalt*" è errata. Il cobalto è un materiale ferromagnetico, ma in questo caso non è magnetizzato, quindi non ha un comportamento simile ad un magnete. Quando un materiale ferromagnetico, come il cobalto, non è magnetizzato, può solo essere attratto (e non respinto) da un magnete.
L'alternativa "*A bar of electrostatically charged aluminium*" è errata, in quanto l'alluminio è un materiale paramagnetico; pertanto, non avverte in modo sensibile la forza del magnete e inoltre non può essere respinto da esso. La carica elettrostatica presente sull'alluminio non ha influenza, poiché le cariche elettrostatiche non interagiscono con i campi magnetici.
L'opzione "*A bar of electrostatically charged copper*" non è valida, in quanto il rame è un materiale diamagnetico; pertanto, non avverte in modo sensibile la forza del magnete e non viene respinto in maniera evidente da esso. La carica elettrostatica presente sul rame non ha influenza, dal momento che le cariche elettrostatiche non interagiscono con i campi magnetici.
La risposta "*A bar of unmagnetised soft iron*" deve essere scartata. Il ferro dolce è un materiale ferromagnetico, ma in questo caso non è magnetizzato, quindi non ha un comportamento simile ad un magnete. Pertanto, non può essere respinto dal magnete. Quando un materiale ferromagnetico, come il ferro, non è magnetizzato, può solo essere attratto (e non respinto) da un magnete.
La risposta "*A bar of magnetised steel*" è corretta. L'acciaio (lega di ferro e carbone) è un materiale ferromagnetico che in questo caso è stato magnetizzato, quindi ha un comportamento simile ad un magnete. Pertanto esso può essere respinto dal magnete.

IMAT
a.a. 2015/2016

General knowledge and logical reasoning

1) Studies are taking place to assess the benefits to dental health of adding fluoride to drinking water, a process known as mass medication. The Health Minister has urged consideration of fluoridation, particularly in deprived areas where dental care is poor. Fluoride can occur naturally in the water because of fluoride containing minerals. Fluoride, if in the water, improves dental health by up to 50 percent. Even so, fluoridation should not take place. A campaign leader opposed to fluoridation has spoken of her experiences of living in a fluoridated area of the USA. She experienced feelings of apathy and depression; her 2 year old son showed autistic tendencies and had white flecks on his teeth. These symptoms disappeared when they returned home from the USA.
Which one of the following is an underlying assumption of the argument above?

A. Fluoridation is cheaper than improving dental facilities
B. Mass medication is always wrong
C. The reported health symptoms were caused by fluoride in the water
D. Fluoridation is only necessary in deprived areas
E. Fluoridation of water is a person's only source of fluoride

2) Climate scientists in Greenland studying patterns of plant growth have suggested that the early arrival of spring in the Arctic threatens to drive down populations of migrating animals such as caribou. However, comparable studies elsewhere show that their fears are unfounded. A recent study of great tits in Oxfordshire showed the birds are capable of adapting to climate change better than many scientists expected. Over the past half century, the birds have brought forward the date they lay their eggs by two weeks, so that young are born when plant-eating grubs are most plentiful.
Which one of the following is an underlying assumption of the above argument?

A. Migrating animals in the Arctic can adapt to climate change as successfully as great tits in Oxfordshire
B. The scientists working in Oxfordshire have greater expertise than those working in Greenland
C. Climate change in Greenland and climate change in Oxfordshire are of the same scale
D. Birds are more adaptable than large mammals such as caribou
E. Unless animals like the caribou produce their young earlier in the year, their population will fall

3) Now, it might be thought an amazing coincidence if Earth were the only planet in the galaxy on which intelligent life evolved. If it happened here, the one planet we have studied closely, surely one would expect it to have happened on a lot of other planets in the galaxy – planets we have not yet had the chance to examine. This objection, however, rests on a fallacy: it overlooks what is known as an 'observation selection effect', so it wouldn't be such a coincidence. Whether intelligent life is common or rare, every observer is guaranteed to originate from a place where intelligent life did, in fact, arise. Since only the successes give rise to observers who can wonder about their existence, it would be a mistake to regard our planet as a randomly selected sample from all planets.

Which one of the following best expresses the main conclusion of the above argument?

A. Our planet is not a randomly selected sample from all planets
B. If life had evolved here on Earth, it would probably have happened on a lot of other planets in the galaxy
C. It would be an amazing coincidence if Earth were the only planet in the galaxy on which intelligent life evolved
D. There would be no amazing coincidence if we discovered that Earth were the only planet in the galaxy on which intelligent life evolved
E. However common intelligent life is, every observer will certainly originate from a place where intelligent life did, in fact, arise

4) Although it is sometimes suggested that the congestion caused by the bunching of cars on motorways could be eased by increasing the speed limit to 150 km/hr, such an increase would not be a good thing. An estimated 35 per cent of drivers exceed the speed limit by 20 km/hr and would continue to do so if the limit were raised. Since bunching is caused by speeding drivers trying to pass those who observe the speed limit, raising the limit to 150 km/hr would result in the same amount of congestion, but at an increased speed. Moreover, a higher speed limit would encourage all drivers to drive faster, and thus would increase the existing danger from those who drive too close to the car in front.

Which one of the following best expresses the main conclusion of the above argument?

A. Congestion on motorways is caused by speeding drivers trying to pass those who observe the speed limit
B. Raising the speed limit to 150 km/hr would not reduce congestion on motorways
C. A higher speed limit on motorways would encourage all drivers to drive faster
D. An increase in the speed limit would increase the existing danger from those drivers who drive too close
E. It would not be a good thing to increase the speed limit to 150 km/hr

5) Food producers are resisting pressure to reduce still further the levels of salt in food. Although it is proven that salt intake must be reduced by those with hypertension, there is no evidence that reducing salt intake prevents hypertension. So why should we all be deprived of the pleasures of salt in food? We certainly need to identify those with hypertension and give them advice on their salt intake, but why should everyone else be deprived of salt? Food producers are right to resist the pressure.

Which one of the following best illustrates the principle underlying the argument above?

A. Adding fluoride to drinking water has reduced tooth decay, but fluoride is unwelcome to some people. Instead, dentists should advise patients with tooth problems on better tooth care
B. Advice to wear sun block to protect the skin from harmful rays is ignored

by some people Those people should be charged for medical treatment for skin cancer
C. Passive smoking is still a problem for people who share a home with a smoker. The law should be extended to make smoking illegal even in the home
D. The requirement to wear seatbelts has reduced deaths in car accidents but was unpopular when first introduced. People eventually accepted such changes even if it has not benefited them personally
E. Retailers cannot sell alcohol to people under 18 years, but providing more general advice on alcohol in schools would be better, as it would encourage young people to be self limiting in their consumption of alcohol

---

6) Sports are played either as a means of getting exercise or as a competition with an opponent. Some sports, such as football, involve a large amount of running and some people are more motivated to run when it is part of a game. Other sports, such as pool, do not involve much physical activity and so it is unlikely that they would be played for the exercise.
Which one of the following conclusions is best supported by the passage above?

A. It is easier to exercise when it is as part of another activity, such as playing sport
B. Since the main reason for playing sports is to get exercise, pool should not be classified as a sport
C. People who play pool are more likely to be interested in the competition than those who play football
D. Football is a better sporting activity than pool
E. There is no point in running as a hobby, since football is more fun

7) Concern about the effects of chemicals upon the environment has led to calls for more re-search. But we should not wait for further research before we ban some of the chemicals used by industry. If anyone has a good reason to think something is harmful, it should not be used until, or unless, the risk is found to be zero. We know enough about past mistakes to be fore-warned. Much of the harm to wildlife and humans is long-term, and the disturbing results we see today reflect the chemical environment 40 years ago. Thousands more chemicals have been released into the environment since then.
Which one of the following most closely matches the reasoning above?

A. Some cars that have passed the annual roadworthiness test would not pass 6 months later. Cars should be tested more than once a year once they pass a certain age
B. People should not be able to adopt children until proper checks have been carried out. Serious consequences may follow if adoptive parents are unsuitable
C. Some homes for the elderly have been found to give dangerously substandard care. Therefore they should be closed down and the residents found acceptable alternatives
D. A suspected terrorist should be arrested at once. Waiting for conclusive evidence in the past has resulted in atrocities that could have been avoided by acting on suspicion, and the threat of terrorism has grown
E. Cyclists should not place too much confidence in the benefits of helmets, because there is no conclusive evidence as yet that helmets prevent serious injuries

8) Children are being encouraged to take up gardening through special events at shows and activities in schools. It is hoped that an interest in gardening, and particularly growing one's own food, will make children more interested in learning about their food and they will therefore be deterred from eating junk food. The initiative should be supported and spread to more schools as quickly as possible.

Which one of the following, if true, would most weaken the above argument?

A. The practical experience of gardening is not a traditional academic subject
B. Most children have enjoyed the events provided, but have not gained an interest in gardening itself
C. It tends to be older people who are interested in gardening and growing their own food
D. Some schools do not have a garden
E. The events to encourage children to garden also included stands where junk food was for sale

9) Although the Earth supports life, it has a mysterious carbon deficit. Compared with other bodies in the solar system the Earth has far less carbon than would be expected for a planet that supports life. Originally it was thought that in the inner region of the dust disc where the Earth formed, temperatures soared high enough for the carbon to boil away. However, observations of developing solar systems have now suggested that the temperature would not have been high enough. It is more likely that fire is to blame. Hot oxygen atoms would have readily combined with carbon, burning to produce carbon dioxide. There would have been fewer of these oxygen atoms further away from the Sun.

Which one of the following, if true, would most strengthen the above argument?

A. The carbon that is present on the Earth could have arrived at a later date from an asteroid
B. There is no theoretical reason why life has to be carbon-based
C. At temperatures that are high enough for carbon to boil away, oxygen would also have boiled away
D. The abundance of carbon in the asteroid belt surrounding the inner planets increases the fur-ther away you get from the Sun
E. There are other solar systems with Earth-like planets that have an abundance of carbon on them

10) Undercover police investigators sometimes commit 'crimes' in order to convince the "real criminals" that they are on the same side as them. Some of these activities have victims, although in the main these are other criminals – rival gang members for example. In committing what are technically offences the officers are preventing many more serious crimes by helping to convict and imprison dangerous criminals who might otherwise remain at liberty. But that is not really the point. A breach of the law is a breach of the law, whoever commits it and for whatever reason. Preventing a crime does not make it right to commit another crime.

Which one of the following is the general principle underlying the above argument?

A. The police have a duty to protect law-abiding citizens from violence
B. Serious crime must be prevented by any reasonable means
C. An act is criminal only if it is committed for criminal reasons

D. The end does not justify the means
E. There is no such thing as a victimless crime

11) Looking in his rearview mirror, Graham sensed that there was something wrong with the number plate of the car behind him. When the car overtook him and he saw its rear plate he realised that the front plate had been upside down.

What had Graham seen in his rearview mirror?

A. 

B. 

C. 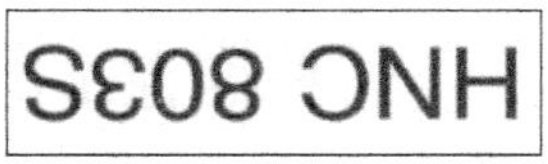

D. 

E. 

12) A local museum wishes to exhibit a collection of butterflies which is mounted in nine narrow (only 0.2 m wide) display cases, each 1.5 m long. The museum wants to arrange four tables, each 2 m long and 1 m wide, in such a way that all the display cases can be placed around the edges.
The room for the exhibition is 6 m by 6 m and there must be at least 1 m of clear floor space around the outside of the tables.

Which one of the five arrangements shown would be satisfactory?

A. 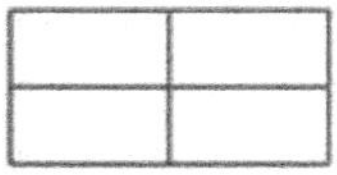

B. 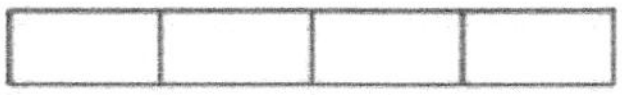

C. 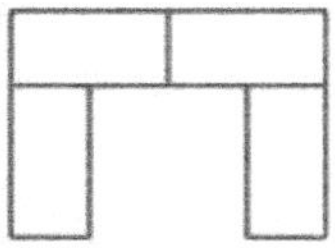

D. 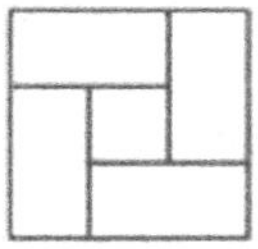

E. 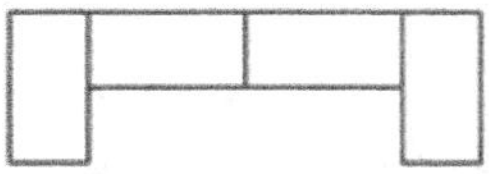

13) Alberto has decided to paint his dining room. Paint comes in 1 litre cans. The paint in one can will cover an area of approximately 24 square metres. The dining room is 4 m × 6 m × 3.5 m high. There is just one window which is in one of the long walls and is 1.5 m × 2 m. All of the walls, door and ceiling are to be painted with the same type of paint. Approximately 20% of the wall area to be painted is wood which will need a second coat of paint.
What is the minimum number of cans of paint that Alberto should buy to have sufficient to complete the room?

A. 3 cans
B. 2 cans
C. 5 cans
D. 4 cans
E. 6 cans

14) A farmer wishes to fix fencing rails to posts which are already in place. The posts are shown in the diagram. The farmer has a supply of rails, each one 2.4 m long. One rail or part of a rail is to be fixed between each pair of posts. (He can cut the rails into smaller lengths).

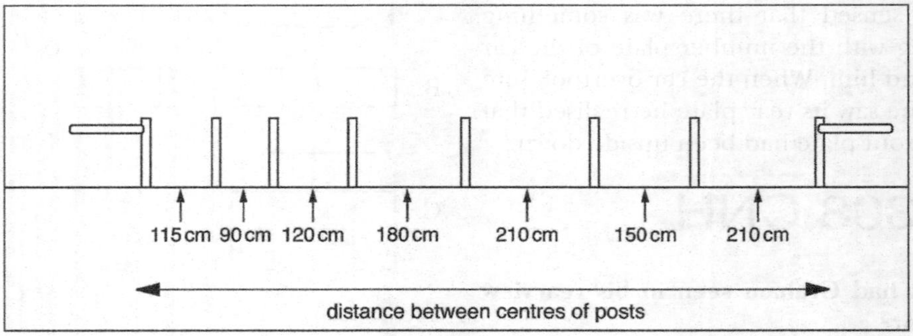

What is the smallest number of rails that he could use?

A. 7
B. 3
C. 4
D. 6
E. 5

15) Tom is having a celebration and needs to send out 50 invitation cards. The cards must be at least 6 cm wide and at least 8 cm high and Tom wants to put a photo on the card. Each type of card has a standard version and a deluxe version. The prices (per card) that have been quoted to Tom are shown in the table below:

Width (cm)	Height (cm)	Photo?	Personalised greeting?	Price (standard)	Price (deluxe)
6	6	Y	N	€0.90	€1.65
6	10	N	Y	€1.00	€1.60
6	10	Y	Y	€1.75	€2.15
7	7	Y	N	€1.40	€1.90
7	10	Y	N	€1.50	€1.95
7	10	Y	Y	€1.60	€2.15
10	10	Y	N	€2.25	€2.95

Tom wants to buy the cheapest type of card possible but is willing to pay for the deluxe version instead of the standard.
What is the total extra that Tom would have to pay to buy the deluxe cards?

A. € 22.50
B. € 25.00
C. € 20.00
D. € 27.50
E. € 30.00

16) The table below shows the average mass of the cerebellum, which is a part of the brain, and total body mass, for a number of animal species. The cerebellum of a cat has an average mass of 5.3 g, while a cat's average body mass is 3.5 kg.

Species	Cerebellum mass (g)	Body mass (g)
Mouse	0.09	58
Pigeon	0.4	500
Squirrel	1.5	350
Rabbit	1.9	1800
Dog	6.0	3500

For which of the species shown is the ratio of cerebellum to total body mass closest to that of the cat?

A. Rabbit
B. Dog
C. Pigeon
D. Mouse
E. Squirrel

17) There are two services between Sandpoint and Genville: a fast hovercraft service which takes 50 minutes and a slow ferry which takes 1 hour 40 minutes. They both stop in port for 20 minutes at each end before starting the return journey. They start out from Sandpoint together at the same time each morning.
For how long has the slow ferry been sailing before it meets the hovercraft coming back?
(Answer to the nearest minute if necessary).

A. 1 hour and 30 minutes
B. 1 hour and 10 minutes
C. 1 hour and 7 minutes
D. 1 hour and 25 minutes
E. 1 hour and 20 minutes

18) Deanna keeps a record of the petrol she puts into her car and the current distance it has covered so she can estimate her fuel consumption. When she puts petrol in, sometimes the tank is filled completely and she marks 'FULL' beside the entry if this is so, otherwise the tank is only partly filled.
Her data for the last month is as follows:

Date	Total km	Fuel added	FULL?
2 June	23,508	5 litres	
6 June	23,805	37 litres	FULL
12 June	24,350	25 litres	
17 June	24,743	21 litres	
23 June	24,989	34 litres	FULL
27 June	25,454	18 litres	

Which one of the following is the best estimate of her fuel consumption?

A. 8.0 litres / 100 km
B. 1.7 litres / 100 km
C. 7.7 litres / 100 km
D. 6.8 litres / 100 km
E. 9.9 litres / 100 km

19) Leroy cycles to work each morning. The first half of his journey is uphill and he can manage only a steady 5 kilometres per hour. The second half, however, is downhill and he covers this at 15 kilometres per hour.
Which one of these graphs could show Leroy's journey?

A.
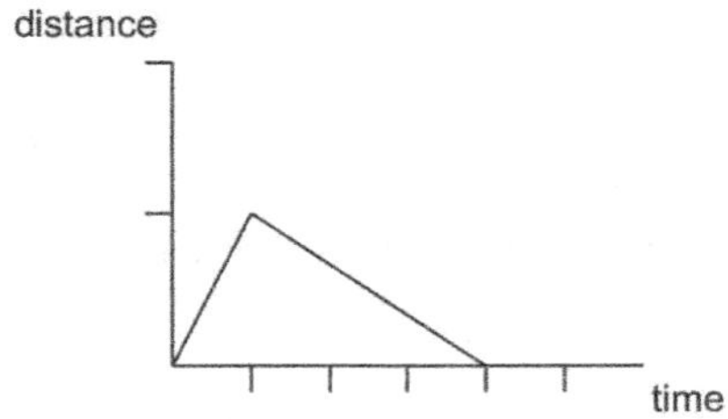

B. 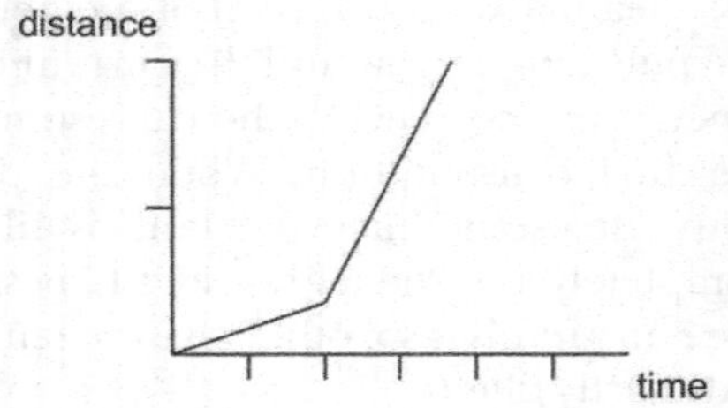

C. 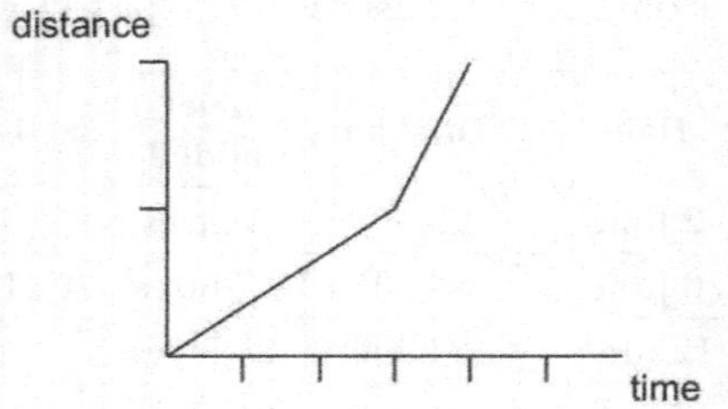

D. 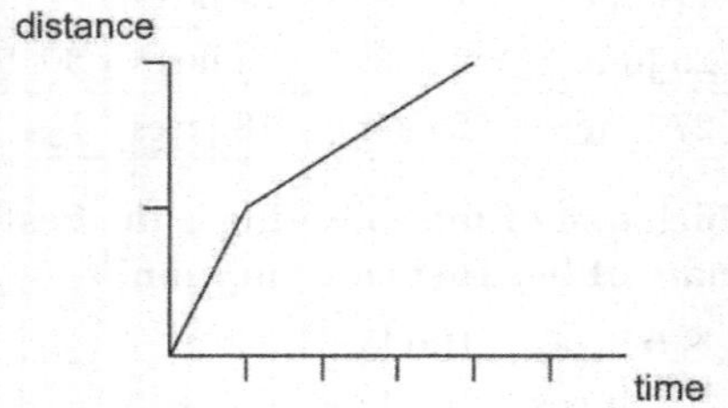

E. 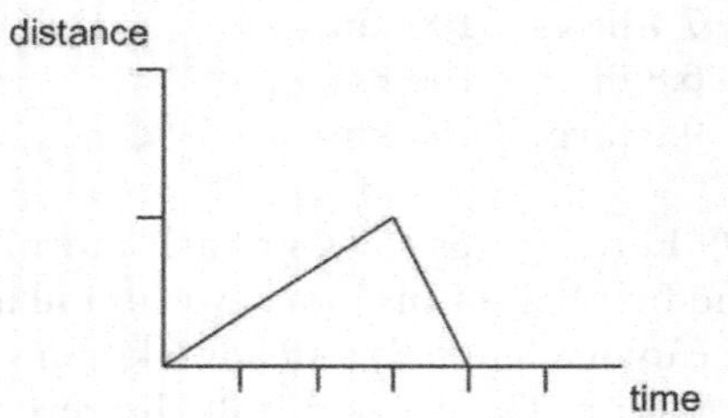

20) When I made a hotel reservation online yesterday I was given an 8-digit booking reference which contained no zeros. It did, however, consist of three 2-digit odd numbers followed by the sum of these three numbers, and all eight digits were different.
The first digit of the booking reference was 4. What was the last digit?

A. 1
B. 7
C. 3
D. 5
E. 9

21) Which one of the following pairs of scholar/field of study is NOT correct?

A. Max Weber – Pedagogy
B. Doris Lessing – Literature
C. Ludwig Wittgenstein – Philosophy
D. Amartya Sen – Economics
E. Konrad Lorenz – Ethology

22) Which one of the following public figures was NOT awarded the Nobel Peace Prize?

A. Aung San Suu Kyi
B. Willy Brandt
C. Mahatma Gandhi
D. Nelson Mandela
E. Martin Luther King

Biology

23) The diagram below shows an amino acid.

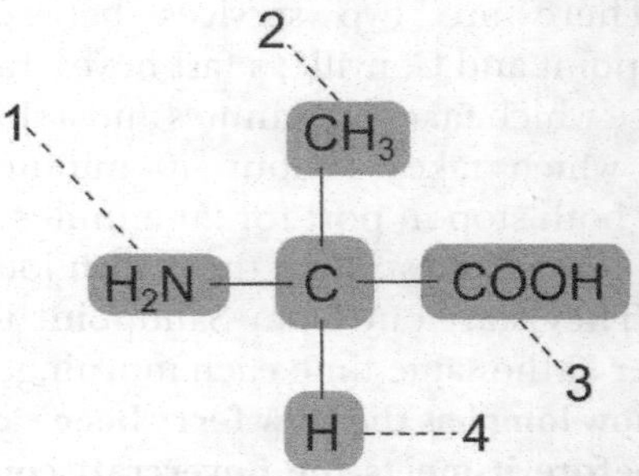

Which option correctly identifies both the variable group (R group) and the acidic group?

A. Variable group = 1; acidic group = 2
B. Variable group = 3; acidic group = 1
C. Variable group = 4; acidic group = 3
D. Variable group = 2; acidic group = 3
E. Variable group = 2; acidic group = 4

24) In a prokaryote, transcription can occur in which of the following?
1. cytoplasm
2. mitochondria
3. ribosomes

A. 1 and 3 only
B. 3 only
C. 2 only
D. 1 and 2 only
E. 1 only

25) Which of the following are directly produced during photolysis of water?
1. oxygen
2. carbon dioxide
3. protons

A. 1 and 2 only
B. 1 and 3 only
C. 2 only
D. 1 only
E. 2 and 3 only

26) The table shows some events of the normal eukaryotic cell cycle.

row 1	nuclear envelope disappears	DNA start to condense	chromosomes line up at the equator	cytoplasm divides
row 2	chromosomes line up at the equator	spindle fibres shorten	DNA starts to condense	nuclear envelope reappears
row 3	chromosomes line up at the equator	spindle fibres shorten	nuclear envelope reappears	cytoplasm divides
row 4	DNA starts to condense	nuclear envelope disappears	spindle fibres shorten	chromosomes line up at the equator
row 5	nuclear envelope disappears	spindle fibres shorten	chromosomes line up at the equator	nuclear envelope reappears

Which row shows the correct sequence of events (left to right) as they occur during part of this cell cycle?

A. Row 3
B. Row 4
C. Row 5
D. Row 1
E. Row 2

27) A double stranded DNA molecule is shown below:

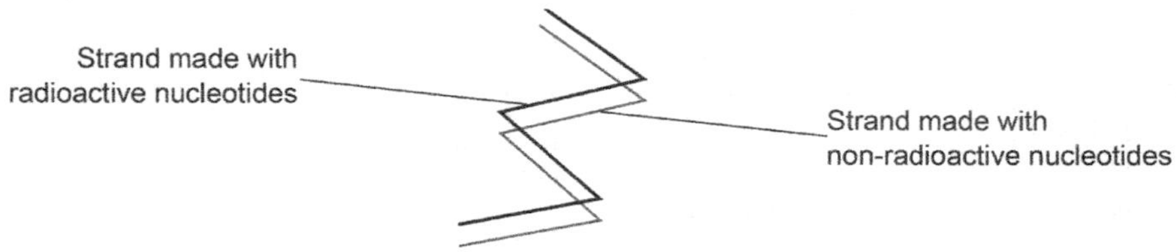

This DNA molecule is allowed to replicate three times in a medium containing nonradioactive nucleotides.

Which answer shows the correct percentages of original DNA and completely nonradioactive DNA?

row	Percentage original DNA	Percentage completely nonradioactive DNA
1	12.5	87.5
2	25	75
3	50	50
4	87.5	12.5
5	75	25

[Assume all radioactive nucleotides remain radioactive throughout, and all nonradioactive nucleotides remain nonradioactive throughout].

A. Row 4
B. Row 2
C. Row 3
D. Row 5
E. Row 1

28) The genotype QqRr produces a certain phenotype. If two individuals with a genotype of QqRr reproduce, how many different possible phenotypes could be created, assuming all allele combinations are equally viable and the phenotypes are the result of complete dominance?

A. 9
B. 5
C. 4
D. 16
E. 8

29) A normal sequence of triplets in a section of DNA is given by: ATCGAACGG. The same section of DNA has been changed by mutation, and is given by: ATCTTGCGG
Some of the triplets below represent the tRNA triplets which code for amino acids. Key:

triplet	amino acid	triplet	amino acid	triplet	amino acid
AUC	□	ATC	■	UAG	⊡
CAA	⊙	UUG	○	GAA	●
CGG	◇	GCC	◈	TTG	◆
AAC	▲	CUU	▽	ACC	△

Using the tRNA triplets, which amino acid sequence given below could be formed from the mutated DNA sequence?

A. ■-◆-◇
B. □-●-◇
C. ■-●-◇
D. □-○-◇
E. ⊡-▲-◈

30) Which of the following could be the outcome of evolution?
1. speciation
2. a change in allele frequency
3. increased biodiversity

A. 1 only
B. 1, 2 and 3
C. 2 and 3 only
D. 1 and 3 only
E. 1 and 2 only

31) Where in a shoulder joint are osteocytes found?

A. Cartilage
B. Muscle tissue
C. Skin
D. Bone tissue
E. Ligament

32) The diagram shows how the pressure changes in the left atrium, left ventricle and the aorta during one heartbeat in a healthy human.

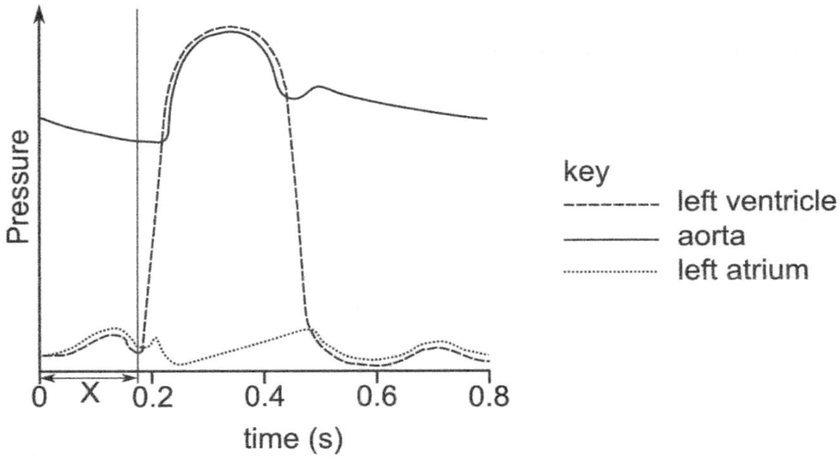

Which row shows the correct events during time period X?

row	volume of blood in left atrium	semi-lunar valve in aorta	muscles of left ventricle wall
1	decreases	closed	relax
2	decreases	open	relax
3	increases	closed	contract
4	decreases	open	contract
5	increases	closed	relax

A. row 3
B. row 2
C. row 5
D. row 1
E. row 4

33) The diagram shows a single sarcomere in a relaxed state.

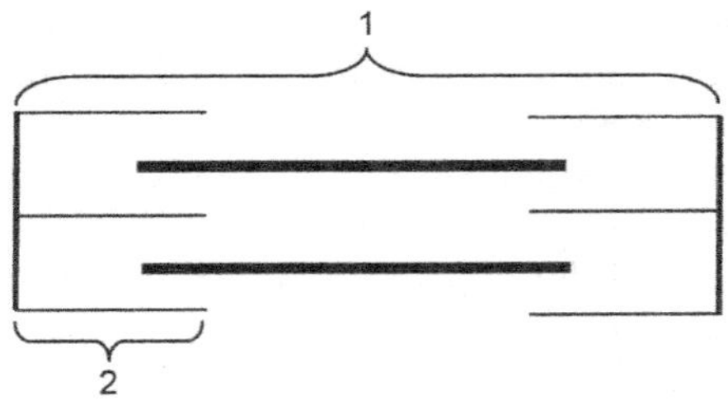

Which answer describes the changes when the sarcomere contracts?

A. 1 does not change and 2 gets wider
B. 1 gets smaller and 2 gets smaller
C. 1 gets longer and 2 gets wider
D. 1 gets longer and 2 gets smaller
E. 1 gets smaller and 2 does not change

34) Some local anaesthetics affect nervous impulse transmission by making it more difficult for voltage-gated sodium channels to open.
In a human patient treated with these anaesthetics which of the following statements would be true?

A. The sodium/potassium pump may need to work faster to maintain the resting potential
B. It would become harder to depolarise the neuron
C. The membrane potential of the neuron at rest would decrease below –90 mV
D. The threshold potential required to generate an action potential would be lowered
E. The axon membrane would become more difficult to repolarise

35) The changes in concentration of hormones in a healthy woman's blood were monitored during several menstrual cycles.
During which stage of the menstrual cycle was the concentration of oestrogen falling, the concentration of luteinising hormone (LH) and follicle-stimulating hormone (FSH) maximal and the progesterone concentration rising?

A. Between the end of menstruation and four days before ovulation
B. At the start of menstruation
C. Four days before ovulation and the time of ovulation
D. After ovulation but before the start of menstruation
E. At the end of menstruation

36) The following events occur during a reflex response to a person placing a hand on a hot object.
1. Myosin binding sites on actin filaments uncovered.
2. ADP and phosphate ion released from myosin head.
3. Sodium voltage-gated channels open.
4. Myosin head detaches from binding site on actin.
5. Calcium ions released by sarcoplasmic reticulum.
Which of the following options places four of these events in the correct order (from left to right)?

A. 5, 2, 1, 4
B. 3, 1, 4, 2
C. 3, 5, 4, 2
D. 1, 2, 4, 3
E. 5, 1, 2, 4

37) The picture below shows a DNA microarray. Each spot (labelled 1–4) contains a different DNA probe. A sample of fluorescently-labelled human DNA, with the sequence TGGTCAAGATTAT, is washed over the array.

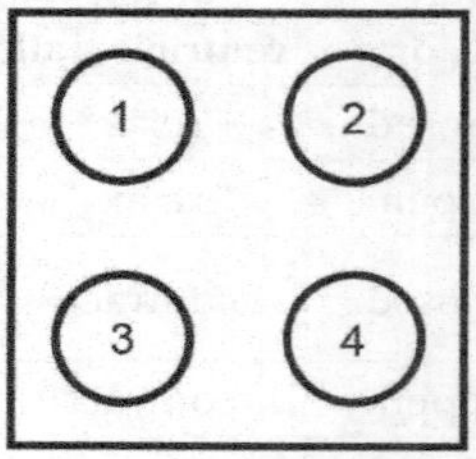

spot	DNA probe
1	GATTAT
2	CTAATA
3	ACCAGT
4	TGGTCA

Which of the spots would show a positive signal because it fluoresces?

A. 1, 2, 3 and 4
B. 1 and 3 only
C. 1 and 4 only
D. 2 and 3 only
E. 2 and 4 only

38) In the nerve cells of a person, one gene has two alleles, 'A' and 'a', present. For this person, which row correctly shows the alleles present in all three different situations given in the table?

row	Situation		
	Stem cell starting to specialise into a liver cell	Cell at the start of mitosis	Cell at the start of mitosis I
1	Aa	AAaa	AAaa
2	AAaa	Aa	AAaa
3	AAaa	AAaa	Aa
4	Aa	Aa	A or a
5	A or a	A or a	Aa

A. Row 4
B. Row 5
C. Row 3
D. Row 1
E. Row 2

39) Place the following structures in a human sperm cell in descending order of size (left to right):
1. mitochondria
2. nucleus
3. ribosome

A. 2, 1, 3
B. 1, 3, 2
C. 2, 1, 3
D. 2, 3, 1
E. 1, 2, 3

40) Which one of the following is NOT a carbohydrate?

A. Amylose
B. Glucagon
C. Amylopectin
D. Ribose
E. Maltose

Chemistry

41) What is the correct formula of propanal?
A. $CH_3CH_2CH_2OH$
B. $CH_3CH_2CO_2H$
C. CH_3COCH_3
D. CH_3CH_2CHO
E. $CH_3CH_2OCH_3$

42) Which two of the following oxides would NOT give acidic solutions in water?

CO, CO_2, SO_2, NO

A. CO and SO_2
B. CO and NO
C. NO and SO_2
D. CO and CO_2
E. NO and CO_2

43) Assume that the oxidation numbers are as shown below:

N = –3 H = +1 Cr = +6 O = –2

Which compound formula given below is correct?

A. $(NH_4)_3CrO_4$
B. $[(NH_4)_3CrO_4]^-$
C. $NH_4Cr_2O_7$
D. $[(NH_4)_2CrO_4]^+$
E. $(NH_4)_2CrO_4$

44) 0.75 g of a hydrocarbon compound contains 0.60 g of carbon.

(A_r : C = 12.0; H = 1.0)

Which one of the following could be the molecular formula of the hydrocarbon compound?

A. CH_4
B. C_2H_3
C. C_2H_6
D. C_3H_8
E. C_2H_4

45) The atomic number of aluminium is 13.
Which electron configuration given below corresponds to the Al^{2+} ion in its ground state?

A. $Is^2 2s^2 2p^6 3s^1$
B. $Is^2 2s^2 2p^6 3s^2 3p^3$

C. $Is^2 2s^2 2p^5 3s^2$
D. $Is^2 2s^2 2p^6$
E. $Is^2 2s^2 2p^6 3s^2 3p^1$

46) When propan-1-ol is burnt in excess oxygen the only products formed are carbon dioxide and water.
In the balanced equation for this reaction what is the ratio of $CO_2 : H_2O$ molecules formed?

A. 2 : 7
B. 3 : 4
C. 3 : 8
D. 4 : 7
E. 5 : 12

47) 2,2 – dimethylpropane, $C(CH_3)_4$, is an isomer of pentane, $CH_3(CH_2)_3CH_3$. Pentane has a boiling point of 36°C whilst the boiling point of 2,2 – dimethylpropane is 10°C.
Which statement below explains the difference in the boiling points for these two substances?

A. Isomers have different chemical properties
B. 2,2 – dimethylpropane has stronger intermolecular forces
C. Pentane has permanent dipoles
D. Longer chain, less branched molecules have stronger spontaneous/induced dipoles
E. The molecules have different relative molecular masses

48) Potassium nitrate was found to have a solubility of 120 g in 100 g of water at 80 °C and 50 g in 100 g of water at 25 °C. 50 g of water was heated to 80 °C and solid potassium nitrate added until the solution was just saturated.
The solution was then cooled to 25 °C when solid potassium nitrate separated out to leave a saturated solution.

Using the information provided in this question, what is the minimum mass of water that must now be added to the mixture of the solution and the solid in order to make this solid potassium nitrate redissolve at 25 °C?

A. 20 g
B. 190 g
C. 70 g
D. 120 g
E. 140 g

49) Pure water self-ionises. This endothermic reaction is represented by the equation:

$$H_2O(I) \rightleftharpoons H^+(aq) + OH^-(aq)$$

Which of the following statements is true for pure water between the temperatures of 0 °C and 100 °C?
1. The concentrations of H^+(aq) and OH^-(aq) are equal between 0 °C and 100 °C.
2. An increase in temperature causes the pH to fall.
3. An increase in temperature causes the electrical conductivity to decrease.

A. 2 only
B. 1 and 2 only
C. 1 and 3 only
D. 1 only
E. 3 only

50) Which one of the following 0.01 M aqueous solutions has a pH > 7.0?

A. Na_2CO_3
B. CH_3CO_2H
C. NH_4Cl
D. $AlBr_3$
E. NaI

51) Atoms X and Y form an ionic compound with formula XY_2.
Which option below could give the correct atomic numbers for X and Y?

A. X = 3; Y = 17
B. X = 11; Y = 16
C. X = 12; Y = 9
D. X = 14; Y = 8
E. X = 6; Y = 16

52) In the reaction

$$C_3H_7Br + KOH \rightarrow C_3H_7OH + KBr$$

24.6 g of 1-bromopropane react with excess potassium hydroxide to produce 8.00 g of propan-1-ol.

M_r : C_3H_7Br = 123
A_r : H = 1.0; C = 12.0; O = 16.0

What is the percentage yield of this reaction?

A. 57.1%
B. 33.3%
C. 93.0%
D. 32.5%
E. 66.7%

Physics and Mathematics

53) The variables x and y satisfy the following two equations:

$x + 3y = 13$
$2x - y = 5$

What is the value of $x + y$?

A. 6
B. 10
C. 9
D. 7
E. 8

54) Evaluate: $(27^2 - 23^2) + (14^2 - 6^2)$

A. 840
B. 360
C. 1680
D. 80
E. 40

55) Given that $2 \log_{10}(x) - 3 = \log_{10}(y)$. Express y in terms of x.

A. $y = \frac{2x}{3}$

B. $y = x^2 - 3$

C. $y = \frac{x^2}{1000}$

D. $y = \frac{2x}{1000}$

E. $y = \frac{x^2}{3}$

56) The arithmetic mean of the three numbers a, b, c is 8.
Find the arithmetic mean of the four numbers: $a + 1$, $b + 2$, $c + 6$, 3.

A. 9
B. 11
C. 7
D. 2
E. 5

57) An aluminium block of mass 2.5 kg is supplied with 9000 J of thermal energy. This causes its temperature to rise by 4 K. Which expression gives the specific heat capacity of this aluminium, from this data? [Assume that the block remains solid throughout, and that no additional energy is exchanged between the block and the surroundings].

A. $\frac{2.5 \times 4}{9000} Jkg^{-1}K^{-1}$

B. $\frac{9000 \times 4}{2.5} Jkg^{-1}K^{-1}$

C. $\frac{9000 \times 2.5}{4} Jkg^{-1}K^{-1}$

D. $9000 \times 2.5 \times 4 Jkg^{-1}K^{-1}$

E. $\frac{9000}{2.5 \times 4} Jkg^{-1}K^{-1}$

58) The diagram shows a car of mass 1000 kg travelling at a constant speed of

30 m/s in the direction shown along a flat, level road which forms a circle of radius 50 m.

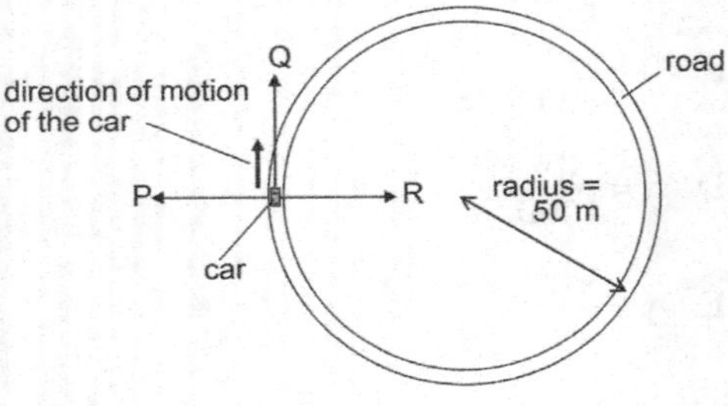

Which row in the table gives both the magnitude of the resultant force on the car and the direction of the acceleration of the car at the instant shown?

row	magnitude of resultant force (kN)	direction of acceleration
1	0	R
2	18	Q
3	18	R
4	30	Q
5	30	P

A. Row 2
B. Row 4
C. Row 5
D. Row 3
E. Row 1

59) Two forces F of equal magnitude act on a beam.
Which diagram shows a couple acting and states the magnitude of the torque (moment) of the couple about the pivot?
[The pivot is at the centre of the beam]

A.

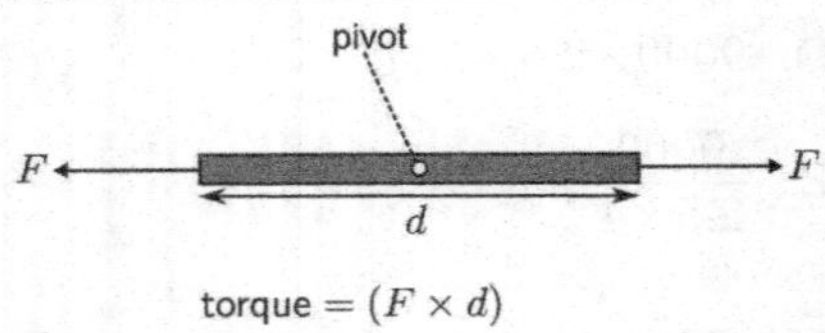

B.

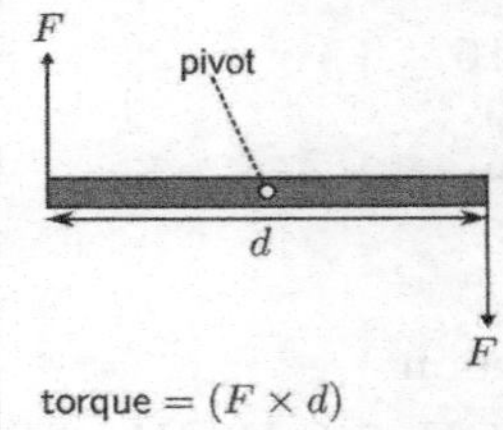

C.

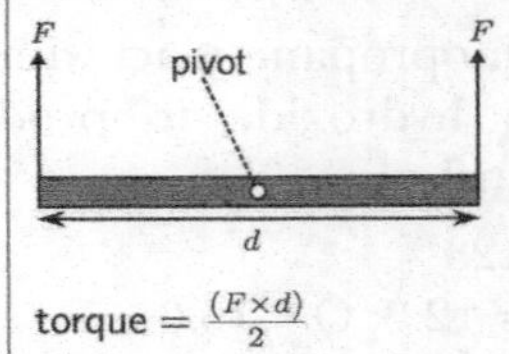

D.

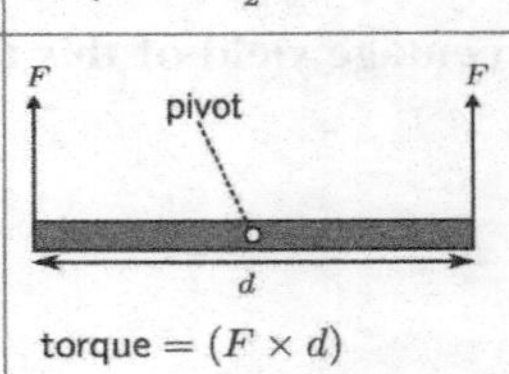

E.

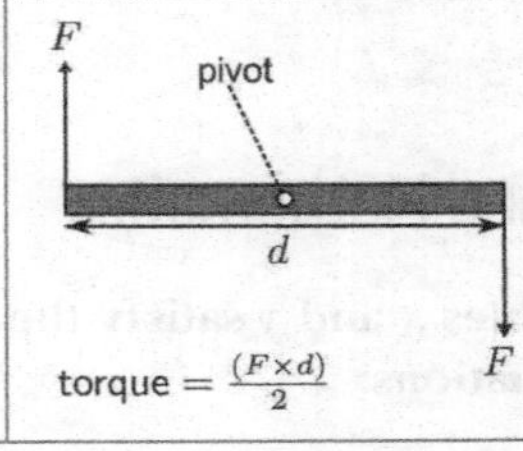

60) Which one of the following equations is dimensionally consistent (has consistent units)?
[All the symbols have their usual meanings: v = velocity; F = force; m = mass; t = time; V = voltage; Q = charge; R_1, R_2, R_3, R_4 = resistance]

A. Energy = $(\frac{1}{2}mv^2) + Fv$
B. Temperature change = energy × m × specific heat capacity
C. Electrical current = $(V/R_1) + (Q/t)$
D. Acceleration = $(\frac{1}{2}vt^2) + (F/m)$
E. Resistance = $R_1 + R_2 + (1/R_3) + (1/R_4)$

RISPOSTE COMMENTATE • IMAT a.a. 2015/2016

Cultura generale e ragionamento logico

1) C. Il quesito richiede di identificare, fra le cinque opzioni di risposta, quella che riporta la supposizione implicita deducibile dalla traccia. È necessario, quindi, analizzare il testo, individuando così le premesse esplicite e la conclusione in esso contenute. Nella parte introduttiva (*Studies are taking place to assess the benefits to dental health of adding fluoride to drinking water, a process known as mass medication. [...] . Fluoride, if in the water, improves dental health by up to 50 percent*) è esposto l'accaduto, mentre la conclusione è riportata nella frase: *Even so, fluoridation should not take place.*
Nella seconda parte del testo, poi, sono esposti i problemi di salute manifestati dalla leader del movimento contro la fluoridazione e da suo figlio durante il soggiorno in un'area soggetta a fluoridazione. Il legame tra i sintomi riferiti e la fluoridazione delle acque messa in atto dal governo è lasciato intendere in maniera implicita, quindi la risposta esatta è: *The reported health symptoms were caused by fluoride in the water.* Infatti, solo presupponendo che i sintomi riferiti fossero causati dal fluoro nell'acqua si può ricavare la conclusione per cui *fluoridation should not take place.*
Le altre opzioni, invece, pur essendo anch'esse implicitamente deducibili, o dalla premessa o dalle argomentazioni esposte in seguito, non sono riconducibili alla conclusione.

2) A. Il quesito richiede di individuare quale tra le cinque alternative di risposta è implicitamente deducibile dal ragionamento esposto nella traccia. È necessario, quindi, analizzare il testo, individuando così le premesse esplicite e la conclusione in esso contenute.
Nella parte introduttiva (*Climate scientists in Greenland studying patterns of plant growth have suggested that the early arrival of spring in the Arctic threatens to drive down populations of migrating animals such as caribou*) è esposta la tesi ipotizzata dagli studiosi impegnati in ricerche di diversa natura, mentre la conclusione cui il brano tende è contenuta nella frase: *However, comparable studies elsewhere show that their fears are unfounded.*
Nella seconda parte del brano, invece, sono riportate le argomentazioni di studi più recenti a conferma della conclusione contenuta nel brano (*A recent study of great tits in Oxfordshire showed the birds are capable of adapting to climate change better than many scientists expected. Over the past half century, the birds have brought forward the date they lay their eggs by two weeks, so that young are born when planteating grubs are most plentiful*).
L'opzione di risposta *Climate change in Greenland and climate change in Oxfordshire are of the same scale* esprime un concetto già esplicitato nel testo, quindi non deducibile implicitamente. Le altre opzioni, invece, contengono concetti lontani da quanto espresso nel brano e, quindi, vanno anch'esse scartate. La risposta corretta è: *Migrating animals in the Arctic can adapt to climate change as successfully as great tits in Oxfordshire,* opzione che, oltre ad essere implicitamente deducibile dal brano, convalida quanto espresso nella conclusione.

3) D. Il quesito richiede di indicare tra le alternative di risposta quella che esprime meglio il concetto esposto nella traccia. È necessario, quindi, analizzare il brano proposto e individuare la frase che ne rappresenta il messaggio principale. Nella premessa si sostiene la tesi per cui sarebbe una coincidenza sorprendente se la Terra fosse il solo pianeta nella galassia su cui si è evoluta la vita intelligente. Tuttavia, più avanti si spiega come tale tesi si basi su un errore. L'affermazione che rappresenta la conclusione del brano è pertanto rintracciabile nella risposta *There would be no amazing coincidence if we discovered that Earth were the only planet in the galaxy on which intelligent life evolved.*
Le altre quattro alternative, infatti, esprimono non il messaggio principale, ma solo concetti posti nelle premesse a sostegno della stessa.

4) E. Per risolvere il quesito è necessario analizzare il brano proposto e individuare la frase che contiene il messaggio principale. Tale affermazione è la seguente: *such an increase* (ossia l'aumento del limite di velocità) *would not be a good thing.* La risposta corretta è, quindi, "*It would not be a good thing to increase the speed limit to 150 km/hr*".
Le altre alternative di risposta sono tutte da scartare, perché riportano non il messaggio principale, ma solo concetti posti nelle premesse a supporto dello stesso.

5) A. Per poter rispondere correttamente al quesito è necessario comprendere il principio su cui si fonda il ragionamento della traccia, in modo da individuare l'opzione di risposta corretta tra le alternative proposte. La tesi sostenuta nel brano proposto è che una qualsiasi misura, nella fattispecie la riduzione dell'assunzione di sale, utile per alcuni, in questo caso coloro che soffrono di ipertensione, non dovrebbe essere estesa a tutti, ossia anche a coloro che non soffrono di ipertensione.
L'alternativa di risposta contenente questo stesso principio è: *Adding fluoride to drinking water has reduced tooth decay, but fluoride is unwelcome to some people. Instead, dentists should advise patients with tooth problems on better tooth care.* Qui, infatti, si esprime l'idea che una misura, nella fattispecie l'aggiunta di fluoro all'acqua potabile, utile per alcuni, cioè coloro che hanno problemi di denti, non dovrebbe essere estesa a tutti, ossia anche a coloro che non soffrono di problemi di denti. È chiaro, quindi, che quest'alternativa è la risposta corretta al quesito.

6) C. La risposta corretta al quesito sarà, tra le alternative proposte, quella che rappresenta la conclusione di quanto argomentato nel brano. In quest'ottica bisogna innanzitutto individuare i passaggi logici del ragionamento esposto:

- "*Sports are played either as a means of getting exercise or as a competition with an opponent*";
- "*Some sports, such as football, involve a large amount of running and some people are more motivated to run when it is part of a game*";
- "*Other sports, such as pool, do not involve much physical activity and so it is unlikely that they would be played for the exercise*".

In base alle argomentazioni su esposte la risposta corretta è: *People who play pool are more likely to be interested in the competition than those who play football.* Infatti, se gli sport sono praticati per due motivi, o per fare esercizio o per competere con gli avversari, e se nel football si fa molto esercizio, mentre è improbabile che chi gioca a biliardo lo faccia per lo stesso motivo, si deve concludere che chi gioca a biliardo probabilmente sia più interessato alla competizione di chi gioca a football.

7) D. Per risolvere il quesito è necessario innanzitutto individuare il principio di fondo del ragionamento nella traccia e poi determinare quale delle alternative di risposta si basa sullo stesso principio.
Nel brano proposto si sostiene che riguardo all'utilizzo delle sostanze chimiche l'esperienza passata dimostra che l'attesa di ulteriori evidenze causa problemi più gravi, cioè il rilascio di una grande quantità di sostanze inquinanti nell'ambiente. Il ragionamento generale che se ne può ricavare è: di fronte al sospetto di un pericolo, nella fattispecie la presenza di sostanze chimiche pericolose, bisogna intervenire subito.
Tra le varie alternative di risposta quella che sottende lo stesso principio della traccia è: *A suspected terrorist should be arrested at once. Waiting for conclusive evidence in the past has resulted in atrocities that could have been avoided by acting on suspicion, and the threat of terrorism has grown.* Da questa opzione, infatti, emerge l'idea che di fronte al sospetto di un pericolo, nella fattispecie un sospetto terrorista, bisogna intervenire subito, in tal caso arrestandolo immediatamente, perché l'esperienza passata dimostra che l'attesa di ulteriori evidenze causa problemi più gravi, ossia la crescita del terrorismo.

8) B. La soluzione del quesito consiste nell'individuare quale tra le alternative di risposta, se vera, indebolisce le argomentazioni del brano.
Analizzando le opzioni, si può subito notare che le affermazioni *The practical experience of gardening is not a traditional academic subject* e *It tends to be older people who are interested in gardening and growing their own food* trattano l'argomento da punti di vista molto diversi rispetto a quello del brano (il primo fa riferimento al mondo universitario e il secondo al mondo degli anziani) e quindi non ne minano il senso.
Le alternative restanti, invece, potrebbero indebolire l'argomentazione della traccia. Ad esempio, il fatto che *some schools do not have a garden* potrebbe essere un problema per la diffusione dell'iniziativa, così come l'affermazione *The events to encourage children to garden also included stands where junk food was for sale* contrasta con il fine ultimo dichiarato nel brano, cioè la dissuasione dal mangiare cibo spazzatura. L'affermazione che rappresenta la risposta corretta, quindi, è *Most children have enjoyed the events provided, but have not gained an interest in gardening itself*, con la quale si indebolisce fortemente il principio alla base di questi eventi speciali nelle scuole: fare interessare i bambini al giardinaggio. Affermando, infatti, che gran parte dei bambini si è divertita agli eventi ma non si è interessata al giardinaggio in sé, è molto difficile concludere che l'iniziativa in esame dovrebbe essere sostenuta e diffusa, non potendo essa ottenere gli obiettivi prefissati: far interessare i bambini al giardinaggio per poi renderli più attenti a ciò che mangiano e dissuaderli dal consumare cibo spazzatura.

9) D. Il quesito chiede di determinare quale delle cinque opzioni di risposta riporta la cosiddetta prova addizionale, cioè l'affermazione che, se fosse aggiunta alle premesse, rafforzerebbe maggiormente l'argomentazione citata nella traccia.
Analizzando le opzioni di risposta, possiamo osservare che l'affermazione *The carbon that is present on the Earth could have arrived at a later date from an asteroid* non aggiunge informazioni riguardo al deficit di carbonio sulla Terra, ma avanza ipotesi sulla prove-

nienza di questo elemento. L'opzione *There is no theoretical reason why life has to be carbon-based*, allo stesso modo, fornisce un dato irrilevante rispetto al contenuto della traccia che non si interroga sul fatto che la vita sia basata o meno sul carbonio. La risposta *At temperatures that are high enough for carbon to boil away, oxygen would also have boiled away* dà un'informazione che sembrerebbe pertinente, ma in realtà riguarda l'ossigeno e non il carbonio.

Allo stesso modo, l'opzione di risposta *There are other solar systems with Earth-like planets that have an abundance of carbon on them* potrebbe rafforzare l'argomentazione del brano ma mette il pianeta Terra a confronto con pianeti simili in altri sistemi solari.

L'opzione corretta è, quindi, *The abundance of carbon in the asteroid belt surrounding the inner planets increases the further away you get from the Sun*, in cui si paragona la Terra *with other bodies in the solar system*, proprio come argomentato nel brano. Si tratta degli asteroidi della fascia che circonda i pianeti interni e che, quindi, è un termine di confronto diretto con la Terra: se in questa fascia la quantità di carbonio aumenta con l'aumentare della distanza dal Sole, un tale fenomeno dovrebbe riguardare anche i pianeti interni, fra i quali la Terra è il penultimo per distanza dal Sole. Ciò rende ancora più misterioso il deficit di carbonio sulla Terra, per cui la conclusione è rafforzata.

10) D. Per rispondere correttamente al quesito è necessario individuare, fra le alternative di risposta, quella che sintetizza il messaggio principale sostenuto dal brano.

Tra le alternative di risposta possiamo scartare subito l'affermazione *An act is criminal only if it is committed for criminal reasons*, che sembra giustificare l'operato dei poliziotti sotto copertura – qualunque esso sia – e in contrasto con quanto concluso dal brano.

Le opzioni *The police have a duty to protect lawabiding citizens from violence* e *Serious crime must be prevented by any reasonable means* potrebbero concordare con alcune affermazioni riportate nel brano, ma non esprimono il concetto chiave in esso sostenuto. Difatti, posto che i mezzi per impedire i crimini devono essere ragionevoli, allora essi non devono violare la legge.

La risposta corretta è *The end does not justify the means*, che rappresenta una formulazione più generale di ciò che è asserito nella conclusione del brano, ossia che per prevenire un crimine non è giusto commetterne un altro.

11) B. Nella traccia la targa dell'auto appare in posizione normale, ma per risolvere il quesito bisogna immaginarla sottosopra (*upside down*) e confrontarla in quest'ultima posizione con ciascuna delle immagini nelle alternative di risposta. Tale operazione è illustrata graficamente di seguito.

Targa in posizione normale **S308 CNH**

↓

Targa sottosopra **Ƨ308 CИH**

Se concentriamo la nostra attenzione sulla lettera C, possiamo notare che è l'unica lettera che, anche se sottosopra, mantiene il suo aspetto costante, quindi le ipotesi SƐ08 ƆNH, Ƨ308 ƆNH e S308 ƆИH sono da escludere. L'alternativa SƐ08 CИH, anche se presenta la lettera C raffigurata in maniera corretta, ha la lettera S non solo sottosopra ma anche al contrario. L'unica alternativa di risposta plausibile è Ƨ308 CИH.

12) C. Analizzando le alternative di risposta, possiamo innanzitutto eliminare le alternative che propongono le seguenti disposizioni:

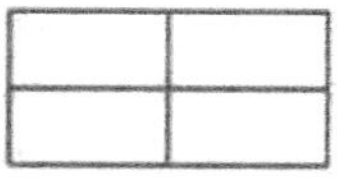

nella quale manca il metro di spazio intorno ai tavoli e

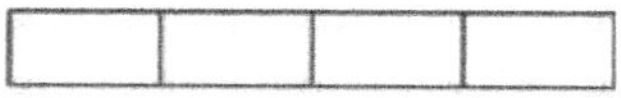

che è lunga 2 m × 4 = 8 m, cioè più dei 6 m di lunghezza della sala.
L'alternativa che propone la disposizione con il perimetro superiore dei tavoli lungo (2 m × 2) + (1 m × 2) = 4 m + 2 m = 6 m, può contenere 6 m ÷ 1,5 m = 4 bacheche. Inoltre, i 2 tavoli che si trovano lateralmente misurano 2 m di lunghezza ciascuno, quindi ognuno potrà contenere una bacheca, e nella parte inferiore dei 2 tavoli centrali, lunga 2 m × 2 = 4 m, possono entrare altre 2 bacheche (1,5 m × 2 = 3 m). In totale, con la disposizione B si riescono a sistemare 4 + 1 + 1 + 2 = 8 bacheche, ma non 9 (vedi disegno).

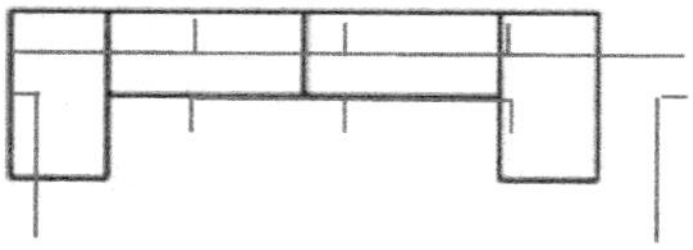

La disposizione che si presenta di forma quadrata, con i 4 lati lunghi 1 m + 2 m = 3 m, e con un'apertura centrale di 1 m × 1 m, può ospitare esternamente lungo 2 lati opposti (per esempio quello superiore e quello inferiore) 2 bacheche per lato (1,5 m × 2 = 3 m), ma lungo gli altri 2 lati, che hanno perso 0,2 m × 2 = 0,4 m, può ospitarne soltanto una. Internamente, inoltre, non è possibile disporre nessuna bacheca, poiché i bordi disponibili sono di 1 m, mentre le bacheche sono lunghe 1,5 m (vedi disegno). In totale con tale disposizione si riescono a sistemare soltanto 2 + 2 + 1 + 1 = 6 bacheche.

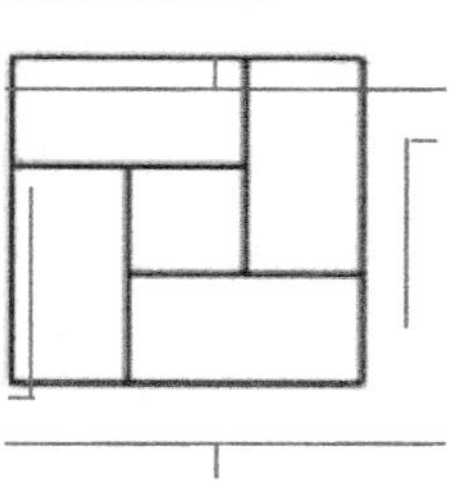

Infine, la disposizione a ferro di cavallo ha il perimetro superiore esterno pari a 2 m × 2 = 4 m, dove si possono disporre 2 bacheche, e i 2 perimetri laterali esterni lunghi ciascuno 1 m + 2 m = 3 m, e adatti, quindi, a contenere 2 bacheche ciascuno. Ma i 2 tavoli inferiori hanno anche 2 m di perimetro interno laterale, su ciascuno dei quali si può disporre 1 bacheca, e i 2 tavoli superiori hanno 2 m di perimetro interno, sul quale si può disporre 1 bacheca (vedi disegno). Allora le bacheche sistemabili in questo caso sono 2 + 2 + 2 + 1 + 1 + 1 = 9.

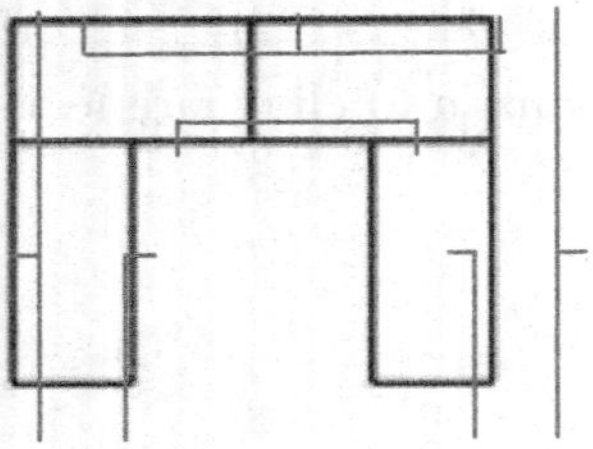

13) C. Per risolvere il quesito si deve innanzitutto calcolare quanta superficie deve essere verniciata. Sono date le dimensioni della sala da pranzo ed è detto che sulla parete più grande, cioè quella che misura 6 m × 3,5 m, c'è una finestra di dimensione 1,5 m × 2 m, che ovviamente non va dipinta. Si dovranno, quindi, dipingere le 4 pareti, esclusa la finestra, più il soffitto, cioè:

(6 m × 3,5 m) – (1,5 m × 2 m) + (6 m × 3,5 m) + (4 m × 3,5 m) × 2 + (6 m × 4 m) =
= 21 – 3 + 21 + 14 × 2 + 24 = 91 m^2

Il 20% dell'area da verniciare, però, è fatta di legno ed ha bisogno di una seconda mano di pittura, per cui si deve calcolare il 20% di 91 m^2 e aggiungerlo alla superficie totale:

$$91\,m^2 \times \frac{20}{100} = 18{,}2\,m^2$$

Allora la superficie da dipingere sarà 91 m^2 + 18,2 m^2 = 109,2 m^2 e quindi, poiché con ciascuna lattina si riescono a dipingere 24 m^2, saranno necessarie 109,2 m^2 ÷ 24 m^2 = 4,55 lattine, vale a dire, visto che non è possibile comprare mezza lattina, 5 lattine di pittura.

14) E. Per sapere qual è il numero minimo di rotaie necessarie a completare il lavoro si deve calcolare in quante parti può essere divisa ogni rotaia per coprire le varie distanze. Innanzitutto si devono trasformare le misure delle distanze da cm a m, poiché la lunghezza delle rotaie è riportata in metri:

115 cm = 1,15 m

90 cm = 0,90 m

120 cm = 1,20 m

180 cm = 1,80 m

210 cm = 2,10 m

150 cm = 1,50 m

Osservando i dati a disposizione, si può notare intuitivamente che le due distanze da 2,10 m necessitano di una rotaia ciascuna, da cui avanzano due pezzi di soltanto 0,30 m, quindi inutilizzabili su altre distanze (2 rotaie).
A questo punto si procede con le altre distanze partendo dalle maggiori: si ipotizza di utilizzare una rotaia per ciascuna distanza, si calcolano di volta in volta le parti rimanenti e il loro possibile riutilizzo.
Per la distanza di 1,80 m si utilizzerà una rotaia dalla quale avanzerà un pezzo di 0,60 m, inutilizzabile altrove (1 rotaia). Per la distanza di 1,5 m si utilizza un'altra rotaia (2,40 – 1,50 = 0,90) da cui avanza un pezzo utilizzabile esattamente per la distanza di 0,90 m (1 rotaia).
Infine, per la distanza di 1,20 m si utilizzerà una rotaia da cui avanza un pezzo di 1,20 m (2,4 – 1,20 = 1,25), riutilizzabile per la distanza di 1,15 m (1 rotaia).
Il numero minimo di rotaie necessarie al contadino per completare il lavoro è, quindi, 5.

---

15) A. Per risolvere il quesito è necessario mettere in relazione i dati forniti nel testo con quelli osservabili nella tabella.
Innanzitutto, Tom desidera che i biglietti di invito siano alti almeno 8 cm, allora si devono subito eliminare i biglietti della prima e della quarta riga, che sono alti rispettivamente 6 e 7 cm.
Inoltre, Tom vorrebbe inserire una foto nell'invito, quindi non può essere considerato nemmeno il tipo di biglietti riportato nella seconda riga della tabella.
Tra i modelli di biglietti rimanenti il più economico è quello della quinta riga, che costa € 1,50 a biglietto, per una spesa totale di € 1,50 × 50 = € 75,00.
Ma Tom è disposto a pagare di più per avere la versione deluxe di questi biglietti, che costa € 1,95 a pezzo, per una spesa totale di € 1,95 × 50 = € 97,50.
Allora, per avere dei biglietti di invito deluxe Tom spenderà in più € 97,50 – € 75,00 = € 22,50.

---

16) D. Il rapporto tra cervelletto e massa corporea totale del gatto è pari a 5,3 g ÷ 3500 g = 0,0015. Per sapere quale tra le altre specie di animali ha il rapporto tra massa del cervelletto e massa corporea totale più vicino a quello del gatto non si deve far altro che calcolarlo specie per specie:

Topo	0,009 g ÷ 58 g = 0,0015
Piccione	0,4 g ÷ 500 g = 0,0008
Scoiattolo	1,5 g ÷ 350 g = 0,004
Coniglio	1,9 g ÷ 1800 g = 0,0010
Cane	6,0 g ÷ 3500 g = 0,0017

Come notiamo, tra tutti gli animali elencati nella tabella, il topo è quello che ha il rapporto tra massa del cervelletto e massa corporea totale esattamente identico a quello del gatto.

---

17) E. Si indichino con A l'aliscafo, con B il traghetto e con S la distanza tra Sandpoint e Genville. Poiché A percorre lo spazio S in 50 minuti, mentre B lo percorre in 1 h e

40 min = 100 minuti, possiamo dire che la velocità dell'aliscafo è doppia rispetto a quella del traghetto, cioè $v_A = 2v_B$.
Inoltre, è noto che quando A riparte da Genville sono passati 50 min + 20 min = 70 minuti, per cui B deve percorrere ancora 30 minuti, ovvero i 30/100 del suo tragitto, cioè gli manca una parte di tragitto R = 30/100 S.
Lungo questo tragitto R il traghetto incontrerà l'aliscafo ad un certo tempo *t*, in cui A avrà percorso un tragitto s_A da Genville verso Sandpoint e B avrà percorso un tragitto s_B verso Genville, con $S_A + s_B = R$. Ma si sa anche che a questo tempo *t*:

$s_A \div s_B = v_A \div v_B$, con $v_A = 2v_B$,

cioè $s_A \div s_B = 2v_B \div v_B$ (1)

Allora, poiché in una proporzione il prodotto dei medi è uguale al prodotto degli estremi,

$s_A = (s_B \times 2v_B) \div v_B = 2\ s_B$

e quindi $R = 2\ s_B + s_B = 3\ s_B$.

Ma R = 30/100 S, quindi si avrà che $3\ s_B = 30/100\ S$, da cui

$s_B = (30/100\ S) \div 3 = S/10$.

Pertanto, poiché B impiega 100 minuti per percorrere S, impiegherà 100/10 = 10 minuti per percorrere s_B, pertanto incontrerà l'aliscafo A dopo 10 min + 70 min = 80 minuti, cioè dopo 1 h e 20 min dalla sua partenza da Sandpoint.
Si osservi che, analogamente, dalla proporzione (1) si ha

$s_B = (s_A \times v_B) \div 2v_B = s_A/2$

e quindi $R = s_A + s_A/2 = 3/2\ s_A$

per cui $3/2\ s_A = 30/100\ S$

da cui $s_A = (30/100\ S) \times 2/3 = S/5$

Pertanto, poiché A impiega 50 minuti per percorrere S, impiegherà 50/5 = 10 minuti per percorrere s_A e, quindi, incontrerà il traghetto B dopo 10 minuti dalla sua partenza da Genville, cioè dopo 10 min + 70 min = 80 minuti dalla partenza di entrambi i mezzi di trasporto da Sandpoint.

---

18) D. Poiché non è possibile sapere quanta benzina ci sia nel serbatoio prima del 2 giugno, l'unico modo per calcolare qual è la migliore stima del consumo di benzina dell'auto di Diana è da considerare il rapporto tra la benzina messa nel serbatoio tra un pieno e l'altro e i relativi chilometri percorsi.
Infatti, tra i 2 pieni, quello che Diana ha messo nel serbatoio corrisponde a quello che l'auto ha consumato. I litri messi tra i 2 pieni sono 25 + 21 + 34 = 80, mentre i chilometri percorsi sono 545 + 393 + 246 = 1184, per cui il consumo dell'auto di Diana è pari a:

80 litri ÷ 1184 km = 0,068 litri per chilometro,

ovvero 6,8 litri / 100 km.

19) E. La distanza percorsa da Leroy da casa al lavoro aumenta con l'aumentare del tempo, per cui i grafici in cui dopo la prima metà di percorso la variabile "distanza" decresce non rappresentano il tragitto da lui compiuto, pertanto sono errati.
Nel testo del quesito, inoltre, si parla di metà percorso fatto in salita alla velocità di 5 km/h e di un'altra metà fatta in discesa alla velocità di 15 km/h, quindi ci sarà un momento, corrispondente al primo tratto della retta, in cui la variabile "distanza" crescerà lentamente, per poi crescere più rapidamente nel secondo tratto della retta, corrispondente alla parte di percorso in discesa.
Per questo, il grafico in cui il tratto in salita (cioè a velocità bassa e durante il quale la variabile "distanza" cresce meno rapidamente della variabile "tempo") è troppo breve rispetto al secondo tratto, e quindi meno della metà, è anch'esso da scartare.
Nella prima metà di percorso, inoltre, la velocità è 5 km/h = 15 km/h ÷ 3, cioè un terzo della velocità della seconda metà di percorso. Allora, poiché velocità e tempo sono grandezze inversamente proporzionali (vale a dire che se la velocità diminuisce, il tempo impiegato a percorrere lo stesso tragitto aumenta proporzionalmente), si avrà che il tempo impiegato a percorrere la prima parte di tragitto sarà il triplo di quello impiegato per arrivare alla fine del percorso. Pertanto, il grafico in cui è rappresentata una retta che cresce molto nel primo tratto per poi rallentare nel secondo esprime una situazione completamente opposta al tragitto di Leroy. Il grafico che mostra perfettamente il tragitto di Leroy è quello con una retta in cui nel primo tratto si ha un rapporto tra distanza e tempo pari a 1:3, mentre nel secondo tratto un rapporto pari a 3:1.

---

20) B. L'ultima cifra è la seconda del numero risultante dalla somma dei primi 3 numeri a due cifre, che sappiamo essere dispari o, più in particolare, la somma delle cifre che nella sequenza si trovano al 2°, al 4° e al 6° posto. Tale cifra, allora, sarà pari alla somma di 3 numeri dispari a una cifra, e quindi, per sapere di che cifra si tratta, basta fare le possibili somme tra 1, 3, 5, 7 e 9 e vedere man mano se viene fuori una cifra plausibile per l'8° posto.
Si procede in questo modo:

- 1 + 3 + 5 = 9, che potrebbe essere un risultato. Si va allora a considerare anche le prime cifre, con le quali si dovrebbe avere una somma del tipo 41 + x3 + y5 = z9, e si cerca di trovare i numeri da sostituire a x, y e z. Poiché la somma di questi 3 numeri deve essere a 2 cifre, si devono scegliere i numeri più piccoli da sostituire a x e y, ovvero, visto che ogni cifra può essere usata una sola volta, 2 e 6, che, sommati a 4, danno come risultato 12, cioè un numero a 2 cifre che non può essere messo al posto della z. Allora il 9 viene scartato e si passa a provare con le altre somme;
- 1 + 3 + 7 = 11, cioè 1 (con riporto di 1), che non va bene perché già utilizzato al 2° posto (le cifre devono essere tutte diverse);
- 1 + 3 + 9 = 13, cioè 3 (con riporto di 1), che non va bene perché già utilizzato al 4° posto;
- 1 + 5 + 7 = 13, cioè 3 (con riporto di 1), che potrebbe essere un risultato.

Si considerano, quindi, anche le prime cifre, con le quali si dovrebbe avere una somma del tipo 41 + x5 + y7 = z3, e si cerca di trovare i numeri da sostituire a x, y e z. Come nel caso precedente, si devono scegliere i numeri più piccoli da sostituire a x e y, ovvero, visto che ogni cifra può essere usata una sola volta, 2 e 6, che, come prima, sommati a 4 e al riporto di 1, danno come risultato 13, cioè un numero a 2 cifre che non può essere messo al posto della z. Allora il 3 viene scartato e si passa a provare con le altre somme;

- 1 + 5 + 9 = 15, cioè 5 (con riporto di 1), che non va bene perché già utilizzato al 2° posto;
- 1 + 7 + 9 = 17, cioè 7 (con riporto di 1), che non va bene perché già utilizzato al 4° posto;
- 3 + 5 + 7 = 15, cioè 5 (con riporto di 1), che non va bene perché già utilizzato al 4° posto;
- 3 + 7 + 9 = 19, cioè 9 (con riporto di 1), che non va bene perché già utilizzato al 6° posto;
- 5 + 7 + 9 = 21, cioè 1 (con riporto di 2), che potrebbe essere un risultato.

Si considerano, allora, anche le prime cifre, con le quali si dovrebbe avere una somma del tipo 45 + x7 + y9 = z1, e si cerca di trovare i numeri da sostituire a x, y e z. In questo caso i numeri più piccoli da sostituire a x e y sono 2 e 3, che, sommati a 4 e al riporto di 1, danno come risultato 10, cioè un numero a 2 cifre che non può essere messo al posto della z. Allora anche l'1 viene scartato e si passa a provare con le altre somme;

- 3 + 5 + 9 = 17, cioè 7 (con riporto di 1), che potrebbe essere un risultato.

Si considerano, quindi, anche le prime cifre, con le quali si dovrebbe avere una somma del tipo 43 + x5 + y9 = z7, e si cerca di trovare i numeri da sostituire ad x, y e z. In questo caso si possono prendere 1 e 2, che, sommati a 4 e al riporto di 1, danno come risultato 8. Allora 43 + 15 + 29 = 87, quindi sono state utilizzate 8 cifre diverse, i primi 3 numeri sono dispari e l'ultimo numero è pari alla loro somma, per cui l'ultima cifra della password è 7.
Si noti che l'ordine delle coppie dei primi 6 numeri è ininfluente, cioè troveremmo lo stesso risultato anche sommando, per esempio, 45 + 19 + 23 = 87.

21) A. Il quesito richiede di individuare tra le coppie "studioso/campo di studi" proposte quella non corretta. Mentre Doris Lessing è una scrittrice, Konrad Lorenz un etologo, Ludwig Wittgenstein un filosofo e Amartya Sen un economista, è certo che Max Weber è un sociologo e non un pedagogista.

22) C. La risposta corretta al quesito è Mahatma Gandhi, l'unico personaggio, tra quelli elencati nelle alternative di risposta, a non aver vinto il premio Nobel per la pace. Willy Brandt lo vinse nel 1971 per il suo impegno nella Ostpolitik; Martin Luther King nel 1964 per aver lottato a favore dei diritti civili; Nelson Mandela nel 1993 insieme a de Klerk per aver svolto un ruolo decisivo nello smantellamento del sistema di segregazione razziale in Sudafrica; Aung San Suu Kyi nel 1991 per il suo impegno nel processo di democratizzazione della Birmania.

Biologia

23) D. Un amminoacido è un composto che contiene sia un gruppo amminico (basico, indicato in figura con il numero 1) sia un gruppo carbossilico (acido, indicato in figura con il numero con 3), legati entrambi al carbonio alfa. Quest'ultimo è legato anche a un atomo di idrogeno (indicato con il numero 4) e al gruppo R (o catena laterale variabile) che nel caso illustrato è CH_3 (indicato con il numero 2). Il gruppo R varia da amminoacido ad amminoacido, andando da un atomo di idrogeno della glicina a più complesse catene carboniose alifatiche o aromatiche. La risposta esatta è, quindi, gruppo variabile = 2; gruppo acido = 3.

24) E. Nei procarioti la trascrizione avviene nel citoplasma, mentre la sintesi delle proteine avviene nei ribosomi. I procarioti sono privi di mitocondri.

25) B. La fotolisi dell'acqua è un processo durante il quale una molecola di acqua viene scissa in due protoni, due elettroni ed un atomo di ossigeno.

26) A. Nel ciclo di una normale cellula eucariotica si verificano i seguenti eventi: i cromosomi si allineano lungo il piano equatoriale, le fibre del fuso si accorciano, ricompare l'involucro nucleare e il citoplasma si divide. La corretta sequenza di eventi è indicata nella riga 3 della tabella.

27) E. La replicazione avviene sempre con meccanismo semiconservativo poiché ciascuna delle doppie eliche figlie è composta da un filamento intero derivato dalla doppia elica parentale e da un filamento completo di nuova sintesi. Nel momento in cui una doppia elica di DNA costituita da un filamento radioattivo e uno non radioattivo viene fatta replicare in un terreno non radioattivo, dopo una prima replicazione il DNA radioattivo sarà al 50%, dopo una seconda divisione al 25% e dopo una terza al 12,5%.

28) C. Dall'incrocio tra due individui con genotipo *QqRr* si ottengono i seguenti fenotipi: Q_R_, Q_rr, qqR_, qqrr.

29) D. La traduzione è il processo mediante il quale diversi amminoacidi vengono uniti per formare una nuova proteina, seguendo le istruzioni contenute in un filamento di RNA messaggero che si forma su uno stampo di DNA. Quindi, l'RNA messaggero è una copia complementare di uno dei due filamenti di DNA che costituiscono un gene, mentre gli RNA transfer (RNA di trasferimento o tRNA), che rappresentano la terza principale classe di RNA richiesta durante la sintesi delle proteine, sono necessari per tradurre le informazioni contenute nella sequenza nucleotidica di un mRNA nella sequenza di amminoacidi di un polipeptide. A ogni codone dell'mRNA (un codone è la sequenza di tre basi azotate, specifica per ogni amminoacido) corrisponde un anticodone del tRNA. Se la sequenza del DNA mutato è ATCTTGCGG, la sequenza del tRNA sarà AUCUUGCGG. Sostituendo alle triplette i simboli degli amminoacidi riportati nella tabella, si ottiene la sequenza indicata di seguito: □–○–◇.

30) B. Uno dei principi della genetica di popolazioni è che non ci può essere evoluzione se non c'è variazione genetica. La speciazione è la divergenza di una specie in una o più specie, oppure la trasformazione di una specie in una nuova specie nel corso del tempo, come risultato ultimo di cambiamenti delle frequenze alleliche e genotipiche nel pool genico.
La biodiversità è la varietà degli ecosistemi, delle specie e delle popolazioni all'interno delle specie e contribuisce anch'essa all'evoluzione.

31) D. Gli osteociti sono le cellule dell'osso maturo; essi controllano la concentrazione di proteine e minerali nella matrice che li circonda e si trovano in piccoli spazi detti lacune, compresi tra gli strati della matrice calcificata, definiti lamelle. All'interno dell'articolazione della spalla, quindi, gli osteociti si trovano nel tessuto osseo.

32) D. Si tratta del ciclo cardiaco e la fase X corrisponde alla diastole, ovvero alla fase di riempimento ventricolare. Durante la seconda metà della diastole, il sangue entra negli atri rilasciati, passa attraverso le valvole AV e riempie i ventricoli (il volume del sangue nell'atrio sinistro, quindi, diminuisce). Durante il riempimento, le valvole polmonare e aortica (semilunari) sono chiuse, perché la pressione ventricolare è più bassa rispetto a quelle vigenti nell'aorta e nelle arterie polmonari. Alla fine della diastole, gli atri si contraggono, spingendo ulteriore sangue nei ventricoli. Dopo poco, gli atri si rilasciano e inizia la sistole. Tutta questa fase in cui il sangue riempie i ventricoli viene chiamata "riempimento ventricolare" e la muscolatura della parete ventricolare sinistra è rilasciata.

33) E. Si tratta di analizzare gli eventi che si verificano nel sarcomero durante la contrazione. Con 1 identifichiamo l'intera lunghezza del sarcomero che durante la contrazione si accorcia. Con 2 indichiamo i filamenti sottili, che durante la contrazione scivolano su quelli spessi senza però variare la loro lunghezza.

34) B. Gli anestetici locali bloccano i canali del sodio voltaggio-dipendenti e riducono l'ingresso di ioni sodio, prevenendo così la normale depolarizzazione della membrana bloccando la conduzione del potenziale d'azione.

35) C. Quattro giorni prima dell'ovulazione si ha una diminuzione di breve durata dei livelli di estrogeni e un incremento degli ormoni FSH e LH. Durante l'ovulazione gli alti livelli di LH responsabili dell'ovulazione stimolano anche la produzione di progesterone.

36) E. La sequenza degli eventi è 5, 1, 2, 4. Nel dettaglio, in seguito ad uno stimolo si instaura un potenziale d'azione che si propaga lungo la membrana plasmatica e i tubuli T; si aprono i canali per il calcio presenti nel reticolo sarcoplasmatico; il calcio si lega alla troponina, spostando la tropomiosina dai siti di legame per la miosina presenti sull'actina. Quando i siti attivi sono esposti, le teste della miosina, a cui è legato l'ATP, si legano ad essi, formando dei ponti trasversali; successivamente la testa della miosina ruota determinando il rilascio di ADP e fosfato. Quando un'altra molecola di

ATP si lega alla testa della miosina, si scinde il legame tra il sito attivo sulla molecola di actina e la testa della miosina.

37) D. Bisogna considerare l'appaiamento delle basi: l'adenina si lega alla timina, la citosina alla guanina. Quindi le sonde che si legano sono la 2 e la 3.

38) D. Per rispondere al quesito occorre conoscere il ciclo cellulare. Nella cellula staminale abbiamo i due alleli A e a del gene in questione. All'inizio della mitosi è avvenuta già la duplicazione del corredo cromosomico e quindi avremo gli alleli in doppia copia. All'inizio della prima divisione meiotica si verifica la duplicazione dei cromosomi e, quindi, il numero degli alleli sarà in doppia copia.

39) C. La sequenza è 2, 1, 3. Il nucleo è l'organulo più grande (5 μm), il mitocondrio misura circa 1500 nm e il ribosoma 20 nm.

40) B. Il glucagone non è un carboidrato, ma un ormone di natura proteica. Invece, il maltosio è un disaccaride, l'amilosio è un componente idrosolubile dell'amido, il ribosio è un monosaccaride e l'amilopectina è un componente insolubile dei granuli di amido.

Chimica

41) D. Il propanale, un composto organico saturo a tre atomi di carbonio, è un'aldeide e possiede il gruppo funzionale —CHO, il quale contiene a sua volta il gruppo C=O, che viene chiamato carbonile o gruppo carbonilico. La formula generale delle aldeidi è RCHO; essa indica che un radicale qualsiasi, indicato con R, è legato al gruppo —CHO che costituisce la parte terminale della molecola. La risposta esatta è CH_3CH_2CHO.

42) B. Gli ossidi dei metalli sono chiamati ossidi basici, perché quando si disciolgono in quantità apprezzabile in acqua danno origine a soluzioni basiche. Gli ossidi dei non metalli, che possono reagire con l'acqua per formare ioni H_3O^+, sono chiamati ossidi acidi e danno luogo a soluzioni acide. NO e CO, non essendo né acidi né basi, non danno luogo in acqua a soluzioni acide o basiche.

43) E. La formula corretta è $(NH_4)_2CrO_4$, in quanto sono bilanciate le cariche (N = –6, H = 8, Cr = 6, O = –8).

44) C. Gli idrocarburi sono composti organici che contengono soltanto atomi di carbonio e di idrogeno. La formula dell'idrocarburo si può rappresentare come C_xH_y. Il composto C_xH_y pesa 0,75 g e il carbonio è 0,60 g. Di conseguenza il peso dell'idrogeno è (0,75 – 0,60) g = 0,15 g. Calcoliamo ora il numero di moli di C e H:

– moli di C = grammi/PM = 0,60/12 = 0,05 mol di C;

– moli di H = grammi /PM = 0,15/1 = 0,15 mol di H.

Per trovare il rapporto tra le moli dividiamo per il numero più piccolo:

C = 0,05/0,005 = 1   H = 0,15/0,05 = 3

C e H sono presenti nel composto nel rapporto di 1 : 3, la formula minima è CH_3.
La formula molecolare è pari a n × (CH_3), quindi C_nH_{3n}, da cui si può ricavare la formula molecolare C_2H_6.

45) A. L'alluminio è presente nel terzo periodo della tavola periodica, ha numero atomico pari a 13 e configurazione elettronica $1s^22s^22p^63s^23p^1$. Al^{2+} ha perso due elettroni, quindi ha la seguente configurazione elettronica: $1s^22s^22p^63s^1$.

46) B. La formula del propan-1-olo è C_3H_8O. L'equazione non bilanciata è $C_3H_8O + O_2 \rightarrow CO_2 + H_2O$.
L'equazione bilanciata è: $2C_3H_8O + 9O_2 \rightarrow 6CO_2 + 8H_2O$.
Il rapporto tra CO_2 e H_2O è 3 : 4.

47) D. La diversa temperatura di ebollizione che si riscontra tra due isomeri dipende dalle forze intermolecolari, dalla lunghezza della catena e da quanto essa sia ramificata.

48) C. Consideriamo la solubilità di KNO_3 nelle due condizioni:
- primo caso 120 g KNO_3/ 100 g H_2O a 80°C;
- secondo caso 50 g KNO_3/ 100 g H_2O a 25°C.

Teniamo presente che la solubilità da considerare è quella del secondo caso ovvero a 25 °C.
A 80 °C, in 50 g di H_2O, il KNO_3 che si scioglierà sarà la metà rispetto al primo caso, quindi 60 g.
Portando la temperatura di questa soluzione a 25 °C troveremo la metà della solubilità del secondo caso, pertanto si sciolgono altri 25 g di KNO_3.
A questo punto il KNO_3 che non si è sciolto sarà pari a 60 g – 25 g = 35 g.
Facendo una proporzione calcoliamo quant'acqua bisogna aggiungere per sciogliere ulteriormente questi 35 g di KN O_3.
50 g di KNO_3 : 100 g di H_2O = 35 g di KNO_3 = x
$x = 100 \times 35/50 = 70$ g di H_2O.

49) B. Le affermazioni corrette sono la 1 e la 2. Le concentrazioni degli ioni H^+ e OH^-, infatti, sono le stesse all'interno dei valori di temperatura compresi tra 0 e 100 °C. Aumentando la temperatura si verifica una diminuzione del pH dovuta alla maggiore produzione di H^+.

50) A. $AlBr_3$, NH_4Cl e NaI sono sali che in soluzione acquosa hanno un pH neutro. Il composto CH_3CO_2H, nel momento in cui si scinde, porta ad una soluzione con pH acido. L'unico composto che in soluzione acquosa determina un pH basico è Na_2CO_3.

51) C. Il legame ionico si realizza per trasferimento di elettroni. Tra le soluzioni elencate, quella corretta è X = 12; Y = 9. L'atomo X ha numero atomico 12 e Y ha numero atomico 9. Dalla loro posizione nella tavola periodica diciamo che Y corrisponde al magnesio (Mg) e presenta 2 elettroni nel livello energetico più esterno; X corrisponde al fluoro (F) e presenta 7 elettroni nel livello energetico più esterno. Tenendo presente la regola dell'ottetto, la condivisione di questi elettroni tra l'atomo X e due atomi Y porta alla formazione del composto XY_2.

52) E. Il rapporto tra la resa reale e la resa teorica (moltiplicato per 100) dà la resa percentuale di quel prodotto nella reazione considerata.
Dai dati forniti sappiamo che il numero di moli di C_3H_7Br è 0,2 e il peso molecolare di C_3H_7OH è 60 g/mol: la resa reale è 8 g.
Il rapporto stechiometrico tra prodotti e reagenti è 1 : 1, quindi le moli teoriche di C_3H_7OH sono proprio 0,2.
La resa teorica di C_3H_7OH = 0,2 mol × 60 g/mol = 12 g.
Ora calcoliamo la resa percentuale:

resa % = resa reale/resa teorica = (8 g /12 g) x 100 = 66.7%.

Fisica e Matematica

53) D. Per rispondere correttamente al quesito, risolviamo il sistema:

$x + 3y = 13$

$2x - y = 5$

Ricaviamo x dalla prima equazione e lo sostituiamo nella seconda:

$x = 13 - 3y$

$2\ (13 - 3y) - y = 5$

Nella seconda equazione possiamo calcolare il valore di y:

$26 - 7y = 5$

da cui $y = 21/7 = 3$

Sostituendo il valore di y nella prima equazione otteniamo il valore di x:

$x = 13 - (3 \times 3) = 13 - 9 = 4$

per cui $x = 4$; $y = 3$; $x + y = 7$.

54) B. Svolgendo i calcoli abbiamo: (729 – 529) + (196 – 36) = 200 + 160 = 360.

55) C. Possiamo scrivere: $2 \log_{10} x = \log_{10} y + 3$
$2 \log_{10} x = \log_{10} y + 3\log_{10} 10 = \log_{10} x^2 = \log_{10} y \cdot \log_{10} 10^3 = \log_{10} x^2 = \log_{10} 10^3 \cdot y\ x^2 = 10^3 \cdot y$ da cui: $y = x^2/1000$, che ci dà y in funzione di x.

56) A. La media dei tre numeri è 8, quindi sostituendo 8 nella sequenza dei quattro numeri otteniamo: (8 + 1) + (8 + 2) + (8 + 6) + 3 = 9 + 10+ 14 + 3 = 36.
Calcoliamo ora la media dei quattro numeri dividendo la loro somma per il numero dei termini: 36/4 = 9.

57) E. La capacità termica specifica (C) è definita come l'energia trasferita in forma di calore necessario per innalzare di 1 Kelvin la temperatura di un grammo di sostanza. La sua unità di misura è Joule su grammo per Kelvin (J/g·K). Sostituendo i valori dati, la risposta corretta sarà $\frac{9000}{2.5 \times 4} Jkg^{-1}K^{-1}$.

58) D. La forza radiale F = m · a che costringe un oggetto di massa m a muoversi di moto circolare uniforme deve avere una direzione centripeta e modulo costante:

$F = m \cdot v^2/r$

In base ai nostri dati abbiamo:

$F = 1000 \text{ kg} \cdot (30 \text{ m s}^{-1})^2/50 \text{ m} = 18000 \text{ kg} \cdot \text{m/s}^2 = 18 \text{ kN}$.

La direzione dell'accelerazione è R in quanto Q = 0, dal momento che l'accelerazione è costante.

59) B. La risposta corretta è:

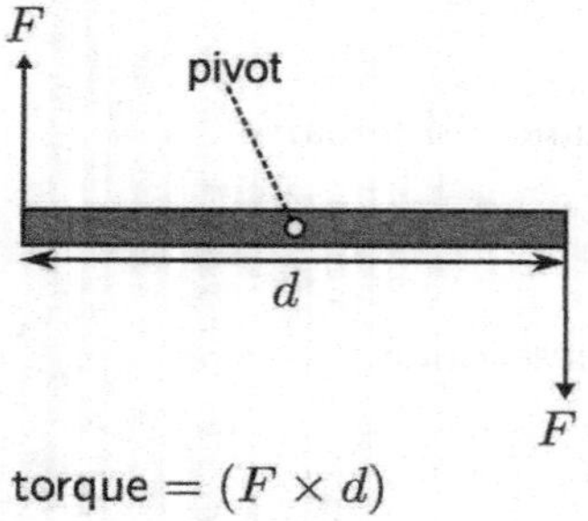

in quanto la coppia è data dal braccio per la forza:

$F \cdot d/2 + F \cdot d/2 = 2 F \cdot d/2 = F \cdot d$

60) C. Escludendo le equazioni riportate nelle altre alternative di risposta, quella corretta è:

electrical current = $(V/R_1) + (Q/t)$

perché l'intensità della corrente i è pari a Q/t e considerando che V = R · i allora i = V/R. Essendo entrambe dimensionalmente coerenti, possono essere sommate.

IMAT
a.a. 2016/2017

General knowledge and logical reasoning

1) Childhood obesity is still a problem. This is often blamed on the fact that children have easy access to a range of unhealthy foods and increasingly have more money available to them to spend on fattening and sugarfilled foods. A solution seems obvious – raise the prices of all these foods so that parents will have more control over what their children eat and will find it more economical to buy healthy foods. Unfortunately, this is unlikely to work as the problem is also caused by the fact that unhealthy foods tend to be more convenient and that is what many parents consider when deciding what foods to provide. A wider range of 'ready to eat' healthy food options would be a good start to solving the problem of child obesity.

Which one of the following best expresses the main conclusion of the above argument?

A. Child obesity is still a problem
B. There should be more 'ready to eat' healthy meals available
C. The price of unhealthy foods should be raised
D. Children have too much access to fattening and sugarfilled foods
E. Parents should have more control over the food that their children eat

2) High profile members of society can raise awareness of worthy causes better than members of the public, because they have their opinions listened to and respected more readily by a larger number of people. Celebrities should not be shy about drawing attention to charities and foundations to which they donate their time and money, because it may encourage other people to do the same.

Which one of the following best illustrates the principle underlying the argument above?

A. If you can help someone else by donating your disposable time and money, it will help improve society
B. People should value their superiors' opinions on all matters because they have been successful in one or more fields
C. If your boss does not commit any virtuous acts then neither should you
D. Companies with the most employees should be put under pressure to commit to the most social change
E. Directors of companies should encourage their employees to recycle more by visibly doing so themselves

3) What is a clone but a twin? What is genetic engineering or selective breeding but assisted evolution? How often do we hear these trite excuses for man's arrogant interference with natural processes? Too often. It is time to call a halt and consider just what limits need to be placed on the breakneck progress of biotechnology, if 'progress' is even the right word for it. The big question for science should not be 'What's in it for us?' but 'Could this have happened naturally?' And if the answer is 'No' then we should not bring it about just because we have found that we can. If we do we may live a bit longer or grow more food per acre, but we don't know where our meddling will end.

Which one of the following is a principle which underlies the above argument?

A. Science should not progress beyond what is natural
B. Cloning, genetic engineering and selective breeding are not 'progress'
C. Meddling with nature could only ever end in disaster
D. It is time to call a halt on biotechnological advances
E. Nature will have its own way in the long run

4) In recent years there has been increased concern that fashion models reflect an unrealistic and unattainable image of femininity and that this has a negative effect on the self-esteem of many young women. Many major designers continue to design for an exceptionally tall and flat-chested female frame. It should be no surprise therefore that there have been several cases recently when designers have favoured male models on their catwalks to model their womenswear. Rather than being a cause of surprise or concern, this should be welcomed as a recognition of the fact that these designs are unsuitable for most women and it draws attention to the major differences between catwalk fashion and clothing for the real world.

Which one of the following statements, if true, would most strengthen the argument above?

A. Some female models struggle to maintain the necessary physique for catwalk modelling
B. Very few observers noticed initially that the male models were not in fact women
C. Some designers have favoured male models simply to generate more media attention for their collections
D. Surveys of young women have suggested that the use of male models makes the typical model physique less desirable to attain
E. Some designers are recognising that the physique of many catwalk models represents an unhealthy ideal for most women

5) The government is considering changing the law to assume consent for the donation of organs after death. People opposed to the idea would have to deliberately 'opt out' of the scheme, although relatives would still be consulted. The supply of healthy organs available for transplant would be vastly increased under this scheme. If the government really wants to improve the lives of people with long-term health problems, this is a measure it must take.

Which one of the following, if true, would most strengthen the argument in the passage above?

A. There would be opposition by civil liberties groups to this measure
B. Bereaved relatives find donation decisions very distressing
C. The number of voluntary organ donors is small and not increasing
D. Not all of the organs donated are suitable for transplant
E. It is not known how many people would 'opt out' of the compulsory scheme

6) Children born in Japan today can expect to live five years longer than their American counterparts. Life expectancy has been rising in all countries, but the slowest rate of increase has been in the USA. What could account for this, given that the percentage of people who smoke is roughly the same in all rich countries? Of course, the USA is the birthplace of fast food restaurants that sell unhealthy food. Moreover, a recent survey of American lifestyles has found that overeating and failure to exercise are widespread amongst the population. So we must assume that obesity and lack of exercise have caused the USA to lag behind in the increase in life expectancy.

Which one of the following, if true, most weakens the above argument?

A. American fast food restaurants are now found in most rich countries
B. Most rich countries have the same standard of medical expertise
C. Japanese children had a healthier diet in the 1960s than they do today
D. In the 1960s and 1970s the USA had the highest percentage of smokers
E. The USA spends more money on fast food than any other nation

7) Children need to play in order to develop their thinking skills. When children play, they are merely going through scenarios, working out the consequences and implications of actions, puzzling out what might happen – the very same processes that adults have learned to do in their heads, the process more commonly known as 'thinking'! It follows that thinking and playing are really one and the same thing.

Which one of the following best expresses the main conclusion of the above argument?

A. Children who do not play will not be good thinkers
B. Playing is just an early version of abstract thinking and reasoning
C. Playing and thinking are essentially two forms of the same activity
D. Children need to be taught how to think about the future
E. Children need to be allowed to play in order to develop their thinking skills

8) While some animal rights activists have long accepted that there is a link between bovine tuberculosis (TB in cattle) and badgers, others have argued that it was not proven. They felt that the culling of badgers to stop the spread of TB in cattle was not justified if a link was unproven. But direct evidence of the transmission of TB between badgers and cattle has now been found. DNA sequencing of the TB bacteria in cattle and in badgers has shown that the disease crosses species barriers. This latest discovery completely undermines the case of those who have opposed badger culling. To protect farmers from severe loss of their cattle and hence their livelihoods – and to protect one of our primary sources of meat and milk – the badger population should be culled.

Which one of the following, if true, would most weaken the argument in the passage above?

A. There may be factors other than badgers, such as the movement of cattle, which contribute to the spread of TB in cattle
B. Not all farmers are convinced that the culling of badgers would stop the spread of TB
C. Animal rights activists are interested in the protection of badgers per se, whatever risk they pose
D. It is too expensive and logistically difficult to vaccinate all cattle against TB
E. Badger culling would be unpopular with a substantial number of people

9) Few linguists would argue against the view that our first language is acquired and not learned. Preschool children do not study their native tongue nor do they learn grammar rules but, by the time they start school at the age of five or six, the vast majority are competent users of their language. Therefore, when learning a second or additional language, studying grammar is a waste of time and all that is required is exposure to the target language in order to acquire competency in its use.

Which one of the following identifies the underlying assumption of the above argument?

A. Only people who know how to read can learn a second or additional language
B. Acquiring a second or additional language is the same process as acquiring a first language
C. Children are better at acquiring languages than adults
D. Learners of second or additional languages should read the target language
E. Languages are fundamentally different from one another

10) In 1688 the Irish philosopher William Molyneux asked whether a blind person who regained their vision could recognise by sight an object they had previously only known by touch. Richard Held and Pawan Sinha of the Massachusetts Institute of Technology attempted to answer this question in an experiment with five children in India who had just had successful surgery which gave them their sight for the first time. Within 48 hours of the operation the children were asked to feel a toy block without looking at it. They were then shown two blocks, one of which they had touched. They identified the original block just over half of the time and this is only a little better than guesswork. Recognising touched objects by sight alone improved within days.

Which one of the following can be drawn as a conclusion of the above passage?

A. Identifying an object by sight alone which had been touched but not seen previously is something which children do better than adults
B. Identifying an object by sight alone which had been touched but not seen previously is innate behaviour and not learned
C. Identifying an object by sight alone which had been touched but not seen previously is learned behaviour and not innate
D. Identifying an object by sight alone which had been touched but not seen previously is something which adults do better than children
E. Using children in experiments such as the one described above is morally wrong

11) The following pattern is made from six square tiles:

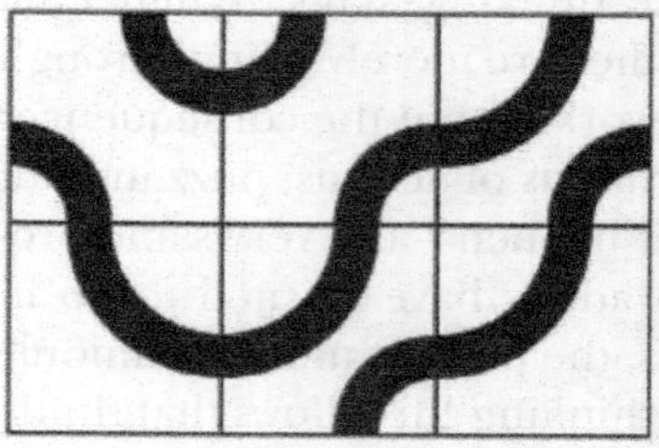

Which one of the following patterns can also be made from the same six tiles?

A.

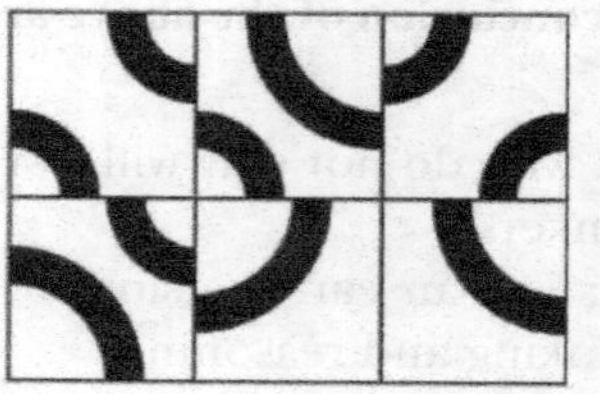

B. 

D. 

C. 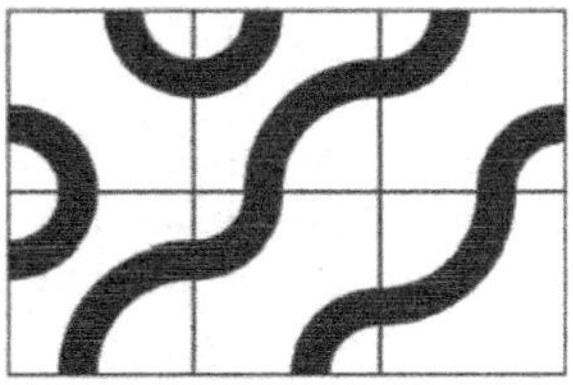

E. 

12) My choice of sandwich will depend on its nutritional content as shown in the following table:

type	price (£)	energy (kJ)	protein (g)	fat (g)	salt equiv (g)
beef	2.00	1220	22	3.4	1.3
chicken	2.10	1327	26	4.1	1.4
ham	1.90	1164	18	3.8	1.7
turkey	2.20	1163	20	2.5	1.5
salad	1.50	931	8	3.3	1.7
tuna	2.00	1579	19	14.3	1.7

I want to have at least 20 g of protein in my sandwich and no more than 4 g of fat. Which is the smallest amount that I will pay for my sandwich?

A. £ 2.10
B. £ 1.50
C. £ 1.90
D. £ 2.00
E. £ 2.20

13) In the foyer of a company in London there are nine clocks showing the local time at each of the Company's nine branches. This is how they appear at present:

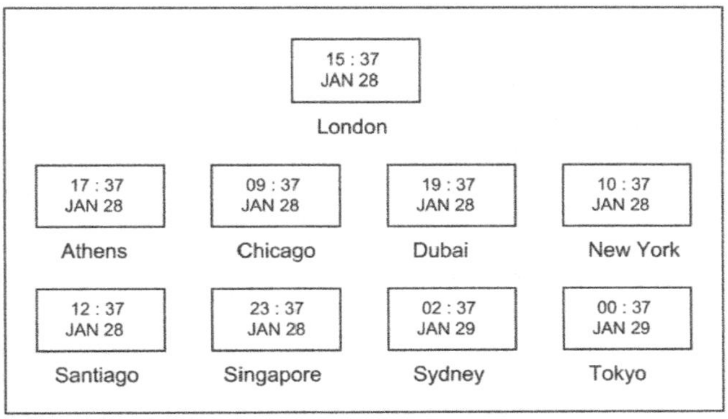

The person in charge of resetting these clocks in March and October has to remember:
1 In Dubai, Singapore and Tokyo clocks remain unchanged all year round.
2 In London, Athens, Chicago and New York clocks are put one hour forward in March and one hour back in October.
3 In Santiago and Sydney clocks are put one hour forward in October and one hour back in March.
When these clocks are next reset, which two will show the same time?

A. Sydney and Tokyo
B. Athens and London
C. Chicago and New York
D. Singapore and Tokyo
E. New York and Santiago

14) A factory has received an order for a product. It takes 9 operations to manufacture it. These may take place in any order and at any time in the manufacturing process but an individual worker stays with one operation from its beginning to its end. The number of hours for one worker to complete each operation is as follows:

Operation	A	B	C	D	E	F	G	H	I
Duration in hours	12	3	8	9	10	2	6	4	10

All workers are able to complete all operations, but can only do one at a time. The product has to be ready in 16 hours.
What is the minimum number of workers required to manufacture the product in the given time?

A. 5
B. 1
C. 4
D. 6
E. 9

15) A delivery company opens its depot at 7:30 am. It uses large and small vans to make deliveries. The smaller vans take 10 minutes to load and then 1 hour to make the deliveries and return. The larger ones have a loading time of 30 minutes and return from deliveries after 2 hours. The driver of a large van starts loading at 8:00 am.
If the driver of a small van is to make the maximum number of deliveries he can, how much later than the driver of the large van can he start loading if they are both to arrive back at the depot for lunch at 1:00 pm?
A. 10 minutes
B. 0 minutes
C. 5 minutes
D. 20 minutes
E. 15 minutes

16) Below is a picture of a biscuit tin with four identical sides. A set of these tins is to be made that are all distinguishable from each other by colour alone. The manufacturer will paint each of the four sides either red or blue. The top and bottom are not painted.

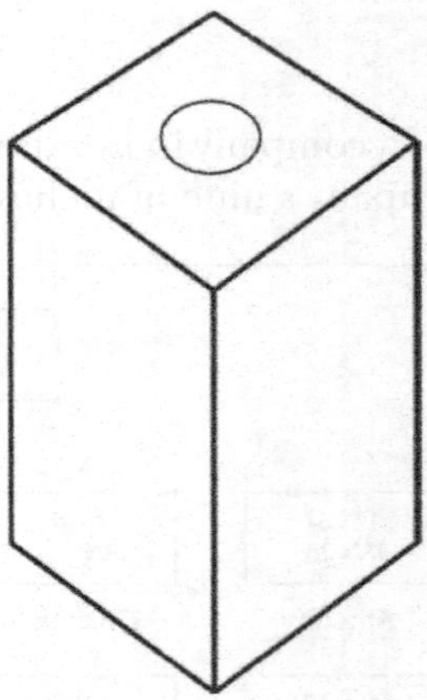

What is the greatest number of different tins that can be made?

A. 8
B. 5
C. 4
D. 7
E. 6

17) In a slalom skiing competition skiers tackle the course one at a time. Each skier makes two runs. The times for the two runs are added and the fastest total time determines the winner. Competitors who fail to finish their first run are not allowed to make a second run.
In the second round, skiers compete in the reverse order of their positions after the first round.

Grace took part in a slalom competition last week. She was the eighth skier to make her first run. At the end of the first round she was in sixth position, so she had to wait for 17 of her rivals to make their second runs before it was her turn again. Three skiers had failed to complete the course in the first round.
How many competitors took part in last week's slalom competition?

A. 23
B. 26
C. 28
D. 31
E. 34

18) A bakery shop makes its own bread in batches to sell on site. Bakers always describe the quantities of other ingredients as a percentage of the weight of flour used. They will then use the percentages in the table below to calculate how much water, salt and fat are required. Today, the baker is planning to use 250 kg of flour to make White Bread.

The Baker's Percentage			
Bread Type	**Water (%)**	**Salt (%)**	**Fat (%)**
Neapolitan Pizza	59	1.5	None
Baguette	60	2	None
French Bread	66	2	None
Ciabatta	80	2	2.5
Focaccia	80	3	3
White Bread	54	2	17
Brioche	22	2	133

What is the total weight of the mixture to be made?

A. 323 kg
B. 182.5 kg
C. 250 kg
D. 432.5 kg
E. 420 kg

19) I have folded a square piece of paper in half, then in half again, then cut three pieces from the resulting smaller square, as indicated below:

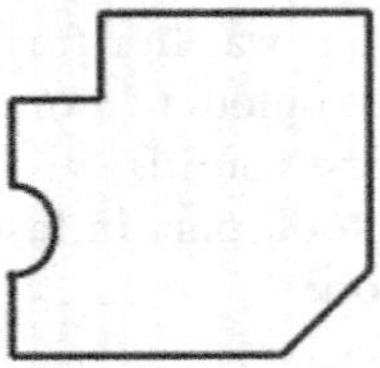

Which one of the following CANNOT possibly be the appearance of the paper after I unfold it?

A.
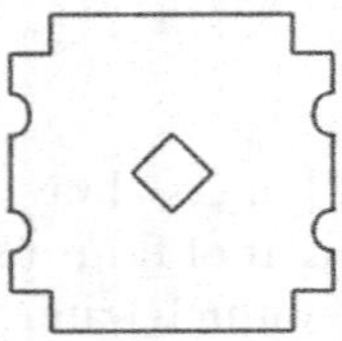

B.
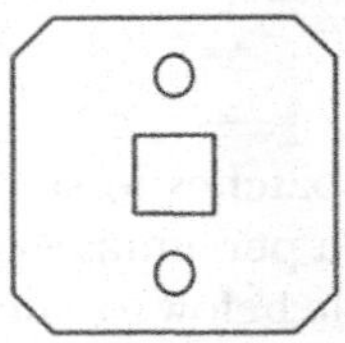

C.
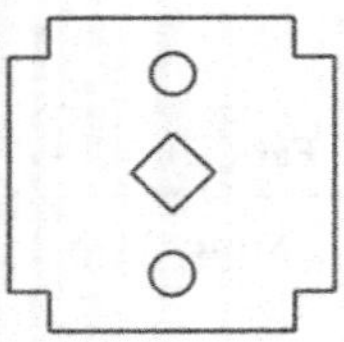

D.
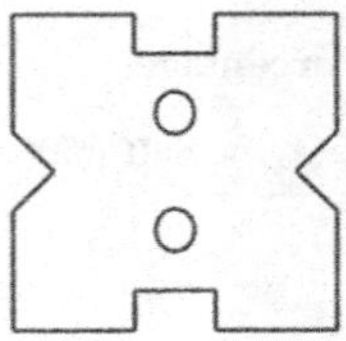

E.
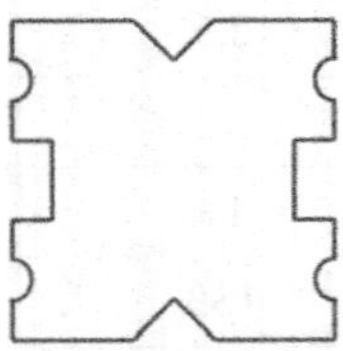

20) This is part of the tiled floor of the magic shop Spell It Out.

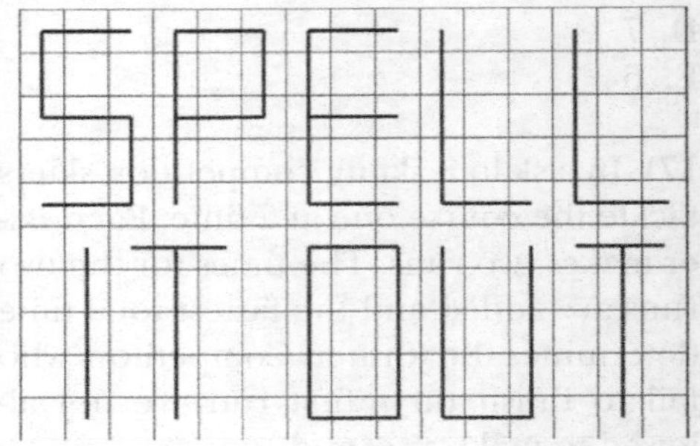

Five different types of tile make up the design. How many of the tiles have the pattern 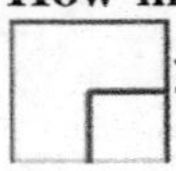 **?**

A. 18
B. 17
C. 19
D. 20
E. 21

21) Which of the following is NOT one of the Seven Wonders of the Ancient World?

A. The Great Pyramid of Giza
B. The Colossus of Rhodes
C. The Hanging Gardens of Babylon
D. The Lighthouse of Alexandria
E. The Parthenon of Athens

22) Which of the following countries is NOT a founding member of NATO?

A. Germany
B. France
C. Italy
D. Canada
E. Belgium

Biology

23) Which row of the table correctly indicates features that are found in both pure extracts of DNA and tRNA molecules?

	pentose sugar	adenine	hydrogen bond	phosphodiester bond	uracil
row 1	✓	✓	X	X	X
row 2	X	✓	✓	✓	✓
row 3	✓	X	X	✓	✓
row 4	✓	✓	✓	✓	X
row 5	X	✓	X	X	✓

✓ = present and X = absent

A. Row 3
B. Row 1
C. Row 2
D. Row 4
E. Row 5

24) The dipeptide represented below is in aqueous solution.

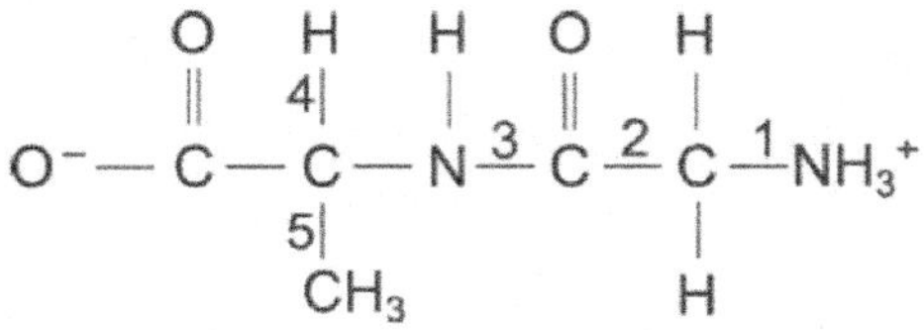

Which numbered bond (1 to 5) needs to be broken (hydrolysed) in this dipeptide to directly form two amino acids?

A. 4
B. 1
C. 2
D. 3
E. 5

25) Which organelle contains RNA but not DNA?

A. Smooth endoplasmic reticulum
B. Mitochondrion
C. Nucleolus
D. Chloroplast
E. Ribosome

26) The following shows the phases in mitosis.

Prophase → Phase two → Anaphase → Phase four

Which row in the table below shows the correct processes occurring in Phase two and Phase four of mitosis?

	Phase two	Phase four
row 1	chromosomes line up	nuclear envelope reforms
row 2	spindle fibres contract	chromosomes reach opposite poles
row 3	DNA duplicates to form sister chromatids	chromosomes are not visible
row 4	DNA starts to condense	chromatids separate and move to opposite poles
row 5	homologous chromosomes line up	cytoplasm of parent cell is divided into two daughter cells

A. Row 1 only
B. Row 4 only
C. Row 1 and row 5 only
D. Row 2 and row 3 only
E. Row 5 only

27) Which sequence shows cells of increasing size (from left to right)?

A. E. coli → onion epidermal cell → human red blood cell
B. E. coli → human red blood cell → onion epidermal cell
C. Onion epidermal cell → E. coli → human red blood cell
D. Onion epidermal cell → human red blood cell → E. coli
E. Human red blood cell → E. coli → onion epidermal cell

28) Which option correctly identifies the site of the lightdependent reactions in photosynthesis (S), the hydrogen carrier (H) used and its end state (N)?

A. S: granum; H: NAD; N: reduced
B. S: stroma; H: FAD; N: oxidised
C. S: stroma; H: NAD; N: reduced
D. S: stroma; H: NADP; N: oxidised
E. S: granum; H: NADP; N: reduced

29) An organism is heterozygous for two genes. These two genes make up part of the same DNA molecule.
For one gene, E represents the dominant allele, e represents the recessive allele.
For the other gene, R represents the dominant allele, r represents the recessive allele.
Assuming there is no mutation, at the end of a mitotic division producing two cells which row(s) is/are possible?

	number of DNA molecules containing these two genes in each cell	alleles present in each cell
row 1	one	only E or only R
row 2	one	E and r
row 3	one	E and R
row 4	one	only E on one molecule, only R on the other
row 5	one	only e on one molecule, only r on the other
row 6	one	E and R on one molecule, e and r on the other
row 7	one	E and r on one molecule, e and R on the other

A. Row 6 only
B. Row 1 only
C. Rows 6 and 7 only
D. Rows 2 and 3 only
E. Rows 4 and 5 only

30) An experiment is set up to study two genes. The two genes assort independently and for each gene the expression of alleles involves complete dominance. In the genetic cross RrTt × RrTt, a number of different phenotypes are seen.
What is the difference between this number of phenotypes and the number of phenotypes seen when the cross RrTt × rrtt is carried out?

A. 0
B. 1
C. 2
D. 4
E. 8

31) The diagram represents a whole DNA plasmid that has been cut open using a single restriction enzyme:

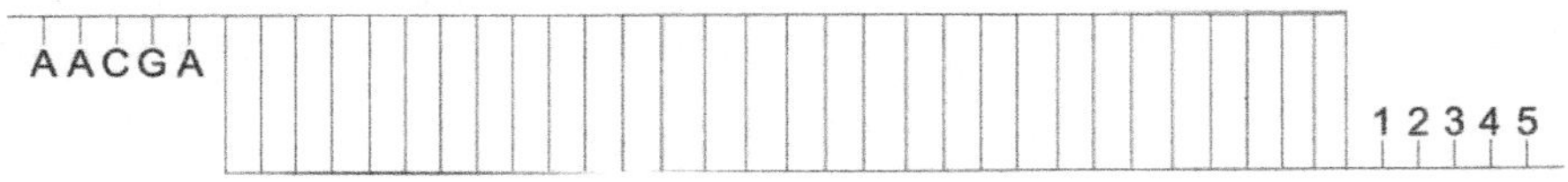

What are the bases in positions 1, 2, 3, 4 and 5 respectively?

A. U G C U U
B. T C G T T
C. U C G U U
D. T T G C T
E. U U G C T

32) Below are some steps involved in the production of transgenic plants.

Step V: Mixing of the required gene and the plasmid with ligases

Step W: Isolation of the required gene using restriction enzymes

Step X: Identification of the recombinant plasmid

Step Y: Injection of plasmid into host plant cell

Step Z: Use of restriction enzymes to produce sticky ends in the plasmid

Which one of the following options gives a correct order for these steps?

A. W → V → Z → X → Y
B. W → Z → X → Y → V
C. Z → W → V → X → Y
D. W → Z → X → V → Y
E. Z → W → V → Y → X

33) Which option shows the structure in humans that produces bile and then the structure that stores bile?

A. gall bladder produces and then gall bladder stores
B. gall bladder produces and then liver stores
C. liver produces and then gall bladder stores
D. liver produces and then liver stores
E. liver produces and then duodenum stores

34) The diagram shows the change in potential difference (pd) across the cell surface membrane of a sensory neurone. During which one of the phases (1–5) are the Na^+ gates of the neurone open?

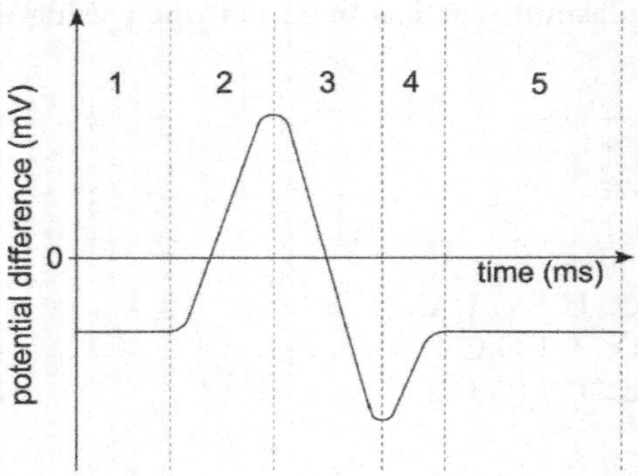

A. 1
B. 2
C. 3
D. 4
E. 5

35) Which labelled structure on the diagram of the brain plays the major role in regulating the nervous control of heart rate?

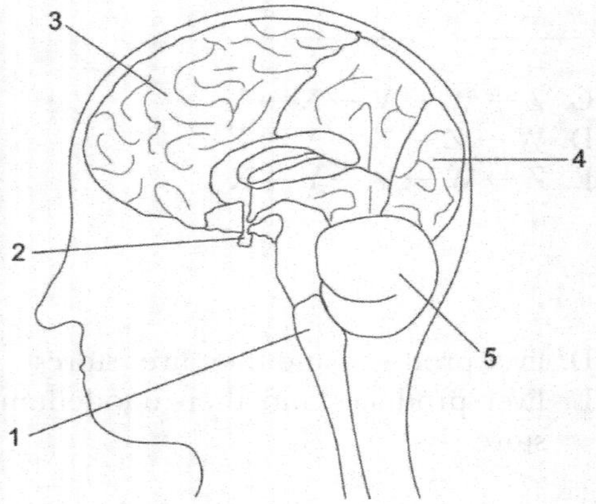

A. 4
B. 2
C. 3
D. 1
E. 5

36) Which row correctly identifies a nucleic acid NOT directly involved in transcription, and a nucleic acid which is NOT directly involved in translation?

row	nucleic acid NOT directly involved in transcription	nucleic acid NOT directly involved in translation
1	tRNA	DNA
2	mRNA	tRNA
3	DNA	mRNA
4	tRNA	mRNA
5	DNA	DNA

A. Row 5
B. Row 2
C. Row 3
D. Row 4
E. Row 1

37) In which of the following organelles do carbohydrates play a relevant role?
1 mitochondria
2 Golgi apparatus
3 chloroplasts

A. 1, 2 and 3
B. 1 and 3 only
C. 2 only
D. 1 and 2 only
E. 2 and 3 only

38) Which of the following are respiratory enzymes?
1 acetyl coenzyme A
2 FAD
3 reduced NAD

A. 1 and 2 only
B. none of them
C. 1 and 3 only
D. 2 and 3 only
E. 1, 2 and 3

39) In the testes of a healthy man there are diploid cells that undergo meiosis to produce gametes.
Which of the following statements is/are correct about meiosis for one of these diploid cells?
1 The diploid cell has doubled its DNA content before the start of meiosis I.
2 The cells at the start of meiosis II are diploid.
3 The total number of chromosomes produced by the end of meiosis II is double that of the original diploid cell.

A. 1, 2 and 3
B. 3 only
C. 1 only
D. 1 and 3 only
E. 2 and 3 only

40) Which of the following can be random processes?
1 genetic drift
2 mutations
3 artificial selection

A. 2 and 3 only
B. 1 and 3 only
C. 1 and 2 only
D. 1, 2 and 3
E. none of them

Chemistry

41) Which of the following molecules contain bond angles of 180° in their gaseous states?
(Atomic numbers: H = 1; Be = 4; C = 6; Cl = 17)
1 $BeCl_2$
2 C_2H_2
3 CCl_4

A. 2 and 3 only
B. 1 only
C. 2 only
D. 1 and 3 only
E. 1 and 2 only

42) Identify the number of protons (p), neutrons (n) and electrons (e) present in the ion:

$^{52}_{24}Cr^{3+}$

A. p = 24 n = 28 e = 21
B. p = 24 n = 28 e = 24
C. p = 27 n = 25 e = 24
D. p = 24 n = 24 e = 21
E. p = 27 n = 25 e = 21

43) Lead(II) nitrate solution and potassium iodide solution react to form potassium nitrate in solution and a bright yellow precipitate of lead(II) iodide.
Which one of the following correctly represents the ionic equation for this chemical reaction?

A. $Pb^{2+}(aq) + 2I^-(aq) \rightarrow PbI_2(s)$
B. $Pb^+(aq) + I^-(aq) \rightarrow PbI(s)$
C. $Pb^{2+}(aq) + I^-(aq) \rightarrow PbI(s)$
D. $Pb^+(aq) + 2I^-(aq) \rightarrow PbI_2(s)$
E. $Pb^{2+}(aq) + I^{2-}(aq) \rightarrow PbI(s)$

44) A sample of lithium was completely reacted with water. The equation for this reaction is:

$$2Li(s) + 2H_2O(l) \rightarrow 2LiOH(aq) + H_2(g)$$

The aqueous lithium hydroxide solution formed has a concentration of 0.10 mol/L.
What is its concentration in g/L?
(A_r: Li = 7.0; O = 16.0; H = 1.0)

A. 240
B. 3.1
C. 4.8
D. 2.4
E. 480

45) The compounds carbon dioxide (CO_2), propane (C_3H_8) and ethanal (CH_3CHO) all have $M_r = 44$.
Which of the following lists correctly shows these compounds in the order that they become gases as their temperature rises from –100°C at the same pressure?

A. CH_3CHO, C_3H_8, CO_2
B. CO_2, CH_3CHO, C_3H_8
C. CO_2, C_3H_8, CH_3CHO
D. C_3H_8, CO_2, CH_3CHO
E. C_3H_8, CH_3CHO, CO_2

46) A mixture of methanol and ethanoic acid is left until equilibrium is reached. The equation for this reaction is given below.

$$CH_3OH(l) + CH_3COOH(l) \rightleftharpoons CH_3COOCH_3(l) + H_2O(l)$$
$$\Delta H = -8.5\ kJmol^{-1}$$

The amount of CH_3OH in this mixture at equilibrium can be increased by:
1 adding more water to the mixture
2 raising the temperature of the mixture
3 adding sodium hydroxide to the mixture
4 adding a catalyst to the mixture

A. 1 and 2 only
B. 1, 2 and 3 only
C. 1 and 3 only
D. 2 and 4 only
E. 4 only

47) An aqueous solution of NaOH has a concentration of 0.01 mol/L.
Given the ionic product of water is $K_w = [H^+][OH^-] = 10^{-14}\ mol^2/L^2$ (at 25°C) and that the equation for pH is $pH = -\log_{10}[H^+]$, calculate the pH of the NaOH solution at 25°C.

A. 11
B. 13
C. 7
D. 12
E. 14

48) Which of the following substances will form an alkaline solution when dissolved in water?
1 Na_2CO_3
2 NaCl
3 $NaHSO_4$

A. 1, 2 and 3
B. 1 and 2 only
C. 1 and 3 only
D. 2 and 3 only
E. 1 only

49) How many unbranched straight chain molecules are there with the molecular formula $C_4H_8F_2$, but with different structural formulas?

A. 6
B. 4
C. 9
D. 12
E. 8

50) Five of the ions of vanadium are listed below:
1 VO_3^-
2 V^{3+}
3 V^{2+}
4 VO^{2+}
5 VO_2^+
Which two ions have vanadium in the same oxidation state?

A. 1 and 5
B. 1 and 3
C. 2 and 5
D. 3 and 4
E. 4 and 5

51) The formula of a molecule is $CH_2CHCH_2CH_2COCH_2CHO$.
Which functional groups given below are present in the molecule?

1 alkene
2 alcohol
3 aldehyde
4 ketone

A. 3 and 4 only
B. 1, 2 and 3 only
C. 2, 3 and 4 only
D. 1 and 4 only
E. 1, 3 and 4 only

52) Which of these particles have the same electronic structure?

1 $_{12}Mg^{2+}$
2 $_{10}Ne$
3 $_{16}S^{2-}$
4 $_{9}F^{-}$
5 $_{3}Li^{+}$

A. 3, 4 and 5 only
B. 1, 2 and 5 only
C. 1, 2 and 4 only
D. 2, 4 and 5 only
E. 1, 2 and 3 only

Physics and Mathematics

53) A right-angled triangle has an area of 18 cm². One of the two shorter sides is twice the length of the other one.
What is the length of the hypotenuse of the triangle?

A. $3\sqrt{10}$ cm
B. $3\sqrt{6}$ cm
C. $3\sqrt{5}$ cm
D. $9\sqrt{2}$ cm
E. $6\sqrt{5}$ cm

54) $x = 3 \times 10^m$ and $y = 5 \times 10^n$ where m and n are integers.

Which of the following is an expression, in scientific notation, for xy?

A. $1.5 \times 10^{mn+1}$
B. $1.5 \times 10^{m+n+1}$
C. $8 \times 10^{m+n}$
D. $15 \times 10^{m+n-1}$
E. 1.5×10^{mn}

55) The straight-line graph given by the equation

$$\frac{x}{4}+\frac{y}{6}=1$$

intersects the x-axis at A (a,0) and the y-axis at B (0,b). A circle passes through A and B and has a diameter AB.
What are the coordinates of the centre of the circle?

A. (6, 4)
B. (0, 0)
C. (3, 2)
D. (4, 6)
E. (2, 3)

56) Which one of the following is a simplification of

$$\frac{2}{x^2-1}-\frac{1}{x-1}$$

[where $x \neq \pm 1$]

A. $\frac{3-x}{(x-1)(x+1)}$

B. $-\frac{1}{x+1}$

C. $\frac{1}{x^2-1}$

D. $\frac{3-x}{(x-1)^2}$

E. $\frac{2}{x-1}$

57) The diagram shows a uniform horizontal beam of negligible mass, 5.0 m long, placed on two supports, one at each end. It has a 300 N weight placed 1.0 m from one end and a 500 N weight placed 1.0 m from the other end. Both weights act vertically on the beam as shown in the diagram.

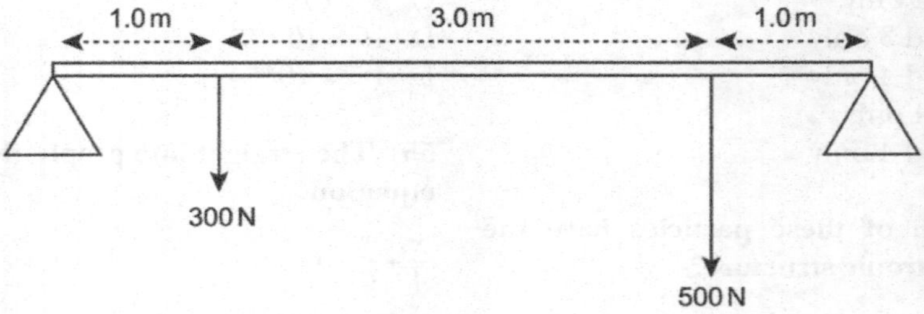

What are the upward forces from the two supports acting on the beam?

A. 240 N and 560 N
B. 400 N and 400 N
C. 300 N and 500 N
D. 360 N and 540 N
E. 340 N and 460 N

58) A student has three 6.0 Ω resistors that can be connected together in any configuration. What are the maximum and minimum resistances that can be obtained by using one or more of these three resistors?
[Assume the connections between the resistors have negligible resistance, the temperature of the resistors is constant, the resistors are used in a d.c. circuit and none of the resistors is short-circuited].

A. Maximum resistance: 18.0 Ω; minimum resistance: 2.0 Ω
B. Maximum resistance: 6.0 Ω; minimum resistance: 0.50 Ω
C. Maximum resistance: 12 Ω; minimum resistance: 0.50 Ω
D. Maximum resistance: 6.0 Ω; minimum resistance: 2.0 Ω
E. Maximum resistance: 18 Ω; minimum resistance: 6.0 Ω

59) Which physical quantity can be measured in joules per metre?

A. Momentum
B. Force
C. Kinetic energy
D. Power
E. Work

60) A ball is projected vertically upwards and then falls back to its original position.
Once projected, the ball experiences only a single force, downwards, due to a constant gravitational field strength of 10 N/kg.
Here are three statements about the ball:
1 When the ball is moving upwards it loses kinetic energy and gains potential energy.
2 The magnitude of the ball's acceleration increases as it falls.
3 No vertical forces act on the ball when it is at its maximum height.
Which of the statement(s) is/are correct?

A. 3 only
B. 1 and 2 only
C. 2 and 3 only
D. 1 only
E. none of them

RISPOSTE COMMENTATE • IMAT a.a. 2016/2017

Cultura generale e ragionamento logico

1) B. Per risolvere il quesito, bisogna individuare quale delle cinque opzioni di risposta esprima meglio la conclusione principale del ragionamento riportato nel brano. Un tale obiettivo può essere raggiunto distinguendo le premesse e la conclusione di tale ragionamento. Nel brano si dice che causa dell'obesità infantile è la facilità con cui i bambini possono accedere a cibi non sani che sono più economici (prima premessa). Aumentare il prezzo di questi cibi non è una soluzione, dal momento che i genitori li preferiscono perché sono più pratici (seconda premessa). Punto di partenza per risolvere il problema è offrire una gamma più ampia di cibi sani "pronti da mangiare" (conclusione).
A questo punto occorre valutare le cinque opzioni di risposta, per stabilire in quale compaia la conclusione principale del discorso appena analizzato.
Le quattro alternative seguenti sono tutte da scartare, perché riportano solo concetti posti nelle premesse:

- "*Child obesity is still a problem*". Ciò è chiaramente espresso all'inizio del brano e indica solo il problema da cui parte il ragionamento;
- "*The price of unhealthy foods should be raised*". Il senso di tale alternativa corrisponde alla frase che sembrerebbe essere la conclusione del ragionamento, in quanto pare proporre una soluzione del problema in questione. Tuttavia, con un po' di attenzione è facile capire che si tratta di un tipico distrattore, perché nella seconda premessa si dice che è improbabile che una tale soluzione funzioni ("*this is unlikely to work*");
- "*Children have too much access to fattening and sugarfilled foods*". Questo è uno degli aspetti del problema da cui parte il ragionamento e di cui, infatti, si parla all'inizio del testo: "*children have easy access to a range of … fattening and sugarfilled foods*";
- "*Parents should have more control over the food that their children eat*". Un concetto del genere richiama ciò che è ipotizzato nel brano: l'aumento del prezzo del cibo che fa ingrassare potrebbe aumentare il controllo dei genitori su ciò che mangiano i loro figli. Tuttavia, più avanti si dice che è improbabile che un tale aumento funzioni.

La risposta corretta è dunque: "*There should be more 'ready to eat' healthy meals available*". Ciò corrisponde a quanto espresso nella conclusione dall'autore del ragionamento che identifica come un buon inizio per risolvere il problema dell'obesità dei bambini una più ampia offerta di cibo sano "pronto da mangiare".

2) E. La soluzione del quesito consiste nel comprendere il principio su cui si fonda il ragionamento della traccia e nel riconoscere, fra le cinque alternative di risposta, quale illustri tale principio di base. Bisogna fare attenzione al fatto che la corrispondenza è formale, ma non necessariamente contenutistica: i due ragionamenti che si fondano sullo stesso principio non per forza affrontano lo stesso argomento.

Innanzitutto, identifichiamo il principio alla base del ragionamento: le persone socialmente più in vista e importanti dovrebbero sfruttare la propria notorietà per sensibilizzare gli altri alle cause meritevoli, impegnandosi in esse in prima persona e dando così l'esempio.
Ora si devono passare al vaglio le cinque alternative di risposta, per riconoscere quale di esse si basi sullo stesso concetto appena individuato. Tale alternativa è: "*Directors of companies should encourage their employees to recycle more by visibly doing so themselves*". In essa, infatti, si esprime l'idea che gli amministratori delle società, che sono più in vista rispetto ai loro dipendenti, dovrebbero sensibilizzare questi ultimi a una specifica causa, ovvero quella del riciclo, impegnandosi in essa in prima persona.

3) A. Per risolvere il quesito, bisogna individuare quale delle cinque alternative di risposta riporti il principio su cui si fonda il ragionamento esposto nella traccia, il quale affronta la questione generale dei limiti che bisogna porre alle possibili applicazioni della scienza. In proposito l'autore ritiene che bisognerebbe evitare di servirsi della scienza, in particolare delle biotecnologie, per realizzare ciò che non può verificarsi in modo naturale.
Sotto tale luce si può ora individuare il principio su cui si fonda l'argomentazione. Esso è espresso dalla seguente alternativa di risposta: "*Science should not progress beyond what is natural*", che è dunque la risposta corretta.

4) D. La domanda chiede di identificare quale delle cinque alternative di risposta riporti la cosiddetta prova addizionale, cioè l'affermazione che, se fosse aggiunta alle premesse dell'argomentazione, ne rafforzerebbe la conclusione. Le seguenti due alternative, se fossero vere, indebolirebbero la conclusione invece di rafforzarla, pertanto devono essere scartate:

- "*Some designers have favoured male models simply to generate more media attention for their collections*". In tal caso l'uso di modelli maschili nelle sfilate, di cui si parla nel brano, non potrebbe più supportare la conclusione per cui gli abiti disegnati dagli stilisti "*are unsuitable for most women*";
- "*Very few observers noticed initially that the male models were not in fact women*". Un fatto del genere non potrebbe incidere sul ragionamento o, al massimo, potrebbe indebolirlo, indicando che gli abiti disegnati dagli stilisti non sono lontani da modelli femminili.

Le opzioni "*Some female models struggle to maintain the necessary physique for catwalk modeling*" e "*Some designers are recognising that the physique of many catwalk models represents an unhealthy ideal for most women*" potrebbero rafforzare l'argomentazione; tuttavia il quesito chiede di individuare l'affermazione che, se vera, rafforzerebbe maggiormente la conclusione, pertanto vanno scartate. L'opzione corretta è dunque la seguente: "*Surveys of young women have suggested that the use of male models makes the typical model physique less desirable to attain*". Un tale dato, collegandosi con quanto espresso nel brano, e cioè che stilisti hanno preferito modelli uomini, renderebbe più forte la conclusione, in particolare riguardo alle grandi "*differences between catwalk fashion and clothing for the real worldi*".

5) C. Per risolvere il quesito, bisogna trovare quale delle cinque opzioni di risposta riporti la cosiddetta prova addizionale, cioè l'affermazione che, se fosse aggiunta alle premesse, renderebbe più forte il ragionamento nella traccia. Le alternative "*There would be opposition by civil liberties groups to this measure*" e "*It is not known how many people would 'opt out' of the compulsory scheme*", anziché rafforzare l'argomentazione la indebolirebbero, perciò vanno scartate.
L'opzione che più di tutte le restanti tre rafforzerebbe l'argomentazione nella traccia è "*The number of voluntary organ donors is small and not increasing*": infatti, il dato per cui il numero di donatori volontari di organi è ristretto e non in crescita chiaramente è ciò che renderebbe più necessaria e urgente l'adozione del provvedimento in discussione nella traccia, che, secondo l'autore del testo, aumenterebbe "*the supply of healthy organs available*".

6) D. La domanda chiede di identificare quale delle cinque alternative di risposta riporti l'affermazione che, se fosse aggiunta alle premesse dell'argomentazione, ne indebolirebbe la conclusione. Secondo quest'ultima dovremmo supporre che l'obesità e la mancanza di esercizio fisico sono le cause principali per cui negli Stati Uniti l'aspettativa di vita cresce in maniera più lenta rispetto agli altri paesi. Analizziamo dunque le cinque alternative per individuare l'affermazione che toglierebbe forza alla conclusione. Le seguenti tre vanno scartate, poiché, se fossero vere, non inciderebbero sulla conclusione del ragionamento:

- "*American fast food restaurants are now found in most rich countries*". Questo è un dato riferito solo al presente, mentre il ragionamento considera un fenomeno iniziato nel passato e con effetti nel presente;
- "*Most rich countries have the same standard of medical expertise*". Un tale dato non si collega alla differente aspettativa di vita negli Stati Uniti e nel resto del mondo;
- "*Japanese children had a healthier diet in the 1960s than they do today*". Un dato riferito solo al Giappone non può inficiare tutto il ragionamento.

L'alternativa "*The USA spends more money on fast food than any other nation*" non può essere presa in considerazione dal momento che se fosse vera rafforzerebbe l'argomentazione piuttosto che indebolirlo, rendendo più valido il ragionamento per cui l'obesità, legata ai *fast food*, è la causa del minore aumento dell'aspettativa di vita negli Stati Uniti rispetto agli altri paesi.
La risposta corretta è pertanto "*In the 1960s and 1970s the USA had the highest percentage of smokers*". Tale affermazione, infatti, smentirebbe quanto affermato nel brano e cioè che la percentuale di fumatori è uguale in tutti i paesi ricchi, indebolendo così la conclusione, dal momento che introduce il fattore fumo quale causa del minore aumento dell'aspettativa di vita negli Stati Uniti rispetto agli altri paesi.

7) E. Il quesito chiede di riconoscere quella che fra le cinque opzioni di risposta esprime meglio la conclusione principale dell'argomentazione esposta nella traccia, cioè l'importanza che riveste il gioco nello sviluppo delle capacità di pensiero nei bambini.

Individuiamo in primo luogo la conclusione e le premesse espresse nel testo:
Conclusione: "*Children need to play in order to develop their thinking skills*".
Prima premessa: "*When children play, they are merely going through scenarios, working out the consequences and implications of actions, puzzling out what might happen*".
Seconda premessa: "*– the very same processes that adults have learned to do in their heads, the process more commonly known as 'thinking'!*"
Terza premessa: "*It follows that thinking and playing are really one and the same thing*".
Le alternative "*Children who do not play will not be good thinkers*" e "*Children need to be taught how to think about the future*" vanno scartate perché riportano concetti assenti nell'argomentazione in esame e che non si possono ricavare dalle informazioni fornite nelle premesse; nel ragionamento, infatti, non c'è mai uno specifico riferimento al futuro dei bambini.
Le alternative "*Playing and thinking are essentially two forms of the same activity*" e "*Playing is just an early version of abstract thinking and reasoning*", invece, sono da scartare perché riportano concetti che sono esposti nelle premesse e non nella conclusione. La risposta corretta è dunque: "*Children need to be allowed to play in order to develop their thinking skills*". Tale affermazione, infatti, corrisponde quasi esattamente alla conclusione.

8) A. Il quesito chiede di individuare quale delle cinque alternative di risposta presenti la cosiddetta prova addizionale, ovvero l'affermazione che, se fosse aggiunta alle premesse, ne indebolirebbe la conclusione. Analizzando le singole alternative è evidente che la risposta corretta è: "*There may be factors other than badgers, such as the movement of cattle, which contribute to the spread of TB in cattle*". Infatti, l'indagine scientifica di cui si parla ha fornito la prova diretta della trasmissione della TBC dai tassi al bestiame. È chiaro, quindi, che se anche altri fattori, diversi dai tassi, contribuissero alla diffusione della TBC nel bestiame, sarebbe indebolita la conclusione per cui la popolazione dei tassi dovrebbe essere abbattuta per impedire la diffusione della malattia.

9) B. Questa tipologia di quesito richiede di determinare quale, fra le cinque opzioni di risposta, costituisca la supposizione implicita del ragionamento, ossia il presupposto che non è affermato nel brano ma sul quale poggia la conclusione. Innanzitutto bisogna individuare le premesse e la conclusione del ragionamento:
Prima premessa: "*Few linguists would argue against the view that our first language is acquired and not learned*".
Seconda premessa: "*Preschool children do not study their native tongue nor do they learn grammar rules but, by the time they start school at the age of five or six, the vast majority are competent users of their language*".
Conclusione: "*Therefore, when learning a second or additional language, studying grammar is a waste of time and all that is required is exposure to the target language in order to acquire competency in its use*".
L'unica alternativa che dà supporto alla conclusione e rappresenta quindi il suo il presupposto è: "*Acquiring a second or additional language is the same process as acquiring a first language*". Infatti, se nelle premesse si spiega che la competenza nell'uso della prima lingua è acquisita già in età prescolare senza che i bambini imparino le regole grammaticali, e se la conclusione sostiene che per acquisire la competenza anche nell'uso di una seconda lingua è necessario essere esposti ad essa, e non studiarne la

grammatica, allora la supposizione implicita deve essere che il processo di apprendimento di una seconda lingua è lo stesso di quello della prima.

10) C. Per rispondere al quesito, bisogna individuare l'affermazione tra quelle proposte che risulta logicamente connessa alle premesse e che da queste può essere tratta come conclusione. Nel brano si parla della possibilità che le persone che tornano a vedere dopo un intervento chirurgico agli occhi siano poi in grado di riconoscere con la vista oggetti che hanno conosciuto in precedenza solo attraverso il tatto. Poiché nel brano si dice che l'esperimento effettuato da due studiosi ha dimostrato che il riconoscimento solo attraverso la vista di oggetti precedentemente toccati migliorò in pochi giorni, ne deriva che tale riconoscimento visivo non è un comportamento innato, ma che può essere man mano appreso, dunque la conclusione è: "*Identifying an object by sight alone which had been touched but not seen previously is learned behaviour and not innate*".

11) A. La risoluzione del quesito è di tipo visivo e si ottiene isolando le 6 mattonelle del disegno iniziale per poi verificare in quale dei 5 disegni sono presenti.

Il disegno di partenza è costituito da 2 mattonelle del tipo , 2 mattonelle , 1 mattonella  e 1 mattonella , che, in ordine differente, costituiscono anche, e solo, il disegno A.

Osserviamo, infatti, che gli altri disegni sono costituiti da combinazioni diverse di mattonelle:

- nel disegno B si nota subito che le mattonelle del tipo  sono 3 invece di 2;
- nel disegno C le mattonelle  sono 3 invece di 2;
- nel disegno D c'è la mattonella  che non è presente nel disegno di partenza;
- nel disegno E, infine, la mattonella  è presente 3 volte invece di 2.

12) D. La soluzione del quesito si ottiene osservando attentamente i dati contenuti nella tabella e metterli in relazione con quelli forniti nel testo.
Innanzitutto, poiché desidero che nel mio sandwich ci siano almeno 20 g di proteine, vado a verificare la quarta colonna della tabella ed elimino immediatamente i tipi *ham*, *salad* e *tuna*, che contengono rispettivamente 18, 8 e 19 g di proteine.

Inoltre, poiché vorrei non più di 4 g di grassi, controllo la quinta colonna della tabella e vado quindi a scartare anche il tipo *chicken*, che ha 4.1 g di grassi.
A questo punto, per sapere qual è il minimo importo che pagherò per il mio sandwich, vado a verificare nella prima colonna il prezzo dei rimanenti, cioè *beef* e *turkey*, e scelgo il primo sandwich, che costa £ 2.00.

13) E. Guardando l'orologio di Londra, sappiamo che oggi è il 28 gennaio, per cui la prossima volta gli orologi saranno regolati a marzo. In particolare, gli orologi di Londra, Atene, Chicago e New York saranno messi un'ora avanti, quelli di Santiago e Sidney saranno messi un'ora indietro e quelli di Dubai, Singapore e Tokyo rimarranno invariati. Possiamo allora fare una simulazione a partire dagli orari attuali, ottenendo gli orari seguenti:

Londra:	16:37
Atene:	18:37
Chicago:	10:37
Dubai:	19:37
New York:	11:37
Santiago:	11:37
Singapore:	23:37
Sydney:	1:37
Tokyo:	00:37

Si vede immediatamente, quindi, che dopo il prossimo riposizionamento gli orologi di New York e Santiago mostreranno lo stesso orario.

14) A. Per individuare la soluzione al quesito è necessario mettere in relazione i dati forniti nel testo con quelli contenuti nella tabella. Sappiamo, infatti, che il prodotto va completato in 16 ore durante le quali, quindi, ovvero in 16 ore vanno effettuate le 9 operazioni riportate in tabella, utilizzando il minimo numero di operai possibile, cercando, cioè, di far compiere a ciascun operaio più di un'operazione durante le 16 ore. Per fare ciò si deve considerare un'operazione alla volta, partendo da quelle di durata maggiore, e "accoppiarla" ad un'altra (o a più altre) tale che la somma delle durate sia uguale, o di poco inferiore, alle 16 ore: in tal modo ogni lavoratore sfrutterà al meglio le 16 ore di manifattura del prodotto e avremo, quindi, utilizzato il minor numero di operai possibile.
Il primo operaio, allora, potrebbe eseguire l'operazione A che, durando 12 ore, può essere unita all'operazione H, che ne dura 4 : $12 + 4 = 16$. Il secondo operaio, poi, potrebbe eseguire l'operazione E, che, durando 10 ore, può essere unita all'operazione G, che ne dura 6 : $10 + 6 = 16$. Ma anche l'operazione I dura 10 ore, per cui il terzo operaio potrebbe compierla insieme alle operazioni B e F, che durano rispettivamente 2 e 3 ore: $10 + 2 + 3 = 15$. Restano, infine, fuori le operazioni C e D, che, durando 8 e 9 ore, non possono essere unite, ma vanno compiute da 2 operai diversi. Pertanto il numero minimo di operai per completare il prodotto in 16 ore è 5.

15) D. Poiché il guidatore del furgone piccolo impiega in totale 1 ora e 10 minuti per ciascuna consegna (10 minuti per caricare e 1 ora per andare e tornare), per sapere a che ora al più tardi deve arrivare la mattina al deposito per effettuare il numero massimo di consegne entro l'1:00 pm, basta sottrarre 1h 10m a 1:00 pm, tante volte finché non si arriva alle 8:00 am. Si ha quindi:

1:00 pm – 1h 10m = 11:50 am

11:50 am – 1h 10m = 10:40 am

10:40 am – 1h 10m = 9:30 am

9:30 am – 1h 10m = 8:20 am

A questo punto, sottraendo ancora 1 ora e 10 minuti dalle 8:20 am si ottiene 7:10 am, orario in cui il deposito non è ancora aperto, per cui il guidatore del furgone piccolo non può compiere più di 4 consegne in una mattina, e quindi può arrivare 20 minuti più tardi del guidatore del furgone grande. Si osservi che, ai fini della risoluzione del quesito, non sono stati utilizzati i tempi di carico e consegna del furgone grande, che costituiscono dei distrattori.

16) E. Per trovare il maggior numero di scatole di biscotti differenti che è possibile ottenere dipingendo le 4 facce laterali di rosso (R) o blu (B), bisogna innanzitutto tenere presente il fatto che la scatola è chiusa, e quindi, per esempio, la sequenza RBBR è uguale alla sequenza RRBB. A questo punto, per contare tutte le possibili scatole, conviene tenere fisso un colore su una o più facce e vedere come possono variare le facce rimanenti. Allora, innanzitutto si possono avere 4 facce rosse: RRRR (caso 1).
Poi, fissate 3 facce rosse, la quarta deve essere necessariamente blu. Se fosse rossa, infatti, ricadremmo nel caso 1 : RRRB (caso 2).
Invece, fissate 2 facce rosse, le restanti possono essere solo entrambe blu, perché nel caso fossero una rossa e una blu ricadremmo nel caso 2: RRBB (caso 3).
Inoltre, fissata 1 faccia rossa, le 3 restanti possono essere: tutte blu, RBBB (caso 4), oppure una blu, una rossa e una blu, RBRB (caso 5), ma non una rossa e 2 blu (RRBB), perché ricadremmo nel caso 3, né 2 rosse e una blu (RRRB) perché ricadremmo nel caso 2.
Resta infine da aggiungere il caso in cui nessuna faccia è rossa, ovvero tutte le facce sono blu: BBBB (caso 6). Pertanto il maggior numero di scatole possibili è 6.

17) B. Sappiamo che gli sciatori che superano il primo turno, al secondo giro gareggeranno in ordine inverso al loro arrivo al primo, quindi, poiché Grace al primo turno è arrivata sesta, al secondo giro ci saranno 5 sciatori che correranno dopo di lei. Inoltre, ci sono 17 sciatori che correranno prima (sappiamo che al secondo giro deve aspettare 17 rivali) e infine 3 sciatori che non hanno superato il primo turno. In totale, quindi, gli sciatori sono: 5 + 17 + 3 + 1 (Grace) = 26.

18) D. Per sapere qual è il peso totale di pane bianco da preparare basta calcolare le percentuali di acqua, sale e grasso da utilizzare rispetto al quantitativo di farina usata. In particolare, servirà il 54% di 250 kg di acqua, il 2% di sale e il 17% di grasso, vale a dire:

$$250\ \text{kg} \times \frac{54}{100} = 135\ \text{kg di acqua}$$

$$250\ \text{kg} \times \frac{2}{100} = 5\ \text{kg di sale}$$

$$250\ \text{kg} \times \frac{17}{100} = 42{,}5\ \text{kg di grasso}$$

Pertanto il peso totale dell'impasto sarà pari a:

250 kg + 135 kg + 5 kg + 42,5 kg = 432,5 kg.

19) C. Per sapere quale dei 5 fogli aperti non può corrispondere a quello chiuso basta simulare la piegatura in 4 di ciascuno di essi e vedere se è uguale o meno alla figura iniziale. Dunque si ha che:

A.
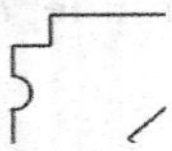
corrisponde alla figura iniziale

B.
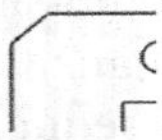
corrisponde alla figura iniziale dopo una rotazione di 180°

C.
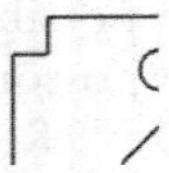
NON corrisponde alla figura iniziale

D.
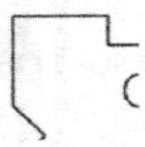
corrisponde alla figura iniziale dopo una rotazione di 90° in senso orario

E.

corrisponde alla figura iniziale dopo averla ribaltata

20) B. Per sapere quante mattonelle della scritta contengono il disegno richiesto basta osservare attentamente ciascuna lettera e contare le mattonelle con il disegno, facendo attenzione a considerare anche i casi in cui la mattonella è ruotata. Si ha quindi quanto segue:

– nella S il disegno è presente 4 volte: a sinistra dall'alto nella prima e terza mattonella e a destra dall'alto nella terza e nella quinta;

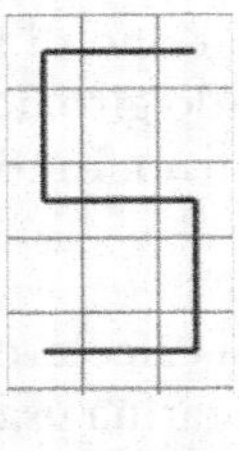

– nella P il disegno è presente 3 volte: a sinistra dall'alto nella prima mattonella e a destra dall'alto nella prima e nella terza;

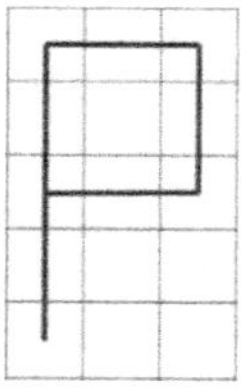

- nella E il disegno è presente 2 volte: a sinistra dall'alto nella prima e nella quinta mattonella;

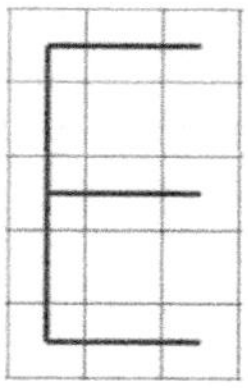

- nelle 2 L il disegno è presente 1 volta ciascuna: nell'angolo in basso a sinistra;

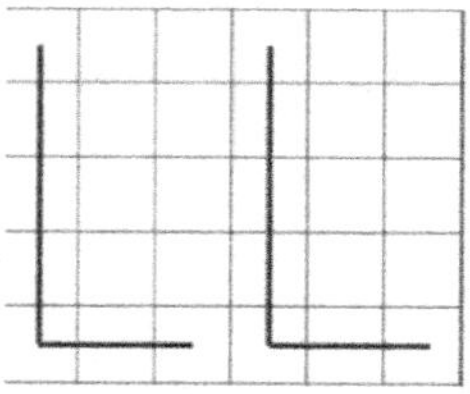

- nella I e nelle T il disegno NON è presente;
- nella O il disegno è presente 4 volte: ai 4 angoli;

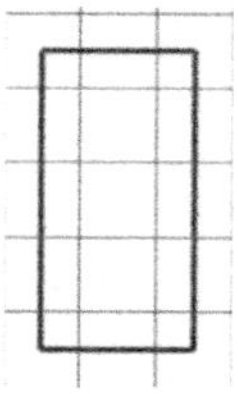

- nella U il disegno è presente 2 volte: ai 2 angoli inferiori;

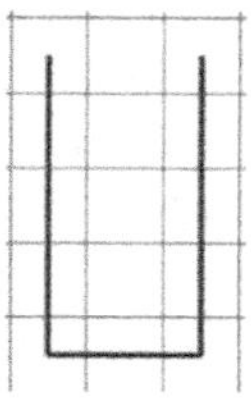

- nella T il disegno NON è presente.

In totale, quindi, il disegno è presente 4 + 3 + 2 + 2 + 4 + 2 = 17 volte.

21) E. Le sette meraviglie del mondo antico sono opere che i Greci e i Romani considerarono spettacolari nella loro epoca. Si tratta di costruzioni imponenti realizzate dall'uomo, annoverate in numerose liste durante l'antichità (il riferimento più antico risale al II secolo a.C.). Il Partenone, tempio realizzato sull'acropoli di Atene nel V secolo a.C. e dedicato alla dea Atena, non fa parte delle sette meraviglie. L'elenco completo comprende: la piramide di Cheope, i Giardini pensili di Babilonia, la statua colossale di Zeus, il tempio di Artemide a Efeso, il Mausoleo di Alicarnasso, il Colosso di Rodi, il Faro di Alessandria d'Egitto.

22) A. Nel 1949 Stati Uniti, Canada e alcuni paesi dell'Europa occidentale (tra cui Regno Unito, Francia, Belgio e Italia) firmarono il Patto Atlantico, trattato istitutivo della NATO (*North Atlantic Treaty Organization*), organizzazione internazionale per la collaborazione nella difesa. La Germania aderì alla NATO nel 1955.

Biologia

23) D. Il DNA e l'RNA sono polimeri di nucleotidi. Un nucleotide è composto da uno zucchero, una base azotata e un gruppo fosfato. Nel DNA lo zucchero è il desossiribosio, nell'RNA invece è il ribosio. Entrambi presentano un legame a idrogeno e fosfodiestereo. Sia il DNA che l'RNA hanno le basi A, C e G; la quarta base è la T per il DNA e l'U per l'RNA.

24) D. Nelle proteine gli amminoacidi sono uniti mediante un legame peptidico (covalente). Tale legame si stabilisce tra il gruppo carbossilico di un amminoacido e il gruppo amminico dell'amminoacido successivo, pertanto il legame numero 3 (nella figura) deve essere rotto per formare due amminoacidi.

25) E. Un ribosoma è un organello sferico estremamente piccolo, composto da proteine e RNA. I ribosomi sono il sito cellulare della sintesi proteica, coordinano in tal modo il funzionamento dell'mRNA e del tRNA, sintetizzando i polipeptidi.

26) C. La fase 2 della mitosi è detta metafase, durante la quale i cromosomi, che hanno raggiunto il massimo grado di condensazione, migrano sul piano equatoriale della cellula in posizione equidistante dai due poli opposti del fuso. In questa fase ogni cromosoma si trova disposto in modo tale da garantire il collegamento dei due cromatidi fratelli ai poli opposti della cellula.
Fin dall'inizio della telofase i due corredi cromosomici delle future cellule figlie hanno raggiunto i poli opposti del fuso. Si ottiene, pertanto, ad ogni polo il ripristino del numero originario di cromosomi. L'involucro nucleare, infine, compare ad avvolgere i due distinti gruppi di cromosomi fratelli completando il processo mitotico.

27) B. L'*E. coli* si presenta sotto forma di cellula bastoncellare di circa 1 μm di lunghezza e di 0,5 μm di diametro. Gli eritrociti hanno una forma di disco biconcavo con un diametro longitudinale di circa 7,2 μm e uno spessore al centro di 1,2 μm. Le cellule epidermiche della cipolla hanno dimensioni dell'ordine di mm.

28) E. La fotosintesi è il processo attuato dagli organismi autotrofi per produrre glucosio a partire da acqua e anidride carbonica, utilizzando come fonte di energia la luce solare assorbita da un particolare pigmento fotosensibile, la clorofilla. Tale processo si svolge all'interno dei cloroplasti e prevede due fasi distinte: fase luminosa e fase oscura. La fase luminosa avviene sulla membrana dei tilacoidi (grana); la luce assorbita dalla clorofilla viene utilizzata come fonte di energia per rompere le molecole di acqua e per sintetizzare ATP (da ADP) e NADPH (da $NADP^+$), un trasportatore ricco di energia.

29) C. Un individuo doppio eterozigote (Ee, Rr) produrrà 4 tipi di gameti: ER, er, Er, eR. Pertanto, alla fine della divisione mitotica si avranno due molecole di DNA per ciascuna cellula: ER, er, Er, eR.

30) A. Incrociando due doppi eterozigoti si ottengono 4 classi fenotipiche sulla base della terza legge di Mendel. Dall'incrocio tra un doppio eterozigote e un omozigote recessivo per due geni, le classi fenotipiche che si ottengono sono sempre 4.

31) D. Nella figura l'enzima di restrizione ha creato tagli sfalsati nella doppia elica di DNA plasmidico, dando luogo a estremità coesive *sticky ends*, in cui uno dei due filamenti presenta nucleotidi non appaiati e sporgenti, quindi le basi nelle posizioni 1, 2, 3, 4, 5 saranno TTGCT, ossia complementari all'altra estremità del filamento opposto.

32) C. Come prima tappa bisogna isolare sia il DNA plasmidico utilizzato come vettore che il DNA contenente il gene d'interesse, tagliati rispettivamente con enzimi di restrizione che producono estremità coesive. Successivamente il DNA plasmidico e il gene d'interesse vengono mescolati e legati mediante l'enzima ligasi, al fine di formare un plasmide ricombinante, identificato con opportune tecniche molecolari. Infine, tale plasmide viene iniettato nella cellula vegetale dell'ospite.

33) C. Una delle funzioni più evidenti del fegato è quella di secernere la bile, sostanza che lascia suddetto organo attraverso un sistema di dotti. La colecisti (o cistifellea) è studiata per raccogliere la bile prodotta dal fegato e per liberarla quando i cibi (in particolare i grassi) raggiungono l'intestino.

34) B. L'apertura dei canali del Na^+ è responsabile della fase di depolarizzazione veloce che porta V_m (ampiezza della risposta), vicino al potenziale di equilibrio del Na^+ (+63 mV). I canali del Na^+ dopo una breve apertura si inattivano e i canali del K^+ iniziano ad aprirsi. I due eventi sono responsabili della fase di discesa del potenziale d'azione che si avvicina al valore di -90 mV, potenziale postumo, prima di ritornare al valore di riposo.

35) D. Come si può osservare dalla figura, il tronco encefalico è costituito da bulbo e ponte, e collega il cervello al midollo spinale; regola la frequenza cardiaca, la respirazione e altri processi.

36) E. Il tRNA è coinvolto nella traduzione ma non nella trascrizione, viceversa il DNA.

37) A. Nei mitocondri i carboidrati sono un essenziale substrato per la produzione di ATP, nell'apparato di Golgi si ha il processo di glicosilazione e infine nei cloroplasti quello di fotosintesi, mediante il quale si ha la formazione di glucosio.

38) B. L'acetil coenzima A è un coenzima del ciclo di Krebs, il FAD e il NAD ridotto sono coenzimi ossidoriduttivi che partecipano a reazioni che comportano il trasferimento di elettroni.

39) D. L'affermazione numero 1 è corretta perché il contenuto di DNA viene duplicato durante la fase S (di sintesi). L'affermazione numero 3 è corretta perché partendo da 46 cromosomi presenti nei testicoli, alla fine della meiosi II si formeranno 4 cellule aploidi con un numero complessivo di 92 cromosomi.

40) C. I processi evolutivi traggono origine da fattori capaci di alterare la stabilità genetica di una popolazione, modificandone il pool genico. Tra i principali fattori evolutivi ci sono le mutazioni e la deriva genetica. Le mutazioni naturali possono avere cause diverse, ma hanno una caratteristica in comune: sono casuali rispetto ai bisogni adattativi dell'organismo.
Nelle popolazioni di piccole dimensioni la deriva genetica che è la riduzione casuale della frequenza di un allele può provocare forti alterazioni nelle frequenze alleliche delle generazioni successive. Può anche accadere che alleli vantaggiosi vadano perduti perché rari, con conseguente aumento della frequenza di alleli nocivi.

Chimica

41) E. Il cloruro di berillio ($BeCl_2$) presenta angoli di legame pari a 180° per la teoria VSEPR (Cl-Be-Cl), mentre l'etino (C_2H_2) presenta legami con angoli pari a 180° a causa dell'ibridazione sp degli atomi di carbonio (H-C≡C-H). Nel tetracloruro di carbonio (CCl_4) il carbonio è ibridato sp^3 e darà quindi luogo ad angoli di legame pari a circa 109.5°.

42) A. Il numero in pedice prima dell'elemento è il numero atomico, pari al numero di protoni (p = 24), mentre il numero in apice è il numero di massa che rappresenta la somma del numero di protoni e neutroni (quindi i neutroni saranno n = 52 – 24 = 28). Dato che lo ione ha 3 cariche positive sarà presente un numero di elettroni pari al numero di protoni meno 3: e = 24 – 3 = 21.

43) A. La reazione descritta è una precipitazione, nella quale non variano i numeri di ossidazione degli elementi coinvolti: il piombo ha un numero di ossidazione pari a +2 (Pb^{2+}), mentre lo ione ioduro –1 (I^-), quindi il composto che si forma è PbI_2.

44) D. Il peso molecolare dell'idrossido di litio è 24 g/mol. Per passare dalla concentrazione molare a quella in g/L è sufficiente moltiplicare il peso molecolare per la concentrazione molare: 24 g/mol × 0.10 mol/L = 2.4 g/L.

45) C. Per prevedere l'ordine con il quale una serie di composti che hanno uguale massa diventa gassosa, è necessario analizzare le forze intermolecolari presenti nei diversi composti. Il diossido di carbonio (CO_2) è una molecola apolare (a causa della simmetria) e le uniche forze intermolecolari saranno quindi le forze di Van der Waals, le più deboli. Il propano è invece lievemente polare e presenterà deboli interazioni dipolo-dipolo. Tali interazioni saranno molto più forti nel caso dell'etanale, che è molto più polare a causa del legame C=O. Più forte è il legame intermolecolare, maggiore è la temperatura che è necessario raggiungere per portare le sostanze allo stato gassoso.

46) B. Per il principio di Le Châtelier ogni sistema tende a reagire a una modifica impostagli dall'esterno diminuendone gli effetti. Se si vuole aumentare il metanolo (uno dei reagenti) si può aggiungere uno dei prodotti (acqua), aumentare la temperatura (in quanto la reazione è esotermica) o diminuire la quantità di un altro dei reagenti (l'aggiunta di NaOH ha l'unico effetto di "rimuovere" dall'equilibrio l'acido acetico). L'aggiunta di un catalizzatore porta alla modifica della velocità con cui si raggiunge l'equilibrio, ma non influisce sulla quantità di reagenti o prodotti presenti in soluzione.

47) D. L'idrossido di sodio (NaOH) è una base forte che si dissocia completamente. In soluzione sarà presente quindi una concentrazione di ioni OH^- pari a 0.01 mol/L. Di conseguenza la concentrazione di ioni H^+ (calcolabile dall'espressione del K_w dell'acqua) sarà pari a 10^{-14} mol^2/L^2 / 0.01 mol/L = 10^{-12} mol/L. Il pH della soluzione sarà pari al logaritmo negativo di questa concentrazione ed è quindi 12.

48) E. Il carbonato di sodio (Na_2CO_3) darà luogo a una soluzione basica a causa dello ione carbonato:

$CO_3^{2-} + H_2O \rightleftharpoons HCO_3^- + OH^-$.

Il cloruro di sodio (NaCl), invece, non altera il pH della soluzione (lo ione Cl^- è la base coniugata di un acido molto forte: HCl). Nel bisolfato di sodio ($NaHSO_4$) lo ione HSO_4^- si comporta da acido, non da base (è anch'esso la base coniugata di un acido molto forte: H_2SO_4).

49) A. Partendo dalla struttura base del *n*-butano, possiamo immaginare di ottenere composti differenti mettendo i due atomi di fluoro:

- Entrambi nel primo atomo di carbonio: $CHF_2CH_2CH_2CH_3$
- In posizione 1,2: $CH_2FCHFCH_2CH_3$
- In posizione 1,3: $CH_2FCH_2CHFCH_3$
- In posizione 1,4: $CH_2FCH_2CH_2CH_2F$
- Entrambi nel secondo atomo di carbonio: $CH_3CF_2CH_2CH_3$
- In posizione 2,3: $CH_3CHFCHFCH_3$

Si noti che porre gli atomi di fluoro in altre posizioni (per esempio entrambi nel carbonio 3) porta a conformazioni equivalenti a quelle già descritte (l'esempio riportato è equivalente alla quinta combinazione considerata).

50) A. Calcolando il numero di ossidazione del vanadio (ricordandosi che l'ossigeno ha numero di ossidazione –2) per i diversi composti, otteniamo rispettivamente: +5; +3; +2; +4; +5. Quindi ad avere lo stesso numero di ossidazione sono gli ioni 1 e 5.

51) E. Il composto possiede sicuramente il gruppo delle aldeidi (CHO) e dei chetoni (CO). Controllando il numero di legami degli atomi di carbonio ci si accorge che i primi due atomi devono formare tra di loro un doppio legame $CH_2{=}CH{-}$, gruppo funzionale degli alcheni.

52) C. Le strutture elettroniche sono:

Mg^{2+}: $1s^2\ 2s^2\ 2p^6$; Ne: $1s^2\ 2s^2\ 2p^6$ S^{2-}: $1s^2\ 2s^2\ 2p^6\ 3s^2\ 3p^6$

F: $1s^2\ 2s^2\ 2p^6$ Li^+: $1s^2$

Si nota che le particelle 1, 2 e 4 hanno esattamente la stessa struttura elettronica.

Fisica e Matematica

53) A. L'area del triangolo rettangolo è $A = (a \times b)/2$, dove a e b sono le lunghezze dei cateti. Sappiamo che $a = 2b$, quindi, sostituendo otteniamo l'espressione $18\ cm^2 = (2b^2)/2$, dalla quale possiamo ricavare la lunghezza del cateto $b = \sqrt{18}$ cm e $a = 2\sqrt{18}$ cm. Dal teorema di Pitagora abbiamo che l'ipotenusa è pari a $\sqrt{18 + 4 \times 18} = \sqrt{90} = 3\sqrt{10}$ cm.

54) B. Per la proprietà delle potenze il prodotto tra due potenze con la stessa base è uguale a una potenza che ha per base la stessa base e per esponente la somma degli esponenti, ovvero $10^m \times 10^n = 10^{m+n}$. Nel caso in esame abbiamo $xy = 3 \times 10^m \times 5 \times 10^n = 15 \times 10^{m+n} = 1.5 \times 10^{m+n+1}$.

55) E. Dall'equazione fornita è facile trovare le coordinate dei punti di interesse: A (4, 0); B (0,6). Dato che tali punti rappresentano anche gli estremi del diametro del cerchio, il centro del cerchio si trova esattamente al centro del segmento che unisce i due punti A e B. Le coordinate di tale punto saranno (4+0)/2, (0+6)/2), cioè C≡(2, 3).

56) B. Il denominatore $x^2 - 1$ è la differenza tra due quadrati e può essere scritto come $(x-1)(x+1)$. Tale prodotto corrisponde al minimo comune denominatore tra le due frazioni, per cui avremo:

$$\frac{2-(x+1)}{(x-1)(x+1)} = \frac{-x+1}{(x-1)(x+1)} = \frac{-(x-1)}{(x-1)(x+1)} = -\frac{1}{(x+1)}$$

57) E. I due supporti si trattano separatamente, come fulcri di leve di secondo genere: il supporto a sinistra è sottoposto a una forza di 300 N × 1 m + 500 N × 4 m = 2300 Nm, ma viene equilibrato dalla forza applicata dal fulcro alla destra (distante 5 m) e pari a 2300 Nm / 5 m = 460 N. Analogamente il supporto a destra è sottoposto a una forza di 300 N × 4m + 500 N × 1 m = 1700 Nm, equilibrato dalla forza applicata dal fulcro a sinistra: 1700 Nm / 5 m = 340 N.

58) A. Se le resistenze sono poste in serie, avremo $R_{tot} = 3\ R = 18.0\ \Omega$, se invece sono poste in parallelo, $1/R_{tot} = 3/R = 0.5\ \Omega^{-1}$ e quindi $R_{tot} = 2.0\ \Omega$; le altre possibili disposizioni avranno resistenze totali intermedie a tali valori.

59) B. Il joule è l'unità di misura dell'energia; 1 joule è definito come il lavoro svolto esercitando la forza di un newton per una distanza di un metro. Il joule per metro è quindi equivalente al newton, unità di misura della forza.

60) D. La palla, muovendosi verso l'alto, rallenta e quindi perde energia cinetica che guadagna come energia potenziale (di posizione). Dato che la forza del campo gravitazionale è costante, l'accelerazione a cui è sottoposta la palla è costante. Quando la palla è alla massima altezza è ferma e sottoposta alla forza del campo gravitazionale (verticale).

IMAT
a.a. 2017/2018

General knowledge and logical reasoning

1) The recently-appointed captain of the national football team has been publicly accused of adultery with several women, including the girlfriend of a former teammate. The newspaper shave made a great deal of his extramarital activities and it has become a scandal. His behaviour has led him to be the subject of crude jokes. He has now been suspended from his duties. It is right that he has been removed from his position so that the team can start to pull together and have the best possible chance of winning the World Cup.

Which one of the following is an underlying assumption of the above argument?

A. This new captain should not have been appointed
B. If the new captain is fired, the national team will win the World Cup
C. The national team will not win the World Cup
D. The new captain's actions have weakened team morale
E. Newspapers have the right to report on people's personal lives

2) E-cigarettes, which provide nicotine without cigarette smoke, have been praised by health campaigners. Research has suggested that success rates for quitting smoking are higher with e-cigarettes than with other methods. However, rather than tackling their nicotine addiction, e-cigarette users have simply replaced one habit with another. It is true that cigarette smoke contains many hazardous compounds, and also that quitting smoking increases life expectancy and reduces the risk of many health problems. But nicotine also has its dangers: it has been associated with a range of conditions that we do not fully understand, and research has yet to establish the long-term effects of nicotine use outside of cigarette smoke.

Which one of the following is a conclusion that can be drawn from the above passage?

A. People should not assume e-cigarettes are a safe alternative to traditional cigarettes
B. Smoking traditional cigarettes still poses a major risk to health
C. Using nicotine patches is an ineffective way to give up smoking
D. E-cigarettes are just as harmful as traditional cigarettes
E. Not everyone is able to give up smoking without nicotine replacement

3) Many children from poor backgrounds would benefit from wearing spectacles but do not have them. Sometimes parents are not aware of their children's poor eyesight, but most often they suffer from financial constraints. The government should provide free glasses to poor children with eyesight problems. A recent study of underprivileged students with poor vision demonstrated that those who were given free glasses enjoyed an improvement in test scores equivalent to almost a year of additional schooling. Using the most conservative estimate of the impact of schooling on salary, this would significantly increase an average school-leaver's annual income and tax contributions, and by far more than the cost of a pair of glasses.

Which one of the following best expresses the main conclusion of the above argument?

A. Parents should be educated about potential eyesight problems in children
B. Children from poor backgrounds with bad eyesight should be given additional schooling
C. Exam marking should take into account any disabilities the student might have
D. People's salaries should reflect whether or not they had eyesight problems during school
E. The government should help financially with the provision of children's glasses

---

4) It is common practice to look online for a loan or a mortgage. This has led to a large number of' comparison websites' where you type in your details and they search a range of companies for you based on these details. Night after night, there are adverts on television emphasising how much time and money comparison sites could save you. The experience of one user should make you consider the wisdom of using such sites. She gave her details to a comparison website and received no useful results. However, for weeks afterwards she was bombarded with emails and phone calls from companies she had never heard of.

Which one of the following is the best statement of the flaw in the above argument?

A. It attacks the website and not what the company does
B. It assumes everyone uses comparison websites
C. It assumes that comparison websites save customers money
D. It draws a conclusion based on one example of how a company operates
E. It assumes using the internet is the only way to get a loan

---

5) Though relatively few people know it by name, palm oil is found in over fifty per cent of processed supermarket goods, from soaps to snacks. This vegetable oil, which is taken from the fruit of the oil palm tree, causes a great deal of environmental concern. The clearing of tropical forests to grow oil palm plantations threatens the survival of orangutans and other endangered species. The land conversion often happens on carbon rich peat soils in a process which releases significant greenhouse gas emissions. Yet even some environmental organizations warn that alternative vegetable oil crops may require much larger areas of forest to be converted to agricultural land.

Which one of the following is a conclusion that can be drawn from the above passage?

A. To produce the most profitable crops, oil palm plantations must be grown on carbon rich peat soils
B. If farmers stopped clearing tropical forests for oil palm plantations, endangered orangutan populations would recover
C. A ban on palm oil alone would not solve all of the environmental problems associated with vegetable oil production
D. The environmental risks associated with oil palm plantations are not well understood in tropical countries

E. There is no motivation for manufacturers to stop using palm oil in their products

6) Next week the European Parliament will vote on whether to ban trawling, a method of fishing that involves pulling large fishing nets behind boats. The fishing industry is opposed to a ban and has argued strongly against it. Trawling is not as damaging to ecosystems as environmentalists claim. Trawling the seabed doesn't always create 'dead zones' in the ocean. It can boost fish numbers, since the species that are more resistant to the effects of trawling can proliferate. So trawling on flat sandy beds in shallow areas can benefit marine life.

Which one of the following, if true, most weakens the above argument?

A. Trawling in deep waters is expensive and an ineffective use of fishing resources
B. Trawling in shallow waters can alter the ecology in beneficial ways
C. Trawling nets have a destructive impact on many endangered species
D. Trawling in shallow waters can damage the bottom of fishermen's boats
E. Trawling creates new habitats by making parts of the sea more habitable

7) Car drivers understandably become very annoyed at high sales taxes on fuel. In the interests of fairness, money raised from fuel taxes should be spent on maintaining roads or even on subsidising public transport. In fact much of it is put to other uses, such as providing healthcare or improving national defence.

Which one of the following is an application of the principle underlying the above argument?

A. Money raised by taxing fuel should be spent on improving roads rather than on public transport
B. Better transport is more important than national defence
C. Maintaining roads should be a higher priority than spending on healthcare
D. There should be no sales taxes on consumer goods
E. Profits from sporting events should be spent on encouraging people to participate in sport

8) Widespread underage drinking in certain countries prompted their governments to place restrictions on selling alcohol to young people. The aim was to protect young people's health, but the result was not as intended. Soon after the restrictions were in place, hospitals saw several cases of young people becoming ill as a result of drinking alcohol-based liquids such as medical spirits, ethanol solutions and perfumes. The young people claimed that the restriction on legal alcohol was the main reason they were drinking other substances. If the restrictions were abolished, the health risk would be reduced.

Which one of the following is the best statement of the flaw in the above argument?

A. It ignores the role of education in encouraging young people to drink alcohol responsibly
B. It assumes that restrictions encourage young people to drink alcohol
C. It does not take into account the social and cultural importance of drinking alcohol
D. It ignores the fact that if there had been no restrictions more young people would have suffered from drinking alcohol

E. It ignores the problem of people drinking dangerous substances because they cannot afford to buy alcohol legally

9) Over the last ten years there has been a huge increase in the number of television programmes involving the work of forensic scientists. This media attention has been matched by a massive increase in the number of courses and qualifications available in this field. Although this new attention has led to greater public awareness, it has not led to the creation of more jobs in this field. The work of forensics professionals has continued unchanged. Therefore, those who choose to study these courses will find that there is fierce competition for difficult and unpleasant work.

Which one of the following, if true, would most weaken the above argument?

A. Many students of forensic science go on to pursue careers in other areas
B. New technologies have brought about a decrease in the number of forensics staff required in laboratories
C. Salaries for forensic scientists compare well with those in other scientific fields
D. The number of university courses in forensic science has grown at an unprecedented rate
E. Each year around 1500 graduates in forensic science compete for 200 jobs in the sector

10) Many banks encourage their customers to buy insurance against credit card fraud and other kinds of "identity theft". But the banks are really protecting themselves. Customers who are victims of credit card fraud suffer inconvenience but they are unlikely to lose money: the costs of any fraudulent transactions are met by the bank. It is therefore unnecessary for customers to spend money on additional insurance services.

Which one of the following is an underlying assumption of the above argument?

A. The banks' additional insurance services protect only against the costs of fraudulent credit card transactions
B. People who are worried about identity theft worry only about their credit cards
C. Credit card fraud is a less serious problem than many people believe
D. Customers whose identities have been stolen would have benefited from the banks' additional insurance services
E. Additional insurance services are widely available for credit card customers

11) I recently received a publications list and order form. I want to order seven items from the list.
However, I noticed that the structure of the postage and packaging charges was very strange, as shown in the table below:

Number of items	Cost of postage and packaging
1	55p
2	70p
3	95p
4	£ 1.30
5	£ 1.60
6 or more	£ 3.30

I have decided that I will ask them to pack my order in the number of parcels that will have thelowest postal charge.
What is the lowest postal charge for my seven items?

A. £ 1.90
B. £ 2.25
C. £ 2.35

D. £ 2.45
E. £ 3.30

12) Luke walks his puppy to a nearby park and lets the puppy off the lead.
As Luke starts walking along the path, the puppy runs on ahead, until it has gone 100 metres.
The puppy then turns and runs back to Luke, who in that time has walked 50 metres. The puppy then goes on ahead again, turns after running 100 metres and runs back to Luke who has now walked another 50 metres. This routine continues until Luke has walked 1 km.
If it takes 12 minutes for Luke to walk 1 km in the park, what is the puppy's average runningspeed during the same time?

A. 5 km/h
B. 10 km/h
C. 15 km/h
D. 12 km/h
E. 14 km/h

13) The diagram below shows how 12 matchsticks can be used to create a grid containing 4 squares, arranged in rows of 2.

I now intend to use matchsticks to create a grid containing 100 squares, arranged in 10 rows of10.
How many matchsticks do I need?

A. 220
B. 200
C. 242
D. 300
E. 400

14) I have a tin of chocolates to share with some friends. In the tin are four types of chocolate – one type in red wrappers, one type in blue, one type in green and one type in yellow, with equal numbers of each.
The tin is passed around in turn from friend to friend. When the tin gets to them:

- John always takes three red chocolates
- Peter always takes one of each colour
- Jane always takes one yellow chocolate
- I always take two green chocolates

After six passings around of the tin, half of the chocolates remaining in the tin are blue.
How many chocolates were there in the tin when it was full?

A. 96
B. 24
C. 48
D. 60
E. 72

15) The table below shows calories burned depending on a person's weight:

Activity (1 hour)	Calories burned by a 60 kg person	Calories burned by a 75 kg person	Calories burned by a 85 kg person	Calories burned by a 100 kg person
Walking slow	150	175	200	240
Walking fast	210	260	310	350
Walking very fast	300	350	400	460
Running slow	360	420	450	510
Running fast	510	540	600	650

Five friends choose the following exercise routine:

	Weight	Activity 1	Activity 2
Harry	85 kg	walks fast for 30 minutes	walks slow for 30 minutes
Holly	60 kg	runs fast for 20 minutes	walks slow for 10 minutes
Jessie	75 kg	runs fast for 10 minutes	runs slow for 20 minutes
Josie	100 kg	walks fast for 30 minutes	walks slow for 30 minutes
Paul	60 kg	runs slow for 20 minutes	walks fast for 20 minutes

Which one of the five friends burns the most calories?

A. Harry
B. Holly
C. Jessie
D. Josie
E. Paul

16) I leave Victoria at 8:07 and arrive at Three Bridges at 8:41. I need to catch a train from Three Bridges at 8:45 to either Arundel or Chichester. I want to spend at least four hours in Chichester and four hours in Arundel. I have no preference in which order I will visit the towns. I then need to return to Victoria.
The tables below show extracts from the train timetables:

Depart	Three Bridges	8:45	Three Bridges	8:45
Arrive	Arundel	9:32	Chichester	9:34

Depart	Arundel	13:02	13:29	14:02	14:29
Arrive	Chichester	13:24	13:50	14:24	14:50

Depart	Chichester	12:25	12:41	13:25	13:41	14:25
Arrive	Arundel	12:46	13:12	13:46	14:12	14:46

Depart	17:12	17:46	18:13	18:52
Arrive	18:47	19:18	19:47	20:20

Depart	17:13	17:21	17:43	18:13	18:37
Arrive	18:47	19:15	19:18	19:47	20:20

What is the earliest possible time I can arrive back at Victoria?

A. 18:47
B. 19:15
C. 19:18
D. 20:20
E. 19:47

17) Shee lagh runs a business from London with regional headquarters located in seven cities – Jakarta, Nairobi, Prague, Ottawa, Moscow, Canberra and Hong Kong. The company also has plants in other cities shown in the table. Her senior managers at regional headquarters work from 8 am to 5.15 pm local time and constantly check their emails between these hours but are not available outside these hours. All her staff have an international time chart displayed at their place of work.
At 12 noon in London it is:

8 pm	Beijing
10 pm	Canberra
8 pm	Hong Kong
8 pm	Jakarta
1 pm	Lisbon
3 pm	Moscow

3 pm	Nairobi
2 pm	Nicosia
7 am	Ottawa
1 pm	Prague
7 am	Quebec
5 pm	Rawalpindi

3 pm	Riyadh
9 am	Rosario
8 am	Santiago
1 pm	Stockholm
4 am	Vancouver
6 am	Winnipeg

At 3 pm in London she sends an urgent email to all her senior managers at her regional head quarters.
What is the longest possible interval between the first and last of her senior managers reading the email?

A. 7 hours
B. 9 hours
C. 14 hours
D. 16 hours
E. 17 hours

18) Alex's bedroom is rectangular. If you stand at the doorway looking into the room, there is a square wardrobe on your right hand side in the corner. The bed is on the same side of the room as the wardrobe and is over half the length of the room. There is a desk along the other wall.
Which one of these aerial views is the view of Alex's bedroom?

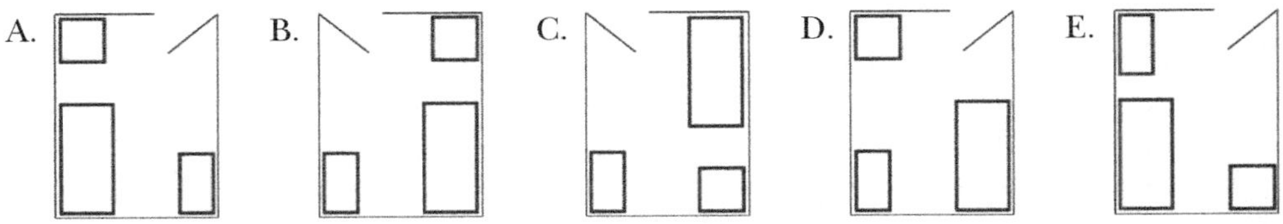

19) The distance from Ardale to Banby is 16 km and from Banby to Carston is a further 8 km in the same direction.
David leaves Ardale at 11.00 and runs for an hour at 6 km/h. He rests for 20 minutes and then completes the rest of the distance to Banby at an average speed of 10 km/h. He chats with some friends in Banby for 20 minutes and then borrows a bicycle from one of them and cycles to Carston at an average speed of 16 km/h. David leaves Carston at 15.00 and cycles back over his route, arriving home at 15.50.

Which one of the following correctly shows David's distance from Ardale as a function of time?

A. 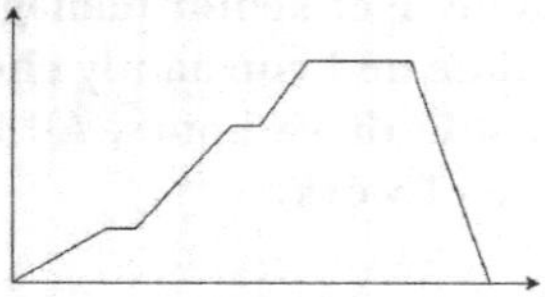

B. 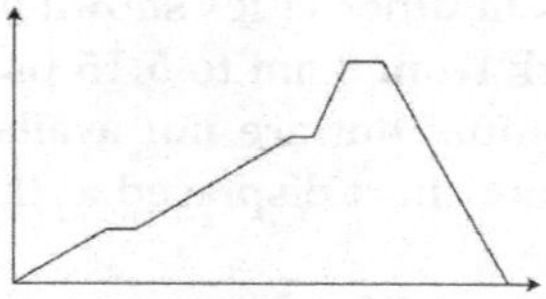

C. 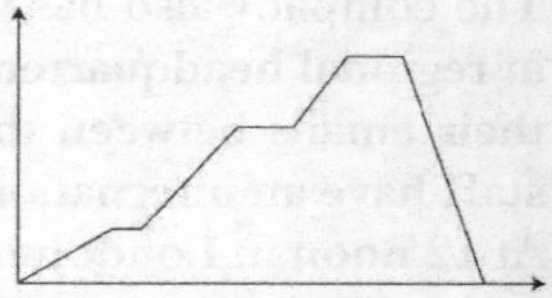

D. 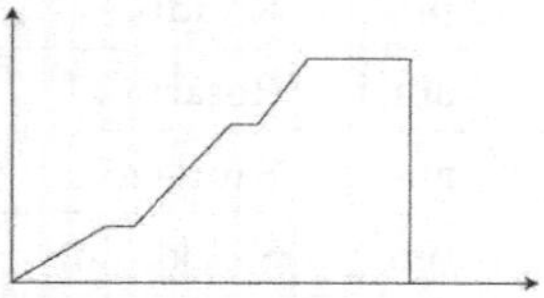

E. 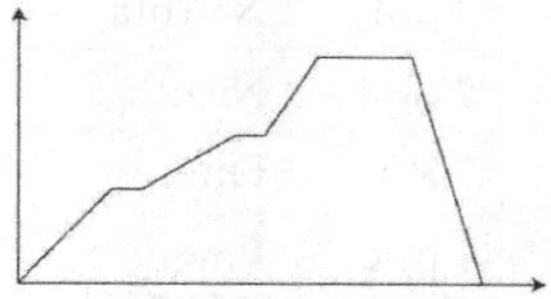

20) This is a view of a cross section of part of an aluminium window frame.

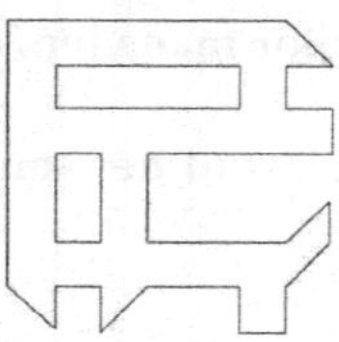

The cross section is uniform throughout its length. Which one of the following is NOT a possible side view of this part of the aluminium window frame?

A. 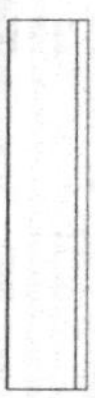
B. 
C. 
D. 
E. 

21) Which one of the following theories was publicly announced to the Prussian Academy of Science on 25th November 1915?

A. String theory
B. Einstein's general theory of relativity
C. Dalton's atomic theory
D. Quantum theory
E. The Big Bang theory

22) Which one of the following introduced the metaphor of the "invisible hand" in relation to a free trade economy?

A. David Ricardo
B. Adam Smith
C. Karl Marx
D. Vilfredo Pareto
E. Thomas Robert Malthus

Biology

23) Which of the following components of a human immunodeficiency virus (HIV) contain peptide bonds?

1. Capsid
2. Envelope
3. Reverse transcriptase

A. 1, 2 and 3
B. 1 and 2 only
C. 1 and 3 only
D. 2 and 3 only
E. 3 only

24) Which one of the following most accurately describes the structure of a human haemoglobin molecule that can bind four oxygen molecules to form oxyhaemoglobin?

A. It has a primary, secondary and tertiary structure only
B. It has a primary, secondary and quaternary structure only
C. It has a primary, tertiary and quaternary structure only
D. It has a primary and secondary structure only
E. It has a primary, secondary, tertiary and quaternary structure

25) A short section of the DNA strand that codes for a protein has the sequence:

CAT TGG GCA TCG

Which of the following statements about this section of the sequence is/are correct?

1. There are a total of 29 hydrogen bonds between this section of DNA and its complementary strand.
2. There are 12 phosphodiester bonds present within this section of DNA.
3. The unmutated tRNA molecules used to translate this sequence contain a total of 3 uracil bases.

A. 2 only
B. 3 only
C. 1 and 2 only
D. 1 and 3 only
E. 2 and 3 only

26) The following structures are found in plant cells:

1. cell wall
2. cell membrane
3. nucleolus
4. mitochondrion

Which cell structures might contain molecules containing carbohydrate monomers?

A. 4 only
B. 2 and 3 only
C. 1 and 4 only
D. 1 only
E. 1, 2, 3 and 4

27) Two adjacent healthy human cells, X and Y, contain the two molecules Q and R. The concentration of molecule Q in cell X is 4 arbitrary units (a.u.) and in cell Y it is 6 a.u.
The concentration of molecule R in both cell X and cell Y is 7a.u.
Which of the following statements about the net movement of ONLY molecules Q and R between cells X and Y could be correct?

1. Molecules of Q move by facilitated diffusion from cell X.
2. Molecules of Q move by active transport into cell Y.
3. Molecules of R move into and out of both cell X and cell Y.

A. 2 only
B. 2 and 3 only
C. 1 and 3 only
D. 1 only
E. 1, 2 and 3

28) Four students, 1, 2, 3 and 4, recorded different structures that they thought were found in ahealthy animal kidney cell and a typical bacterial cell.

Student	Animal cell	Bacterial cell
1	DNA found in a nucleus	70S ribosomes present
2	cell wall present	mitochondria present
3	70S ribosomes present	DNA found in a nucleus
4	circular DNA	plasmids present

Which students gave totally correct answers?

A. Students 2 and 4 only
B. Students 2 and 3 only
C. Students 1 and 2 only
D. Students 1, 2, 3 and 4
E. Students 1 and 4 only

29) Which one of the following is a correct outline of some main events in photosynthesis in a healthy wheat plant?

A. Light joins carbon dioxide to an acceptor compound which is then reduced by hydrogen obtained from water
B. Light splits carbon dioxide and the resulting carbon then combines with oxygen and hydrogen obtained from water
C. Light splits water and the resulting hydroxyl group combines with a compound which has reacted with carbon dioxide
D. In the presence of light, oxygen reacts with a carbohydrate to produce water and carbon dioxide
E. Carbon dioxide combines with an acceptor compound which breaks into two and each is reduced by hydrogen split from water by light

30) Which of the following molecules is/are directly produced during BOTH glycolysis and pyruvate decarboxylation in a healthy human cell?

1. ATP
2. carbon dioxide
3. reduced NAD

A. 3 only
B. 1 only
C. 1 and 2 only
D. 1 and 3 only
E. 2 and 3 only

31) The pathway shows some of the cells produced during oogenesis in the ovary of a healthy human female. Which of the following cells in the pathway are diploid?

1. germinal epithelial cells in the ovary
↓
2. oogonia
↓
3. primary oocyte
↓
4. secondary oocyte

A. 1, 2 and 3 only
B. 4 only
C. 1 only
D. 2, 3 and 4 only
E. 1, 2, 3 and 4

32) Which of the following occurs in a healthy human testis cell before it undergoes meiosis?

1. DNA content of the nucleus doubles
2. spindle fibres form the spindle
3. crossing over

A. 1 and 2 only
B. 1 and 3 only
C. 2 and 3 only
D. 1, 2 and 3
E. 1 only

33) A mother and a father, neither of whom has cystic fibrosis, conceive a child who has the condition.
What is the likelihood that the same parents will have another child who is a boy without cystic fibrosis?

A. 3 in 8
B. 1 in 2
C. 3 in 4
D. 1 in 8
E. 1 in 4

34) Which one of the following statements about unmutated nucleic acids is correct?

A. mRNA is made up of a single nucleotide with a codon of uracil, cytosine and guanine bases
B. Prokaryotic DNA is a single strand which forms a loop
C. Bases in DNA may form hydrogen bonds with uracil bases
D. rRNA has anticodons which bind to tRNA
E. tRNA is made up of one phosphate-sugar backbone and may have adenosine and thymine bases

35) Which combinations of DNA could be present in a transgenic organism?

1. invertebrate animal DNA in mammal DNA
2. prokaryotic DNA in plant DNA
3. plant DNA in animal DNA

A. 1, 2 and 3
B. 1 and 2 only
C. 1 and 3 only
D. 2 and 3 only
E. 2 only

36) Which of the following could be a consequence of a reduction in pituitary function in an otherwise healthy human?

1. more urine produced in a male or female
2. infertility in a female
3. infertility in a male

A. 1 and 2 only
B. 2 and 3 only
C. 1, 2 and 3
D. 1 and 3 only
E. 2 only

37) Which of the following statements is/are correct for all enzyme inhibitors?

1. They alter the shape of the active site
2. They denature the enzyme
3. They increase the activation energy of the reaction
4. They reduce the rate of the enzyme catalysed reaction

A. 4 only
B. 1, 2 and 4 only
C. 2 and 4 only
D. 3 only
E. 1, 2 and 3 only

38) A person was admitted to hospital suffering from a loss of memory.
Which part of the central nervous system is most likely to have been affected?

A. Cerebellum
B. Hypothalamus
C. Cerebrum
D. Medulla
E. Spinal cord

39) Which of the following processes take place during the establishment of a resting potential in the axon of a healthy human neuron?

1. active transport
2. facilitated diffusion
3. respiration

A. 1 and 2 only
B. 1 and 3 only
C. 1, 2 and 3
D. 2 and 3 only
E. 2 only

40) Which of the following statements is/are correct in a healthy human?

1. During inspiration, the pressure within the chest cavity is lower than outside the body
2. During ventricular systole, the pressure in the atrium is lower than in the ventricles
3. During ventricular systole, the pressure in the aorta is lower than the pressure in the atrium

A. 1 and 2 only
B. 2 only
C. 3 only
D. 1 only
E. 2 and 3 only

Chemistry

41) Consider the following list of particles:

1. molecules
2. ions
3. single atoms
Which one of the following options correctly describes the particles that are

present in an aqueous solution of sodium chloride?

A. 2 only
B. 3 only
C. 1 only
D. 1, 2 and 3
E. 1 and 2 only

42) Element X is a grey solid.
It combines with chlorine to form a polar molecule with the formula XCl. In this compound, element X has an oxidation state of +1.
In potassium iodide solution, it dissolves to form a coloured solution.
At 500 °C, it becomes a coloured vapour.
What is the identity of element X?

A. Iodine
B. Lithium
C. Manganese
D. Fluorine
E. Carbon

43) Which option correctly describes the following features of a silane (silicon tetrahydride) molecule?
• Number of bonding pairs (bp) of electrons
• Number of lone/non-bonding pairs (lp) in the valence shell of the silicon atom
• Bond angle
[Atomic number: Si = 14; H = 1]

A. 3bp; 1lp; 109.5°
B. 3bp; 1lp; 107°
C. 4bp; 0lp; 109.5°
D. 4bp; 0lp; 90°
E. 4bp; 2lp; 90°

44) Which one of the following options gives the correct electron structure of the particle $^{16}_{8}O^{2-}$?

A. $1s^22s^22p^4$
B. $1s^22s^22p^2$
C. $1s^22s^22p^6$
D. $1s^22s^22p^63s^23p^4$
E. $1s^22s^22p^63s^23p^6$

45) The solubility of potassium nitrate in water increases with temperature.
A saturated solution of potassium nitrate at 80 °C is cooled to 25 °C in a closed container.
Which of the following statements is/are correct?

1. The mass of undissolved potassium nitrate will increase
2. The concentration of the potassium nitrate solution remains the same
3. The total mass of solvent present remains the same

A. 1 and 3 only
B. 1 only
C. 2 only
D. 2 and 3 only
E. 1, 2 and 3

46) Which one of the following statements correctly describes the type of mixture and the most appropriate method used to separate the specified component from the mixture?

A. Chlorophyll from a solution of different plant pigments – homogeneous; chromatography
B. Gasoline/petrol from crude oil – heterogeneous; simple distillation
C. Red blood cells from blood – homogeneous; centrifuge
D. Salt from salt solution – homogeneous; paper filtration
E. Water from salt solution – heterogeneous; simple distillation

47) In which one of the following reactions is the <u>underlined</u> species acting as an oxidising agent?

A. $\underline{Cl_2} + 2KBr \rightarrow 2KCl + Br_2$
B. $\underline{Zn} + CuSO_4 \rightarrow ZnSO_4 + Cu$

C. $3CO + Fe_2O_3 \longrightarrow 3CO_2 + 2Fe$
D. $H_2SO_4 + 2NaOH \longrightarrow Na_2SO_4 + 2H_2O$
E. $2Mg + O_2 \longrightarrow 2MgO$

48) In an experiment involving the reaction shown below, 150 cm³ of F_2 reacts with 100 cm³ of Cl_2.

$$3F_2(g) + Cl_2(g) \longrightarrow 2ClF_3(g)$$

On completion of the reaction, what is the final gaseous volume at the same temperature and pressure?

A. $100\ cm^3$
B. $200\ cm^3$
C. $150\ cm^3$
D. $250\ cm^3$
E. $350\ cm^3$

49) Which one of the following molecules is a structural isomer of methylcyclopentane?

A. Cyclohexene
B. 2-methylpentane
C. Hexane
D. Hex-2-ene
E. 2,2-dimethylbutane

50) Which one of the following statements about the four atoms/ions below is correct?

$$^{23}_{11}Na^+ \quad ^{16}_{8}O^{2-} \quad ^{18}_{8}O \quad ^{32}_{16}S$$

A. $^{16}_{8}O^{2-}$ has the same number of electrons but four fewer neutrons than $^{23}_{11}Na^+$
B. Both $^{16}_{8}O^{2-}$ and $^{32}_{16}S$ each have an equal number of protons, neutrons and electrons
C. $^{16}_{8}O^{2-}$ and $^{18}_{8}O$ have exactly the same number of protons and electrons but not neutrons
D. Out of the four atoms/ions, only $^{23}_{11}Na^+$ has two more electrons than $^{18}_{8}O$
E. $^{32}_{16}S$ has twice the number of neutrons that $^{18}_{8}O$ has but only four more than $^{23}_{11}Na^+$

51) Which one of the following samples of gases contains the most particles?
All gases are at 0 °C and 1 atm pressure, when 1 mole of gas has a volume of 22.4 L.
[Relative atomic mass, Ar: H = 1, He = 4, C = 12, O = 16, Cl = 35.5]

A. 66.0 g of carbon dioxide gas
B. 64.0 g of oxygen gas
C. 22.4 L of hydrogen gas
D. 10.0 g of helium gas
E. 33.6 L of chlorine gas

52) A solution of hydrochloric acid has a concentration of 1.0 mol/L. If 10 mL of this acid is added to water and made up to a total volume of 1.0 L, what is the pH of the resulting solution?

A. 0
B. 2
C. 5
D. 6
E. 9

Physics and Mathematics

53) What is the gradient of the straight line passing through the points with coordinates(2, –3) and (–1, 6)?

A. –9
B. –1
C. $-\frac{1}{3}$
D. $-\frac{1}{9}$
E. –3

54) Given that:
$\log_{10}7 = x$
$\log_{10}2 = y$

$\log_{10}3 = z$

What is $\log_{10}\left(\frac{14}{3}\right)$ expressed in terms of x, y, and z?

A. $x + y - z$
B. $\frac{x+y}{z}$
C. $xy - z$
D. $\frac{xy}{z}$
E. $xy + z$

55) Which one of the following is an expression for the mean of $\frac{x}{3}$, x, and $x + 6$?

A. $\frac{7x+18}{9}$
B. $7x + 2$
C. $\frac{7x+6}{3}$
D. $7x + 18$
E. $\frac{7x+6}{9}$

56) How many ways are there to order the letters 'AABBC'? (For example, 'ACABB' and 'AABBC' are two ways.)

A. 5
B. 60
C. 116
D. 120
E. 30

57) A car starts at point X. It travels 3.0 km due east, then 4.0 km due south, then 6.0 km due west and finally 8.0 km due north.
How far away is the car from point X when it has reached the end of this journey?
[Assume that all distances moved are on a flat horizontal surface, and that point X is on the equator. You may ignore any curvature of the Earth.]

A. 5.0 km
B. 2.0 km
C. 7.0 km
D. 10.0 km
E. 21.0 km

58) A solid wooden cube has sides of length *a*. The density of the wood is ρ. The cube is completely immersed in a beaker of oil, which has a density σ. The top surface of the cube is horizontal. The gravitational field strength is *g*.
What is the upward force (up thrust) on the cube due to the oil?
[Assume that no oil is absorbed by the wood.]

A. $\rho a^3 g$
B. σa^3
C. $\sigma a^3 g$
D. ρa^3
E. $(\sigma - \rho) a^3 g$

59) A fixed mass of an ideal gas undergoes a change in which it is supplied with 3500 J of thermal energy. At the same time this gas does 3500 J of work on its surroundings.
Which type of change does the gas undergo during this time?

A. Isothermal
B. Isobaric
C. Isochoric
D. Isomeric
E. Adiabatic

60) A resistor has a resistance of 5.0 Ω. There is a direct current of 10 A in the resistor. What is the power dissipated by the resistor?

A. 500 W
B. 50 W
C. 250 W
D. 20 W
E. 2500 W

RISPOSTE COMMENTATE • IMAT a.a. 2017/2018

Cultura generale e ragionamento logico

1) D. Il ragionamento nella traccia trae una conclusione basandosi su una premessa esplicita e su una implicita che il quesito richiede di individuare tra le cinque alternative di risposta presenti. A tale scopo si devono individuare innanzitutto la premessa esplicita e la conclusione:
Premessa esplicita: "*The recently-appointed captain of the national football team has been publicly accused of adultery with several women, including the girlfriend of a former teammate. The newspapers … his duties*".
Conclusione: "*It is right that he has been removed from his position so that the team can start to pull together and have the best possible chance of winning the World Cup*".
Esaminando le cinque alternative di risposta, le seguenti introducono concetti non collegabili alla premessa esplicita e alla conclusione e vanno dunque scartate:

- "*The national team will not win the World Cup*". Questa frase esprime la certezza della mancata vittoria della Coppa, ma contrasta con la conclusione, in cui invece si parla di possibilità di vittoria;
- "*If the new captain is fired, the national team will win the World Cup*". Questa opzione esprime la certezza della vittoria della Coppa, ma contrasta anch'essa con il fatto che nella conclusione si parla solo di possibilità di vittoria;
- "*Newspapers have the right to report on people's personal lives*". Tale affermazione potrebbe essere al massimo un presupposto della premessa esplicita, in cui si parla di "*newspapers*", ma non della conclusione, in cui non c'è alcun accenno ai giornali;
- "*This new captain should not have been appointed*". Pur collegandosi all'idea espressa nella conclusione per la quale il nuovo capitano è stato rimosso, questa opzione non si collega esplicitamente all'altra nozione fondamentale della conclusione, ossia che la rimozione del capitano darà alla squadra "*the best possible chance of winning the World Cup*".

La risposta corretta è dunque "*The new captain's actions have weakened team morale*". Questa frase rappresenta la premessa implicita perché, da un lato, fa riferimento alle azioni deplorevoli compiute dal capitano, di cui si parla nella premessa esplicita, e, dall'altro, spiega l'idea, espressa nella conclusione, che la rimozione del capitano darà alla squadra "*the best possible chance of winning the World Cup*".

2) A. Il quesito chiede quale delle cinque alternative di risposta rechi l'affermazione che può fungere da conclusione del ragionamento esposto nella traccia. Per trovare la risposta, bisogna innanzitutto riconoscere quelle che sono le premesse di tale ragionamento:
Prima premessa: "*E-cigarettes, which provide nicotine without cigarette smoke, have been praised by health campaigners. Research has suggested that success rates for quitting smoking are higher with e-cigarettes than with other methods. However… problems*".

Seconda premessa: "*But nicotine also has its dangers: it has been associated with a range of conditions that we do not fully understand, and research has yet to establish the long-term effects of nicotine use outside of cigarette smoke*".
Ora non resta che passare in rassegna le cinque alternative di risposta, per riconoscere quella che riporta l'affermazione supportata dalle premesse come conclusione del ragionamento in questione. Le seguenti opzioni si basano tutte su concetti non collegabili o non coerenti con le due premesse. Poiché si cerca l'opzione che è logicamente connessa alle premesse e che da queste può essere tratta come conclusione, tali alternative vanno dunque scartate:

- "*Using nicotine patches is an ineffective way to give up smoking*". In nessun punto del ragionamento si parla di "*nicotine patches*", cioè di cerotti alla nicotina;
- "*Smoking traditional cigarettes still poses a major risk to health*". Tale concetto contrasta con quanto espresso nella seconda premessa, ovvero che "la ricerca non ha ancora stabilito gli effetti a lungo termine dell'uso della nicotina al di fuori del fumo di sigaretta". Tale incertezza non consente di concludere che le sigarette tradizionali siano più nocive di quelle elettroniche e nemmeno di concludere che i due tipi di sigarette siano nocivi nella stessa misura come espresso nell'opzione "*E-cigarettes are just as harmful as traditional cigarettes*";
- "*Not everyone is able to give up smoking without nicotine replacement*". Nelle premesse si fa un confronto tra i rischi delle sigarette elettroniche e quelli delle sigarette tradizionali. La conclusione, quindi, deve riguardare tale confronto, non la sostituzione della nicotina, che è presente in entrambe le tipologie.

La risposta corretta è pertanto "*People should not assume e-cigarettes are a safe alternative to traditional cigarettes*". Nella prima premessa sono descritti gli aspetti positivi che le sigarette elettroniche hanno rispetto a quelle tradizionali, nella seconda, però, si dice che le sigarette elettroniche comportano l'uso della nicotina al di fuori del fumo di sigaretta, un uso i cui effetti a lungo termine sono ancora incerti. La conclusione, quindi, è quella espressa dall'opzione in esame: data l'incertezza, gli aspetti positivi delle sigarette elettroniche non dovrebbero far supporre che esse siano un'alternativa sicura a quelle tradizionali.

3) E. La soluzione del quesito consiste nell'individuare quale delle cinque opzioni di risposta corrisponda alla conclusione principale del ragionamento esposto nella traccia. Un tale obiettivo può essere raggiunto facilmente distinguendo le premesse e la conclusione di tale ragionamento.
Nel brano si dice che molti bambini provenienti da ambienti poveri trarrebbero beneficio dall'indossare gli occhiali ma non li hanno perché i genitori non sono consapevoli dei problemi di vista dei figli e spesso hanno difficoltà economiche (prima premessa). Il governo dovrebbe provvedere a fornire gratuitamente occhiali ai bambini poveri che non vedono bene (conclusione). Uno studio recente condotto su studenti svantaggiati con problemi di vista ha dimostrato che coloro ai quali sono stati dati occhiali gratuiti hanno ottenuto un miglioramento nei risultati dei test scolastici, elemento che avrebbe anche un impatto positivo sul salario (seconda premessa).

Dall'analisi delle cinque alternative l'unica che corrisponde alla conclusione del brano è: "*The government should help financially with the provision of children's glasses*"; tutte le altre opzioni esprimono concetti assenti nel ragionamento.

4) D. Il ragionamento esposto nella traccia ha un difetto che fa sì che il passaggio logico dalle premesse alla conclusione non sia accettabile. È dunque indispensabile individuare innanzitutto le premesse e la conclusione dell'argomentazione. Nel brano si dice che è pratica comune cercare online un prestito o un mutuo e che ciò ha portato a un gran numero di siti web in cui vengono comparate diverse compagnie sulla base dei dati inseriti. L'esperienza negativa di un utente che non ha ottenuto risultati utili ma è stata solo bombardata di pubblicità via mail dovrebbe far considerare l'importanza di un uso saggio di tali siti. Il difetto nel ragionamento consiste nel fatto che si mette in guardia dall'usare i siti web per chiedere un prestito o un mutuo, ma tale avvertimento è basato dichiaratamente su un solo caso negativo, "*the experience of one user*". La risposta corretta è dunque "*It draws a conclusion based on one example of how a company operates*".

5) C. Il quesito chiede quale delle cinque alternative di risposta riporti l'affermazione che supportata dalle premesse costituisca la conclusione del ragionamento in questione. Analizziamo di seguito le premesse:
Prima premessa: "*Though relatively few people know it by name, palm oil is found in over fifty per cent of processed supermarket goods, from soaps to snacks. This vegetable oil … gas emissions.*
Seconda premessa: "*Yet even some environmental organizations warn that alternative vegetable oil crops may require much larger areas of forest to be converted to agricultural land*".
Poiché si cerca l'opzione che è logicamente deducibile dalla connessione delle due premesse e che da queste può essere tratta come conclusione, le alternative seguenti vanno scartate:

- "*To produce the most profitable crops, oil palm plantations must be grown on carbon rich peat soils*". Tale affermazione contrasterebbe con l'"environmental concern" di cui si parla nella prima premessa con riferimento al fatto che la coltivazione di olio di palma proprio su suoli ricchi di carbonio rilascia significative emissioni di gas serra;
- "*If farmers stopped clearing tropical forests for oil palm plantations, endangered orangutan populations would recover*". Tale affermazione si concentra solo sull'olio di palma di cui si parla nella prima premessa, ma non concorda con la seconda in cui si avverte che le colture di oli vegetali alternativi potrebbero essere ancora più disastrose per l'ambiente e le specie a rischio;
- "*The environmental risks associated with oil palm plantations are not well understood in tropical countries*". Questo concetto non emerge affatto dalle premesse, in cui non si parla mai di paesi tropicali.
- "*There is no motivation for manufacturers to stop using palm oil in their products*". Ciò contrasta con l'"environmental concern" di cui si parla nella prima premessa con riferimento alla coltivazione di olio di palma.

La risposta corretta è "*A ban on palm oil alone would not solve all of the environmental problems associated with vegetable oil production*". Quest'affermazione è la conclusione del ragionamento perché concorda sia con la preoccupazione espressa nella prima premessa per i rischi sull'ambiente causati dalla coltivazione di olio di palma, sia con l'avvertimento nella seconda premessa che le colture di oli vegetali alternativi potrebbero causare danni ancora più gravi per l'ambiente. Bandire solo l'olio di palma, quindi, non risolverebbe i rischi per l'ambiente.

6) C. La domanda chiede di identificare quale delle cinque alternative di risposta riporti l'affermazione che, se fosse aggiunta alle premesse dell'argomentazione, ne indebolirebbe la conclusione. Nel brano si parla della pesca a strascico, metodo di pesca osteggiato dagli ambientalisti perché ritenuto dannoso per gli ecosistemi. L'industria della pesca, invece, si oppone fortemente alla possibilità di vietare tale metodo ritenendo piuttosto che possa portare benefici alla vita marina, dal momento che le specie che sono più resistenti agli effetti della pesca a strascico possono proliferare. Le seguenti alternative, se fossero vere, rafforzerebbero la conclusione invece di indebolirla. Perciò, vanno scartate:

- "*Trawling creates new habitats by making parts of the sea more habitable*", se ciò fosse vero, sarebbe ancora più valido ricavare la conclusione che la pesca a strascico "can benefit marine life";
- "*Trawling in shallow waters can alter the ecology in beneficial ways*", anche questa affermazione se fosse vera, renderebbe ancora più valida la conclusione che la pesca a strascico porta benefici.

L'alternativa "*Trawling in shallow waters can damage the bottom of fishermen's boats*", invece, deve essere ugualmente scartata poiché, se fosse vera, non inciderebbe sulla conclusione e, dunque, non la indebolirebbe: nel brano, infatti, sono in discussione gli effetti della pesca a strascico sull'ambiente marino, non sul fondo delle barche dei pescatori.
L'opzione "*Trawling in deep waters is expensive and an ineffective use of fishing resources*" non è valida poiché se fosse vera potrebbe in qualche modo indebolire la conclusione, ma la domanda richiede di individuare l'affermazione che indebolirebbe DI PIÙ il ragionamento della traccia; tale affermazione non può non essere l'alternativa "*Trawling nets have a destructive impact on many endangered species*": sostenere che le reti da pesca a strascico hanno un impatto distruttivo su molte specie in via di estinzione contrasterebbe del tutto con la conclusione che la pesca a strascico "can benefit marine life".

7) E. Per risolvere il quesito, bisogna individuare quale delle cinque alternative di risposta riporti il principio su cui si fonda il ragionamento esposto nella traccia, il quale affronta la questione dei profitti derivanti da un certo ambito o settore economico (nella fattispecie quello automobilistico) che devono essere spesi in quello stesso ambito o settore (ad es. per la manutenzione delle strade o per sovvenzionare i trasporti pubblici). A questo punto si possono esaminare le cinque alterative e stabilire quale si basi sul principio appena individuato. Tale alternativa è quella che afferma: "*Profits from sporting events should be spent on encouraging people to participate in sport*". Il principio di fondo, infatti, è lo stesso: i profitti derivanti da un certo ambito o settore economico (nella fattispecie quello sportivo) devono essere spesi in quello stesso ambito o settore (ad es. per incoraggiare le persone a partecipare allo sport).

8) D. L'argomentazione della traccia ha un difetto, per cui non è accettabile il passaggio logico dalle premesse alla conclusione. È dunque indispensabile individuare innanzitutto le premesse e la conclusione dell'argomentazione. Nel brano si afferma che in alcuni paesi le restrizioni alla vendita di alcolici ai giovani non ha avuto gli effetti benefici previsti sulla loro salute dal momento che, in seguito a tali restrizioni, negli ospedali si sono registrati numerosi casi di giovani che si sono ammalati a causa del consumo di soluzioni di etanolo e profumi come alcolici. Dunque, l'autore del brano conclude che se le restrizioni fossero abolite, il rischio per la salute sarebbe ridotto.
L'opzione che riporta il difetto del ragionamento è: "*It ignores the fact that if there had been no restrictions more young people would have suffered from drinking alcohol*". Stando alla conclusione del ragionamento, dovrebbero essere abolite le restrizioni sulla vendita di alcolici ai giovani, al fine di evitare il consumo giovanile di altre sostanze a base di alcol nocive per la salute. Tuttavia, il ragionamento si limita a considerare che se le restrizioni non ci fossero state, non ci sarebbe stato il consumo di altre sostanze nocive da parte di un certo numero di giovani, ma ignora che in tal caso il rischio sarebbe stato maggiore, perché ci sarebbe stato l'uso di alcolici da parte di un numero maggiore di giovani.

9) A. Per risolvere il quesito si deve stabilire in quale delle cinque alternative di risposta vi sia la cosiddetta prova addizionale, cioè l'affermazione che, se aggiunta alle premesse, indebolirebbe di più l'argomentazione nella traccia. Nel brano si parla dell'aumento registrato negli ultimi dieci anni della presenza di programmi televisivi in cui sono presenti scienziati forensi. Sebbene l'attenzione dei media sia stata accompagnata da un massiccio aumento del numero di corsi e di qualifiche disponibili, ciò non ha portato alla creazione di più posti di lavoro in questo campo. Pertanto, coloro che studiano questi corsi scopriranno che esiste una forte competizione per un lavoro difficile.
Le seguenti alternative, se fossero vere, rafforzerebbero la conclusione invece di indebolirla, pertanto vanno scartate:

- "*New technologies have brought about a decrease in the number of forensics staff required in laboratories*". La diminuzione del numero di personale forense richiesto nei laboratori aumenterebbe la "fierce competition", di cui si parla nella conclusione del ragionamento, per i pochi posti rimasti;
- "*Each year around 1500 graduates in forensic science compete for 200 jobs in the sector*". Un numero di 200 posti nel settore forense per 1500 laureati all'anno, più quelli degli anni precedenti ancora senza lavoro, confermerebbe la conclusione per la quale c'è una "fierce competition" nel settore.

L'alternativa "*The number of university courses in forensic science has grown at an unprecedented rate*", invece, non è valida perché esprime un concetto – quello dell'aumento dei corsi in scienze forensi – già presente in una delle premesse e, quindi, non potrebbe indebolire il ragionamento.

L'opzione "*Salaries for forensic scientists compare well with those in other scientific fields*" se fosse vera in qualche modo potrebbe indebolire la conclusione: infatti, se i salari degli scienziati forensi sono comparabili a quelli di altri campi scientifici, ciò non renderebbe la scienza forense economicamente più appetibile di altri settori scientifici e, quindi, non sarebbe molto forte la "fierce competition" di cui si parla nella conclusione. La domanda, però, richiede di individuare l'affermazione che indebolirebbe di più il ragionamento della traccia, pertanto tale alternativa va scartata. La risposta corretta è "*Many students of forensic science go on to pursue careers in other areas*". Se ciò fosse vero, non ci sarebbero molti candidati a contendersi i pochi posti disponibili per i laureati in scienze forensi, giacché molti di questi ultimi potrebbero intraprendere carriere in altri settori.

---

10) A. Questa tipologia di quesito richiede di determinare quale, fra le cinque alternative di risposta, contiene la supposizione implicita del ragionamento, ossia il presupposto che non è affermato nel brano ma sul quale poggia la conclusione. Nel testo si parla del fatto che molte banche incoraggiano i loro clienti ad acquistare un'assicurazione contro le frodi con carta di credito e altri tipi di "furto d'identità". Si tratta però di una forma di protezione per le banche stesse e non per i clienti dal momento che i costi di eventuali transazioni fraudolente sono a carico della banca; pertanto, per i clienti non è necessario investire denaro in servizi assicurativi aggiuntivi.
Le due opzioni seguenti introducono concetti non collegabili alla premessa e alla conclusione perciò vanno scartate:

- "*People who are worried about identity theft worry only about their credit cards*". Tale affermazione contrasta con la premessa esplicita, dove si parla non solo di "*credit card fraud*", ma anche di "*other kinds of 'identity theft*";
- "*Customers whose identities have been stolen would have benefited from the banks' additional insurance services*". Anche ciò contrasta con la premessa, in cui si spiega che sono le banche a beneficiare dei loro stessi servizi assicurativi addizionali.

Queste altre due opzioni, invece, presentano concetti già espressi nel ragionamento, per cui non possono riportarne il presupposto implicito e anch'esse non possono essere prese in considerazione:

- "*Credit card fraud is a less serious problem than many people believe*". Tale concetto emerge nella premessa, soprattutto quando si dice che "*customers who are victims of credit card fraud suffer inconvenience but they are unlikely to lose money*";
- "*Additional insurance services are widely available for credit card customers*". Ciò emerge nella premessa, dove si dice che "*many banks encourage their customers to buy insurance*".

La risposta corretta è: "*The banks' additional insurance services protect only against the costs of fraudulent credit card transactions*". Nella premessa si dice che "i costi di eventuali transazioni fraudolente sono a carico della banca". Si deve presupporre l'alternativa di risposta in esame, cioè che "i servizi assicurativi aggiuntivi delle banche proteggono solo contro i costi delle transazioni fraudolente con carta di credito", per dedurre la conclusione, ossia che "non è necessario che i clienti spendano denaro in servizi assicurativi aggiuntivi".

11) B. Dalla tabella si evince che la spedizione di 7 articoli in un unico pacco costa £ 3.30; è necessario ora verificare se ci sono combinazioni di pacchi, contenenti un numero inferiore di articoli, che costano meno di £ 3.30. Poiché la spedizione di 1 singolo articolo costa £ 0.55, è sicuramente più conveniente spedire:

- un pacco con 5 articoli a £ 1.60 piuttosto che 5 pacchi con 1 solo articolo a £ 0.55 × 5 = £ 2.75;
- un pacco con 4 articoli a £ 1.30 piuttosto che 4 pacchi con 1 solo articolo a £ 0.55 × 4 = £ 2.20;
- un pacco con 3 articoli a £ 0.95 piuttosto che 3 pacchi con 1 solo articolo a £ 0.55 × 3 = £ 1.65;
- un pacco con 2 articoli a £ 0.70 piuttosto che 2 pacchi con 1 solo articolo a £ 0.55 × 2 = £ 1.10.

Analogamente, poiché la spedizione di 2 articoli costa £ 0.70, è più conveniente spedire un pacco con 4 articoli a £ 1.30 piuttosto che 2 pacchi con 2 articoli a £ 0.70 × 2 = £ 1.40.
Allora, le possibili combinazioni di pacchi più economiche per spedire 7 articoli sono le seguenti:

- un pacco da 3 articoli più un pacco da 4 articoli, al costo di £ 0.95 + £ 1.30 = £ 2.25
- un pacco da 2 articoli più un pacco da 5 articoli, al costo di £ 0.70 + £ 1.60 = £ 2.30
e quindi la tariffa postale più bassa per spedire 7 articoli è £ 2.25.

12) C. Dal momento che per due volte di seguito, mentre Luke percorre 50 metri, il cucciolo ne percorre 100 ad andare più 50 a tornare, per un totale di 150 metri = 50 metri × 3, si ha che il cucciolo di Luke corre a velocità tripla rispetto al suo padrone. Inoltre, poiché la velocità di Luke è di 1 Km ogni 12 minuti e 1 h = 60 minuti = 12 minuti × 5, la sua velocità oraria è di:

$$1 \text{ km/h} \times 5 = 5 \text{ km/h}.$$

La velocità del cucciolo è allora di 5 km/h × 3 = 15 km/h.

13) A. Osservando il disegno dei 4 quadrati si nota che vengono usati 4 bastoncini per il primo quadrato di una riga, 3 bastoncini per i quadrati ad esso adiacenti, cioè appartenenti alla riga e alla colonna a cui appartiene il quadrato stesso, e 2 bastoncini per il quadrato rimanente. Ripetendo lo stesso ragionamento per i 100 quadrati divisi in 10 righe da 10 (ovvero in 10 righe e 10 colonne), si avrà che serviranno 4 bastoncini per il primo quadrato, 3 bastoncini per tutti i quadrati appartenenti alla prima riga e alla prima colonna, cioè 9 + 9 = 18 quadrati, e 2 bastoncini per tutti i quadrati rimanenti, che saranno 100 – 19 = 81. Allora per costruire una griglia di 100 quadrati in 10 righe da 10 si avrà bisogno di:

4 + (3 × 18) + (2 × 81) = 4 + 54 + 162 = 220 bastoncini.

14) A. Poiché dopo 1 giro sono stati presi in totale 4 cioccolatini con l'involucro rosso, 1 cioccolatino con l'involucro blu, 3 cioccolatini con l'involucro verde e 2 cioccolatini con l'involucro giallo, dopo 6 giri saranno stati presi:

- $4 \times 6 = 24$ cioccolatini con l'involucro rosso;
- $1 \times 6 = 6$ cioccolatini con l'involucro blu;
- $3 \times 6 = 18$ cioccolatini con l'involucro verde;
- $2 \times 6 = 12$ cioccolatini con l'involucro giallo.

È noto che ciascun colore è presente in numero uguale nella scatola di cioccolatini, quindi, poiché dopo 6 giri sono stati presi 24 cioccolatini con l'involucro rosso, anche i cioccolatini degli altri colori dovranno essere almeno 24, cioè ne saranno rimasti almeno:

- $24 - 6 = 18$ con l'involucro blu;
- $24 - 18 = 6$ con l'involucro verde;
- $24 - 12 = 12$ con l'involucro giallo.

Inoltre, poiché la metà dei cioccolatini rimasti ha l'involucro blu e $18 = 12 + 6$, è possibile che nella scatola dopo 6 giri siano rimasti solo questi cioccolatini. Ogni cioccolatino in più, infatti, corrisponderebbe a 4 cioccolatini in più, uno per ogni colore, e non sarebbe più vero che i cioccolatini blu rimasti sono la metà del totale. Allora, quando era piena, la scatola conteneva $24 \times 4 = 96$ cioccolatini.

---

15) D. Per sapere quale dei 5 amici ha bruciato più calorie basta calcolare quante calorie sono state bruciate da ciascuno, utilizzando correttamente i dati presenti nelle due tabelle, ovvero considerando per ognuno il peso, il tipo di attività e la durata. Poiché 1 ora = 60 minuti, e quindi 10, 20 e 30 minuti sono pari rispettivamente a 1/6, 1/3 e 1/2 di un'ora, si ha che:

- Harry, pesando 85 kg, con l'attività 1 brucia $\frac{310}{2}$ calorie e con l'attività 2 brucia $\frac{200}{2}$ calorie, per un totale di 255 calorie;
- Holly, pesando 60 kg, con l'attività 1 brucia $\frac{510}{3}$ calorie e con l'attività 2 brucia $\frac{150}{6}$ calorie, per un totale di 195 calorie;
- Jessie, pesando 75 kg, con l'attività 1 brucia $\frac{540}{6}$ calorie e con l'attività 2 brucia $\frac{420}{3}$ calorie, per un totale di 230 calorie;
- Josie, pesando 100 kg, con l'attività 1 brucia $\frac{350}{2}$ calorie e con l'attività 2 brucia $\frac{240}{2}$ calorie, per un totale di 295 calorie;
- Paul, pesando 60 kg, con l'attività 1 brucia $\frac{360}{3}$ calorie e con l'attività 2 brucia $\frac{210}{3}$ calorie, per un totale di 190 calorie.

È Josie, quindi, l'amica che ha bruciato più calorie di tutti.

16) E. Per sapere quale combinazione di treni consente il ritorno a Victoria il prima possibile è necessario simulare i due possibili tragitti, prestando attenzione alle tabelle degli orari:

- tragitto n°1 – prendendo da Three Bridges il treno delle 8:45 per Arundel, si giunge alla cittadina alle 9:32, quindi, volendo restare in visita almeno 4 ore, cioè fino ad almeno le 13:32, il primo treno utile per Chichester parte alle 14:02 e arriva alle 14:24. Volendo visitare anche Chichester almeno 4 ore, vale a dire fino alle 18:24, si può prendere il treno per Victoria che parte alle 18:37 e arriva alle 20:20;
- tragitto n°2 – prendendo, invece, da Three Bridges il treno delle 8:45 per Chichester, si giunge alla cittadina alle 9:34, quindi, volendola visitare per almeno 4 ore, ovvero fino alle 13:34, sarà possibile ripartire per Arundel alle 13:41, giungendo lì alle 14:12. Volendo poi restare in visita anche ad Arundel per almeno 4 ore, cioè fino alle 18:12, si può prendere il treno delle 18:13, che arriva a Victoria alle 19:47.

Il primo orario in cui è possibile ritornare a Victoria, dopo essere stati nelle due cittadine il numero di ore previste, è le 19:47.

17) C. Poiché la mail è stata spedita alle 3 pm da Londra, aggiungendo 3 ore all'orario di ciascun senior manager dei quartier generali delle città presenti nella tabella, si verrà a conoscenza degli orari in cui è stata ricevuta la mail:

- a Giakarta alle 11 pm;
- a Nairobi alle 6 pm;
- a Praga alle 4 pm;
- a Ottawa alle 10 am;
- a Mosca alle 6 pm;
- a Canberra all'1 am;
- a Hong Kong alle 11 pm.

Considerato, allora, che l'orario di lavoro è dalle 8 am alle 5.15 pm dell'ora locale di ciascun quartier generale, nelle città di Praga e Ottawa i manager stanno lavorando e ricevono l'email immediatamente. Nelle altre città, invece, l'email arriva fuori dall'orario di lavoro e, in particolare, gli ultimi che leggeranno l'email saranno i senior manager di Nairobi e Mosca, per i quali la giornata di lavoro è finita da poco, e che leggeranno l'email tra 14 ore: è questo il massimo intervallo possibile tra il primo e l'ultimo senior manager che leggerà l'email.

18) A. Poiché entrando nella stanza di Alex dalla porta si ha alla destra un armadio quadrato, nei disegni della stanza presenti nel quesito bisogna trovare tale armadio quadrato alla sinistra della porta. Allora sicuramente le viste B e C che non hanno niente in quell'angolo e la vista E che ha un mobile rettangolare non possono essere vedute aeree della stanza di Alex. Poiché, inoltre, sullo stesso muro dell'armadio è presente il letto, che è sicuramente più grande della scrivania, che gli si trova giusto di fronte, l'esatta veduta aerea della stanza di Alex è la A.

19) A. Tutti i grafici hanno, a partire dall'origine, una linea obliqua che rappresenta la prima ora di corsa di David, alla velocità di 6 km/h. Dopo tale corsa David fa una sosta di 20 minuti, rappresentata nei grafici da un piccolo segmento orizzontale, durante il quale il tempo aumenta (sull'asse *x* ci si sposta verso destra), ma lo spazio no (sull'asse *y* si rimane fermi). Dopo essersi riposato, David riprende a correre a 10 km/h, cioè ad una velocità maggiore di prima, che deve essere rappresentata nei grafici da un segmento obliquo con una pendenza superiore a quella del primo segmento: ciò è ben riportato nei grafici A, C e D, ma non nel grafico B, nel quale la pendenza del secondo segmento è uguale alla prima, e nel grafico E, in cui la pendenza è addirittura inferiore. Alla fine di tale corsa David arriva a Banby, dove si ferma a parlare con un amico per 20 minuti, per cui nei grafici si deve trovare un segmento orizzontale uguale a quello precedente, cosa che accade nei grafici A e D, ma non nel C, nel quale il periodo di sosta sembra maggiore. Poi David prende una bicicletta e si rimette in marcia verso Carston a 16 km/h, cioè ad una velocità ancora superiore, per poi fermarsi e ripartire per casa, cioè tornare indietro: nei grafici quindi dopo il secondo segmento orizzontale ce ne devono essere uno obliquo di pendenza superiore ai precedenti, un altro orizzontale ed infine uno obliquo che riporta sull'asse delle *x*, dove la *y* è nulla, in quanto c'è un ritorno all'origine. Ciò è rappresentato perfettamente nel grafico A, ma non nel D, in cui l'ultimo segmento, essendo verticale, fa presupporre un ritorno in 0 minuti, e non in 50 come avvenuto in realtà.

20) B. Per sapere se ciascuna delle visuali proposte corrisponde effettivamente ad una vista laterale del telaio bisogna considerare i quattro lati della sezione trasversale e vedere le parti come si alternano:

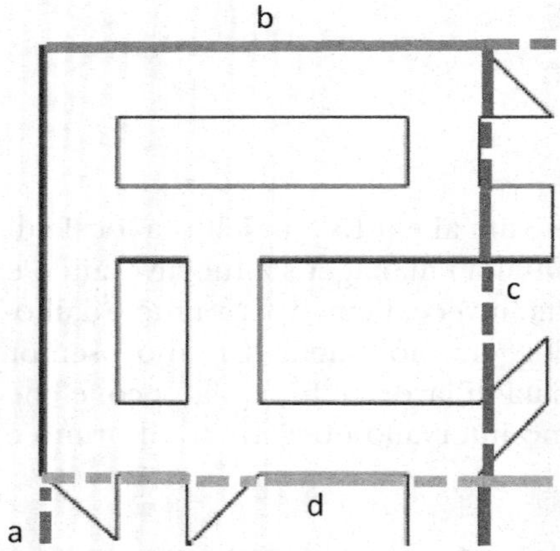

I quattro lati sono indicati con le lettere a, b, c, d e si sono alternate linee intere e linee tratteggiate per evidenziare il cambio di parte. I lati a e b sono divisi in 2 parti, una lunga segnata dalla linea intera ed una molto corta segnata dalla linea tratteggiata, come nelle visuali A ed E. La linea d, invece, ha 3 parti corte, 1 lunga ed altre 2 corte, come la visuale D e la linea c, infine, è formata da 7 parti, come la visuale C. L'unico disegno che non rappresenta nessuna vista laterale del telaio è la figura B.

21) B. La risposta corretta è "*Einstein's general theory of relativity*". Si tratta della teoria della relatività generale, che Einstein presentò mediante una serie di lezioni presso l'Accademia Prussiana delle Scienze a partire dal 25 novembre 1915. Un aiuto per rispondere al quesito può consistere nel procedere per esclusione. Dalton è un fisico vissuto tra XVIII e XIX sec., dunque non nel 1915. La teoria della meccanica quantistica vera e propria risale agli anni '20 del XX sec. La teoria del Big Bang è stata dedotta dalle equazioni della relatività generale, per cui è a questa successiva. Infine, la teoria delle stringhe tenta di conciliare la relatività generale con la meccanica quantistica, quindi è posteriore a entrambe le due teorie sopra citate.

22) B. La risposta corretta è Adam Smith. Infatti, la "mano invisibile" è una metafora usata da Smith per indicare una dinamica economica in un libero mercato: pur perseguendo il proprio interesse egoistico, ciascun individuo, come se fosse spinto da una mano invisibile, finisce per giovare all'interesse di tutta la collettività di cui egli stesso fa parte (ad es., la concorrenza nasce da una pluralità di venditori egoisti, ma finisce per abbassare i prezzi, cosa di cui beneficia tutta la società).

Biologia

23) A. L'HIV è un retrovirus costituito da un genoma a RNA racchiuso in un capside proteico e avvolto da un involucro membranoso formato da proteine, lipidi e carboidrati. Essendo un retrovirus, contiene anche l'enzima trascrittasi inversa, una DNA polimerasi RNA-dipendente che, usando come stampo l'RNA genomico, sintetizza una copia di DNA che si integra nel genoma della cellula ospite. Poiché il capside ha natura proteica, l'involucro esterno contiene proteine e la trascrittasi inversa è un enzima proteico, tutti i tre costituenti contengono legami peptidici.

24) E. In una proteina, la struttura primaria è la sequenza di amminoacidi uniti da legami peptidici, la struttura secondaria è un pattern regolare dovuto alla formazione di legami idrogeno tra amminoacidi non consecutivi, la struttura terziaria è la conformazione tridimensionale assunta dalla catena dovuta alla formazione di legami tra le catene laterali degli amminoacidi, la struttura quaternaria è l'architettura delle proteine costituite da più catene polipeptidiche. L'emoglobina, una proteina globulare, è formata da quattro catene polipeptidiche (due catene α e due catene β), ciascuna delle quali lega un gruppo eme contenente ferro. L'atomo di ferro presente in ciascun gruppo eme ha la capacità di formare un legame debole con l'ossigeno. Pertanto, la molecola di emoglobina in grado di legare quattro molecole di ossigeno per convertirsi in ossiemoglobina presenta tutti i quattro livelli di struttura delle proteine.

25) B. Nell'appaiamento tra basi complementari, citosina e guanina formano tre legami idrogeno, adenina e timina soltanto due. Nella sequenza indicata sono presenti 3 C e 4 G, che nell'appaiamento con il filamento complementare formano un totale di 21 legami idrogeno, mentre le 2 A e le 3 T formano un totale di 10 legami idrogeno: i legami idrogeno sono in totale 31. I legami fosfodiesterici che si stabiliscono tra i 12 nucleotidi adiacenti della sequenza sono 11. Gli anticodoni delle molecole di tRNA che traducono l'mRNA trascritto dalla sequenza contengono un numero di uracili corrispondente al numero di timine presenti nella sequenza di DNA, quindi 3.

26) E. In una cellula vegetale, la parete cellulare è costituita da una serie di strati di cellulosa, un polisaccaride formato da unità di glucosio. Una parte delle proteine presenti nella membrana cellulare è rappresentata da glicoproteine, che hanno catene di carboidrati legate alla molecola proteica di base. Nel nucleolo avviene la sintesi degli rRNA, che contengono monomeri di ribosio. I mitocondri contengono il DNA mitocondriale, che include monomeri di deossiribosio.

27) B. Le molecole Q si trovano a più alta concentrazione nella cellula Y che nella cellula X; pertanto, il loro passaggio dalla cellula X alla cellula Y dovrebbe avvenire contro gradiente di concentrazione. Ciò non si realizza mediante diffusione facilitata, trattandosi di una forma di trasporto passivo, mentre è possibile mediante trasporto attivo. Il flusso di molecole R tra le due cellule avviene in egual misura nelle due direzioni, non sussistendo un gradiente di concentrazione che porti all'instaurarsi di un flusso netto.

28) E. Entrambe le affermazioni dello studente 1 sono corrette, in quanto il DNA nelle cellule animali è contenuto all'interno di un nucleo e i ribosomi delle cellule batteriche hanno un coefficiente di sedimentazione di 70S. Entrambe le affermazioni dello studente 2 sono errate, in quanto le cellule animali non posseggono una parete cellulare e le cellule batteriche non contengono mitocondri. Anche le affermazioni dello studente 3 sono entrambe errate, in quanto i ribosomi delle cellule animali hanno un coefficiente di sedimentazione di 80S e il DNA delle cellule batteriche non contenuto all'interno di un nucleo. Entrambe le affermazioni dello studente 4 sono corrette, in quanto le cellule animali contengono DNA circolare all'interno dei mitocondri e le cellule batteriche contengono DNA extracromosomico in forma di plasmidi.

29) E. Nella fase luce-dipendente della fotosintesi, l'energia luminosa porta alla scissione dell'acqua in ossigeno molecolare e ioni idrogeno; questi ultimi vengono utilizzati per ridurre il coenzima $NADP^+$ a $NADPH + H^+$. Nella fase luce-indipendente della fotosintesi avviene il ciclo di Calvin, nel quale l'anidride carbonica reagisce con il ribulosiobisfosfato formando un intermedio a sei atomi di carbonio instabile, che si scinde immediatamente in due molecole di fosfoglicerato; queste vengono ridotte a gliceraldeide 3-fosfato utilizzando il potere riducente del $NADPH + H^+$ prodotto grazie alla scissione dell'acqua.

30) A. La glicolisi, una via metabolica che conduce alla scissione di una molecola di glucosio a 6 atomi di carbonio in due molecole di piruvato a 3 atomi di carbonio, produce sia ATP che NAD ridotto, ma non anidride carbonica. La successiva decarbossilazione ossidativa del piruvato ad acetil-CoA produce sia anidride carbonica sia NAD ridotto, ma non ATP.

31) A. Durante il processo di oogenesi, le cellule germinali dell'ovaio (diploidi) si dividono per mitosi, dando origine a una popolazione di oogoni (diploidi); questi si dividono per mitosi, producendo una popolazione di cellule che si differenziano in ooциti primari (diploidi). Gli oociti primari sono le cellule che vanno incontro alla prima divisione meiotica, producendo gli oociti secondari (aploidi).

32) E. Dei tre eventi elencati, soltanto la replicazione del DNA avviene prima che abbia inizio la meiosi, precisamente durante la fase S dell'interfase. Invece, la formazione del fuso a partire dalle fibre del fuso e il crossing over si verificano nella tarda profase della meiosi.

33) A. La fibrosi cistica è una malattia genetica ereditaria a trasmissione autosomica recessiva. Nel caso presentato, i genitori, essendo sani e avendo avuto un figlio affetto dalla malattia, sono entrambi eterozigoti per il gene-malattia. La probabilità che essi concepiscano un figlio non affetto è pari a ¾ e la probabilità che concepiscano un figlio maschio è pari a ½. Trattandosi di due eventi indipendenti, la probabilità che la coppia abbia un figlio maschio non affetto da fibrosi cistica è pari al prodotto delle probabilità, ovvero $3/4 \times 1/2 = 3/8$.

34) C. L'mRNA è una catena polinucleotidica formata da una sequenza di codoni contenenti le basi adenina, uracile, guanina e citosina. Il DNA procariotico è una molecola circolare di DNA a doppio filamento. Nell'appaiamento tra DNA e RNA, i residui di adenina presenti nel DNA formano un appaiamento complementare con i residui di uracile dell'RNA mediante due legami idrogeno. L'rRNA non contiene anticodoni; gli anticodoni sono triplette nucleotidiche presenti nei tRNA che si appaiano con i codoni complementari presenti nell'mRNA durante la traduzione. I tRNA, come tutti gli RNA, contengono la base uracile in luogo della base timina presente nel DNA.

35) A. Un organismo transgenico è un organismo nel cui genoma sono stati inseriti geni provenienti da un'altra specie. Un organismo transgenico può essere un mammifero nel cui genoma è inserito DNA di un invertebrato, una pianta nel cui genoma è inserito DNA procariotico, un animale nel cui genoma è inserito DNA vegetale, ecc.

36) C. La neuroipofisi secerne ossitocina e ormone antidiuretico (ADH); poiché quest'ultimo stimola il riassorbimento dell'acqua a livello dei reni, una disfunzione ipofisaria può determinare un aumento della quantità di urina prodotta sia nei maschi che nelle femmine. L'adenoipofisi secerne numerosi ormoni, tra cui le gonadotropine, ovvero l'ormone follicolo-stimolante (FSH) e l'ormone luteinizzante (LH). Le gonadotropine sono essenziali per il corretto funzionamento delle gonadi sia nei maschi che nelle femmine; pertanto, una disfunzione ipofisaria può causare infertilità in entrambi i sessi.

37) A. Tutti gli inibitori enzimatici riducono la velocità della reazione catalizzata dall'enzima bersaglio. L'inibizione enzimatica può essere reversibile o irreversibile. Nell'inibizione reversibile, l'efficienza dell'enzima torna normale con l'allontanamento dell'inibitore. Gli inibitori reversibili possono essere competitivi, se competono con il substrato per il legame al sito attivo, e non competitivi, se legano un sito diverso e causano un cambiamento conformazionale nel sito attivo che inibisce la sua capacità di legare il substrato. Nell'inibizione irreversibile, l'enzima non torna efficiente dopo l'allontanamento dell'inibitore, in quanto questo ne causa l'inattivazione o la denaturazione permanente. L'energia di attivazione non è influenzata dagli inibitori.

38) C. La memorizzazione è il processo attraverso il quale le informazioni vengono codificate e immagazzinate in una forma che consente di recuperarle all'occorrenza. La memoria sembra risiedere in varie regioni encefaliche, ma di certo la sede principale di immagazzinamento è rappresentata dalla corteccia cerebrale. Infatti, a seguito della distruzione di aree della corteccia cerebrale di mammifero, si verifica una perdita di informazioni la cui entità è pressoché proporzionale all'estensione dell'area distrutta.

39) C. Il potenziale di riposo di una cellula è la differenza di potenziale esistente a cavallo della membrana plasmatica quando la cellula non trasmette né riceve segnali elettrici. Tale potenziale ha un valore negativo, perché l'interno della cellula risulta carico negativamente rispetto all'esterno; nello specifico, nei neuroni ha un valore di –70 mV. Il potenziale di riposo si stabilisce grazie alla combinazione dei flussi passivi degli ioni sodio e potassio secondo gradiente di concentrazione attraverso canali ionici di membrana e il trasporto attivo contro gradiente degli stessi ioni a opera della pompa sodio/potassio. Inoltre, considerando che la pompa sodio/potassio opera un trasporto attivo, per il suo funzionamento necessita di idrolizzare ATP, che viene prodotto dal processo di respirazione cellulare.

40) A. Nel corso della ventilazione polmonare, l'inspirazione si verifica quando la pressione all'interno della cavità toracica è inferiore alla pressione atmosferica, cosicché sussiste un gradiente pressorio che richiama aria dall'esterno verso l'interno dei polmoni. Durante la sistole ventricolare, la pressione sanguigna all'interno dei ventricoli raggiunge il picco massimo ed è molto più elevata di quella all'interno degli atri, che sono in fase di diastole. In questa fase del ciclo cardiaco, la pressione aortica è più bassa di quella ventricolare, ma più elevata di quella atriale.

Chimica

41) E. In una soluzione acquosa di cloruro di sodio sono presenti molecole di acqua, gli ioni idronio e gli ioni idrossido derivanti dalla dissociazione dell'acqua, gli ioni sodio e gli ioni cloruro derivanti dalla dissociazione del cloruro di sodio. Non sono presenti, invece, singoli atomi neutri.

42) A. L'elemento X è lo iodio, un elemento appartenente al gruppo degli alogeni che si presenta in forma di solido grigio a temperatura ambiente. Lo iodio si combina con il cloro a formare cloruro di iodio (ICl), un composto polare nel quale il suo numero di ossidazione è pari a +1. In una soluzione di ioduro di potassio (KI), lo iodio si scioglie e reagisce con gli ioni ioduro (I^-) derivanti dalla dissociazione di KI, formando ioni triioduro (I_3^-), che conferiscono alla soluzione un colore marrone. A 500 °C, lo iodio sprigiona vapori di colore violetto.

43) C. Il silano (tetraidruro di silicio) ha formula SiH_4. L'atomo di silicio forma 4 legami sigma con i 4 atomi di idrogeno, per cui le coppie di elettroni di legame sono 4. Poiché il silicio possiede 4 elettroni di valenza, nella molecola di silano non presenta doppietti elettronici non condivisi. I 4 legami sigma si formano tra gli orbitali *s* degli atomi di idrogeno e i 4 orbitali ibridi sp^3 dell'atomo di silicio; la geometria della molecola è pertanto tetraedrica, con angoli di legame di 109,5°.

44) C. La configurazione elettronica dell'ossigeno elementare, che ha numero atomico 8, è $1s^22s^22p^4$: 2 elettroni si collocano nell'orbitale 1*s*, 2 nell'orbitale 2*s* e 4 nei 3 orbitali 2*p*. Lo ione O^{2-} possiede 2 elettroni in più rispetto all'atomo neutro, per cui la sua configurazione elettronica è $1s^22s^22p^6$: i 2 elettroni aggiuntivi trovano posto nei 3 orbitali 2*p*, che nel complesso possono ospitare 6 elettroni.

45) A. Poiché la soluzione di nitrato di potassio è satura, un abbassamento della temperatura, determinando una diminuzione della solubilità, causa la precipitazione di una parte del sale disciolto. Pertanto, la massa di nitrato di potassio non disciolto aumenta, mentre la concentrazione della soluzione diminuisce, poiché diminuisce la quantità di sale disciolto in una massa di solvente che resta invariata.

46) A. Nel processo di estrazione della clorofilla, la soluzione omogenea contenente i pigmenti estratti dalle foglie di una pianta viene sottoposta a cromatografia su strato sottile. Il petrolio greggio è una miscela omogenea di diversi idrocarburi; la separazione di benzina e gasolio dal petrolio si effettua per distillazione frazionata. Il sangue è un miscuglio eterogeneo dal quale i globuli rossi possono essere separati per centrifugazione. Una soluzione salina è una miscela omogenea che, sottoposta a distillazione semplice, viene separata nelle componenti salina e acquosa.

47) A. Nella reazione (A), il cloro si riduce (agente ossidante) e il bromo si ossida. Nella reazione (B), lo zinco si ossida (agente riducente) e il rame si riduce. Nella reazione (C), il monossido di carbonio si ossida (agente riducente) e il ferro si riduce. Nella reazione (D) non avvengono processi di ossido-riduzione. Nella reazione (E), il magnesio si ossida (agente riducente) e l'ossigeno si riduce.

48) C. Nell'esperimento descritto, il fluoro è il reagente limitante; infatti, dai coefficienti stechiometrici della reazione si ricava che 150 cm^3 di F_2 consumano solo 50 cm^3 dei 100 cm^3 di Cl_2 presenti, con produzione di 100 cm^3 di ClF_3. Il volume finale della miscela di reazione è dato dalla somma del volume del prodotto e di quello di Cl_2 che non ha reagito, ovvero $V = (100 + 50)\ cm^3 = 150\ cm^3$.

49) D. Due composti si definiscono isomeri strutturali se hanno la stessa formula molecolare, ma diversa connettività. La formula molecolare del metilciclopentano è C_6H_{12}, che è uguale a quella del 2-esene; i due composti sono, quindi, isomeri strutturali. La formula molecolare del cicloesene è C_6H_{10}. Il 2-metilpentano, l'esano e il 2,2-dimetilpentano sono isomeri strutturali con formula molecolare C_6H_{14}.

50) A. Lo ione $^{23}_{11}Na^+$ contiene 10 elettroni, 11 protoni e 12 neutroni. Lo ione $^{16}_{8}O^{2-}$ contiene 10 elettroni, 8 protoni e 8 neutroni. L'atomo $^{18}_{8}O$ contiene 8 elettroni, 8 protoni e 10 neutroni. L'atomo $^{32}_{16}S$ contiene 16 elettroni, 16 protoni e 16 neutroni.

51) D. Poiché 1 mole di qualsiasi sostanza contiene lo stesso numero di particelle (numero di Avogadro), basta calcolare il numero di moli di gas contenute in ciascun campione. La massa molare del diossido di carbonio (CO_2) è pari a 12 + (16 × 2) = 44 g/mol. In 66,0 g di CO_2 sono contenute 66/44 = 1,5 mol. La massa molare dell'ossigeno gassoso (O_2) è pari a 16 × 2 = 32 g/mol. In 64,0 g di O_2 sono contenute 64/32 = 2 mol. 22,4 L di idrogeno gassoso (H_2) contengono 1 mol. La massa molare dell'elio gassoso (He) è 4 g/mol. In 10,0 g di He sono contenute 10/4 = 2,5 mol. 33,6 L di cloro gassoso (Cl_2) contengono 33,6/22,4 = 1,5 mol. Pertanto, il campione che contiene il maggior numero di particelle è quello costituito da 10,0 g di elio gassoso.

52) B. Calcoliamo il numero di moli di HCl contenute in 10 mL della soluzione di acido: mol = 1 mol/L × 0,001 L = 10^{-2} mol. Poiché HCl è un acido forte, in acqua esso si dissocia completamente negli ioni H^+ e Cl^-. Pertanto, in 1 L di soluzione finale, la concentrazione di ioni H^+ sarà $[H^+] = 10^{-2}$ mol/L. Calcoliamo adesso il pH della soluzione: $pH = -\log[H^+] = -\log(10^{-2}) = 2$.

Fisica e Matematica

53) E. Per conoscere la pendenza della retta passante per i due punti indicati nel quesito, basta applicare la formula per scrivere l'equazione esplicita della retta $y = mx + q$, in cui m indica appunto la pendenza della retta. La formula della retta passante per 2 punti è

$$\frac{x-x_1}{x_2-x_1}=\frac{y-y_1}{y_2-y_1}$$

che in questo caso diventa

$$\frac{x-2}{-1-2}=\frac{y+3}{6+3}$$

da cui

$$-\frac{9}{3}(x-2)=y+3$$

e quindi

$$y=-3x+3$$

e la pendenza della retta è –3.

54) A. Ricordando che il logaritmo del rapporto tra due numeri è uguale alla differenza tra il logaritmo del numeratore e il logaritmo del denominatore, si ha che:

$$\log_{10}\left(\frac{14}{3}\right)=\log_{10}14-\log_{10}3$$

Poiché, inoltre, 14 può essere visto come 7 × 2 e il logaritmo del prodotto di due numeri è uguale alla somma dei logaritmi dei due fattori, si ha anche che:

$$\log_{10}(7\times 2)=\log_{10}7+\log_{10}2$$

Allora, considerate le corrispondenze elencate nel testo, si ha che:

$$\log_{10}\left(\frac{14}{3}\right)=\log_{10}7+\log_{10}2-\log_{10}3=x+y-z$$

55) A. Ricordando che la media di n numeri è data dalla loro somma divisa per n, si ha che la media di $\frac{x}{3}$, x e $x+6$ è:

$$\frac{\frac{x}{3}+x+x+6}{3}=\frac{x+3x+3x+18}{9}=\frac{7x+18}{9}$$

56) E. Per sapere in quanti modi è possibile ordinare le lettere "AABBC" basta contare le possibili permutazioni di n oggetti su k posti, con $n = k$, e r ripetizioni, la cui formula è:

$$\frac{n!}{r_1!\times r_2!\times\ldots\times r_k!}$$

In questo caso particolare, poiché le lettere sono 5, $n = k = 5$, e poiché la A e la B si ripetono ciascuna 2 volte, le ripetizioni sono $r_1 = 2$ e $r_2 = 2$. Allora le possibili permutazioni di "AABBC" sono:

$$\frac{5!}{2!\times 2!}=\frac{120}{4}=30$$

57) A. Alla fine del viaggio, l'automobile ed il punto X di partenza si trovano alle 2 estremità dell'ipotenusa di un triangolo rettangolo, i cui cateti sono lunghi 3 km e 4 km, come si vede dal disegno seguente, nel quale sono tracciati il percorso dell'automobile, la distanza dell'automobile dal punto X (a) e, tratteggiato, il cateto (b) utile alla risoluzione del quesito:

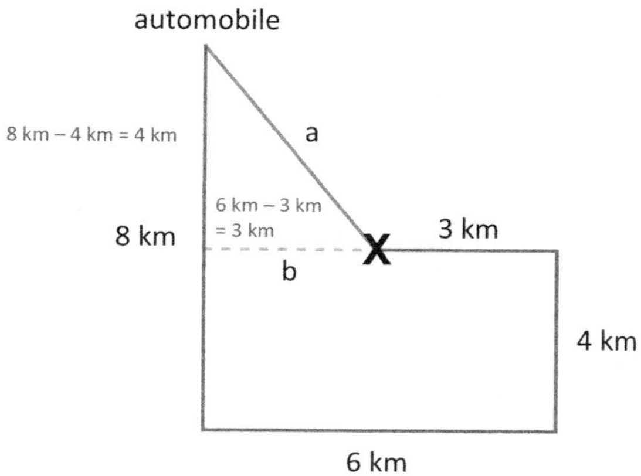

Allora è possibile trovare la distanza tra l'automobile e il punto di partenza applicando il teorema di Pitagora al triangolo rettangolo, trovando che è uguale a:

$$\sqrt{3^2 + 4^2} = \sqrt{25} = 5\ km$$

58) C. Per sapere qual è la forza verso l'alto esercitata dall'olio sul cubo basta ricordare la formula della spinta di Archimede, che assicura che tale spinta è pari al prodotto tra la densità del fluido (in questo caso σ), il volume del solido (in questo caso a^3) e l'accelerazione di gravità (in questo caso g). Allora la spinta sul cubo è pari a $\sigma a^3 g$.

59) A. Per il primo principio della termodinamica la variazione di energia interna, cioè di temperatura, durante un passaggio di stato, è pari alla differenza tra il calore assorbito e il lavoro compiuto dal sistema durante la trasformazione. In questo caso, poiché il calore fornito ed il lavoro effettuato sono uguali, non c'è stata variazione di temperatura, e quindi la trasformazione è stata isotermica.

60) A. Poiché per la terza legge di Ohm la potenza dissipata dal resistore è pari al prodotto tra la differenza di potenziale e l'intensità di corrente

$$P = V \times \underline{I}$$

e, per la prima legge di Ohm, la differenza di potenziale è pari al prodotto tra l'intensità di corrente elettrica e la resistenza

$$V = I \times \underline{R},$$

la potenza dissipata dal resistore sarà pari a:

$$P = I^2 \times R = 10^2\ A \times 5\ \Omega = 500\ W$$

IMAT
a.a. 2018/2019

General knowledge and logical reasoning

1) You want to buy a house in your local area with three bedrooms and a garage. However, you only want to spend € 150,000. Houses in your local area with three bedrooms and a garage never sell for less than € 200,000. You will have to spend more to get the house you want.
Which one of the following most closely matches the logical structure of the above argument?

A. You want to study mathematics but you don't like numerical reasoning. Mathematics is essentially numerical reasoning, so you should choose a different subject
B. You want a large powerful car that is fuel efficient. Large powerful cars are never fuel efficient, so you will have to spend more on fuel if you want a large powerful car
C. You want either the green jacket or the blue jacket. The green jacket looks good and the blue jacket is a bargain, so there are advantages in buying either one
D. You want a well-paid job with lots of holiday and the chance to retire early. Such jobs do not exist, so you need to adjust your expectations
E. You want to buy the painting at the auction. Lots of other people want to buy it, so you have to be prepared to bid a lot of money to be successful

2) Competition between restaurants is fierce and restaurateurs are trying to gain recognition for the quality of their food. Research from Oxford University might just give them that edge over their competitors. More than a hundred people participated in a series of experiments to see if the taste of food was affected by the cutlery used to eat it. The study found that desserts tasted better when eaten using small spoons. Similarly yoghurt tasted creamier when eaten with a black spoon. Cheese cut with a heavy knife tasted more expensive than cheese cut with a lighter knife.
Which one of the following is a conclusion that can be drawn from the above passage?

A. Restaurants should think carefully about what cutlery they use.
B. Customers pay attention to the cutlery they are using.
C. Variety of cutlery is more important than quality of food.
D. People choose restaurants only because of the quality of the food.
E. Restaurants should pay less attention to food presentation.

3) Food manufacturers should reduce sugar levels in processed foods. This is because there are too many overweight and obese people. Since people are unable or unwilling to make sensible decisions for themselves, manufacturers must take responsibility for rectifying a problem to which they contribute.

Which one of the following illustrates the principle used in the above argument?

A. Cigarette packets should have plain packaging and display government health warnings
B. In order to reduce sugar intake, foods with high sugar content should be taxed more heavily
C. To reduce the number of deaths caused by excessive speed, car manufacturers should incorporate speed limiters in vehicles
D. Labelling on food should be improved so that consumers are clear about the level of sugar in a product
E. Power tools should have clear instructions in order to reduce the number of accidents caused by incorrect use

4) Action has to be taken now to stop the spread of bovine tuberculosis (TB). Experts agree that reducing the number of badgers in the most heavily infected areas will help to break the cycle of infection between badgers and cattle and begin to reduce TB in both species. Although badgers can be vaccinated, there is no vaccine available to protect our cattle, and best estimates suggest it will be ten years before one is available. The only way to stop bovine TB spreading is to kill badgers.
Which one of the following, if true, most strengthens the above argument?

A. Less than ten per cent of the dairy cows destroyed each year are destroyed because of bovine TB
B. Shooting large numbers of badgers is more expensive than vaccinating them
C. In a trial, killing ten thousand badgers reduced the TB rate in cattle by only fifteen per cent
D. When efforts are made to remove badgers, many are injured rather than killed outright
E. Five annual vaccinations are necessary to protect a badger fully against bovine TB

5) Sperm whales have the largest brains on the planet, although both humans and dolphins have larger brains relative to their body size. But why should relative brain size be important? If one thinks of a brain as a computer, there is no obvious reason why it must be sized in proportion to the body it lives in. Why for example should a whale need an especially large brain, when a hummingbird – which has complex tasks to perform – manages with a tiny one?
Which one of the following is a conclusion that is supported by the above passage?

A. Dolphins are more intelligent than whales
B. Brain size and the ability to perform complex tasks are not necessarily related
C. Hummingbirds and whales have equally complex tasks to perform, despite huge difference in brain size
D. Whales need larger brains than either dolphins or humans because of their enormous size
E. There is no important difference between a brain and a computer

6) Recent research in the USA has found that areas with more dentists per person have much lower rates of obesity than neighbouring areas of similar population size. Clearly, public health authorities concerned with obesity rates should focus more resources on the provision of dental care. Dentists are a neglected asset in the struggle against the serious health problems associated with obesity.
Which one of the following is the best statement of the flaw in the above argument?

A. It assumes that a higher number of dentists causes lower obesity rates
B. It assumes dental care in the USA is somewhat similar to that found elsewhere
C. It ignores factors that might prevent public health authorities from spending more on obesity and related conditions
D. It assumes that obesity rates should be a priority concern for public health authorities
E. It ignores the fact that help and advice concerning obesity can be delivered in a variety of ways

7) It's better for your children's health to give them a video game to play than to let them watch television. Researchers at Queensland University examined the effects of video gaming and watching television on children between the ages of two and five. They found that the children burned more calories when they were gaming than when they were watching television; higher blood pressure was associated with watching television, but not with video gaming. The scientists believe that the difference comes from two distinct kinds of screen time: passive screen time, where you are simply viewing programmes or films, and active screen time, where you are engaging both your mind and your body.
Which one of the following is the main conclusion of the above argument?

A. Video gaming engages both the mind and the body
B. Children burn more calories when they play video games than when they watch television
C. Playing video games helps to reduce children's blood pressure
D. Video gaming is better for children's health than watching television
E. Watching television does not stimulate children's minds

8) "Internet addiction" is about to be classified as a recognised psychiatric disorder. Internet addiction is characterised by a number of signs: excessive use of the internet; anger or depression if access is lost; isolation from friends and family; and, most significantly, poor educational achievement. This should make us cautious about incorporating computer-based learning into all aspects of education. Educationalists should consider the long-term problems associated with extensive internet use as well as its immediate attractions.
Which one of the following is an assumption of the above argument?

A. Classifying internet addiction as a recognised psychiatric disorder will help lead to a cure
B. Students are unable to regulate their internet use
C. Excessive internet use is the only cause of poor educational achievement
D. All computer-based learning includes internet use
E. It is a bad idea to incorporate computer-based learning into education

9) One of the populations with the highest life expectancy is Iceland. The people there are very healthy, as indicated by the low incidence of diabetes, obesity, heart disease and diet related cancers. Their diet is rich in good quality local fish, and meat and dairy products from grass fed animals. The fish and meat is all caught, produced and processed on a small scale. If we want to live long and healthy lives we should adopt the Icelanders' diet.
Which one of the following is the best statement of the flaw in the above argument?

A. Vegetarians may not be able to live on an Icelandic diet
B. There may be other reasons for the Icelanders' health and longevity
C. There may be insufficient space in many countries to raise grass fed animals
D. The Icelandic diet may be prohibitively expensive elsewhere
E. People may not like being told what they should eat

10) A leaking undersea oil well in the USA caused massive damage to wildlife and was extremely expensive to clear up. Worst of all, it destroyed the livelihoods of poor people living in the area. Despite this, in the developed world we still don't take seriously the risks of deepwater drilling. Until we can be satisfied that regulation is effective and that oil companies are operating safely, deepwater drilling should be banned.
Which one of the following, if true, most weakens the above argument?

A. Oil companies will operate more safely in future than they did before the accident in the USA
B. The risks of deepwater drilling were known prior to the accident in the USA
C. Oil companies involved in the accident in the USA paid money to compensate the victims
D. Alternatives to fossil fuels may eventually be able to meet our energy needs
E. A ban on deepwater drilling would cause oil prices to rise, which would affect poor people most

11) A train is travelling at 30 mph towards a terminus which is 120 miles away. At the same time, a pigeon starts flying from the terminus towards the train. When it meets the train, it turns and flies back towards the terminus and, when it arrives there, it turns and flies back towards the train again. The pigeon flies at an average speed of 40 mph. The pigeon continues to do this until the train reaches the terminus.
Assuming that no time was lost in each turnaround, how far (to the nearest 10 miles) does the pigeon fly altogether?

A. 140 miles
B. 120 miles
C. 160 miles
D. 180 miles
E. 240 miles

12) Mr and Mrs Massa's rectangular lawn measures 10 metres by 6 metres. They pay Giovanni to cut the grass and trim the edges. Giovanni charges a fixed rate per square metre of grass to be cut and another fixed rate per metre of edge to be trimmed. For Mr and Mrs Massa's lawn, this results in a charge of $12 to cut the grass and $8 to trim the edges.
Now, Mr and Mrs Costa next door want Giovanni to do the same for them. Their lawn is also rectangular and measures 15 metres by 9 metres.
If he charges them at the same rate as the Massas, how much will Giovanni charge Mr and Mrs Costa, in total, for cutting their grass and trimming their edges?

A. $39
B. $30
C. $35
D. $36
E. $45

13) David normally takes 45 minutes to walk at a steady speed in a straight line from his house, past his friend Barry's house and then past a shop to reach his college.
Today, however, he stopped at Barry's house on the way and had to wait 3 min-

utes for him to be ready to leave. They stopped at the shop to buy their lunch, which took another 3 minutes. It normally takes David 20 minutes to walk from his home directly to the shop and Barry normally takes 32 minutes to walk directly from his home to the college and they both walk at the same steady speed.
How long does it take them to walk from Barry's house to the shop?

A. 1 minute
B. 4 minutes
C. 10 minutes
D. 7 minutes
E. 13 minutes

14) In a family, each of the six children has one packet of crisps on each weekday (Monday to Friday) for their packed lunch. The triplets have Cheese flavoured crisps, the twins have Paprika flavoured crisps, and the oldest child always has Chilli flavoured crisps. The exact number of packets of crisps needed are purchased at the same time for the four-week period.

The table below shows the price of single packets of crisps and multipacks of crisps of the same flavour. A multipack is a discounted collection of a number of single packets of one flavour.

packet type	*price*
single packet	£0.50
multipack of 6	£2.50
multipack of 12	£4.50
multipack of 24	£8.50
multipack of 36	£12.50

What is the most money that can be saved for the four weeks by purchasing the appropriate combination of multipacks and single packs of the different flavours rather than all single packs?

A. £8.00
B. £16.50
C. £18.00
D. £23.50
E. £43.50

15) The table below shows how to choose an appropriate glue for different materials you may want to bond together. For example, to bond cork and rubber you can use either rubber contact glue or epoxy glue.

	balsa wood	*plywood*	*acrylic*	*card*	*fabric*	*polystyrene*	*metal*	*cork*	*glass*	*rubber*
rubber	G	G	I	F I	G	H	F I	G I	G I	F G
glass	I	I	F I	F I	G	D H	F I	G I	G I	
cork	G I	G I	F I	F I	G	D H	G I	D G J		
metal	I	I	F I	F I	G	D H	F I			
polystyrene	D	D	D H	D	D H	D H				
fabric	G H	G H	G	G	D H					
card	C D	C D	D F I	C D						
acrylic	F I	F I	B							
plywood	D E	D E								
balsa wood	C D									

Key
B – acrylic cement
C – balsa cement
D – PVA glue
E – synthetic resin glue
F – cyanoacrylate (superglue)
G – rubber contact glue
H – latex glue
I – epoxy glue
J – polyester resin

Which one of the following statements is supported by the information in the table?

A. Polystyrene and card can only be bonded with rubber contact glue
B. The only materials that are suitable for bonding together with three different types of glue are cork with cork
C. Acrylic can be bonded to polystyrene using cyanoacrylate
D. Balsa cement can only be used to glue balsa wood to another material
E. Synthetic resin glue can only be used to glue wood materials together

16) The bar chart below shows the number of endangered species between 2000 and 2002 per animal class.

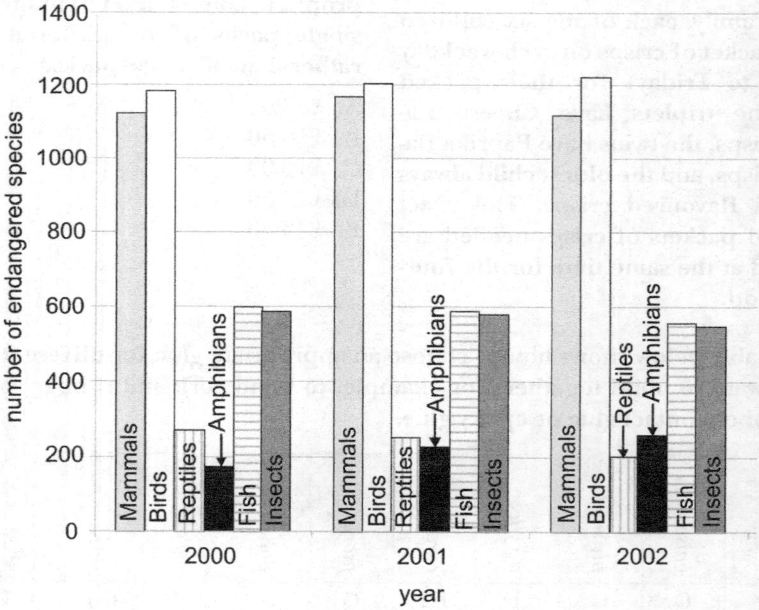

Which one of the following pieces of information can be inferred from the bar chart above?

A. The number of endangered species of mammals remained constant over the three-year period
B. More species of bird became endangered over the three-year period than any other animal class
C. The number of species of insects that were endangered was almost equal to the number of species of fish that were endangered over the three-year period
D. The number of endangered species of reptiles increased over the three-year period while that of amphibians decreased

E. In 2001, there were exactly four times as many endangered species of birds as there were endangered species of reptiles

17) A 300 g packet of Scottish oatcakes has the following information on the side of the packet:

typical value	*per 100 g*	*per oatcake*
energy	462 kcal	60 kcal
protein	10.78 g	1.4 g
carbohydrate total	56.0 g	7.27 g
carbohydrate sugars	2.31 g	0.3 g
fat total	20.79 g	2.7 g
fat saturates	5.4 g	0.7 g
fibre	6.9 g	0.9 g

How many oatcakes are there in the packet?

A. 23
B. 18
C. 21
D. 24
E. 29

18) A regular tetrahedron is made by fastening together four triangles made from card coloured on one side only, as shown in the diagram below.

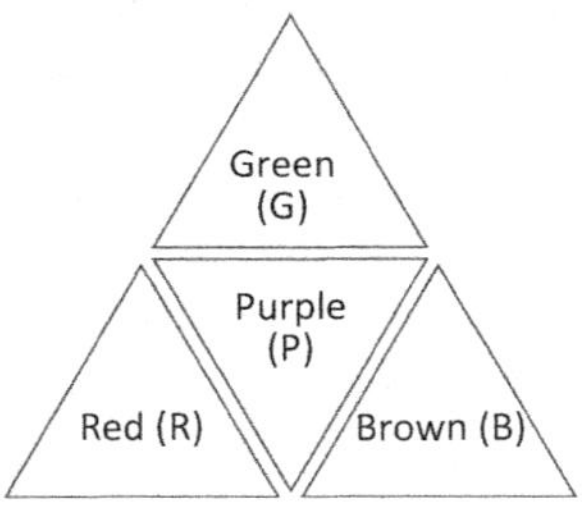

Which one of the following is NOT a possible view of this tetrahedron when looked at from above?

A.
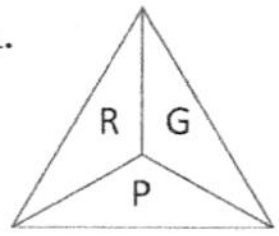

B.
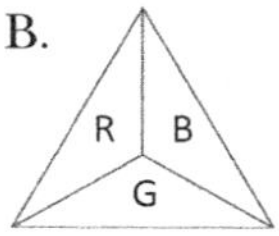

C.
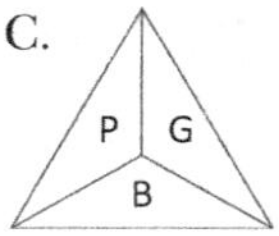

D.
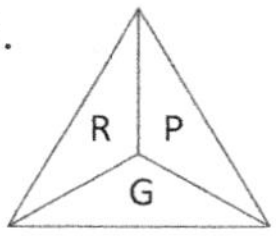

E.
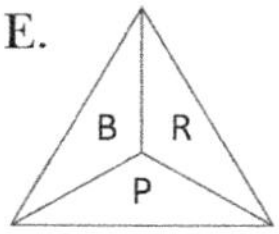

19) Alpha, Beta and Gamma are the three political parties in the Parliament. There are 360 seats in the Parliament. Before last week's General Election, each party held 120 seats.
In last week's election:
There was no change in 216 seats.
Alpha gained 15 seats from Beta and 23 seats from Gamma.
Beta gained 31 seats from Alpha and 41 seats from Gamma.
Gamma gained 24 seats from Alpha and 10 seats from Beta.
Which pie chart, suitably labelled, shows the current state of the parties in the Parliament?

A.
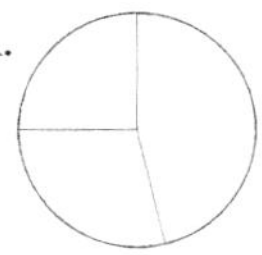

B.
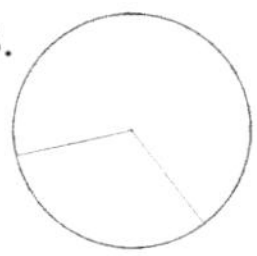

C.
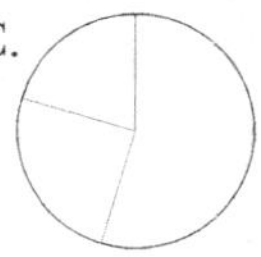

D.
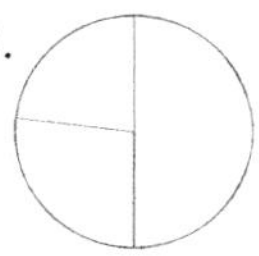

E.
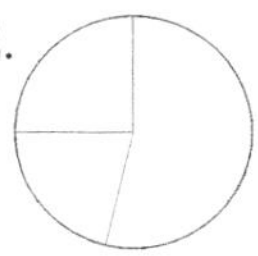

20) A puzzle is made up of these three pieces. The pieces can be flipped and rotated, but they cannot overlap.

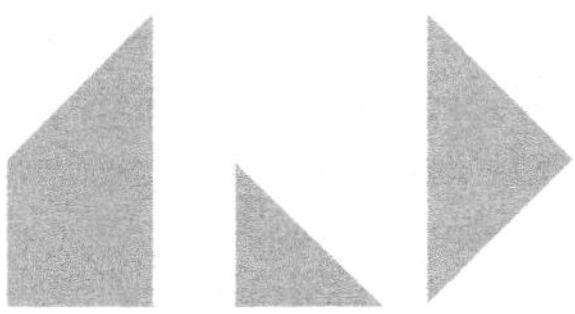

Which one of the following shapes CANNOT be made using these three pieces?

A. 
B. 
C. 

D. 
E. 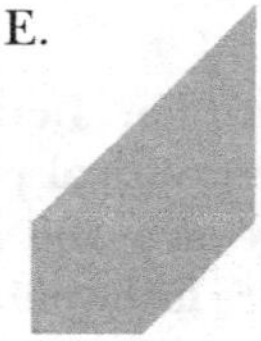

21) The *Almagest* is the common title of a mathematical and astronomical treatise written by:

A. Aristotle
B. Nicolaus Copernicus
C. Pythagoras
D. Johannes Kepler
E. Claudius Ptolemy

22) Which of these pairs of nation and national newspaper name is wrong?

A. Germany – Süddeutsche Zeitung
B. Denmark – De Telegraaf
C. France – Le Monde
D. Slovakia – Nový Čas
E. United Kingdom – The Times

Biology

23) Reverse transcriptase is mainly found in retroviruses such as HIV. Four nucleotides are needed for the reaction catalysed by this enzyme.
A group of molecules may inhibit this enzyme. These molecules are structurally similar to the nucleotides but slightly altered so that bonds normally formed in the reaction cannot be made.
Which of the following statements may be correct?

1. The four inhibitor molecules will resemble adenine, thymine, guanine and cytosine.
2. The inhibitor molecules can prevent the formation of phosphodiester bonds.
3. The inhibitor molecules can result in a reduction in the number of new virus particles produced.

A. 1, 2 and 3
B. 1 and 2 only
C. 1 and 3 only
D. 2 and 3 only
E. 3 only

24) The enzyme HIV-1 protease is produced by the HIV virus.
The enzyme is formed from two identical chains of 99 amino acids. In each chain, amino acids 25, 26 and 27 in the sequence form part of the active site.
Which levels of structure control the shape of the active site of the HIV protease?

A. Primary, secondary and tertiary only
B. Primary and quaternary only
C. Secondary and tertiary only
D. Primary, secondary, tertiary and quaternary
E. Quaternary only

25) A section of unmutated double-stranded DNA contains 100 nucleotides and 38% of these nucleotides contain thymine.
Which one of the following correctly identifies the number of hydrogen (H) bonds and phosphodiester bonds present in this section of DNA?

A. 112 H bonds present and 98 phosphodiester bonds present
B. 112 H bonds present and 99 phosphodiester bonds present
C. 138 H bonds present and 98 phosphodiester bonds present

D. 138 H bonds present and 99 phosphodiester bonds present
E. 224 H bonds present and 98 phosphodiester bonds present

26) Which of the following statements about a neurone in a healthy human is/are correct?

1. Transport across its cell membrane can occur by exocytosis.
2. It contains the gene that codes for insulin.
3. It contains circular DNA.

A. 1 and 2 only
B. 1 and 3 only
C. 1, 2 and 3
D. 2 and 3 only
E. 1only

27) Squamous epithelium, ciliated epithelium and cartilage are tissues found in healthy humans.
Which one of the following structures is made up of at least TWO of these tissues?

A. Alveoli
B. Oviduct
C. Capillaries
D. Bowman's capsule
E. Trachea

28) Which of the following contain peptide bonds?

1. Ribosomes in human liver cells
2. Antibodies in human plasma
3. Cilia on human bronchial cells
4. Cholesterol in the membrane of human kidney cells

A. 2 and 4 only
B. 1 and 3 only
C. 1 and 4 only
D. 1, 2 and 3 only
E. 2, 3 and 4 only

29) An organism, in bright sunlight, has the following features:

• Consists of some cells with organelles which contain grana.
• All cells contain molecules of ATP, ADP and NAD.
• Some cells release carbon dioxide by diffusion all the time.

Which one of the following statements about the organism is correct?

A. It is prokaryotic and only carries out respiration
B. It is eukaryotic and all cells carry out photosynthesis
C. It is photosynthetic but has some cells which only respire
D. It is made up of cells which all contain mitochondria and chloroplasts
E. It is an anaerobic organism which only releases carbon dioxide

30) Which of the following can be a result of exercise in a healthy human?

1. A decrease in muscle pH
2. An increase in blood pH
3. More blood flows to certain organs

A. 1 and 2 only
B. 1 and 3 only
C. 3 only
D. 2 and 3 only
E. 1, 2 and 3

31) Which of the following could explain why the phenotype of a healthy female child may show differences from her healthy biological brother (apart from the gender)?

1. Independent assortment after the formation of the female zygote
2. Crossing over between a chromosome from the sperm and a chromosome from the egg
3. Random alignment of homologous chromosomes at the equator of the cell during metaphase I

A. 3 only
B. 2 only
C. 1 only
D. 1 and 2 only
E. 2 and 3 only

32) The genes P, Q, R and S occur on the same chromosome. The COV (crossover values) for the pairs of genes are:
P and Q 35%
P and R 5%
R and Q 40%
Q and S 10%
R and S 30%
Which one of the following sequences of letters represents a correct order of genes on the chromosome?

A. PRSQ
B. PQSR
C. RSQP
D. RPSQ
E. PQRS

33) A eukaryotic cell undergoes division. At one point it has pairs of chromosomes being separated by spindle fibres and moving towards the poles of the cell. What stage of division is this?

A. Telophase in Meiosis I
B. Anaphase in Meiosis I
C. Metaphase in Mitosis
D. Metaphase in Meiosis II
E. Anaphase in Mitosis

34) A condition caused by the dominant allele of a gene on the X chromosome is passed down through a family. Individual Z inherits the condition.
For this family, which of the following statements must be correct, assuming no spontaneous mutations have occurred?

1. If Z is a boy, then he must have inherited the dominant allele from his father.
2. If Z is a boy, then one of his mother's parents must have also had the condition.
3. If Z is a girl, then both of her parents must have had the allele.
4. If Z is a boy, and has children, then all of his daughters will have the condition.

A. 1 and 4 only
B. 2 and 3 only
C. 1 and 3 only
D. 1, 3 and 4 only
E. 2 and 4 only

35) Part of a polypeptide sequence consists of four amino acids –1–2–3–4–. The tRNA anticodons for each amino acid are:

amino acid	anticodon
1	GCA
2	ACA
3	UUG
4	GGU

Which one of the following is the correct sequence, in a 3′ to 5′ direction, for the bases on the template strand of the DNA?

A. CGUUGUAAGCCA
B. GCAACAUUCCCU
C. GCAACATTGGGT
D. CGTTGTAAGCCA
E. ATGGTGCCTTTC

36) Mutations in the CFTR gene cause cystic fibrosis (CF). The non-mutated allele of the gene can be obtained and then introduced into the lung cells of a person with CF using liposomes as a vector. This treatment gives only short-term relief from the symptoms of CF.
Which of the following statements would be a correct explanation of this treatment?

1. Genes are unstable and break down over time in the cell.
2. Lung cells are constantly being replaced and new cells will have the faulty allele.

3. The non-mutated allele is recessive.

A. 2 only
B. 1 only
C. 1 and 2 only
D. 1 and 3 only
E. 2 and 3 only

37) A Petri dish contains populations of two different species of bacteria (V and W). Both are growing and reproducing at the same rate, using the same resources. The conditions are then changed and the rate of growth and reproduction of the population of species V increases.
Which of the following, acting independently, could cause this increase in growth and reproduction rate?

1. A decrease in temperature
2. A change in pH
3. The addition of an antibiotic

A. 1, 2 and 3
B. 1 and 2 only
C. 2 and 3 only
D. 1 and 3 only
E. 2 only

38) Which one of the following statements is correct when the pressure in the ventricles of a healthy human heart is at its highest?

A. The semi-lunar valves will be closed
B. The heart will be in atrial systole
C. The atrioventricular valves will be open
D. The atria of the heart will be filling
E. A wave of electrical activity will be reaching the atrioventricular node

39) Which of the following structures make a solution that can raise the pH in the digestive system of a healthy human?

1. Gallbladder
2. Pancreas
3. Stomach

A. 1 only
B. 2 only
C. 3 only
D. 1 and 2 only
E. 2 and 3 only

40) B lymphocytes are involved in the human immune response to a bacterial infection. Which of the following processes would TYPICALLY be carried out by these lymphocytes in response to the infection?

1. Cell division by mitosis
2. Transcription producing mRNA
3. Engulfing and digesting bacteria

A. 3 only
B. 1 only
C. 2 and 3 only
D. 1 and 3 only
E. 1 and 2 only

Chemistry

41) What is the molecular formula of the compound shown below?

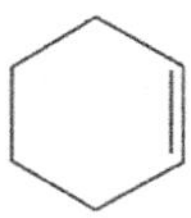

A. C_6H_{10}
B. C_6H_{12}
C. C_6H_{14}
D. C_6H_6
E. C_6H_8

42) Five atoms are shown below. The letters are NOT chemical symbols. Which one of the following atoms has the highest first ionization energy?

A. $^{19}_{9}V$

B. $^{20}_{10}W$

C. $^{21}_{9}X$

D. $^{22}_{11}Y$

E. $^{23}_{11}Z$

43) Which of the following species have the same number and arrangement of electrons in their lowest energy states?

$_{19}K^+$ $_{11}Na^+$ $_{8}O^-$ $_{8}O^{2-}$ $_{16}S^-$

A. $_{8}O^-$ and $_{8}O^{2-}$
B. $_{8}O^-$ and $_{16}S^-$
C. $_{19}K^+$ and $_{16}S^-$
D. $_{19}K^+$ and $_{11}Na^+$
E. $_{11}Na^+$ and $_{8}O^{2-}$

44) Which of the following statements, if any, are correct for the properties of Group I elements?

1. They form hydrides where the hydrogen has an oxidation state of –1.
2. They can reduce iodine to iodide.
3. Their outer electrons are delocalized when in the liquid state.

A. 2 and 3 only
B. 1 and 3 only
C. 1 and 2 only
D. 1, 2 and 3
E. none of them

45) Compounds of chlorine include:

Cl_2O KCl KClO
$KClO_3$ $KClO_4$ Cl_2O_7

Which one of the following options correctly lists the oxidation states of chlorine that are shown in these compounds?

A. –1, +1, +5 and +7 only
B. 1, 0 and +1 only
C. –1 only
D. –1, 0, +1, +5 and +7 only
E. –1, +1, +3, +5 and +7 only

46) Which row correctly shows the shape of each molecule and whether the molecule is polar (i.e. has a permanent dipole moment) or non-polar?
[Atomic numbers: H = 1; B = 5; C = 6; N = 7; O = 8; F = 9; P = 15; Cl = 17]

	molecule	*shape*	*polar or not polar*
1	BF_3	trigonal planar	polar
2	CH_2Cl_2	tetrahedral	non-polar
3	CO_2	linear	polar
4	NH_3	trigonal planar	polar
5	PCl_5	trigonal bipyramidal	non-polar

A. row 2
B. row 5
C. row 4
D. row 1
E. row 3

47) Which one of the following substances has the highest solubility in the specified liquid at a temperature of 298 K and 1 atm pressure?

A. Sodium chloride in liquid cyclohexane
B. Hydrogen in liquid water
C. Silicon dioxide in liquid water
D. Potassium bromide in liquid tetrachloromethane
E. Bromine in liquid hexane

48) When nitrogen and hydrogen are mixed under suitable conditions of temperature and pressure, and in the presence of a catalyst, an equilibrium state is attained:

$$N_2(g) + 3H_2(g) \rightleftharpoons 2NH_3(g)$$

ΔH is negative

Which of the following statements explain(s) why, when the pressure on a mixture of nitrogen and hydrogen is increased while the temperature remains constant, the time taken to attain equilibrium is decreased?

1. The molecules have a higher collision frequency.
2. The yield of ammonia ($NH_3(g)$) decreases.
3. A greater proportion of molecules in the mixture have energy greater than the activation energy.

A. 3 only
B. 1 only
C. 2 only
D. 1 and 3 only
E. 1, 2 and 3

49) Consider this ionic equation in aqueous solution:

$$CH_3O^- + H_2O \rightarrow CH_3OH + OH^-$$

Which statement about this reaction is correct?

A. CH_3OH is the conjugate acid of CH_3O^-
B. The hydroxide ion is the conjugate acid of the water
C. Water is acting as a Brønsted–Lowry base
D. The final mixture of solutions would have a pH below 7
E. The CH_3O^- ion is a Lewis acid

50) What is the correct IUPAC name of this compound?

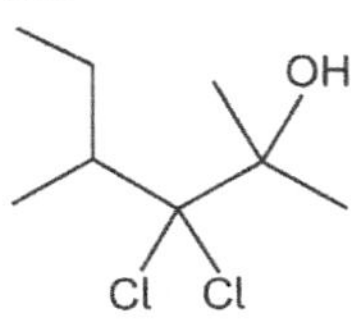

A. 4,4-dichloro-3,5-dimethylhexan-5-ol
B. 3,3-dichloro-4-ethyl-2-methylpentan-2-ol
C. 3,3-chloro-4-ethyl-2-methylpentan-2-ol
D. 3,3-dichloro-2,4-dimethylhexan-2-ol
E. 3,3-chloro-2-ethyl-4-methylpentan-4-ol

51) A sealed container contains 1.00 mol of hydrogen gas, which behaves as an ideal gas. Which of the following changes increase(s) the total kinetic energy of the hydrogen gas molecules initially within the container?

1. Changing the amount of hydrogen from 1.0 mol to 1.2 mol whilst keeping the pressure and volume constant.
2. Changing the pressure from 1.0 atm to 1.2 atm whilst keeping the volume and number of moles constant.
3. Changing the volume from 1.0 L to 1.2 L whilst keeping the pressure and number of moles constant.

A. 3 only
B. 1 and 2 only
C. 1 only
D. 2 and 3 only
E. 1, 2 and 3

52) Consider a fixed volume and amount of an ideal gas at 10°C. What temperature would it have to be changed to in order for the pressure to be doubled?

A. 293 °C
B. 20 °C
C. 278 °C
D. 5 °C
E. 566 °C

Physics and Mathematics

53) Evaluate

$$(3 \times 10^3)^3 \times (2 \times 10^{-5})$$

A. 5.4×10^1
B. 5.4×10^5
C. 5.4×10^2
D. 5.4×10^4
E. 5.4×10^{-1}

54) Which one of the following is an equation of the line that passes through (4, 3) and is perpendicular to the line $y = 2x + 4$?

A. $2x + y = 11$
B. $2y - x = 2$
C. $2y + x = 10$
D. $2x - y = 5$
E. $2y + x = 11$

55) A pentagon has one line of symmetry. All five sides are 6 cm, and the interior angles, in anticlockwise order, are 60°, 150°, 90°, 90° and 150°. What is the area of this pentagon?

A. $3(5 + \sqrt{3})\ cm^2$
B. $9(2 + \sqrt{3})\ cm^2$
C. $3(12 + \sqrt{3})\ cm^2$
D. $9(4 + \sqrt{3})\ cm^2$
E. $3(4 + \sqrt{3})\ cm^2$

56) The equation below has two roots.

$$\frac{x+4}{x+1} = x$$

What is the sum of the two roots?

A. –2
B. –4
C. 2
D. 4
E. 0

57) Three spherical particles have the following diameters: 1650 pm, 1.5 nm and 0.0036 μm. What is their order of diameter (smallest first)?

A. 1.5 nm, 1650 pm, 0.0036 μm
B. 1.5 nm, 0.0036 μm, 1650 pm
C. 0.0036 μm, 1.5 nm, 1650 pm
D. 0.0036 μm, 1650 pm, 1.5 nm
E. 1650 pm, 1.5 nm, 0.0036 μm

58) An electric train is travelling on a straight, horizontal track. A constant resultant force (greater than zero) acts on the train in the direction of the train's motion. What happens to the magnitude of the acceleration and to the magnitude of the velocity of the train while this force is acting?

A. The acceleration increases and the velocity remains constant
B. The acceleration decreases and the velocity increases
C. The acceleration remains constant and the velocity increases
D. The acceleration increases and the velocity increases
E. The acceleration remains constant and the velocity remains constant

59) The Earth's atmosphere contains oxygen and nitrogen. The mass of an oxygen molecule is greater than the mass of a nitrogen molecule. The temperature of air in a room on a particular day is 300 K. Below are four statements about the motion of the two types of molecule in this room.

1. They have an equal mean square velocity $(\overline{v^2})$.

2. A nitrogen molecule has a greater mean square velocity $(\overline{v^2})$ than an oxygen molecule.

3. A nitrogen molecule has a greater mean kinetic energy than an oxygen molecule.

4. An oxygen molecule has a greater mean kinetic energy than a nitrogen molecule.

Which of the statements is/are correct?

A. Statement 1 only
B. Statement 1 and 3 only
C. Statement 2 only
D. Statement 2 and 4 only
E. None of them

60) A wire made of a metal of uniform resistivity 1.0×10^{-6} Ωm is 2.0 m long and has a diameter of 2.0×10^{-3} m. What is the electrical resistance of this length of the wire?

A. $\frac{2.0}{\pi}\Omega$

B. $\frac{1.0}{2\pi}\Omega$

C. $\frac{2.0\times 10^{-3}}{\pi}\Omega$

D. $5.0 \times 10^{-13}\ \pi\Omega$

E. $2.0 \times 10^{-12}\ \pi\Omega$

RISPOSTE COMMENTATE • IMAT a.a. 2018/2019

Cultura generale e ragionamento logico

1) B. Questo genere di quesito chiede di determinare quale delle cinque alternative di risposta contenga il ragionamento che ricalca più fedelmente quello esposto nella traccia. L'analogia non va intesa dal punto di vista del contenuto, ma della forma, ovvero della struttura logica.
Analizziamo innanzitutto la forma logica del ragionamento della traccia:

- per avere A (= una casa con tre camere da letto e un garage), bisogna spendere almeno X (= € 200,000);
- per avere A, vuoi spendere Y (= € 150,000), minore di X;
- per avere A, dovrai spendere più di Y.

Adesso bisogna passare in rassegna le cinque opzioni di risposta e trovare quella il cui ragionamento ha la struttura logica maggiormente corrispondente alla forma poc'anzi individuata. Così facendo, osserviamo che la risposta corretta è: "*You want a large powerful car that is fuel efficient. Large powerful cars are never fuel efficient, so you will have to spend more on fuel if you want a large powerful*". Infatti, la struttura logica di questo ragionamento è:

- per avere A (= una grande macchina potente), bisogna spendere almeno X (= un'alta somma di denaro per il carburante);
- per avere A, vuoi spendere Y (= una bassa somma di denaro per il carburante), minore di X;
- per avere A, dovrai spendere più di Y.

2) A. Il quesito chiede quale delle cinque alternative di risposta rechi l'affermazione che può fungere da conclusione del ragionamento esposto nella traccia. Per trovare la risposta, bisogna innanzitutto individuare i passaggi logici del ragionamento esposto: i ristoratori cercano un modo per esaltare la qualità del loro cibo. In base a una ricerca, un modo consiste nell'usare specifiche tipologie di posate per ogni pietanza. Ora bisogna rintracciare l'opzione che è logicamente connessa alle premesse del ragionamento e che da queste può essere tratta come conclusione. Tutte le alternative si basano su concetti non collegabili o non coerenti con le premesse tranne "*Restaurants should think carefully about what cutlery they use*", ossia "i ristoranti dovrebbero pensare attentamente a quali posate usare" che è dunque la risposta corretta.

3) C. Per risolvere il quesito, bisogna individuare quale delle cinque alternative di risposta si basi sul principio su cui si fonda il ragionamento esposto nella traccia. A tal fine la prima cosa da fare è esaminare quest'ultimo per comprendere il principio su cui si basa: *se i consumatori di un certo prodotto* (nella fattispecie, il cibo contenete zucchero) *non possono o non vogliono farne un uso sicuro, che eviti loro danni* (nel caso in

esame, l'obesità), *allora i produttori devono assumersi la responsabilità di correggere preventivamente il problema che essi contribuiscono a creare* (nella traccia, riducendo i livelli di zucchero negli alimenti lavorati).
A questo punto si possono esaminare le cinque alterative di risposta e stabilire quale si basi sul principio appena individuato. Tale alternativa è quella che afferma: "*To reduce the number of deaths caused by excessive speed, car manufacturers should incorporate speed limiters in vehicles*". Il principio di fondo, infatti, è lo stesso: *se i consumatori di un certo prodotto* (in questo caso, le automobili) *non possono o non vogliono farne un uso sicuro, che eviti loro danni* (cioè la morte in incidenti per eccesso di velocità), *allora i produttori devono assumersi la responsabilità di correggere preventivamente il problema* (nell'alternativa, incorporando limitatori di velocità nelle automobili).

4) E. La domanda chiede di identificare quale delle cinque alternative di risposta riporti la cosiddetta prova addizionale, cioè l'affermazione che, se fosse aggiunta alle premesse dell'argomentazione, ne rafforzerebbe la conclusione. In tal senso bisogna innanzitutto riconoscere le premesse e la conclusione del ragionamento. Nella traccia si parla della tubercolosi bovina e della possibilità di arrestarne la diffusione unicamente abbattendo, nelle aree più colpite, i tassi, animali che trasmettono la malattia al bestiame, dal momento che ci vorranno almeno dieci anni prima che sia disponibile un vaccino per proteggere i bovini. A questo punto bisogna esaminare le cinque opzioni di risposta. Le seguenti alternative, se fossero vere, indebolirebbero l'argomentazione invece di rafforzarla, perciò vanno tutte scartate:

- "*Less than ten per cent of the dairy cows destroyed each year are destroyed because of bovine TB*". Una percentuale così bassa – meno del 10% – di vacche abbattute per via della tubercolosi renderebbe poco pericolosa la tubercolosi bovina e, quindi, non sarebbe così urgente, come invece emerge dalla traccia prendere provvedimenti contro la sua diffusione.
- "*Shooting large numbers of badgers is more expensive than vaccinating them*". Se fosse vero che abbattere i tassi è un'operazione più costosa che vaccinarli, la loro vaccinazione rappresenterebbe un altro modo, più conveniente rispetto alla loro uccisione, per impedire la diffusione della tubercolosi bovina, contrariamente a quanto spiegato nella traccia.
- "*In a trial, killing ten thousand badgers reduced the TB rate in cattle by only fifteen per cent*". Anche in questo caso una percentuale così bassa – la riduzione di appena il 15% del tasso di tubercolosi nel bestiame – non renderebbe l'uccisione dei tassi, come invece si dice nella conclusione, l'unico modo per fermare la diffusione della malattia.
- "*When efforts are made to remove badgers, many are injured rather than killed outright*". Se i tentativi di uccidere i tassi portassero solo al loro ferimento, chiaramente questi animali, anche se feriti, continuerebbero a diffondere la tubercolosi tra i bovini, pertanto tale affermazione indebolirebbe la conclusione del ragionamento.

La risposta corretta è dunque: "*Five annual vaccinations are necessary to protect a badger fully against bovine TB*". Un tale dato indicherebbe che la vaccinazione dei tassi, richiedendo ben cinque iniezioni all'anno, è un modo troppo laborioso per difendere il bestiame dalla tubercolosi. Ciò rafforzerebbe l'idea, espressa nella conclusione, per cui l'uccisione dei tassi è il solo modo per proteggere il bestiame dalla malattia.

5) B. La domanda chiede di riconoscere tra le cinque alternative di risposta quella in cui compare l'affermazione che può fungere da conclusione dell'argomentazione della traccia, nella quale si parla della relazione tra grandezza del cervello e intelligenza.
Le seguenti alternative si basano tutte su concetti non collegabili o non coerenti con quanto esposto nella traccia, pertanto devono essere scartate:

- "*Dolphins are more intelligent than whales*". Nel quesito si dice solo che rispetto ai capodogli i delfini hanno un cervello più grande in proporzione al corpo, ma non ci sono elementi che permettano di confrontare i rispettivi livelli di intelligenza.
- "*Hummingbirds and whales have equally complex tasks to perform, despite huge difference in brain size*". Nella traccia si afferma unicamente che i colibrì hanno compiti complessi da eseguire, ma non vi è alcun dato sul fatto che colibrì e balene hanno compiti ugualmente complessi da svolgere, nonostante l'enorme differenza nelle dimensioni del cervello.
- "*Whales need larger brains than either dolphins or humans because of their enormous size*". Tale affermazione è in contrasto con quanto espresso nella traccia in cui si dice che non c'è alcuna ragione ovvia per cui il cervello debba essere dimensionato in proporzione al corpo in cui vive.
- "*There is no important difference between a brain and a computer*". Il confronto tra cervello e computer è solo un esempio fatto nella traccia, quindi non si può concludere che non ci siano importanti differenze tra i due.

La risposta corretta è dunque: "*Brain size and the ability to perform complex tasks are not necessarily related*". Infatti, che le dimensioni del cervello e la capacità di eseguire compiti complessi non siano necessariamente correlate si ricava dal passaggio in cui si dice che i colibrì hanno compiti complessi da eseguire pur avendo un cervello minuscolo.

6) A. Il ragionamento esposto nella traccia ha un difetto che fa sì che il passaggio logico dalle premesse alla conclusione non sia accettabile. È dunque indispensabile individuare innanzitutto le premesse e la conclusione dell'argomentazione:

- recenti ricerche negli Stati Uniti hanno rilevato che le aree con più dentisti a persona hanno tassi di obesità molto più bassi rispetto alle zone vicine di dimensioni simili della popolazione (prima premessa);
- i dentisti sono una risorsa trascurata nella lotta contro i gravi problemi di salute associati all'obesità (seconda premessa);
- le autorità sanitarie pubbliche che si occupano dei tassi di obesità dovrebbero concentrare maggiori risorse sulla fornitura di cure dentistiche (conclusione).

L'alternativa corretta è: "*It assumes that a higher number of dentists causes lower obesity rates*". Infatti il ragionamento è basato su una corrispondenza statistica tra un minore tasso di obesità e una maggiore percentuale di dentisti per persona, corrispondenza che viene considerata come una relazione causale, ma questo ovviamente è un errore.

7) D. Per risolvere il quesito, bisogna individuare quale delle cinque opzioni di risposta esprima meglio la conclusione principale del ragionamento esposto nella traccia. Dall'analisi del quesito è evidente che si parte dalla conclusione del ragionamento ossia dal concetto che è meglio per la salute dei bambini dargli un videogioco piuttosto che permettere loro di guardare la televisione dal momento che alcune ricerche hanno evidenziato che i bambini bruciano più calorie quando giocano che quando guardano la televisione e che l'aumento della pressione sanguigna è associato alla visione della televisione, ma non ai videogiochi. Tra le alternative proposte l'unica che ripete quanto espresso nella conclusione è "*Video gaming is better for children's health than watching television*" che è dunque la risposta corretta.

8) D. Questa tipologia di quesito richiede di determinare quale, fra le cinque alternative di risposta, contiene la supposizione implicita del ragionamento, ossia il presupposto che non è affermato nel brano ma sul quale poggia la conclusione del ragionamento. Nel testo della traccia si parla della dipendenza da internet, disturbo psichiatrico riconosciuto, per il quale è importante fare un impiego limitato dell'apprendimento basato sul computer. Per giungere a tale conclusione è necessario partire dal presupposto che tutti gli apprendimenti basati sul computer includano l'uso di Internet; la risposta esatta è dunque "*All computer-based learning includes internet use*".

9) B. Nell'argomentazione della traccia c'è un difetto, per cui il passaggio logico dalle premesse alla conclusione non è accettabile. Il quesito chiede quale delle cinque alternative di risposta contenga tale difetto. Nella traccia si afferma che una delle popolazioni con la più alta aspettativa di vita è l'Islanda dove le persone sono molto sane grazie al tipo di alimentazione che seguono; la conclusione del ragionamento è che se vogliamo vivere una vita lunga e sana dovremmo adottare la dieta degli islandesi. Dunque, nel passaggio dalle premesse alla conclusione si assume che la dieta degli islandesi sia la ragione della loro longevità in buona salute, ma questo è un errore, perché potrebbero esserci anche altre ragioni, pertanto la risposta corretta è "*There may be other reasons for the Icelanders' health and longevity*".

10) E. La soluzione del quesito consiste nell'identificare la risposta che, se fosse aggiunta alle premesse dell'argomentazione, ne indebolirebbe la conclusione. Tema del ragionamento sono i rischi per l'ambiente e per l'uomo legati alle trivellazioni in acque profonde, rischi che spesso vengono sottovalutati mentre sarebbe opportuno che in mancanza di una regolamentazione efficace e in assenza di sicurezza da parte delle compagnie petrolifere, le trivellazioni in acque profonde fossero vietate. La risposta corretta è "*A ban on deepwater drilling would cause oil prices to rise, which would affect poor people most*". Questa affermazione, infatti, se fosse vera indebolirebbe l'intera deduzione del ragionamento, che parte dalla costatazione che l'incidente negli USA ha distrutto i mezzi di sostentamento delle persone povere che vivono nella zona e giunge alla conclusione di bandire momentaneamente le trivellazioni in acque profonde.

11) C. Per sapere quante miglia vola il piccione in totale, bisogna calcolare dopo quante miglia l'uccello e il treno si incontrano la prima volta, raddoppiare tale numero, dato che il piccione ritorna al capolinea, calcolare poi dopo quante miglia si incontrano la seconda volta (se c'è il tempo per un secondo incontro), raddoppiare anche questo numero e così via. Poiché la velocità è data dal rapporto tra spazio e tempo

$$velocità = \frac{spazio}{tempo},$$

lo spazio è dato dal prodotto tra velocità e tempo

$$spazio = velocità \times tempo$$

e quindi, indicando con s_p lo spazio percorso dal piccione, con s_t lo spazio percorso dal treno e con t il tempo impiegato per incontrarsi, varrà il seguente sistema di 3 equazioni in 3 incognite, che risolto darà il primo quantitativo di miglia percorse dal piccione:

$$\begin{cases} s_p = 40\ mph \times t \\ s_t = 30\ mph \times t \\ s_p + s_t = 120\ m \end{cases}$$

Sostituendo s_p ed s_t nella terza equazione si ha

$$40\ mph \times t + 30\ mph \times t = 120\ m$$

da cui è possibile ricavare t:

$$t = \frac{120\ m}{70\ mph} = 1{,}7\ h$$

Si ha allora che

$$s_p = 40\ mph \times t = 40\ mph \times 1{,}7\ h = 68\ m \quad \text{e quindi} \quad s_t = 120\ m - 68\ m = 52\ m,$$

ovvero che il piccione incontra il treno dopo aver percorso 68 miglia. Per tornare al capolinea ne percorrerà altre 68, durante le quali il treno ne percorrerà 52, per cui, quando l'uccello partirà dal capolinea la seconda volta, lo spazio che lo separa dal treno sarà pari a

$$120 - (52 \times 2) = 16 \text{ miglia.}$$

Per sapere quante miglia percorrerà ancora il piccione per incontrare il treno una seconda volta si deve risolvere lo stesso sistema di equazioni precedente, dove la terza equazione è però

$$s_p + s_t = 16\ m.$$

Come prima, allora, è possibile ricavare t dal seguente rapporto

$$t = \frac{16\ m}{70\ mph} = 0{,}23\ h$$

e a seguire si ha che

$$s_p = 40\ mph \times 0{,}23\ h = 9{,}2\ m \quad \text{e quindi} \quad s_t = 16\ m - 9{,}2\ m = 6{,}8\ m.$$

Quando il piccione tornerà nuovamente al capolinea, il treno avrà percorso altre 6,8 miglia, per cui lo separeranno dal capolinea soltanto:

$$16 - (6{,}8 \times 2) = 2{,}4 \text{ miglia,}$$

cioè un numero inferiore a 10, che è l'approssimazione richiesta dal quesito. In totale, quindi, il piccione ha percorso

$$68 \times 2 + 9{,}2 \times 2 = 154{,}4 \text{ miglia,}$$

per cui la risposta esatta è 160 miglia.

---

12) A. Per sapere quanto pagheranno in totale i signori Costa è necessario conoscere i costi applicati da Giovanni sia per metro quadro di erba da tagliare che per metro di bordo da rifilare, per poi moltiplicarli rispettivamente per l'area e il perimetro del prato dei Costa.
Sapendo quanto hanno pagato i signori Massa per tagliare l'erba e rifilare il bordo del loro giardino, è possibile dividere tali cifre per area e perimetro del prato e conoscere così le tariffe applicate da Giovanni.
Poiché il prato dei Massa è un rettangolo, si ha che l'area è pari a

$$10\ m \times 6\ m = 60\ m^2$$

mentre il perimetro è pari a

$$(10\ m + 6\ m) \times 2 = 32\ m,$$

per cui la tariffa per tagliare l'erba sarà pari a

$$12\ \$ \div 60\ m^2 = 0{,}2\ \$ \text{ per metro quadro}$$

e la tariffa per rifilare i bordi del prato sarà uguale a

$$8\ \$ \div 32\ m = 0{,}25\ \$ \text{ per metro.}$$

L'area e il perimetro del prato dei signori Costa sono invece dati da

$$15\ m \times 9\ m = 135\ m^2 \quad \text{e} \quad (15\ m + 9\ m) \times 2 = 48\ m,$$

per cui la cifra totale che essi spenderanno sarà

$$\left(135\ m^2 \times 0{,}20 \frac{\$}{m^2}\right) + \left(48\ m \times 0{,}25 \frac{\$}{m}\right) = 27\ \$ + 12\ \$ = 39\ \$$$

---

13) D. È possibile visualizzare il tragitto da casa di David al college nel modo seguente:

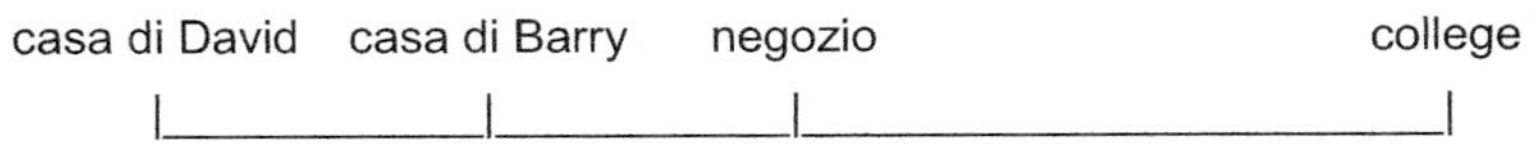

Poiché David impiega 45 minuti per il tragitto totale e 20 minuti per il tragitto da casa sua al negozio, impiegherà 45 – 20 = 25 minuti dal negozio al college:

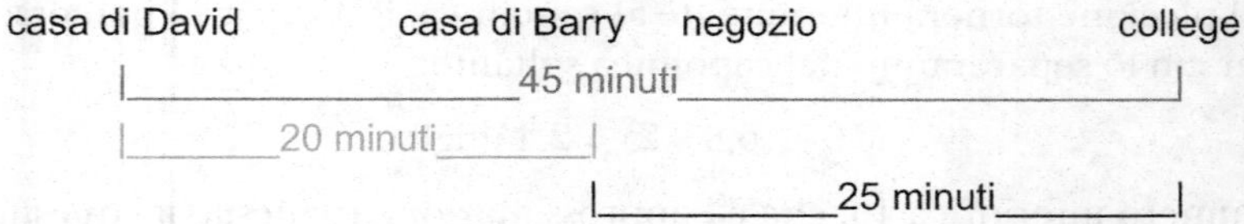

Visto che, inoltre, Barry e David camminano alla stessa velocità e Barry impiega 32 minuti da casa sua al college, si ha immediatamente che David impiegherà 32 – 25 = 7 minuti da casa di Barry al negozio:

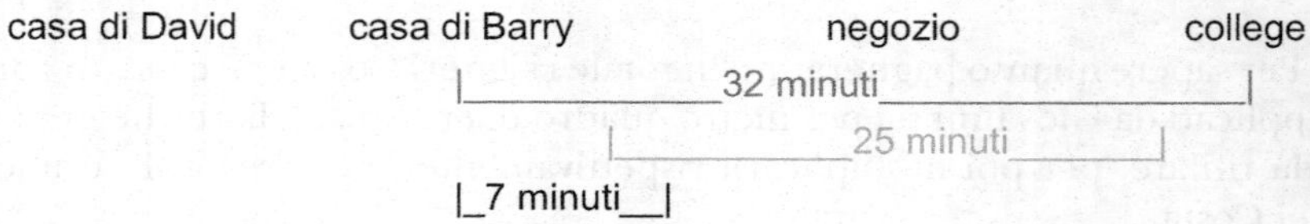

Si osservi che i 3 minuti che David aspetta fuori casa di Barry ed i 3 minuti che impiega ad acquistare il pranzo non sono utili al fine della risoluzione del quesito, ma sono stati inseriti nel testo come distrattori.

---

14) B. Il numero di totale di pacchetti di patatine da acquistare è dato dal prodotto tra il numero di bambini, i giorni in cui mangiano le patatine e le settimane per le quali vanno acquistate le stesse, ed è quindi pari a

$$6 \times 5 \times 4 = 120 \text{ pacchetti di patatine.}$$

Allora si ha immediatamente che la spesa per acquistarle, nel caso di pacchi singoli, è pari a

$$120 \times 0{,}50\ £ = 60\ £$$

Per risparmiare è però possibile acquistare una combinazione di confezioni multiple e pacchi singoli, tenendo ben presente i 3 diversi gusti di patatine scelti dai bambini. Poiché 3 figli mangiano le patatine al formaggio, tali pacchetti saranno in totale

$$3 \times 5 \times 4 = 60$$

e potranno essere acquistati in due confezioni multiple, una da 24 e una da 36, per una spesa di

$$8{,}50\ £ + 12{,}50\ £ = 21\ £$$

I gemelli, invece, preferiscono le patatine alla paprika, i cui pacchetti dovranno essere allora

$$2 \times 5 \times 4 = 40$$

e potranno essere acquistati nella confezione multipla da 36 più 4 confezioni singole, per una spesa di

$$12{,}50\ £ + 4 \times 0{,}50\ £ = 14{,}50\ £$$

Il figlio più grande, infine, vuole le patatine al Chili, che saranno quindi

$$1 \times 5 \times 4 = 20 \text{ pacchetti,}$$

acquistabili in una confezione multipla da 12, una da 6 e 2 confezioni singole, per una spesa di:

$$4{,}50\ £ + 2{,}50\ £ + 2 \times 0{,}50\ £ = 8\ £$$

La spesa totale in questo caso sarà allora pari a

$$21\ £ + 14{,}50\ £ + 8\ £ = 43{,}50\ £$$

per un risparmio di 60 £ – 43,50 £ = 16,50 £.

15) E. Per risolvere il quesito bisogna analizzare ogni affermazione e verificare se è supportata dalle informazioni fornite dalla tabella oppure no, facendo attenzione a leggere i dati correttamente. Per ogni affermazione è cioè necessario incrociare i materiali elencati sia nella prima colonna a sinistra che nella prima riga in alto, e verificare al loro incrocio quali colle sono presenti, leggendo correttamente la corrispondenza tra le lettere maiuscole B, C, D, ... e le colle. Analizziamo di seguito le singole opzioni:

- "*Polystyrene and card can only be bonded with rubber contact glue*": affermazione errata; il polistirolo e la carta non possono essere incollati con la colla a contatto in gomma (G), ma con la colla PVA (D);
- "*The only materials that are suitable for bonding together with three different types of glue are cork with cork*": affermazione errata dal momento che il sughero non è l'unico materiale che può essere incollato con tre diversi tipi di colla (DGJ), perché guardando attentamente la tabella si nota che anche all'incrocio tra acrilico e carta sono presenti tre colle (DFI);
- "*Acrylic can be bonded to polystyrene using cyanoacrylate*": affermazione non vera poiché l'acrilico non può essere incollato al polistirolo con il cianoacrilato (F), ma con la colla PVA (D) e con la colla di lattice (H);
- "*Balsa cement can only be used to glue balsa wood to another material*": affermazione non vera, il cemento balsa (C) può essere usato anche per incollare la carta con la carta;
- "*Synthetic resin glue can only be used to glue wood materials together*": affermazione corretta, la colla di resina sintetica (E) può essere infatti usata per incollare soltanto il compensato con il compensato e il compensato con il legno di balsa, cioè soltanto materiali legnosi.

16) C. Per risolvere il quesito bisogna analizzare ogni affermazione e verificare se può essere desunta dal grafico a barre o meno. Analizziamo di seguito le singole opzioni:

- "*The number of endangered species of mammals remained constant over the three-year period*": affermazione errata, il numero di specie di mammiferi in via di estinzione (prima barra del grafico in ciascun anno) non è rimasto costante nel corso del triennio, ma è aumentato nel 2001 e poi diminuito nel 2002;
- "*More species of bird became endangered over the three-year period than any other animal class*" affermazione errata, dal grafico si osserva immediatamente che la barra delle specie di anfibi in via di estinzione (quarta barra in ciascun anno) è aumentata

considerevolmente di più rispetto a quella delle specie di uccelli (seconda barra in ciascun anno);

- "*The number of species of insects that were endangered was almost equal to the number of species of fish that were endangered over the three-year period*": affermazione vera, il numero di specie di insetti e di specie di pesci in via di estinzione (quinta e sesta barra in ciascun anno) è rimasto quasi uguale nel corso del triennio;
- "*The number of endangered species of reptiles increased over the three-year period while that of amphibians decreased*": affermazione falsa, il numero di specie di rettili in via di estinzione (terza barra in ciascun anno) è diminuito nel corso del triennio, mentre quello di specie di anfibi (quarta barra) è aumentato;
- "*In 2001, there were exactly four times as many endangered species of birds as there were endangered species of reptiles*": affermazione falsa, nel 2001 le specie di rettili in via di estinzione (terza barra del grafico) erano circa 250, mentre quelle di uccelli (seconda barra) erano 1200 e $250 \times 4 = 1000 \neq 1200$.

17) A. I dati della tabella forniscono il quantitativo totale di calorie per 100 grammi, ovvero 462 kcal, e per singolo dolcetto, ovvero 60 kcal. Si ha quindi immediatamente che le calorie totali di un pacco di dolcetti di 300 grammi è pari a $462 \times 3 = 1386$ kcal, e dividendo tale cifra per le calorie di un singolo pezzo si ottiene il numero di dolcetti del pacco: $1386 \div 60 = 23$.

18) D. Per risolvere il quesito bisogna immaginare di chiudere i triangoli in modo da formare un tetraedro conforme a quello di ciascuna figura e verificare se tale figura è possibile o meno.
Nella visione proposta nell'alternativa A il triangolo Purple è alla base, per cui, immaginando di chiudere i triangoli con vertice superiore tra Red, Green e Brown, si ha che questi sono disposti in senso orario, cioè il lato destro di Red tocca il lato sinistro di Green, proprio come in figura.
Nella visione dell'opzione B il triangolo Green è alla base, per cui, immaginando di chiudere i triangoli con vertice superiore tra Red, Brown e Purple, si ha che questi sono disposti in senso orario, cioè il lato destro di Red tocca il lato sinistro di Brown, proprio come in figura.
Nella visione dell'opzione C il triangolo Brown è alla base, per cui, immaginando di chiudere i triangoli con vertice superiore tra Red, Purple e Green, si ha che questi sono disposti in senso orario, cioè il lato destro di Purple tocca il lato sinistro di Green, proprio come in figura
Nella visione proposta nell'alternativa D il triangolo Green è alla base, per cui, immaginando di chiudere i triangoli con vertice superiore tra Red, Brown e Purple, si ha che questi sono disposti in senso orario, cioè il lato destro di Red tocca il lato sinistro di Brown e il lato destro di Purple, l'opposto di ciò che si vede in figura. Dunque la figura D non è una possibile vista del tetraedro.
Nella visione dell'opzione E il triangolo Purple è alla base, per cui, immaginando di chiudere i triangoli con vertice superiore tra Red, Green e Brown, si ha che questi sono disposti in senso orario, cioè il lato destro di Brown tocca il lato sinistro di Red, proprio come in figura.

19) A. Per sapere quale dei grafici a torta mostra l'attuale situazione del Parlamento è necessario verificare quanti seggi hanno gli Alfa, i Beta e i Gamma dopo le elezioni della settimana scorsa.
Il testo del quesito fornisce il numero di seggi di partenza di ciascun partito (120 per tutti), quanti seggi sono stati guadagnati e quanti persi, quindi, aggiungendo a 120 seggi quelli guadagnati e sottraendo quelli persi da ciascun partito, si può conoscere la situazione odierna del parlamento. In particolare gli Alfa hanno

$$120 + 15 + 23 - 31 - 24 = 103 \text{ seggi},$$

i Beta hanno

$$120 + 31 + 41 - 15 - 10 = 167 \text{ seggi},$$

e i Gamma hanno

$$120 + 24 + 10 - 23 - 41 = 90 \text{ seggi}.$$

Per verificare quale grafico a torta rappresenti tale divisione in seggi bisogna innanzitutto osservare che, poiché i seggi totali sono 360, metà della torta rappresenta 180 seggi, traguardo non raggiunto da nessun partito. Vanno allora scartati i grafici C, D ed E, nei quali è sempre presente una fetta maggiore o uguale alla metà, ovvero un partito con numero di seggi maggiore o uguale a 180. Poiché, inoltre, il partito Gamma ha ottenuto solo 90 seggi, cioè un quarto di tutto il parlamento, il grafico B va scartato, perché nessuna delle tre fette corrisponde a un quarto del totale. Il grafico che mostra l'attuale stato delle parti in Parlamento è quindi il grafico A, etichettato come segue:

A

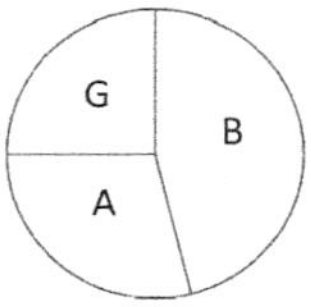

---

20) E. La risoluzione del quesito consiste nel verificare se ciascuna figura è divisibile nei tre pezzi di partenza. Come si evince dal disegno riportato di seguito, ciò è possibile per tutte le figure tranne la E, nella quale sarebbe necessario aggiungere un secondo triangolo piccolo:

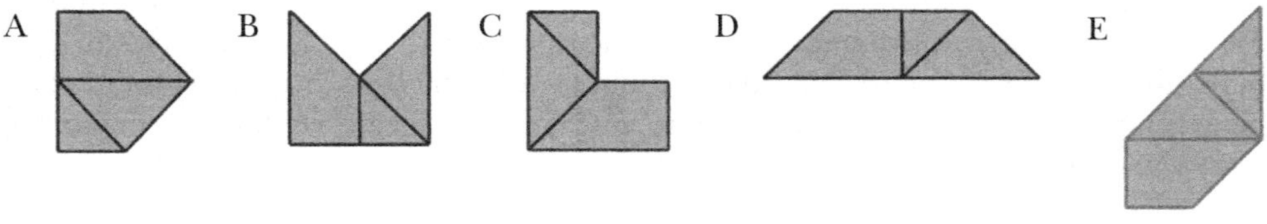

La figura che non può essere costruita utilizzando i tre pezzi di partenza è quindi la E.

---

21) E. Scritto intorno al 150 a. C. dall'astronomo greco Claudio Tolomeo, l'*Almagesto* (titolo originale *Mathematikè sýntaxis*, ossia *Trattato matematico*) è un'importante opera di carattere astronomico-matematico in cui viene formulato il modello geocentrico che si impose nell'antichità e nel Medioevo. Il nome con cui è conosciuta l'opera, Almagesto, è frutto della sua traduzione araba avvenuta nel IX secolo.

22) B. L'accoppiamento errato è Denmark – De Telegraaf, infatti il De Telegraaf, fondato nel 1893, è il principale quotidiano dei Paesi Bassi. Tra i più importanti quotidiani danesi segnaliamo il Berlingske Tidende che, nato a Copenaghen nel 1749, rappresenta una delle testate più antiche del mondo.

Biologia

23) B. La trascrittasi inversa è un enzima che catalizza la sintesi di un filamento di DNA complementare a un filamento stampo di RNA. Gli inibitori della trascrittasi inversa sono molecole molto simili ai nucleotidi presenti nel DNA (contenenti le basi azotate adenina, timina, guanina e citosina) (affermazione 1), ma se ne differenziano in un modo che impedisce la formazione di legami fosfodiesterici tra essi (affermazione 2). Poiché il DNA sintetizzato dalla trascrittasi inversa utilizzando come stampo l'RNA del retrovirus viene utilizzato per produrre sia l'RNA sia le proteine dei nuovi virioni, la presenza degli inibitori determina la produzione di un minor numero di nuove particelle virali (affermazione 3).

24) D. La struttura primaria di una proteina consiste nella sequenza degli amminoacidi che la compongono. La struttura secondaria dipende dallo schema di formazione dei legami idrogeno tra i gruppi carbossilici e amminici degli amminoacidi. La struttura terziaria è determinata dai legami che si instaurano tra le catene laterali degli amminoacidi. La struttura quaternaria riflette l'assemblaggio delle subunità che compongono le proteine oligomeriche. Tutti i quattro livelli di struttura contribuiscono alla forma tridimensionale del sito attivo della proteasi dell'HIV, formato da due tratti corrispondenti sulle due catene polipeptidiche componenti l'enzima.

25) A. Ciascuno dei due filamenti di questo tratto di DNA è composto da 50 nucleotidi, uniti tra loro da legami fosfodiesterici. Ciascun nucleotide forma un tale legame con quello successivo; pertanto, il numero di legami fosfodiesterici su ciascun filamento è pari al numero di nucleotidi meno uno, in quanto l'ultimo nucleotide non ne ha un altro a valle con cui formare il legame. In totale, sui due filamenti sono presenti $49 \times 2 = 98$ legami fosfodiesterici. Il 38% dei nucleotidi contiene timina e quindi il 38% contiene adenina; per le regole di Chargaff, il 12% dei nucleotidi contiene guanina e il 12% citosina. Poiché timina e adenina presenti sui filamenti complementari formano due legami idrogeno, mentre guanina e citosina ne formano tre, il numero complessivo di legami idrogeno è pari a $(38 \times 2) + (12 \times 3) = 112$.

26) C. A livello del terminale sinaptico dei neuroni avviene l'esocitosi delle vescicole contenenti il neurotrasmettitore (affermazione 1). I neuroni, come tutte le altre cellule umane, contengono tutti i geni che costituiscono il genoma umano (affermazione 2), i quali vengono espressi in maniera differenziale nei diversi tipi cellulari. I neuroni sono dotati di mitocondri, i quali contengono DNA mitocondriale circolare (affermazione 3).

27) E. La trachea è un condotto cilindrico costituito da una serie di anelli cartilaginei uniti tra loro da tessuto connettivo. Essa è tappezzata da un epitelio pseudostratificato ciliato, detto epitelio respiratorio.

28) D. I legami peptidici sono legami covalenti tra il gruppo carbossilico e il gruppo amminico di amminoacidi adiacenti nelle catene polipeptidiche. I legami peptidici sono presenti nelle proteine ribosomali costituenti i ribosomi (1). Sono anche presenti negli anticorpi (2), essendo questi ultimi delle glicoproteine. Le ciglia che rivestono le cellule dell'epitelio bronchiale possiedono una struttura centrale formata da microtubuli, polimeri della proteina tubulina, associati a diverse proteine; quindi, anche nelle ciglia sono presenti legami peptidici (3). Questi ultimi sono invece assenti nel colesterolo (4), un lipide appartenente alla classe degli steroidi.

29) C. L'organismo descritto è fotosintetico, in quanto alcune delle cellule che lo compongono contengono cloroplasti, organelli dotati di grana in cui avviene la fotosintesi. Le altre cellule, che non contengono cloroplasti, effettuano solo la respirazione cellulare, un processo comune a tutte le cellule che produce anidride carbonica come sottoprodotto.

30) B. Durante l'esercizio fisico, nei muscoli avviene la produzione di acido lattico, che determina un abbassamento del pH sia a livello del muscolo sia a livello del plasma sanguigno. Inoltre, si assiste a un aumento del flusso ematico diretto ai muscoli che stanno lavorando e al cuore.

31) A. L'assortimento indipendente dei cromosomi e il crossing over tra i cromosomi omologhi che avvengono dopo la formazione dello zigote femminile hanno effetti sui gameti prodotti dalla femmina, non sul fenotipo della stessa. L'allineamento casuale dei cromosomi omologhi sulla piastra equatoriale nella metafase I della meiosi cui vanno incontro le cellule germinali del padre e della madre fa sì che il figlio maschio e la figlia femmina ricevano un diverso assortimento di cromosomi paterni e materni, che si riflette nelle differenze fenotipiche.

32) D. La frequenza di crossing over tra due geni associati è una misura della distanza fisica tra essi; infatti, più due geni sono distanti, maggiore è la probabilità che nel tratto di cromosoma compreso tra i due si verifichi un crossing over. Tra i quattro geni considerati, la frequenza di crossing over più elevata sussiste tra i geni R e Q (40%), per cui questi vanno posizionati ai due estremi della sequenza, essendo i più distanti. Il gene P è molto più vicino a R (5%) che a Q (35%), quindi va posizionato subito dopo R. Il gene S è molto più vicino a Q (10%) che a R (30%), per cui va posizionato subito prima di Q. La sequenza è pertanto RPSQ.

33) B. La fase della divisione cellulare in cui i membri delle coppie di cromosomi omologhi vengono tirati verso i poli dalle fibre del fuso è l'anafase della meiosi I. In metafase i cromosomi sono posizionati sulla piastra equatoriale, mentre in telofase sono già segregati ai due poli del fuso. Invece, nell'anafase della mitosi, le fibre del fuso tirano verso i poli i cromatidi fratelli di ciascun cromosoma.

34) E. Poiché si tratta di un allele dominante, è sufficiente possederne una sola copia per manifestare il carattere (l'affermazione 3 è falsa). Essendo un gene X-linked, gli individui di sesso maschile possono ereditarlo esclusivamente dalla madre (l'affermazione 1 è falsa), mentre quelli di sesso femminile possono ereditarlo sia dal padre che dalla madre. Se Z è maschio, deve aver ereditato l'allele dalla madre, la quale a sua volta l'ha ereditato da uno dei suoi genitori; essendo un allele dominante, il genitore della madre portatore dell'allele manifestava il carattere (l'affermazione 2 è vera). L'individuo Z trasmetterà il suo cromosoma X a tutte le sue figlie, le quali manifesteranno il carattere (l'affermazione 4 è vera).

35) C. L'anticodone sul tRNA per un determinato amminoacido è complementare al codone dell'mRNA codificante quell'amminoacido (in direzione $5' \rightarrow 3'$). Poiché il codone è complementare alla tripletta corrispondente sul DNA stampo (in direzione $3' \rightarrow 5'$), la tripletta di DNA in direzione $3' \rightarrow 5'$ ha la stessa sequenza dell'anticodone, ma presenta la timina al posto dell'uracile. La sequenza di DNA richiesta è pertanto GCAACATTGGGT.

36) A. I liposomi sono vescicole formate da un doppio strato lipidico utilizzate come vettori di DNA plasmidico nella terapia genica somatica. I geni introdotti nei liposomi non sono instabili e non si degradano nel tempo (l'affermazione 1 è falsa). Il DNA plasmidico contenuto nei lisosomi penetra nel nucleo della cellula ospite e viene espresso insieme al DNA della cellula. Se l'allele non mutato veicolato fosse recessivo, non avrebbe alcun effetto, in quanto continuerebbe a manifestarsi il fenotipo determinato dall'espressione dell'allele mutato dominante (l'affermazione 3 è falsa). Gli effetti benefici di questo tipo di terapia genica sono temporanei in quanto, con la rigenerazione delle cellule del polmone, le cellule contenenti il gene non mutato prima o poi muoiono, mentre le nuove cellule sono prive di tale allele (l'affermazione 2 è vera).

37) A. Ciascuna specie batterica presenta una crescita ottimale in determinate condizioni del mezzo di crescita. Sia una diminuzione della temperatura sia una variazione del pH possono favorire la crescita della specie V rispetto a quella della specie W (le affermazioni 1 e 2 sono vere). Inoltre, le diverse specie batteriche presentano sensibilità differenti ai vari antibiotici; pertanto, anche l'aggiunta di un antibiotico che uccide i batteri della specie W e non ha effetti sui batteri della specie V favorisce la specie V a discapito della specie W (l'affermazione 3 è vera).

38) D. La pressione nei ventricoli raggiunge il suo valore massimo nella fase di sistole ventricolare, quando le valvole semilunari si aprono e il sangue viene pompato nelle arterie. Contemporaneamente inizia il riempimento degli atri, dove la pressione è al suo valore minimo, e si chiudono le valvole atrioventricolari, cosicché il sangue non può refluire dai ventricoli agli atri. Lo stimolo elettrico investe il nodo atrioventricolare in concomitanza della contrazione degli atri, quindi prima della fase di sistole ventricolare.

39) B. Il pancreas produce e secerne nel duodeno il succo pancreatico, una miscela alcalina composta da enzimi digestivi, acqua e ioni (l'affermazione 2 è vera). La cistifellea ha il compito di immagazzinare la bile alcalina prodotta dal fegato e di rilasciarla nel duodeno dietro stimolazione ormonale; tuttavia, la bile non è prodotta in essa (l'affermazione 1 è falsa). Lo stomaco secerne il succo gastrico, fortemente acido (l'affermazione 3 è falsa).

40) E. Quando i linfociti B incontrano un antigene batterico capace di legarsi agli anticorpi esposti sulla loro superficie, vanno incontro a un processo di attivazione in cui si dividono per produrre linfociti B della memoria e plasmacellule capaci di produrre anticorpi (l'affermazione 1 è vera). La produzione massiccia di anticorpi da parte delle plasmacellule prevede l'aumento della trascrizione dei geni delle immunoglobuline negli mRNA corrispondenti (l'affermazione 2 è vera). I linfociti B non agiscono, invece, fagocitando e digerendo i batteri (l'affermazione 3 è falsa).

Chimica

41) A. La molecola è il cicloesene; rispetto all'alcano corrispondente (esano, C_6H_{14}) ha 4 idrogeni in meno a causa delle due insaturazioni (il doppio legame e la formazione del ciclo).

42) B. L'energia di ionizzazione è l'energia che è necessario fornire a un atomo affinché perda un elettrone, formando un catione. Il numero a sinistra in pedice (il numero atomico) ci permette di identificare il numero di protoni dell'elemento, da cui possiamo ricavare la configurazione elettronica. Per esempio l'elemento "W" ha 10 protoni, la sua configurazione elettronica è $1s^22s^22p^6$: si tratta di un gas nobile, quindi l'elemento che sicuramente presenta l'energia di ionizzazione maggiore.

43) E. Occorre scrivere la configurazione elettronica per tutti gli ioni:

$_{19}K^+$: $1s^22s^22p^63s^23p^6$ $_{11}Na^+$: $1s^22s^22p^6$ $_8O^-$: $1s^22s^22p^5$

$_8O^{2-}$: $1s^22s^22p^6$ $_{16}S^-$: $1s^22s^22p^63s^23p^5$

È evidente che i due ioni che hanno lo stesso arrangiamento di elettroni sono $_{11}Na^+$ e $_8O^{2-}$.

44) D. Gli elementi del primo gruppo formano idruri (come NaH) in cui l'idrogeno ha numero di ossidazione –1; sono elementi che si ossidano facilmente e sono quindi in grado di ridurre lo iodio (I_2) in ioduro (I^-); infine sono dei metalli, e il legame metallico è caratterizzato da una condivisione degli elettroni, che sono quindi delocalizzati tra tutti gli atomi.

45) A. In questo caso, per ricavare il numero di ossidazione del cloro, occorre ricordarsi che l'ossigeno (in questi composti) ha numero di ossidazione –2, che il potassio ha sempre numero di ossidazione +1 e che la somma dei numeri di ossidazione degli atomi deve essere pari a 0 (in questi casi non abbiamo a che fare con ioni). Il cloro presenta numero di ossidazione –1 in KCl, +1 in KClO e Cl_2O, +5 in $KClO_3$ e +7 in $KClO_4$ e Cl_2O_7.

46) C. Tra le forme delle molecole riportate, l'unica errata è quella dell'ammoniaca (NH_3), dove l'azoto ibridato sp^3 dà luogo a una geometria tetraedrica. Per la polarità occorre far attenzione alla simmetria delle molecole: CH_2Cl_2 non è simmetrica è mostrerà un certo momento di dipolo dovuto alla diversa elettronegatività tra cloro e carbonio; BF_3, CO_2 e PCl_5 sono molecole simmetriche, in cui la somma dei momenti di dipolo porta a delle molecole complessivamente non polari.

47) E. Per stimare la solubilità di una sostanza in un liquido si deve tenere presente il principio "simile scioglie simile": solo nel caso del bromo in esano liquido si prendono in considerazione due sostanze simili (entrambi apolari), negli altri casi una sostanza è polare e l'altra no, per cui ci si aspetta una solubilità molto limitata.

48) B. L'aumento della pressione a temperatura costante influisce sulla frequenza di collisione (in uno spazio più piccolo lo stesso numero di molecole ha più probabilità di collidere), mentre non influisce sull'energia media delle collisioni (che è influenzata solo dalla temperatura).

49) A. In questa reazione l'acqua si comporta da acido di Brønsted–Lowry (perde lo ione H^+), CH_3O^- da base di Brønsted–Lowry (acquista lo ione H^+). Lo ione OH^- è la base coniugata dell'acqua e CH_3OH è l'acido coniugato di CH_3O^-. Dato che si producono ioni OH^-, il pH sarà sicuramente maggiore di 7.

50) D. La catena più lunga contiene sei atomi di carbonio. Tenendo in considerazione le priorità di numerazione dei gruppi, in posizione 2 è presente il gruppo alcolico, in posizione 3 due gruppi cloro e nelle posizioni 2 e 4 sono presenti due gruppi metile. Il nome del composto risulta quindi 3,3-dicloro-2,4-dimetilesan-2-olo.

51) D. L'energia cinetica totale delle molecole dipende dalla temperatura del sistema. Tenendo conto della legge dei gas ideali PV = nRT, l'aumento di pressione tenendo costante il volume può avvenire solamente con l'aumento della temperatura; discorso analogo si può fare con l'aumento del volume a pressione costante. L'aumento del numero di moli a pressione e volume costante, invece, porterebbe a una diminuzione della temperatura.

52) A. Si deve ricordare la seconda legge di Gay-Lussac, secondo la quale a volume costante, la pressione di un gas è direttamente proporzionale alla sua temperatura assoluta. 10 °C = 283 K; per raddoppiare la pressione occorre arrivare a $2 \times 283 = 566$ K = 293 °C.

Fisica e Matematica

53) B. $(3 \times 10^3)^3$ può essere scritto come $3^3 \times 10^9 = 27 \times 10^9$; tale valore, moltiplicato per 2×10^{-5} porta a $54 \times 10^4 = 5.4 \times 10^5$.

54) C. Affinché la retta sia perpendicolare a $y = 2x + 4$, il coefficiente angolare (m) deve essere l'inverso e l'opposto di 2, cioè -1/2. Per fare in modo che la retta passi per il punto (4, 3), essa deve soddisfare la condizione $3 = 4m + q$; dal valore imposto di m si ricava $q = 5$. La retta è quindi $y = -1/2x + 5$, equivalente a $2y + x = 10$.

55) D. Disegnando la figura ci si accorge che si tratta di un quadrato di lato 6 (area 36 cm^2) attaccato a un triangolo equilatero i cui lati misurano 6 cm. Per il teorema dei seni l'altezza di questo triangolo è pari a 6 sen(60) = $3\sqrt{3}$, e la sua area pari a $(6 \times 3\sqrt{3})/2 = 9\sqrt{3}$. L'area totale è $36 + 9\sqrt{3} = 9(4 + \sqrt{3})$ cm^2.

56) E. Questa equazione può essere scritta più semplicemente come $x + 4 = x(x + 1)$; con pochi semplici passaggi si arriva a $x^2 = 4$, che ha due soluzioni +2 e –2, la cui somma è pari a 0.

57) A. Per ordinare correttamente questi numeri conviene convertirli nella stessa unità di misura, per esempio in metri:

1.5 nm = 1.5×10^{-9} m   0.0036 μm = 3.6×10^{-9} m   1650 pm = 1.65×10^{-9} m

58) C. Dato che sul treno insiste una forza costante nella stessa direzione in cui si muove, la sua accelerazione sarà costante (ricordare $F = m \times a$); un corpo che viaggia con accelerazione costante aumenta di velocità.

59) C. La velocità quadratica media delle molecole è direttamente proporzionale alla loro temperatura e inversamente proporzionale al loro peso molecolare. A parità di temperatura l'azoto ha una $\overline{v^2}$ minore dell'ossigeno. L'energia cinetica delle molecole, invece, dipende solamente dalla temperatura e quindi avrà lo stesso valore per l'azoto e l'ossigeno.

60) A. La resistenza di un conduttore è definita come $R = \rho L/S$, dove L è la lunghezza del cavo, S la sua area di sezione e ρ la sua resistività. L'area di sezione è $S = \pi d^2/4 = \pi\ 1.0 \times 10^{-6}\ m^2$ e la resistività risulta quindi $(1.0 \times 10^{-6} \times 2.0)/\pi\ 1.0 \times 10^{-6} = 2.0/\pi\Omega$.

IMAT
a.a. 2019/2020

General Knowledge and Logical Reasoning

1) A study involving a brain-training exercise was carried out on more than a thousand adults aged 65 and over, some of whom later developed dementia. Results showed that the benefits of the five-week mental agility course undertaken by some of the adults lasted for at least five years. This led to an improvement in everyday activities such as money management and the ability to2 do housework. If those with trained brains developed dementia, they did so later than those in the control group. The results also showed that, for those people in the study who developed dementia, after the diagnosis their mental decline occurred faster than for those who had not undertaken the training.
Which one of the following can be drawn as a conclusion from the above passage?

A. All over-65s who undertake brain training live for at least five years afterwards
B. Keeping the mind active delays the onset of dementia
C. Older people do not perform mentally challenging tasks unless forced to do so
D. People do a decreasing amount of housework as they grow older
E. It is preferable to have swift mental decline once dementia develops

2) Once again it has become fashionable for householders to replace their carpets with wooden floors. Sales of laminate and solid floors, such as oak, have seen a massive increase in the last ten years. This trend seems more in tune with our eco-friendly aspirations: carpets are often plastic-based and use vast quantities of underlying material, or underlay, made from petrochemicals. For this reason, it seems unlikely that wooden floors will go out of fashion in the near future.
Which one of the following, if true, most weakens the above argument?

A. Carpets can harbour dust mites and allergens
B. Not all wooden floors need a layer of underlay
C. Most types of laminate and wood floors use petrochemicals in their manufacture
D. Sales of carpets made of synthetic materials have decreased in the last ten years while woollen carpets have seen an increase
E. Wooden floors may look longer-lasting but can be more easily damaged than carpets

3) According to the current mainstream scientific view, Near Death Experiences (NDEs) are explicable in purely physiological terms. Specifically, they are caused by cerebral anoxia (oxygen deficiency in brain tissue), which occurs in a dying brain. On the other hand, recent research on hundreds of successfully resuscitated cardiac patients found that only twenty per cent reported NDEs. If NDEs had purely medical causes then most of

the patients should have experienced them, since they had all been clinically dead and experienced cerebral anoxia. NDEs therefore do not have purely physiological causes.
Which one of the following best expresses the main conclusion of the above passage?

A. NDEs are caused by oxygen deficiency in the brain
B. Not all clinically dead patients have NDEs
C. NDEs are a physical property of the human brain
D. NDEs are not necessarily caused by physical events alone
E. Not all successfully resuscitated cardiac patients have NDEs

4) Increasingly, the quality of a teacher, and of his or her lessons, is to be judged by feedback from their pupils. This is dangerous, as pupils have a tendency to focus too much on whether or not they enjoyed the lesson, in other words, on how much 'fun' they found it. The purpose of education, however, is not to keep children entertained; it is not to make their lives more fun. Arguably, it is not even to make them happier, per se. The purpose of schools is to make their pupils better, more educated people. This is all that matters, and therefore it is whether the teacher succeeds at this – not at being a children's entertainer – that counts.
Which one of the following is a flaw in the above argument?

A. It fails to consider that enjoying lessons could result in pupils ending up better educated
B. By simply asserting that the purpose of education is not even to make people happier, the argument rests on a questionable contention
C. It patronises young people by thinking that their judgement will be based solely on how much fun they found the lesson
D. It doesn't specify precisely what it means by making someone a better, more educated person
E. The comparison with being a children's entertainer is an unfair exaggeration of what a teacher tries to do by making lessons more fun

5) Researchers have tried to establish reasons for a recent drop in the catch of marlin near the Madeira coast. This drop cannot be explained by environmental conditions; there was no significant change in the temperature or composition of the region's water. Nor could one blame the human factor, because the size of the fishing fleet, catch quotas and pollution levels have been strictly observed. The environmentalists then analysed the records of the fishing catch of marlin over the last six centuries. This research identified that regular five-year periods of significant decrease in the catch alternated with fifteen-year periods of gradual growth of the catch. In view of this, the study concluded that the current drop in the marlin catch is part of a long-term cycle related to fish migration and food-chain balance.
Which one of the following is an underlying assumption of the above argument?

A. The change in fishing technology has affected the change in the fishing catch
B. The records provide accurate information about the catch of marlin off the Madeira coast
C. There is no correlation between the fishing catch today and the deep-sea stock of marlin in the sixteenth century
D. The fishing catch of marlin around Madeira does not depend on the condition of the water around the island

E. Climate change did not affect the temperature of ocean water off the Madeira coast

6) A student packs books into a box which is 20 cm high, 30 cm wide, and 40 cm long. She ties string around the box in the pattern shown. A further 20 cm of string is needed for a knot.

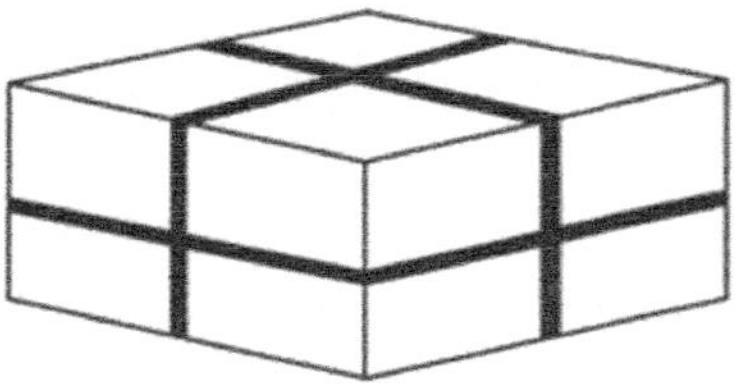

What length of string is needed to tie up her box?

A. 5.4 m
B. 3.8 m
C. 2.0 m
D. 2.6 m
E. 2.9 m

7) The plan of a domestic lawn with dimensions in metres is shown below.

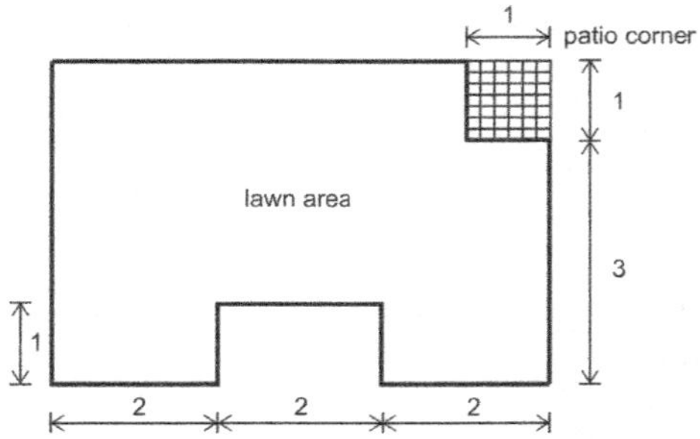

The lawn area is to be reseeded. Seed must be applied at the rate of 50 grams per square metre. Appropriate grass seed is available only in the following quantities:

grass seed packet prices			
1.6 kg	£20.00	500 g	£8.00
1.2 kg	£16.50	200 g	£3.00
1.0 kg	£14.00	100 g	£2.00

What is the least amount of money that needs to be spent to buy sufficient seed to reseed the lawn?

A. £16.00
B. £13.50
C. £14.00
D. £16.50
E. £22.00

8) Five girls competed in five events at their sports day. The following scoring system was used for each event:

1st place	6 points	3rd place	1 point
2nd place	3 points	4th/5th place	0 points

Before the events started, each girl nominated the event in which they wished to play their joker card – this doubled the number of points gained in that event.

The table below shows the results of each event and the athletes' final points scores:

competitor	800 m run	100 m hurdles	high jump	long jump	shot put	total points scored
Tia	4th	1st	5th	3rd	3rd	14
Jessica	1st	3rd	1st	5th	4th	19
Carolina	3rd	4th	2nd	1st	2nd	14
Kelly	2nd	2nd	4th	2nd	5th	12
Helena	5th	5th	3rd	4th	1st	13

How many of the girls won the event in which they had elected to play their joker?

A. 4
B. 1
C. 2
D. 3
E. 5

9) At the Shawilde Theatre, tickets are priced as follows:

Front stalls	£35
Centre stalls	£28
Rear stalls	£20

Every row in the theatre contains 30 seats. Last night's performance was a sell-out and the ticket sales were £21 000. Exactly 60% of this income came from tickets for the centre stalls, and the rest was split equally between the front stalls and the rear stalls. **How many rows of seats make up the centre stalls at the Shawilde Theatre?**

A. 19
B. 11
C. 15
D. 22
E. 26

10) 

Four of the following five pieces can be fitted together to make the above pattern. Which one of the pieces is NOT needed?

A. 

B. 

C. 

D. 

E. 

11) Which one of the following literary works does NOT originate in the corresponding country?

A. The Tale of Genji – Japan
B. The Poems of Rumi – China
C. Oedipus Rex – Greece
D. The Divine Comedy – Italy
E. Don Quixote – Spain

12) Which one of the following composed the opera *Madama Butterfly*?

A. Richard Wagner
B. Giuseppe Verdi
C. Gioachino Rossini
D. Georges Bizet
E. Giacomo Puccini

13) Which one of the following plays by William Shakespeare is NOT set in Italy?

A. A Midsummer Night's Dream

B. Much Ado About Nothing
C. Othello
D. The Taming of the Shrew
E. Romeo and Juliet

14) Which one of the following writers is the author of the novel *To Kill a Mockingbird*?

A. Iris Murdoch
B. Georges Simenon
C. Harper Lee
D. Elena Ferrante
E. Ernest Hemingway

15) The 'prisoner's dilemma' is a common example analysed in the field of:

A. Network theory
B. Chaos theory
C. Asymptotic theory
D. Game theory
E. Quantum theory

16) Who was the first woman to be awarded a Nobel Prize?

A. Mother Teresa
B. Marie Curie
C. Grazia Deledda
D. Selma Lagerlöf
E. Doris Lessing

17) Which one of these events in world history happened most recently?

A. The October Revolution in the Russian Empire
B. The fall of the Western Roman Empire
C. The Taiping Rebellion in China
D. The building of the Taj Mahal
E. The crowning of Charlemagne

18) Which one of the following religions is NOT considered to have been revealed to or founded by an individual?

A. Confucianism
B. Hinduism
C. Islam
D. Christianity
E. Buddhism

19) The governance of modern states is often based on the separation of which three powers?

A. Legislative – elective – executive
B. Legislative – elective – jurisprudential
C. Electoral – regulatory – jurisprudential
D. Regulatory – executive – judicial
E. Legislative – executive – judicial

20) The Constitution of the Italian Republic was enacted on 22 December 1947 by:

A. The Ministry of Justice
B. The Supreme Court
C. The Constituent Assembly
D. The Ministry of Defence
E. The Government

21) Which one of the following is NOT a stated purpose of the United Nations?

A. To encourage peaceful trade between nations
B. To maintain international peace and security
C. To develop friendly relations among nations
D. To achieve international co-operation in solving international problems
E. To be a centre for harmonizing the actions of nations

22) Which one of the following countries did NOT adopt the coins and banknotes of the Euro as its currency on 1 January 2002?

A. Finland
B. Austria
C. Portugal
D. Luxembourg
E. Sweden

Biology

23) Which of the following rows are correct about these naturally occurring biological molecules?

	biological molecule	presence of carboxylic acid groups	presence of 2 or more hydroxyl groups
row 1	ALL amino acids	yes	no
row 2	glucose	no	yes
row 3	glycerol	no	no
row 4	ALL fatty acids	yes	no

A. 1, 2 and 3 only
B. 1, 3 and 4 only
C. 2, 3 and 4 only
D. 1, 2, 3 and 4
E. 1, 2 and 4 only

24) Which of the following is/are tissues?

1 cartilage
2 skin
3 endothelium

A. 1, 2 and 3
B. 1 and 2 only
C. 2 and 3 only
D. 1 only
E. 1 and 3 only

25) Which of the following statements about the metabolism of plants is/are correct?

1 CO_2 is produced during the day.
2 CO_2 is produced at night.
3 The CO_2 produced can be used by the plant.

A. 1 only
B. 2 only
C. 1, 2 and 3
D. 2 and 3 only
E. 1 and 2 only

26) Which one of the following occurs during anaphase of mitosis in a healthy human liver cell?

A. Chromatin condenses so that the chromosomes are visible under the microscope
B. Chromosomes move towards the equator of the cell and attach to the spindle fibres
C. DNA replicates so that each chromosome is made up of two sister chromatids
D. Sister chromatids are pulled by the spindle fibres towards opposite poles of the cell
E. Centrioles migrate to opposite poles of the cell and help to assemble the spindle fibres

27) Which row shows a correct component of each of the three structures listed?

	viral envelope	capsid	genetic material
row 1	glycogen	glycosidic bonds	adenine
row 2	glycosidic bonds	glycogen	ester bonds
row 3	phosphodiester bonds	hydrogen bonds	amino acids
row 4	fatty acids	amino acids	phosphodiester bonds
row 5	phosphate	phosphodiester bonds	cytosine

A. row 2
B. row 3
C. row 4
D. row 1
E. row 5

28) Beetroot is a root vegetable with cells that contain a red pigment. Normally the pigment cannot pass out of the cells because it cannot diffuse through their cell surface membranes. An investigation was carried out into the effect of various chemicals on the permeability of the cell surface membranes of beetroot cells. 1 cm^3 samples were cut from the beetroot and washed in running water for 20 minutes to remove any pigment that was released from the damaged cells.
Five experiments were carried out. In each experiment, one cube of beetroot was placed in liquid P and one cube placed in liquid Q, and the results were observed. Which row shows the correct results and conclusions?

		result	conclusion		result	conclusion
	liquid P	**liquid P turns red**	**phospholipids dissolve**	**liquid Q**	**liquid Q turns red**	**protein denatures**
row 1	dilute HCl	x	x	water at 20°C	✓	✓
row 2	dilute HCl	✓	✓	ethanol	✓	✓
row 3	ethanol	✓	✓	dilute HCl	✓	✓
row 4	ethanol	x	x	water at 20°C	✓	✓
row 5	water at 20°C	✓	✓	dilute HCl	x	x

Key
✓ does happen
x does not happen

A. row 4
B. row 2
C. row 1
D. row 3
E. row 5

29) If a cell divides by mitosis ten times, what is the number of cells at the end of the process? [Assume that all cells remain alive.]

A. 1024
B. 10
C. 100
D. 64
E. 11

30) Familial hypercholesterolaemia (FH) is an inherited disease caused by a dominant allele. People with FH have high concentrations of cholesterol in the blood, which can lead to an increased risk of coronary heart disease. The family tree shows the inheritance of this disease in one family.

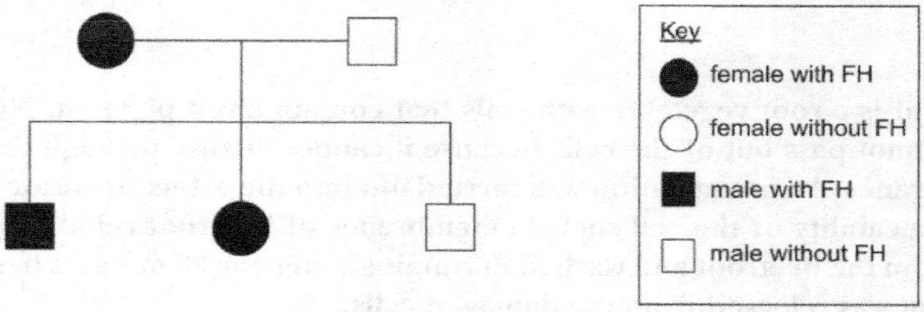

Which row shows the number of individuals in the family tree with each genotype?

	genotype		
	homozygous dominant	**homozygous recessive**	**heterozygous**
row 1	3	2	0
row 2	2	3	0
0	0	2	3
row 4	0	3	2
row 5	3	0	2

A. row 2
B. row 3
C. row 1
D. row 4
E. row 5

31) The diagrams show some pathways between the central nervous system and effector organs in a healthy human. Which pathway is a possible route for impulses passing along a parasympathetic neuron?

A.

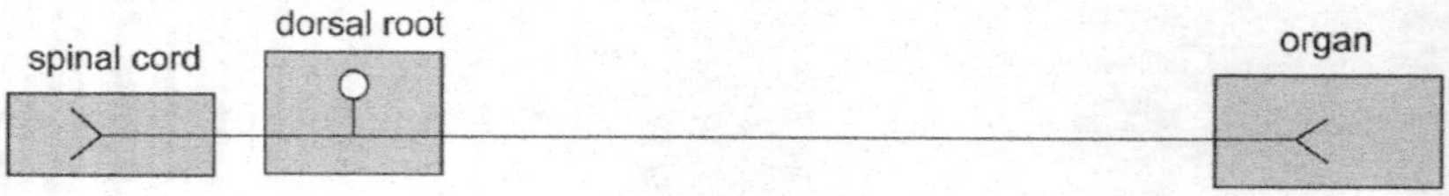

B.

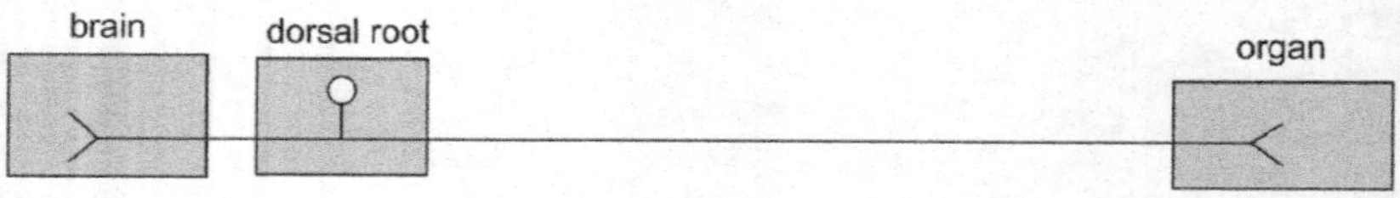

C.

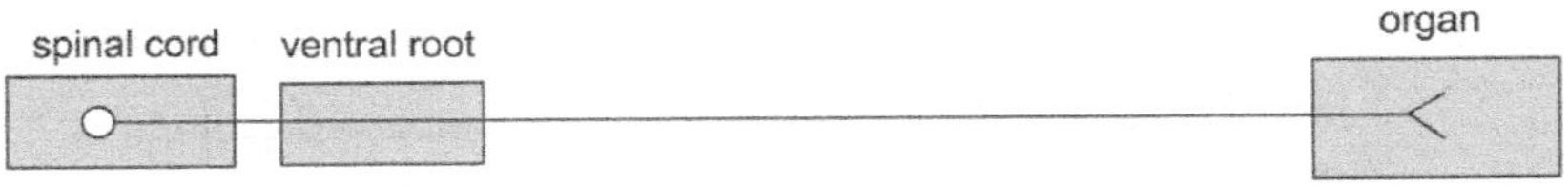

D.

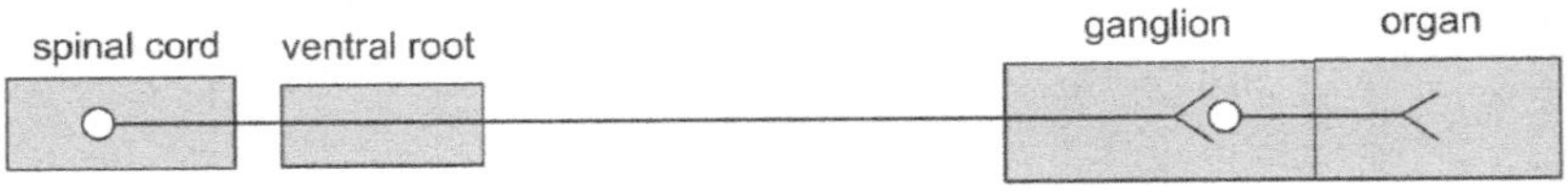

E.

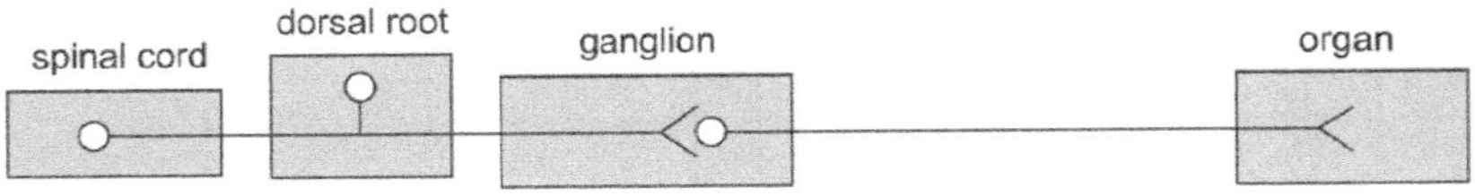

32) The diagrams show some pathways between the central nervous system and effector organs in a healthy human.
Which pathway is a possible route for impulses passing along a parasympathetic neuron?
An electron microscope (EM) was used to view a cell.
The maximum dimension of the cell was observed at a magnification ×30 000. The image on the EM screen showed a maximum length of 30 mm. Which of the following mature healthy cells was being magnified?

A. One coccus bacterium in a Staphylococcus cluster
B. One lymphocyte from a human
C. One mature human red blood cell
D. One sensory neuron from a human
E. One palisade cell from a wheat plant

33) Which statement about an enzyme involved in genetic modification is correct?

A. A ligase causes phosphodiester bonds to be broken
B. A restriction enzyme causes H-bonds to form between sticky ends
C. A restriction enzyme causes phosphodiester bonds to be broken
D. A restriction enzyme causes only H-bonds to be broken
E. A ligase causes H-bonds to form between sticky ends only

34) Which statement is correct in healthy humans?

A. Blood leaving active muscles that are respiring aerobically will contain hydrogencarbonateions and raised levels of lactic acid
B. In active tissues where the carbon dioxide concentration is high, haemoglobin has a low affinity for oxygen
C. At a low partial pressure of oxygen, myoglobin is less saturated with oxygen thanhaemoglobin
D. Increasing the partial pressure of oxygen makes it more likely that haemoglobin willrelease its oxygen
E. The majority of carbon dioxide transported in the blood is in the form ofcarbaminohaemoglobin

35) Which of the following regions within a sarcomere remain UNCHANGED in length when a healthy human muscle cell contracts?

1 A-band
2 I-band
3 H-zone/band

A. 2 only
B. 1 only
C. 3 only
D. 1 and 3 only
E. 2 and 3 only

36) Which row is correct for the three given features of typical human B lymphocytes?

	formed from bone marrow stem cells	processed in the thymus	contain genes coding for antibodies
row 1	✓	✓	✓
row 2	✓	✓	x
row 3	✓	x	✓
row 4	x	x	✓
row 5	x	✓	x

Key
✓ correct
x incorrect

A. row 1
B. row 2
C. row 3
D. row 4
E. row 5

37) Which of the following processes involve ions?

1 contraction of a muscle
2 transmission of a nerve impulse across a synapse
3 transfer of light energy into chemical energy in photosynthesis
4 oxidative phosphorylation in a mitochondrion

A. 3 and 4 only
B. 2 and 3 only
C. 1, 2, 3 and 4
D. 1, 2 and 3 only
E. 1 and 2 only

38) An animal has a coat that has some patches of white hair and some patches of black hair. Cells that make up a hair follicle form a single hair, which is either white or black.
Assume that there are no mutations following formation of the zygote.
A student wrote the following statements:

1 The cells in all the hair follicles contain the same genes.
2 The alleles in a hair follicle forming a white hair are different from the alleles in the hair follicle forming a black hair.
3 Each white hair follicle cell contains two recessive alleles.

Which statement(s) is/are correct?

A. 1 only
B. 2 only
C. 1 and 2 only
D. 2 and 3 only
E. 1, 2 and 3

39) The diagram shows a nephron with collecting duct from a healthy human.

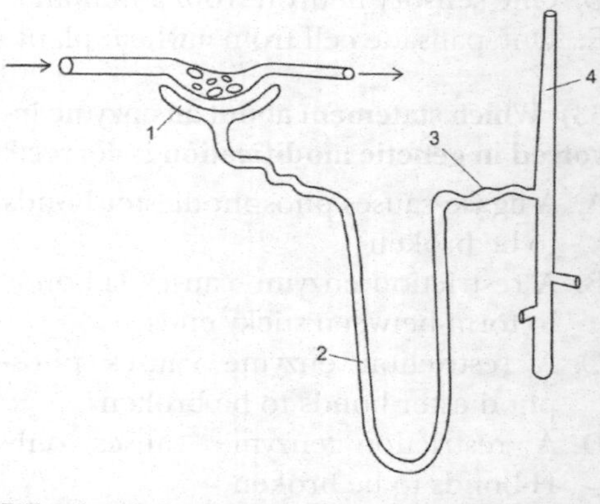

Which of the regions (1- 4) contain a liquid with no urea?

A. 1 only
B. 1 and 2 only
C. none of them
D. 2 and 3 only
E. 2, 3 and 4 only

40) The same section of an allele coding for five amino acids from two different individuals, P and Q, is shown.

P ATTCCGGGATTCCCT
Q ATTCCGGATTGCACT

Which of the following types of mutation could explain the differences between P and Q?

1 addition
2 deletion
3 substitution

A. 1 only
B. 1 and 3 only
C. 2 and 3 only
D. none of them
E. 1, 2 and 3

Chemistry

41) Which statement about a positive ion explains why it is positively charged?

A. The ion has more electrons than neutrons.
B. The ion has more electrons than protons.
C. The ion has more protons than neutrons.
D. The ion has the same number of protons and neutrons.
E. The ion has more protons than electrons.

42) A few drops of universal indicator solution were added to exactly 50 mL of sodium hydroxide solution, NaOH, of concentration 1 mol/L. Exactly 50 mL of hydrochloric acid, HCl, of concentration 1 mol/L, was added drop by drop to the sodium hydroxide solution containing the universal indicator solution.
What colour changes would be observed as the hydrochloric acid was added?

A. red × orange × yellow × green
B. violet × blue × green × yellow × orange × red
C. blue × red
D. violet × blue × green
E. red × orange × yellow × green × blue × violet

43) A student observed that when powdered sugar at –1 °C was added to ice at –1 °C all of the ice melted. Which of the following statements explain this observation?

1 Sugar has given the water molecules energy.
2 The melting point of the mixture is higher.
3 The melting point of the mixture is lower.

A. 1 only
B. 2 only
C. 3 only
D. 1 and 2 only
E. 1 and 3 only

44) Which of the following pairs of structural formulae represent structural isomers?

1 CH_3CH_2OH and CH_3OCH_3
2 $CH_3CH(CH_3)CH_2CH_2CH_3$ and $CH_3CH_2CH_2CH(CH_3)CH_3$
3 $CH(OH){=}CHCH_2OH$ and CH_3CH_2COOH

A. 1, 2 and 3
B. 2 only
C. 1 only
D. 2 and 3 only
E. 1 and 3 only

45) Element Z reacts with water at room temperature and hydrogen gas is relea-

sed. The oxide of element Z is a solid at room temperature and does not conduct electricity. The oxide reacts with acids and has the formula ZO. To which group/part of the Periodic Table does element Z belong?

A. Group II
B. Group I
C. Group III
D. Transition metals
E. Group VII

46) Which of the following equations represent(s) a redox reaction?

1 $4LiH + AlCl_3 \rightarrow 3LiCl + LiAlH_4$
2 $N_2O_3 + 3H_2O \rightarrow 2H_3O^+ + 2NO_2^-$
3 $NH_4NO_3 \rightarrow 2H_2O + N_2O$

A. 2 only
B. 1 and 2 only
C. 1 and 3 only
D. 1, 2 and 3
E. 3 only

47) Which of the following molecules have an overall permanent dipole moment?

1 CO_2
2 H_2O
3 NH_3
[C is in Group IV, N is in Group V, O is in Group VI]

A. 1 and 3 only
B. 1 and 2 only
C. 2 and 3 only
D. none of them
E. 1, 2 and 3

48) Why does hydrogen iodide (HI) have a higher boiling point than hydrogen bromide (HBr)?
[Atomic numbers: bromine = 35; iodine = 53]

A. The permanent dipole-permanent dipole forces between HI molecules are stronger than those between HBr molecules
B. There are hydrogen bonds between HI molecules but not between HBr molecules
C. The H–I covalent bond is stronger than the H–Br covalent bond
D. The iodide ions in HI are larger than the bromide ions in HBr
E. The induced dipole-induced dipole (dispersion) forces between HI molecules are stronger than those between HBr molecules

49) What is the minimum mass of sulfur dioxide needed to make 500 mL of a solution of concentration 3.0 mol/L?
[A_r values: O = 16; S = 32]

A. 96 g
B. 48 g
C. 32 g
D. 192 g
E. 384 g

50) A compound consists of carbon, hydrogen and oxygen only. 8 g of this compound contains 3 g of carbon and 1 g of hydrogen. Which one of the following could be the molecular formula of the compound?
[A_r values: C = 12; H = 1; O = 16]

A. CH_2O
B. C_2H_4O
C. CH_4O
D. C_2H_8O
E. C_3HO_4

51) Hydrogen has a radioactive isotope called tritium. Tritium atoms have two neutrons. The most abundant naturally occurring isotope of hydrogen has a relative atomic mass of 1.0. What is the value for the relative atomic mass of a sample of hydrogen gas that has an equal amount of these two isotopes of hydrogen?

A. 4.0
B. 1.0
C. 1.5
D. 3.0
E. 2.0

52) Consider the following reversible reaction at temperature *T*.

$$A + 2B \rightleftharpoons 2C + D$$

At equilibrium, there are 0.5 moles of A, 0.2 moles of B, 0.5 moles of C and 0.8 moles of D, all in a vessel of volume *V*. What is the value of the equilibrium constant, K_c, at this temperature?

A. 10
B. 4
C. 2
D. 0.25
E. 0.1

Physics and Mathematics

53) Which of the following expressions is equal to $\frac{8^{2n} \times 4^n}{2^n}$ for all integers *n*?

A. 2^{6n+1}
B. 2^{6n}
C. 2^{7n}
D. 2^{2n+5}
E. 2^{14n}

54) The mean mass of three babies is 2.1 kg. The range of their masses is 0.7 kg. The lightest baby has a mass of 1.8 kg. What is the median mass of the three babies?

A. 2.0 kg
B. 1.95 kg
C. 2.1 kg
D. 2.15 kg
E. 2.3 kg

55) What is the highest common factor of 360, 500 and 700, given as the product of powers of its prime factors?

A. $2^3 \times 3^2 \times 5^3 \times 7$
B. 2×5
C. $2^3 \times 5^3$
D. $2^2 \times 3^2 \times 5 \times 7$
E. $2^2 \times 5$

56) What is the sum of the solutions to the equation $\frac{3}{x} + \frac{2}{x-2} = 1$ where *x* is a real number and $x \neq 0$ and $x \neq 2$?

A. 2.4
B. 5
C. –7
D. 7
E. –3

57) A car, which is initially stationary, accelerates for 5.0 seconds at 4.0 m/s^2 along a straight road. It then continues in the same direction for 20 seconds at a constant speed. What is the maximum speed of the car, and what is the distance travelled by the car in the final 20 seconds of its motion?

A. maximum speed = 9.0 m/s; distance = 200 m
B. maximum speed = 20 m/s; distance = 80 m
C. maximum speed = 9.0 m/s; distance = 180 m
D. maximum speed = 20 m/s; distance = 400 m
E. maximum speed = 24 m/s; distance = 480 m

58) A stone of density 5.20 g/cm^3 and volume 200 cm^3 is completely submerged in a liquid of density 1.20 g/cm^3. What is the magnitude of the upthrust acting on the stone? [gravitational field strength = 10.0 N/kg]

A. 6.40 N
B. 2.40 N
C. 8.00 N
D. 10.4 N
E. 2.00 N

59) Two charged particles P and Q are 0.10 m apart. The charge on P is 1.50×10^{-7} C and the charge on Q is 1.50×10^{-7} C. Particle P experiences an electrostatic force of magnitude F because it is near to the charge on particle Q.
The distance between the two particles is increased to 0.20 m. The charge on P is increased to 4.50×10^{-7} C and the charge on Q is increased to 6.00×10^{-7} C. What is the magnitude of the force that particle P experiences now?

A. $3F$
B. $12F$
C. $6F$
D. $\frac{F}{4}$
E. $\frac{3F}{4}$

60) A fixed mass of an ideal gas is compressed at constant temperature. The pressure is recorded continuously as the volume decreases. The pressure (*y*-axis) and volume (*x*-axis) are plotted on a linearly scaled graph. Which statement describes the plotted line?

A. a straight line parallel to the pressure axis
B. a straight line of positive gradient starting at the origin of the graph
C. a curved line with negative gradient of decreasing magnitude
D. a straight line parallel to the volume axis
E. a curved line of increasing positive gradient starting at the origin of the graph

RISPOSTE COMMENTATE • IMAT a.a. 2019/2020

Cultura generale e ragionamento logico

1) B. Il quesito chiede quale delle cinque alternative di risposta rechi l'affermazione che può fungere da conclusione del ragionamento esposto nella traccia. Per questo scopo è sufficiente osservare che nel passo in esame sono illustrati i risultati di uno studio secondo cui un allenamento mentale svolto dai 65 anni in poi ha effetti positivi sull'eventuale sviluppo della demenza. È chiaro, quindi, che la conclusione che può essere tratta dal passo deve essere che "*Keeping the mind active delays the onset of dementia*".

2) C. La soluzione del quesito consiste nell'identificare la risposta che, se fosse aggiunta alle premesse dell'argomentazione, ne indebolirebbe la conclusione. Argomento del brano è la tendenza particolarmente diffusa negli ultimi anni a sostituire i tappeti con i pavimenti in legno essendo i tappeti realizzati con prodotti petrolchimici; per questo motivo, l'autore del brano conclude che sembra improbabile che i pavimenti in legno passino di moda nel prossimo futuro. Analizziamo dunque le cinque alternative per individuare l'affermazione che toglierebbe forza alla conclusione.
L'alternativa "*Carpets can harbour dust mites and allergens*" evidenzia un altro aspetto negativo dei tappeti, che rappresenterebbe un ulteriore motivo a sostegno dell'importanza di sostituirli con pavimenti in legno. Analogamente anche "*Not all wooden floors need a layer of underlay*" indica un altro vantaggio dei pavimenti in legno rispetto ai tappeti e sarebbe un ulteriore ragione per preferirli. È chiaro, quindi, che se una di queste due opzioni fosse aggiunta all'argomentazione della traccia, invece di indebolirne la conclusione la rafforzerebbe. Per quanto riguarda le restanti tre alternative di risposta, tutte potrebbero indebolire l'argomentazione, ma in grado diverso. "*Wooden floors may look longer-lasting but can be more easily damaged than carpets*" mostra uno svantaggio dei pavimenti in legno rispetto ai tappeti, i quali, perciò, potrebbero essere rivalutati rispetto ai primi. Tuttavia, tale opzione non indebolisce nessun passaggio specifico dell'argomentazione della traccia, come invece fanno le altre due alternative. Queste ultime, infatti, mostrano motivi che si collegano alle "*eco-friendly aspirations*" di cui si parla nel brano. "*Sales of carpets made of synthetic materials have decreased in the last ten years while woollen carpets have seen an increase*" attenua ma non elimina del tutto i motivi ambientalisti che portano a scegliere i pavimenti in legno al posto dei tappeti, perché tale opzione significa che in vendita c'è ancora una percentuale di tappeti sintetici la cui produzione è dannosa per l'ambiente. Invece, "*Most types of laminate and wood floors use petrochemicals in their manufacture*" elimina quasi del tutto i motivi ambientalisti in questione ed è, quindi, l'alternativa che indebolisce di più l'argomentazione esposta nella traccia.

3) D. Per risolvere il quesito, bisogna riconoscere quale delle cinque opzioni di risposta esprima meglio la conclusione principale del ragionamento esposto nella traccia.

Poiché tale conclusione, supportata da tutto il discorso che la precede, è "*NDEs therefore do not have purely physiological causes*", è chiaro che l'opzione ricercata è "*NDEs are not necessarily caused by physical events alone*".

4) A. Il ragionamento riportato nella traccia ha un difetto, che fa sì che il passaggio logico dalle premesse alla conclusione non sia accettabile. Il quesito chiede di stabilire quale fra le cinque alternative di risposta indichi questo difetto. La risposta corretta è "*It fails to consider that enjoying lessons could result in pupils ending up better educated*". Infatti, nel brano si afferma che è sbagliato valutare la qualità di un insegnante e delle sue lezioni sulla base dei feedback degli allievi perché questi ultimi tendono a considerare positivamente solo le lezioni che li hanno divertiti, mentre scopo della scuola non è rendere allegri i ragazzi ma renderli persone più istruite. L'errore del ragionamento risiede nel fatto di non considerare, dunque, che il divertimento prodotto da una lezione possa contribuire alla sua efficacia educativa.

5) B. Per spiegare il recente calo nella pesca del marlin vicino alla costa di Madeira, il ragionamento della traccia cita uno studio che ha analizzato i registri riguardanti la pesca di questo pesce negli ultimi sei secoli. Da tali registri è emerso un andamento ciclico dell'aumento e della diminuzione della pesca del marlin. In base a queste premesse il ragionamento conclude che "*the current drop in the marlin catch is part of a long-term cycle related to fish migration and food-chain balance*". Una tale conclusione, però, può basarsi sull'analisi dei registri solo presupponendo che essi forniscano informazioni precise sul fenomeno in questione. Pertanto, l'alternativa di risposta corretta è "*The records provide accurate information about the catch of marlin off the Madeira coast*".

6) B. La scatola in cui lo studente ha messo i libri è un parallelepipedo, ovvero un solido costituito da 6 facce uguali a due a due, di cui in figura sono mostrate le 3 facce differenti, delle quali sono note le dimensioni:

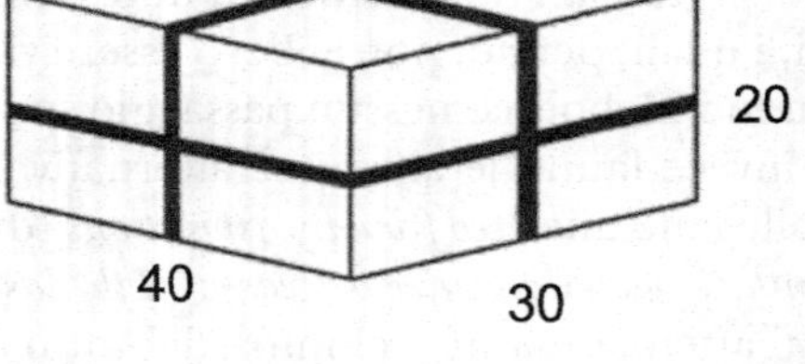

Il nastro dovrà allora essere lungo:

$$(20+40)\times 2+(30+20)\times 2+(30+40)\times 2=120+100+140=360 \text{ cm}$$

a cui devono essere sommati i 20 cm di lunghezza del nodo, per un totale di 380 cm = 3,8 m.

7) A. Osservando con attenzione la pianta del prato è possibile calcolarne l'area, per poi conoscere il quantitativo di semi necessario a riseminare tutto il prato.

Il prato è un rettangolo, lungo 6 metri e profondo 4, a cui manca un rettangolo centrale davanti di 2 m^2 e un angolo di 1 m^2. L'area sarà allora pari a:

$$(6 \times 4) - (2 + 1) = 24 - 3 = 21\, m^2$$

e serviranno

$$21 \times 50 = 1050\, g = 1.05\, kg$$

di semi per riseminare tutto il prato. Guardando con attenzione il listino prezzi si nota innanzitutto che un pacco da 1 kg, costando £14, è più conveniente di 2 pacchi da 500 g, che costerebbero £8 × 2 = £16. Inoltre, per avere un 1.05 kg si potrebbe acquistare un sacco da 1.2 kg a £16.50, ma, guardando nuovamente il listino, si nota che sono sufficienti un pacco da 1 kg e un pacco da 100 g per un totale di £16, che è quindi la minima quantità di denaro necessaria per riseminare il prato.

---

8) D. Per risolvere il quesito è necessario calcolare il punteggio ottenuto da ciascuna ragazza nelle cinque gare, sulla base del sistema di punteggio utilizzato, e paragonarlo con il totale riportato in tabella, per vedere in quale delle cinque gare sono stati usati i jolly. Considerando solo le gare in cui le ragazze sono finite sul podio (visto che il 4° e il 5° posto non danno diritto a punti), la situazione è quella che segue:

- Tia ha ottenuto un 1° posto (6 punti) e due volte un 3° posto (1 + 1 = 2 punti), per un totale di 8 punti. Allora la differenza con il punteggio finale è di 14 – 8 = 6 punti, per cui Tia aveva scelto di giocare il jolly nella gara dei 100 m a ostacoli, che ha effettivamente vinto;
- Jessica ha ottenuto due volte il 1° posto (6 + 6 = 12 punti) e un 3° posto (1 punto), per un totale di 13 punti. Allora la differenza con il punteggio finale è di 19 – 13 = 6 punti, per cui Jessica aveva scelto di giocare il jolly in una delle due gare che ha effettivamente vinto;
- Carolina ha ottenuto un 1° posto (6 punti), due volte un 2° posto (3 + 3 = 6 punti) e un 3° posto, per un totale di 13 punti. Allora la differenza con il punteggio finale è di 14 – 13 = 1 punto, per cui Carolina aveva scelto di giocare il jolly nella gara degli 800 m di corsa, nella quale è arrivata terza;
- Kelly non ha vinto nessuna delle cinque gare;
- Helena ha ottenuto un 1° posto (6 punti) e un 3° posto (1 punto), per un totale di 7 punti. Allora la differenza con il punteggio finale è di 13 – 7 = 6 punti, per cui Helena aveva scelto di giocare il jolly nella gara di lancio del peso, che ha effettivamente vinto.

Le ragazze che hanno vinto una gara in cui avevano deciso di giocare il jolly sono allora 3.

---

9) C. Il ricavato dei biglietti per le poltrone centrali di platea è stato pari a:

$$£21000 \times \frac{60}{100} = £12600$$

per cui i biglietti venduti per questo tipo di posti sono stati

$$12600 \div 28 = 450$$

Poiché ciascuna fila del teatro contiene 30 poltrone, le file della platea centrale sono

$$450 \div 30 = 15$$

10) E. Osservando i cinque pezzi si nota subito che quello A e quello E non sono compatibili tra loro per realizzare il disegno, quindi è necessario provare a incastrare i pezzi B, C e D con A o E, al fine di verificare quale dei due sia adatto a completare il disegno. Il pezzo B, costituendo una delle barre verticali scure, è compatibile sia con A che con E; analogamente il pezzo C può essere posizionato sia accanto al pezzo A che accanto al pezzo E.

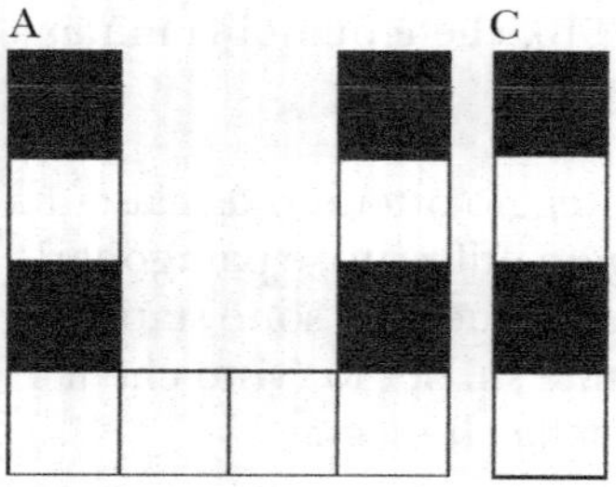

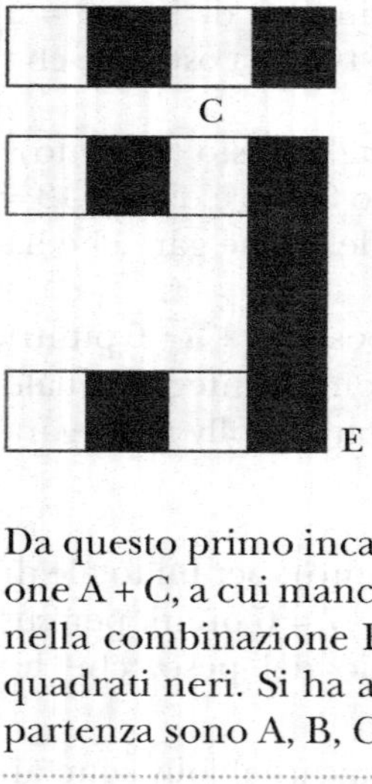

Da questo primo incastro, si nota subito che D può essere contenuto nella combinazione A + C, a cui mancano quattro quadrati neri separati due quadrati bianchi, ma non nella combinazione E + C, a cui mancano quattro quadrati bianchi separati da due quadrati neri. Si ha allora che i pezzi combinabili tra loro per formare il disegno di partenza sono A, B, C e D, e il pezzo E è quindi l'unico non necessario.

11) B. In tutte le coppie presenti nella alternative c'è corrispondenza tra l'opera letteraria e il paese di origine dell'autore ad eccezione dell'alternativa "*The Poems of Rumi – China*"; tale testo infatti fu scritto dal teologo e poeta mistico persiano Gialal al-Din Rumi, nato nel 1207 a Balkh, oggi parte dell'attuale Afghanistan.
The Tale of Genji, letteralemete "Il racconto di Genji", è un romanzo della dama di corte giapponese Murasaki Shikibu vissuta nell'XI secolo e considerato uno dei capolavori della lingua e cultura nipponica; *Edipo re* è la più famosa tragedia del drammaturgo greco Sofocle (496-406 a.C.), ambientata a Tebe; la *Divina Commedia* è opera del sommo poeta fiorentino Dante Alighieri (1265-1321); il *Don Quixote*, in italiano

Don Chisciotte, è il capolavoro letterario dello scrittore e romanziere ispanico Miguel de Cervantes (1547-1616) ed è ambientato in Spagna.

12) E. *Madama Butterfly* è un'opera in 3 atti del compositore italiano Giacomo Puccini, nato a Lucca nel 1858, e rappresentata per la prima volta al Teatro della Scala di Milano nel 1904. Ambientata in Giappone, e pertanto definita "tragedia giapponese", è la storia dell'amore straziante tra la giovane geisha Cho Cho-san e l'ufficiale di marina americano Pinkerton. I due si sposano ma poco dopo Pinkerton abbandona la donna per fare ritorno in patria. La geisha continuerà ad aspettarlo fiduciosa per tre lunghi anni, fino a quando l'uomo tornerà in Giappone con un nuova moglie intenzionato a portare via con sé il figlio avuto con Cho Cho-san; quest'ultima distrutta dal dolore si toglie la vita affondandosi un pugnale nel petto.

13) A. L'unica tra le opere di Shakespeare citate nelle alternative a non essere ambientata in Italia è la commedia *Sogno di una notte di mezza estate* (*A Midsummer Night's Dream*) la cui storia si svolge ad Atene, in un bosco abitato da fate e folletti, dove dominano gli incantesimi operati dal dispettoso folletto Puck. *Molto rumore per nulla* (*Much Ado About Nothing*) è ambientata a Messina, *Otello* a Venezia, *La bisbetica domata* (*The Taming of the Shrew*) a Padova, *Romeo e Giulietta* (*Romeo and Juliet*) a Verona

14) C. *To Kill a Mockingbird*, conosciuto in Italia con il titolo *Il buio oltre la siepe*, è un romanzo della scrittrice americana Nelle Harper Lee nata a Monroeville, in Alabama, nel 1926. L'opera, che valse alla Harper Lee il premio Pulitzer, è ambientata in Alabama negli anni Trenta, all'epoca della segregazione razziale, in cui la rigida divisione tra bianchi e neri fa del razzismo una realtà indiscutibile, accertata e fortemente identitaria. La protagonista è una bambina di sei anni, Scout, orfana di madre e figlia di un avvocato, la quale, attraverso l'esperienza dell'ingiustizia e della diversità tra gli uomini, vedrà necessariamente cambiare la sua percezione del mondo, finendo per crescere prima del tempo nonostante il racconto finisca quando Scout ha appena compiuto nove anni.

15) D. La "teoria dei giochi" è la scienza del cosiddetto *ragionamento strategico*, in quanto studia il comportamento e la decisione di un soggetto (il giocatore) in una situazione di conflitto con altri soggetti (anch'essi giocatori), a lui rivali, in un contesto di interdipendenza strategica.

Il *prisoner's dilemma*, in italiano "dilemma del prigioniero", è uno dei problemi più noti della teoria dei giochi, inventato dal matematico statunitense A.W. Tucker negli anni Cinquanta del Novecento,

Il dilemma si basa su una situazione in cui due persone sono imprigionate, accusate di aver commesso un crimine. Il giudice le confina in due locali separati, senza possibilità di consultarsi, e informa separatamente ciascuna delle conseguenze della sua decisione, che può essere quella di *confessare* o di *negare* di aver commesso il crimine. Gli scenari possibili sono i seguenti:

- se entrambi confessano, sarà comminata loro una pena di 6 mesi di reclusione;
- se entrambi negano, la pena per entrambi sarà di soli 3 mesi, poiché le prove sono di natura indiziaria;

- se uno confessa e l'altro nega, la pena sarà ridotta a chi ha ammesso la responsabilità del crimine a 1 mese di reclusione, mentre sarà di 12 mesi per chi nega.
- La pena preannunciata dal giudice costituisce il cosiddetto *pay off* che ciascun prigioniero sa di dover attendere da ciascun possibile profilo di strategie adottate.

La *soluzione* del dilemma si ottiene considerando che ciascuno dei giocatori adotta una strategia non strettamente dominata da un'altra, il che accade se sceglie una strategia che offre *pay off* comunque non inferiori rispetto a quelli di una strategia alternativa.

16) B. La prima donna ad aver vinto il premio Nobel è stata la chimica e fisica polacca Marie Curie, nata a Varsavia nel 1867. In realtà, la Curie fu insignita due volte del prestigioso riconoscimento: la prima nel 1903, insieme al marito Pierre Curie, fisico e matematico, e al fisico francese Antoine Herni Becquerel, per gli studi sulle radiazioni; la seconda volta, da sola, nel 1911, per la scoperta del radio e del polonio.
MadreTeresa fu premiata con il Nobel per la pace nel 1979; Selma Lagerlöf, Grazia Deledda e Doris Lessing, sono state tutte insignite del Nobel per la letteratura, rispettivamente nel 1909, nel 1926 e nel 2007.

17) A. L'avvenimento accaduto più di recente nella storia mondiale, tra quelli proposti nelle alternative, è la Rivoluzione Russa del 1917, detta "di ottobre" in base alla datazione del calendario giuliano. Essa decretò la fine della dinastia zarista dei Romanov e portò poi alla nascita dell'Unione sovietica.
La caduta dell'Impero Romano d'Occidente è fissata dagli storici alla data 476 d.C., quando il re barbarico Odoacre occupò Ravenna costringendo l'imperatore Romolo Augusto ad abdicare; l'incoronazione di Carlo Magno avvenne nella notte di Natale dell'800 d.C. a Roma, e segnò l'inizio del Sacro Romano Impero; i lavori per la costruzione del celeberrimo e imponente mausoleo del Taj Mahal, situato nella cittadina indiana di Agra, ebbero inizio nel 1632; infine, la rivolta dei Taiping fu una cruenta guerra popolare avvenuta in Cina tra il 1851 e il 1864.

18) B. Tra le alternative proposte, l'unica religione che non è stata rivelata né fondata da un uomo è l'Induismo, caratterizzato da un insieme di correnti religiose, diffusissimo in India, che non ha, appunto, un fondatore, né un unico testo sacro né un'organizzazione istituzionale. Si basa sull'osservazione della legge morale, detta *dharma*, che serve principalmente a salvaguardare e mantenere l'ordine sociale.
Il Confucianesimo è stato fondato dal filosofo cinese Confucio; l'Islam è una religione monoteista rivelata dal profeta Maometto, il cui testo sacro è il Corano; il Cristianesimo, il cui testo sacro è la Bibbia, è una religione fondata sulla rivelazione, cioè sulla venuta e predicazione di Gesù; il Buddismo, tra le più antiche religioni, fu fondato dall'asceta indiano Siddharta, cui fu attribuito il nome di Buddha, che significa "il Risvegliato".

19) E. Il sistema politico comune a molti Stati moderni è di sovente basato sulla separazione dei seguenti 3 poteri: legislativo, ovvero il potere di creare leggi, che spetta al Parlamento o ad analoghi organi di altri enti territoriali; esecutivo, che si occupa dell'applicazione delle leggi, in capo agli organi di governo; giudiziario, regolato e applicato dalla Magistratura e, quindi, dai giudici e dai pubblici ministeri. Tale separazione costituisce il principio fondamentale di uno Stato liberale e democratico.

20) C. La Costituzione della Repubblica Italiana fu approvata dall'Assemblea Costituente il 22 dicembre 1947 e resa esecutiva dall'allora capo provvisorio dello Stato Enrico De Nicola, in seguito primo Presidente della Repubblica. Nata subito dopo la seconda guerra mondiale e dopo il referendum del 2 giugno 1946 con il quale gli Italiani furono chiamati a scegliere tra monarchia e repubblica, conta 139 articoli e 18 disposizioni transitorie finali. Questa Legge fondamentale dello Stato italiano vanta una serie di caratteristiche che la differenziano da quella di altri Paesi, essendo: "votata, lunga, scritta, rigida, compromissoria, democratica, laica e programmatica". Entrò in vigore il 1° gennaio 1948.

21) A. Tra quelli elencati nelle alternative, non costituisce uno scopo né un compito dichiarato delle Nazioni Unite favorire o incoraggiare il commercio pacifico tra le Nazioni. Lo Statuto dell'ONU, firmato a San Francisco il 26 giugno 1945 ed entrato in vigore il successivo 24 ottobre dello stesso anno, riporta negli articoli 1 e 2 che fini delle Nazioni Unite sono "*mantenere la pace e la sicurezza internazionale; sviluppare le relazioni amichevoli tra le Nazioni sulla base del rispetto del principio di uguaglianza tra gli Stati; promuovere la soluzione delle controversie internazionali e risolvere pacificamente le situazioni che potrebbero portare ad una rottura della pace; promuovere il rispetto dei diritti umani e delle libertà fondamentali a vantaggio di tutti gli individui*".

22) E. Tra quelle proposte nelle alternative, la Nazione che non ha adottato l'euro, valuta ufficiale dell'Unione Europea, la cui circolazione ha debuttato il 1° gennaio 2002, è stata la Svezia, Stato che, pur facendo parte dell'UE, non ha riconosciuto l'euro come moneta unica di scambio e continua a utilizzare la sua valuta nazionale, ovvero la corona svedese.

Biologia

23) E. La formula generale degli amminoacidi è $NH_2CHRCOOH$; un atomo di carbonio centrale lega un atomo di idrogeno, un gruppo amminico, un gruppo carbossilico e un gruppo laterale, che differenzia i diversi amminoacidi. Il glucosio ($C_6H_{12}O_6$), un monosaccaride, è un aldoesoso che presenta 4 gruppi idrossilici, ma nessun gruppo carbossilico. Il glicerolo ($C_3H_8O_3$) è un alcool a tre atomi di carbonio che presenta 3 gruppi idrossilici e nessun gruppo carbossilico. Gli acidi grassi sono costituiti da lunghe catene idrocarburiche che terminano con un gruppo carbossilico e non presentano gruppi idrossilici.

24) E. Un tessuto si definisce come un insieme di cellule specializzate e di prodotti cellulari che svolgono un numero relativamente limitato di funzioni. Esistono quattro tipi fondamentali di tessuti: epiteliale, connettivo, muscolare e nervoso. La cartilagine è un tessuto connettivo di sostegno, mentre l'endotelio è un tessuto epiteliale che riveste le superfici interne di cuore e vasi sanguigni. La cute, invece, è un organo formato da due tipi di tessuti: un tessuto epiteliale (epidermide) e un tessuto connettivo (derma).

25) C. Le cellule vegetali, come quelle animali, effettuano costantemente la respirazione cellulare per ricavare energia dall'ossidazione delle molecole organiche, con produzione di CO_2. Le piante sono organismi autotrofi, ovvero capaci di fissare il carbonio grazie al processo di fotosintesi; esse, quindi, possono utilizzare il carbonio inorganico della CO_2 per sintetizzare molecole organiche, a differenza degli organismi eterotrofi, che necessitano del carbonio in forma organica per i loro processi anabolici.

26) D. Durante la fase S dell'interfase, il DNA dei cromosomi viene replicato; pertanto, nel momento in cui la cellula affronta la mitosi, i suoi cromosomi risultano costituiti da due cromatidi identici uniti a livello del centromero. La mitosi consta di 5 fasi: profase, prometafase, metafase, anafase e telofase. L'anafase è lo stadio della mitosi in cui i cromatidi fratelli di ciascun cromosoma vengono separati e tirati ai poli opposti della cellula a opera delle fibre del fuso, in modo da segregare ciascuno in una delle due cellule figlie.

27) C. I virus sono formati da un acido nucleico racchiuso in un capside di natura proteica. Il materiale genetico può essere costituito da DNA o RNA e in entrambi i casi presenta legami fosfodiesterici tra i nucleotidi che lo compongono. Il capside è costituito da molecole proteiche, a loro volta formate da catene di amminoacidi. Alcuni virus sono dotati anche di un involucro membranoso, che deriva dalla membrana plasmatica della cellula ospite da cui sono stati liberati; pertanto, l'involucro contiene gli acidi grassi che compongono i fosfolipidi di membrana.

28) D. Quando il liquido diventa rosso, significa che le membrane plasmatiche delle cellule sono state danneggiate e il pigmento rosso intracellulare è fuoriuscito dalle cellule. Le membrane plasmatiche sono formate da proteine e fosfolipidi, per cui il loro danneggiamento può essere dovuto alla dissoluzione dei fosfolipidi (come avviene in etanolo) o alla denaturazione delle proteine (come avviene a seguito del trattamento con acido cloridrico diluito).

29) A. Quando una cellula si divide per mitosi, produce due cellule figlie identiche alla cellula madre. Poiché a ogni divisione successiva il numero di cellule raddoppia, l'aumento del numero di cellule segue un andamento esponenziale. Il numero di cellule prodotto da n mitosi a partire da una singola cellula madre si calcola come 2^n, nel caso specifico $2^{10} = 1024$.

30) B. Trattandosi di un carattere dominante, gli individui non affetti hanno genotipo omozigote recessivo, mentre quelli affetti possono avere genotipo omozigote dominante oppure eterozigote. Poiché nella progenie c'è un figlio omozigote recessivo e anche il padre è omozigote recessivo, la madre non può che essere eterozigote. I due figli affetti sono anch'essi eterozigoti, essendo nati da madre eterozigote e padre omozigote recessivo.

31) D. Nella divisione parasimpatica del sistema nervoso autonomo, i corpi dei neuroni pregangliari sono localizzati nel tronco encefalico e nei segmenti sacrali del midollo spinale. Gli assoni dei neuroni posti nel midollo spinale fuoriescono da esso attraverso le radici ventrali dei nervi pelvici e contraggono sinapsi con i corpi cellulari dei neuroni gangliari localizzati nei gangli intramurali, posti in prossimità degli organi bersaglio, rappresentati dai visceri della parte inferiore della cavità addominopelvica.

32) A. La cellula osservata ha mostrato una lunghezza massima di 30 mm con un ingrandimento ×30.000. Questo significa che la dimensione reale della cellula in esame è pari a 30 mm/30.000 = 1/1000 mm = 1 mm. Tale dimensione è tipica di molte cellule procariotiche, mentre è inferiore alle dimensioni delle cellule eucariotiche. Pertanto, al microscopio si sta osservando una cellula di stafilococco.

33) C. Gli enzimi di restrizione sono endonucleasi di derivazione batterica che tagliano il DNA a doppio filamento in corrispondenza di sequenze specifiche, dette siti di restrizione. Il taglio consiste nell'idrolisi dei legami fosfodiesterici tra i nucleotidi del DNA. La ligasi, invece, è un enzima che forma legami fosfodiesterici tra nucleotidi adiacenti.

34) B. Nei tessuti metabolicamente attivi, che producono grandi quantità di CO_2, l'emoglobina ha elevata affinità per la CO_2 e bassa affinità per l'O_2, cosicché in tali tessuti essa rilascia ossigeno e lega anidride carbonica. Viceversa, nei polmoni, dove la concentrazione di CO_2 è bassa, l'emoglobina ha elevata affinità per l'O_2 e bassa affinità per la CO_2, cosicché rilascia anidride carbonica e lega ossigeno.

35) B. All'osservazione microscopica, nel sarcomero, l'unità contrattile del tessuto muscolare striato, si distinguono una banda A scura, corrispondente alla zona di sovrapposizione di filamenti sottili (di actina) e spessi (di miosina), una banda H al centro della banda A, un po' più chiara, corrispondente ai soli filamenti spessi, e due bande I chiare laterali alla banda A, corrispondenti ai soli filamenti sottili. Dato che la contrazione prevede lo scorrimento dei filamenti sottili su quelli spessi, l'unica delle tre bande che non si accorcia è la banda A.

36) C. I linfociti B sono le cellule del sistema immunitario responsabili dell'immunità anticorpo-mediata (o umorale). Sono prodotti nel midollo osseo rosso a partire da cellule staminali progenitrici e in questa sede maturano. Essi esprimono geni che codificano per gli anticorpi (o immunoglobuline), attraverso i quali legano antigeni specifici nel corso della risposta immunitaria specifica.

37) C. La contrazione muscolare è mediata dagli ioni Ca^{2+}, che vengono rilasciati nel citoplasma della fibra muscolare dal lume del reticolo sarcoplasmatico all'arrivo di un potenziale d'azione; gli ioni Ca^{2+} si legano alla troponina, portando alla liberazione dei siti di legame per la miosina sui filamenti di actina. La trasmissione degli impulsi nervosi a livello delle sinapsi è mediata dagli ioni Ca^{2+}, che inducono il rilascio del neurotrasmettitore dalle vescicole presenti nel terminale presinaptico. La conversione dell'energia luminosa in energia chimica nel processo di fotosintesi e la fosforilazione ossidativa nei mitocondri si basano sull'uso di gradienti protonici (di ioni H^+) per la sintesi di ATP.

38) A. Il fatto che non siano avvenute mutazioni somatiche successivamente alla formazione dello zigote implica che tutte le cellule dell'organismo adulto, derivando da divisioni mitotiche, sono tutte geneticamente identiche tra loro e allo zigote. Tutte le cellule contengono gli stessi geni, ma li esprimono in maniera differenziale.

39) C. La regione 1 corrisponde alla capsula di Bowman, la regione 2 al tratto discendente dell'ansa di Henle, la regione 3 al tubulo contorto distale e la regione 4 al dotto collettore. Nella regione 1, l'ultrafiltrato glomerulare ha una composizione analoga a quella del plasma deproteinato. Nella regione 2 avviene principalmente il riassorbimento dell'acqua. Il tubulo contorto distale riassorbe ioni, ma è impermeabile all'acqua e all'urea. Nel dotto collettore viene riversata l'urina.

40) E. Partendo dalla sequenza dell'individuo P, quella dell'individuo Q si genera per delezione della terza G di P, inserzione della terza G di Q e sostituzione della seconda C di P con la terza A di Q.

Chimica

41) E. Le particelle elementari che costituiscono gli atomi sono i protoni (carichi positivamente), i neutroni (privi di carica elettrica) e gli elettroni (carichi negativamente). Protoni e neutroni sono contenuti nel nucleo atomico, mentre gli elettroni orbitano intorno a esso. Gli atomi neutri possiedono lo stesso numero di protoni e neutroni, i cationi (ioni positivi) contengono un numero di protoni maggiore del numero di elettroni e gli anioni (ioni negativi) posseggono più elettroni che protoni.

42) D. Un indicatore universale è una soluzione costituita da una miscela di diversi indicatori acido-base di uso comune con intervalli di viraggio differenti; una simile soluzione ha la proprietà di cambiare colore in modo pressoché continuo al variare del pH della soluzione in cui è immerso. Esso conferisce una colorazione verde alle soluzioni neutre (pH 7), mentre vira verso il blu-violetto a pH basici e verso il giallo-rosso a pH acidi. Pertanto, poiché in questo caso si parte da una soluzione basica e si aggiunge acido fino a raggiungere la neutralità, il viraggio è dal violetto al blu al verde.

43) C. Una delle proprietà colligative delle soluzioni è l'abbassamento crioscopico: l'aggiunta di un soluto non volatile a un solvente determina l'abbassamento del punto di fusione della soluzione rispetto a quello del solvente puro. In questo caso, l'aggiunta di zucchero al ghiaccio determina un abbassamento della temperatura di fusione del ghiaccio al di sotto di –1 °C, per cui a –1 °C il ghiaccio si converte in acqua liquida.

44) E. Gli isomeri strutturali (o costituzionali) sono composti che presentano la stessa formula bruta, ma differente connettività tra gli atomi di carbonio. Nei casi 1 e 3, i due composti sono formati dagli stessi atomi, ma questi sono legati in modo diverso. Nel caso 2, invece, le due formule indicano lo stesso composto.

45) A. L'elemento Z appartiene al Gruppo II della Tavola Periodica, quello dei metalli alcalino-terrosi. Si tratta di elementi che posseggono 2 elettroni nel guscio di valenza, per cui reagiscono con l'ossigeno formando ossidi di formula ZO che sono solidi a temperatura ambiente, non conducono l'elettricità e reagiscono con gli acidi. Quando reagiscono con l'acqua a temperatura ambiente, i metalli alcalino-terrosi producono i relativi idrossidi ZOH e idrogeno gassoso.

46) E. Soltanto l'equazione 3 rappresenta una reazione redox: al primo membro l'azoto ha numeri di ossidazione (n.o.) –3 e +5, mentre al secondo membro ha numero di ossidazione +1. Nella reazione 1, sia al primo che al secondo membro, il litio ha n.o. +1, l'idrogeno –1, l'alluminio +3 e il cloro –1. Nella reazione 2, sia al primo che al secondo membro, l'azoto ha n.o. +3, l'idrogeno +1 e l'ossigeno –2.

47) C. Una molecola è dotata di momento dipolare permanente quando la risultante dei dipoli di legame all'interno di essa è diversa da zero. Un legame è dotato di momento di dipolo quando i due atomi tra cui si instaura hanno elettronegatività diverse, per cui gli elettroni di legame sono attratti più fortemente dall'atomo maggiormente elettronegativo, che assume una carica parziale negativa, generando una carica parziale positiva sull'atomo meno elettronegativo. Sia l'ammoniaca che l'acqua hanno geometria tetraedrica, con l'atomo centrale (N e O, rispettivamente) più elettronegativo, per cui sono molecole dotate di momento di dipolo permanente. Al contrario, l'anidride carbonica, pur presentando due legami dotati di momento di dipolo, ha geometria lineare, cosicché i due momenti di dipolo opposti si neutralizzano a vicenda e la molecola risulta nel complesso non polare.

48) E. Il punto di ebollizione degli alogenuri di idrogeno (fatta eccezione per HF) è influenzato principalmente dall'intensità delle forze di dispersione di London (dipolo indotto-dipolo indotto) tra le molecole; tali interazioni deboli sono tanto più intense quanto maggiore è la grandezza delle molecole. Pertanto, essendo la molecola di HI più grande di quella di HBr, HI ha un punto di ebollizione superiore a quello di HBr.

49) A. Per preparare 500 mL di una soluzione di diossido di zolfo (SO_2) 3.0 mol/L, sono necessarie 3.0 mol/L × 0.5 L = 1.5 mol. La massa molecolare di SO_2 si calcola come $A_r(SO_2) = A_r(S) + 2A_r(O) = 32 + 32 = 64$ g/mol. La massa di SO_2 richiesta è pari a $A_r(SO_2) \times mol(SO_2) = 64$ g/mol × 1.5 mol = 96 g.

50) C. 8 grammi del composto in esame contengono 3 g di C, 1 g di H e, di conseguenza, (8 – 3 – 1) = 4 g di O. Le moli di carbonio sono (3 g)/(12 g/mol) = 0.25 mol, quelle di idrogeno (1 g)/(1 g/mol) = 1 mol e quelle di ossigeno (4 g)/(16 g/mol) = 0.25 mol. Pertanto, il rapporto molare tra C:H:O è pari a 0.25:1:0.25, equivalente a 1:4:1. La formula molecolare del composto è quindi CH_4O.

51) E. Sia il protone che il neutrone hanno una massa di circa 1 u.m.a., mentre l'elettrone ha massa trascurabile. L'isotopo più comune dell'idrogeno, che contiene un protone e un elettrone, ma è privo di neutroni, ha massa atomica relativa pari a 1.0 u.m.a. Il trizio, che contiene un protone, un elettrone e due neutroni, ha massa atomica relativa pari a 3.0 u.m.a. La massa atomica relativa di un campione di idrogeno che contiene eguali quantità dei due isotopi è pari alla media aritmetica delle masse dei due isotopi, ovvero (1 + 3) u.m.a./2 = 2 u.m.a.

52) A. La costante di equilibrio di una reazione si calcola come il rapporto tra il prodotto delle concentrazioni dei prodotti all'equilibrio elevate ai rispettivi coefficienti stechiometrici e il prodotto delle concentrazioni dei reagenti all'equilibrio elevate ai rispettivi coefficienti stechiometrici. Pertanto, in questo caso, $K_c = ([C]^2[D])/([A][B]^2) = [(0.5 \text{ mol}/V)^2\ (0.8 \text{ mol}/V)]/[(0.5 \text{ mol}/V)\ (0.2 \text{ mol}/V)^2] = 10$.

Fisica e Matematica

53) C. Ricordando che $(am)^n = a^{m \cdot n}$ e $a^m \cdot a^n = a^{m+n}$, si ha:

$$\frac{8^{2n} \cdot 4^n}{2^n} = \frac{(2^3)^{2n} \cdot (2^2)^n}{2^n} = \frac{2^{6n} \cdot 2^{2n}}{2^n} = 2^{6n+2n-n} = 2^{7n}.$$

54) A. Il range è dato da:

$$\Delta m = m_{max} - m_{min},$$

da cui:

$$m_{max} = m_{min} + \Delta m = 1{,}8 + 0{,}7 = 2{,}5 \text{ kg}.$$

Poiché il valore medio $\bar{m}$ si ottiene come:

$$\bar{m} = \frac{m_1 + m_2 + m_3}{3} = \frac{m_{min} + m_{med} + m_{max}}{3} = \frac{1{,}8 \text{ kg} + m_{med} + 2{,}5 \text{ kg}}{3} = \frac{4{,}3 \text{ kg} + m_{med}}{3},$$

si ha:

$$m_{med} = 3 \cdot \bar{m} - 4{,}3 \text{ kg} = 3 \cdot (2{,}1 \text{ kg}) - 4{,}3 \text{ kg} = 2{,}0 \text{ kg}.$$

55) E. I tre numeri, scomposti in fattori primi, sono: $360 = 2^3 \cdot 3^2 \cdot 5$, $500 = 2^2 \cdot 5^3$ e $700 = 2^2 \cdot 5^2 \cdot 7$. Il massimo comun divisore si ottiene prendendo i fattori comuni con minore esponente:

$$2^2 \cdot 5.$$

56) D. Risolviamo l'equazione fratta, avendo posto x diversa da 0 e 2 così da moltiplicare a destra e a sinistra per $x(x-2)$ dopo avere fatto il minimo comune multiplo in entrambi i membri:

$$\frac{3}{x}+\frac{2}{x-2}=1$$

$$\frac{3(x-2)}{x(x-2)}+\frac{2x}{x(x-2)}=\frac{x(x-2)}{x(x-2)}$$

$$3(x-2)+2x=x(x-2)$$

$$3x-6+2x=x^2-2x$$

$$x^2-7x+6=0.$$

Si tratta di un trinomio notevole la cui somma delle radici corrisponde all'opposto del coefficiente del termine lineare, in particolare a 7. Non è necessario, pertanto, trovare le singole soluzioni calcolando il discriminante.

57) D. La velocità massima è: $v = v_0 + at = 0 + (4{,}0\ \text{m/s}^2) \cdot 5{,}0\ \text{s} = 20\ \text{m/s}$.
Questa è la velocità con cui viene percorso l'ultimo tratto di moto rettilineo uniforme:

$\Delta s = vt_2 = (20\ \text{m/s}) \cdot (20\ \text{s}) = 400\ \text{m}$.

58) B. La spinta di Archimede è data da:

$$F_A = m_0 g = \rho_0 V g = (1{,}20\ \text{g/cm}^3)(200\ \text{cm}^3)(10{,}0\ \text{N/kg}) = (240\ \text{g})(10{,}0\ \text{N/kg}) =$$
$$= (0{,}240\ \text{kg})(10{,}0\ \text{N/kg})$$
$$F_A = 2{,}40\ \text{N}.$$

59) A. La forza di Coulomb è direttamente proporzionale a ciascuna carica e inversamente proporzionale al quadrato delle due cariche. Se la prima carica triplica e la seconda quadruplica, allora la forza aumenta di un fattore 12. Ma poiché la distanza raddoppia, allora tale fattore va moltiplicato per 1/4, essendo inversamente proporzionale al quadrato della distanza, ottenendo così un fattore 3. La forza, quindi, triplica.

60) C. La trasformazione in questione è una trasformazione isoterma, rappresentata nel piano *pV* di Clapeyron da un ramo di iperbole equilatera posto sul primo quadrante. Tale funzione è decrescente e tende asintoticamente a zero, per cui la derivata è negativa e decresce al crescere di *x*.

IMAT
a.a. 2020/2021

General Knowledge and Logical Reasoning

1) Thousands of books and blogs – and quite a bit of legitimate science – sing the praises of positivity. Optimistic, happy people tend to be healthier, more physically active and more successful. They may even live longer. But as shown by research, positivity, when deployed at the wrong time or in the wrong amount, can have negative effects. For example, when it comes to waiting for the results of an exam or a job interview, 'being prepared for the worst' is shown to be a better strategy for protecting ourselves than categorical optimism. When it comes to health, negative thinking spurs people into seeking information and engaging in healthy behaviour. Finally, relentlessly positive people may seem dismissive or insensitive to friends who are having difficulties, seeming to make light of their problems. Which one of the following best expresses the main conclusion of the above argument?

A. Research into positivity has so far ignored its potential downsides
B. Positive thinking is not always helpful
C. Being overly positive can damage our relationships with friends
D. Negative thinking about health can be beneficial
E. People who think positively live longer

2) Although the idea of a driverless vehicle seems like the stuff of science fiction, we are moving very close to the reality of self-driving cars. But we are so engrossed in the technology that we are ignoring the legal implications – and legislating for new scenarios takes time. A whole new set of questions is raised by the development of these machines. One example is the question of who takes responsibility when an accident happens. Given that the vast majority of crashes are caused in part at least by human error, self-driving cars should have the capacity to save lives. But they will not be perfect. So if an accident happens, who is responsible? The owner of the car, or the manufacturer of the car? The car itself cannot be prosecuted or made to pay damages. Which one of the following can be drawn as a conclusion from the above passage?

A. New laws are needed to determine liability for accidents involving driverless cars
B. We should not continue to develop self-driving cars
C. All the technology needed to create a self-driving car is already available
D. It will be impossible to determine liability for accidents involving driverless cars
E. The design of driverless cars will continue to improve with time

3) In 1938 the Dutch artist Piet Mondrian left Paris to escape the threat of German invasion and went to live in London, where he painted what are now regarded as his best works. Mondrian had the option of moving to a more rural area in

England, but chose London because of his love of the diverse and vibrant culture of big cities. This explains why London has more artists living in it than any other city in England.
Which one of the following is an underlying assumption of the above passage?

A. Other big cities in England have the same attractive features as London
B. Artists can only create great works if they are happy and relaxed
C. Other artists make the same choice as Mondrian for the same reasons
D. London is a big city because all the artists who live there boost its size and population
E. There is less inspiration for artists in rural areas

4) In some countries, prisoners may purchase books with the money they earn by working. Hence receiving gifts of books may discourage prisoners from undertaking paid work while in prison. This work is important in building self-esteem and encouraging a work ethic among prisoners. In any case, prisoners have access to books through the prison library. Therefore prisoners should not be allowed to receive parcels containing books from friends or relatives while they are serving their sentence.
Which one of the following, if true, most strengthens the above argument?

A. The range of books available in prison libraries is limited
B. Many prisoners have difficulty finding work when they are released because of their low level of literacy
C. Prisoners have to purchase a range of items from their wages, including a television licence
D. Many parcels of books sent by relatives or friends have been found to contain illegal drugs
E. Prisoners often read detective stories which may encourage them to glamorise crime

5) People who take their holidays in Las Vegas love to gamble. Gerry will be going to France for his holiday so he must not like gambling.
Which one of the following most closely parallels the reasoning used in the above argument?

A. You always walk when you are visiting your sister. You are not visiting your sister so that's why you are taking the car
B. In England cars are driven on the left side of the road. We are driving on the left, so we must be in England
C. People who eat a lot of sweets have rotten teeth. You eat a lot of sweets, so your teeth must be rotten
D. You have to find the password to complete the game. You haven't finished the game yet so you can't have found the password
E. People who live in the city hate traffic jams. You live in the country so you must like traffic jams

6) LoCost sells three different types of washing powder: Zoom, Zap and Ownbrand. Zoom is a double concentrate brand needing only half the amount of powder used by the other two brands. Which one of the boxes of powder below represents best value for money?

A.
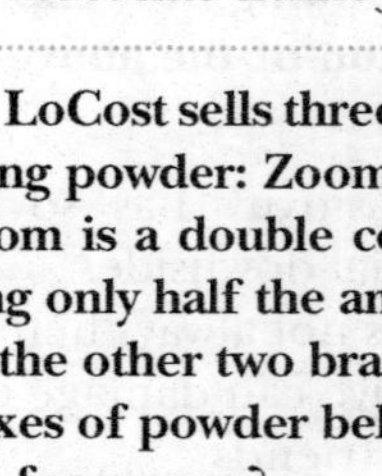

B.
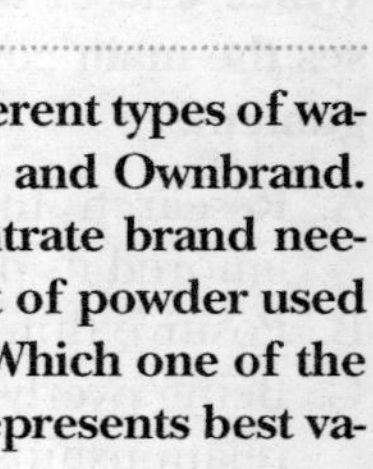

C.

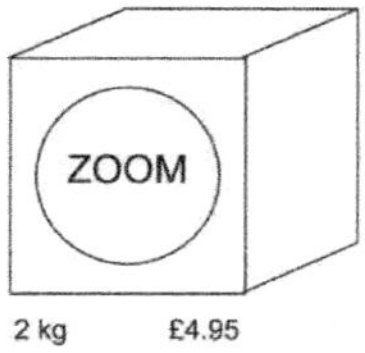

D.

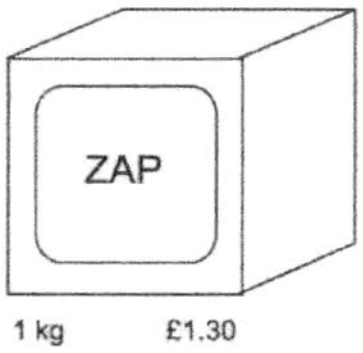

E.

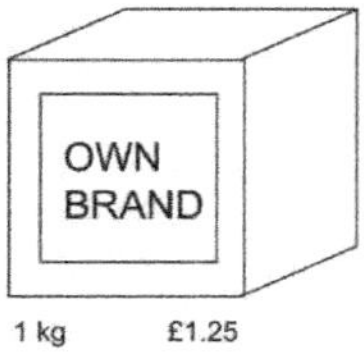

7) 36% of the contents of a tin of sweets have been eaten. Today, 25% of the remaining sweets will be eaten. The same number of sweets will be eaten on each of the following 2 days.
What % of its original contents will it then contain?

A. 9
B. 16
C. 15
D. 24
E. 25

8) As part of a maths project, a class of 30 children conduct a survey amongst themselves of how many brothers and sisters they have. They each write their name in the appropriate space on the chart below. No one in the class has a brother or sister who is also in the class.

		BROTHERS			
		0	1	2	3
SISTERS	0	Sara Jordan Ben Ellie	Kylie Gita Tamsin Sam Adam Bethany Craig	Leroy Gemma	Callum
	1	Kate Jessica Robin Vikram Sally Scott Chloe Oliver	Rajiv Emily Fatima	Paul	
	2	Aruna	Candice Marvin		
	3		Phoebe		

How many of the 30 families involved in the survey have a total of 3 or more children?

A. 7
B. 6
C. 11
D. 8
E. 10

9) Jeff is looking to buy a new car. He will only be using it for commuting to his workplace for 1 year and will have a total annual mileage of 20 000. He wants to buy the car which would make his total spend over the year, including the initial cost of the car, the lowest.

type of car	*cost to fill or charge tank* ($)	*distance on full tank or charge (miles)*	*car cost* ($)
autogas	30	200	10000
diesel	50	500	12000
petrol	50	400	10000
hydrogen	50	200	9500
electric	5	200	12500

Using the table above, which type of car should he buy?

A. autogas
B. diesel
C. hydrogen
D. petrol
E. electric

10) A piece of paper is laid on a table in landscape orientation (i.e. the longer side running left to right and the shorter side running top to bottom).
This piece of paper is then folded in half four times, alternately by moving the left hand side across over the right hand side and folding, and by moving the top half down over the bottom half and then folding. After each fold a dot is made with a pen in the centre of the face showing on the table.
After the four folds and four dots, the paper is unfolded in the reverse sequence and is then turned over so that the four dots are showing.
What is the pattern of the dots on the paper? (Dotted lines represent the fold marks)

A.
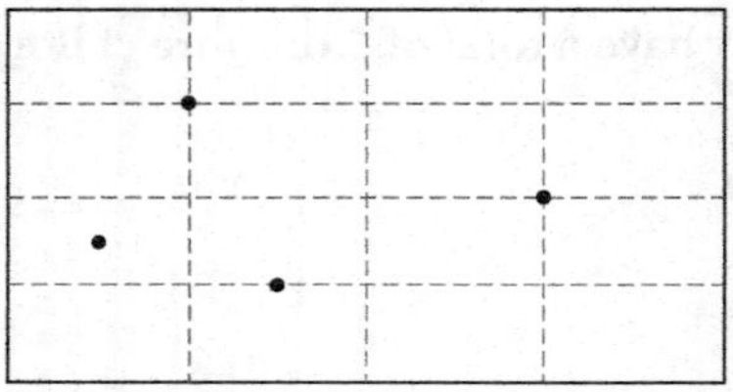

B.
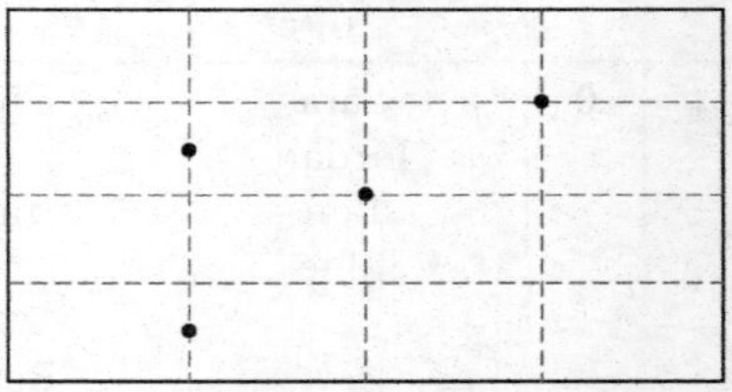

C.
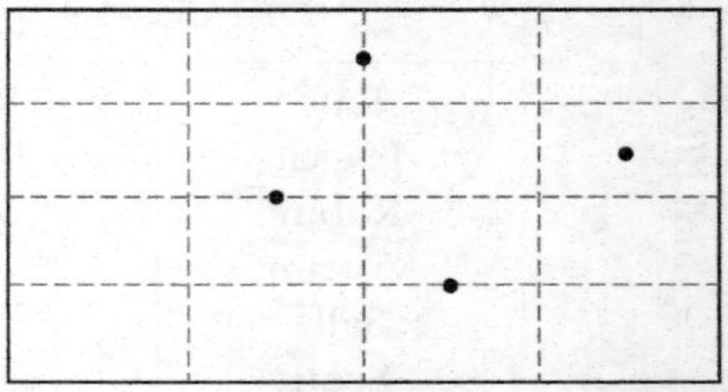

D.
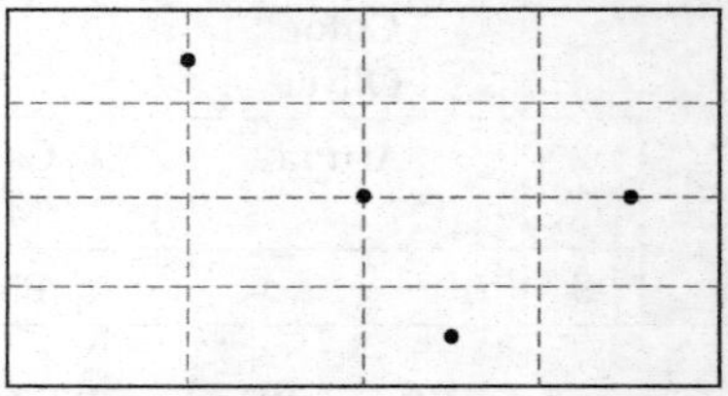

E.
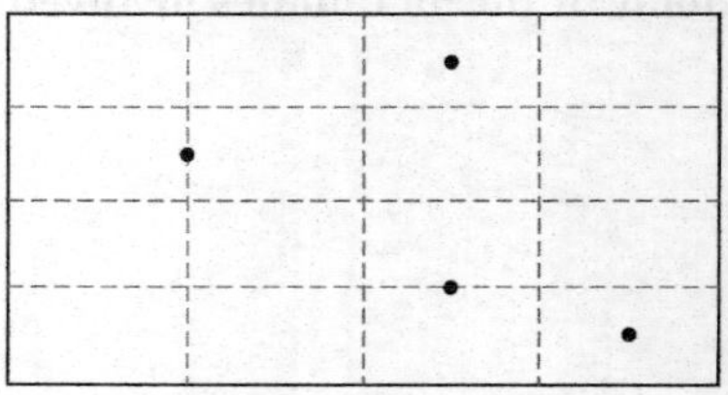

11) Which of the following languages is not a member of the 'Romance' language family?

A. Spanish
B. Catalan
C. French
D. Bulgarian
E. Romanian

12) Which of these people did NOT win the Nobel Prize in Literature?

A. Bob Dylan
B. Charles Dickens
C. Pablo Neruda
D. Harold Pinter
E. Thomas Mann

13) Which one of the following is the director of the film *Amarcord*?

A. François Truffaut
B. Alfred Hitchcock
C. Francis Ford Coppola
D. Stanley Kubrick
E. Federico Fellini

14) Which of the following books was NOT written by Primo Levi?

A. *If This Is a Man*
B. *The Truce*
C. *If Not Now, When?*
D. *Beyond Good and Evil*
E. *The Drowned and the Saved*

15) The name of the German mathematician Carl Friedrich Gauss is famously associated with:

A. the sine function
B. Bayes' theorem
C. the normal distribution curve
D. the law of supply and demand
E. the uncertainty principle

16) Which one of the following was the first human to complete an orbit of the Earth in 1961?

A. Yuri Gagarin
B. Neil Armstrong
C. Buzz Aldrin
D. Valentina Tereshkova
E. John Glenn

17) Which one of the following pairs of archipelago/country is NOT correct?

A. Hawaii – United States of America
B. Azores – Portugal
C. Canary Islands – Spain
D. Galapagos Islands – Ecuador
E. Cape Verde – Brazil

18) Which one of the following international organisations maintains a list of the World Heritage Sites of outstanding cultural or natural importance?

A. WHO
B. UNESCO
C. UNICEF
D. OECD
E. WTO

19) Which one of the following pairs of currency/country is NOT correct?

A. Rupee – India
B. Peso – Argentina
C. Baht – Thailand
D. Rand – South Africa
E. Euro – Hungary

20) Which of the following institutions of the Republic of Italy is democratically elected by direct universal suffrage?

A. Government
B. President of the Republic
C. Senate of the Republic
D. President of the Council of Ministers
E. High Council of the Judiciary

21) Which one of the following is NOT a principle of the sharing economy?

A. Access is preferable to ownership

B. Transparent and open data increases innovation
C. Stranger danger can be overcome
D. Competition is dangerous
E. Unused value is wasted value

22) The *Fields medal* is a prestigious award in the field of:

A. Mathematics
B. Psychology
C. Biology
D. Economics
E. Music

Biology

23) The diagram represents the fluid mosaic model of a cell membrane.

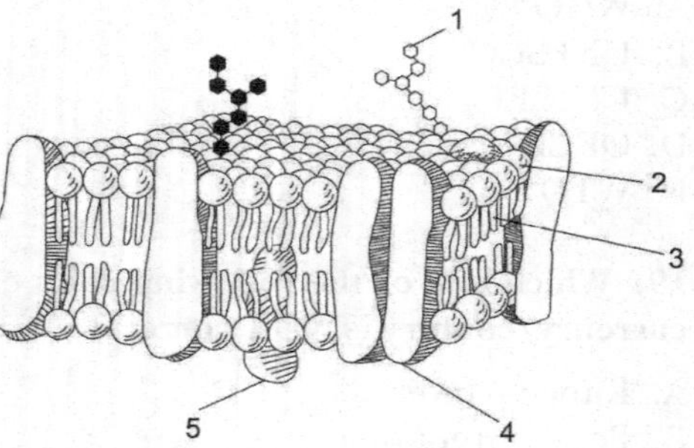

Which one of the labels 1-5 shows a hydrophobic region of a molecule?

A. 2
B. 3
C. 1
D. 4
E. 5

24) The structure of the amino acid asparagine is shown. In each image (V-Z) a part of the structure is enclosed by a line.

V

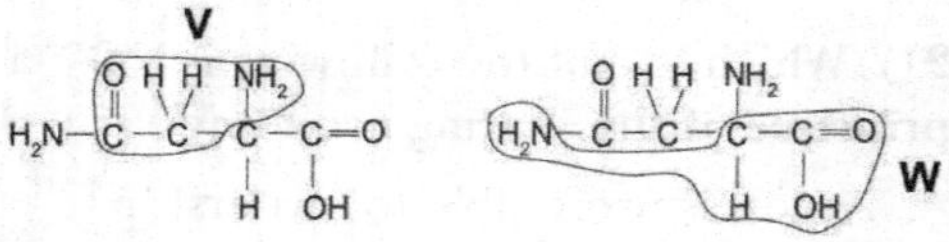

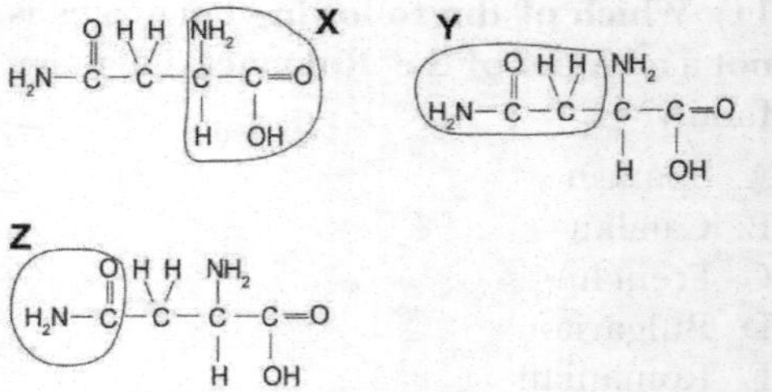

Which line completely encloses the part of the molecule that is common to all naturally-occurring amino acids and the R-group for this amino acid?

row	*common to all amino acids*	*R-group for this amino acid*
1	X	Z
2	Y	X
3	W	V
4	V	W
5	X	Y

A. row 5
B. row 2
C. row 3
D. row 4
E. row 1

25) Which of the following statements about healthy living organisms are correct?
1 They are made up of one or more cells
2 They have DNA as the genetic material
3 They use energy to stay alive when their surroundings change
4 They undergo phases of growth

A. 1, 2 and 4 only
B. 1, 3 and 4 only
C. 2, 3 and 4 only
D. 1, 2 and 3 only
E. 1, 2, 3 and 4

26) The diagram shows how recombinant DNA can be used to make cotton plants produce an insect toxin. The insect toxin kills any insect that can damage the cotton crop.

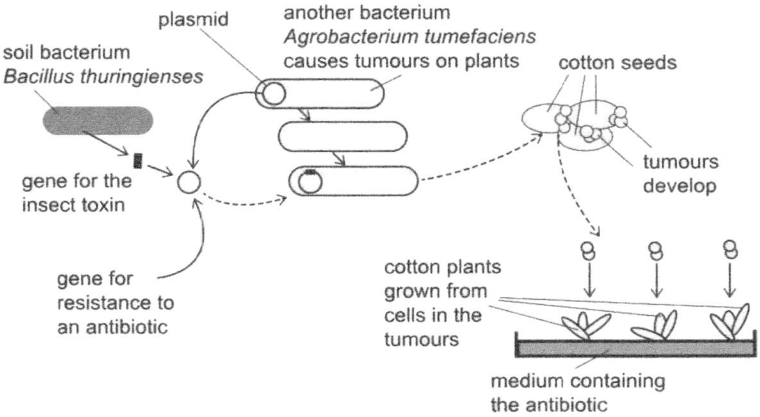

What are the TWO functions of the *Agrobacterium tumefaciens* bacteria in this process?
1 They stimulate cell division in cotton plant seeds
2 They supply the plasmid vector
3 They are the source of the gene for the production of the insect toxin
4 They are the source of the gene for antibiotic resistance

A. 1 and 3 only
B. 1 and 4 only
C. 2 and 3 only
D. 1 and 2 only
E. 2 and 4 only

27) Which one of the structures listed is NOT involved in the reabsorption of water in a healthy human?

A. Distal convoluted tubule
B. Glomerulus
C. Collecting duct
D. Loop of Henle
E. Proximal convoluted tubule

28) Which of the following statements about bile in the digestive system are correct?
1 It emulsifies fat globules
2 It dilutes the contents of the small intestine
3 It lowers the activation energy of lipase
4 It helps to reduce the acidity of the contents leaving the stomach

A. 1, 2 and 3 only
B. 1 and 4 only
C. 2 and 3 only
D. 1 and 2 only
E. 1, 2 and 4 only

29) The heart of a developing human fetus normally has a hole in the septum. The septum separates the right atrium and the left atrium.
Which one of the statements about the circulation in the developing fetus with a hole in the septum is correct?

A. Blood entering the right atrium can bypass the lungs and go to the rest of the body
B. Blood in the right atrium may return directly to the vena cava

C. Blood in the pulmonary artery will go directly to the aorta
D. The maximum pressure in the aorta is the same as the maximum pressure in the contracting atrium
E. The atrioventricular node will not cause ventricular systole

30) Which row shows three structures found in a healthy human male liver cell, in order of size from largest to smallest?
[Assume that there are no mutations in the cell.]

row	*structures from largest to smallest*				
1	Y chromosome	→	nucleosome	→	histone
2	nucleosome	→	X chromosome	→	Y chromosome
3	histone	→	nucleosome	→	X chromosome
4	Y chromosome	→	X chromosome	→	histone
5	X chromosome	→	histone	→	nucleosome

A. row 4
B. row 2
C. row 3
D. row 1
E. row 5

31) What is the correct order of the following events that occur immediately after acetylcholine binds to postsynaptic receptors of a muscle fibre, causing the muscle to contract?

1 Ca^{2+} ions diffuse into the sarcoplasm

2 The muscle fibre membrane is depolarised

3 The myosin binding site on the actin filament is uncovered

A. 3, 2, 1
B. 2, 3, 1
C. 1, 2, 3
D. 1, 3, 2
E. 2, 1, 3

32) Which of the following is/are features of HIV?
1 It has a capsid
2 It contains DNA
3 It has ribosomes

A. 2 only
B. 1 only
C. 3 only
D. 1 and 2 only
E. 2 and 3 only

33) The diagrams show five different microscopic structures. The structures are not drawn to the same scale. Which of these structures is the smallest?

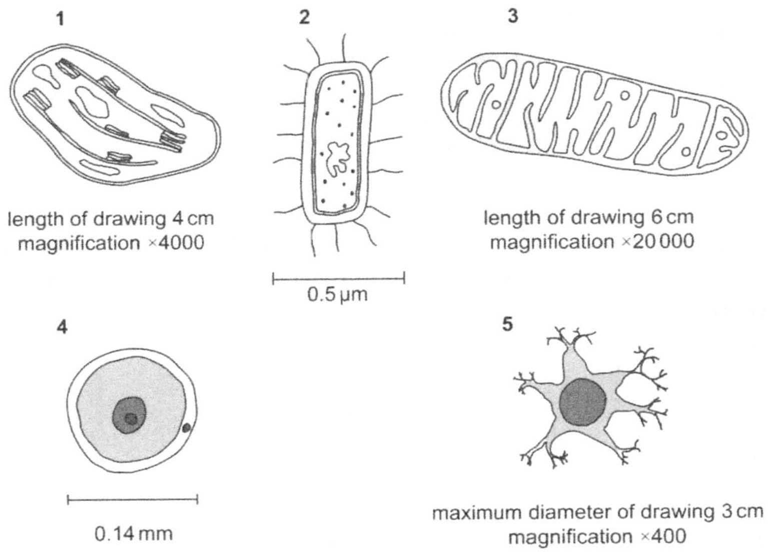

A. 3
B. 1
C. 2
D. 4
E. 5

34) Which of the following healthy cells contain circular DNA?
1 *Escherichia coli*
2 *Saccharomyces cerevisiae* (yeast)
3 human liver cell

A. 2 only
B. 1 and 2 only
C. 2 and 3 only
D. 1, 2 and 3
E. 1 only

35) The occurrence of which of the following could allow you to distinguish between the processes of DNA replication and transcription?
1 The breaking of hydrogen bonds
2 The formation of hydrogen bonds
3 The formation of phosphodiester bonds

A. 2 only
B. 3 only
C. 1 and 2 only
D. 1 only
E. none of them

36) In 1981, an immature male finch (*Geospiza conirostris*) arrived on an island in the Galapagos.
This male finch was similar to finches of the species (*G. fortis*) living on the island. However, *G.conirostris* was 70% larger than *G. fortis* and had a distinctly different song.

The diagram shows how, after observing further generations, a new species has evolved.

G. conirostris immigrant male X *G. fortis* female

↓

one of F_1 X *G. fortis* female

↓

from F_2 further generations have bred only with F_1 or F_2 finches

↓

population of new species

The success of the new species is due to its larger bill and body size and its unique song. Which of the following terms is/are illustrated by this information?
1 sympatric speciation
2 reproductive isolation
3 post-zygotic isolationv

A. 1 only
B. 2 only
C. 3 only
D. 1 and 2 only
E. 2 and 3 only

37) A single base mutation occurs in a gene. Which of the following is/are possible effects on the protein produced as a result of this mutation?
1 The protein has an altered tertiary structure
2 The protein is shorter in length
3 The protein is unchanged

A. 1 and 2 only
B. 1 and 3 only
C. 2 and 3 only
D. 1, 2 and 3
E. 1 only

38) Which one of the following is an example of catabolism in healthy human cells?

A. Attachment of tRNA to mRNA
B. Formation of RuBisCo
C. Oxidation of NADH
D. ATP made during glycolysis
E. Replication of DNA

39) The diagrams show animal cells from organisms that sexually reproduce. Each diagram shows a single cell containing chromosomes during cell division. Which one of the following diagrams has a correct description for a cell from an organism with a haploid number of 4? [Assume that the sex of the organism is inherited in the same way as in humans.]

A.

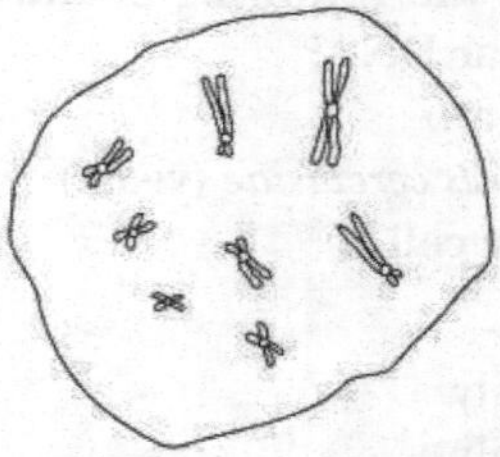

Cell from a male organism with 16 chromatids during prophase of meiosis

B.

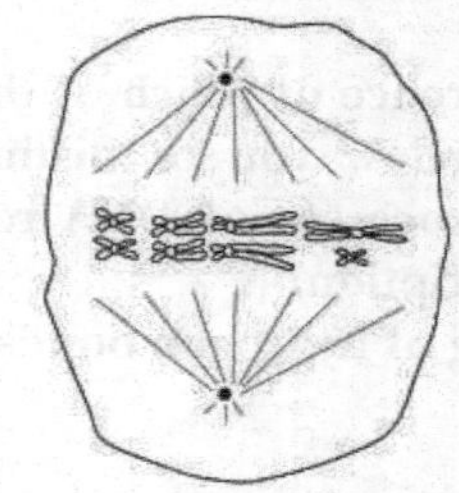

Cell from a female organism with 8 chromosomes during metaphase of mitosis

C.

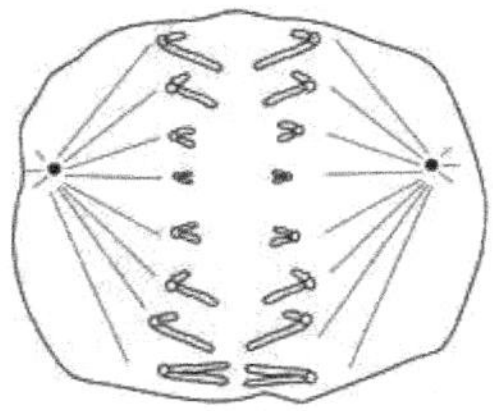

Cell from a male organism with a diploid number of 8 during anaphase of first division of meiosis

D.

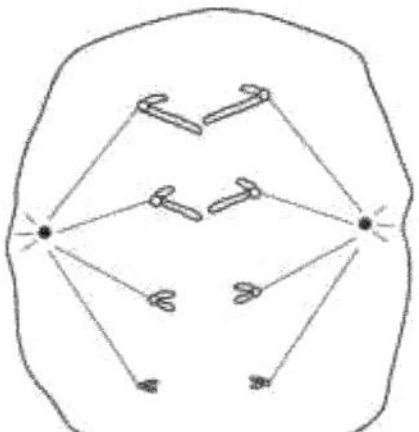

Cell has a diploid number of 8 showing the chromosomes during anaphase of mitosis

E.

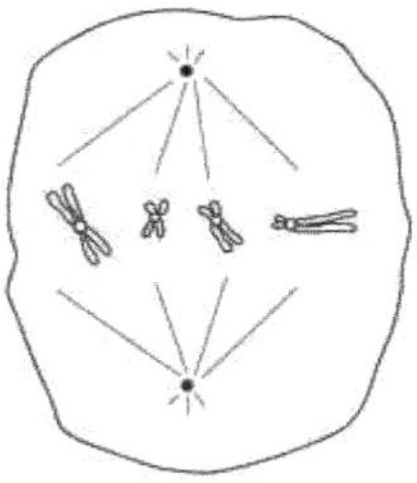

Cell from a female organism with 4 chromatids during metaphase of mitosis

40) Which one of the following will be caused by an appropriate stimulus of a rod cell in the retina of a healthy human eye?

A. An opsin and retinol will form rhodopsin
B. Rhodopsin will form an opsin and retinol
C. Rhodopsin will form opsonin and retinol
D. Rhodopsin will form an opsin and retinal
E. An opsin and retinal will form rhodopsin

Chemistry

41) What does the formula Br_2 represent?

A. A compound of the element bromine
B. Two separate atoms of the element bromine
C. A molecule of the element bromine
D. A molecule of the compound bromine
E. Two bromide ions

42) Sucrose, $C_{12}H_{22}O_{11}$, is added to water at 20 °C until no more sucrose will dissolve. Four statements are made about sucrose and the solution that is produced:
1 A saturated solution of sucrose is produced
2 The freezing point of the solution is 0 °C
3 Sucrose is a non-polar substance
4 Sucrose is the solute
Which two statements are correct?

A. 3 and 4 only
B. 1 and 4 only
C. 1 and 2 only
D. 2 and 3 only
E. 3 and 1 only

43) Which of the following is the equation for there action of magnesium with excess cold water?

A. $2Mg + 2H_2O \rightarrow 2MgOH + H_2$
B. $Mg + H_2O \rightarrow MgO + H_2$
C. $2Mg + H_2O \rightarrow Mg_2O + H_2$
D. $Mg + 2H_2O \rightarrow Mg(OH)_2 + H_2$
E. $Mg + H_2O \rightarrow Mg(OH)_2 + H_2$

44) Which of the following substances has the weakest overall intermolecular forces?

[atomic numbers: H = 1; C = 6; N = 7; O = 8; F = 9]

A. CH_4
B. CO_2
C. HF
D. H_2O
E. NH_3

45) An atom has atomic number *x* and a mass number of 2*x* + 6. How many neutrons are in the nucleus of this atom?

A. $x+3$
B. $x-6$
C. $x+6$
D. $x-3$
E. 6

46) In which of the following pairs of species does the vanadium, V, have the same oxidation state?

A. VO_2 and VO_3^-
B. VO_2 and V_2O_5
C. V_2O_5 and VO^{2+}
D. VCl_4 and VO^{2+}
E. VCl_4 and VO_3^-

47) Which of the following pairs of molecules are structural isomers?

1, 2

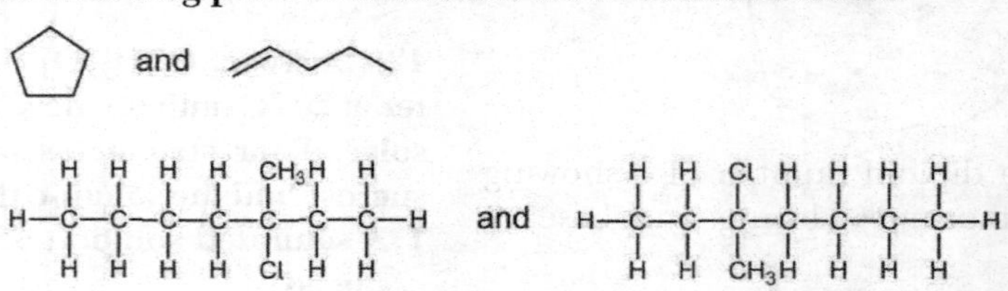

3 $CH_3CH_2CH_2CN$ and $CH_2{=}C{=}CHCH_2NH_2$

A. 1, 2 and 3
B. 1 and 3 only
C. 3 only
D. 2 only
E. 2 and 3 only

48) Which of the following functional groups is present in cysteine?

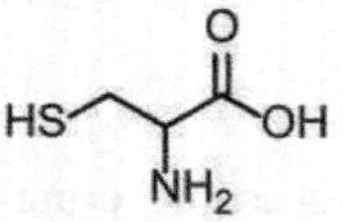

cysteine

A. Alcohol
B. Ketone
C. Amide
D. Ester
E. Thiol

49) *P*, *Q* and *R* represent substances involved in a gaseous reaction. The equilibrium constant (K_c) and the sign of the enthalpy change for the reaction are:

$$K_c = \frac{[P]^2}{[Q][R]^3} \quad \Delta H \text{ is negative}$$

Assuming that all other conditions remain constant, a change in which factor results in an increase of the value of the equilibrium constant, K_c?

A. A decrease in pressure
B. An increase in temperature
C. A decrease in temperature
D. An increase in pressure
E. Use of a suitable catalyst

50) Which of the following molecules has a permanent overall dipole moment? [C is in Group IV; N and P are in Group

V; O and S are in Group VI; F and Cl are in Group VII]

A. PCl_5
B. NF_3
C. CO_2
D. SF_6
E. CCl_4

51) X and Y are acidic solutions. X has a pH of 2 and Y has a pH of 4. Which of the following statements about the hydrogen ion concentrations of X and Y is correct?

A. Y has a hydrogen ion concentration 2 times greater than X
B. X has a hydrogen ion concentration 4 times greater than Y
C. X has a hydrogen ion concentration 2 times greater than Y
D. X has a hydrogen ion concentration 100 times greater than Y
E. Y has a hydrogen ion concentration 100 times greater than X

52) 40 cm^3 of a solution of sodium hydroxide is exactly neutralised by 25 cm^3 of 0.40 mol L^{-1} sulfuric acid.

$$2NaOH + H_2SO_4 \rightarrow Na_2SO_4 + 2H_2O$$

What is the concentration, in g L^{-1}, of the sodium hydroxide solution?
[M_r value: NaOH = 40]

A. 0.25 g L^{-1}
B. 10 g L^{-1}
C. 5 g L^{-1}
D. 0.5 g L^{-1}
E. 20 g L^{-1}

Physics and Mathematics

53) Given that $8^{2x+3} \times \frac{1}{4^{3x}} = 2^{x+3}$ what is the value of x?

A. $\frac{1}{2}$
B. 6
C. $\frac{3}{2}$
D. 3
E. 0

54) Which of the following is equal to $\frac{2}{2+\sqrt{3}}$?

A. $\frac{4}{7}-\frac{2\sqrt{3}}{7}$
B. $4+2\sqrt{3}$
C. $4-2\sqrt{3}$
D. $\frac{4}{7}+\frac{2\sqrt{3}}{7}$
E. $1-\frac{\sqrt{3}}{2}$

55) What are the coordinates of the turning point of the graph of the quadratic equation $y = 2x^2 + 5x - 2$?

A. $\left(-\frac{5}{2},-\frac{41}{8}\right)$
B. $\left(-\frac{5}{2},-\frac{41}{16}\right)$
C. $\left(\frac{5}{4},-\frac{41}{16}\right)$
D. $\left(-\frac{5}{4},-\frac{41}{8}\right)$
E. $\left(-\frac{5}{4},-\frac{41}{16}\right)$

56) 39 male students and 36 female students were asked how many meals they had eaten in the school cafeteria during the first week of the term. The results are shown in the table:

	male	*female*	*all students*
mean number of meals eaten	2	x	$3\frac{1}{5}$

What is the value of x?

A. $3\frac{4}{5}$

B. $4\frac{1}{2}$

C. $4\frac{2}{5}$

D. $2\frac{3}{5}$

E. $4\frac{2}{3}$

57) The diagram represents a concave mirror, where F is the principal focus and *f* is the focal length.

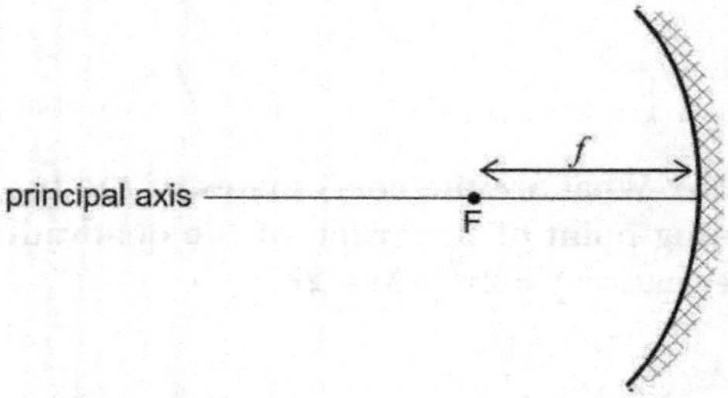

The mirror is used to produce an image of an object. Which of the following statements are correct?
[Assume the mirror is parabolic.]

1 Incident rays travelling parallel to the principal axis always pass through F after reflection
2 Incident rays passing through F always travel parallel to the principal axis after reflection
3 The image formed is always inverted
4 The image formed is always real
5 The image formed is always larger than the object

A. 3, 4 and 5 only
B. 1 and 2 only
C. 1 and 3 only
D. 2 and 4 only
E. 1, 3 and 4 only

58) A beaker contains 1000 g of a liquid that is stirred at its boiling point. A 100 W electric heater is completely immersed in the liquid. The heater provides the liquid with thermal energy, and 200 g of the liquid changes to vapour in 1600 s.
What is the specific latent heat of evaporation of the liquid?
[Assume that no thermal energy is transferred to or from the surroundings, and no vapour condenses.]

A. 3200 J/g
B. 12.5 J/g
C. 800 J/g
D. 160 J/g
E. 16000 J/g

59) A rocket is launched vertically from the surface of the Earth. As it leaves the launch pad, the total mass of the rocket and its contents is *m*. The gravitational field strength at the Earth's surface is *g*. The rocket motor provides an upward vertical thrust *T* to the rocket.

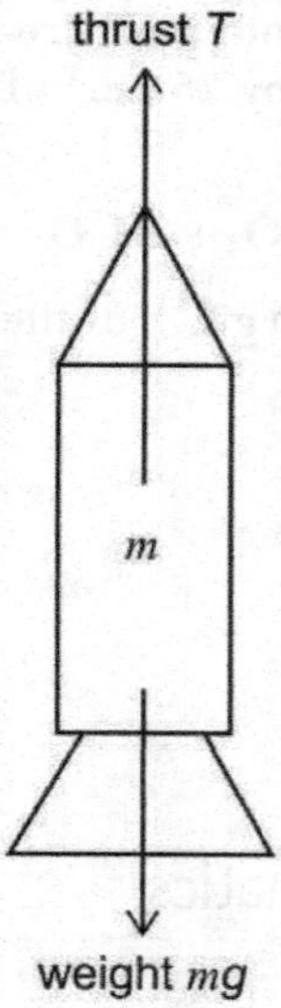

What is the initial vertical acceleration of the rocket as it leaves the launch pad?

A. $\frac{T}{m} - mg$

B. mg

C. $\frac{T}{m}$

D. $T - mg$

E. $\frac{T}{m} - g$

60) A boat crosses a river that has straight, parallel sides. In still water, the boat has a maximum speed of 4.0 m/s at maximum power. The boat is aimed at a point directly across the river from its starting point. The river flows at a constant speed of 3.0 m/s parallel to its sides.

What is the speed of the boat as measured by a person stationary on the bank, and what is the angle at which the boat travels, measured from a line at 90° to the bank?

[The boat travels at maximum power throughout its journey.]

A. Speed of boat = 7.0 m/s; angle = $\cos^{-1}\left(\frac{4.0}{7.0}\right)$

B. Speed of boat = 5.0 m/s; angle = $\cos^{-1}\left(\frac{3.0}{5.0}\right)$

C. Speed of boat = 5.0 m/s; angle = $\cos^{-1}\left(\frac{3.0}{4.0}\right)$

D. Speed of boat = 5.0 m/s; angle = $\cos^{-1}\left(\frac{4.0}{5.0}\right)$

E. Speed of boat = 7.0 m/s; angle = $\cos^{-1}\left(\frac{3.0}{7.0}\right)$

RISPOSTE COMMENTATE • IMAT a.a. 2020/2021

Cultura generale e ragionamento logico

1) B. La soluzione del quesito consiste nel trovare quale delle cinque alternative di risposta esprima meglio la conclusione principale del ragionamento riportato nella traccia. A tale scopo si deve innanzitutto riconoscere che il ragionamento in esame è composto da due premesse fondamentali P_1 e P_2: P_1 asserisce che l'ottimismo ha molteplici effetti positivi, mentre P_2 ne evidenzia anche gli effetti negativi in determinate circostanze, che sono illustrate attraverso vari esempi. Perciò, la migliore conclusione che si può dedurre dalla connessione concettuale di P_1 e P_2 è che "*Positive thinking is not always helpful*". Al contrario, "*People who think positively live longer*" è un concetto ricavabile solo da P_1; "*Being overly positive can damage our relationships with friends*" e "*Negative thinking about health can be beneficial*" sono concetti deducibili solo da P_2; "*Research into positivity has so far ignored its potential downsides*" è in contrasto con il passaggio di P_2 in cui, con riferimento al fatto che l'ottimismo può avere effetti negativi in certe circostanze, si precisa che ciò è "*shown by research*".

2) A. La traccia contiene le premesse di un ragionamento la cui conclusione è invece riportata in una sola delle cinque opzioni di risposta. Per individuare tale conclusione, la prima cosa da fare è riconoscere che nella traccia vi sono due premesse P_1 e P_2. In P_1 si asserisce che le auto a guida autonoma ormai stanno per diventare realtà, ma sollevano varie questioni di cui ancora si trascurano le implicazioni legali. P_2 si collega a P_1 prendendo ad esempio una di tali questioni, quella di chi sia la responsabilità in incidenti che coinvolgono le auto a guida autonoma. Dalla connessione logica di P_1 e P_2 si deduce come conclusione che "*New laws are needed to determine liability for accidents involving driverless cars*". Tutte le altre opzioni di risposta sono da escludere: "*The design of driverless cars will continue to improve with time*" riguarda un aspetto, quello del design delle auto a guida autonoma, di cui non si parla mai nella traccia; "*All the technology needed to create a self-driving car is already available*" è in contrasto con il passaggio di P_1 in cui si dice che "*we are moving very close to the reality of self-driving cars*"; "*It will be impossible to determine liability for accidents involving driverless cars*" non è in accordo con il fatto che in P_2 già si ipotizza chi possa essere responsabile di tali incidenti, cioè "*the owner of the car, or the manufacturer of the car*"; "*We should not continue to develop self-driving cars*" contrasta con il fatto che in P_2 si evidenzia un aspetto positivo delle auto a guida autonoma, ossia che esse "*should have the capacity to save lives*".

3) C. Il ragionamento della traccia parte dalla premessa che il motivo per il quale l'artista Piet Mondrian, costretto a trasferirsi da Parigi in Inghilterra nel 1938 per sfuggire all'occupazione tedesca, preferì soggiornare a Londra piuttosto che in un'area più rurale, fu l'amore per la cultura varia e vibrante delle grandi città. Lo stesso ragionamento giunge poi alla conclusione che tale motivo spiega perché a Londra soggiornino molti più artisti che in una qualsiasi altra città inglese. Per giungere a tale conclusione è necessario partire dal presupposto che la motivazione degli altri artisti di vivere a Londra sia la stessa di Mondrian e che dunque "*Other artists make the same choice as Mondrian for the same reasons*".

4) D. La domanda chiede di identificare quale delle cinque alternative di risposta riporti la cosiddetta prova addizionale, cioè l'affermazione che, se fosse aggiunta alle premesse dell'argomentazione, ne rafforzerebbe la conclusione. In vista di tale obiettivo bisogna distinguere innanzitutto le premesse e la conclusione. Nel brano si parla del fatto che ai detenuti non dovrebbe essere consentito ricevere da amici e parenti pacchi contenenti libri perché il ricevere i libri in regalo scoraggerebbe i detenuti dall'intraprendere un lavoro retribuito, mentre sono in prigione, per acquistare libri con i soldi che guadagnano lavorando. Analizzando le cinque opzioni di risposta è evidente che l'unica alternativa che rafforzerebbe l'argomentazione è "*Many parcels of books sent by relatives or friends have been found to contain illegal drugs*" in cui si parla degli stessi pacchi, evidenziando un altro grave motivo, ossia la presenza di droghe illegali, per il quale bisogna vietarne l'invio ai detenuti.

5) E. Questa tipologia di quesito chiede di determinare quale delle cinque alternative di risposta contenga il ragionamento che ricalca più fedelmente quello esposto nella traccia. La corrispondenza non va intesa dal punto di vista del contenuto, ma della forma, ovvero della struttura logica, prescindendo dalla correttezza e verità dell'argomentazione. Pertanto, la prima cosa da fare è individuare la struttura logica del ragionamento della traccia. La frase "*People who take their holidays in Las Vegas love to gamble*" costituisce la prima premessa (P_1) ed equivale logicamente a "per ogni *x*, se *x* trascorre le proprie vacanze a Las Vegas, allora *x* ama giocare d'azzardo", dove '*x*' sta per un qualsiasi individuo. La frase "*Gerry will be going to France for his holiday*" costituisce la seconda premessa (P_2) e significa logicamente "Gerry non trascorrerà le proprie vacanze a Las Vegas". La frase "*he must not like gambling*" costituisce la conclusione (C) e logicamente significa "Gerry non ama giocare d'azzardo".
Indicando "trascorrere le proprie vacanze a Las Vegas" con il simbolo 'LV', "amare il gioco d'azzardo" con 'G', il quantificatore "per ogni" con il simbolo '∀', l'implicazione "se ..., allora ..." con '→' e la negazione con '¬', la struttura logica del ragionamento della traccia è la seguente:

P_1: $(\forall x)(\text{LV}\ x \rightarrow \text{G}\ x)$

P_2: $\neg\ \text{LV}\ \textit{Gerry}$

C: $\neg\ \text{G}\ \textit{Gerry}$

A questo punto bisogna esaminare le cinque alternative di risposta per trovare quale presenti una struttura logica analoga a quella della traccia. Così facendo, si osserva che l'alternativa cercata è "*People who live in the city hate traffic jams. You live in the country so you must like traffic jams*". Infatti, la prima premessa (P_1) è "*People who live in the city hate traffic jams*", che equivale logicamente a "per ogni *x*, se *x* vive in città, allora *x* odia gli ingorghi"; la seconda premessa (P_2) è "*You live in the country*", che logicamente significa "Tu non vivi in città"; la conclusione (C) è "*you must like traffic jams*", che logicamente significa "tu non odi gli ingorghi". Indicando "vivere in città" con il simbolo

'LC' e "odiare gli ingorghi" con 'T', si ricava la seguente struttura logica, chiaramente analoga a quella poc'anzi individuata nella traccia:

$$\begin{array}{ll} \mathbf{P_1}: & (\forall x)(\text{LC } x \to \text{T } x) \\ \mathbf{P_2}: & \neg \text{ LC } you \\ \hline \mathbf{C}: & \neg \text{ T } you \end{array}$$

6) A. Per sapere quale delle scatole di detersivo sia più conveniente basta confrontare il prezzo al chilogrammo di ciascuna di esse. Si ha che:

- lo scatolo Zap di 2 kg a £2.40 costa £1.20 al chilogrammo
- lo scatolo Zoom di 1 kg a £2.50 costa ovviamente £2.50 al chilogrammo
- lo scatolo Zoom di 2 kg a £4.95 costa £2.475 al chilogrammo
- lo scatolo Zap di 1 kg a £1.30 costa £1.30 al chilogrammo
- lo scatolo OwnBrand di 1 kg a £1.25 costa £1.25 al chilogrammo.

Allora lo scatolo più conveniente è lo Zap di 2 kg.

7) B. Avendo già mangiato il 36% delle caramelle, oggi ne è rimasto il 100 – 36 = 64%. Poiché per 3 giorni verrà mangiato il 25% del contenuto di oggi, in totale verrà mangiato il 25 × 3 = 75% del contenuto di oggi, cioè $\frac{75 \times 64}{100} = 48\%$

Allora resta il 64 – 48 = 16% del contenuto iniziale.

8) C. Dalla tabella riassuntiva è possibile sapere quanti figli ci sono nella famiglia di ciascun bambino guardando il numero scritto in corrispondenza della riga per le sorelle o della colonna per i fratelli, e poi sommarli tra di loro e aumentare il totale di 1 (il bambino stesso). Allora per sapere quante famiglie hanno 3 o più figli basta contare i bambini segnati nelle caselle all'incrocio tra le colonne di 1, 2 o 3 fratelli e le righe di 1, 2 o 3 sorelle (cioè Rajiv, Emily, Fatima, Paul, Candice, Marvin e Phoebe) e quelli nelle caselle all'incrocio tra 0 fratelli e 2 o 3 sorelle (solo Aruna) e tra 0 sorelle e 2 o 3 fratelli (cioè Leroy, Gemma e Callum). In totale, quindi, le famiglie con 3 o più figli sono 11.

9) D. Per sapere quale automobile dovrebbe acquistare Jeff per spendere di meno durante l'anno basta calcolare il costo di ciascun tipo di auto, sommando alla spesa iniziale il prodotto tra il costo di un pieno del serbatoio e il numero di pieni che dovrà fare per percorrere 20.000 miglia, cioè il rapporto tra 20.000 e la distanza percorsa con un pieno. Si ha allora:

- auto a gas: 10.000 + 30 × (20.000 ÷ 200) = 10.000 + 3.000 = 13.000
- auto diesel: 12.000 + 50 × (20.000 ÷ 500) = 12.000 + 2.000 = 14.000
- auto a benzina: 10.000 + 50 × (20.000 ÷ 400) = 10.000 + 2.500 = 12.500
- auto a idrogeno: 9.500 + 50 × (20.000 ÷ 200) = 9.500 + 5.000 = 14.500
- auto elettrica: 12.500 + 5 × (20.000 ÷ 200) = 10.000 + 500 = 13.000

Per spendere meno durante l'anno Jeff dovrebbe acquistare l'auto a benzina.

10) A. Considerando il foglio diviso in 16 rettangoli, il primo dei 4 punti si deve trovare al centro degli 8 rettangoli di destra, visto che la prima piega è stata fatta da sinistra verso destra lungo la dimensione maggiore (e alla fine il foglio è stato girato), e in tali 8 rettangoli non devono essere presenti altri punti:

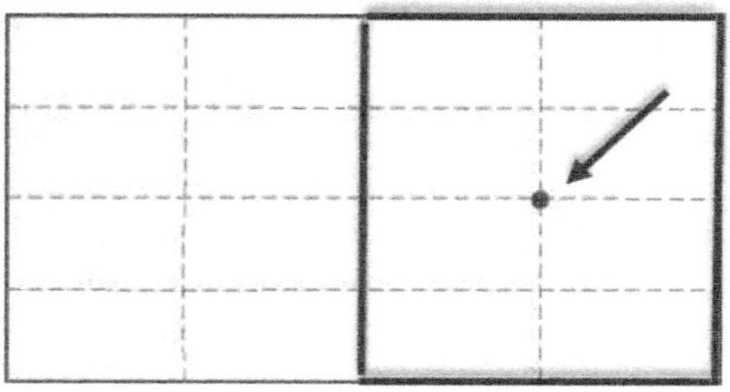

Considerati, invece, gli 8 rettangoli di sinistra, un punto deve andare al centro dei 4 rettangoli superiori, dato che la seconda piega è stata fatta dalla parte superiore sulla parte inferiore:

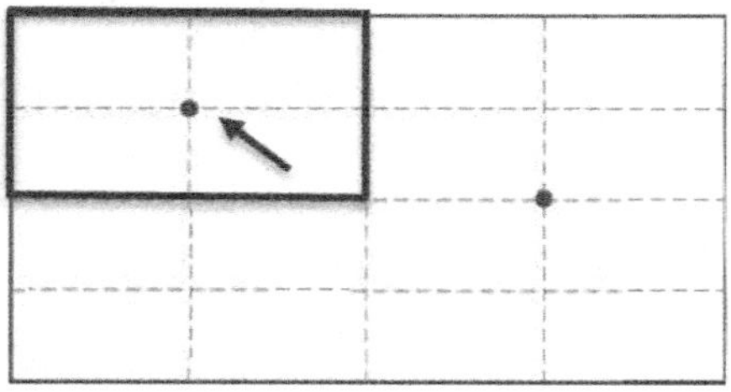

Analogamente, considerando i 4 rettangoli inferiori, il terzo punto dovrà trovarsi al centro dei 2 rettangoli di destra:

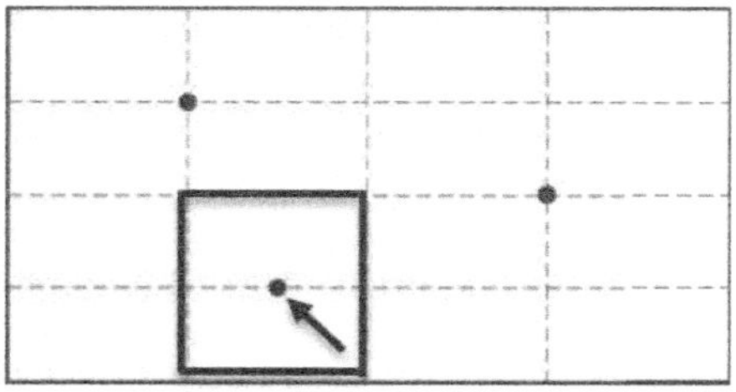

mentre il quarto e ultimo punto deve essere al centro del rettangolo in alto a sinistra:

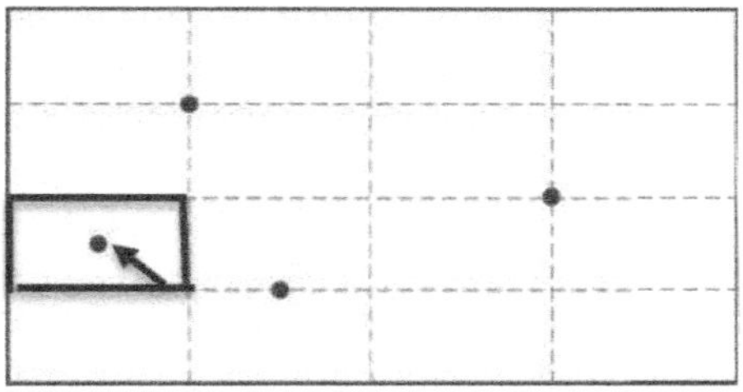

Una suddivisione di punti di questo tipo è nella prima figura proposta nelle alternative.

11) D. Non appartiene al ceppo delle lingue romanze il bulgaro, diversamente dalle altre elencate nelle alternative, e di cui fanno parte anche l'italiano, il portoghese, il gallego e altre lingue minori. La lingua bulgara, infatti, è una lingua slava del gruppo meridionale appartenente al ceppo indoeuropeo, di cui fanno parte anche lo sloveno, il serbo e il croato. Il bulgaro è, tra l'altro, la più antica lingua scritta e letteraria fra le lingue slave.

12) B. Tra gli autori citati nelle alternative, l'unico a non aver vinto il Premio Nobel per la Letteratura è stato il romanziere inglese Charles Dickens (1812 – 1870). Bob Dylan (1941), cantautore e musicista statunitense, ha ricevuto il prestigioso premio nel 2016; il poeta cileno Pablo Neruda (1904 – 1973) nel 1971; il drammaturgo inglese Harold Pinter (1930 – 2008) nel 2005; lo scrittore e saggista tedesco Thomas Mann (1875 – 1955) nel 1929.

13) E. A dirigere il film *Amarcord* (1973) fu l'italiano Federico Fellini (1920 – 1993), uno dei maggiori registi della storia del cinema. La pellicola, vincitrice del premio Oscar nel 1975 come miglior film straniero, ha ricevuto numerosi altri premi, tra i quali il David di Donatello, il Nastro d'Argento e il Globo d'Oro. Film in parte autobiografico, *Amarcord*, che in dialetto romagnolo vuol dire "io mi ricordo", è ambientato nella Rimini degli anni Trenta, abitata da una galleria di personaggi piuttosto stravaganti (il matto del paese, la procace parrucchiera Gradisca, oggetto del desiderio degli adolescenti, la ninfomane Volpina, il suonatore cieco ecc.) appartenenti a quella memoria reinventata e fantastica tipicamente felliniana.

14) D. Tra i libri citati nella alternative, l'unico a non essere stato scritto dal torinese Primo Levi (1919 – 1987) è *Al di là del bene e del male* (*Beyond Good and Evil*), saggio filosofico in 9 capitoli del filosofo tedesco Friedrich W. Nietzsche (1844 – 1900). *Se questo è un uomo, La tregua, Se non ora, quando?, I sommersi e i salvati* sono, ognuno a suo modo, testimonianza del vissuto dell'autore e della sua tragica esperienza di deportato nel campo di sterminio di Auschwitz, in quanto ebreo, dal quale Levi fece ritorno dopo la liberazione da parte dell'Armata Rossa nel gennaio del 1945.

15) C. La distribuzione normale è una distribuzione di probabilità continua, chiamata anche "curva a campana", perché il grafico della funzione di densità di probabilità associata somiglia proprio a una campana. È nota anche come "campana di Gauss" o "distribuzione gaussiana" derivando il nome dal matematico e astronomo tedesco Carl Gauss (1777 – 1855) che per primo la descrisse. La distribuzione gaussiana è una delle distribuzioni di probabilità più comunemente utilizzate nelle applicazioni pratiche, in quanto semplice modello per spiegare e risolvere fenomeni complessi ed è spesso impiegata in statistica e nelle scienze naturali e sociali.

16) A. Tutti quelli menzionati nelle alternative sono stati famosi cosmonauti, ma il primo a entrare in orbita e a compiere un intero giro attorno alla Terra in 108 minuti, avendo la possibilità di osservare il nostro pianeta dallo spazio, è stato il russo Jurij Gagarin (1934 – 1968). Era il 12 aprile 1961 e la prima navicella spaziale, la Vostok 1, decollò dalla base di Baikonur, in Kazakistan. All'epoca Gagarin aveva appena ventisette anni e fu scelto per la missione tra 3.461 candidati. Neil Armstrong (1930 – 2012) è stato, invece, il primo uomo a mettere piede sulla Luna nel 1969, seguito da Buzz Aldrin (1930) nell'ambito della missione "Apollo 11". Valentina Tereshkova (1937) comandò la navicella spaziale "Vostok 6" per una missione nello spazio nel 1963; John Glenn (1921 – 2016) fu il primo statunitense a viaggiare nello spazio, nel 1962.

17) E. L'abbinamento sbagliato è Capo Verde – Brasile in quanto l'arcipelago di Capo Verde, formato da dieci isole vulcaniche, è situato nell'Oceano Atlantico, al largo della costa occidentale dell'Africa, continente di cui fa parte, mentre il Brasile è uno stato dell'America meridionale.

18) B. L'UNESCO (*United Nations Educational, Scientific and Cultural Organization* – Organizzazione delle Nazioni Unite per l'Educazione, la Scienza e la Cultura) è un'agenzia fondata nel 1946 a Parigi, città in cui ha sede, con l'obiettivo fondamentale di promuovere la pace e la comprensione tra le nazioni attraverso l'istruzione, la scienza, la cultura, la comunicazione e l'informazione. Si occupa, però, anche di favorire la comprensione interculturale attraverso la protezione e la salvaguardia di siti di particolare e notevole valore e bellezza dal punto di vista culturale o naturalistico, iscritti nel Patrimonio Mondiale dell'Umanità, la cui custodia e protezione sono considerate importanti per il mondo intero.

19) E. Nonostante l'Ungheria faccia parte degli Stati membri dell'Unione Europea dal maggio 2004, non ha adottato la moneta comune; in Ungheria viene infatti usato il fiorino ungherese.

20) C. Come sancito dall'art. 58 della Costituzione Italiana, sono i senatori ad essere eletti a suffragio universale e diretto da elettori che abbiano superato il venticinquesimo anno d'età. Possono essere eletti senatori soltanto gli elettori che abbiano compiuto il quarantesimo anno d'età. Il Governo, formato dal Presidente del Consiglio dei Ministri e dai ministri, è nominato dal Presidente della Repubblica che designa anche i ministri indicati dal premier. Il Presidente della Repubblica, invece, è eletto dal Parlamento, ovvero da Camera e Senato riuniti in seduta comune. Infine, il CSM, Consiglio Superiore della Magistratura consta di 3 membri di diritto (Presidente della Repubblica, Primo Presidente della Corte di Cassazione, Procuratore Generale presso la Corte) mentre gli altri componenti vengono eletti, in proporzioni diverse, dai magistrati ordinari e dal Parlamento, nelle persone di professori universitari di materie giuridiche e di avvocati.

21) D. L'economia della condivisione o economia collaborativa è un particolare sistema per scambiare beni e servizi e che si caratterizza per il contatto diretto tra domanda e offerta, attraverso piattaforme digitali: in tal modo, un individuo può affittare o condividere con altre persone un bene personale, che sia la propria casa, la propria auto, la propria bicicletta ecc. Le parti in gioco di questo scambio, che si basa necessariamente su meccanismi di relazione, condivisione e fiducia, sono rappresentate dai prestatori di servizi, dagli utenti e dalle piattaforme di collaborazione (intermediari). Tra gli altri, i principi alla base di questa economia sono:

- "l'accesso è preferibile alla proprietà": cambiano le modalità di godimento dei beni, per cui si passa dall'idea di avere la proprietà di un bene a quella di poter usare quel bene;
- "dati trasparenti e aperti aumentano l'innovazione": condividendo le informazioni sui beni e servizi (in genere tramite un mercato online), il valore degli stessi può aumentare per l'azienda, per gli individui e per la società in generale;
- "il pericolo sconosciuto può essere superato": tale tipo di economia è basata sull'impegno a costruire e convalidare relazioni di fiducia tra i membri della comunità, per cui gli utenti possono condividere, scambiare, superando pericoli sconosciuti;
- "il valore non utilizzato è un valore sprecato": la messa in comune di informazioni e di beni, resa possibile dalle piattaforme digitali, permette di aumentare la loro produttività e di ridurre al minimo gli sprechi.

Non rientra tra questi, quindi, il principio secondo cui "la concorrenza è pericolosa".

22) A. La medaglia Fields, che prende il nome dal matematico canadese John Charles Fields (1863 – 1932) che la ideò, viene assegnata ogni 4 anni in occasione del Congresso Internazionale dei Matematici della *International Mathematical Union*, associazione di cui fanno parte circa 50 nazioni. Si tratta della massima onorificenza assegnata a 2 o 4 matematici di età inferiore ai 40 anni che si sono particolarmente distinti nel loro ambito di attività e ciascuno in un settore diverso della disciplina.

Biologia

23) B. Secondo il modello a mosaico fluido, la membrana plasmatica è costituita da un doppio strato di fosfolipidi in cui sono immerse le proteine. I fosfolipidi sono molecole anfipatiche che presentano una testa polare e una coda apolare. Nell'ambiente acquoso in cui si trova la cellula, i fosfolipidi formano un doppio strato esponendo le teste idrofiliche verso l'ambiente acquoso e rivolgendo le code idrofobiche verso l'interno del doppio strato, le une verso le altre, in modo da allontanarle dall'acqua. Nell'immagine proposta, 2 rappresenta la testa idrofilica di un fosfolipide e 3 la sua coda idrofobica; 1 rappresenta una catena carboidratica appartenente a un glicolipide o a una glicoproteina; 4 una proteina integrale e 5 una proteina periferica, tutte molecole idrofiliche.

24) A. Gli amminoacidi, i monomeri che costituiscono le proteine, sono molecole in cui un atomo di carbonio lega un atomo di idrogeno (H), un gruppo amminico (NH_2), un gruppo carbossilico (COOH) e una catena laterale (R) caratteristica di ciascun amminoacido. Nella molecola di asparagina, $NH_2CHCOOH$ (parte X in figura) è in comune con tutti gli altri amminoacidi, mentre CH_2CONH_2 (parte Y in figura) è la catena laterale caratteristica di questo composto.

25) E. Gli organismi viventi sono costituiti da una sola cellula (unicellulari) o da più cellule (pluricellulari). La cellula, infatti, è l'unità morfo-funzionale di tutti gli organismi viventi. Il materiale genetico è sempre costituito da DNA (solo alcuni virus hanno un genoma a RNA, ma i virus non sono annoverati tra i viventi). Quando le condizioni ambientali cambiano, gli organismi viventi consumano energia per adattarsi alle nuove condizioni. Tutti gli organismi viventi vanno incontro a fasi di crescita.

26) D. Il plasmide Ti di *Agrobacterium tumefaciens* contiene i geni necessari per l'infezione delle cellule vegetali e per l'induzione della loro proliferazione, che porta alla genesi di un tumore, detto galla del colletto. Con le tecniche del DNA ricombinante, nel plasmide Ti vengono inseriti un gene che codifica una tossina contro gli insetti e un gene che codifica la resistenza a un antibiotico. Il plasmide Ti ricombinante, inserito nei semi di una pianta di cotone, causa la crescita di un tumore, costituito da una massa di cellule che producono la tossina. La selezione dei semi produttori della tossina avviene con un mezzo contenente l'antibiotico cui i semi con il plasmide ricombinante sono resistenti.

27) B. Il glomerulo renale è responsabile della produzione del filtrato glomerulare attraverso un processo di filtrazione del plasma sanguigno; il filtrato così prodotto entra nel tubulo contorto prossimale, nel quale avviene il riassorbimento di acqua, ioni e nutrienti organici, attraversa poi l'ansa di Henle, dove avviene un ulteriore riassorbimento di acqua (tratto discendente) e ioni sodio e cloruro (tratto ascendente), quindi passa nel tubulo contorto distale, in cui avviene un riassorbimento di acqua, sodio e calcio sotto controllo ormonale, per riversarsi infine nel dotto collettore, dove si assiste a un riassorbimento variabile di acqua e a riassorbimento o secrezione di ioni sodio, potassio, bicarbonato e idrogeno.

28) E. La bile, prodotta dal fegato, immagazzinata nella cistifellea ed escreta nel duodeno, è una miscela costituita da acqua, ioni, bilirubina e sali biliari. L'acqua e gli ioni contribuiscono alla diluizione e alla neutralizzazione degli acidi del chimo quando questo entra nell'intestino tenue; i sali biliari emulsionano i lipidi del chimo, rendendo possibile l'attacco delle lipasi, gli enzimi che scindono tali lipidi in acidi grassi assorbibili.

29) A. Nel cuore umano, il setto interatriale separa l'atrio destro dall'atrio sinistro, in modo che non vi sia ricircolo di sangue tra il circolo sistemico e quello polmonare. A partire dalla quinta settimana di sviluppo embrionale fino alla nascita, il setto è reso pervio da un'apertura ovale, detta foro di Botallo, che consente al sangue di passare direttamente dall'atrio destro all'atrio sinistro, bypassando i polmoni, che non sono ancora funzionanti.

30) D. Ciascun cromosoma umano consiste in un'unica enorme molecola di DNA associata a proteine (cromatina). La cromatina interfasica ha una struttura a filo di perle, nella quale le perle sono i nucleosomi e il filo è costituito da DNA linker. Ogni nucleosoma consiste in un ottamero istonico attorno al quale è avvolto un tratto di DNA di 166 bp ed è stabilizzato da una molecola di istone H1. L'ottamero istonico è formato da due molecole di ciascuno degli istoni H2A, H2B, H3 e H4.

31) E. A livello della giunzione neuro-muscolare, a seguito del legame dell'acetilcolina ai suoi recettori sulla membrana post-sinaptica, la membrana della fibra muscolare si depolarizza e si genera un potenziale d'azione, che si propaga lungo la superficie della fibra e i tubuli T. Il reticolo sarcoplasmatico rilascia nel sarcoplasma gli ioni calcio immagazzinati; questi ultimi si legano alla troponina, causando un cambiamento di orientamento del complesso troponina-tropomiosina e l'esposizione dei siti di legame per la miosina sul filamento di actina.

32) B. L'HIV (virus dell'immunodeficienza umana) è l'agente eziologico dell'AIDS (sindrome da immunodeficienza acquisita). Si tratta di un retrovirus costituito da un genoma a RNA racchiuso in un capside proteico e in un rivestimento esterno. Nella particella virale sono contenuti anche alcuni enzimi essenziali per l'infezione, che sono codificati dal genoma virale. Uno di questi enzimi è la trascrittasi inversa, una DNA polimerasi RNA-dipendente che retrotrascrive l'RNA genomico in DNA, il quale si integra nel genoma dell'ospite. L'HIV, come tutti gli altri virus, non contiene ribosomi.

33) C. L'immagine della struttura 1 ha una lunghezza di 4 cm ed è stata ingrandita 4000 volte; pertanto, la dimensione reale è 4/4000 cm = 10 μm. L'immagine della struttura 2 ha una lunghezza di 0,5 μm. L'immagine della struttura 3 ha una lunghezza di 6 cm ed è stata ingrandita 20.000 volte; pertanto, la dimensione reale è 6/20.000 cm = 3 μm. L'immagine della struttura 4 ha una lunghezza di 140 μm. L'immagine della struttura 5 ha un diametro massimo di 3 cm ed è stata ingrandita 400 volte; pertanto, la dimensione reale è 3/400 cm = 75 μm. Dunque, la struttura più piccola è la 2.

34) D. *Escherichia coli* è un batterio; in quanto tale, presenta un genoma costituito da un'unica grande molecola circolare di DNA e contiene plasmidi, piccole molecole circolari di DNA extracromosomico. Il lievito unicellulare *Saccharomyces cerevisiae* e l'epatocita umano sono cellule eucariotiche, che presentano il genoma organizzato in cromosomi lineari. Tuttavia, i mitocondri delle cellule eucariotiche contengono un proprio genoma (mtDNA), che si presenta in forma circolare.

35) E. Tutti i tre passaggi indicati si verificano sia nella replicazione del DNA sia nella sua trascrizione in RNA. Infatti, in entrambi i processi, affinché sia disponibile uno stampo, avviene la separazione dei due filamenti complementari che costituiscono la doppia elica del DNA, grazie alla rottura dei legami idrogeno tra le basi appaiate. Alle basi del filamento stampo si appaiano le basi complementari inserite nel filamento di nuova sintesi (DNA o RNA), grazie alla formazione di legami idrogeno tra esse. Nel filamento di nuova sintesi (DNA o RNA), i nucleotidi via via incorporati vengono legati ai precedenti mediante legami fosfodiesterici.

36) B. La speciazione simpatrica consiste nella nascita di una nuova specie, a partire da una popolazione appartenente alla specie originaria, nello stesso areale geografico. L'isolamento riproduttivo consiste nell'assenza di accoppiamento tra individui appartenenti a popolazioni diverse. L'isolamento post-zigotico consiste nella mancata vitalità degli ibridi nati dall'accoppiamento tra individui che appartengono a popolazioni diverse.

37) D. Gli effetti di una mutazione genica per sostituzione di una singola base possono essere diversi. Se la mutazione determina la sostituzione di un amminoacido con un altro (mutazione missense), ne può derivare un'alterazione della struttura terziaria della proteina; tuttavia, se il nuovo amminoacido ha proprietà simili a quelle dell'amminoacido originario, la mutazione può risultare silente a livello fenotipico. In alcuni casi, per la degenerazione del codice genetico, la sostituzione di una base produce un codone che continua a codificare lo stesso amminoacido; in tal caso, si parla di mutazione neutra. La sostituzione può anche generare un codone di stop della traduzione (mutazione nonsense), che porta alla sintesi di una proteina tronca.

38) C. Il metabolismo di un organismo comprende il catabolismo e l'anabolismo. Il catabolismo è l'insieme delle reazioni chimiche di demolizione di molecole complesse in molecole più semplici, con liberazione di energia. L'anabolismo è l'insieme delle reazioni chimiche di sintesi di molecole complesse a partire da molecole più semplici, con consumo di energia. L'ossidazione del NADH a $NAD^+ + H^+$ è una reazione catabolica, che determina rilascio di energia.

39) A. Il disegno A rappresenta una cellula appartenente a un organismo maschile con 16 cromatidi (8 cromosomi duplicati) durante la profase meiotica. Il disegno B rappresenta una cellula appartenente a un organismo maschile, poiché si vede che i cromosomi sessuali sono X e Y (hanno dimensioni diverse). Il disegno C illustra una cellula con numero diploide pari a 16. Il disegno D rappresenta una cellula con numero diploide pari a 4. Il disegno E illustra una cellula con 8 cromatidi (4 cromosomi duplicati).

40) D. I bastoncelli dell'occhio umano contengono rodopsina, un fotopigmento formato da opsina e retinale. Quando un bastoncello riceve uno stimolo luminoso appropriato, la luce è assorbita dalla rodopsina. Il retinale subisce un cambiamento conformazionale e si dissocia dall'opsina. Quest'ultima attiva la trasducina, che a sua volta attiva l'enzima fosfodiesterasi, che catalizza la scissione del GMP ciclico. Gli eventi a valle determinano un'iperpolarizzazione del bastoncello, con riduzione del rilascio di neurotrasmettitore.

Chimica

41) C. Il termine molecola indica il più piccolo insieme di atomi (uguali o diversi e uniti da legami chimici) capace di esistere come unità discreta. La specie Br_2 è, quindi, una molecola costituita dagli stessi atomi legati tramite un legame covalente. Si parla di composto quando la sostanza è costituita da atomi di due o più elementi diversi presenti in rapporti ben definiti.

42) B. Il saccarosio è un disaccaride costituito da fruttosio e glucosio legati tramite un legame α-1,2-glicosidico. È una molecola molto solubile in acqua grazie alla presenza dell'elevato numero di funzioni ossidriliche (–OH) libere. Tuttavia, esiste un valore limite della sua solubilità, che dipende dalla temperatura. Superato tale valore limite, si formerà un corpo di fondo, e si instaurerà un equilibrio dinamico fra le molecole di saccarosio che passano in soluzione e quelle che ritornano a far parte del reticolo cristallino. Una soluzione satura di saccarosio in acqua congelerà al di sotto di 0 °C (temperatura di congelamento dell'acqua pura a pressione atmosferica) e bollirà al di sopra di 100 °C (temperatura di ebollizione dell'acqua pura a pressione atmosferica), per effetto dell'abbassamento della tensione di vapore della soluzione rispetto a quella del solvente puro.

---

43) D. Il magnesio (Mg) è un metallo alcalino terroso che fa parte del secondo gruppo della tavola periodica. L'atomo di magnesio ha una configurazione elettronica esterna $2s^2$; a seguito dell'espulsione dei due elettroni dall'orbitale 2s raggiunge la configurazione elettronica del gas nobile neon (Ne). Il magnesio è, quindi, ossidato dall'acqua a ioni Mg^{2+}, secondo la reazione $Mg \rightarrow Mg^{2+} + 2e^-$, e contemporaneamente l'acqua si riduce, sviluppando idrogeno gassoso (H_2) e ioni idrossido (OH^-), secondo la reazione $2H_2O + 2e^- \rightarrow H_2 + 2OH^-$. Gli ioni OH^- si combinano con gli ioni Mg^{2+}, secondo la reazione $Mg^{2+} + 2OH^- \rightarrow Mg(OH)_2$. Sommando le tre reazioni membro a membro e semplificando i termini uguali, si ottiene:

$$Mg \rightarrow Mg^{2+} + 2e^-$$
$$2H_2O + 2e^- \rightarrow H_2 + 2OH^-$$
$$Mg^{2+} + 2OH^- \rightarrow Mg(OH)_2$$
$$\overline{Mg + 2H_2O \rightarrow Mg(OH)_2 + H_2}$$

---

44) A. Le forze intermolecolari sono forze di attrazione che determinano lo stato di aggregazione di una sostanza. Quando due atomi si uniscono per formare una molecola, a seconda della loro differenza di elettronegatività si possono generare momenti dipolari elettrici più o meno intensi, che determineranno la polarità della molecola (se i due atomi sono uguali il momento dipolare è nullo). Questo ragionamento è valido solo se la molecola è costituita da due atomi; se, invece, la molecola è poliatomica, bisogna considerare anche la forma che essa assume nello spazio (geometria molecolare). Le molecole polari si legheranno tramite interazioni dipolo permanente – dipolo permanente, mentre quelle apolari tramite interazioni dipolo istantaneo – dipolo indotto. Nella molecola di anidride carbonica (CO_2) l'atomo di carbonio è legato a due atomi di ossigeno molto elettronegativi; tuttavia, per effetto della geometria molecolare lineare, la somma vettoriale dei momenti di dipolo è nulla e la molecola non è polare. In un dato istante, il centro delle cariche positive può non coincidere con quello delle cariche negative e si forma, così, un dipolo istantaneo che induce un dipolo in una molecola adiacente nello spazio. Le molecole di CO_2 sono tenute insieme in fase gassosa tramite le attrazioni dipolo istantaneo – dipolo indotto. Nella molecola di metano (CH_4), la differenza di elettronegatività tra gli atomi di carbonio e idrogeno è molto più piccola rispetto a quella fra carbonio e ossigeno nella CO_2. La molecola di CH_4, a causa della sua geometria tetraedrica, non è polare (la somma vettoriale dei momenti di dipolo è nulla). Le molecole di CH_4 sono tenute insieme in fase gassosa da forze dipolo istantaneo – dipolo indotto, la cui intensità è minore rispetto a quelle che tengono insieme le molecole di CO_2. Il fluoruro d'idrogeno (HF), l'acqua (H_2O) e l'ammoniaca (NH_3) presentano ciascuno un atomo molto elettronegativo (F, O e N rispettivamente) legato ad atomi di idrogeno. Le tre molecole assumono nello spazio geometrie (rispettivamente lineare, angolata e piramidale) tali da generare dipoli permanenti, e si legano fra loro mediante forti legami a idrogeno.

45) C. Il numero di massa di un atomo è la somma del numero dei suoi protoni e neutroni, nel caso in esame $2x + 6$. Sapendo che il numero atomico è x, il numero di neutroni sarà dato dalla differenza fra $(2x + 6)$ e x, ossia: numero di neutroni = $2x + 6 - x = x + 6$.

46) D. Il numero di ossidazione di un atomo in una molecola o ione molecolare si calcola impostando un'equazione di primo grado, attribuendo l'incognita x all'atomo di cui si vuole calcolare lo stato di ossidazione. La somma dei numeri di ossidazione degli atomi sarà pari a zero se si tratta di una molecola neutra o, se si tratta di uno ione molecolare, sarà pari alla carica di quest'ultimo. L'ossigeno ha numero di ossidazione –2 negli ossidi mentre il cloro –1 nei cloruri. In base a questi dati, si può facilmente calcolare che il vanadio (V) ha numero di ossidazione +4 in VO_2, +5 in VO_3^-, +5 in V_2O_5, +4 in VO^{2+} e +4 in VCl_4.

47) B. Gli isomeri strutturali sono molecole che condividono la stessa formula bruta ma una diversa struttura. Essi possono differire per la diversa posizione dei singoli atomi o dei gruppi presenti sulla catena di atomi di carbonio o dei legami multipli presenti nella molecola. Il ciclopentano e l'1-pentene sono isomeri strutturali perché hanno la stessa formula bruta (C_5H_{10}); il 3-cloro-3-metileptano è rappresentato nei suoi due isomeri configurazionali, ossia due molecole che hanno la stessa formula bruta, la stessa disposizione degli atomi all'interno dello scheletro molecolare ma una diversa disposizione nello spazio; il butirronitrile e il 3-ammino-1,2-butadiene sono due isomeri strutturali perché hanno la stessa formula bruta (C_4H_7N), ma sono due molecole diverse.

48) E. La cisteina è un α-amminoacido polare che in catena laterale reca un gruppo funzionale tiolo (–SH).

49) C. La costante di equilibrio di una reazione è una grandezza che dipende solo dalla temperatura. La reazione in esame è esotermica perché ha un ΔH negativo. Potendo considerare la quantità di calore liberata a pressione costante (ΔH) alla stregua di un prodotto di reazione, per spostare l'equilibrio della reazione verso destra (aumentare il valore della costante di equilibrio) è necessario sottrarre calore al sistema (principio di Le Chatelier). Tale condizione può essere realizzata abbassando la temperatura.

50) B. Quando due atomi si uniscono per formare una molecola, a seconda della loro differenza di elettronegatività si possono generare momenti dipolari elettrici più o meno intensi, che determineranno la polarità della molecola (se i due atomi sono uguali il momento dipolare è nullo). Questo ragionamento è valido solo se la molecola è costituita da due atomi; se, invece, la molecola è poliatomica, bisogna considerare anche la forma che essa assume nello spazio (geometria molecolare). Nella molecola di PCl_5 l'atomo di fosforo è legato a cinque atomi di cloro più elettronegativi; tuttavia, per effetto della geometria molecolare trigonale bipiramidale, la somma vettoriale dei momenti di dipolo è nulla e la molecola non è polare. Anche la molecola di CO_2, in cui l'atomo di carbonio è legato a due atomi di ossigeno più elettronegativi non è polare, in virtù della sua geometria molecolare lineare. La molecola di SF_6 non è polare, nonostante la differenza di elettronegatività tra gli atomi di S e F, poiché la disposizione geometrica degli atomi di F intorno all'atomo di S è ottaedrica e la somma vettoriale dei momenti di dipolo è nulla. La molecola di CCl_4, a causa della sua geometria tetraedrica, non è polare perché, anche in questo caso, la somma vettoriale dei momenti di dipolo è nulla, nonostante i legami C-Cl siano polarizzati. L'unica molecola polare è NF_3, perché i momenti di dipolo generati dai legami N-F non si cancellano a vicenda, presentando la molecola una geometria molecolare piramidale.

51) D. Se la soluzione X ha un pH = 2, allora $[H^+] = 10^{-2}$ M = 0,01 M; se la soluzione Y ha un pH = 4, allora $[H^+] = 10^{-4}$ M = 0,0001 M. In conclusione, la soluzione X ha $[H^+]$ 100 volte maggiore della soluzione Y.

52) E. 25 cm^3 = 0,025 L di una soluzione 0,40 M di H_2SO_4 contengono 0,010 moli di acido ($[H_2SO_4] = mol_{H_2SO_4}/V_{soluzione\ in\ L}$). Dall'equazione di reazione, si evince che sono necessarie 0,020 moli di NaOH per neutralizzare completamente l'acido (mol NaOH : mol H_2SO_4 = 2 : 1, ossia mol NaOH = 2 mol H_2SO_4). La concentrazione in mol/L di NaOH è, quindi, M_{NaOH} = 0,020 mol/0,040 L = 0,50 mol/L. Per trasformare la concentrazione da mol/L a g/L, basta moltiplicare il numeratore per il peso formula dell'NaOH (M_r = 40 g/mol), ottenendo [(0,50 mol/L) × (40 g/mol)] = 20 g/L.

Fisica e Matematica

53) B. $$8^{2x+3}\cdot\frac{1}{4^{3x}}=2^{x+3}\rightarrow\left(2^3\right)^{2x+3}\cdot\frac{1}{\left(2^2\right)^{3x}}=2^{x+3}\rightarrow 2^{6x+9}\cdot\frac{1}{2^{6x}}=2^{x+3}$$

$$2^{6x+9}\cdot 2^{-6x}=2^{x+3}\rightarrow 2^{6x+9+6x}=2^{x+3}\rightarrow 9=x+3$$

$$x=6.$$

54) C. Razionalizzando il denominatore si ha:

$$\frac{2}{2+\sqrt{3}}\cdot\frac{2-\sqrt{3}}{2-\sqrt{3}}=\frac{4-2\sqrt{3}}{4-3}=4-2\sqrt{3},$$

dove si è utilizzato il prodotto notevole $(A+B)(A-B)=A^2-B^2$ e si è tenuto conto che $\left(\sqrt{3}\right)^2=3$.

55) D. L'ascissa del vertice della parabola è data da:

$$x_V=-\frac{b}{2a}=-\frac{5}{2\cdot 2}=-\frac{5}{4}.$$

Per trovare l'ordinata del vertice possiamo utilizzare la formula $y_V = \frac{4ac - b^2}{4a}$ o, alternativamente, sostituire l'ascissa x_V appena trovata nell'equazione della parabola:

$$y_V = 2x_V^2 + 5x_V - 2 = 2\left(-\frac{5}{4}\right)^2 + 5\left(-\frac{5}{4}\right) - 2 = \frac{25}{8} - \frac{25}{8} - 2 = -\frac{41}{8}.$$

Il vertice ha, quindi, coordinate $\left(-\frac{5}{4}; -\frac{41}{8}\right)$.

56) B. Dalla definizione di media pesata si ha:

$$\frac{2 \cdot N_{maschi} + x \cdot N_{femmine}}{N_{maschi} + N_{femmine}} = 3 + \frac{1}{5}$$

$$\frac{2 \cdot 39 + x \cdot 36}{39 + 36} = \frac{16}{5}$$

$$\frac{2 \cdot 39 + x \cdot 36}{75} = \frac{16}{5}.$$

Semplifichiamo la prima frazione dividendo il numeratore e il denominatore per 3:

$$\frac{2 \cdot 13 + x \cdot 12}{25} = \frac{16}{5}$$

$$\frac{26 + x \cdot 12}{25} = \frac{80}{25}$$

$$12x = 80 - 26 \rightarrow 12x = 54 \rightarrow x = \frac{54}{12} = \frac{9}{2}.$$

Infine possiamo riscrivere il risultato finale nella notazione proposta nelle alternative possibili:

$$\frac{9}{2} = \frac{8}{2} + \frac{1}{2} = 4 + \frac{1}{2} = 4\frac{1}{2}.$$

57) B. Poiché si tratta di uno specchio concavo, tutti i raggi paralleli all'asse ottico principale vengono riflessi passando per il fuoco F e viceversa. Nulla si può dire sull'orientazione, realtà e dimensioni dell'immagine formata, in quanto dipendono tutte dalla posizione dell'oggetto rispetto allo specchio. Infatti, se l'oggetto è più vicino del fuoco la sua immagine risulterà virtuale e dritta, mentre se è più lontano risulterà reale e capovolta.

58) C. L'energia somministrata risulta:

$$E = P \cdot \Delta t = 100 \cdot 1600 = 160\,000 \text{ J}$$

per cui il calore latente di vaporizzazione è:

$$c_L = \frac{E}{m_{vaporizzata}} = \frac{160\,000}{200} = 800 \text{ J/g}$$

59) E. Dalla seconda legge di Newton:

$$a_y = \frac{\sum F_y}{m} = \frac{T - mg}{m} = \frac{T}{m} - g.$$

60) D. La velocità della barca per una persona ferma a terra si ottiene sommando vettorialmente la velocità della barca rispetto all'acqua e la velocità dell'acqua rispetto alla terraferma:

$$\vec{v}_{barca,\,terra} = \vec{v}_{barca,\,acqua} + \vec{v}_{acqua,\,terra}$$

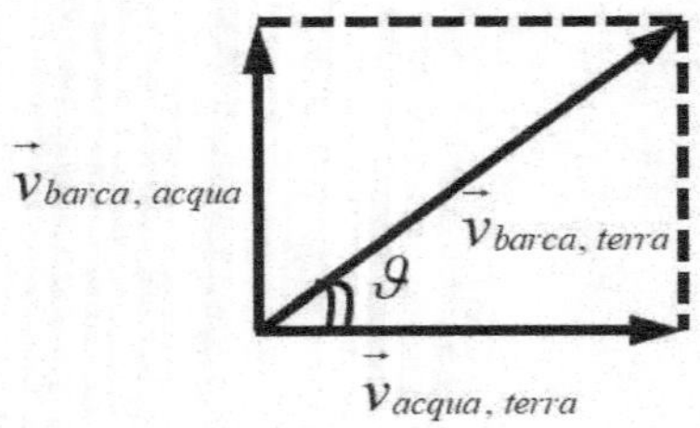

Poiché questi due vettori sono tra loro perpendicolari, il modulo del vettore somma è dato dal Teorema di Pitagora:

$$v_{barca,\,terra} = \sqrt{v^2_{barca,\,acqua} + v^2_{acqua,\,terra}} = \sqrt{3^2 + 4^2} = 5\ \text{m/s}.$$

Infine, l'angolo di navigazione della barca risulta:

$$\vartheta = \arccos\frac{v_{barca,\,acqua}}{v_{barca,\,terra}} = \arccos\frac{4}{5}.$$

IMAT
a.a. 2021/2022

General Knowledge and Logical Reasoning

1) A young woman (A), knowing that she was dying, requested that her mother (B), who was awaiting a kidney transplant, should be allowed to receive her kidneys after her death. The request was not allowed, and A's kidneys were received by another patient (C), who was higher up the waiting list than B because his medical need for a transplant was more urgent. The committee overseeing transplant decisions argued that the system it used had to be administered solely in accordance with the rationale behind its waiting list. Their decision seemed to others unduly bureaucratic, especially as B will be left to care for A's young child.
Which one of the following best illustrates the principle behind the committee's decision?

A. Decisions on transplants cannot be influenced by emotions
B. Decisions on transplants should focus on the medical need of the potential recipient
C. Donations between family members are not allowed
D. Decisions on transplants should include social considerations
E. The donor's wishes should not be considered

2) From ever younger ages, people are reporting symptoms of anxiety due to the pressure to be 'perfect' in all areas of life. It seems that, in many cultures, there is an increasing sense of competition in everything from school results to the job market to personal appearance and even how one's social life looks on social media. As a result, many people experience problems associated with low self-confidence. But rather than reach for a pill or a self-help book to tackle their problems, more of these individuals should just go outside for a run or a walk. While it sounds simplistic, this recommendation is supported by the research finding that people who do a lot of outdoor activities tend to have high self-esteem.
Which one of the following is the best statement of the flaw in the above argument?

A. It assumes that high levels of self-confidence or self-esteem are all that are needed for a person to enjoy good mental health
B. It ignores the fact that not everyone with low self-esteem has the desire to go for a run or a walk outside
C. It assumes that people who manage to appear 'perfect' in the different parts of their lives will not suffer from problems with self-confidence
D. It ignores the likelihood that many people with varying levels of self-confidence would benefit from the advice of a mental health professional
E. It ignores the possibility that people with higher self-esteem might be more inclined to take part in outdoor activities

3) For many years, children and young people have been protected from exploitation by the entertainment industry. In recent years, however, the number of young people suddenly thrust into the limelight has increased, and many of them feel that they must seize any opportunity to achieve recognition before this window passes them by. Dealing with fame, performing in front of large audiences, the rigours of rehearsal and the general stresses of what is a difficult occupation take maturity and can rob children of their childhood. Rejection, disappointment and failure are felt more keenly by young people because they lack wider experience and this can make for a very unhappy childhood. These factors would indicate that young performers need further protection by law.
Which one of the following best expresses the main conclusion of the above argument?

A. Young performers need further protection by law
B. Young people can be suddenly thrust into the limelight
C. Young performers are robbed of their childhood by the demands of performing
D. Young people feel rejection, disappointment and failure more because they lack wider experience
E. Young people have been protected from exploitation by the entertainment industry for many years

4) Our three local universities have agreed that they will offer a place to everyone from our school who applies to them. Because you attend a different school, you are not guaranteed an offer from these universities.
Which one of the following most closely parallels the reasoning used in the above argument?

A. Everyone who becomes a student at our college has achieved a high score in their high school examinations. You have a high score, and therefore you are sure to be accepted as a student at our college
B. Everyone who has a free bus pass is entitled to travel on buses after 9:30 am without payment. Since it is after 9:30 am and you have a free bus pass, you do not have to pay for this bus journey
C. Everyone over the age of 60 is entitled to a bus pass, which gives them free travel on buses after 9:30 am. Since you are younger than 60, you are not entitled to free bus travel
D. In our country, everyone who becomes a teacher must have a university degree. Since you do not have a degree, you are not qualified to become a teacher
E. The only way to stand for election to Parliament is to be nominated by voters in a geographical constituency. Since you have not been nominated, you cannot stand for election.

5) Of all the food we buy, bread suffers the worst fate when it comes to waste. 32% of it ends up being thrown away. We value other types of food a lot more, as the average for all food and drink being wasted is 15%. The proportion of meat and fish thrown away is below average (13%) and our most precious item is alcohol – we throw away just 6% of it.
Which one of the following is an underlying assumption of the above argument?

A. Bread is a low-quality food
B. We should be more moderate when it comes to buying bread
C. The more expensive a food or drink is, the less likely it is that it will be wasted

D. The main reason why we throw food away is that we do not value it much
E. Bread goes stale faster so is more likely to be thrown away

6) In a survey of cats' eating habits, 10% of the cats tested showed a clear preference for Moggiemeat, 20% preferred Fuss-a-Puss and 40% preferred Yummy Paws. An additional 6 cats did not seem to care at all which of the three foods they ate, while the remaining 27 cats in the survey would not touch any of these foods.
How many cats were involved in the survey?

A. 110
B. 33
C. 63
D. 90
E. 103

7) It is usual, when seating people round a table at a social function, to alternate males with females, but if there are unequal numbers of each, this is impossible. At one party, 14 women and only 6 men were present. They were seated round a circular table so that as few women as possible had no male sitting directly next to them.
How many women had no male sitting directly next to them?

A. 7
B. 4
C. 6
D. 2
E. 8

8) Simon plans to send Christmas cards to 35 friends. He is going to choose a single design to send to them all and knows that some of the recipients really do not like glitter cards so he will not buy this type. He wants 2-fold cards so that he can write a letter on the inside for 5 of them.
The following table shows the possibilities that he is considering.

card type	*no. in pack*	*glitter*	*1-fold*	*2-fold*	*pack price*
religious	5	no		yes	£1.80
robins	8	no	yes		£1.95
village scene	20	yes		yes	£2.50
cartoon	12	no	yes		£2.20
father xmas	10	no		yes	£3.10

What is the lowest amount of money that Simon could spend on his cards?

A. £12.60
B. £12.40
C. £5.00
D. £6.00
E. £9.75

9) When I first woke up early this morning the display of my bedside digital clock showed:

I presumed that it was faulty, but, after drifting off to sleep again, when I next awoke and saw the clock I realised that someone must have turned the clock upside down and that it was exactly an hour and a half since I had looked at it before.

What did I see when I woke up the second time?

A.
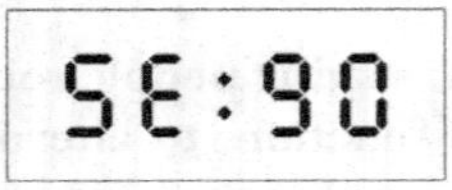

B.
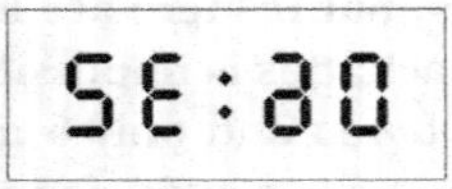

C.

D.
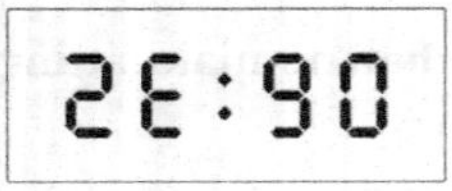

E.
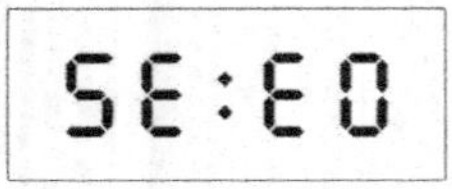

10) Teams from five US states have reached the final of a competition. The event organisers are trying to design a sign for each state. One idea involves the name, in capital letters, being placed vertically on a sign board which spins when one of the team presses their buzzer to answer a question. They want the sign to read correctly regardless of whether it is read from the front or the back.
Unfortunately they realise that most of the states for which this would have worked have not reached the final.
Which one of the following is the only state in the final for which this style of sign would work?

A. Alabama
B. Idaho
C. Montana
D. Oklahoma
E. Hawaii

11) Which one of the following pairs of scholar/field of study is NOT correct?

A. John Maynard Keynes – economics
B. Maria Montessori – pedagogy
C. Hans Jonas – medicine
D. Max Planck – physics
E. B. F. Skinner – psychology

12) Which one of the following writers is the author of the best-selling novel *My Brilliant Friend*?

A. Khaled Hosseini
B. Ian McEwan
C. Paulo Coelho
D. Elena Ferrante
E. Kazuo Ishiguro

13) What does the letter A stand for in the international organisation FAO?

A. Architecture
B. Aerospace
C. Automotive
D. Agriculture
E. Aesthetics

14) Which of the following pairs of theatre/city is the only correct one?

A. San Carlo – Venice
B. Metropolitan Opera House – New York
C. The Bolshoi Theatre – Saint Petersburg
D. La Fenice – Florence
E. The Palais Garnier Opera House – Brussels

15) The Rosetta Stone provided the key to decipher:

A. characters of the Phoenician alphabet
B. characters of the Ancient Greek alphabet
C. Egyptian hieroglyphs
D. the Code of Hammurabi
E. the Sumerian language

16) Which one of the following institutions of the European Union is elected by direct universal suffrage?

A. European Parliament

B. European Commission
C. Court of Justice of the European Union
D. European Economic and Social Committee
E. Council of the European Union

17) Which one of the following directors directed the films that make up *The Godfather* trilogy?

A. Martin Scorsese
B. Sergio Leone
C. Brian De Palma
D. Matteo Garrone
E. Francis Ford Coppola

18) Which one of the following pairs of scholar/scientific discovery is NOT correct?

A. Dmitri Mendeleev – periodic table of elements
B. Niels Bohr – electron microscope
C. Wilhelm Conrad Röntgen – x-ray
D. Hans Wilhelm Geiger – particle detector
E. Evangelista Torricelli – mercury barometer

19) Which one of the following treaties established the European Coal and Steel Community (ECSC)?

A. Lisbon
B. Amsterdam
C. Paris
D. Nice
E. Rome

20) Which one of the following global organisations sets and enforces rules of trade between nations?

A. World Bank
B. WTO
C. IMF
D. OECD
E. World Economic Forum

21) Which one of the following pairs of Russian writers/works is NOT correct?

A. Vladimir Nabokov – Lolita
B. Fyodor Dostoyevsky – The Brothers Karamazov
C. Leo Tolstoy – Anna Karenina
D. Mikhail Bulgakov – Uncle Vanya
E. Boris Pasternak – Doctor Zhivago

22) The expression 'perfect bicameral system' refers to:

A. the legislative procedure that assigns identical powers to the two chambers of a parliament
B. the judicial system whereby the first sentence must be confirmed by the first round of appeal
C. the form of government that assigns identical power to two institutional figures.
D. the kind of parliamentary monarchy where monarch and parliament have the same powers
E. the perfect separation of the magistrate judge and public prosecutor

Biology

23) Which of the following types of nucleic acid is/are found in viruses?
1 single-stranded DNA
2 double-stranded DNA
3 RNA

A. 1 and 2 only
B. 2 only
C. 1 and 3 only
D. 2 and 3 only
E. 1, 2 and 3

24) Which one of the diagrams (not drawn to scale) represents a structure that is formed by mitosis?

A.
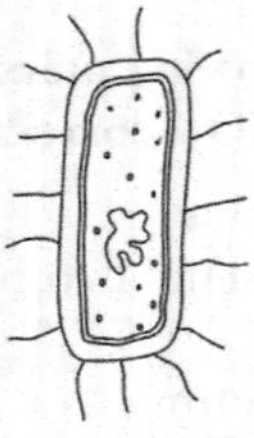

B.
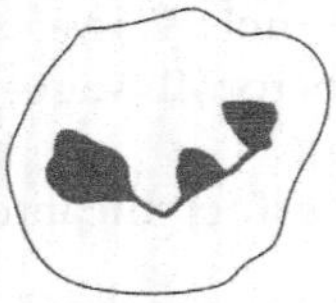

C.

D.
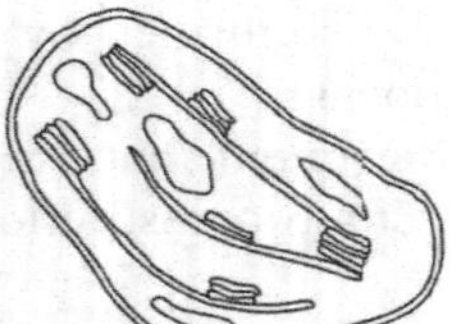

E.
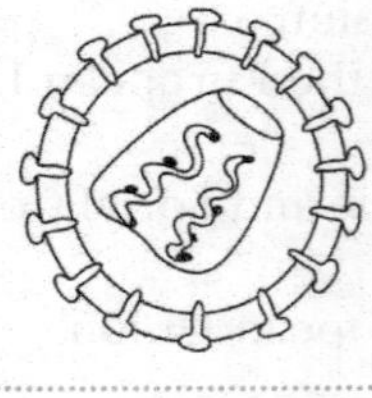

25) Three fatty acids with the formula $C_8H_{16}O_2$ react with glycerol ($C_3H_8O_3$) to form a triglyceride. Which of the following is the correct formula for the triglyceride?

A. $C_{27}H_{48}O_5$
B. $C_{27}H_{48}O_6$
C. $C_{27}H_{50}O_6$
D. $C_{27}H_{52}O_7$
E. $C_{27}H_{56}O_9$

26) Which of the following is correct for cholesterol in humans?

A. It is used to make all hormones
B. It is a good source of energy because of the number of hydrogen atoms
C. It forms hydrogen bonds with water which stabilises the cell membrane
D. It transports fatty acids around the body
E. It maintains the fluidity of the cell membrane

27) The diagram represents an animal cell with five organelles labelled P, Q, R, S and T.

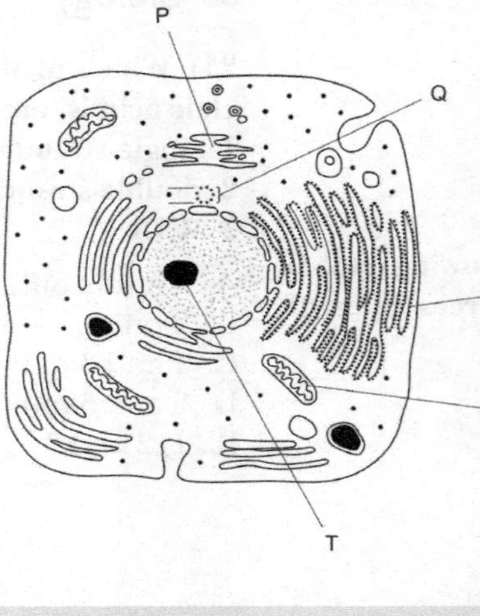

Which row correctly matches the label with the name and function of the cell organelle?

	label	*name of cell organelle*	*funcion of cell organelle*
row 1	P	mitochondrion	protein synthesis
row 2	Q	centrioles	holds sister chromatids together
row 3	R	ribosome	formation of lysosomes
row 4	S	Golgi apparatus	anaerobic respiration
row 5	T	nucleolus	formation of ribosomal sub-units

A. row 3
B. row 2
C. row 5
D. row 4
E. row 1

28) Which of the following cell structures contain(s) biological catalysts?
1 cytoplasm
2 nucleus
3 mitochondria

A. 1, 2 and 3
B. 2 only
C. 3 only
D. 2 and 3 only
E. 1 only

29) Which of the following reactions or biological processes involves a redox reaction?

A. glucose + glucose $\rightleftharpoons$ maltose + water
B. $NAD^+ + H_2 \rightleftharpoons NADH + H^+$
C. a cytosine and guanine pairing
D. polymerisation of amino acids
E. depolarisation of a neuron

30) The SRY gene is normally located on the human Y chromosome. This gene initiates the development of male characteristics.
Using this information, which of the following statements about the SRY gene is/are correct?

1 Insertion of the SRY gene into an X chromosome of a female zygote could give it male characteristics.
2 A sperm cell arising from incorrect division, which has a functional SRY gene, could give rise to a female with a sex chromosome trisomy following fertilisation with a normal ova.
3 During meiosis, crossing over could result in the formation of 'X' sperm with the SRY gene, which could cause male characteristics after fertilisation.

A. 2 only
B. 3 only
C. 1 and 2 only
D. 1 and 3 only
E. 1 only

31) A cell containing four pairs of homologous chromosomes divides by meiosis. Which row shows the cells produced and the number of chromosomes that they contain?

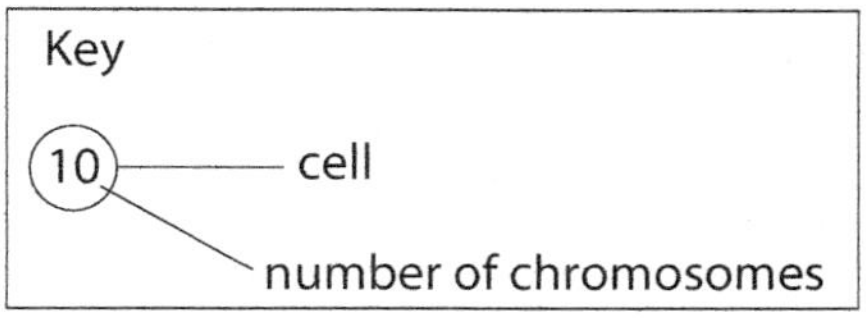

row	parent cell	end of meiosis I		after meiosis II			
1	④	②	②	②	②	②	②
2	④	④	④	②	②	②	②
3	⑧	④	④	④	④	④	④
4	⑧	⑧	⑧	④	④	④	④
5	⑧	⑯	⑯	⑧	⑧	⑧	⑧

A. row 5
B. row 2
C. row 1
D. row 4
E. row 3

32) The sequence of bases in part of a DNA strand is:

TATGATCTTAGGCAACAT

A strand of mRNA is transcribed using this sequence of bases.
Which one of the following charts shows the correct proportions of the bases in the mRNA?

A.
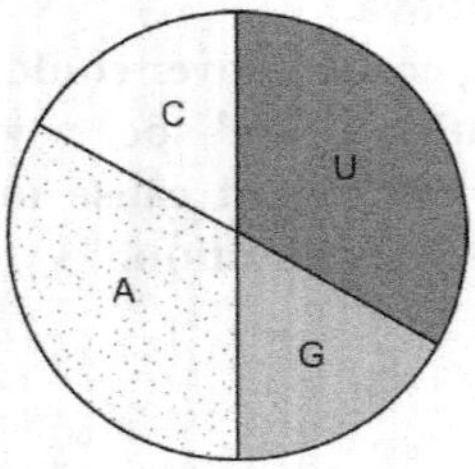

B.
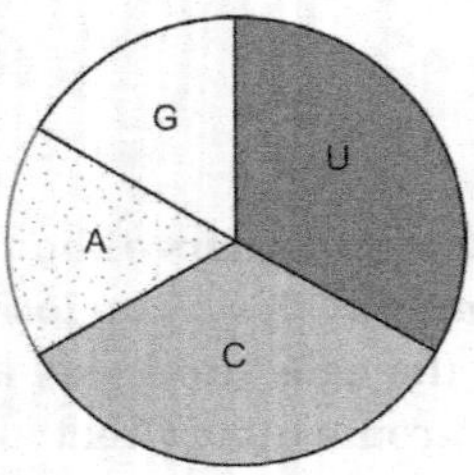

C.
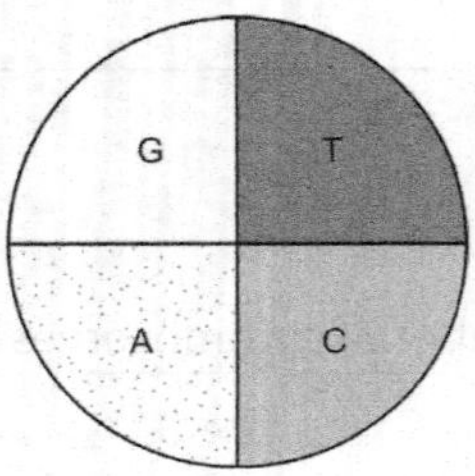

D.
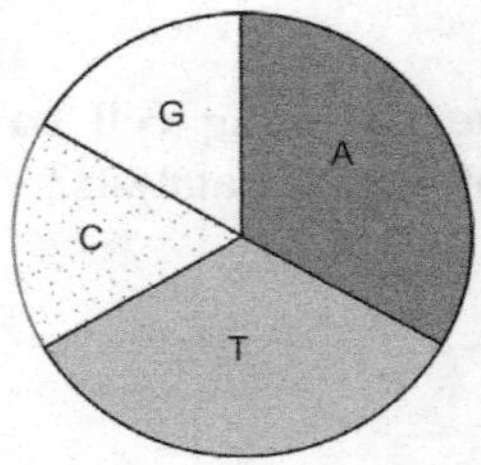

E.
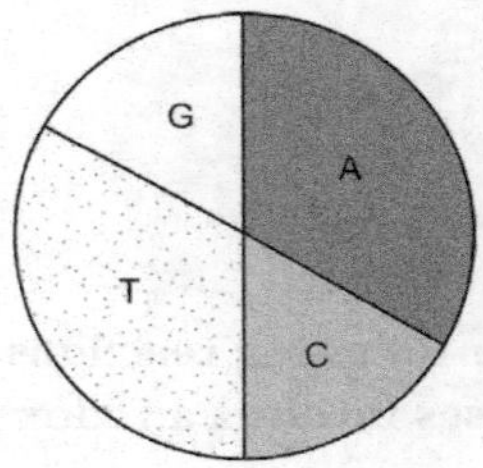

33) Polydactyly is a condition caused by a gene mutation. Animals affected by polydactyly have extra digits on one or more limbs.
Five inheritance patterns of polydactyly in a species are shown in the diagrams.

Key
□ male without condition
■ male with condition
○ female without condition
● female with condition

1

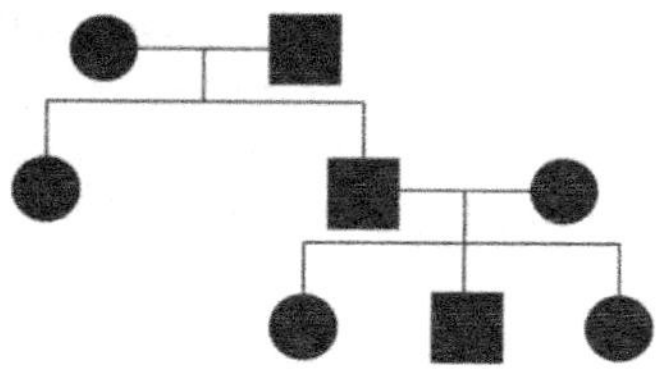

2

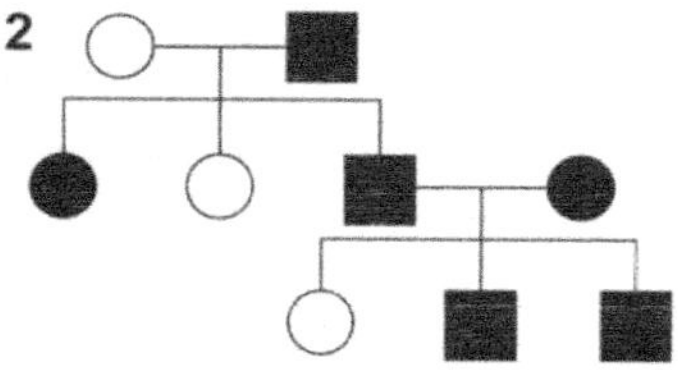

3

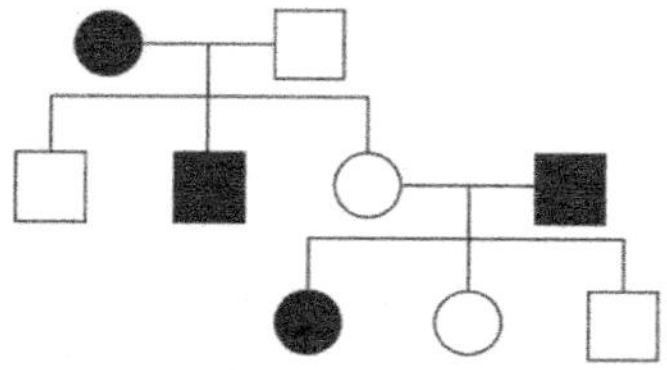

4

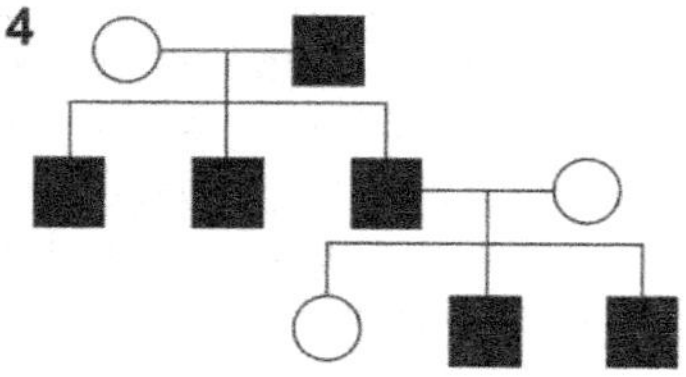

5

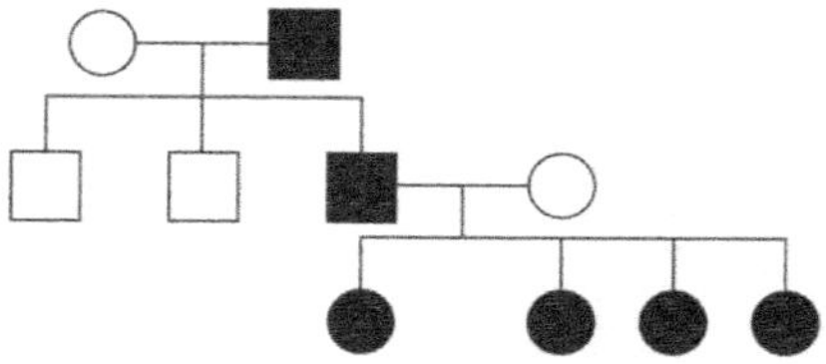

Which inheritance pattern can ONLY occur when polydactyly is caused by an autosomal dominant allele and NOT when it is caused by an autosomal recessive allele?
[Assume normal cell divisions in all individuals.]

A. 1
B. 2
C. 3
D. 4
E. 5

34) In which of the following places are proton pumps found?
1 the chloroplast stroma
2 the gap between the thylakoid membranes
3 the membrane of the granum

A. 2 only
B. 1 only
C. 1 and 2 only
D. 3 only
E. 1 and 3 only

35) Which row could be correct for directional selection?

Key
✓ yes
✗ no

	a low-frequency phenotype is selected	*a predator could be the cause*	*the frequency of a recessive allele increases*
row 1	✓	✗	✗
row 2	✗	✓	✗
row 3	✗	✗	✓
row 4	✗	✓	✓
row 5	✓	✓	✓

A. row 2
B. row 3
C. row 5
D. row 4
E. row 1

36) Which one of the following statements is correct about the cardiac cycle of a healthy human?

A. When the left ventricle relaxes, the aortic valve closes
B. When the left atrium contracts, the aortic valve opens
C. When the right atrio-ventricular valve closes, the left atrio-ventricular valve opens
D. When the right atrium contracts, the left ventricle contracts
E. When the right ventricle contracts, the right atrio-ventricular valve opens

37) The graph below shows the change in blood cell count of a human over time.

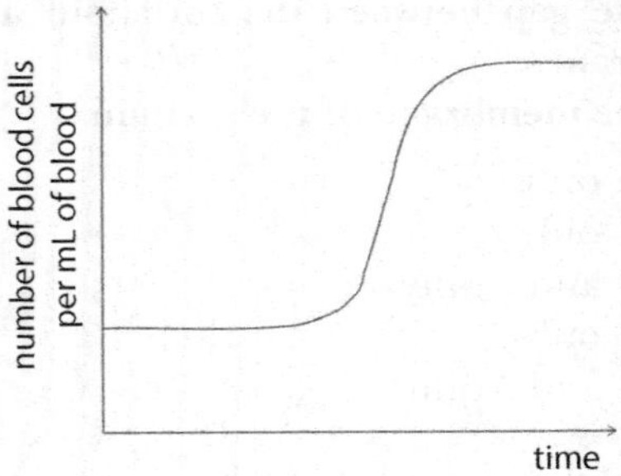

Which of the following could explain the shape of the above graph?

1 a reduction in the concentration of oxygen in the atmosphere
2 a response to a bacterial infection
3 increased differentiation of bone marrow stem cells

A. 1, 2 and 3
B. 1 and 2 only
C. 2 and 3 only
D. 1 only
E. 2 only

38) The diagram shows a cross section through a human eye. Some parts of the eye are labelled 1 to 5 with notes. Which one of the following notes is correct?

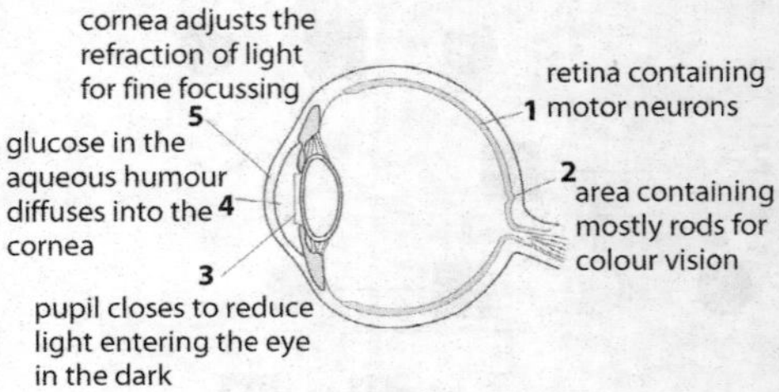

A. note 1
B. note 2
C. note 3
D. note 4
E. note 5

39) Organ or tissue transplants normally require that the donor's antigens must be closely matched to those of the recipient. Which one of the following types of transplant can typically be carried out WITHOUT the need for a match between donor and recipient?

A. Liver
B. Lung
C. Cornea
D. Heart
E. Kidney

40) The diagram shows the relationship between the features of two substances involved in digestion: bile and amylase.

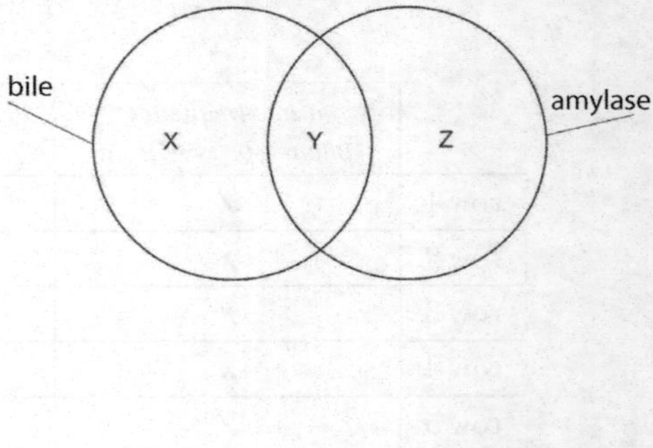

	X	Y	Z
row 1	assimilates lipid	stored in the gall bladder	digests maltose
row 2	digests lipid	works in the small intestine	digests starch
row 3	digests lipid	produced by the pancreas	produces maltose
row 4	emulsifies lipid	produced by the pancreas	digests maltose
row 5	emulsifies lipid	works in the small intestine	digests starch

Which of the following rows is correct for X, Y and Z?

A. row 2
B. row 5
C. row 3
D. row 4
E. row 1

Chemistry

41) As Group VII of the Periodic Table (F to I) is descended, which of the following properties of the elements DECREASE?
1 melting points
2 electronegativities
3 first ionisation energies

A. 2 only
B. 1 only
C. 1 and 3 only
D. 1, 2 and 3
E. 2 and 3 only

42) An atom has a mass number of 18 and contains 10 neutrons. A common ion of this atom has a charge of –2. What is the electron configuration of this ion in its lowest energy state?

A. $1s^2 2s^2 2p^4$
B. $1s^2 2s^2 2p^2$
C. $1s^2 2s^2 2p^6 3s^2$
D. $1s^2 2s^2 2p^6 3s^2 3p^4$
E. $1s^2 2s^2 2p^6$

43) Which of the following changes is/are correct?

1 The addition of 1 g of salt to 100 g water will increase the freezing point.
2 A change in temperature from 150 °C to 120 °C will increase the average kinetic energy of water molecules.
3 A change in the surrounding air pressure from 100 kPa to 120 kPa will increase the boiling point of water.

A. 1 only
B. 2 only
C. 3 only
D. 1 and 3 only
E. 1, 2 and 3

44) Which of the following hydrocarbons are structural isomers of hexane?

1 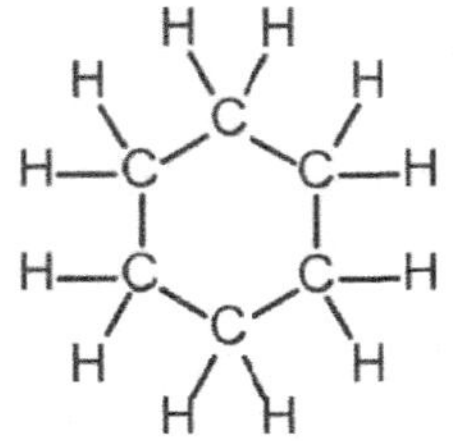

2 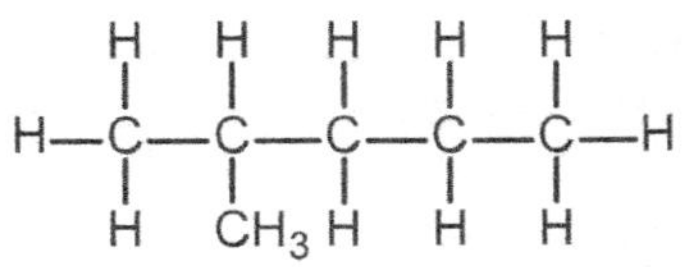

3 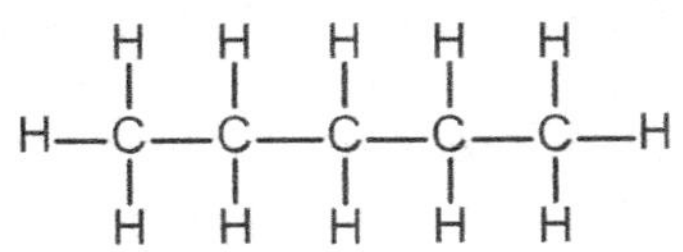

A. 1 only
B. 3 only
C. 1 and 2 only

D. 2 only
E. 1 and 3 only

45) Which of the following equations is associated with the first electron affinity of chlorine?

A. $Cl(g) + e^- \rightarrow Cl^-(g)$
B. $Cl(g) \rightarrow Cl^-(g) + e^-$
C. $Cl_2(g) + 2\,e^- \rightarrow 2\,Cl^-(g)$
D. $2\,Cl^-(g) - 2\,e^- \rightarrow Cl_2(g)$
E. $Cl^-(g) + e^- \rightarrow Cl(g)$

46) Vitamin B5 has the structure:

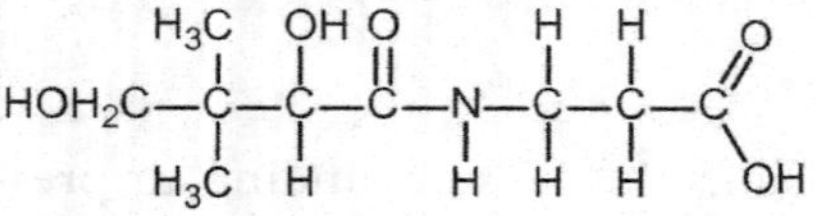

Which of the following functional groups are contained in a molecule of vitamin B5?
1 alcohol
2 aldehyde
3 amide
4 amine
5 carboxylic acid
6 ketone

A. 1, 2 and 4 only
B. 1, 3 and 6 only
C. 2, 4 and 6 only
D. 1, 3 and 5 only
E. 4, 5 and 6 only

47) X is 50.0 mL of a 0.050 mol L^{-1} aqueous solution of nitric acid (HNO_3). Y is 100 mL of a 0.050 mol L^{-1} aqueous solution of sulfuric acid (H_2SO_4). Which of the following statements about these solutions is/are correct?
1 The hydrogen ion concentration in Y is four times greater than the hydrogen ion concentration in X.
2 Only the acid in Y will be completely dissociated into ions.
3 Y has a pH value of less than 2 at 25 °C.

A. none of them
B. 1 only
C. 3 only
D. 1 and 3 only
E. 2 and 3 only

48) Which row gives the correct shapes around the aluminium centres in Al Cl_3 and Al_2Cl_6 molecules?

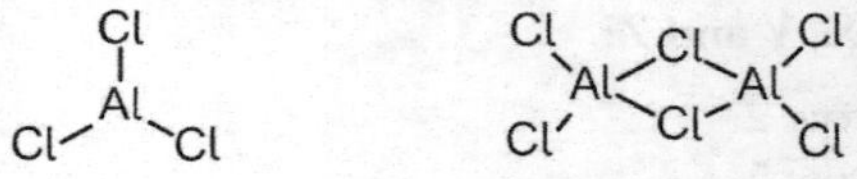

$AlCl_3$ Al_2Cl_6

	$AlCl_3$	Al_2Cl_6
row 1	trigonal planar	square planar
row 2	trigonal pyramidal	tetrahedral
row 3	tetrahedral	square planar
row 4	trigonal planar	tetrahedral
row 5	trigonal pyramidal	square planar

[atomic numbers: Al = 13; Cl = 17]

A. row 2
B. row 4
C. row 3
D. row 1
E. row 5

49) At room temperature and pressure, which of the following substances has the strongest hydrogen bonds between their molecules?

A. propanal, CH_3CH_2CHO
B. fluoromethane, CH_3F
C. trimethylamine, $(CH_3)_3N$
D. hydrogen sulfide, H_2S
E. ethanoic acid, CH_3COOH

50) 100 mL of a solution contained 3.2 g of potassium nitrate. 25 mL of this solution was added to an empty 250 mL volumetric flask. Distilled water was added up to the 250 mL mark and the flask was shaken to ensure that mixing was com-

plete. A pipette was used to transfer 25 mL of the resulting solution from the volumetric flask to an empty conical flask. What is the concentration of the potassium nitrate solution, in g L^{-1}, in the conical flask?

A. 3.20 g L^{-1}
B. 0.80 g L^{-1}
C. 0.32 g L^{-1}
D. 8.00 g L^{-1}
E. 0.08 g L^{-1}

51) The general formula of an oxoacid is H_mXO_n. Which of the following expressions gives the oxidation state of element X?

A. $m - 2n$
B. $2n - m$
C. $m + 2n$
D. $2m - n$
E. $n - 2m$

52) A sample of an oxide of iron contains 1.68 g of iron and 0.64 g of oxygen only.
What is the formula of this oxide? [A_r values: Fe = 56; O = 16]

A. Fe_4O_3
B. Fe_2O_3
C. Fe_3O_2
D. Fe_3O_4
E. FeO

Physics and Mathematics

53) Which one of the following is a simplification of

$$\frac{(x+2)^2}{x^2+x-2}$$

A. -4

B. $\frac{(x+2)^2}{(x-2)(x+1)}$

C. $\frac{4x+4}{x-2}$

D. $\frac{x+2}{x-2}$

E. $\frac{x+2}{x-1}$

54) Find the complete set of values of x which satisfy the inequality

$$\frac{1}{2}(2x+3)-\frac{2}{3}(x+1)<2x$$

A. $x > \frac{1}{2}$

B. $x > \frac{5}{14}$

C. $x > \frac{7}{8}$

D. $x > \frac{5}{4}$

E. $x < -5$

55)

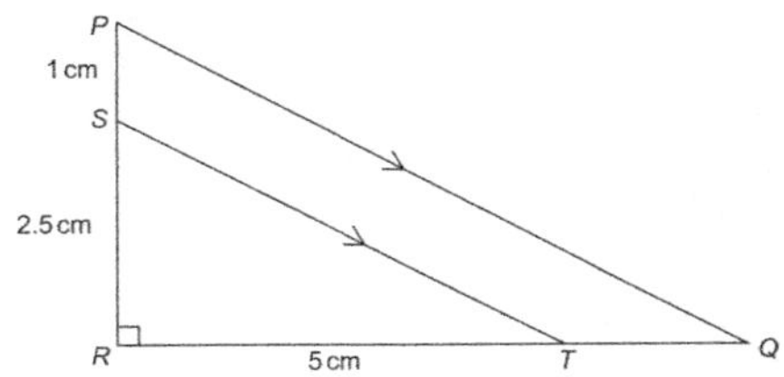

[diagram not to scale]

***PQR* is a right-angled triangle with angle *PRQ* equal to 90°.**
Point *S* is on the side *PR*.
Point *T* is on the side *RQ*.
The line *ST* is parallel to the line *PQ*.
***RS* = 2.5 cm**
***PS* = 1 cm**
***RT* = 5 cm**
What is the perimeter of the trapezium *PQTS* in cm?

A. $2(1+3\sqrt{3})$

B. $3(1+2\sqrt{5})$

C. $3(1+2\sqrt{3})$

D. $2(1+3\sqrt{5})$

E. $2(1+3\sqrt{6})$

56) 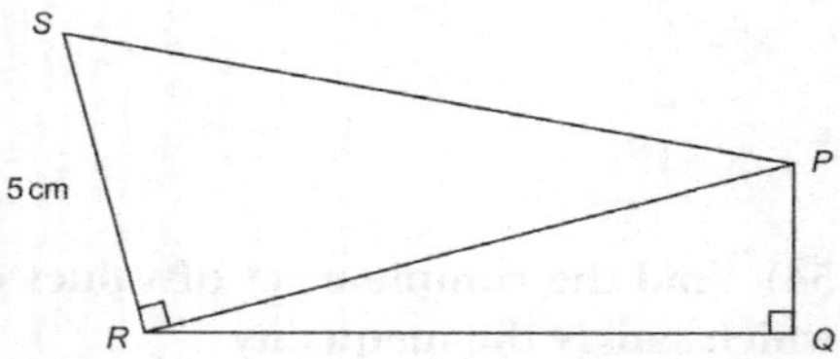

[diagram not to scale]

***PQR* and *PRS* are right-angled triangles.**
Angle *PRS* = Angle *PQR* = 90°
***RS* = 5 cm**
The area of triangle *PQR* is 14 cm^2 and $\tan PRQ = \frac{1}{7}$
What is the value of cos*RPS*?

A. $\frac{2\sqrt{2}}{3}$

B. $\frac{\sqrt{2}}{4}$

C. $\frac{\sqrt{2}}{2}$

D. $\frac{\sqrt{6}}{3}$

E. $\frac{1}{3}$

57) At an athletics competition, a hammer thrower swings a hammer in a horizontal circle.
Immediately before releasing the hammer, the ball at the end of the hammer is moving at a constant angular velocity of 10 rad / s in a horizontal circular path of radius 2.5 m.
Which row in the table gives the speed and the magnitude of the acceleration of the ball just before release?

	speed (m/s)	*acceleration* (m/s^2)
row 1	25	250
row 2	25	40
row 3	15	50
row 4	10	40
row 5	10	0

A. row 2
B. row 3
C. row 4
D. row 1
E. row 5

58) A hydraulic jack consists of a piston with a small cross-sectional area connected by a tube to a piston with a larger cross-sectional area. The cylinders of the pistons and the tube contain oil.

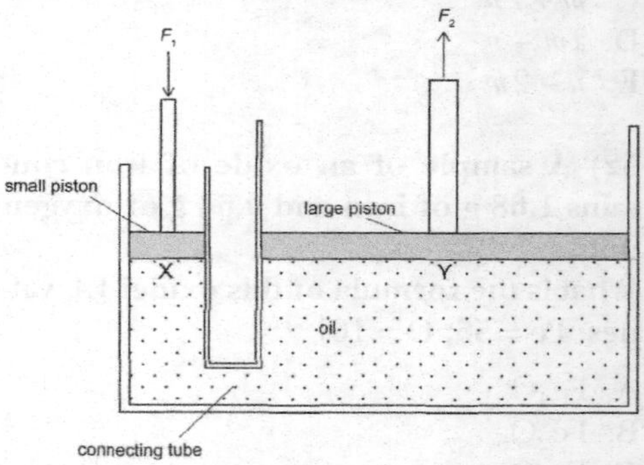

A downward force F_1 is applied to the smaller piston, which results in an upwards resultant force F_2 being exerted on the larger piston. Points X and Y are in the oil, immediately underneath the pistons, which are at the same height.
Which of the following statements about the pressure and forces in the hydraulic jack is/are correct?

1 The pressure at Y is less than the pressure at X.

2 The pressure at Y is equal to the pressure at X.
3 F_2 is greater than F_1.
4 F_2 is less than F_1.

A. 3 only
B. 1 only
C. 2 and 3 only
D. 2 and 4 only
E. 1 and 4 only

59) A metal has a specific heat capacity of 500 J/(kg °C). A block of this metal has a mass of 1.20 kg and is provided with thermal energy by a heater for 5.00 minutes. The temperature of the block increases from 40.0°C to 90.0°C without a phase change.
What is the power of the heater?
[Assume that no thermal energy is lost to or gained from the surroundings and that the metal is at a uniform temperature at all times.]

A. 6000 W
B. 100 W
C. 180 W
D. 10 800 W
E. 80 W

60) Which of the following expressions gives a quantity that can be measured in joules (J)? [Assume that all quantities are magnitudes.]

A. momentum × velocity
B. $(\text{charge})^2 \times \text{resistance}$
C. $(\text{mass})^2 \times \text{resistance}$
D. $\dfrac{\text{specific heat capacity}}{\text{mass} \times \text{temperature change}}$
E. $\dfrac{\text{voltage}}{\text{current} \times \text{time}}$

RISPOSTE COMMENTATE • IMAT a.a. 2021/2022

Cultura generale e ragionamento logico

1) B. Nella traccia si illustra come una giovane donna (A), sapendo di stare per morire, avesse chiesto l'autorizzazione a donare *post mortem* i propri reni a sua madre (B), in attesa di un trapianto. Inoltre, nel testo si spiega come la richiesta non fosse stata accolta e i reni di (A) fossero stati donati a un altro paziente (C), essendo questi più in alto di (B) nella lista d'attesa a causa di una necessità medica più urgente di trapianto di reni. Proprio questa urgenza dovuta alle necessità mediche rappresenta il motivo della donazione dei reni a (C) e non a (B) addotto dal comitato responsabile delle decisioni sui trapianti. Pertanto, il principio dietro la decisione del comitato è che "*decisions on transplants should focus on the medical need of the potential recipient*".

2) E. L'argomentazione esposta nella traccia contiene un passaggio logico difettoso dalle premesse (P_1 e P_2) alla conclusione (C). La domanda richiede di individuare quale delle cinque opzioni di risposta indichi al meglio tale difetto. A tale scopo esaminiamo innanzitutto l'argomentazione. In P_1 si afferma che molte persone sperimentano problemi di ansia e bassa autostima a causa della crescente pressione per essere "perfetti" in tutti gli ambiti della vita. In P_2 si espongono i risultati di una ricerca, secondo la quale le persone che fanno molte attività all'aperto tendono ad avere un'alta autostima. Da P_1 e P_2 si deduce C: quanti stanno sperimentando i suddetti problemi di ansia e bassa autostima dovrebbero semplicemente uscire a fare una corsa o una passeggiata. Se ora analizziamo le cinque opzioni di risposta, osserviamo come "*it ignores the possibility that people with higher self-esteem might be more inclined to take part in outdoor activities*" indichi la possibilità che i risultati della ricerca di cui si parla in P_2 siano inattendibili. Infatti, se le persone con una maggiore autostima fossero quelle più inclini a prendere parte ad attività all'aperto, la loro maggiore autostima non dipenderebbe dalle stesse attività all'aperto e ciò renderebbe difettose sia la ricerca esposta in P_2 sia la deduzione di C da P_2. Abbiamo quindi trovato l'opzione di risposta corretta, mentre le altre sono tutte da scartare. Infatti, "*it ignores the fact that not everyone with low self-esteem has the desire to go for a run or a walk outside*" indica un possibile difetto che riguarda sostanzialmente solo C, mentre le restanti tre opzioni non riguardano propriamente il passaggio logico da P_1 e P_2 a C.

3) A. Il ragionamento riportato nella traccia è costituito da almeno tre premesse fondamentali (P_1, P_2 e P_3): in P_1 si spiega come negli ultimi anni stia aumentando il numero di giovani che cercano il successo nell'industria dello spettacolo; in P_2 si segnala il rischio che la ricerca del successo in questo settore "*can rob children of their childhood*"; in P_3, infine, si sottolinea come i rifiuti, le delusioni e i fallimenti, frequenti nel mondo dello spettacolo, vengano percepiti in modo più acuto dai giovani. Da queste tre premesse il ragionamento giunge alla conclusione che "*young performers* *need further protection by law*". Tale conclusione è ripresa parola per parola in una delle cinque opzioni di risposta, che, quindi, è la soluzione del quesito.

4) C. Per risolvere il quesito, bisogna individuare quale delle cinque opzioni di risposta riporti un ragionamento che riproduce maggiormente quello contenuto nella traccia. La corrispondenza va intesa non dal punto di vista del contenuto, ma da quello della forma logica, indipendentemente dalla correttezza e dalla verità degli stessi ragionamenti. Perciò, bisogna stabilire innanzitutto la struttura logica del ragionamento della traccia. La frase "*our three local universities have agreed that they will offer a place to everyone from our school who applies to them*" è la prima premessa (P_1) e, con buona approssimazione, significa logicamente che "*TUTTI i futuri iscritti a una delle nostre tre università locali SE frequentano la nostra scuola, ALLORA riceveranno l'offerta di un posto da tali università*". La frase "*you attend a different school*" è la seconda premessa (P_2) e da un punto di vista logico significa "*tu NON frequenti la nostra scuola*". La frase "*you are not guaranteed an offer from these universities*" è la conclusione (C) e logicamente significa "*tu NON riceverai l'offerta di un posto da tali università*". Indicando con '*x*' "i futuri iscritti a una delle nostre tre università locali", con FNS "frequentare la nostra scuola", con ROP "ricevere l'offerta di un posto da una delle nostre tre università locali", con '∀' il quantificatore universale "TUTTI", con '¬' la negazione "NON" e con '→' l'implicazione "SE ..., ALLORA ...", la struttura del ragionamento della traccia è così simbolizzabile:

$$\begin{array}{ll} \mathbf{P_1:} & (\forall x)\ (\text{FNS}\ x \rightarrow \text{ROP}\ x) \\ \mathbf{P_2:} & \underline{\neg\ \text{FNS}\ tu \qquad\qquad\qquad} \\ \mathbf{C:} & \qquad\qquad \neg\ \text{ROP}\ tu \end{array}$$

Adesso non resta che analizzare le cinque opzioni di risposta, per individuare quella con il ragionamento la cui struttura logica è analoga a quella della traccia. Così facendo, si rileva che l'opzione cercata è "*everyone over the age of 60 is entitled to a bus pass, which gives them free travel on buses after 9:30 am. Since you are younger than 60, you are not entitled to free bus travel*". Infatti, la frase "*everyone over the age of 60 is entitled to a bus pass, which gives them free travel on buses after 9:30 am*" è la prima premessa (P_1) e da un punto di vista logico significa che "*TUTTE le persone SE hanno più di 60 anni, ALLORA hanno diritto a una tessera dell'autobus, che garantisce viaggi gratuiti sugli autobus dopo le 9:30 del mattino*". La frase "*you are younger than 60*" è la seconda premessa (P_2) e logicamente significa "*tu NON hai più di 60 anni*". La frase "*you are not entitled to free bus travel*" è la conclusione (C) e logicamente significa "*tu NON hai diritto a una tessera dell'autobus, che garantisce viaggi gratuiti sugli autobus (dopo le 9:30 del mattino)*". Indicando con '*x*' "le persone", con APS "avere più di 60 anni", con DTA "avere diritto *a una tessera dell'autobus, che dà viaggi gratuiti sugli autobus (dopo le 9:30 del mattino)*", si ottiene la seguente struttura logica, evidentemente analoga a quella individuata prima nella traccia:

$$\begin{array}{ll} \mathbf{P_1:} & (\forall x)\ (\text{APS}\ x \rightarrow \text{DTA}\ x) \\ \mathbf{P_2:} & \underline{\neg\ \text{APS}\ tu \qquad\qquad\qquad} \\ \mathbf{C:} & \qquad\qquad \neg\ \text{DTA}\ tu \end{array}$$

5) D. L'argomentazione della traccia parte da quattro premesse esplicite (P_1, P_2, P_3 e P_4), che riportano le percentuali con cui vari tipi di cibo sono buttati via: in P_1 si dice che il 32% del pane finisce per essere buttato via; in P_2 che la media di cibo e bevande sprecate è del 15%; in P_3 che la percentuale di carne e pesce buttati è al di sotto della media (13%); in P_4 che solo il 6% di alcol è buttato via. Da queste premesse si giunge alla conclusione che, rispetto al pane, apprezziamo molto di più altri tipi di cibo. Per poter giungere a tale conclusione, che ricava il grado di apprezzamento di un cibo in confronto a un altro dalle rispettive percentuali di spreco, l'argomentazione deve assumere implicitamente la premessa che "*the main reason why we throw food away is that we do not value it much*".

6) A. Il totale dei gatti coinvolti nel sondaggio costituisce il 100%, di cui il 10% + 20% + 40% = 70% ha espresso chiare preferenze per i tre tipi di cibo Moggiemeat, Fuss-a-Puss e Yummy Paws. La restante percentuale, invece, ovvero il 100% – 70% = 30%, è costituita dai 6 gatti che non sono sembrati interessati ai tre tipi di cibo assaggiati e dai 27 che non hanno toccato nessuno dei tre cibi, per un totale di 33 gatti. Indicando con X il numero totale di gatti, e ricordando che la percentuale è una possibile rappresentazione del rapporto tra due numeri in cui uno viene espresso in centesimi dell'altro, si ha allora la seguente uguaglianza:

$$33 = 30\%X = \frac{30}{100}X$$

da cui

$$X = \frac{33 \times 100}{30} = 110$$

Pertanto, il totale dei gatti coinvolti nel sondaggio è 110.

7) D. Per sapere quante donne non hanno avuto uomini seduti accanto durante la festa, basta dividere il numero di donne per il numero di uomini partecipanti e valutare il resto della divisione: se la divisione non dà resto c'è stata una perfetta alternanza tra donne e uomini alla tavola, se invece dà resto, esso costituisce il numero di donne che sono state sedute avendo un'altra donna sia a destra sia a sinistra. In questo caso

$14 \div 6 = 2$ con il resto di 2

pertanto, 2 donne non avevano un uomo seduto direttamente accanto a loro.

8) B. Poiché ad alcuni amici di Simon non piacciono le carte glitterate e Simon vuole acquistare carte doppie, gli unici tipi di carta che prenderà in considerazione sono *religous* e *father xmas.* Allora, dato che i biglietti d'auguri sono 35, potrebbe comprare 7 confezioni di carta *religous,* spendendo 7 × 1,80£ = 12,60, oppure 4 confezioni di carta *father xmas,* spendendo 4 × 3,10£ = 12,40£. Pertanto, la somma di denaro più bassa che Simon potrebbe spendere per le sue carte è 12,40£.

9) D. Poiché alla prima sveglia il display dell'orologio digitale era stato capovolto, erano le 05:02, pertanto alla seconda sveglia erano le 06:32, orario che, visto nel display al contrario, appare come 2Ɛ:90.

10) E. Per risolvere il quesito in modo agevole, conviene rappresentare graficamente le indicazioni fornite nella traccia. Perciò, disegniamo 5 coppie di rettangoli. Scriviamo poi nel primo rettangolo di ciascuna coppia il nome di uno dei 5 Stati delle alternative di risposta, facendo attenzione a usare le lettere maiuscole e a disporle in verticale. Scriviamo quindi nel secondo rettangolo di ciascuna coppia lo stesso nome sempre a lettere maiuscole e in verticale, ma in modo da ruotarle di 180°. Il primo rettangolo raffigura il lato anteriore e il secondo quello posteriore di ciascuna insegna dei 5 Stati:

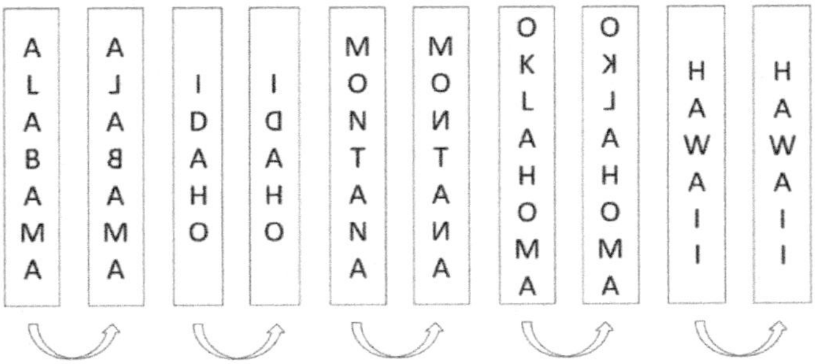

È facile costatare che solo il nome "Hawaii" si legge nello stesso modo sia anteriormente sia posteriormente.

11) C. L'abbinamento errato è "*Hans Jonas – medicine*", in quanto Jonas è stato un filosofo tedesco, e non un medico, allievo di Heidegger, che si è dedicato allo studio dello gnosticismo mettendone in discussione le tradizionali interpretazioni legate alla cultura greco-ellenistica e giudaico-cristiana, ritrovandone piuttosto l'essenza in matrici orientali autonome.

12) D. *My Brilliant Friend*, in italiano *L'amica geniale*, romanzo di successo ambientato a Napoli da cui è stata tratta l'omonima serie televisiva è opera della scrittrice napoletana Elena Ferrante, sulla cui reale identità non si ha alcuna notizia certa. Il romanzo narra la storia dell'amicizia tra due donne, Lila ed Elena, a partire dall'infanzia negli anni '50 del Novecento fino a oggi, seguendo passo passo la loro crescita individuale. Khaled Hosseini è l'autore, tra gli altri, de *Il cacciatore di aquiloni*; Ian McEwan ha scritto successi come *L'amore fatale* ed *Espiazione*; Paulo Coelho è un prolifico autore e tra i suoi lavori figura il best-seller *L'alchimista*; Kazuo Ishiguro, premio Nobel per la letteratura 2017, ha scritto, tra gli altri, *Quel che resta del giorno* e *Non lasciarmi*.

13) D. Nell'acronimo FAO (*Food and Agriculture Organization of the United Nations*, Organizzazione delle Nazioni Unite per l'Alimentazione e l'Agricoltura), la lettera *A* sta appunto per *Agricoltura*. L'Ente mondiale, fondato nel 1945 in Canada, ha sede a Roma e conta 194 Stati membri. Sin dalla sua fondazione ha come obiettivo quello di sviluppare e rendere accessibili a tutti informazioni e dati fondamentali su cibo, agricoltura e risorse naturali.

14) B. L'unico abbinamento teatro/città corretto è Metropolitan Opera House – New York; infatti, il Teatro San Carlo non si trova a Venezia ma a Napoli, il Bolshoi si trova a Mosca e non a San Pietroburgo; La Fenice è uno storico teatro veneziano e non fiorentino e, infine, l'Opéra Garnier è un monumento storico con sede a Parigi e non a Bruxelles.

15) C. La cosiddetta Stele di Rosetta è una lastra monolitica in pietra rinvenuta nel 1799 da Pierre-François Bouchard, capitano nella Campagna d'Egitto di Napoleone Bonaparte, nei pressi della città egiziana di Rashid il cui nome latinizzato è Rosetta. Sul reperto è inciso un decreto emesso nel 196 a.C. in onore del faraone Tolomeo V Epifane in tre differenti grafie: egizio geroglifico, egizio demotico e greco antico, lingua ufficiale del governo tolemaico. La sua importanza di reperto storico si deve al fatto che consentì agli studiosi di decifrare per la prima volta i geroglifici egizi partendo dal greco antico.

16) A. Tra le istituzioni dell'Unione Europea menzionate, l'unica ad essere eletta direttamente dai cittadini è il Parlamento Europeo, formato da rappresentanti dei cittadini dell'UE eletti a suffragio universale diretto ai quali viene conferito un mandato di cinque anni. Attualmente, questo organo è composto da 705 deputati di cui 76 italiani.

17) E. La pluripremiata e pluriacclamata trilogia intitolata *The Godfather*, in italiano *Il padrino*, (1972, 1974, 1990) è il capolavoro del regista statunitense Francis Ford Coppola, tratta dall'omonimo romanzo dello scrittore Mario Puzo. La trilogia narra le vicende della potente famiglia newyorkese dei Corleone, divenuta nel tempo una delle principali organizzazioni criminali della Grande Mela, in un arco di tempo di 96 anni, dal 1901 al 1997, e vanta un cast stellare con interpreti del calibro di Marlon Brando, Al Pacino, Robert De Niro.

18) B. L'abbinamento errato studioso/scoperta scientifica è Niels Bohr – microscopio elettronico, in quanto Bohr è stato un fisico danese, creatore della Scuola di Copenhagen, che ha dato un contributo fondamentale alla comprensione della struttura atomica e alla fisica quantistica, tanto da essere considerato il "padre" dell'atomo quantistico. I suoi studi gli valsero il Premio Nobel nel 1922. Il microscopio elettronico fu inventato, invece, dal fisico Ernst Ruska e dall'ingegnere Max Knoll.

19) C. La Comunità Europea del Carbone e dell'Acciaio (CECA) nacque con il Trattato di Parigi nell'aprile del 1951 con lo scopo di facilitare gli scambi di prodotti quali carbone, ferro e acciaio, senza diritti doganali o tasse, tra i sei paesi aderenti: Belgio, Francia, Germania Occidentale, Italia, Lussemburgo e Paesi Bassi. Avendo durata di 50 anni, il Trattato è terminato nel 2002 e contestualmente si è avuta la graduale integrazione delle competenze della CECA in quelle dell'Unione Europea.

20) B. L'organizzazione mondiale che ha il compito di stabilire le regole commerciali tra le Nazioni è la WTO (*World Trade Organization*, Organizzazione Mondiale del Commercio) che dal 1995 si occupa di vigilare sulle regole del commercio globale. Composta da 164 Paesi, tra cui l'Italia che ne fa parte fin dalla sua fondazione, quest'organizzazione inter-governativa formata da professionisti – economisti, avvocati, esperti di statistica – si occupa, tra l'altro, di garantire che le pratiche commerciali si svolgano in modo corretto e trasparente.

21) D. L'abbinamento sbagliato tra scrittori russi/opera è Mikhail Bulgakov – *Zio Vanya*. Bulgakov, tra i più autorevoli autori del Novecento, è, infatti, autore, tra gli altri, del celebre romanzo *Il maestro e Margherita*, pubblicato tra il 1966 e il 1967 e che narra la storia d'amore tra uno scrittore, detto il "Maestro", vittima di persecuzioni politiche da parte delle autorità sovietiche negli anni '30 del Novecento, e Margherita. *Zio Vanya* è, invece, un'opera drammatica di Anton Pavlovič Čhecov.

22) A. L'espressione "bicameralismo perfetto" o "paritario" prevede l'esercizio del potere legislativo assegnato a due camere rappresentative legislative paritarie, cioè con gli stessi poteri, stessi compiti e medesima importanza costituzionale. Tra gli Stati che esercitano tale forma figurano la Svizzera e l'Italia dove, per esempio, Camera dei Deputati e Senato della Repubblica hanno gli stessi poteri e funzioni dal punto di vista costituzionale seppur con differenze di composizione e tecniche.

Biologia

23) E. I virus sono piccole particelle formate da un genoma incluso in un capside di natura proteica. Il genoma virale può essere costituito da DNA a singolo filamento (es. virus della gastroenterite), da DNA a doppio filamento (es. virus della varicella), da RNA a singolo filamento (es. virus del morbillo) o da RNA a doppio filamento (es. virus dell'encefalite). I virus con genoma a singolo filamento di RNA includono i retrovirus (es. HIV).

24) B. La mitosi è la modalità di divisione delle cellule eucariotiche somatiche, attraverso la quale da una cellula madre si originano due cellule figlie con corredo cromosomico identico a quello della cellula di origine. L'immagine A rappresenta una cellula procariotica, che si divide per scissione binaria. L'immagine C rappresenta un mitocondrio e l'immagine D il complesso di Golgi, entrambi organelli delle cellule eucariotiche. L'immagine E rappresenta un virus.

25) C. La sintesi di un trigliceride a partire da una molecola di glicerolo e tre molecole di acidi grassi avviene attraverso tre reazioni di condensazione, in ciascuna delle quali un gruppo ossidrilico del glicerolo reagisce con il gruppo carbossilico di un acido grasso con eliminazione di una molecola d'acqua. Pertanto, la formula del trigliceride si ottiene sommando gli atomi del glicerolo e dei tre acidi grassi e sottraendo gli atomi di tre molecole d'acqua, ovvero 6 atomi di idrogeno e 3 atomi di ossigeno (27 C + 56 H + 9 O – 6 H – 3 O = 27 C + 50 H + 6 O). La formula richiesta è pertanto $C_{27}H_{50}O_6$.

26) E. Il colesterolo, uno steroide presente nella membrana plasmatica delle cellule animali, ha la capacità di stabilizzare la fluidità della membrana. Infatti, la molecola di colesterolo è idrofobica ma, in ragione della presenza di un gruppo ossidrilico, è leggermente anfipatica. Il gruppo ossidrilico si associa alle teste idrofiliche dei fosfolipidi di membrana, mentre la parte idrofobica della molecola si incastra tra le catene idrocarburiche degli acidi grassi.

27) C. La riga che riporta l'associazione corretta è la 5, in quanto T rappresenta il nucleolo, responsabile della sintesi delle subunità ribosomali. P rappresenta il complesso di Golgi, a cui è ascrivibile la formazione dei lisosomi. Q rappresenta la coppia di centrioli, da cui dipende la formazione del fuso mitotico durante la divisione cellulare. R rappresenta i ribosomi adesi al reticolo endoplasmatico ruvido, responsabili della sintesi proteica. S rappresenta il mitocondrio, la sede in cui viene sintetizzato ATP attraverso la respirazione aerobica.

28) A. Tutte le tre strutture cellulari indicate contengono catalizzatori biologici, ovvero enzimi. Per citarne alcuni, nel citoplasma sono presenti gli enzimi che catalizzano le varie reazioni della glicolisi; nel nucleo sono contenute la DNA polimerasi, che catalizza la replicazione del DNA, e la RNA polimerasi che catalizza la trascrizione del DNA in RNA; nei mitocondri sono presenti gli enzimi che catalizzano le reazioni del ciclo di Krebs.

29) B. Le reazioni redox, o di ossido-riduzione, sono reazioni in cui una o più specie si ossidano e una o più specie si riducono in conseguenza del trasferimento di elettroni. La specie che si ossida perde elettroni e la specie che si riduce li guadagna. La risposta $NAD^+ + H_2 \rightleftharpoons NADH + H^+$ rappresenta la reazione di riduzione del coenzima NAD^+, con formazione del coenzima ridotto $NADH_2$; il NAD^+ si riduce grazie al trasferimento di elettroni da parte dell'idrogeno, che si ossida.

30) D. Il gene *SRY* è responsabile dello sviluppo sessuale in senso maschile. L'inserzione di tale gene in un cromosoma X di uno zigote femminile (XX) sarebbe sufficiente a determinare lo sviluppo di caratteri sessuali maschili (affermazione 1). La formazione di uno spermatozoo portatore di un cromosoma X contenente il gene *SRY* condurrebbe, con la fecondazione, alla formazione di uno zigote contenente il gene, con conseguente sviluppo di caratteri sessuali maschili (affermazione 3). Nel caso di una divisione non corretta, il gene *SRY* funzionale contenuto nello spermatozoo darebbe in ogni caso origine a uno zigote di sesso maschile con la fecondazione (l'affermazione 2 è errata).

31) E. La meiosi è la modalità di divisione cellulare con cui le cellule germinali diploidi danno origine ai gameti aploidi. Si tratta di una divisione riduzionale, che porta al dimezzamento del numero di cromosomi, poiché avviene una sola duplicazione dei cromosomi seguita da due divisioni cellulari consecutive. Nel caso in questione, la cellula madre possiede 4 coppie di cromosomi omologhi, per un totale di 8 cromosomi (4 di origine materna e 4 di origine paterna), ciascuno formato da 2 cromatidi fratelli. Al termine della meiosi I, i due membri di ciascuna coppia di omologhi segregano nelle due cellule figlie, che pertanto conterranno ciascuna 4 cromosomi, ancora costituiti da 2 cromatidi fratelli. Al termine della meiosi 2, i cromatidi fratelli di ciascun cromosoma segregano nelle due cellule figlie, che quindi conterranno ciascuna 4 cromosomi formati da un singolo cromatidio. Il risultato finale è, pertanto, la formazione di 4 gameti aploidi.

32) A. La sequenza di DNA TATGATCTTAGGCAACAT viene trascritta nella sequenza di RNA AUACUAGAAUCCGUUGUA, complementare a essa e contenente l'uracile in luogo della timina. Contando il numero delle singole basi, si trova A = 6, U = 6, C = 3, G = 3. Pertanto, il numero di A e il numero di U, entrambi pari a 6, sono il doppio del numero di C e del numero di G, entrambi pari a 3.

33) B. L'unico pattern di ereditarietà compatibile esclusivamente con la trasmissione di un tratto autosomico dominante è il 2. Detto *A* l'allele dominante e *a* l'allele recessivo, nel caso in cui la polidattilia fosse dovuta a un allele autosomico recessivo, gli individui affetti avrebbero genotipo *aa* e quelli non affetti genotipo *AA* o *Aa*. In questo caso, nell'albero genealogico 2, l'accoppiamento tra il maschio affetto (*aa*) e la femmina affetta (*aa*) della prima generazione filiale non potrebbe generare prole non affetta, in quanto tutti i figli avrebbero genotipo *aa*.

34) D. Le pompe protoniche del cloroplasto sono situate soltanto nelle membrane tilacoidali. In presenza di luce, vi è un continuo flusso di elettroni attraverso una catena di trasporto degli elettroni posta nella membrana tilacoidale. Nel trasferimento di elettroni da un accettore a un altro, si ha una perdita di energia che è in parte utilizzata per pompare protoni attraverso la membrana tilacoidale. Un enzima (ATP sintasi), localizzato nella membrana tilacoidale, sfrutta l'energia del gradiente protonico per sintetizzare ATP.

35) B. Se un ambiente cambia nel tempo, la selezione direzionale può favorire i fenotipi a uno degli estremi della distribuzione normale. Con il passare delle generazioni, un fenotipo ne rimpiazza gradualmente un altro. La riga 5 prospetta il seguente scenario: nel caso in cui un fenotipo a bassa frequenza, determinato da un allele recessivo, risulti vantaggioso nello sfuggire a un nuovo predatore, allora il predatore potrebbe essere il motore di una selezione direzionale nella quale è favorito il fenotipo a bassa frequenza così come l'allele recessivo che lo determina. Gli individui con tale costituzione genotipica e fenotipica hanno così una fitness superiore agli altri e la loro prole ha maggiori probabilità di sopravvivenza; ne consegue che nella popolazione aumenta la frequenza dell'allele recessivo e del fenotipo da esso determinato.

36) A. Il ciclo cardiaco è il periodo compreso tra l'inizio di un battito cardiaco e l'inizio del successivo e si articola in fasi alternate di sistole (contrazione) e di diastole (rilasciamento) degli atri e dei ventricoli. Quando il ventricolo sinistro si rilascia, la pressione ventricolare scende e il sangue refluisce verso le cuspidi della valvola aortica, chiudendola (l'opzione "*When the left ventricle relaxes, the aortic valve closes*" è corretta). Quando l'atrio sinistro si contrae, il ventricolo sinistro è in diastole e la valvola aortica è chiusa (l'opzione "*When the left atrium contracts, the aortic valve opens*" è errata). I due atri, così come i due ventricoli, si contraggono simultaneamente; pertanto, le valvole AV destra e sinistra si aprono e si chiudono insieme (l'ozione "*When the right atrio-ventricular valve closes, the left atrio-ventricular valve opens*" è errata). Quando gli atri si contraggono, i ventricoli sono rilasciati (l'opzione "*When the right atrium contracts, the left ventricle contracts*" è errata). Quando i ventricoli si contraggono, le valvole AV sono chiuse (l'opzione "*When the right ventricle contracts, the right atrio-ventricular valve opens*" è errata).

37) A. Il grafico ha un andamento sigmoidale: inizialmente l'emocromo (conta delle cellule del sangue) è costante, dopodiché accade qualcosa che ne determina un incremento fino al raggiungimento di una fase di plateau, nella quale l'emocromo resta costante al nuovo valore raggiunto. Una diminuzione della pressione parziale di ossigeno nell'aria determina un meccanismo compensatorio che porta a una maggiore produzione di eritrociti (globuli rossi), responsabili del trasporto dell'ossigeno ai tessuti. Un'infezione batterica induce una risposta immunitaria che comporta l'aumento della conta di leucociti (globuli bianchi). Le cellule del sangue vengono prodotte mediante il processo di emopoiesi, che consiste nel differenziamento delle cellule staminali del midollo osseo negli elementi corpuscolati del sangue.

38) D. Nella retina sono contenuti neuroni sensitivi per la trasmissione delle informazioni visive alla corteccia visiva attraverso il nervo ottico (nota 1 errata). Nella fovea, una piccola area al centro della retina, vi è la massima concentrazione di coni, mentre i bastoncelli sono più numerosi in periferia (nota 2 errata). In condizioni di buio, la pupilla si dilata per consentire un maggiore ingresso di luce (nota 3 errata). Dalla camera anteriore, l'umor acqueo, che contiene glucosio, diffonde nella cornea, svolgendo una funzione trofica (nota 4 corretta). La cornea è una lente fissa, mentre il cristallino consente di mettere a fuoco le immagini sulla retina modificando la propria curvatura a seconda della distanza degli oggetti da osservare (nota 5 errata).

39) C. Quando viene effettuato un trapianto d'organo, le cellule dell'organo trapiantato vengono riconosciute come estranee e attaccate dai linfociti T. Allo scopo di ridurre al minimo le differenze negli antigeni di istocompatibilità, occorre effettuare una tipizzazione accurata sia del donatore che del ricevente, ma quanto maggiori sono le differenze, tanto maggiore è la probabilità del rigetto. Per prevenirlo o per ridurne le conseguenze, vengono somministrati ai pazienti che ricevono un trapianto farmaci immunosoppressori. Fanno eccezione alcuni organi, tra cui la cornea, che, essendo praticamente priva di vasi sanguigni, può essere trapiantata senza rischio di rigetto.

40) B. La bile, una miscela complessa sintetizzata dal fegato, immagazzinata e concentrata dalla cistifellea e riversata da questa nell'intestino tenue, ha la funzione di emulsionare i grassi, riducendoli in piccole goccioline lipidiche facilmente attaccabili dalla lipasi pancreatica. L'amilasi pancreatica, contenuta nel succo pancreatico riversato nell'intestino tenue, degrada a disaccaridi quasi tutti i polisaccaridi, ad eccezione della cellulosa.

Chimica

41) E. Il punto di fusione è la temperatura alla quale un solido si trasforma in un liquido; esso aumenta scendendo lungo il VII gruppo della tavola periodica degli elementi (la proprietà 1 è errata). L'elettronegatività è la tendenza di un atomo ad attrarre a sé gli elettroni condivisi nei legami covalenti; essa diminuisce scendendo lungo il VII gruppo della tavola periodica degli elementi (la proprietà 2 è corretta). L'energia di prima ionizzazione è l'energia necessaria per sottrarre un elettrone a un atomo neutro; essa diminuisce scendendo lungo il VII gruppo della tavola periodica degli elementi (la proprietà 3 è corretta).

42) E. Il numero di massa di un atomo è pari alla somma dei protoni e dei neutroni contenuti nel suo nucleo. L'atomo in questione possiede, pertanto, 8 protoni. Dato che in un atomo neutro il numero di protoni eguaglia il numero di elettroni, l'atomo possiede 8 elettroni; perciò, il corrispondente ione con carica –2 contiene 10 elettroni. Partendo dal principio di esclusione di Pauli, secondo il quale ciascun orbitale atomico può contenere al massimo 2 elettroni, nel primo guscio elettronico, costituito dal solo orbitale 1*s*, si collocano 2 elettroni, mentre nel secondo guscio elettronico, costituito dall'orbitale 2*s* e dai 3 orbitali 2*p*, si collocano 2 elettroni nel 2*s* e 2 elettroni in ogni orbitale 2*p*. La configurazione elettronica dello ione è, pertanto, $1s^2 2s^2 2p^6$.

43) C. L'aggiunta di un soluto a un solvente puro determina l'abbassamento del punto di congelamento della soluzione rispetto al solvente puro (l'affermazione 1 è errata). L'energia cinetica è associata al moto casuale delle molecole (maggiore è la temperatura, maggiore è la velocità delle molecole); pertanto, un abbassamento della temperatura determina una riduzione dell'energia cinetica media delle molecole (l'affermazione 2 è errata). Il punto di ebollizione di un liquido è la temperatura alla quale la tensione di vapore del liquido eguaglia la pressione esterna; un aumento della pressione esterna fa sì che sia richiesta una temperatura superiore affinché ciò si realizzi (l'affermazione 3 è corretta).

44) D. Gli isomeri strutturali sono composti aventi la stessa formula molecolare, ma diversa formula di struttura. Ciò significa che gli isomeri strutturali sono formati dagli stessi atomi, che però risultano legati in maniera differente. L'esano ha formula molecolare C_6H_{14}, proprio come il composto 2. Invece, il composto 1 ha formula molecolare C_6H_{12} e il composto 3 C_5H_{12}. Pertanto, solo il composto 2 è un isomero strutturale dell'esano.

45) A. L'affinità elettronica di un elemento è la variazione di energia che si osserva quando un atomo neutro e isolato di quell'elemento acquista un elettrone nel suo orbitale di valenza libero di energia più bassa. Essa rappresenta la tendenza di un atomo a formare un anione. L'affinità elettronica del cloro è associata all'equazione in cui un atomo di cloro neutro acquista un elettrone, formando un anione cloruro.

46) D. Il gruppo alcolico è un residuo ossidrilico (–OH) legato a un atomo di carbonio tetraedrico. Il gruppo aldeidico è un gruppo carbonilico (C=O) legato a due atomi di idrogeno o a un atomo di carbonio e a un atomo di idrogeno. Il gruppo ammidico (O=C–N) è un derivato del gruppo carbossilico per sostituzione dell'ossidrile con un'ammina. Il gruppo amminico (C–N) consiste in un atomo di azoto legato a uno, due o tre atomi di carbonio. Il gruppo carbossilico (–COOH) consiste in un atomo di carbonio che lega un atomo di ossigeno con un doppio legame e un gruppo ossidrilico. Il gruppo chetonico è un gruppo carbonilico (C=O) legato a due atomi di carbonio. Dei gruppi funzionali elencati, la vitamina B5 contiene il gruppo alcolico, il gruppo ammidico e il gruppo carbossilico.

47) C. L'acido nitrico si dissocia in acqua secondo la seguente reazione: $HNO_3 \rightarrow H^+ + NO_3^-$. Pertanto, la concentrazione di H^+ è uguale alla concentrazione di acido nitrico (0,050 mol/L). L'acido solforico si dissocia in acqua secondo la seguente reazione: $H_2SO_4 \rightarrow 2\ H^+ + SO_4^{2-}$. Pertanto, la concentrazione di H^+ è il doppio di quella di acido solforico (0,100 mol/L). Quindi, la concentrazione di H^+ nella soluzione Y è il doppio di quella nella soluzione X (l'affermazione 1 è errata). L'acido nitrico è un acido forte, per cui si dissocia completamente in acqua (l'affermazione 2 è errata). Il pH della soluzione Y a 25°C si calcola come $-\log [H^+] = -\log (0{,}100) = 1$ (l'affermazione 3 è corretta).

48) B. L'atomo di alluminio possiede 3 elettroni di valenza e quello di cloro 7; pertanto, in $AlCl_3$, Al forma un legame covalente con ciascun atomo di cloro. In $AlCl_3$, l'atomo di alluminio centrale è quindi circondato da 3 coppie di elettroni di legame, che si dispongono alla massima distanza reciproca, ovvero con una geometria trigonale planare (angoli di legame di 120°). In Al_2Cl_6, ciascun atomo di alluminio lega 3 atomi di cloro mediante legami covalenti e un altro atomo di cloro in qualità di accettore in un legame covalente dativo. Ciascun atomo di alluminio è quindi legato a 4 atomi di cloro, che si dispongono in una geometria tetraedrica (angoli di legame di 109°).

49) E. Il legame a idrogeno è una forza intermolecolare attrattiva che si stabilisce tra un atomo di idrogeno legato covalentemente a un atomo molto elettronegativo e un altro atomo elettronegativo. Il legame tra l'idrogeno e un atomo elettronegativo, ad esempio l'ossigeno, è un legame covalente polare; pertanto, sull'ossigeno si crea una parziale carica negativa e sull'idrogeno una parziale carica positiva. In virtù di tali cariche parziali, si stabiliscono forze attrattive tra i suddetti dipoli, cosicché l'idrogeno di un gruppo polare è attratto da un atomo con parziale carica negativa. Nell'acido etanoico, le molecole formano tra loro legami a idrogeno grazie all'OH dei gruppi carbossilici, che sono molto polarizzati; invece, negli altri composti elencati, l'idrogeno è legato ad atomi (C e S) non fortemente elettronegativi e, di conseguenza, le molecole di questi composti non stabiliscono forti legami a idrogeno.

50) A. In 100 mL della soluzione di nitrato di potassio (KNO_3) sono contenuti 3,2 g di sale; pertanto, nei 25 mL prelevati ne sono contenuti 3,2/4 = 0,8 g. Questi vengono disciolti nei 250 mL della soluzione finale, che risulta avere una concentrazione di KNO_3 pari a 0,8 g/0,25 L = 3,2 g/L. Nei 25 mL prelevati con la pipetta e trasferiti, la concentrazione di KNO_3 è, pertanto, pari a 3,2 g/L.

51) B. Trattandosi di un composto neutro, il numero di ossidazione complessivo della molecola deve essere pari a zero. Poiché il numero di ossidazione dell'idrogeno è +1 e quello dell'ossigeno è –2 e poiché la molecola contiene *m* atomi di idrogeno e *n* atomi di ossigeno, detto *x* il numero di ossidazione dell'atomo X, deve essere $+1m - 2n + x = 0$, ovvero $x = 2n - m$.

52) D. Conoscendo i valori delle masse molari dei due elementi che compongono l'ossido, è possibile calcolare il numero di moli di ciascuno di essi nel campione come segue: mol(Fe) = 1,68 g/56 g mol^{-1} = 3 mol; mol(O) = 0,64 g/16 g mol^{-1} = 4 mol. Pertanto, l'ossido di ferro indicato ha formula molecolare Fe_3O_4.

Fisica e Matematica

53) E. $\dfrac{(x+2)^2}{x^2+x-2}=\dfrac{(x+2)^{\not 2}}{\cancel{(x+2)}(x-1)}=\dfrac{x+2}{x-1}.$

54) A. Moltiplicando entrambi i membri per 6, che è il minimo comune multiplo dei due denominatori, si ottiene:

$$3(2x+3)-4(x+1)<12x$$

$$6x+9-4x-4<12x$$

$$6x-4x-12x<-9+4$$

$$-10x<-5.$$

Infine, dividiamo entrambi i membri per −10, cambiando di verso la disequazione:

$$\frac{-10x}{-10}>\frac{-5}{-10}$$

$$x>\frac{1}{2}.$$

55) B. Poiché i due triangoli dati sono simili, allora i loro lati sono in proporzione:

$$\overline{RQ}:\overline{RT}=\overline{RP}:\overline{RS},$$

da cui:

$$\overline{RQ}=\frac{\overline{RT}\cdot\overline{RP}}{\overline{RS}}=\frac{5\cdot 3,5}{2,5}=7\text{ cm},$$

quindi:

$$\overline{TQ}=\overline{RQ}-\overline{RT}=7-5=2\text{ cm}.$$

Per il teorema di Pitagora:

$$\overline{ST}=\sqrt{\overline{RT}^2+\overline{RS}^2}=\sqrt{5^2+2,5^2}=\sqrt{25+\frac{25}{4}}=\sqrt{\frac{125}{4}}=\frac{5}{2}\sqrt{5}\text{ cm},$$

da cui, sempre in virtù della proporzionalità tra i lati:

$$\overline{QP}=\frac{\frac{5}{2}\sqrt{5}\cdot 7}{5}=\frac{7}{2}\sqrt{5}\text{ cm}.$$

Il perimetro richiesto risulta, infine:

$$P=\overline{PS}+\overline{ST}+\overline{TQ}+\overline{QP}=1+\frac{5}{2}\sqrt{5}+2+\frac{7}{2}\sqrt{5}=(3+6\sqrt{5})\text{ cm}$$

$$P=3(1+2\sqrt{5})\text{ cm}.$$

56) A. Siano $\overline{QR} = x$ e $\overline{PQ} = y$. Dalle informazioni del testo:

$$\begin{cases} A = \frac{1}{2}xy = 14 \\ \tan\widehat{PRQ} = \frac{y}{x} = \frac{1}{7}, \end{cases}$$

da cui:

$$\begin{cases} xy = 28 \\ y = \frac{x}{7} \end{cases} \rightarrow \begin{cases} x\frac{x}{7} = 28 \\ '' \end{cases} \rightarrow \begin{cases} x^2 = 196 \\ '' \end{cases} \rightarrow \begin{cases} x = \sqrt{196} = 14 \\ y = \frac{14}{7} = 2 \end{cases}$$

Per il teorema di Pitagora:

$$\overline{PR} = \sqrt{x^2 + y^2} = \sqrt{14^2 + 2^2} = \sqrt{200} = 10\sqrt{2}\text{ cm},$$

così come:

$$\overline{SP} = \sqrt{\overline{PR}^2 + \overline{RS}^2} = \sqrt{200 + 25} = \sqrt{225} = 15\text{ cm}.$$

Infine:

$$\cos\widehat{RPS} = \frac{\overline{PR}}{\overline{SP}} = \frac{10\sqrt{2}}{15} = \frac{2\sqrt{2}}{3}.$$

57) D. La velocità è data da:

$v = \omega r = 10 \cdot 2{,}5 = 25$ m/s,

mentre l'accelerazione centripeta da:

$a = \omega^2 r = 10^2 \cdot 2{,}5 = 250$ m/s^2.

58) C. Per il principio di Pascal le pressioni nei punti X e Y sono uguali, in quanto una variazione di pressione si ripercuote inalterata in tutti i punti di un fluido confinato e in tutti i punti delle pareti del suo contenitore. Inoltre, poiché la forza risulta direttamente proporzionale alla superficie del pistone, F_2 risulta più grande di F_1.

59) B. La potenza fornita in 5 minuti, che equivalgono a 300 secondi, risulta:

$$P = \frac{Q}{\Delta t} = \frac{mc\Delta T}{\Delta t} = \frac{1{,}2 \cdot 500 \cdot (90 - 40)}{300} = 100\text{ W}.$$

60) A. L'espressione (quantità di moto) × (velocità) è pari a:

$mv \cdot v = mv^2$,

che ha la stessa unità di misura dell'energia cinetica $\frac{1}{2}mv^2$.